The Business of Walt Disney and the Nine Principles of His Success

Barry Linetsky

Theme Park Press
www.ThemeParkPress.com

Editor: Bob McLain
Layout: Artisanal Text

ISBN 978-1-68390-058-0
Printed in the United States of America

Theme Park Press | www.ThemeParkPress.com
Address queries to bob@themeparkpress.com

*This book is dedicated
to my loving wife and children:
Marlaine, Corinna, and Leanne;
and my loving parents,
Carl and Helen Linetsky*

Contents

PART TWO
The Nine Principles of Walt Disney's Success

Introduction

It has been my challenge in writing this book to bring together information from diverse sources to describe, in appropriate detail, the challenges and issues that Walt Disney faced as a businessman in doing his work of growing and leading a major film studio in the mid-twentieth century. With a solid foundational understanding of Walt Disney's career challenges and achievements as presented in Part 1, I then set out in Part 2 to identify inductively a number of business-related principles that could account for Walt's success, and that may serve as instructive lessons for other entrepreneurs and entrepreneurial executives and managers.

The information and stories contained herein rests on an immense amount of research and work done by previous Disney historians and authors over the past 75 or so years, to whom I am grateful for providing the depth of resource material as the backbone for this book. It is from this material that leaders, students, and general readers can draw the appropriate lessons from this entrepreneurial maverick; lessons that worked for Walt given his particular temperament, capabilities, and circumstances.

As authors write about the events in Walt Disney's career that played out along a temporal path, there are only so many ways to convey much of the same factual information, originating from the same historical sources. Sometimes the most appropriate and just thing to do is to let other Disney historians and experts speak for themselves. Where they have done an exemplary job conveying the same information I needed to convey, I rely on their telling of the story. I think of it as my way of honoring their work. The sources I cite are the same sources I would recommend to readers who wish to delve deeper into the colorful history of Walt Disney and his illustrious career. They can be found throughout the text and in a bibliography.

While the book of necessity follows the narration of events in Walt Disney's career, my primary focus is on relating some of the business challenges Walt faced and decisions he made at key points in his career to drive these events.

Events exist in a social context, but are driven by the choices of individual actors based on their own knowledge, values, philosophies, and psychologies. As always with people, including when acting within organizations, things happen because people make them happen. They don't happen on their own. They don't happen inevitably. Actions are purposeful, and are taken in pursuit of goals to achieve a defined end. Whether they are the right actions, or only actions, or best actions, to achieve any given end are always open to debate.

A business is a specific kind of organization with a specific purpose and function to produce goods and services in exchange for profit. To function effectively, a business requires leaders who are accountable for driving success. The focus here is on Walt Disney's story: the creation and leadership of his business rather than the artistic or esthetic aspects of animation, or his and other Disney artists' growth.

Even though at times Walt Disney Productions had more than 1,000 employees, it can still be said that as an entity it was Walt's business in the sense that he was the prime architect of events—he was the prime mover that generated and sustained a forward vector. It was his imagination, his vision, his courage, his thinking, his values, his will to achieve specific ends, that focused and guided the thinking and work of those he employed to help him create a successful business.

Walt Disney wasn't the only leader. Many people Walt employed were visionaries in their creative fields and engaged in pioneering work, but their creative work and their tasks as managerial leaders were by necessity subordinate to Walt's leadership, applying themselves as independent agents to serve the needs and ends defined by the organization's top executive.

In retelling a story that has been told many times before, I have tried to highlight Walt Disney's progression as an entrepreneur and managerial leader of a business, who was engaged as a businessman, a manager of people and performance, a builder of organizations, and a strategist. I have tried to selectively focus on those aspects that should be of interest to those with a desire to understand Walt Disney as one of the world's leading businessmen, as well as an artist. To do so I have of necessity selectively chosen some events in Walt's biography while ignoring others, focusing heavily on some things while quickly passing over or not mentioning others.

I have also tried to be meticulous in setting out a proper chronology in order to understand Walt Disney and his capabilities for managing complex challenges and processing information over long periods of time and throughout his career. The narratives of too many Disney histories are focused around individual events such as the creation of *Snow White and the Seven Dwarfs*, or the studio strike, or the 1964–1965 World's Fair in New York City, among others, as if they occur in isolation. In fact, these events all occur in a dynamic context, while Walt and the studio have to simultaneously manage all of their other business commitments. One has to understand this if one is to attempt to understand Walt Disney. I have tried to tell the story in a way that the reader has some semblance of the context and weight of responsibility felt by Walt and Roy Disney as they encounter new challenges and figure out how best to overcome them.

In too many Disney histories, information is overly compressed such that events occurring months or years apart occur in the same sentence, leaving the reader with the impression that these events just happen by themselves rather than that they are made to happen by means of the purposeful thinking and choices of actors. In many books, it is impossible to follow the chronology, which jumps forwards and backwards, as if chronology plays no role in the telling of history or the understanding of the subject matter, in this case, Walt Disney. In this regard, I tried to follow the advice of the great contemporary historian Paul Johnson, who said: "I think it is terribly, terribly important to get chronology right. Remember the dates. Fix people with the dates. I think a weakness in chronology [makes it] impossible to write good history." I have endeavored to untangle the various threads and to present the key business elements of the Walt Disney story chronologically, wherever possible, although there are a few exceptions.

There is one final note of personal historic interest. This book began as an extended essay I wrote and published in 2006. A client and friend of mine, Chuck Hawley, had the pleasure of knowing and working with Roy E. Disney. Both were avid sailors, and for many years worked together as board members of the Transpacific Yacht Club. Chuck had agreed to assist Roy in the capacity of a marine safety expert to train a group of teenage rookie sailors as they prepared to sail Roy's boat *Morning Light* and participate in the 2,225 mile Transpacific Yacht Race from Los Angeles to Hawaii. Without my knowledge, Chuck was kind enough to forward my roughly fifty-page essay to Roy E. Disney. In a personal correspondence to Chuck on January 9, 2007, Roy thanked him for his tremendous work and dedication to teaching and preparing his crew for their journey, and contributing in his small way to the making of the Disney documentary *Morning Light*. Roy also wrote: "And thanks, too, for the Disney piece. Very interesting, and informative…and pretty accurate, too!"

I'm very appreciative that Roy E. Disney took time out of his busy schedule to read and comment on an early version of what has now been transformed into this book. It is my hope that if he was still with us today to read it, he would respond with the very same kind words.

Barry Linetsky
Toronto, Canada
November 7, 2016

PART ONE

The Business of Walt Disney

CHAPTER ONE

Growing Up Walt

Like so many self-made men of his time, Walt Disney had very little schooling and no formal business education. He didn't start school until he was seven years old, and ended his formal education after the eighth grade.

Walter Elias Disney was born in Chicago on December 5, 1901. In April 1906, when Walt was four, his father Elias Disney bought a forty-acre farm near the rural town of Marceline, Missouri, and close to his brother Robert's farm. Toward the end of 1910—four-and-a-half years after they arrived in Marceline—Elias Disney sold the family farm due to his poor health (typhoid fever and pneumonia), and in the spring of 1911 moved with his family to bustling Kansas City, Missouri.

To generate family income in Kansas City, Elias Disney purchased two paper routes. The morning route had almost 700 customers and the afternoon and Sunday routes had more than 600 customers.

Each day before and after school, nine-year-old Walt and sixteen-year-old Roy were required by their father to deliver newspapers to help support the financially struggling family.

Walt recalled his experience forty-five years later:

> When I was nine, my brother Roy and I were already businessmen. We had a newspaper route...delivering papers in a residence area every morning of the year, rain, shine, or snow. We got up at 4:30 a.m., worked until the school bell rang and did the same thing again from four o'clock in the afternoon until supper time. Often I dozed at my desk, and my report card told the story.[1]

For the two Disney boys, there was no throwing of newspapers from the street to the stoop. These newspapers belonged to customers, so each paper had to be carried to the front door and delivered properly. Elias insisted that quality and reputation mattered. In the dark mornings of icy and snowy winters of the Midwest, Walt remembered, "I was so darn cold I'd slip, and I could cry, so I cried." In the warmer weather, Walt would sometimes sneak some time to play with the "wonderful toys" like "electric trains or wind-up trains" that the children of wealthier families had left outside.[2] When done playing, Walt was careful to leave everything exactly as he had found it.

Elias refused to pay his sons any money for delivering papers. Helping out was considered a family obligation even though other boys would be paid to help when needed. As a means to earn his own spending money, and without his father's knowledge, Walt arranged to deliver medicine for a drug store while doing his route. Also, when he could, he would order and sell extra papers.

Walt continued to deliver newspapers twice a day, every day, for six years, until the summer of 1917 when his father and mother moved back to Chicago. Walt stayed in Kansas City for the summer, living with his two older brothers, Roy and Herbert, along with Herbert's wife and baby daughter.

When Walt wasn't in school he was working. According to Roy, Walt wasn't very good "at attending to the business" side of work. Walt took a summer job selling newspapers and candies as a "news butcher" on the trains. At the end of the summer, Walt found himself in a negative financial situation, having to borrow money from his parents to pay his employer. He would come back at the end of the day, said Roy, "and he couldn't account for all that merchandise he took out so he'd run into a loss and who do you think paid his losses? ... He was always that way. He never had any knack for business ... It just annoyed him."[3]

Walt's recollection was that while he loved the excitement of traveling on the train every day, interacting with the travelers, and traveling to the surrounding states, passengers were constantly stealing his empty soda bottles and thus robbing him of his profits. Also, admitted Walt, he couldn't resist eating the candy bars he was selling.[4]

As the summer of 1917 drew to a close, fifteen-year-old Walt joined his parents in Chicago in time to attend high school. He also took a job at the O-Zell Jelly factory where his father now worked and had a small ownership stake. Walt did a number of manual labor tasks including washing bottles and crushing apples. He also attended art classes three nights a week at the Chicago Academy of Fine Arts.

A year later, in the summer of 1918, Walt worked for the Chicago post office, arriving at work each day at 7 a.m. to sort mail and fill in as a substitute carrier. When his shift ended mid-afternoon, he did additional work for about an hour carrying special-delivery letters or picking up mail from boxes, then he went across town to work as a "gate man" to assist in controlling rush-hour passenger traffic on the city's elevated train line.[5] Walt enjoyed his employment and valued making productive use of his time. Perhaps he enjoyed the contrast of working for pay after so many years of delivering newspapers for his father and having no money to show for it. Walt would later use the money he saved to start his own short-lived commercial art business.

While Walt must have lived a harsh childhood by the idealized standards of today, it wasn't that different from many other boys growing up in early 20th century middle America, and certainly not from his peers. Nostalgic romanticism may have somewhat colored Walt's later recollections of his childhood years, yet overall, he had a positive and optimistic perspective about life's challenges and opportunities. "I don't regret having worked like I've worked," Walt said later when reflecting back on these youthful years. "I can't even remember that it ever bothered me. I mean, I have no recollection of ever being unhappy in my life. I look back and I worked from way back there and I was happy all the time. I was excited. I was doing things."[6] Still, at other times Walt contemplated the benefits of living a simpler, less burdensome life, but it is unlikely that he would have preferred it. Most people who knew him were in agreement that Walt had boundless energy for moving forward. He enjoyed his work and made it his play, and found it very difficult to just relax away from his work. Work was about solving problems, and Walt, who was curious by nature, enjoyed the personal challenge of applying himself to finding practical and profitable solutions.

In the summer of 1918 the United States was engaged in World War I. Roy was in training as a recruit in the U.S. Navy. Walt signed up to be a Red Cross driver in the American Ambulance Corps, and was posted to France. The war had ended by the time his unit arrived overseas in December of 1918, but there was still work to be done. Walt provided driving services while in France, moving personnel and delivering supplies, and with his extra time he would draw cartoons and submit them to humor magazines back in the United States. He also earned some extra money by drawing caricatures for "the guys." His time in Europe introduced him to patriotic duty and provided him with a sense of independence and worldly experience.

Walt returned to Chicago in the fall of 1919, just prior to his eighteenth birthday. Having spent a year overseas contributing to the nation's war effort, he felt more mature and had a greater sense of purpose to get on with his life as an adult and make his way in the world.

Walt perceived that the only real talent he had was drawing, so he decided he would look for a job as a commercial artist and cartoonist. He was eager to learn what was needed to succeed and to exuberantly apply himself to his newly chosen career. By all accounts, there was nothing unusual or peculiar about Walt to indicate that he was starting down a road that would eventually earn him a place as a leading iconoclast, visionary, and entrepreneurial genius of the twentieth-century.

1. Walt Disney quoted in Barrier, *The Animated Man*, 18–19.
2. Barrier, *The Animated Man*, 19.
3. Barrier, *The Animated Man*, 21.
4. Barrier, *The Animated Man*, 20.
5. Barrier, *The Animated Man*, 22.
6. Walt quoted in Barrier, *The Animated Man*, 23.

CHAPTER TWO

Starting a Career in Kansas City, Missouri: Learning Animation

Walt returned to Chicago from France via New York in early October 1919.[1] He had grown in height to five feet ten inches, filled out to 165 pounds, and had taken up cigarette smoking. He was now eager to start a new phase in his life and to face the challenge and excitement of adulthood.

Having spent a year away from his family doing his part for the American war effort, he quickly recognized that his independence would require he separate himself from his father, who wanted Walt to take a manual labor job at the O-Zell jelly factory. Walt refused.

Instead Walt chose to return to Kansas City to seek work and once again take up residence with Herbert and Roy in the Disney family home. Roy had received a discharge from the navy in February 1919, and taken a job as a bank teller in Kansas City. As was the case when they were growing up, Roy continued to look out for Walt and Walt continued to look up to Roy and view him as his best friend.

Soon after Walt's return to Kansas City, Roy learned that a company called Pesmen-Rubin Commercial Art Studio was seeking an apprentice and sent Walt over to apply for the job. After an unpaid one-week trial period, Walt was hired at fifty dollars a month, and couldn't believe his luck to have a real job where he was paid to do what he loved most—drawing. Walt worked on catalogues for the Christmas holiday season, but after six weeks, when that work came to an end, he was dismissed from his job and again found himself without work.

Walt was able to find temporary work at the post office delivering mail during the Christmas rush and began thinking about going into business for himself as a commercial artist. Walt reflected on what he had observed and learned about the commercial art trade during his short time at Pesmen-Rubin: that speed and efficiency were important practical aspects that customers expected and sometimes, to satisfy customers, quality had to take a back seat to practicality, that "when you get into the commercial art shop you cut things out and paste over and scratch out with razor blades.... Cutting corners" to get the work done quickly.[2]

Early into the new year of 1920, a fellow worker that Walt had struck up a friendship with at Pesmen-Rubin named Ubbe Iwwerks was also laid off. Iwwerks, who was the son of a Dutch immigrant (and who would change the spelling of his name to Ub Iwerks), would come to play an important role in the early part of Walt Disney's successful career. Walt suggested they go into business together and Iwwerks reluctantly agreed. Walt bootstrapped the startup with $250 of his savings to purchase two desks, drawing boards, and other necessary supplies.[3] The Iwerks-Disney commercial art studio was formed.

Things started off well, with Walt able to leverage his connections with friends and acquaintances into $135 in revenue in the first month, a substantial amount and more than his and Ub's combined monthly salaries at Pesmen-Rubin.

While the prospects of building a successful commercial partnership looked promising to Walt, before their first month in business was over Ub spotted an ad of interest in the *Kansas City Star*. The Kansas City Slide Company was seeking a cartoon artist to draw ads on slides that were shown to movie theatre audiences to advertise local businesses and products.

Always eager to pursue an opportunity, Walt approached the company's owner, A. Verne Cauger, and tried to convince him to outsource the work to Walt and Ub. Instead, Cauger offered Walt forty dollars a week to come work for him, which was far more than Iwerks-Disney had taken in together, while at the same time eliminating the risks inherent in owning and operating a small independent business.

After discussing Cauger's offer with Ub, Walt accepted the job, while Ub continued to run their commercial art venture. Unfortunately, in the absence of Walt's driving ambition, business suffered due to Ub's shy and quiet nature, which wasn't conducive to advancing sales or servicing clients. In March, Walt convinced Cauger to hire Ub, and Iwerks-Disney ceased operating. Soon thereafter, the Kansas City Slide Company changed its name to Kansas City Film Ad Company.

It was at Film Ad that Walt first learned how to animate and how animated films were made. Film Ad worked with cutout figures with moveable joints and used stop-action animation to create the illusion of movement. Walt found the mechanics of animation intriguing, and took it upon himself to learn as much about it as he could.

He began by going to the public library and seeking everything he could about animation. He was able to find a small book that had just been published in February 1920 and had recently arrived, describing the animation techniques being used by the leading New York cartoon studios, *Animated*

Cartoons: How They Are Made, Their Origin and Development, by Edwin G. Lutz. Walt was likely the first person in Kansas City to read the Lutz book, and through his own curiosity and initiative had become the foremost local expert in animation after less than two months on the job.

Walt was eager to try out for himself what he had learned about animation. He tried to convince Film Ad owner Cauger to make changes to his animation processes, encouraging the idea of doing hand-drawn animation to create more realistic movements instead of using cut-outs, but Cauger resisted. Walt formally reported to the manager of the art department, who was weary of Walt's enthusiasm for new and untried ideas, although he did welcome some incremental process improvements suggested by Walt.[4]

In early 1921, almost a year after joining Film Ad, a nineteen year-old Walt was still enthusiastic about experimenting with animation, and was able to convince Cauger to let him borrow one of their old, unused cameras so that he could experiment with the animation methods expounded by Lutz.

By this time Walt's father and mother had returned to Kansas City from Chicago and had taken up residence in the Disney family home, and Elias had built a garage. With the help and support of Roy, Walt turned the space into a small animation studio. Walt would return home from work and make his way to the garage studio where, as he put it later, he could experiment "with this other method, which is the method that was then being employed by the theatrical cartoonists."[5]

Walt's experiments to create animation from his own drawings proved to be a success. At once he could see the aesthetic improvement of hand-drawn animation over Film Ad's antiquated use of moving cutout figures, and immediately recognized the commercial opportunity this provided. If successful, Walt's ambitious experimentation could possibly put him in direct competition with his employer.

To test the viability of his idea, Walt wasted little time. He created a one-minute demonstration sample reel titled "Newman Laugh-O-grams." With his outgoing personality and entrepreneurial flair, Walt approached Milton Feld, the manager of the most prestigious movie theatre in town, Newman's Theater in downtown Kansas City, to show him what he had created and explore its appeal. Because Newman's was not a client of Film Ad, Walt felt comfortable that he was not competing directly with Cauger.

Walt's sales pitch to Feld was that he could produce a weekly series of Newman's Laugh-O-grams that could be shown in all four of Newman's Kansas City theatres. Each film would mix a humorous animated cartoon commentary of local current affairs with on-screen advertising promoting local business services to moviegoers. Walt was so nervous that when Feld asked what they would cost, Walt blurted out his own production cost of $60, neglecting to add in his profit.

In an interview almost thirty-five years later, Walt recalled their meeting:

> I was sitting behind him in the theatre, just the two of us. I was nervous as a cat, wondering what he would think of it, and when he whirled around and snapped, 'I like it. Is it expensive?' I blurted quickly, 'No, sir; I can make it for thirty cents a foot.' He said, 'It's a deal; I'll buy all you can make.' I went out walking on air, and it must have been an hour before I realized I had forgotten one small detail—the profit. Thirty cents a foot was exactly what it cost me to make it."[6]

It thus came to be that Walt Disney's first theatrical film was a Newman's Laugh-O-gram that was animated and produced entirely by nineteen-year-old Walt in his father's garage. The cartoon premiered at the ritzy 1,900 seat Newman's Theater in downtown Kansas City on March 20, 1921, as one segment included with a number of other newsreel segments.[7]

Walt continued to produce Newman's Laugh-O-grams single-handedly on an interim basis as quickly as he could, which turned out to be every few months rather than every week.[8]

Newman's Laugh-O-grams and a Taste of Entrepreneurship

It didn't take long for Walt to realize that working at Film Ad by day and animating at night was a problem for timely production. What he needed was assistance in completing the movies more quickly, but he had no money to pay wages. Operating on the premise that where there's a will, there's a way, Walt devised a creative solution. He placed a newspaper ad under the company name Kaycee Studios, in which he promised to teach animation to aspiring cartoonists in exchange for their work. To Walt's delight, the ad was answered by "two or three boys."[9]

A working system was developed to advance the speed at which Newman's Laugh-O-grams could be produced. Each evening Walt would sketch the drawings in a light-blue pencil that would not be captured when photographed on the film. In the morning he would leave a big pile of drawings for his apprentices to work on during the day in the garage of the Disney family home. Together, Walt and his helpers would draw, ink, and photograph the sketches to create the Laugh-O-grams.

The Newman's Laugh-O-grams never became a source of profit for Walt, but they were a success in their own small way. By developing and selling the Laugh-O-gram idea to Newman's, Walt was able to create and manage a small business in his spare time, although it was really more like a hobby given that he wasn't making any money from them.

Walt looked at the whole affair as an educational experiment, and derived value from learning and practicing the fundamentals of animation, apart from any monetary reward. In addition, having his movies shown at the most prestigious movie house in town brought attention his way, and made Walt a bit of a local hotshot and celebrity to his friends and acquaintances.

The Newman's Laugh-O-grams were also a calling card that allowed him to begin to connect to other community business owners and leaders as a young up-and-coming man with ambition and the ability to organize people and tasks to get things done. Even Walt's boss, A.V. Cauger at Film Ad, proudly introduced Walt to his clients as the Laugh-O-gram artist, and his minor celebrity status at the studio may have contributed to Walt receiving a raise in salary from fifty to sixty dollars a week.

Around this time, Walt's brother Herbert, a U.S. postal worker, requested and received a transfer to Portland, Oregon, leaving Kansas City in July 1921. His parents and sister Ruth followed in November 1921, selling the family home and causing Walt to abandon his garage animation studio. Roy had left in October 1920 after being diagnosed with tuberculosis and sent by the Veteran's Administration to Santa Fe, New Mexico, eventually making his way to warmer weather near Los Angeles. Walt stayed in Kansas City with his friends and job, as the only remaining member of the immediate family.[10]

Walt's initial success in animation along with the encouragement of others gave him the confidence to expand his horizons. As a young man just starting out in his career, he was beginning to realize that his talent, skill, and ideas were valuable enough to earn a living for himself while pursuing his own ambitions.

Walt envisioned that he would soon be running his own studio. He contemplated quitting his job at Film Ad, but his father advised against it, predicting that it could never succeed and would inevitably lead to bankruptcy. Walt rejected his father's pessimism in favor of his own optimism, convinced and determined that things would be otherwise.

Always ambitious and curious to find new challenges and better ways to do things, Walt began to think about how he could build on his current achievement in setting his next goal. Up until this point, the Newman's Laugh-O-grams were only one to two minutes in length.

On the heels of his success, Walt was convinced that he could make a longer animated cartoon of the quality he was seeing in movie theatres produced by the best New York City animation studios. He set for himself the goal of creating a six- to seven-minute film to illustrate a narrative story line as his next challenge. At the same time, he wanted to continue creating Newman's Laugh-O-grams. Walt's problem was that between his Film Ad job and his commitment to Newman's, he didn't have any additional time to devote to this task.

Shortly after his parents sold their house and moved to Oregon, thereby cutting off Walt's access to his garage studio, Walt decided that it was now time to take a chance in business and in life. Demonstrating his confidence and boldness, Walt invested $300 of savings from his work at Film Ad to purchase his own professional quality movie camera and tripod, He quit his job at Film Ad, rented office space in the Kansas City business district as Kaycee Studios, and began devoting his full attention to becoming a cartoon film producer.[11]

After a short time, Walt began losing interest in the solitary and tedious act of repetitive drawing that animation required. He was impatient for results and felt that it would take him too long to create a fully animated cartoon of six to seven minutes on his own. Walt realized that dividing up the tasks and delegating them to helpers was a more productive and effective way to achieve results; but to do so, he would first need more helpers.

Spending less time animating would also allow Walt to lead from the front as a business manager and producer responsible for directing the business, rather than as a technician wedded to his desk with a narrower focus on animating a story scene or action sequence. Walt was a solutions-oriented problem-solver who had a good way with people, and was more comfortable leading others along *his* chosen path than he was at conforming to precedents and adhering to preferences decided by others *on* his behalf.

Around February of 1922, Walt placed an ad in the local newspapers with an offer to teach aspiring cartoonists the art of animation. At this point Walt had personal experience with animation but was neither an expert in animation nor in movie making. He did, however, trust his own judgment about how to get things done, and was one step ahead of everybody else in Kansas City when it came to animation. If there were other aspiring local cartoonists and filmmakers seeking a leader and local celebrity to inspire and teach them, Walt was their man. It wasn't long before several young men started stopping by Walt's Kaycee studio in the evenings to join in the drawing and be part of the fraternity, including aspiring artists Hugh Harman and Rudolf Ising.[12] Together they worked with Walt on his various film projects.

Walt decided that for his new series of longer narrative films, he would try his hand at creating spoofs of traditional children's stories modeled after the very popular Aesop's Fables cartoons. It took months for Walt and his team of aspiring unpaid animators to create their first silent black and white cartoon version of *Little Red Riding Hood* (the innovation of color film and recorded sound in movies were still many years off). Walt was very impressed with the finished result, which was completed in the spring of 1922, and quickly began a second story, *The Four Musicians of Bremen*.[13]

While Walt posed as a successful young businessman with dreams of grandeur who kept himself busy making films, he was now also without a steady income not only to pay for his business expenses, but also to pay for his own rent and groceries. He quickly depleted his savings and his debts were mounting. It didn't take long before a process server was tracking him down to issue a summons to appear in court to have his debts adjudicated before a judge. Rudy Ising recalled, "Walt and I and a couple of the guys were still working for practically nothing for a long time."[14] When Ising learned about the extent of Walt's financial troubles, he chose to help by lending him $500 from money he had saved up over three or four years of working.[15]

In what was to become the start of a recurring theme in his career, Walt didn't look upon a lack of money as a barrier to carrying on with his endeavors. Rather, he looked for ways to improve the situation at hand through creative problem solving. For Walt, money was a means to an end, as was productive work. He didn't measure work by what it cost; he measured work by what it achieved.

Walt's business challenge was how to put cost and achievement together to produce something of commercial value.

---

1. Gabler, *Walt Disney*, 41.

2. Barrier, *The Animated Man*, 24, quoting what Walt said in 1956.

3. Barrier, *The Animated Man*, 25.

4. Barrier, *The Animated Man*, 7.

5. Barrier, *The Animated Man*, 28, quoting Walt from 1956.

6. Jackson, *Walt Disney: Conversations*, 50, "The Amazing Secret of Walt Disney," Don Eddy, 1955, From *The American Magazine*, Vol. 160, August 1955, 29, 110-115. Also in Timothy S. Susanin, *Walt Before Mickey: Disney's Early Years, 1919-1928*, 9; Barrier, *The Animated Man*, 29.

7. Barrier, *The Animated Man*, 29.

8. Merritt & Kaufman, *Walt in Wonderland*, 38; Gabler, *Walt Disney*, 57.

9. Barrier, *The Animated Man*, 29. According to Gabler, Rudolph Ising was one of the boys, but Barrier says they didn't meet until later.

10. Barrier, *The Animated Man*, 30, 39.

11. Barrier, *The Animated Man*, 31.

12. Barrier, "Walt Disney's Errors and Ambiguities," http://www.michael-barrier.com/Commentary/Gabler/GablerErrata.htm, see note for page 58, accessed July 19, 2016.

13. Susanin, *Walt Before Mickey*, 31.

14. Ising quoted in Merritt & Kaufman, *Walt in Wonderland*, 40.

15. Merritt & Kaufman, *Walt in Wonderland*, 40.

CHAPTER THREE

Laugh-O-gram Films, Inc., 1922–1923, and the Challenges of Corporate Leadership

Having quit his job at Film Ad to become an independent film producer, Walt sought and found a solution for how to carry on in business without immediate revenue.

In order to keep moving forward, Walt decided that he would create a new company—Laugh-O-gram Films—and incorporate. He may have been encouraged to do so by enthusiastic friends and supporters who looked favorably upon Walt's films and entrepreneurial character traits as a unique investment opportunity. He most assuredly leveraged his local reputation as the creator of Newman's Laugh-O-grams to his advantage, and likely used the completed *Little Red Riding Hood* as part of his sales pitch to potential investors. In an interview in 1932, Elias Disney, Walt's father, stated, "The neighbors urged Walter to form an independent company, which he did."[1]

Walt was able to organize affairs and garner enough interest and support from local merchants and friends to raise about $2,700 in cash. According to Ising, who had earlier lent money to Walt, he was a good salesman; good enough to convince Ising "that rather than pay me back, he'd give me stock in the corporation. And he talked me into it."[2]

Disney historian Michael Barrier, author of *The Animated Man*, provides his assessment of Walt at this point in his burgeoning career:

> Disney was becoming a filmmaker and entrepreneur. ... He had created a business even though he had limited experience and financial capital, trusting the strength of his desire for independence to make up for those shortcomings. That any investor should have been attracted to the new venture may seem surprising, but Disney had already enjoyed modest success as a filmmaker, thanks to the Newman Laugh-O-grams, and he had shown by making *Little Red Riding Hood* that he could produce a longer film as presentable as many of the short cartoons being made in the East. Add to that record the

young Disney's enthusiasm and self-confidence, and investors could reasonably conclude that the risks attending a small investment in Laugh-O-gram Films were acceptable.[3]

Laugh-O-grams Films, Inc. was incorporated on May 23, 1922, and was capitalized at $15,000, with 300 shares of stock at a par value of $50 each. At the time of incorporation, reports Barrier in *The Animated Man*, "51 percent of the stock issue was subscribed, giving the company assets of $7,700. Only $2,700 was in cash, though, with the remaining $5,000 in physical assets."[4] The assets included the not-yet-completed *Four Musicians of Bremen* but not *Little Red Riding Hood*, three experimental short animated films Walt called *Lafflets*, plus office furniture and equipment from Walt's Kaycee Studios, including his camera, stand, lights, and other photographic accessories.[5] Walt, at age 20, was president of the company and its largest shareholder with 70 shares. Ising received 8 shares of Laugh-O-gram stock one month after incorporation, representing $400 of his earlier $500 loan to Walt.

With the bank account seemingly flush with cash and optimism all-around for future success based on a series of incomplete modern fairy-tale cartoons, Walt began to staff up his operation by hiring local talent through newspaper ads, many of whom would eventually follow Walt to Hollywood in a few years.[6] As with start-ups of today, youthful optimism, exuberance, camaraderie, and a sense of mission and adventure carried the day.

"The Laugh-O-gram office was an exhilarating place to work," writes Disney biographer Bob Thomas in *Walt Disney: An American Original*. "The president of the company was twenty years old, and he declined to act the role of executive. He did some of the animation, operated the camera, washed the celluloid sheets—'cels'—for reuse. Many of his employees were still in their teens, and they shared his zest for the cartoon medium, often working past midnight. They were unconcerned when they received only half of their salaries on weeks when the company treasury was low."[7]

The Four Musicians of Bremen was completed in the summer of 1922, and was followed by *Jack and the Beanstalk*. Everyone was enthusiastically working hard and applying themselves fully to any task that needed to be done. The films were packed with gags and story ideas, and the backgrounds were minutely detailed with a full-range of gray tones. No effort was spared. Authors Russell Merritt and J.B. Kaufman note in *Walt in Wonderland: The Silent Films of Walt Disney* that while employees were given titles when they were hired, "the division of labor was highly informal. All of them were learning a new craft and a new business together, by trial and error, and whatever needed doing was done without regard to strict job classifications."[8]

As work to complete the cartoons proceeded according to plan, the company was still without any revenues to support its efforts. The operating capital in the bank was dwindling week by week.

With two installments now complete, Laugh-O-gram Films received some trade press in June 1922, and in July placed its first trade advertisement in *Motion Picture News*, promising a series of twelve cartoons and seeking buyers.[9] When the ad failed to draw any serious inquiries, Walt decided that he needed to send the company salesman, Leslie Mace, to New York City for a month in late August to find a theatrical distributor for the films and secure a contract.

Despite the high quality product that Walt and his studio team had created, Mace was unable to convince a single East Coast distributor to buy the films. Meanwhile, without any offsetting revenues, the New York City hotel bills and living expenses were taking their toll on the company's financial situation and consuming the last of the money in the bank.

Mace's time in New York was running out and he was feeling increasingly desperate to land a deal. The fate of the company depended on it. Finally, on September 16, 1922, Mace signed a contract with the Tennessee branch of a group called Pictorial Clubs, Inc., to deliver six Laugh-O-grams. Pictorial Clubs was a non-theatrical film distributor that provided films exclusively to schools and churches. It wasn't what Mace was seeking, but it was the only offer that he had, so he took it.

Merritt and Kaufman in *Walt in Wonderland* describe what happened next:

> The Laugh-O-gram forces were clearly desperate by this time, and Pictorial Clubs must have appeared a savior. But the resulting agreement reinforces the impression of naïve youngsters being conned by city slickers, for the contract was outrageous. The agreed-upon price seemed fair enough: $11,000 for six films, or $1850 apiece. But only $100 of that amount was specified as a down payment. Pictorial Clubs was not required to pay the balance until 1 January 1924, 15 months later! This lengthy interval with no prospect of income would have been a crippling setback, even if the contract had been followed to the letter—but as it happened, the Tennessee branch of Pictorial Clubs went out of business shortly after the contract was signed. The New York branch acquired the assets of the Tennessee branch (including the Laugh-O-grams, all of which had been delivered by then), but was not obligated for any of its liabilities. In short, Disney and company were swindled, and their contract with Pictorial Clubs became a death grip that virtually guaranteed Laugh-O-gram's demise.[10]

With the signing on of Pictorial Clubs, Walt now had his first major studio contract, but when Mace returned to Kansas City, Walt immediately understood that the deal was a potential disaster. In addition to his obligation to fulfill the contractual terms and deliver the six films, Walt now also faced the challenge of generating immediate cash flow by some alternate means to cover operating expenses including staff salaries, and to fund future operations long enough to receive payment from Pictorial Clubs. Laugh-O-gram Films was already under severe financial pressure, with the situation quickly deteriorating.

Salesman Mace quit shortly after returning from New York, perhaps feeling some pressure due to his perceived lack of business judgment. At the time he was owed $511 in back pay, which he received through a loan made to Laugh-O-gram Films by local surgeon and Laugh-O-gram treasurer and benefactor, Dr. John V. Cowles. Others were also owed back pay.[11]

Disney biographer Timothy Susanin writes in *Walt Before Mickey* that in October 1922, as Walt and his staff worked on finishing up the remaining films for Pictorial Clubs, employee Red Lyon wrote a letter to his mother in which he informed her that the company was "turning out some real pictures," but was "worse than broke" being "about two thousand dollars in the hole and going in for about four hundred more each week. ... We have the business in sight and orders to put this place over, but we lack the ready cash. ... I am going to try and sell my stock, loan the money to the company [and] possibly quit and get me something more sure."[12]

Walt was never one to fear hard work and bold action—in fact, that would become his usual response when facing a crisis—and he quickly set himself to the task of figuring a way forward.

The first thing Walt did was redouble his efforts to complete the balance of the six films. The first four Laugh-O-grams—*Little Red Riding Hood*, *Jack and the Beanstalk*, *The Four Musicians of Bremen*, and *Goldie Locks and the Three Bears*—had been completed by the time Mace returned from New York.[13]

Even though Walt didn't acquire movie-house distribution for his Laugh-O-grams and didn't have to concern himself with movie-audience acceptance per se, nonetheless he previewed each of his films locally at the Isis Theater with musician and composer Carl Stalling providing the musical accompaniment on the pipe organ.[14] By doing so, Walt and his young staff were able to enjoy the thrill of watching their creative work on the silver screen, observe the audience reaction, and gather valuable direct feedback on what was successful and what wasn't.

And while the financial prospects of the company were moving in the wrong direction, the enthusiasm and pride of accomplishment felt by Walt and his associates remained high. The working atmosphere in the office wasn't one of doom and gloom, but rather one of opportunity and youthful adventure. Walt and his staff continued to press forward with an appetite to learn and improve.

Through Nadine Simpson, whom Walt would hire as a bookkeeper and office assistant for $25 a week, the studio was able to acquire cartoon reels that had been discarded by the film exchange and were destined for the city dump because of excessive wear. This was extremely valuable to Walt and his animators, allowing them to carefully study the timing and action of cycles and chases in Paul Terry's Aesop's Fables cartoons and other leading popular releases. By doing so they were able to learn the most advanced animation techniques of the leading New York animation studios, experiment with them, and incorporate these more advanced techniques into their own productions.[15]

In a desperate effort to do something that might generate cash quickly, Walt looked to his assets for leverage, and, in particular, his movie camera. As one tactic to diversify, Walt announced the expansion of the company's offerings to include the filming of children and family events. The offering included three private screenings in the family's home because home movie equipment didn't exist at the time. Walt found a few customers to create a small amount of revenue, but even if the idea had been more successful, it could never have been enough to sustain the studio payroll.[16]

Walt also returned to the idea at the root of the short Laugh-O-gram reels he produced for Newman's Theaters when he was operating under the Kaycee Studios banner, revitalizing something called Lafflets. According to Ising, Lafflets were "a joke reel about timely local topics of the day" such as a decision by the Kansas City Police Department to have "horse police" or the Shriners coming to town.[17] They were often simplified and experimental animation, including clay modeling and matchstick animation. Walt hoped Lafflets could be something fun to be inserted into pre-feature newsreels to entertain movie house audiences and turned into a revenue-generating vehicle to fund the studio until final payment was received from Pictorial Clubs.

In November 1922, Walt hired Elitha Reynolds to assist as an inker and painter and speed up the production process of his last few Pictorial Clubs productions, and also to find and develop ideas for the Lafflets. He also hired his former business partner Ub Iwerks at a salary of $50 per week. Hearing the good news of the Pictorial Clubs deal in September convinced Iwerks that Laugh-O-gram was on solid ground and its future would be good.[18]

Around the same time Iwerks was hired, Walt was able to extend the life of the corporation by again securing a loan from Laugh-O-gram treasurer Dr. Cowles, this time for the much larger amount of $2,500. The loan was used to pay salaries owing and past-due bills, and was to be paid back with interest in 90 days. With no immediately identifiable source of revenues, Walt must have been banking on the future success of the Lafflets.[19] Even with this influx of borrowed cash, after paying his bills the studio was still broke, as was Walt.

Walt was fully committed to his investors and the work of keeping his company viable. If others had to go without their weekly paychecks, then

Walt was doing the same, leading by example. With no salary, Walt was forced to live off the generosity of others. This included his brother Roy who would occasionally send him small amounts of money from the disability allowance he received while recovering from tuberculosis contracted when serving in the navy in World War I. Walt was also humble enough to accept handouts and good-will gestures of friends and acquaintances.

Walt was about to learn firsthand and at an early age the special challenges and difficulties of managing and leading a business capitalized by outside investors. The weight of responsibility and fiduciary obligation feels much heavier and burdensome when accountability for success of the overall business rests on one's own shoulders. As a salaried employee, one's obligations are much more limited to doing the work assigned to the best of one's ability. Successfully managing a business as a profit-generating system is to assume a much higher order of problem-solving capability and management of complexity than taking on responsibility for any narrower element of that system as part of one's salaried role. This was something Walt didn't have to give much thought to in his previous employment at Film Ad and with his home-based entrepreneurial endeavors.

To generate the revenue needed to pay his staff, landlord, and suppliers, and keep the business operational to protect the financial interests of investors who put their faith in his abilities, Walt needed new ideas that he could implement quickly.

Toward the end of 1922, a live-action movie opportunity came Walt's way that resulted in the creation of an instructional film explaining the concepts of proper dental-care principles. Dr. Thomas B. McCrum, a dentist affiliated with the Kansas City Dental Institute, approached Walt to discuss the cost of making an animated film to help children learn to properly care for their teeth. Walt said he would do it for $500. A short time later, Walt received a phone call from Dr. McCrum and the good news that he was able to raise the money and was looking forward to meeting Walt right away to strike the deal. As Walt's daughter, Diane Disney Miller, tells the story in *The Story of Walt Disney*, Walt responded:

> "I can't. I haven't any shoes." Walt's shoes were falling apart, so he left them at the shoemaker's shop, and Walt didn't have $1.50 to pay for the repair. "'I'll be right over,' Dr. McCrum said. He paid the shoemaker, took Father back to his office, and together they worked out an agreement to make the film he had in mind. It was called *Tommy Tucker's Tooth*."[20]

The film combined live action with animation, and provided Walt with some early experience directing children in a live-action setting. The studio's profit on the venture amounted to just fifty dollars.[21] Walt would return to the idea of producing entertaining educational films twenty years later.

By the end of 1922, Laugh-O-gram Films had run out of cash and had to stop paying its employees. Walt carried on in his role as the unshakable entrepreneur, providing leadership and motivation to the remaining staff as the corporation he led continued to take on debt. The work was still fun and filled with potential, and many of his friends were receiving support from their families. Movie making was creative, glamorous, and romantic. And there was still the exciting prospect of receiving the large payment from Pictorial Clubs owed to Laugh-O-gram on January 1, 1924, for the hard work and effort that had been invested into the creation of the six Laugh-O-grams, if they could keep the company going.

Reflecting on those times, the people who were part of it looked back with fond memories. "We used to eat, drink and sleep cartoons," said Walt Pfeiffer, often arriving at the office at 9 a.m. and working until midnight.

The staff was "completely enthused with animation," recalled Rudy Ising.[22] Ising remembers Walt starting an art class for his staff to improve their drawing abilities: "Walt thought that we should all have more of a training in art and he got the idea of having a night class once a week, a life class. ... It didn't last too long."[23]

"We sure had a lot of fun," said Carman Maxwell. Adolph Kloepper remembered the "happy spirit that existed" through the creativity of stories and development of gags. And Walt Disney, recalled Kloepper, was "always full of fire and energy."[24]

Walt and his team were able to successfully complete the remaining Laugh-O-grams, *Puss in Boots* and *Cinderella*, before the end of the year and deliver them to Pictorial Clubs to fulfill his side of the contractual obligation. (The studio may also have produced a seventh Laugh-O-gram, *Jack, the Giant Killer*, which may have been sent as the sixth film, rather than *Little Red Riding Hood*, which was never listed as an asset of Laugh-O-gram Films upon incorporation.[25])

Unaware that Pictorial Clubs was not going to fulfill its obligations, Walt's primary task now was to sustain the business for one more year to complete the terms of the contract and receive payment.

Desperation and Corporate Restructuring

If Walt had any hopes that *Tommy Tucker's Tooth* was a good omen for his company as it headed into 1923, they were quickly dashed. The first week of January saw Walt being sued by his landlord for $384 in back rent. The courts ruled against Walt, who again had to rely on the generosity of company treasurer Dr. Cowles to pay the judgment plus interest and court costs. Dr. Cowles and his wife were very supportive of Walt in these tough times, and were known to bring sandwiches for the staff in the evenings, and even let Walt live with them for a short time when he had no place else to stay.

The company also owed money to its employees, who were Walt's friends. Many, if not most of the staff had been working for weeks without pay, and were now quitting. Those who lived on their own no longer had money to buy food. The owners of a small restaurant in the building that housed the Laugh-O-gram Film offices cut off Walt's credit when his bill exceeded $60. But when they later discovered Walt eating picnic leftovers of beans and bread, they invited him back for something to eat. Walt's assistant, Nadine Simpson, recalled how another struggling photographer with whom Walt was acquainted would "buy a can of pork and beans—they would cost 10 cents then—and a loaf of bread for 5 cents and he would share it with Walt. And that was about the only meal they had all day."[26]

Roy Disney's girlfriend and future wife, Edna, would also provide help to Walt on occasion. "Walt used to come out to our house," she recalled. "He was having a kind of struggle, financially, and when he'd get hungry he'd come over. We'd feed him a good meal and he'd talk until almost midnight about cartoon pictures, mostly, and things he wanted to do."[27]

It is unclear as to when Walt learned about the demise of the Tennessee branch of Pictorial Clubs, but it was likely somewhere in January or February of 1923 based on the recollection of Nadine Simpson that when Walt discovered that the Pictorial contract was "worthless," Dr. Cowles refused to lend any more money to support the business.[28] It remains unclear whether Walt knew at the time that the New York branch of Pictorial Clubs would refuse to honor the Tennessee branch's debt obligations, and there is some evidence that Walt and the board of directors still expected to be paid.

As the president of Laugh-O-gram, Walt remained committed to finding new ideas and coordinating the work of the remaining staff along a profitable path when it all must have seemed hopeless. Not one to give up, he continued to assume responsibility for finding additional financing to keep the business going with the hope of earning back the investors' money. As debts piled up, this task became more difficult. Investors want to fund future success, not past debts. Nonetheless, Walt was able to acquire some additional investment in February 1923 by way of a chattel mortgage against some of the company's hard assets, including the camera equipment, to a successful local hardware store owner named John Fredrick Schmeltz. The $506.86 mortgage was signed by president Walt Disney and secretary A. H. Kloepper without the authority of the board of directors, and was to be repaid within six months at six percent interest.[29]

In March 1923, with Laugh-O-gram Films on the edge of bankruptcy, a stockholders meeting was held to recapitalize the corporation. Walt was made chairman and Rudy Ising became secretary. The capital stock was raised from $15,000 to $50,000, based on a reassessment of the corporation's assets, with 1,000 shares worth $50 each to be issued. Walt and Dr. Cowles were the largest owners with 350 shares each. "Services rendered" by Walt valued at $1,000 was recognized, which likely consisted of some or all of his back pay which Walt had foregone in his efforts to keep the company solvent.[30]

That same month, after having corresponded with at least three distributors,[31] a Lafflets sample reel was prepared and shipped out to Universal and other New York movie studios to pitch the idea, and while they liked what they saw, they weren't interested in acquiring the distribution rights.

With the ideas of family films and Lafflets failing to find a market, Walt finally hit on a new idea with which he was genuinely enthusiastic.

Living in *Alice's Wonderland*

After some experimentation in the preparation of Lafflets, Walt had discovered that he was able to combine live action with cartoons, and do so in such a way as to have the live actor enter the cartoon world. This was a reversal of a popular series at the time called *Out of the Inkwell*, which featured cartoon characters interacting with the real world.

Walt decided to go all out by putting everything he had on the line to make this new and innovative idea work. He moved forward with his usual confidence, finding a way to side step the economic barriers that would have hindered most other entrepreneurs. In Walt's mind, the idea of combining live action and animation by inserting a little girl into a cartoon fantasy world was ripe with possibilities. He envisioned creating a product with national appeal rather than the parochial appeal of family photography and local editorial page newsreel events.

The creation of a new series of films out of nothing, to be named *Alice's Wonderland*, had raised Walt's sights, and he became fully engaged in the enthusiastic pursuit of a finished product of sufficient quality to land a distribution deal with a leading movie house distributor or film studio.

Walt began scouting for a young child to play the role of Alice, and came across a local Kansas City four-year-old child model and performer named Virginia Davis, having seen her in an on-screen ad in a movie theatre.[32]

Walt contacted her parents, described his plans, and in April 1923 signed a contract through Laugh-O-gram Films for Virginia to play the role of Alice, guaranteeing the Davis' five percent of Laugh-O-grams' receipts from *Alice's Wonderland*.

"Aware that this film might be his last chance," write Merritt and Kaufman in *Walt in Wonderland*,

> Disney plunged into it in an all-or-nothing gamble. No resource of his studio was spared. An elaborate script was prepared, flaunting the most stunning trick effects the artists could devise. Some of

Alice's dream scenes were so intricate that they could be achieved only by making still photographs of the little girl, and "animating" them alongside the drawings. Other scenes featured such embellishments as a live-action cat harassed by an animated mouse with a sword. The finished film showed clearly the effort that had gone into it; if the fairy-tale cartoons had been lavish, *Alice's Wonderland* was downright extravagant.[33]

At the same time, due to the corporation's ongoing inability to make payroll, staff attrition continued. Aletha Reynolds quit in April having accumulated $200 in back pay owing to her. Nadine Simpson quit at the start of May, with $75 being owed to her. Ub Iwerks quit a few days later being owed $1,003 in unpaid salary, and was rehired by Film Ad. Ising was owed in excess of $500, and the company was almost $500 behind in its rent.

On the personal front, Walt was no longer able to afford the three-dollar rent for his apartment, and was evicted. To save money, he moved into the studio and slept on a sofa chair. Once a week he would pay ten cents to take a bath at the Union Station train depot, which included soap and use of a towel. Walt Disney, president of Laugh-O-gram Films, Inc., and struggling entrepreneur, was living the lifestyle of a pre-depression-era hobo, while at the same time, awaking each morning to enthusiastically pursue his dreams and ambitions.

A small break came Walt's way when Carl Stalling, the musical director at the Isis Theater, approached Walt to produce a "follow-the-bouncing-ball" type sing-along movie through an agreement with a Kansas City music publisher. Only one film was made, from which Walt made a bit of money, and the project was quickly abandoned.[34]

Walt began work on the new Alice's Wonderland project. Because the film was silent, he was able to provide instructions and direct Virginia Davis during filming.[35] Davis later recalled that Walt would tell her stories and she would act them out. "All the work was done in pantomime. He'd say 'A bear is chasing you!' or 'Look sad—you've just been hit over the head!' He'd tell me these things and I'd react." The scenes in which Alice would appear in Cartoonland would then be animated around the live-action footage.[36]

As the film progressed, Walt prepared and sent letters to the major cartoon distributors in New York to inform them of his venture and solicit their interest. "We have just discovered something new and clever in animated cartoons!" he wrote in an excited tone, hoping to appeal to their sense of curiosity. He was offering "a new idea that will appeal to all classes, and is bound to be a winner, because it is a clever combination of live characters and cartoons, not like *Out of the Inkwell*...." Walt indicated he would be "using a cast of live child actors who carry on their action on cartoon scenes with cartoon characters."[37]

To help distributors appreciate the quality of the work being offered, they were directed to "get in touch with Mr. W.R. Kelley, of Pictorial Clubs ... as he will gladly screen several of our [Laugh-O-gram fairy-tale] subjects for you. We will not try to tell you any more about this new idea; instead we will send you a print upon the completion of the first one, if you so desire."[38] Implied here is that the relationship between Laugh-O-gram Films and Pictorial Clubs was still intact.

In very short order, Walt received a single reply, from Margaret J. Winkler, a well-known and respectable distributor of two of the most popular cartoon series at the time, *Felix the Cat* and *Out of the Inkwell*. Winkler had a reputation for taking a personal interest in her properties to ensure their success through aggressive promotion and publicity. Gaining the interest of Winkler was a good sign, and Walt energetically nourished the relationship as best he could through mail correspondence.

Walt was eager to complete *Alice's Wonderland*, but was faced with the challenge of trying to balance the need to produce a top-quality product that was good enough to land a highly prized Winkler contract, with a race against his depleting assets.

By now Walt was almost certainly expecting further deterioration in the corporation's financial position despite his general optimism and strong outward appearance. In mid-May 1923, the landlord locked the Laugh-O-gram Film offices with their film equipment inside, barring access until the past-due rent was paid.

With nowhere to turn for additional capital, Walt again appealed to hardware store owner Schmeltz for help. Schmeltz refused to lend any more money without the loan being secured with the remaining Laugh-O-gram assets, including an assignment of the Pictorial Films contract. Seeing no other way to complete *Alice's Wonderland* and perhaps seeing this as his best and final chance to succeed in the animation business and save Laugh-O-gram Films, Walt acquiesced, but not without getting back something of importance to him in return. In addition to acquiring the money to pay the rent owing and rent new space to complete *Alice's Wonderland*, Walt secured the back pay of Nadine Simpson and former secretary Adolph "Jack" Kloepper, as well as the $2,500 loaned by Dr. Cowles the previous November to extend Laugh-O-gram's solvency.

By the end of June 1923, all of Laugh-O-gram's equipment and the Pictorial Clubs contract were committed through chattel mortgages to Schmeltz.[39]

With just over a month having elapsed since Margaret Winkler's expression of interest in seeing Walt's new cartoons, Walt was finally in a position to respond: "Owing to the numerous delays and backsets [setbacks] we have encountered in moving into our new studio, we will not be able to complete the first picture of our new series by the time we expected. However, it will be finished very soon, and the writer expects to be in New York about the first of July with a print of same, and an outline of our future program...."[40]

The letter was warmly received by Winkler who wrote back expressing an interest in meeting with Walt and inquiring as to when she could see a sample reel. Unfortunately for Walt, *Alice's Wonderland* wasn't yet completed and Walt lacked the money to travel to New York anyway, so the meeting didn't take place.

Also in June, Rudy Ising left, with back pay of $711 owing, as did Carman Maxwell, who was owed just over $200.

In the first week of July 1923, Jack Kloepper quit, and immediately sued the company for $499 in back salary. Schmeltz once again paid the July rent. The studio was collapsing and it looked like Alice would not be completed. Walt had hoped that with the interest of Winkler, a contract for a series of Alice movies could save the company, but that hopeful aspiration was now gone. According to Hugh Harman, Walt's optimism had faded, and he had become "really disconsolate...just completely dejected."[41] Walt felt that he was letting down everyone who worked so hard, and especially the investors who believed in him and supported his ambition to produce successful films, including, said Harman, "Doc Cowles...[and] Schmeltz... and quite a few others."[42]

Through sheer determination and perhaps a final effort to demonstrate his commitment, integrity, and appreciation to Dr. Cowles and John Schmeltz, *Alice's Wonderland* was finally completed in July 1923 through the hard work of Hugh Harman and Walt, who continued working to complete it after the others had left. Harman and Walt were able to carry on through the generosity of Harman's father who would send Harman money that was used in part to support and feed Walt.[43]

Even this personal victory of completing the film came with adversity. Because of the hot summer weather, the emulsion on the film began to run, ruining the negative, and some scenes had to be re-filmed. When they first saw the spotted negative, said Harman, "it nearly killed us."[44] It's a testament to Walt Disney and Hugh Harman's tenacity and perseverance that the twelve-minute and twenty-five second film was completed at all, at a time when Walt's Kansas City world was disintegrating around him. Perhaps it provided a cathartic outlet, a positive distraction, and a final achievable goal to bring closure for Walt to the Laugh-O-gram Films chapter.

With all Walt had done as the now twenty-two-year-old president and chairman of Laugh-O-gram Films, he had now run out of time, and all hope for saving the company was gone. There was too much debt and no real prospect of being able to finance a complete series of Alice pictures, in spite of Winker's continued expression of interest. Having done his best to make something out of nothing and to sustain the company through the fairy-tale Laugh-O-grams, Lafflets, and the innovative *Alice's Wonderland*, there was nothing more that Walt could do to prevent an inevitable bankruptcy.

Kansas City Exit: Nothing More To Do

Walt had spent the past two-and-a-half years doing everything he could think of to build upon the small personal success of his Newman's Laugh-O-grams. Disney historian Timothy Susanin, in his book *Walt Before Mickey*, summarizes this busy and trying time for Walt:

> He attempted to parlay that first success into a series. A short time later, he started his first movie studio. At Kaycee Studios, he attempted to sell the *Kansas City Journal* on a film companion series, animate *The Little Artist*, market his and Fred Harman's Film Ad experience to local move theaters, use aerial filming to break into the news footage business, jumpstart his animation portfolio with the *Lafflets* series, and, with Red's [Lyon] and Rudy's help, animate modern versions of the fairy tales *Little Red Riding Hood* and *The Four Musicians of Bremen*.
>
> Later, at Laugh-O-gram, he sought to build a thriving business by selling a series of animated fairy tales, marketing home movies of children, producing an educational film, revising and remarketing the *Lafflet* series, experimenting with a mix of live action and animation through the proposed Alice series, producing a Song-O-Reel, and trying to again entice a local daily newspaper into a joint newsreel series. At one point, Walt even tried to sell a mail-order course on animation. After all these efforts, he now realized that there were no more avenues open to him—his efforts to make it as a film producer in Kansas City had failed.[45]

Walt wrote to his brother Roy in California to explain his situation, and Roy wrote back: "Kid, I think you should get out of there. I don't think you can do any more for it."[46] Roy encouraged Walt to move to Los Angeles, where Roy was recuperating from tuberculosis in a veterans' hospital, and where he could better keep watch over Walt's best interests.

Walt was offered a job in Kansas City, but he no longer had any reason to stay. He was the only member of his immediate family remaining in Missouri. He seriously considered moving to New York to pursue his career as an animator but concluded, "I had missed the boat. I had got in [to the animated cartoon field] too late."[47]

Instead, Walt followed his brother Roy's advice, settling on moving to Hollywood, the movie capital of the world, where he could stay for a while with his father's brother, Uncle Robert, and pursue a career as a film director. Walt began planning his departure.

The same month Walt completed *Alice's Wonderland*, July 1923, he went knocking door-to-door seeking customers interested in a film of their baby as a way to earn travel money.

Before he left, Walt had the foresight to make a print of *Alice's Wonderland* and obtain permission from his creditors, who owned the rights to the movie, to use it as a sample reel to sell the prospect of a series of Alice films. Surely he had Margaret Winkler in mind. He also put in a good word for Hugh Harman and Rudy Ising at Film Ad where Harman, but not Ising, was hired.

As Walt made preparations to leave Kansas City, notes author Neal Gabler in his book *Walt Disney: The Triumph of the American Imagination*, "he visited the people to whom he owed money, telling them he had resolved to go west and offering small partial payments. He gave most of his personal belongings to the Harman brothers with the directive they be sold and the proceeds distributed to his creditors, including Jerry Raggos [the restaurant owner who extended $60 in credit to Walt that Walt could not repay]. ... The other creditors, according to Walt, wished him well, told him he would need a grubstake for California, and graciously said he could send the money when he succeeded."[48]

Walt said goodbye to his friends and associates and prepared to leave town. He did not file a claim against the company for his back salary.[49]

Toward the end of July 1923, Walt packed what little belongings he had into a frayed cardboard suitcase, dressed himself in a borrowed suit, carried three bagged meals that his brother Herbert's mother-in-law prepared for his train ride, bought a first-class train ticket to Los Angeles, and was on his way, "just free and happy," and "with that wonderful audacity of youth," Walt later recalled.[50]

The one other thing Walt carried with him on that train ride from Missouri to California was a burning ambition to make it big in Hollywood.

As a postscript, in October 1923 bankruptcy proceedings against Laugh-O-gram Films commenced. By this time, the Tennessee branch of Pictorial Clubs had ceased operations, and the New York branch had acquired its assets, including the six Laugh-O-grams. The New York branch claimed it had no obligation to pay the debts accrued by the Tennessee branch. Only after three-and-a-half years of aggressive legal action were the Laugh-O-gram mortgage holders able to collect some of what was owed to them from Pictorial Clubs.

1. Susanin, *Walt Before Mickey*, 34.
2. Merritt & Kaufman, *Walt in Wonderland*, 40.

3. Barrier, *The Animated Man*, 32.

4. Barrier, *The Animated Man*, 32.

5. Susanin, *Walt Before Mickey*, 34–35.

6. Barrier, *The Animated Man*, 31.

7. Thomas, *Walt Disney*, 62.

8. Merritt & Kaufman, *Walt in Wonderland*, 44.

9. Barrier, *The Animated Man*, 32.

10. Merritt & Kaufman, *Walt in Wonderland*, 46.

11. Susanin, *Walt Before Mickey*, 51.

12. Susanin, *Walt Before Mickey*, 51; Barrier, *The Animated Man*, 34.

13. Susanin, *Walt Before Mickey*, 54.

14. Susanin, *Walt Before Mickey*, 65.

15. Barrier, *The Animated Man*, 33; Susanin, *Walt Before Mickey*, 34.

16. Barrier, *The Animated Man*, 34; Susanin, *Walt Before Mickey*, 51–52.

17. Susanin, *Walt Before Mickey*, 30.

18. Susanin, *Walt Before Mickey*, 53; Barrier, *The Animated Man*, 34.

19. Susanin, *Walt Before Mickey*, 55.

20. Diane Disney Miller, *The Story of Walt Disney*, 71-72.

21. Susanin, *Walt Before Mickey*, 57.

22. Ising quoted in Susanin, *Walt Before Mickey*, 48, 49.

23. Ising quoted in Ghez, *Walt's People, Vol. 1*, 55.

24. Susanin, *Walt Before Mickey*, 48, 49.

25. Susanin, *Walt Before Mickey*, 54.

26. Nadine Simpson quoted in Susanin, *Walt Before Mickey*, 59.

27. Edna Disney quoted in Susanin, *Walt Before Mickey*, 60.

28. Susanin, *Walt Before Mickey*, 61.

29. Susanin, *Walt Before Mickey*, 61.

30. Susanin, *Walt Before Mickey*, 63.

31. Susanin, *Walt Before Mickey*, 61.

32. Susanin, *Walt Before Mickey*, 64.

33. Merritt & Kaufman, *Walt in Wonderland*, 49.

34. Susanin, *Walt Before Mickey*, 65.

35. Susanin, *Walt Before Mickey*, 64.

36. Susanin, *Walt Before Mickey*, 64.

37. Thomas, *Walt Disney*, 65.

38. Susanin, *Walt Before Mickey*, 67.

39. Susanin, *Walt Before Mickey*, 61.

40. Thomas, *Walt Disney*, 66; Susanin, *Walt Before Mickey*, 69.

41. Susanin, *Walt Before Mickey*, 72.

42. Susanin, *Walt Before Mickey*, 72.

43. Susanin, *Walt Before Disney*, 70.

44. Susanin, *Walt Before Disney*, 70

45. Susanin, *Walt Before Mickey*, 72-73.

46. Thomas, *Walt Disney*, 66.

47. Susanin, 73, Walt quoted from "Showman of the World Speaks" Speech, see Jim Korkis, "Walt in His Own Words," jimhillmedia.com/alumni1/b/wade_sampson/archive/2005/04/06/1256.aspx, accessed July 20, 2016.

48. Gabler, *Walt Disney*, 74.

49. Susanin, *Walt Before Mickey*, 99.

50. Susanin, *Walt Before Mickey*, 74.

CHAPTER FOUR

Hollywood Dreaming: Building the Disney Brothers Studio

When Walt arrived in Hollywood, recalled Roy, he was "skinny as a rail from his harrowing experience in Kansas City where he spent everything on the shop and not on himself. He looked like the devil. I remember he had a hacking cough, and I used to tell him, 'For Christ's sake, now don't you get TB!'"[1]

Walt took up temporary residence at his uncle Robert's house paying rent of $5 a week. He had decided that he was done with cartoons. "I was fed up with cartoons," he said, looking back in 1961. "I was discouraged and everything. My ambition at that time was to be a director."[2] Walt felt he had his chance to succeed at cartoons and had failed. It was time to move on.

Looking at the bigger picture, Walt concluded that he wasn't in the cartoon business; he was in the movie business. His area of expertise just happened to be animation. And he wasn't just a cartoonist; he also had experience as a live-action director. If Walt couldn't be successful in animation, he would instead turn his attention to becoming a Hollywood director or writer.

As soon as he was settled, Walt sought employment at the major film studios in Los Angeles. Ready to prove his worth, he was willing to take any studio job as a way to get started. Once in, he would figure out a career path. "It was hard to get jobs then at studios," Walt recalled. "I wanted anything. .... That was my feeling. Get in. Not choose, but get in. Be a part of it and then move up. I've always had that feeling about things. It upsets me so much when people want to get into something but they're too darn choosy about what they do. What the hell, sweep the floor. I don't care, you know what I mean? ... I went from one studio to another and I went to the personnel departments and it was pretty cold."[3]

The weeks passed and Walt still wasn't working. Roy recalled, years later, that if Walt had wanted a job he could have had one, though perhaps not at a movie studio. Said Roy, "He could have got a job, I'm sure, but he didn't want a job. He'd get into Universal, for example, on the strength of applying for a job, and then when he'd get out of the office, he'd just hang around the studio lot all day, watching sets and what was going on and so on. MGM was another favorite spot where he could work that gag."[4]

Walt wasn't just looking for a job. The time he spent observing on studio lots provided an invaluable first-hand education into how a professional film studio works, which he would later put to good use.

To get into the studios, Walt had ordered business cards proclaiming that he was the Kansas City representative of Universal and Selznick Newsreels, which he self-assuredly presented to the studio receptionists while declaring that he wanted a pass to the studio. Once allowed in, Walt would carefully wander around the sets for hours watching movies being made. He would make his way to the employment office, cite his Kansas City experience, and inquire about work as a director.[5]

"For two months," said Walt, "I tramped from one studio to another, trying to sell myself as a writer, a director, a day laborer—anything to get through those magic gates of big-time show business. But nobody bought."[6]

Playing the role of some star-struck Hollywood dreamer and having no source of income, Walt soon ran out of money and had to borrow from Roy to pay his $5 weekly rent.

With Uncle Robert pressing the happy-go-lucky Walt to find work, Roy encouraged Walt to reconsider a return to animation. Walt resisted. "I'm too late," he told Roy. "I should have started six years ago. I don't know how I can top those New York boys now."[7]

Nevertheless, without any prospects in the movie-making capital of the world, Roy's prudent advice caused Walt to again consider animation. With nobody doing animation in Los Angeles, Walt saw that there was an opportunity to break into the movie business with cartoons. "Things looked pretty black at that time," Walt recalled. "I couldn't get a job, so I went into business for myself,"[8] and "[b]efore I knew it, I was back with my cartoons."[9]

Recalling his Newman's Laugh-O-gram joke reels, Walt headed to the downtown Los Angeles offices of vaudeville and movie theatre owner Alexander Pantages where he was able to secure a meeting with Pantages himself. To Walt's surprise and delight, Pantages expressed his interest in Walt's idea "to create a joke reel for his theatres on the order of 'topics of the day'" with "the name of Pantages splashed all over it, to add prestige and keep the name Pantages before his theatre patrons," recalled Walt.[10] Before Pantages would buy, however, he first wanted to see a sample.

Walt now found himself back in animation, with a potential prominent customer who owned a string of west coast movie theatres. With Uncle Robert's permission, he once again found himself setting up a garage-based animation studio. To speed up the production cycle from what he was able to achieve back in Kansas City, Walt simplified the animation process by using stick figures against simple backgrounds. The comedy was derived through the telling of jokes using word bubbles over the characters' heads rather than the more labor-intensive and time-consuming creation of gags through the animation of character action.

Around this same time, Walt started flogging the *Alice's Wonderland* pilot he had brought from Kansas City to L.A.-based film distributors, but found no takers. "I tried to sell [Alice] in Hollywood without any luck," he said. "With the print of that cartoon under my arm, I tramped the streets of Hollywood for several weeks, trying to interest someone in my picture. I couldn't make a sale."[11] Walt did receive some advice, however. The distributers felt he would have better luck finding a buyer in New York.

This was hardly encouraging news. Walt didn't have money to go to New York. Instead, he took the initiative to seek out and mail his Alice sample reel to a New York film agent. That way, if someone showed an interest, the agent could be instructed to deliver the reel for a showing.

Next Walt created official-looking stationary with "Walt Disney, Cartoonist" printed on it and the inclusion of Uncle Robert's Hollywood address, and once again sent letters out to New York cartoon distributors.

With a garage as a movie studio but no secured work, no money, and no friends to lean on other than Roy, Walt wrote a very creative letter that put a positive spin around the Laugh-O-gram Films bankruptcy, and mailed it to Margaret Winkler, the New York distributor who had already expressed an interest, with the hope of ensuring a positive and enthusiastic response. He may have seen this letter as his final opportunity and last remaining lifeline to create something positive out of his work in Kansas City, and perhaps engineer a happy ending for his Laugh-O-gram colleagues and the friends he left behind.

On August 25, 1923, Walt wrote:

Dear Miss Winkler:

This is to inform you that I am no longer connected with the Laugh-O-Gram Films, Inc., of Kansas City, Mo., and that I am establishing a studio in Los Angeles for the purpose of producing the new and novel series of cartoons I have previously written you about.

The making of these new cartoons necessitates being located in a production center that I may engage trained talent for my casts, and be within reach of the right facilities for producing.

I am taking with me a select number of my former staff and will in a very short time be producing at regular intervals. It is my intention of securing working space with one of the studios, that I may better study technical detail and comedy situations and combine these with my cartoons.

In the past all cartoons combining live actors have been produced in an amateur manner with cartoonists doing the acting, photographing, etc. It is my intention to employ only trained and experienced people for my casts and staff that I may inject quality, humor, photography and detail into these comedies.

The first picture of this new idea [*Alice's Wonderland*] which I have just completed was made in Kansas City under big difficulties owing to lack of necessary equipment and experienced talent.

I would appreciate an interview with your representative here that I may screen several comedies and explain my new idea.[12]

On Friday, September 7, Winkler wrote back to Walt that she currently was handling two of the most popular theatrical cartoons of the time, Pat Sullivan's *Felix the Cat* and Max Fleischer's *Out of the Inkwell*, and indicated that she could only handle one more, but it had to be of equally high standards. Having set up the challenge, Winkler wrote: "If your comedies are what you say they are and what I think they should be, we can do business. If you can spare a couple of them long enough to send me so that I can screen them and can see just what they are, please do so at once. It is necessary for me to have this information without delay so that I can lay my plans properly for immediate and next year's contracts."[13]

Walt immediately dispatched his New York agent to arrange a screening for Winkler.

In the meantime, Walt found working in the garage not to his liking, and sought more conventional office space to rent, paying $10 a month for enough space "to swing a cat" in the rear of a real estate office.[14] He also wrote to his friend, Kansas City theatre musician Carl Stalling, inviting him to assist in bootstrapping his new venture, which resulted in a loan from Stalling to Walt of $75.[15]

Walt had settled into his new studio space and began to work on a prototype joke reel for Alexander Pantages, when on Monday, October 15, 1923, a telegram from Margaret Winkler was delivered to Uncle Robert's house.

When Walt arrived home that night, five months after he first contacted Winkler from Kansas City and just over two years from the signing of his prior ill-fated distribution deal with Pictorial Films, he read Winkler's telegram.

"BELIEVE SERIES CAN BE PUT OVER," she wrote, providing that the quality of the photography was improved. Because the series was new, and theatre owners needed to be convinced to accept the film for exhibition, money would have to be spent on "exploitation and advertising" which would require Walt's cooperation. Thus, with regards to financial terms, Winkler wrote: "WILL PAY FIFTEEN HUNDRED EACH NEGATIVE FOR FIRST SIX AND TO SHOW MY GOOD FAITH WILL PAY FULL AMOUNT ON EACH OF THESE SIX IMMEDIATELY ON DELIVERY OF NEGATIVE...."[16]

After years of hard work, Walt's luck was changing. Attracting a New York distributor for his "new and clever" Alice series was something that he had been coveting since he first wrote to New York distributors back in May. Had it happened months sooner, he would have been able to save Laugh-O-gram Films from its demise.

Walt immediately wired Winkler his acceptance of her offer. He then hopped on a bus and headed out to the hospital at which Roy was staying, gained unauthorized access, and woke Roy with the great news. Roy's recollection was that Walt "found his way to my bed.... It was eleven or twelve o'clock at night, and he shaked me awake and showed me a telegram of acceptance of his offers. He said, 'What can I do now? Can you come out of here and help me to get this started?'"[17]

Walt recalled sitting on Roy's bed unable to contain his excitement: "We're in! It's a deal. Golly! Fifteen hundred smackers a reel," he said. "For how many?" asked Roy. Twelve, replied Walt. "Let's go, Roy!" With Walt pleading for his help, Roy paused to slow Walt down, not wanting to act only on Walt's impulse: "But can we do it?" he asked Walt. Roy had been receiving a government stipend of $85 a month, some of which he had been giving to Walt to help support him while he made the sample reel for Pantages.[18]

Roy was mostly concerned about the terms of the contract. He was well aware of Walt's proclivity not to pay enough attention to important business details. In the discussion that ensued, Roy was assured by Walt he could deliver the films on schedule, and that by Walt's calculations, each reel could be produced for $750, generating 100% profit.[19] Walt's reassurance that he and Roy could do it together, and Roy's desire to help see Walt through with this project that had caused Walt so much grief and meant so much to him, was enough to convince Roy to join forces with his almost nine-years-younger kid brother.

Roy was certainly motivated by his love and support for Walt, but, as is usually the case, his motives were far from altruistic. Roy was eager to get out of the hospital and marry Edna Francis, his long-time sweetheart who remained in Kansas City. But Roy felt his tuberculosis would prevent him from working a regular office job (he had been working as a bank teller previously), and couldn't see a way to leave the hospital and also find appropriate work to support a family. In its own way, Walt's hard work and good fortune serendipitously brought opportunity of a different sort to Roy.

Winkler's offer to Walt required delivery of six Alice cartoons for which Walt would be paid $1,500 each upon receipt, plus an option for a further six at $1,800 each. She stipulated that "Alice must be used in all subjects," and the first must be received by December 15, which was only eight weeks away. In his acceptance response to Winkler's offer, Walt pushed out the initial delivery date to January 1, 1924.

With no time to spare, Roy checked out of the hospital the next day, and he was never troubled by tuberculosis again. He and Walt were now in business together as equal partners, with Walt in charge of the artwork and creative side of the venture, and Roy as the business manager. Together they were focused on a single mission: establish an animation studio to produce and deliver twelve Alice shorts of a consistently high quality to match the standards of the leading New York cartoon studios, or risk losing the contract.

On Monday, October 15, 1923, Walt had received Winkler's telegram and entered into a business partnership with Roy. On Tuesday, said Walt, "I dropped the Pantages idea and went to work on the Alice Series."

Brothers, Partners, and a New Start

In many ways, Walt's life on Monday, October 15, 1923, was much simpler than life the following day.

When Walt awoke on Monday, he had the problem of being without an income and producing a simple animated joke reel for Pantages. When he awoke on Tuesday, his problem had grown immensely in scope and complexity. He was now responsible for having to produce an Alice cartoon from scratch with no animation help, no money to fund the production, and perhaps the greatest obstacle of all, no actress to play Alice. And if that wasn't enough of a challenge, he had until January 1, 1924—about ten weeks—to deliver a completed film equal in quality to the most beloved cartoons in the world. In addition, as Walt was well aware, he would have to carry most of the weight of responsibility himself, because at that time, according to Walt, "Roy didn't know anything about the motion picture business...."[20]

The work of filmmaking and building an organization capable of delivering a new Alice picture every four weeks would have to occur simultaneously.

As Walt and Roy set to work on their immediate problems, Margaret Winkler was preparing contracts in New York. Based on Walt's enthusiastic response, Winkler set the date of delivery for the first Alice as January 2, 1924, and enlarged the option to include twelve Alices in each of 1925 and 1926, bringing the contract potential to 36 movies. She also asked for photos and biographies of both him and Virginia Davis, who played Alice in the sample reel of *Alice's Wonderland*, on the assumption that it would be the same actress. Winkler wired Walt that the contract had been drafted and mailed, and offered up Harry M. Warner, a founder of Warner Bros. Studios, as a reference.[21] Winkler had previously worked for Warner, and it was Warner himself who years earlier had set Winkler up in the cartoon distribution business.

Brimming with excitement and enthusiasm, Walt and Roy began to put the foundational pieces in place. The first thing was to secure financing to allow them to invest in the initial production and hold them over until receipt of payment.

Winkler was being extremely generous and accommodating by agreeing up-front to provide payment upon receipt of each of the first six films, rather than waiting until they were sold to theatre owners as a check on quality and assurance of revenue. The time from receipt of the negative by the distributor until placement and theatrical release could be months. Without Winkler's offer to pay up-front, Walt and Roy would likely have had to find independent funding to support the studio's operating and production costs for at least six months until the first payment arrived.

Roy contributed $200 in savings as initial seed money, and then applied for bank loans but was repeatedly turned down due to excessive risk in movie making. Uncle Robert was the next prospect, and while it took some convincing on Roy's part, once production was underway Uncle Robert eventually loaned $500 to his nephews in installments at eight percent annual interest to support their new business enterprise. Roy deposited the first $200 on November 15, followed by another $150 two weeks later.[22]

For his part, Walt wasted no time trying to convince the parents of Virginia Davis that opportunity had knocked for their daughter's show business career, and that the Davis family should immediately leave Kansas City, Missouri, and move to Hollywood, California. Just two months earlier, in August, the Davis' had already taken Virginia to Hollywood looking for an entry into show business, but were unable to get an appointment at any of the studios, and were already planning for a second try in November. Walt's letter played on this desire, and he promised a one-year contract at $100 a month to cast Virginia in twelve pictures, with an option on additional services. As reported by Timothy Susanin in *Walt Before Mickey*, Walt wrote to Margaret Davis on Tuesday, October 16, 1923:

> I have at last succeeded in arranging for distribution of a series of "Alice" productions—twelve in all—with a very reliable distributor in New York.
>
> I screened "Alice's Wonderland" several times in Hollywood and every one seemed to think that Virginia was real cute and thought she had wonderful possibilities—and I was wondering if you would arrange to come out here so I could star her in this series. It would be a big opportunity for her and would introduce her to the profession in a manner that few children could receive....
>
> [I]f Virginia was used in the series it would be the making of her...so you see the big possibilities that await Virginia....
>
> If you desire to come out and let me star Virginia in this series it will be necessary that you answer immediately as in all probability

I will have to start production within fifteen or twenty days so I will know wheather [sic] or not I will use Virginia or have to get a little girl here in Hollywood. If you decide to come answer immediately so I can count on you. I will want a year[']s contract with option on further services at a very reasonable salary.... [M.J. Winkler] demands that who ever I star in the series must be under contract to me for a series of twelve pictures with option on further services...therefore you understand the necessity of a contract. However if Virginia can secure other work between pictures she can do so without any complications and I believe I can secure her work myself—In all probability I will do most of my shooting in one of the studios near here—I am dickering with several[.][23]

By the end of their first full day in business together, the Disney Brothers Studio was in operation and had hired their first employee, sixteen year-old Kathleen Dollard, to ink and paint cels of Walt's animation.

Having been burned in his previous Laugh-O-gram Films distribution deal with Pictorial Clubs, this time Walt was more cautious. That weekend he wrote to Harry Warner to check on Winkler's credentials. A few days later he received a positive response and some unsolicited advice from one of the giants of the Hollywood movie scene:

Miss M.J. Winker was my secretary for a number of years, and since she has gone into business for herself, she has done very well, and I believe she is responsible for anything she may undertake.

In my opinion, the main thing you should consider is the quality of goods you are going to give her, and if that is right, I don't think you need have any hesitancy in having her handle your merchandise.[24]

Harry Warner's letter plus some additional inquiries, and the fact that she was already distributing some very successful cartoons, satisfied Walt that Winkler was reputable. By this time Walt had received Winkler's contract, and the day after receiving Warner's endorsement, Wednesday, October 24, he signed and returned it.

Walt then wrote to Margaret Davis again, informing her that the distribution contract had been signed, that everything was in order to proceed, and that he awaited her acceptance of his offer, which he had increased by providing a graduated raise of $25 every two months until it leveled off at $200 per month until the end of the first series. Walt set November 15 as the start date, hoping that Virginia Davis would be available by then. That weekend, the Davis family finalized their decision to move to Hollywood, and on Sunday, October 28, Margaret Davis wired Walt with their decision, and soon after made the move to California.[25]

Within just a few days, in early November, work on the *first* Disney Brother's Studio film, *Alice's Day at Sea*, began. Walt and Roy shared the work, with Walt doing the writing, directing, and animating, and Roy operating the camera to film the live-action segments. Walt was required to create hundreds of drawings a day, which he did both in the rented office space and when he returned home to an apartment the brothers were now renting near the studio. According to Walt, "Roy did the cooking while I drew as late as possible every night."[26]

The number one priority for Walt and Roy was now the completion and delivery of *Alice's Day at Sea* according to the terms of the contract. Eating well and sleeping comfortably were treated as luxuries. Within a few weeks of taking an apartment together, the brothers found a way to save money by renting and sharing a single room in a boardinghouse, with no cooking facilities. Walt recalled that "we took just a sleeping room and got our meals at a cheap cafeteria to save time. We worked out a system in that cafeteria. Roy and I always went in together. One would get a meat order, the other a vegetable. When we reached our table we would divide up." While the food was "dreary," most importantly it was inexpensive, and was often the only meal the brothers would eat in a day.[27] Occasionally, they would splurge for an ice cream.

Establishing the Disney Brothers Studio

In late November, Margaret Winkler was wed to Charles B. Mintz, who soon began to exert more influence over M. J. Winkler's business operations. Margaret's brother George Winkler was both the office manager and the West Coast production supervisor overseeing Winkler's interest in Walt's Alice series production. From this point forward, Walt's business dealings with M.J. Winkler Productions would be mostly though Charles Mintz and George Winkler.

With Walt working full out and pressure mounting to complete the picture on time, the brothers hired their second employee, Ann Loomis, as a part-time inker and painter. Uncle Robert provided his last two loan installments of $75 each to the boys by mid-December. To raise additional debt capital, they reached out to everyone they knew who might be willing to lend to them. They borrowed $200 from Carl Stalling, $200 from Margaret Davis, $50 from the husband of Walt's aunt, $25 dollars from Roy's girl friend Edna Francis (whom Walt approached in spite of Roy telling him not to), and most significantly, $2,500 from their parents, who took out a mortgage on their house to help, and which Roy made sure they paid back as quickly as possible.[28]

Walt successfully completed and shipped *Alice's Day at Sea* to Winkler on December 15, 1923, two weeks ahead of his January 1, 1924, deadline. Work on the next production in the Alice Comedies series, *Alice Hunting in*

Africa, began immediately. With Winkler having agreed to pay upon delivery for each of the first six films, the sooner they could be satisfactorily completed, the sooner payment would be received.

On December 26, 1923, Margaret Winkler received *Alice's Day at Sea* and immediately wired the agreed-upon $1,500 fee to the Disneys, along with a letter suggesting future improvements. It was a momentous occasion in Walt's life and an affirmation of his creativity and tenacity. Roy later recalled that when the money had arrived at their bank, "We thought we were rich."[29] They had spent $750 on the film, just as Walt had predicted, leaving a $750 profit.[30] To celebrate, they headed out to a restaurant where each brother ordered his own meat dish.

In January 1924, 22-year-old Walt hired his third inker and painter, Lillian Bounds, for $15 a week. The two would fall in love and be married the following year. Production of *Alice Hunting in Africa* was completed and sent to Winkler, and payment was again promptly received. Uncle Robert's loan was repaid in full with interest.

As the year progressed, Walt's costs increased as he made improvements to the quality of his pictures, including larger live-action casts, and Margaret Winkler continued to provide improvement advice. Virginia Davis recalled that Walt and Roy were efficient in their work to ensure they met their tight production deadlines. "They worked very, very hard. They were the whole studio crew—set makers, carpenters, cameramen, writers, and directors. Money shortages dictated that all live-action shots be completed in one take."[31]

Walt was very supportive and motivating to his actors. He would provide specific directorial instructions, often acting out exactly what he was looking for in the performance: "They didn't have enough film for more than one take," recalled Davis. "It had to be right the first time. Walt was always very pleased that I could do what he told me to do in that first take."[32]

For the most part, Walt completed the first six Alice cartoons on his own, although he had help on some of these when, in February 1924, while working on the third movie, *Alice's Spooky Adventure*, he hired an animation assistant, Rollin "Ham" Hamilton, to lend a hand.

With each production, Walt was determined to improve the audience response to his movies. To gauge this, he made arrangements with local theatres to run previews. Upon shipping *Alice's Spooky Adventure*, he wrote to Margaret Winkler, "I am trying to comply with your instructions by injecting as much humor as possible and I believe I have done better on this production. I have had professional critics at all pre-views and have been informed that we are making big improvements on each one. ... It is my intention to be a little different from the usual run of slap stick and hold them more to a dignified line of comedy."[33]

By the end of February, Walt and Roy had proven to themselves that they were capable of managing the production schedule. There were now six employees including Walt and Roy, but plans were in the works to hire more. It was important to Walt that the studio be its own distinct entity, so they moved out of the rear of the real estate office and rented storefront space nearby and a separate garage for a total of $42 per month. "Disney Bros. Studio" was painted prominently and proudly on the front window.

Walt had sent the first three installments of the Alice Comedies to Margaret Winkler, but it wasn't until March 1, 1924, that the first one, *Alice's Day at Sea*, was finally released to theatres. The industry trade paper *Motion Picture News* wrote that the cartoon was a "novel idea...very unique and entertaining enough to satisfy any sort of audience."[34]

Winkler was extremely pleased with how things were progressing and with Walt's desire to continue to improve each picture. As quality improved and she could trust Walt to deliver what he promised, she was more confident in seeking wider distribution. On March 4, Winkler wrote to Walt:

> [A]llow me to compliment you on "Alice's Spooky Adventure." As long as you have reached that standard please try your utmost to maintain it and if possible go a little bit further. ... I will be frank with you and say that I have been waiting for just such a picture... before using every effort to place it in all the territories throughout the world. ... I am very optimistic about the future and believe that we have something here of which we will all be proud....[35]

Alice's Spooky Adventure was followed by *Alice's Wild West Show*. Winkler was very happy with the continuity in quality. The series was starting to gain wider attention and was receiving positive reviews in the most prestigious industry trade papers. *Moving Picture World* was particularly complimentary, writing:

> In this reel...produced by Walter Disney and distributed on the state right market by M. J. Winkler, clever use is made of photography and cartoon work in combination. There is considerable novelty in which this is handled, the photographed characters and cartoon characters working together against a cartoon background; there are also a number of scenes in which straight camera work is employed. A pretty and talented little tot, Alice, is the feature player, and she will make a hit with almost any audience."[36]

Motion Picture News wrote that "Walt Disney, the cartoonist, produced a novel combination of an actual acting cast and cartoons in this single reeler and it is highly amusing and wholly entertaining."[37]

Walt was acutely aware of his limitations as an animator. To achieve the higher standards he was striving for, he needed the help of others with more talent than himself to fill specialized roles. The only animators he knew were his former associates back in Kansas City. He had kept in touch with them since his move to California and soon began recruiting. Ub Iwerks was his top priority.

In May 1924, Ub wrote to Walt to let him know that he had decided to head west to join him. Walt was thrilled to hear it and wrote back: "I can give you a job—as artist-cartoonist and etc. with the Disney Productions. Most of the work would be cartooning. Answer at once and let me know when you want to start and I will write more details."[38]

Work at the Disney Brothers Studio had settled into a routine, and things seemed to be going well. The production process had been established, and six movies had been successfully completed running on a four-week schedule, with Walt doing all or most of the story development, directing, and animating. Margaret Winkler and her husband Charles Mintz were on their way to California on a business trip and would meet with the Disneys. Walt was thinking that with Ub on board, and perhaps also his other former Laugh-O-gram animators from Kansas City to work with him, he might be able to double his output by operating to a twice-monthly schedule instead of a single film. Scaling up would allow him to double his revenues and profits and, of the utmost importance to Walt, give him the means to try new and better things.

Learning to Manage Business Growth

Since moving to California, Walt kept in touch with his former colleagues, Hugh Harman, Rudy Ising, and Carman "Max" Maxwell, who remained in Kansas City trying to follow Walt's path by establishing their own animation studio called Arabian Nights Cartoons.

As Walt had done when working on his Newman's Laugh-O-grams, they would get together in the evenings to work on a pilot for their own animated series. They had even gone so far as to contact Margaret Winkler to introduce themselves, to which she responded favorably. When Walt learned of this, he wrote to Winkler on May 9, 1924, to vouch for them: "I would like to say a word or two for them, as they are three very clever, clean-cut, young fellows and I would like very much to have them out here with me."[39]

Winkler and Mintz arrived in California and met with Walt and Roy in early June, and seemed to be impressed with Walt and his small studio. Walt excitedly reported on the meetings in a letter to Ub Iwerks: "We have been making arrangements with them for the future. We are trying in every way to improve our picture as intend[ed] to make them the most popular single reel on the film market. ... They are well satisfied with our stuff and are figuring on taking them twice a month, instead of once a month."[40]

Walt also indicated to Ub that he had spoken to Margaret Winkler about Harman, Ising, and Maxwell—the Arabian Nights—and was eager to pass on some advice to promote their success. "They seemed interested," wrote Walt, "and said if they had the right pep and humor they might talk business. So tell the boys to forget unnecessary detail and cram it full of ridiculous and impossible comedy. It[']s what they like. We've had to learn that by degree and at the present are doing everything impossible in the[m] that we can."[41] The Arabian Nights apparently failed to heed Walt's advice, for a film was eventually sent to Winkler, and by Harman's own assessment, while the animation was "advanced technically" it was "not very funny."[42]

The fifth and sixth Alice films, *Alice's Fishy Story* and *Alice and the Dog Catcher*, were completed in May 1924,[43] for which Walt received prompt payment when he delivered them to Winkler. Because of rising production and operating costs attributable to Walt's investment in quality, the cost of making the films had almost risen to the level of their selling price. This was putting a severe strain on the studio's ability to operate profitably.

To make matters worse, the terms of the original distribution agreement were such that after the sixth film, Walt would no longer be paid $1,500 upon delivery, but rather would receive $1,800 upon each subsequent film's *release*. For the seventh film, *Alice the Peacemaker*, the scheduled release date and payment wasn't until August. That left the studio with no revenue for months, the lag time between delivery of the completed film and its theatrical release. The inability of the studio to bank substantial profits on its last few films to fund its cash needs left it with a shortfall of working capital, a situation that is a classic problem for start-up and growth companies, and one that Walt and Roy hadn't adequately prepared for.

Meanwhile, Iwerks wrapped up his affairs in Kansas City and headed to California. He started work toward the end of July, earning the highest salary at the studio at $40 per week, which was $10 less than he had been earning at Film Ad. Walt also gave his animation assistant, "Ham" Hamilton, a 33% raise from $15 to $20 a week.

With the hiring of Iwerks to assume Walt's animation duties, at the age of 22 Walt brought his three-year career as an animator to an end. He recognized that drawing was not his strongest suit; that this wasn't his area of comparative advantage. "It reached a point," Walt noted in a 1959 interview, "that I had so many working with me, and there was so much time and attention demanded that I had to drop the drawing end of it myself. But I've never regretted it, because drawing was always a means to an end with me. And so through these other boys, who were good draftsmen and artists in many different phases of the business...very talented people—and coordinating their talents is what has built this business.

And if I hadn't dropped the drawing end of it myself, I don't think I'd have built this organization."[44]

In August, Charles Mintz, began to take a noticeably more active role managing M. J. Winkler Productions and leading the relationship between the two companies.

From Walt's perspective, the approach Charles Mintz took to managing the business was distinctly different from that of Margaret Winkler. Where Winkler and Walt were aligned in their ambitions to develop "the most popular single reel on the film market" and films "of which we will both be proud," Mintz was more inclined to trade off quality and pride for short-term bottom-line profits. This difference in business philosophy and approach regarding the best way to create economic value and enhance one's prospects for securing future business success would, over time, become an ongoing point of tension between the Disneys and Mintz. Mintz also brought a more antagonistic and brusque New York approach to business relationships that was at odds with the more congenial, polite, and gentlemanly Midwest approach that Walt respected and preferred.

In his autobiography *Talking Animals and Other People*, former Disney animator and industry veteran James "Shamus" Culhane recalled distributor Mintz's visits to the Krazy Kat Studio in New York in the late 1920s, where Culhane was working at that time, and provides his observations of Mintz:

> Mintz made infrequent visits to the studio. When he did, he made a slow inspection of the premises with [producers Ben] Harrison and [Manny] Gould following one step behind. A grim-faced man, with a pair of cold eyes glittering behind a pince-nez, Mintz never talked to the staff. He looked us over like an admiral surveying a row of stanchions."[45]

When the seventh installment, *Alice the Peacemaker*, was received by Mintz, he indicated he was satisfied with its quality and instructed Walt to "please see that all future subjects are up to at least the standard of this one."[46] He also chose to complain to Walt about the second Alice, *Alice Hunting in Africa*, which Winkler had received and accepted months prior. Mintz informed Walt via letter that it was losing money for the company and that "our people will positively not accept that subject." Mintz dispatched Margaret Winkler's brother, George, to Los Angeles to work with Walt to "fix up this subject" so that the film was in acceptable condition for distribution. Ensuring the acceptability of the film to exhibitors was just as important to Walt as to Winkler.[47]

By August 1924, just ten months after signing with Winkler, the Disney Brother's Studio was facing a cash crunch, in part because Mintz, pleading financial difficulties, began to delay payment and at times provide reduced payments of $900.[48] Walt and Roy were learning first-hand that the economics of the cartoon business was precarious. Their ability to remain in business was being squeezed by marketplace demands for high quality pictures, pressure from their distributor, competition from other studios, and Walt's over-exuberance to comply with every improvement opportunity. In desperation, Walt wrote Mintz to explain his predicament and to ask for more money, appealing to the business interests of both parties:

> We need money. .... We have been spending as much as you have been paying us for [the films] in order to improve and make them as good as possible, and now that we are receiving only $900.00, it puts us in a "ell of a 'ole." I am not kicking about that, however, I am perfectly willing to sacrifice a profit on this series, in order to put out something good, but I expect you to show your appreciation by helping us out. As you know, we haven't had the money to spend on them, we will have to skimp, and at this time, it would not be best to do that. So please, for our sake as well as your own, give this more consideration and instead of sending us $900.00, make it the full amount [$1,800] excepting a fair discount which will enable us to pull through this period.[49]

Mintz advanced the requested funds to the studio after confirming with George Winkler that the money was needed. He was also very complimentary of the quality of the new films Walt was turning out, and informed Walt that they continued to be received enthusiastically by audiences and movie theatre managers.[50] The money received was used to fund the studio or pay back money owed. The most important thing was to keep the operation running. Walt and Roy paid themselves the minimum they needed to get by.

Having survived the cash flow lag caused by the switch in payment from delivery to release dates, Walt was able to hire a third animator, Carl Thurston Harper, Jr., to assist Iwerks and Hamilton.[51] To help reduce costs, Walt believed that the live-action bookends on the Alice films that Mintz liked should be dropped to concentrate on cartoon gags and animation quality, which is what Walt said audiences really wanted. After about the fifth Alice, Walt began previewing each film at a local L.A. theatre to observe the audience reaction. Only then would he send it east to Winkler for final editing. As a test, he completed *Alice the Piper*, the tenth in the series, without the live-action opening and closing sections. By observing the audience reception and enjoyment of the cartoon, he concluded that the live action wasn't needed.

In a letter to Winkler in early November, Walt tried to argue his case that a trade-off of lower value for higher value could be made: less live action for higher quality animation. George Winkler had been to the preview screening and could vouch for Walt's position: "We have talked this over with George," Walt wrote to Mintz, "and believe that after you have talked it over with him, you will see the advantage of leaving out the gang of kids, because after all these are cartoon comedies and not kid comedies. ... There are not enough logical live-action openings and closings to go around and besides, the public would soon tire of them."[52] George Winkler went to bat for Walt and was able to convince Mintz to give it a go, as long as Walt made sure to follow through with great pictures. They had to be "100% good," George Winkler wrote to Walt, or "Lord help me!!"[53]

Toward the end of 1924, Ub Iwerks began to demonstrate his value as a technological innovator. Iwerks was well respected by everyone at the studio for his many talents. He was the studio's lead animator, drawer of backgrounds and promotional posters, letterer of all titles and subtitles, and the go-to person for the other animators when they needed training and advice. Iwerks also demonstrated his talent for developing innovative technological solutions by rigging up a motor drive to the studio's hand-cranked camera to improve the quality of photographing the animation. By pressing a telegraph key, Iwerks enabled the camera to trigger a single frame of exposure for animation. This eliminated the need for hand cranking, a key cause of camera shake, resulting in visibly improved quality of the exposures.

Walt wasted no time bringing this to the attention of Mintz to ensure that his distributor and "boss" recognized the advances Walt was making in creating and delivering a product of superior quality: "You will, no doubt, notice a great improvement in the cartoon photography. This is due to the fact that we have equipped our camera with a motor drive, which will give us A-1 photography throughout."[54]

As the year closed out, on December 31, 1924—New Year's Eve—Walt and Mintz signed a new contract for eighteen additional Alice Comedies at $1,800 each. Payment was to be made upon receipt of each film, at three-week intervals. Walt and Roy now started to pay themselves a salary of $50 per week. They also recognized the importance of Iwerks to the studio and the additional work required to produce six additional pictures, and raised his salary to $50 as well. Hamilton was also given a 50% raise from $20 to $30 per week in recognition of his contribution.[55]

Success and Ambition Bring New Challenges

In April 1925, significant and important additions were made in the staffing of the Disney Brothers Studio. Walt was able to entice his former colleagues from Kansas City—Hugh Harman, his younger brother Walker Harman, and Rudy Ising—to come to work with him. They arrived at the studio in June 1925. As Hugh Harman recalled, "Rudy and I decided that it would be a good thing to come [to California], and find out what the Hollywood scene was like, because we intended it anyway and we thought we'd work for Walt for a while, quit, and form our own company."[56]

With new staff on the way, Iwerks received another salary increase to $55 a week, making him the highest paid person at the studio. Hamilton's pay was increased to $35 a week.

It was easy for the new Kansas City imports to adapt, with Ising recalling that the setup was almost identical to what they were used to in Kansas City. They brought a wealth of animation studio experience with them that allowed them to immediately start working. Between them, they could animate, ink, and operate the camera. What they didn't bring, and what they lacked, was the creativity of story development and directing, which was Walt's specialty. Ising recalled that Walt "was the one who really sort of put the story together. ... He was always thinking and acting pictures."[57]

The unsuccessful Arabian Nights Cartoons Studio of Kansas City had effectively merged with the Disney Brothers Studio of Hollywood. Hugh Harman was hired at $45 a week, Rudy Ising at $35, and Walker Harman at $20. Soon thereafter, just before Walt's July 13 wedding to employee Lillian Bounds, Walt raised his own salary from $50 to $75, while Roy's remained at $50.

With the current street-front location running out of space, Walt and Roy agreed that a larger studio was needed to accommodate their growth in staff. They found a suitable piece of property on Hyperion Avenue, made a down payment, and began developing plans to build a new studio.

By mid 1925, Walt's methodology for developing stories hadn't changed very much from years earlier. They still began with story meetings to set the stage and develop gags, which Ising recalled were almost always at night and on weekends, usually at Walt's house or the apartment shared by Ising and the Harmans, and sometimes at the studio.[58]

Ising described a typical "gag" meeting:

> [W]e would sit in the office and would have story meetings, Walt, Ham, Hugh and me would all work over various gags. Walt would have an idea: let's let Alice be a fireman in this one...then we'd work up fire gags. ... [We'd] come up with an idea of continuity, and Walt would work that out, figure out about how long a scene should be and who was the animator. Or maybe one evening when we met at his house, or our apartment, we'd also talk a story gag over. There was no story department as such, or separate storymen. Eventually, as we started making more and more cartoons we had to have a story department. Walt used to make all the early story sketches, but then it got to where Ub was making them out, and then some of them, like Hugh, would make them.[59]

One of Walt's strengths was his ability to take the various gag ideas and connect them all together to tell a story. As quickly as ideas would come up, Walt recalled, they would have them animated. According to Hugh Harman, Walt rarely made changes to the animators' work.[60]

While Ising and Hugh Harman continued to do excellent work for Walt and apply their talents fully, they kept their ambitions to start their own studio in direct competition with Disney. Ising wrote in a letter to a friend in Kansas City two months after he starting working for Walt that "we think in a year we will be able to begin production on our own pictures with the experience and information we are gaining here...."[61]

The studio staff was working long hours, but they were also having a lot of fun together, playing tennis each morning at 6 a.m. and hanging out at each other's homes in evenings and on weekends. Ising described the situation as a "little closed group."[62]

The playfulness of the friends didn't affect their productivity, which had increased to the point where they were able to put out a new film every two weeks, one week faster than the three-week release to which Winkler was working. Walt was delivering his films faster than Mintz was expecting them, and he was now demanding faster payment, upon delivery as promised. Mintz found this completely unacceptable and thought Walt's demands were unreasonable and disrespectful. He responded forcefully:

> Don't you think it is about time for you to put on your brakes? We are supposed to get one picture from you which is satisfactory to us every three weeks. When we get your pictures we always send you a check....
>
> "Alice Chops the Suey" reached here Aug. 28th. You were sent your check. "Alice the Jail Bird" reached here Sept. 12th which is fourteen days after "Chops the Suey." This, as you know, is positively contrary to all our arrangements and we may as well tell you now rather than later that we cannot handle your pictures in that manner....
>
> If every one with whom you deal with will pay you as surely and as promptly as we do, take my word for it, your life will be one sweet song. There is nothing further that I have to say to you, excepting please use a little of the common sense which you displayed when I met you on the Coast last summer.[63]

Emboldened by his success, Walt refused to back off, electing to hold firm to his position. He responded to Mintz by registered mail, writing in part:

> The important point is that, according to the contract, we must make final delivery *not later than January 15, 1926*. However, there is positively nothing in the contract which prevents making final delivery before that date. ... I intend to continue shipping pictures to you as fast as completed, which is about every sixteen days. I will expect you to take them up as delivered and remit immediately. Your failure to do so will constitute a breach of contract and will force me to seek other distributors.[64]

Walt's aggressive stance was driven by the ongoing business need of the studio for working capital to fund its operations, a lack of discipline in managing the cost structure, and the refusal of bankers to lend the studio money. Walt and Roy provided a very sound business rationale for demanding quicker payment, having to do with ramping up production in preparation for the potential requirements of a contract renewal for 26 films over the year, which would entail deliveries every two weeks.

The dispute amounted to a timing and coordination problem between production and distribution, and an issue of who should carry the inventory costs. Walt explained his rationale to Mintz:

> Our contract calls for final delivery by January 15, 1926, with your option calling for twenty-six pictures the following year. I have built up my organization to where I can complete my deliveries on this contract by the specified time and be able to make deliveries of every two weeks, the following year, should you choose to exercise your option. With my present payroll, on a three-week schedule, I would absolutely be loosing (sic) money, and to cut down my force is out of the question. You well know, yourself, how hard it is to get men trained in this line of work. My artists are all experienced, capable men, difficult to replace at any salary. How can I afford the loss which a delayed schedule would mean?[65]

It's unclear how this issue was resolved in the short term, except that the Disney Brothers Studio continued to operate so it is likely that Mintz made some kind of advance, perhaps for $1,800, and by November, communications were much more cordial as Walt and Mintz entered into negotiations for a third series of Alice Comedies. Raises were again handed out to keep the staff motivated: Iwerks to $60 a week, and Hamilton and Ising to $40.

In the meantime, Mintz had entered into a deal with a national distributor, Film Booking Offices (FBO). Prior to this, Winkler Productions had operated its distribution business on a state-by-state basis. FBO had agreed to take fifty-two M. J. Winkler Productions contracted films in 1926, half of which would be Krazy Kat shorts. Mintz was hoping to fill the remaining obligation with Alice shorts if, according to Mintz, he and Walt could "get together on a good healthy basis" and Walt "not insist on too much."[66]

Negotiations started off friendly, but very quickly deteriorated as Walt continued to press for more beneficial terms. To the credit of Mintz, he was exceedingly transparent about the financial aspects of his deal with FBO to show that he was being fair and reasonable in his offer to the Disneys. After all, reaching a deal was to the mutual interests of both he and Walt.

Initially, Mintz offered Walt a seven-year contract. Mintz would take delivery of thirteen reels at three-week intervals followed by thirteen additional reels at two-week intervals. For each of the first thirteen, Mintz would pay $900 upon receipt plus $600 in sixty days. For the final thirteen, he would pay $900 upon receipt plus $600 in ninety days. Walt would receive fifty percent of the profits above $5,000.

After going back and forth by letter a number of times and still failing to come to an agreement, pressure was mounting on Mintz to come up with twenty-six more shorts to fulfill his agreement with distributor FBO. Walt and Roy were surely leveraging this to their advantage. According to Disney historian Timothy Susanin in *Walt Before Mickey*:

> On New Year's Eve, Charlie [Mintz] wrote Walt that he thought a new contract with Disney Brothers Studio was "a hopeless task" since he and Walt "wasted just about enough time, energy and money in trying to get together." Charlie threatened that if he and Walt could not "get together … this is my last letter to you, [and] I don't intend to argue any further." Walt's counter offer of $2,250 per reel was unworkable for Charlie because, if a reel earned $5,000, Walt's take of $2,250 plus overhead of $1,500, left only $1,250 for the Winkler company. Charlie would "positively not work along those lines."
>
> Charlie offered Walt two options: $1,500 per reel plus half of profits in excess of $3,000, or $1,750 per reel plus half of profits over $4,500. Charlie was running out of patience, and needed Walt's answer "very, very quickly … as soon as you receive this letter." Charlie was through arguing, and offered to release Walt from their contract if he had a better offer elsewhere. Charlie preferred not to do business with Walt if Walt had "a doubt in your mind as to my intentions[.]" Charlie pointed out that Walt's advances, and Charlie's delayed profits pay-out, meant that Charlie "must keep paying money and holding the bag for fourteen months, while you are happily working along getting your earnings as you finish your pictures. If you have not considered this angle of it you have been unfair."[67]

Walt may have left this offer unanswered, because a week later a new offer arrived: the delivery dates for the completed films remained as in the prior offer, but Winkler would pay $1,500 per reel for twenty-six Alices, providing $900 upon delivery and $600 in ninety days. Walt would receive $350 when profits reached $4,000 and then share equally in any additional profits.

Walt found these financial terms acceptable, but wanted three additional matters added to the agreement: 1) the right to inspect the Winkler books; 2) all pictures must be a minimum of 600 feet and all matters related to making the films left to Walt ("I agree to make each picture in a high class manner and of a standard equal to that of the series of 1925"); and that Walt share equally in any profits from "toys, novelties, newspaper strips, etc."[68]

Mintz was concerned about ensuring the requisite quality, having entered into an important national distribution agreement with FBO, and was nervous about leaving final say to Walt. He rejected Walt's proposition.

When Walt and Roy learned that this was unacceptable to Mintz, Walt sent a telegram notifying Mintz that "upon the delivery of the next subject the final one of the nineteen twenty five series I will consider all my contractual obligations fulfilled."[69]

Three weeks later, and five days after Walt delivered the final Alice of the 1925 series, *Alice's Mysterious Mystery*, Walt sent another counter offer to Mintz that varied in the profit-sharing, in which Walt would get $500 after the first $4,000 in profits, with the next $500 going to Winkler Productions, followed by a fifty-fifty split thereafter. Mintz accepted this offer, but pleaded with Walt to "please use special efforts on your first few subjects so that we can really call them knock-outs."[70] Winkler's new distribution deal would mean an expanded audience for the Disney films, including audiences in Europe. The final contracts were signed on March 30, 1926.

Walt delivered the last film of the 1925 series in February 1926, but FBO would not begin releasing the 1926 series until September. Mintz allowed Walt to begin deliveries in March, thereby ensuring that Disney Brothers Studios had at least some continuity of revenue to pay for production, while allowing M. J. Winkler Productions to build an inventory of future releases.[71] Nonetheless, as Merritt and Kaufman note in their book *Walt in Wonderland*, this transition from the 1925 series to the 1926 series once again created lean times for the Disneys. The financial pressure was severe enough to force Walt to seek outside projects to help fund the studio and keep his staff working, including some contracted animation projects and a second dental hygiene movie for Kansas City dentist Dr. McCrum, called *Clara Cleans Her Teeth*.

The Move from Disney Brothers to Walt Disney Productions

In February 1926, with a production break between contracts, Walt and Roy rented a truck and everyone at the studio helped to facilitate the move to the newly completed studio on Hyperion Avenue. Along with the move came a name change from Disney Brothers Studio to Walt Disney Productions.[72]

Walt's obsession for quality and being the recognized leader in the cartoon industry continued, even as the studio struggled financially. Having completed dozens of Alice cartoons, Walt continued to seek new opportunities to improve and deliver a better product to movie house audiences. When he received an unsolicited compliment from Mintz in the spring of 1926 for the quality of *Alice the Fire Fighter*, Walt replied: "I want to say right here that I will not be satisfied until I am able to make them all as good, or better. I am putting every effort toward this end and hope that in a very short time our average will be above them all. (Including Krazy Kat.)

I sincerely believe you are a well-qualified judge of what a good cartoon is and will expect you to give us your opinion, from time to time, as to what you think is best for the good of all."[73]

Walt closed the studio down for two weeks' vacation in September 1926. With Walt's approval, Hugh Harman and Rudy Ising, along with Ub Iwerks and "Ham" Hamilton, tried their hand again at developing an Arabian Nights cartoon titled *Aladdin's Vamp*. As with their earlier attempts in Kansas City, they were unable to interest any distributors. Nonetheless, it demonstrates the continued desire of Ising and Harman to break away from Walt to start their own studio. What Walt didn't know was that they were hoping to take Walt's star animator and studio handyman, Ub Iwerks, with them had their venture been a success. Harman and Ising wrote to Carman "Max" Maxwell in Kansas City that when they finally start their own studio, it "will leave Walt in a mellava hess but business is business."[74]

As Winkler's distributor FBO began to release the Alice movies in September, additional funds again began to flow into the studio coffers, and Walt once again provided raises to his staff. Walt continued to earn $75 per week and Roy $50, but he raised Ub's salary to $70 from $60, and Hugh Harman's to $60. The disparity of salaries between the creative talent of the animators and the important but more mundane and repetitive tasks of those who inked and painted cels continued to grow. Walt hired a new cel painter around this time at $18 a week.[75]

As Walt and Roy continued to raise salaries to acknowledge and reward the good work of their key people, they continued to keep their own salaries in check, thereby investing in the future rather than starving the needs of the business for their own short-term gain. Nonetheless, Walt's ability or willingness to keep costs under control to drive up profits was noticeably absent. Margins in 1926 fell from a high of $300 per short to as little as $100 by year-end.[76]

In what seemed to have become an ongoing narrative, the studio was suffering another cash-flow crisis. Walt again wrote to Winkler just after Christmas in the final week of 1926 that the studio was "in very tight circumstances at this time. ...I have been on a two-week schedule since last October while you only recently started accepting on the two-week schedule. This has cramped me to such an extent that I have borrowed to my capacity and have to squeeze very hard to make things come out right."[77]

Secret Plans and the Roots of Conspiracy

On December 5, 1926, Walt turned 25. Less than four years previously he was the president of the now bankrupt Laugh-O-gram Films in Kansas City. Now he was running a successful but struggling animation studio in

Hollywood. The silent Alice Comedies had become quite popular with movie audiences, both for their novelty and their quality. Walt Disney's name was becoming known in animation circles, and those who were more serious-minded about seeking work in animation began to approach the studio.

Walt had come a long way in a short period of time to get to where he was. Every step forward seemed to bring new and threatening challenges. While he was doing his best to influence events and keep everything under control, there seemed to be no easy path to success and no indication that 1927 would be any different.

In early January 1927 one of the future legends of animation, Isadore "Friz" Freleng, was hired by Walt to join the studio. Freleng would later become famous for his work with Chuck Jones on the Looney Tunes and Merrie Melodies cartoons of the 1940s and 1950s, and as the creator of legendary characters like Porky Pig, Sylvester the Cat, Yosemite Sam, and the Pink Panther. In his long career, Freleng directed and produced more than 300 cartoons and was the winner of five Academy Awards.

Hugh Harman had worked with Freleng at Film Ad in Kansas City, as did Ub and Maxwell. Harman was looking to reunite his United Film Ad Services team under the Disney studio roof. Walt was looking for another animator to replace Rollin "Ham" Hamilton, his very first hire at the Disney Brothers Studio in 1924. Based on the encouragement of Harman, Walt invited Freleng to leave Kansas City and work for him in California.

Freleng indicated to Walt that he really didn't know much about animation because he was mostly self-taught, although he did receive some animation training from Hugh Harman at Film Ad. If he would come to California to work, Walt told Freleng, they would teach him. Walt knew that on-the-job training was the only way to develop animators. Animation was a new and specialized novelty. There were no schools of animation or easily available sources of instruction and training materials. *Everybody* in the business was self-taught. The only place to see animation was at a movie theatre, in a pre-feature cartoon or a pre-show ad, such as those made by Film Ad, where Walt, Ub, and Hugh had worked, experimented, and learned from each other. Freleng was swayed by the encouragement of Hugh and Walt, and made the move to be with his former co-workers.

When Freleng arrived in Los Angeles, Walt met him at the train station and drove him to the studio to meet everybody. For Freleng, it was like a reunion of the Kansas City animators. "I knew practically everybody there except Walt; I had never met Walt or Roy," Freleng recalled.[78] Iwerks became Freleng's mentor, teaching him the basics of character animation.

As Walt continued to pursue his vision of better animation and to build the competencies of his studio to raise the quality and entertainment value of animation in the industry and win screen time from theatre managers ahead of the competition, Ising and Harman continued to use the Disney Brothers Studio as an incubator for their own ambitions, secretly seeking an opportunity to leave Walt to start their own independent animation studio.

At the same time Hugh Harman was encouraging Walt to invite Freleng to join him in Hollywood, he was writing Maxwell in Kansas City that he and Ising were highly confident their Arabian Nights cartoon would land them a contract, "as we are corresponding with Metro Goldwyn, Fox, Universal and Paramount."[79] Ising also wrote to his sister, informing her "we have a secret shop all equipped and can start immediate production on our own pictures in the event of obtaining a contract. I hope this will be soon as we shall not make a name and fortune for ourselves working for Walt."[80]

With Freleng now in California and Maxwell ready to join them, the Arabian Knights were ready and eager to break away and, by doing so, leave Walt in a precarious situation.

---

1. Roy Disney quoted in Ghez, *Walt's People, Vol. 6*, 151–152.

2. Walt Disney quoted in Barrier, *The Animated Man*, 39.

3. Walt quoted in Katherine and Richard Greene, *Inside The Dream: The Personal Story of Walt Disney*, 28.

4. Ghez, *Walt's People, Vol. 6*, 152.

5. Thomas, *Walt Disney*, 70.

6. Walt Disney quoted in Susanin, *Walt Before Mickey*, 81.

7. Walt Disney quoted in Susanin, *Walt Before Mickey*, 80.

8. Walt Disney quoted in Susanin, *Walt Before Mickey*, 85.

9. Walt Disney quoted in Greene and Greene, *Inside the Dream*, 28.

10. Walt Disney quoted in Susanin, *Walt Before Mickey*, 86.

11. Walt Disney quoted in Susanin, *Walt Before Mickey*, 81.

12. Susanin, *Walt Before Mickey*, 82.

13. Susanin, *Walt Before Mickey*, 84.

14. Barrier, *The Animated Man*, 41; Susanin, *Walt Before Mickey*, 86.

15. Susanin, *Walt Before Mickey*, 86.

16. Thomas, *Walt Disney*, 72; Holliss & Sibley, *The Disney Studio Story*, 13; Susanin, *Walt Before Mickey*, 87.

17. Roy Disney quoted in Susanin, *Walt Before Mickey*, 87.

18. Diane Disney Miller, *The Story of Walt Disney*, 78–79.

19. Thomas, *Walt Disney*, 72.

20. Walt Disney quoted in Susanin, *Walt Before Mickey*, 88.

21. Susanin, *Walt Before Mickey*, 88.

22. Thomas, *Walt Disney*, 72; Susanin, *Walt Before Mickey*, 92.

23. Susanin, *Walt Before Mickey*, 89.

24. Susanin, *Walt Before Mickey*, 90.

25. Susanin, *Walt Before Mickey*, 90–91.

26. Susanin, *Walt Before Mickey*, 93.

27. Susanin, *Walt Before Mickey*, 94.

28. Susanin, *Walt Before Mickey*, 95; Gabler, *Walt Disney*, 83; Barrier, *The Animated Man*, 41.

29. Roy O. Disney, in Ghez, *Walt's People, Vol. 6.* 151.

30. Susanin, *Walt Before Mickey*, 96.

31. Susanin, *Walt Before Mickey*, 102.

32. Greene and Greene, *Inside the Dream*, 30.

33. Susanin, *Walt Before Mickey*, 102–103.

34. Susanin, *Walt Before Mickey*, 104.

35. Susanin, *Walt Before Mickey*, 104.

36. Susanin, *Walt Before Mickey*, 106.

37. Susanin, *Walt Before Mickey*, 106.

38. Susanin, *Walt Before Mickey*, 108.

39. Susanin, *Walt Before Mickey*, 107.

40. Susanin, *Walt Before Mickey*, 109.

41. Susanin, *Walt Before Mickey*, 109.

42. Harman quoted in Susanin, *Walt Before Mickey*, 107.

43. Merritt & Kaufman, *Walt in Wonderland*, 133.

44. Jackson, *Walt Disney Conversations*, interview by Tony Thomas, 63.

45. Culhane, *Talking Animals and Other People*, 25; also quoted in Susanin, *Walt Before Mickey*, 93.

46. Susanin, *Walt Before Mickey*, 112.

47. Susanin, *Walt Before Mickey*, 112.

48. Holliss & Sibley, *The Disney Studio Story*, 13.

49. Susanin, *Walt Before Mickey*, 113.

50. Susanin, *Walt Before Mickey*, 114.

51. Susanin, *Walt Before Mickey*, 114.

52. Susanin, *Walt Before Mickey*, 115.

53. Susanin, *Walt Before Mickey*, 116.

54. Susanin, *Walt Before Mickey*, 117.

55. Susanin, *Walt Before Mickey*, 118.

56. Hugh Harman quoted in Susanin, *Walt Before Mickey*, 124.

57. Susanin, *Walt Before Mickey*, 128.

58. Ghez, *Walt's People, Vol. 1*, 41.

59. Ghez, *Walt's People, Vol. 1*, 50–51.

60. Susanin, *Walt Before Mickey*, 129.

61. Susanin, *Walt Before Mickey*, 129.

62. Ghez, *Walt's People, Vol. 1*, 41.

63. Susanin, *Walt Before Mickey*, 131.

64. Susanin, *Walt Before Mickey*, 132.

65. Susanin, *Walt Before Mickey*, 133.

66. Mintz quoted in Susanin, *Walt Before Mickey*, 135.

67. Susanin, *Walt Before Mickey*, 136–137.

68. Susanin, *Walt Before Mickey*, 137.

69. Susanin, *Walt Before Mickey*, 137.

70. Merritt & Kaufman, *Walt in Wonderland*, 79.

71. Merritt & Kaufman, *Walt in Wonderland*, 79.

72. Barrier, *The Animated Man*, 50.

73. Susanin, *Walt Before Mickey*, 144.

74. Susanin, *Walt Before Mickey*, 145.

75. Susanin, *Walt Before Mickey*, 148

76. Susanin, *Walt Before Mickey*, 147.

77. Susanin, *Walt Before Mickey*, 147.

78. Freleng quoted in Susanin, *Walt Before Mickey*, 150.

79. Susanin, *Walt Before Mickey*, 150.

80. Susanin, *Walt Before Mickey*, 150.

CHAPTER FIVE

From Alice to Oswald

By 1927, Walt had come to possess considerable filmmaking and animation studio management skill and experience. He had been creating Alice Comedies cartoons for three years, bringing them to a consistently high standard on a tight two-week release schedule. As noted by authors Merritt and Kaufman in *Walt in Wonderland*, Walt "graduated from ambitious beginner to experienced producer, with a studio and staff capable of producing animated films that rivaled the best in the business."[1]

With studio operations and production running relatively smoothly, Walt had aspirations of expanding his output by establishing a second series of cartoons in addition to the Alice series, of which he was tiring. In Walt's mind, the concept of placing a live actress in a cartoon world had become stale and had run its course. According to Disney historian Charles Solomon, "They had basically exploited all the situations and gags that the live-action little girl could play with the animated characters, and it was becoming formulaic."[2] Walt was itching for something new, something that was aligned with his fascination for the possibilities of pure animation without live actors.

Unbeknownst to Walt, in the fall of 1926 Universal Pictures set into motion the creation of a new animated series to feature a rabbit, eventually to assume the name Oswald. Charles Mintz used his New York industry connections to push hard for the opportunity to provide the new series, and was able to convince Universal that he was the right man for the job. Mintz and his company, now named Winkler Pictures, Inc., were well respected, having been a leader in the production and distribution of the highest quality and most popular animated shorts for a number of years. As the quality of silent black-and-white cartoons continued to advance, they were becoming increasingly popular with movie audiences. Mintz had managed the strengths of his properties well by moving them to major global distributors. Krazy Kat went to Paramount and the Alice Comedies to Universal. This gave Walt's films improved distribution in more prestigious theatres with more aggressive marketing.[3]

Before Universal would award the contract to Mintz and Winkler Pictures, they demanded to see sample drawings. Margaret Winkler suggested to Mintz that he contact Walt. Walt could be obstinate and a tough negotiator, but he was also seen as fair and reasonable by Winkler, and had justly earned a reputation for quality filmmaking. More importantly, he was always able to keep to the rigorous production schedule of completing a high-quality reel every two weeks with few exceptions. The Alice Comedies continued to receive good reviews in the trade press for being innovative and funny. With an important new client like Universal Pictures, Winkler and Mintz knew they needed a partner they could trust to deliver the goods. The obvious choice was Walt Disney.

In January 1927, Mintz approached Walt with the challenge of designing and submitting sketches for a new rabbit character. Walt welcomed the challenge and his animators set about designing something suitable. Iwerks experimented with designs that featured smooth lines and round shapes that were easy to animate. The sample drawings were submitted by Walt to Mintz, who presented them to Universal. Universal liked what they saw and were comfortable with Mintz contracting the Disney studio to do the animation.

Working to a two-week delivery schedule of high quality films, and in hopeful anticipation of acquiring the rabbit cartoons, Walt felt the need to hire a few more artists as assistants to lend a helping hand and learn the art of animation. In February he hired Les Clark, Norm Blackwell, and Ben Clopton.[4] For the most part, Ub trained the new hires.

On March 4, 1927, Universal contracted Mintz to provide twenty-six Oswald the Lucky Rabbit cartoons. It was only after the deal was signed that Walt learned the company Winkler had been negotiating with was Universal.

The deal was structured such that Walt was subcontracted by Winkler to produce the cartoons for Universal, who owned the rights to the character. Disney was working for Winkler, and Winkler was working for Universal. The Disney studio was to be advanced $2,250 each for twenty-six shorts, which was an increase over the advance negotiated for the third series of twenty-six Alice shorts.

There was very little planning for the Oswald series prior to Walt completing his deal with Mintz in mid-March 1927. Disney animator Hugh Harman remembered arriving one morning at the studio and Walt announcing that they were starting production on Oswald. "We all got together in Walt's little office," according to Harman, "...and dreamed up this first story. ... [W]e began to build on it, and about 11 o'clock, Walt said, 'Why don't we start animating?'"[5]

As Walt's animators began working on the first Oswald, the final four Alice shorts were also being put into production, after which that series would be brought to a close. All told, the Alice Comedies were reasonably successful, although they typically didn't appear in premier first-run theaters. Walt produced a total of 56 silent Alice films from late 1923 to 1927.

It is also notable that in March, Walt fired Rudy Ising because of his ongoing problem of falling asleep on the job. Mel Shaw, who worked for Harman-Ising and later Walt, tells the story as he heard it, in his memoir, *Animator on Horseback*:

> As the story goes, one afternoon while Rudy was shooting some tests at the camera stand, he fell asleep. His head had rested on the drawings that he was shooting, which were held in place by two pegs. All drawings, backgrounds, and cels had to fit on the pegs so that everything was kept in registration for the camera. Walt walked in on him snoring away. In a burst of fury, he shouted to Rudy, "You're fired!" Rudy awoke with a start and the imprints from the pegs clearly visible on his forehead.[6]

Ising's propensity to sleep on the job wasn't a minor or one-time event. Surprisingly, Hugh Harman was sympathetic to Walt's decision: "I don't blame Walt, because Rudy would sleep during the day, when he should have been working."[7] Ising later recalled that his firing was done without animosity, as a "friendly, almost casual parting."[8] The friendliness and mutual agreement on the issue may have reflected Ising's anticipation of his own imminent studio startup.

To better manage the additional work coming to the studio, in early April Walt hired two additional employees, one of which was his sister-in-law, Hazel Sewell, to supervise the inking and painting. Iwerks received another significant raise from $70 to $120 a week in recognition of the importance of his contribution, making him the highest paid employee at the studio, surpassing both Walt and Roy's salaries.[9]

The first Oswald attempt, *Poor Papa*, was quickly completed and shipped on Sunday, April 10, 1927.[10] Universal was not impressed and cited a number of complaints, including the lack of story and the appearance of Oswald as "old, sloppy and fat. Audiences like their characters young, trim and smart," chastised Universal, adding, "This one is practically decrepit."[11]

Walt accepted the criticisms humbly, apologized, and made immediate changes. But he also asserted confidence in his own independent judgment, pushing back on some of the suggestions put forward by Mintz and Universal, including one of presenting the rabbit wearing a monocle. "Forget the monicle [sic]," Walt wrote back to Mintz. Walt was also somewhat offended at the suggestion by Universal that some of the animation was "jerky." The animation at the start of the movie was likely animated by Hugh Harman, who indicated that Walt had assigned him the first half of the movie and Iwerks the latter half. Nonetheless, Walt fired back in defense of his animators by noting that Ub was "a man of experience whom I am willing to put alongside any man in the business today."[12]

Around May 1927, Carman Maxwell made the trip to California to reunite with Walt and his fellow Arabian Nights as an animator at the Walt Disney Studios.

Oswald the Lucky Rabbit was a big success from the start, confirming that brash Walt Disney on the West Coast was able to compete with the established studios and more experienced talent operating in New York.

The second Oswald production was the first Oswald theatrical release. *Trolley Troubles* premiered in Los Angeles on July 4, 1927, and impressed the critics. *The Film Daily* wrote: "As conductor on a 'Toonerville' trolley, Oswald is a riot. This ... you can book on pure faith, and our solemn word that they have the goods." *Moving Picture World* proclaimed that Oswald was "good for a lot of smiles and real laughs." *Motion Picture News* wrote:

> If the first of these new cartoon comedies for Universal release is an indication of what is to come, then this series is destined to win much popular favor. They are cleverly drawn, well executed, brimful of action and fairly abounding in humorous situations. Oswald the Lucky Rabbit is all of that. Some of his experiences are hilarious and breath taking. He is the conductor of the suburban trolley in this one and it is a trick car that provides plenty of humor. Oswald and the car encounter all sorts of obstacles. They flatten out to run under a cow and they hurdle others, much to the consternation of the bewildered passengers. The laughs are spontaneous and there are plenty of them."[13]

As the series progressed under Walt's direction, the Oswald cartoons continued to garner excellent reviews. *Moving Picture World* wrote: "[T]hese Disney cartoon creations are bright, speedy and genuinely amusing. ... The animation is good and the clever way in which Disney makes his creatures simulate the gestures and expressions of human beings adds to the enjoyment. They should provide worthwhile attractions in any type of house."[14]

By the end of 1927, *Moving Picture World* had proclaimed Oswald to be the first-run favorite.[15] The studio was also now posting a net profit. Walt had grown his staff to about twenty, and the studio was clearing about $500 per cartoon after expenses. Walt's weekly salary had risen to $100. Roy's was $65.

With Oswald, the Walt Disney Studios, under Walt's leadership and direction, had become the world's leading animation studio. After five years in animated cartoons in Hollywood, and having just turned 26, Walt had made it to the top.

---

1. Merritt & Kaufman, *Walt in Wonderland*, 55.

2. Greene & Greene, *Inside the Dream*, 30.

3. Merritt & Kaufman, *Walt in Wonderland*, 86.

4. Susanin, *Walt Before Mickey*, 151.

5. Susanin, *Walt Before Mickey*, 154.

6. Shaw, *Animator on Horseback*, 47.

7. Harman quoted in Susanin, *Walt Before Mickey*, 152.

8. Barrier quoted in Susanin, *Walt Before Mickey*, 283, n.152.

9. Susanin, *Walt Before Mickey*, 155.

10. Susanin, *Walt Before Mickey*, 155.

11. Susanin, *Walt Before Mickey*, 156.

12. Susanin, *Walt Before Mickey*, 156.

13. Susanin, *Walt Before Mickey*, 160.

14. Susanin, *Walt Before Mickey*, 164.

15. Susanin, *Walt Before Mickey*, 164.

CHAPTER SIX

The Oswald Conspiracy of 1928

The year 1927 had been a good one for Walt and his studio staff, but there were also growing undercurrents of trouble brewing.

By the summer of 1927, as the last of the Alice Comedies were being completed and with the production of the first series of Oswald cartoons underway, tensions within the studio were rising. The staff from Kansas City, whom had now worked under Walt's leadership for a few years, was still looking for a viable way to break away and start their own studio. At the same time, Charles Mintz was looking for new ways to expand Winkler Pictures.

Knowing of the desire of Rudy Ising and Hugh Harman to start their own studio, Mintz carefully approached Harman about joining with Winkler to establish a new studio and take over the production of Oswald. This strategic act of backward integration through the acquisition of the Oswald animators working in a Winkler-owned studio would allow Winkler to control both the production and distribution of the Oswald series for Universal and increase Winkler Pictures' bottom line by cutting Walt Disney Studios out of the cost structure.

Hugh Harman received Mintz's probes positively, and actively pursued the prospect with the other animators. Harman recalled: "I was interested right away, because I was very disappointed in Walt, and wanted to get away from him. I would have quit anyway, one way or another. ... Rudy [Ising] and I had been planning to go into production for ourselves for quite some time, and I saw this as a possibility. Against that, I didn't want to be in a position of stealing the deal with Walt, so I thought I'd just go to work for Winklers[.]"[1]

In August 1927, Ising wrote to a friend in Kansas City: "Winklers have made us a definite offer for a next years [sic] release. Winklers are thoroughly disgusted with the Disneys and with the expiration of their present contract will have no more dealings with them. Their present contract expires in April 1928." According to Ising's letter, Iwerks also had aspirations to leave "to engage in a private enterprise."[2]

The whole affair turned into a full-blown conspiracy between Mintz and Walt's animation staff. The scheme was pretty basic. At the time of contract renewal, Mintz would fail to come to terms with Walt and fire him, and Walt's animators would jump ship to Mintz and continue on as before, except they'd be working for a new boss, hopefully one that wasn't as demanding as Walt. The conspirator animators had all been sworn to secrecy. Hugh Harman indicated that he felt bad about stealing the Oswald deal from Roy, whom he liked, although "I could have kicked the carpet from under [Walt] without any qualms."[3]

While the conspirators eagerly awaited the time when they could join up with Mintz, they were getting restless, and throughout the latter period of 1927 were actively and secretly seeking opportunities to quit. In spite of their apparent commitment to Mintz, on November 15, 1927, Ising wrote to Friz Freleng, who had been fired on September 1, 1927, after Walt caught him skipping work and going to the movies, and who had returned to Kansas City. Ising wrote that a friend was trying to secure a contract for he and the others to start up an animation studio with the Cecil B. DeMille Studios.[4]

In early 1928, the Disney conspirators continued to plot with Charles Mintz and his California representative and brother-in-law, George Winkler. They would talk by phone and meet in various locations to discuss potential arrangements. Mintz and Winkler were depending on assurances that Walt's animation team would enter into a contract directly with Winkler and break their ties with Walt when Walt's current contract with Winkler Pictures expired, but no contracts between Winkler and the conspirators had been signed.[5] Winkler was taking a huge risk. If Winker pulled the rug out from under Walt and Walt's animators failed to follow through with continuity on the Oswald series, Winker would be in trouble with Universal and left scrambling to meet his contractual obligations.

Iwerks, who had been Walt's first business partner in their short-lived Iwerks-Disney commercial artist venture back in Kansas City, became suspicious of George Winkler's motives, and confronted him. Apparently, the situation was explained to Iwerks in some manner, perhaps as a hypothetical situation in case Winkler and Walt were unable to negotiate agreeable terms for a contract renewal. This wasn't far-fetched, as Walt's negotiations with Winkler had been acrimonious in the past. Iwerks found the explanation unconvincing and warned Walt several members of the staff were "renegades" who had decided to sign with Winkler, and that he, Iwerks, wasn't amongst them.

With the Oswald series rising quickly to become the most popular cartoon in the country and one of its best-selling short subject series, Universal signed Winkler Pictures to a new three-year contract.

It had now been almost nine months since Mintz had first broached the topic with Hugh Harman of the Disney animators jumping ship. With the Oswald series a hit and a three-year renewal contract with Universal now in place, everything was aligned for Mintz to set his plan in motion. All he needed was assurances by means of signed contracts with Harman and his colleagues before he could dispose of his need for Walt Disney himself.

In early February of 1928, Rudy Ising wrote to Friz Freleng in Kansas City: "Our plans to get a contract to make our own pictures this year fell through, so we are taking the next best thing. Hugh [Harman], Max [Carman Maxwell], Ham [Rollin Hamilton], and I are signing a one-year employment contract with George Winkler to make 'Oswald the Lucky Rabbit.'"[6]

Ten days later, Walt traveled to New York with his wife Lillian to meet with Winkler and negotiate renewal terms for the second year of the Oswald contract before the expiration of the first contract in April 1928.

Walt and Roy had agreed that based on the success of Oswald and the never-ending pressure to improve the product, they would ask for a modest increase to $2,500 per picture from the current $2,250. Years later, Walt told a reporter: "At the end of the first year with Oswald, because of his success, I expected to be allowed a little more money to build the series up to a higher standard."[7]

Having been put on notice by Iwerks that Mintz may be up to something, Walt was fully aware that the negotiations with Charles Mintz might not go well. Walt thought carefully about the various possible outcomes and planned ahead for foreseeable contingencies. He packed two Oswald reels and some press clippings into his luggage and left with Lillian for New York with the intention of approaching other distributors to assess their interest should the need arise to seek out another distributor. Walt also wanted to assess and, if possible, enhance his own bargaining leverage before meeting and negotiating with Mintz.

The Oswald Negotiations

Walt's first meeting upon arriving in New York on Tuesday, February 21, 1928, was with a prior acquaintance of his, Jack Alicoate, the publisher of industry trade paper *Film Daily*. As an East Coast industry insider, Alicoate was able to provide Walt with a better understanding of the players and his take on the market for cartoons, as well as provide advice to Walt with regards to Mintz and Winkler Pictures.[8] It was Alicoate's assessment that the short subject market was struggling and that Walt's best prospects for finding an alternative distributor were with MGM or Fox.[9]

Walt left his meeting with Alicoate and immediately called both studios to set up appointments.

Two days later, on Thursday, Walt met with Fred Quimby at MGM. Quimby informed Walt that it was MGM's opinion that the public's interest in cartoons was on the wane. For this reason, MGM was not interested in Oswald. Not willing to forgo any opportunity, Walt was able to convince Quimby to allow him to leave one of the Oswald prints behind so they could screen it. Interestingly, Quimby was fairly certain that someone had recently screened a few Oswald shorts for him. Based on Iwerks' warnings, Walt immediately suspected his "renegade" team of animators.[10]

Later that day, Walt met with Charles Mintz at the Winkler offices, where they agreed to have lunch together with their wives the next day. Lunch on Friday was pleasant, but Mintz avoided any business talk. He invited Walt to come by the office the following day, Saturday, to discuss the contract renewal.

On Saturday morning Walt called Quimby at MGM, who by this time had screened the Oswald film left by Walt and confirmed that he had been previously shown Oswald shorts. Quimby again told Walt that MGM wasn't interested in such low-grossing short subjects.[11] With MGM now out as an alternate distributor, Walt called Fox and was able to secure an appointment for that coming Wednesday.

Back at his hotel, Walt received a telegram from Roy that "renegade" Carman "Max" Maxwell, whom Walt had worked with at Laugh-O-gram in Kansas City and who had joined Walt in Hollywood nine months previously, had been fired by Roy, and that Roy was happy to be rid of him.

Walt met with Mintz that Saturday afternoon, during dinner on Monday, and again on Tuesday afternoon, February 28. Their negotiations began with Walt asking for $2,500 per reel, and Mintz countering by offering to pay for Disney's production costs, roughly $1,400 per film, plus an equal share in the profits and "substantial salaries."[12] Walt rejected the offer. He needed credit to fund production, and a more definite offer of cash per movie along with profit sharing.

Walt left the meeting frustrated that they weren't making more headway after being in New York for a week, and characterized his time spent with Mintz to Roy as "the same old stuff." Most offensive to Walt was the suggestion implicit in the terms offered that Walt's organization should become an animation shop for Winker Productions rather than a studio in its own right with Walt as the studio owner; that essentially Walt and Roy should be become salaried employees of Winkler Pictures. Walt feared that under these terms his leadership authority and commitment to quality would be compromised.[13]

Walt was becoming weary of Mintz's "bluffing" and game playing, and wrote Roy that he now felt his best course of action was to leave Mintz and try to contract with Fox or try again with MGM.

Walt again contacted Quimby at MGM to discuss opportunities for working together, and was again told that MGM wasn't interested. His meeting with Fox revealed that their cartoon productions were all made in-house, and that they weren't interested in distributing third-party productions.

Without an immediate alternate distribution channel option open to him, and a growing distrust of Charles Mintz' intentions, Walt was weighing possible alternative paths and was increasingly contemplating the inevitability of a split with Winkler Pictures. Walt wired Roy, "BREAK WITH CHARLIE LOOMING."[14]

Fearing and anticipating that Mintz was stalling negotiations in order to ensure he had Walt's animators under contract to Winkler Pictures, Walt instructed Roy to prepare new contracts for the Disney studio animators to prevent Mintz from signing them and to force their hand. By doing so, he would find out what the real situation was.

Timothy Susanin, author of *Walt Before Mickey*, writes that Walt wired Roy to tell him:

> "Contracts with the boys [are] necessary to prevent [Charlie from] undermining" the Disneys by hiring away their staff. Walt instructed Roy to get a lawyer to prepare "ironclad" staff contracts for a one-year term with a 10-percent raise after six months, and options for two additional years with a 10-percent raise each year. Walt wanted the contracts to...be "absolute[ly] legal[.]" Walt told Roy not to present the contracts to the staff until Walt gave Roy the word to do so, and reminded Roy that "absolute secrecy [is] necessary" but that "everything [i]s OK[.]"[15]

While coming to an amicable arrangement with Mintz was still a possibility, Walt was now actively engaged in developing and working on the creation of alternative options in case one was needed.

The next day, Thursday, March 1, Walt and Lillian had lunch with Bill Nolan, considered to be New York's top animator. Nolan was the producer of Winkler's long-time popular leading series, Krazy Kat. It was from Nolan that Walt learned that Mintz was actively recruiting for a top animator to move to California to work with Charles' brother-in-law, George Winkler, in setting up a new Winkler studio in Hollywood that would be staffed with Walt's animators. After lunch, Walt was given a tour of Nolan's studio, later writing to Roy that "it is sure a dump," while also noting that the staff was "glad to see me and treated me royal."[16]

Walt's suspicions about Mintz were now confirmed. Recognizing that he would need new animators to continue in the cartoon business if the Mintz takeover scheme were to come to fruition, Walt encouraged Nolan and his staff to come out to California to work with him. Walt figured that two could play at the recruitment game, and recruiting the leading East Coast animators for his studio and away from Mintz would be a major Disney coup. He wrote to Roy about his conversation with Nolan, adding that the possibility existed "to get plenty of good men" from the Krazy Kat.[17]

After ten days in New York, Walt was getting tired of Mintz's continued stalling and lack of progress in negotiating a contract renewal. He would much prefer to be back at this studio in California working on projects and to escape the cold New York winter. He was certain by now that there would be no deal forthcoming with Mintz and wanted to quickly bring this episode to an end.

On Friday, March 2, Walt and Lillian again had lunch with Margaret Winkler and Mintz at the Hotel Aster. Mintz refused to talk business, putting such talk off until a meeting in his office the following day. What little he did say made Walt highly suspicious. "I could see that he had something up his sleeve," Walt wrote to Roy.[18]

With the meeting over, Walt returned to his hotel and immediately wired two telegrams to Roy in an attempt to head off Mintz before he caught wind that Walt was on to him.

The first telegram contained instructions to Roy to have the "boys sign contracts...immediately" in an attempt to pre-empt their signing on with Mintz through George Winkler, who was in California.[19] If they refused to sign, Roy was to find out why "before allowing them to leave." Walt would soon have his answer about whether or not to end his dealings with Mintz and a very successful four-year business relationship with Winkler Pictures.

The second telegram was prepared for Roy to show to all of the animators, but was aimed toward the six whose loyalties were in question: Hugh Harman, Rollin Hamilton, Paul Smith, Norm Blackburn, Ben Clopton, and Ray Abrams. In a strategically worded telegram, Walt portrayed a sense of calm and the possibilities of a bright and prosperous future for the Disney studio and its employees, while at the same time providing just enough details to create confusion and doubt if there was a conspiracy afoot. Walt held out the possibility of Krazy Kat's Bill Nolan joining the studio, which would have raised concerns about Winkler Pictures' future stability, given that Winkler Pictures was the Krazy Kat distributor. He also hinted to the others that he knew of their scheme with Mintz in a way that would be innocuous if it weren't true. Walt wrote that he "[l]unched with Bill Nolan today [and I] may be able to bring him out [to California and join the staff. H]ave those of present crew that are going to stay sign contracts[.]"[20] This had to be done right away, wrote Walt, because if some of his animators were leaving, he needed to sign on others in New York to fill their positions before he headed back home.

That afternoon, Walt met again with Jack Alicoate of *Film Daily* whom Walt consulted as an informal advisor throughout his visit to New York.

Given the unstable state of the industry and Walt's lack of alternative distribution options, Alicoate advised Walt to "bluff Charlie." Given the precarious situation Walt was in, he had nothing to lose.[21]

Rather than wait until their scheduled meeting for the following day, Walt returned to the Winkler offices to confront Mintz. In an effort to force Mintz's hand, Walt bluffed that he had two unsolicited offers that he would consider if he and Mintz couldn't come to an agreement. Mintz indicated that he, too, wanted an agreement, but couldn't afford to pay more than $1,750 per short, essentially enough to cover Walt's production costs to produce the negatives, plus 50% of the profits. In a letter to Roy, Walt indicated that he "offered to compromise because I said I hated to leave Oswald after getting it started," but as it stood, Mintz's offer was not acceptable.[22]

Walt then told Mintz he would accept his terms if they could sign the contract immediately. Mintz was unprepared to do so, and indicated that Walt would have to take him on his word. Walt responded by indicating he was going to entertain his other offers, and Mintz encouraged him to do so. The meeting ended cordially, and Mintz asked Walt to sleep on the offer and to return the next day, Saturday, so they could "get down to business."[23]

With the Mintz meeting over, Walt returned to Alicoate, telling him that he was finished with Mintz. Walt told Alicoate that he wasn't going to meet with Mintz as planned the next day, and that if Mintz didn't call him by Monday, Walt was going to complain directly to Universal about Mintz's shady business practices.

By coincidence, Alicoate had been to a boxing match with the treasurer of Universal Pictures, Emmanuel H. Goldstein, the night before, and they had discussed Walt's situation. Walt learned that Universal was paying Mintz a $3,000 advance for each Oswald short, and Goldstein had told Alicoate that Universal would like to talk to Walt. Alicoate called Goldstein, who instructed Walt to come right over.

Walt arrived at Universal where he met Goldstein and was introduced to a very senior executive whose name Walt couldn't in later years recall, perhaps even one of the owners. Universal appeared to be surprised at Walt's difficulty in finalizing a new contract with Mintz, with whom Universal had just signed a new three-year distribution deal. Walt indicated to Roy by letter that Universal's concern was picture quality: "They want good pictures and...they won't stand for Mr. Mintz cutting down costs in any way that might lower the standard."[24]

The Universal executive expressed regret over Walt's situation with regards to Winkler Pictures, and held out hope for a better possible future. Their hands were contractually tied to Winkler at the moment, they said, but perhaps in a year they could deal directly with Walt and eliminate Winkler as the intermediary. Universal's advice to Walt: take the best offer he could negotiate with Mintz and "work like hell" in 1928 so that they could talk business directly in 1929. Walt appreciated the consideration and advice, but was well aware that in the troubled world of film shorts, these kinds of future promises weren't worth much.

Later that night, back at his hotel, Walt learned from Roy that only Ub Iwerks, Les Clark, and Johnny Cannon had signed contracts. It was as Ub had warned him: all six of the remaining animators refused to sign. Walt concluded that because of the scarcity of animation jobs, their refusal to sign "means only one thing—they are hooked up with Charlie. ... I know how the rest of the market is and they haven't a smell."[25]

Walt indicated to Roy that he was hurt by their lack of loyalty, although he must have experienced it as a more substantial and personal betrayal.

Surprisingly, in some ways, Walt seemed to be at ease with the current state of affairs. "I feel very confident that we will come out allright [sic] even if it is a bit disillusioning [sic]...," he wrote Roy.[26]

After two hectic weeks of uncertainty and stress about his future, at least he now knew where he stood, both in terms of his studio in Hollywood, and his chances for carrying on with the Oswald series. He remained optimistic that Mintz's effort would fail in the sense that without Walt's leadership, expertise, and most of all demand for the highest standards of quality, Mintz would not be able to maintain the standard that Universal demanded and would eventually lose the deal. At least that held out some hope that there was opportunity for Universal to come back to Walt, even if that possibility was a year away. On the other hand, he had to be worried that he would be heading back to California worse off than when he left, with a very clear message from everyone he spoke with in New York that the shorts business was in dire straits and the future looked bleak for the industry as a whole.

On Saturday, Walt called Mintz who was not home; and Walt was out when Mintz returned his call.[27]

Then, on Sunday, Walt spent the day with Krazy Kat's Bill Nolan, who indicated he was prepared to leave Mintz and come to work for Walt in June, and was looking forward to working with Ub Iwerks. Walt thought it would be terrific to have the two best animators working together and that by joining forces they'd be able to produce great work.

Walt and Mintz were able to connect by phone on Monday, March 5, and agreed to get together. When they met, Mintz revealed his hand. He had signed Walt's animators; Universal owned the rights to the Oswald cartoons; and Walt now had no choice but to accept the terms Mintz was offering. Mintz would take over Walt's studio, including payment of the taxes, and pay Walt $1,400 per negative plus a weekly salary of $200 and 50% of the Winkler Pictures profits on the Oswald films. Walt objected, indicating that with that deal, it would be impossible for the studio to earn a profit. Mintz replied that further investment to improve the series didn't make good business sense, that the Oswalds were good enough as is, and that the animated cartoon industry was unlikely to overcome its economic and structural obstacles. In other words, Mintz's message to Walt was that it was time to cash in by putting a freeze on value creation and innovation to please customers, and instead to focus on squeezing higher profits from the business while the going is good—a classic cash-cow strategy.

Walt's vision wasn't on the cost of films. It was on building and operating a successful animation studio. Walt was looking for more money per film from Mintz to "plus" Oswald with improvements that would create more value and delight for customers, thereby winning their loyalty in the marketplace and creating consumer demand for Oswald and Walt Disney cartoons. It was the love of the cartoons and the Oswald character by audiences that would drive demand, put pressure on movie houses to prominently feature the cartoons, and increase Disney studio revenues.

Mintz had his sights set on a different business model and road to success, one that looked to "minus" his product as a more effective and rational path to profits. From Walt's way of thinking, these two perspectives—one may even call them business philosophies—on how to succeed in business and earn profits were diametrically opposed.

When Walt refused Mintz's offer that he give up his studio and become a Winkler employee, there was nothing more to talk about. Walt wrote Roy that as they parted ways, he "left [Charlie] with a good bye and wishes for luck in his new venture."[28]

A Clash of Business Philosophies

Walt was finished with New York. He returned to his hotel burning with anger and told Lillian the news: that Winkler controlled the rights to Oswald even though Walt's studio had created the character and made the series a success, and that Mintz intended to continue on with or without him. Walt would never work for Mintz under the terms offered, and now found himself and his studio in a precarious position.

To say things didn't turn out well for Walt is an understatement. Yet he was surprisingly relieved that the whole ordeal had played itself out and was now over. Now Walt knew exactly where things stood and could focus on what he needed to do to move forward.

With four Oswald shorts still to complete under the terms of his existing Winkler contract, one might be sympathetic to Walt had he withdrawn his efforts to put out top-quality product now that the Winkler Pictures relationship was coming to an end. But that wasn't the Disney way. Walt continued to give first consideration to his reputation with the public. After all, it was his name that was on each picture.

Before he left New York, Walt provided guidance and ideas for the fourth-from-last Oswald film to be produced by the studio, *The Fox Chase*. Walt sent instructions that the film should begin the chase scene action right away and that Oswald himself should be involved in as many of the gags as possible so that "[Oswald] will be brought into the story more."[29]

After trying unsuccessfully to arrange a few more meetings with potential distributors, Walt and Lillian boarded a train and set off to Los Angeles on the evening of Tuesday, March 13. Walt was eager to get back to California and back to work making movies. He told Lillian, "Let's get the first train out of here. I can't do any good in New York. I have to hire new artists and get a new series going. I can't sell a new series with talk. I've got to have it on film."[30]

Not wanting to provide the painful details, he wired Roy: LEAVING TONIGHT STOPPING OVER KC ARRIVE HOME SUNDAY MORNING SEVEN THIRTY DON'T WORRY EVERYTHING OK WILL GIVE DETAILS WHEN ARRIVE.[31]

Walt's drive to carry on was most certainly motivated by his anger, but also by his confidence and knowledge that there was nobody better in the industry than he was. Lillian later told a reporter that Walt was like a "raging lion" on the train ride home. "He had gambled everything we had—which wasn't much, but seemed a lot to us—on the Oswald series. All he could say, over and over, was that he'd never work for anyone again as long as he lived; he'd be his own boss."[32]

If Walt had been "the naïve boy from Kansas City," as Notre Dame professor of film Donald Crafton writes in *Before Mickey: The Animated Film 1898–1928*,[33] then his loss of Oswald was a trial-by-fire grown-up education about business opportunism and the need to protect one's own commercial business interests. Freleng, who eventually rejoined his colleagues Harman, Ising, and the others in California to work on Winkler's Oswald, recalled that the atmosphere around animation in the 1920s was extremely competitive. "Everybody was conspiring against the other one. … Everybody had ambition; everybody wanted to be a producer and there was no one to work with."[34] Walt later described the business atmosphere at the time as an "out-and-out cutthroat business" where the same people you were "laughing and having a drink with" would be "putting a knife in your back."[35]

Neal Gabler writes in his biography *Walt Disney: The Triumph of the American Imagination*, that when Walt and Lillian boarded the train home, "[Walt] had nothing—no Nolan, no character, no contract except the one for the Oswalds that he was obligated to animate under the terms of his deal with Mintz, no staff save for a few who remained loyal like Iwerks, [and] no plan...."[36]

And yet through all of this, Walt was uncharacteristically optimistic and forward-looking. He was as analytical as he was creative. He was future-focused on "dissolving" problems and identifying opportunities. But he was also vigilant not to let the past go by without analysis and extraction of the key lessons to be learned and applied going forward.

Up until the Oswald setback, the Winkler Pictures connection had provided Walt with an unprecedented opportunity unavailable to his later followers. Walt had been very fortunate to come across Margaret Winkler when he did at a time when she was trying to expand her animation distribution business in 1923, and, through a confluence of events, was willing to take a chance by contracting six Alice pictures from an unknown twenty-two year-old green upstart who had recently moved to California. Walt gained his practical education in the world of animation under the initial guidance of Margaret Winkler and her coaching, constructive criticism, and tolerance of Walt's errors, even when they cost her business money because of the need for re-editing or rejection by distributors due to product quality issues. Her husband, Charles Mintz, and brother, George Winkler, also assumed this helpful attitude by sharing their understanding of how to create quality cartoons that had distributor and audience appeal. Walt always showed appreciation for, and proactively solicited, their criticism in order to learn how to improve, and of course, Winkler and Mintz were equally satisfied with Walt's desire to improve and to always follow through on his word.

Unfortunately, over time, as Margaret Winkler focused her attention on raising a family, she removed herself from running the first-class business she had built into the premier distributor of animated films, and turned control over to her husband. As Crafton notes, Margaret Winkler was a "straightforward business person," of honorable character with an eye to cordial relations and a win-win outcome, while her husband was more of "a wheeler-dealer in the grand style."[37] Charlie Mintz used more aggressive tactics of persuasion and adopted questionable business ideas that over time transformed into "win-lose" outcomes and predatory practices that eventually destroyed the reputable first-class business that Margaret Winkler spent so many years building.

After just one year without Walt's leadership on the Oswald series, Universal fired Winkler by refusing to renew their option on his Oswald contract.

While working for Mintz, the ever ambitious Hugh Harman and Rudy Ising approached the head of Universal, Carl Laemmle, suggesting that Mintz be removed from the series so that Harman and Ising could head up the operation. Laemmle turned them down, terminated Mintz's contract, and proceeded to produce Oswald cartoons themselves on the Universal lot under the direction of Walter Lantz.[38]

By the time the renegades were back on the street looking for animation work and still dreaming of starting their own studio, Walt had overcome his immediate problems, and was riding high on the success of his latest creation: Mickey Mouse. For Walt Disney and Walt Disney Productions, Oswald was old news.

Once again Walt Disney would create something remarkable out of nothing.

Walt arrived in Los Angeles by train and was met by Roy. Forty years later, Roy recalled the event. "What kind of a deal did you make, kid," Roy asked Walt. "'We haven't got a deal,' Walt admitted. 'The distributor copyrighted Oswald and he's taking over the series himself.' Strangely," wrote Roy, "Walt did not seem downhearted. 'We're going to start a new series,' he enthused. 'It's about a mouse. And this time, we'll own the mouse.'"[39]

1. Susanin, *Walt Before Mickey*, 162.

2. Barrier, *The Animated Man*, 55.

3. Susanin, *Walt Before Mickey*, 162.

4. Susanin, *Walt Before Mickey*, 164; Barrier, *The Animated Man*, 55.

5. Barrier, *The Animated Man*, 55.

6. Barrier, *The Animated Man*, 55.

7. Susanin, *Walt Before Disney*, 165.

8. Susanin, *Walt Before Mickey*, 166.

9. Susanin, *Walt Before Mickey*, 167.

10. Susanin, *Walt Before Mickey*, 167.

11. Susanin, *Walt Before Mickey*, 168.

12. Gabler, *Walt Disney*, 107.

13. Gabler, *Walt Disney*, 107.

14. Gabler, *Walt Disney*, 107; Susanin, *Walt Before Mickey*, 170.

15. Susanin, *Walt Before Mickey*, 170; Gabler, *Walt Disney*, 107.

16. Susanin, *Walt Before Mickey*, 170.

17. Susanin, *Walt Before Mickey*, 170.

18. Gabler, *Walt Disney*, 107.

19. Susanin, *Walt Before Mickey*, 171.

20. Susanin, *Walt Before Mickey*, 171.

21. Susanin, *Walt Before Mickey*, 170.

22. Susanin, *Walt Before Mickey*, 171.

23. Susanin, *Walt Before Mickey*, 171.

24. Susanin, *Walt Before Mickey*, 172.

25. Susanin, *Walt Before Mickey*, 173.

26. Susanin, *Walt Before Mickey*, 173.

27. Susanin, *Walt Before Mickey*, 174.

28. Susanin, *Walt Before Mickey*, 174.

29. Susanin, *Walt Before Mickey*, 176.

30. Susanin, *Walt Before Mickey*, 176-177.

31. Susanin, *Walt Before Mickey*, 176.

32. Susanin, *Walt Before Mickey*, 177.

33. Crafton, *Before Mickey*, 208.

34. Crafton, *Before Mickey*, 208.

35. Walt Disney, quoted in Susanin, *Walt Before Mickey*, 176.

36. Gabler, *Walt Disney*, 109.

37. Crafton, *Before Mickey*, 208.

38. Wikipedia, entry for Oswald The Lucky Rabbit, accessed February 11, 2014.

39. Roy O. Disney, "Unforgettable Walt Disney," *Reader's Digest*, February 1969.

CHAPTER SEVEN

Third Time Lucky: Mickey the Lucky Mouse

When Walt arrived back in L.A. on March 18, 1928, he explained his current situation to Roy and his plan for going forward: "We're going to start a new series."[1] The lead character would be a mouse.

As noted by Disney biographer Bob Thomas in *Walt Disney: An American Original*, in working through the creation and development of Mickey Mouse, Walt applied the lessons he had learned from his experience on both the Alice and Oswald films: "that a strong, attractive central character was essential; and that a good storyline was needed, but too much plot could destroy laughter. He also learned that film-company committees could throttle creativity."[2]

Walt and Iwerks developed a story based on the recent transatlantic flight of Charles Lindbergh and titled it *Plane Crazy*. In recognizing Iwerks' important contribution and loyalty to the business, and surely to secure his animation talent, on March 24, 1928, Iwerks was offered and accepted an arrangement whereby he would contribute $20 a week and later $35 a week from his salary, to eventually secure a twenty percent share of ownership and partnership in the studio.[3]

Walt still had his defecting cartoonists working at the studio until June, when the final Oswald cartoons would be completed and delivered to Mintz, thereby bringing Walt's contractual obligation to an end. Unable to trust his staff, he tried to keep his new mouse character and the work they were doing on *Plane Crazy* a secret. *That* Walt was working on a new project was not a secret to the other studio staff; *what* he was working on allegedly was.

At the studio, Ub would come to work, sit alone in a separate room, and draw. The speed at which Ub animated *Plane Crazy* is legendary in the history of animation, producing about seven hundred drawings a day. At the end of each day, Walt would bring the drawings home, and Lillian, her sister Hazel, and Roy's wife Edna all pitched in to do the inking and painting in a makeshift workshop built in Walt's garage. At night, Walt would take the completed cels back to the studio to be photographed, and everything would be removed by morning.

As a result of Iwerks' speed and determination, *Plane Crazy* was completed in record time, which was important. Time was of the essence. Walt only had a few months to create a new product and place it with a distributor before the inflow of revenue from the last few Oswald pictures would stop.

Walt secretly arranged a preview of *Plane Crazy* to a fully packed Sunset Boulevard movie house with piano accompaniment on May 15, 1928, enabling him to observe the audience reaction to his new character for the first time.[4] It was good enough in Walt's estimation to warrant the production of a second Mickey Mouse picture. On May 29, 1928, Walt held a story meeting for *The Gallopin' Gaucho* with his loyal animation staff of Ub Iwerks, Les Clark, and new hire Wilfred Jackson. Walt acted out the story in his usual hammed-up and corny manner. The high-pitched squeaky falsetto voice that he used as the voice of Mickey had everyone rolling with laughter.[5]

Confident that Mickey would go over well with audiences, Walt wasted no time in seeking a distributor. He approached Metro-Goldwyn-Mayer Studios in Beverly Hills. They were impressed and congratulated him on his work, but weren't prepared to offer a distribution deal. They told Walt that he would have to go to New York to find a reputable distributor.

Given Walt's recent bad experiences in New York, he didn't have the inclination, money, or time to return. Instead of going himself he engaged the services of a New York film dealer named E.J. Denison to seek out a distributor. Walt instructed Denison that he was asking for an advance of $3,000 per cartoon, the same as Universal was paying Mintz for his Oswald cartoons, and would offer a one- or two-year option for twenty-six cartoons per year. "It is our intention," Walt wrote to Denison, to heavily promote the series in order to "make the name of 'Mickey Mouse' as well known as any cartoon on the market."[6]

The general consensus in the industry at the time was that the popularity of cartoons was waning. The quality of most of it was sub-standard compared to the Disney level of quality, and the overall entertainment value was slipping. Low audience interest meant low theatre owner interest, which translated into low distributor interest. As a result, Denison's best efforts were completely unsuccessful and he soon withdrew.

Walt was now in possession of an unsold series with no immediate or foreseeable opportunities to convert his product into future income. As with the Alice Comedies, what he needed was a breakthrough idea or distinguishing feature that would gain the attention of movie-going audiences and set his product apart from the competition.

The date of October 6, 1927, was an historic and momentous day in the history of motion pictures. It marked the world premiere in New York of *The Jazz Singer*, the first motion picture with synchronized dialogue. At the time, Walt immediately recognized that a new level of audience expectations would be set in motion, and he began to think about adding sound to his cartoons. While most theatres were still showing silent pictures and were not equipped with the technology to show "talkies," Walt envisioned the possibilities of cartoons with sound, and along this road saw a bright emerging future for what others saw as a slow-fading industry. As a studio with no existing commitments and driven by the need to take a risk rather than avoid one, he found himself in the best position to move first onto the next wave of movie-making innovation.

In June 1928, as Mintz was just beginning his next series of silent Oswald cartoons for Universal using Walt's former animators, Walt began writing to New York companies to inquire what it would cost to add synchronized sound to cartoons, while at the same time familiarizing himself with the competing sound-recording processes being offered. *The Jazz Singer* used a "sound-on-disc" system, which Walt rejected as unsuitable. In the short time since then, the technology had advanced, allowing sound to be recorded directly to film itself, thereby establishing perfect synchronization.

Without fanfare, Walt arrived one day at a Mickey Mouse gag meeting that Wilfred Jackson recalled years later:

> Walt said, "I've just heard that they've invented a way to put sound on film." He said, "Now that they can get sound on film, they're not going to have the trouble that they had with those discs. If the film breaks and gets patched wrong, it'll still fit, because the sound will be right on the same piece of film with the picture. Before long, there are not going to be any more silent films. Before long, everything will be sound. I wonder if there's a way we can put sound with cartoons. I know how fast the film is going to go. The film is going to go ninety feet per minute. But how in hell do you tell how fast the music is going to go? How do you know how fast the sound is going to go?"[7]

The challenge Walt faced was to match the sound with the action of the cartoon. Jackson's mother was a music teacher and he had some idea of how it might be done. Jackson recalled that the next day, "I brought my mother's metronome down to the studio and I could set it so it would 'tick' every eight frames, every twelve frames, etc. It was just mathematics. I could also play a few tunes on a mouth organ, so I could set the thing ticking and play my mouth organ and Walt could see how fast the music would go. It was on this basis that *Steamboat Willie* was planned."[8] As Jackson played the music, Walt was able to easily calculate how many drawings would be required to match the music.

What may seem obvious to us today had never been done before. A method for creating a cartoon in which the images were a succession of drawings, and assigning synchronized sound to those images so that they exactly matched the action on the screen, was a problem that had yet to be worked out. Until this time, nobody had a reason to give it any thought.

Adding sound required a fundamental rethinking of the entire animation process. Without sound, the timing details of the animation sequences could be left to the animators, and exposure sheets to provide instructions to the cameraman on how the animation is to be shot would be created *after* the animation. But with the addition of sound, the timing of the animation became more critical. Exposure sheets now had to come *first* to provide instructions to the animators to ensure proper sound and picture synchronization.

Upon reviewing the available technology options to synchronize sound and pictures, Walt's preference was to record the sound directly to a thin strip that ran along the edge of the film, known as a "soundtrack." When the idea was presented to Roy, he reluctantly agreed that they should try it, but left it up to Walt and Ub to select an appropriate story suitable for recorded sound.[9]

With two unsold Mickeys in the can, Walt and Iwerks began work on a third Mickey film that was intended for sound—*Steamboat Willie*—with ideas borrowed from a Buster Keaton comedy. With no pre-existing commitments, and no requirement to negotiate approval with a reluctant distributor concerned only about maximizing profits on each new release rather than strategic positioning for a changing marketplace, Walt had the luxury of moving quickly to gain first-mover advantage.

Mickey Mouse Breaks the Sound Barrier

Apart from technical innovations and process changes that were required to solve emerging production challenges brought on by sound synchronization, the addition of sound constituted a complete paradigm shift indicative of all technological change. The famous animated characters which audiences had come to love, such as Krazy Kat and Oswald the Rabbit, were pantomime characters that had never uttered a word aloud. Successful producers of silent movies worried that the illusion would be broken if the characters themselves had voices. For this reason, within the industry, the advent of talkies was initially resisted and treated with a high degree of skepticism.

At the time, studios were uncertain as to whether audiences would accept sound in movies as more than a passing fad. Even in 1929, nine out of ten letters to the editor of *Photoplay* indicated that the general public would prefer a first-rate silent picture, which was typically accompanied by live music, over a second-rate talking picture.[10] Walt's childhood hero, Charlie Chaplin, was himself an outspoken opponent of talking films. Audiences and the studios were of divided opinions, and the industry as a whole was proceeding very cautiously.

One other aspect indictating caution was the high cost of new sound equipment and its installation into existing theatres, as well as the high quality of the sound fidelity required to maintain the audience illusion of being inside the movie. Distribution and accompanying box office receipts would be severely limited without a network capable of showing sound movies. *The Jazz Singer* itself had been released in both sound and silent versions for this reason.

Against this backdrop, Walt needed to know for himself whether the illusion of sound would be compelling. Animator Wilfred Jackson, who was working with Walt at the time, recalled Walt's curiosity. Walt recognized that cartoons aren't like regular studio live-action films. Audiences are used to people talking and the sound a slamming door makes, but people aren't used to hearing drawings make a noise. What Walt needed to know, said Jackson, was, "will people believe that the sound is coming from the drawing or will they just think there's somebody up there behind the screen talking while the picture is running? Will this be effective? Will they believe in cartoons?"[11]

To find out, Walt set up his own experiment. On a warm July night, almost ten months after *The Jazz Singer*'s debut, Walt invited his animators along with their wives and some friends to the studio. Roy projected the silent *Steamboat Willie* through the glass pane in Walt's office door to eliminate projector noise, and onto a bed sheet strung so that the picture could be seen from both sides. Iwerks had rigged a microphone to a speaker so that the audience in another room could hear the sound played in one room through the speaker.

Jackson, Iwerks, Cannon, and Walt worked from the music and sound-effects score to test whether the synchronization would work, providing sound with a harmonica, washboards, sliding whistles, sound effects, and some dialogue. Each man took turns watching the sound-enabled film from inside the studio to observe the movie combined with sound projected from the speaker, and each concluded that the illusion was effective. All agreed that the experiment was a success, and that history was being made.[12]

Walt later recalled, "It was terrible, but it was wonderful! And it was something new!" Iwerks said of that night, "It was wonderful; there was no precedent of any kind. I've never been so thrilled in my life. Nothing since has ever equaled it. That evening proved that an idea could be made to work."[13] Jackson said he was so excited about the idea of animation with sound that "I could hardly sleep that first night after that gag meeting."[14]

With a viable proof of concept, Walt, Roy, and Ub agreed that having come this far, they owed it to themselves to finish what they had started and use the last of the money in the bank to send Walt to New York to record a soundtrack for *Steamboat Willie*.

On his way to New York by train, Walt stopped in Kansas City to ask a favor of friend, theatre organist and composer Carl Stalling: could he compose and retrofit a musical score for *Steamboat Willie*, timing it to the beats that Iwerks had marked on the film? Stalling was excited by the challenge of the project and agreed to help.

With Stalling's completed score in hand, Walt set off to New York City with his studio's future riding on his success. He had left copies of the first two silent Mickeys, *Plane Crazy* and *The Gallopin' Gaucho*, with Stalling to compose a musical score. If things went well in New York, Stalling would join up with Walt to participate in the recording sessions.[15]

Walt arrived in New York on September 4, 1928, and immediately reconnected with Jack Alicoate, the trade paper editor who had provided him with support in his final contract negotiation with Charles Mintz. Alicoate was able to refer Walt to credible sound-recording experts.[16]

Walt discovered that the New York film community was still looking upon movies with sound as a fad, and were not yet convinced that audiences would accept talkies. Walt wrote to Roy:

> None of them [movie executives] are positive how it is all going to turn out, but I have come to this definite conclusion: sound effects and talking pictures are more than a mere novelty. They are here to stay and in time will develop into a wonderful thing. The ones that get in on the ground floor are the ones that will more likely profit by its future development. That is, providing they work for quality and not quantity and quick money. Also, I am convinced that the sound on film is the only logical thing for the future. At the present it is necessary to have both in order to cover the field one hundred percent."[17]

Walt had already rejected the idea of recording to a phonograph record, as some of the movie companies were doing. He concluded that separating the recording from the film was a sure road to trouble because it would be difficult to ensure synchronization between the sound and the visuals, and the intended illusion of bringing animation to life would be destroyed. Instead, Walt was convinced that the sound had to be recorded directly to the film itself, and set about looking for an appropriate solution.[18] He had difficulty finding one that matched up to his high quality standards and expectations.

Walt approached Fox to engage their assistance, but they were busy adding sound to feature films with their system, and weren't interested in a small job of Walt's size. RCA, on the other hand, was very interested.

When Walt asked for a demonstration, they showed him a test recording they had done on an Aesop's Fables cartoon, *Dinner Time*. Walt wrote to Roy and Ub expressing his extreme disappointment:

> MY GOSH—TERRIBLE—A lot of racket and nothing else. I was terribly disappointed. I really expected to see something half-way decent. BUT HONESTLY—it was nothing but one of the rottenest fables I believe that I ever saw, and I should know because I have seen almost all of them. It merely has an orchestra playing and adding some noises. That talking part does not mean a thing. It doesn't even match. We sure have nothing to worry about from these quarters.[19]

Walt concluded that RCA wanted too much money for an inferior product—a $600 fee, plus the cost of an orchestra, plus a $1,000 royalty, plus a "music tax" to the publisher, etc.,—and Walt "dropped them from my mind entirely."[20]

In the end, he found and settled on working with a former movie executive and film industry entrepreneur named Pat Powers, who owned the Cinephone recording system.

Walt met with Powers and was introduced to Carl Edouarde, the conductor of the orchestra at the Strand Theater, and was impressed with both. Edouarde was excited about the opportunity to record for Walt, and indicated he could do the whole thing with five or six players and a couple of sound-effects men. Powers offered to handle the recording for $1,000 plus a royalty on the Disney films. Also, of great importance to Walt, Powers said he would use his many industry connections to help Walt secure distribution.

Walt cut a check to Powers for $500, and in a letter to Roy expressed his dislike for New York and his inability to "mix with strangers and enjoy myself like some people. ... I have so much time to kill at night that I almost go nuts."[21] He also instructed Ub to begin the next Mickey Mouse cartoon, *The Barn Dance*.

The recording session was scheduled for September 15, 1928. Edouarde arrived with seventeen musicians, three drummers, and sound-effects men, each to be paid ten dollars an hour for three hours work.[22] Walt argued for less, but in the end agreed to proceed. "This is our first picture," he wrote to Roy. "It has got to be a wow. On the strength of it we are going to sell the entire series."[23]

Unfortunately, the recording session was a complete failure. Edouarde ignored Walt's synchronization system, consisting of a film that Walt had hired a theatrical-trailer company to make depicting a ball bouncing metronome-like to the tempo of the music.[24] Edouarde insisted that he could synchronize the orchestra to the movie projected on the wall by watching the cartoon, and ignored the bouncing ball. It turned out that the action was too fast and the musicians weren't able to keep pace while discerning and maintaining the meter.[25]

Having spent the last of the studio's money, Walt had no funds for a second recording. He was discouraged that their thousand dollars was wasted, but having come this close, and knowing exactly how to do it right now that he had seen it done wrong, he wasn't prepared to give up. He saw this as a defining moment and a time to muster his tenacity. He sent a telegram to Roy:

> TONE VALUE PERFECT BUT RESULTS ARE NOT SATISFACTORY STOP ALL CONCERNED DESIRE BEST RESULTS OBTAINABLE THEREFORE ARE REMAKING IT...I AM VERY OPTIMISTIC ABOUT RESULTS AND OUR FUTURE LOOKS BRIGHT STOP GAVE POWERS CHECK ONE THOUSAND BE SURE IT IS OK.

From New York City, Walt instructed Roy in California to find the money for a second recording session, in which Walt insisted on using his sound-to-film synchronization method for the recording. When Walt learned that Roy was having trouble raising money, Walt gave Roy permission to sell Walt's beloved Moon Cabriolet roadster, and wrote a letter of optimism and encouragement to Roy and Iwerks to ease the disappointment:

> I am figuring on a good release. I don't think we will have any trouble getting it; this may mean the making of a big organization out of our little dump. Why should we let a few dollars jeopardize our chances? I think this is Old Man Opportunity rapping at our door. Let's don't let the jingle of a few pennies drown out his knock. See my point? So slap as big a mortgage on everything we got and let's go after this thing in the right manner.[26]

Walt was confident that this was worth an all-or-nothing bet.

Walt spent the next two weeks in New York taking charge and planning everything out to ensure that the recording session would be a success. He was determined to get what he came for, hoped for, and paid for. Back at the Disney studio, Walt had Iwerks create another print with a bouncing ball across the bottom to visually indicate to Edouarde the exact placement of each beat.[27] Walt also persuaded Edouarde to reduce the orchestra to a more manageable size and hire only two special-effects men. Walt himself participated by supplying the vocal sounds of Mickey, Minnie, and the parrot.

The second recording session on September 30, 1928, was a complete success. With conductor Edouarde following the beats marked on the screen, the sound was perfectly synchronized to the animated action.

A Mouse in Search of a House

Walt now had a product that was truly unique and sensational. He was also fully aware that it really wasn't worth anything unless he could sell it to a distributor and get it placed in movie theatres so it could make money for him.

Pat Powers was able to get him appointments for showings, but even Walt, with his unbounded enthusiasm for selling his own cartoons, found it to be a weary, tiring, and uninspiring process. Walt found himself waiting around outside projection rooms until Mickey Mouse could be given a showing, and then receiving a variation of the same reply when he asked potential distributors for an opinion: "We'll call you about it," or "We'll be in touch with Pat Powers."[28] When he heard that, it was inevitably the last he would hear from them.

Walt had now been in New York for almost seven weeks. Three weeks had passed since the successful recording session. Walt was convinced that there wasn't anything out there better than *Steamboat Willie*, leaving him perplexed that nobody seemed to be interested in taking on distributorship.

Through the assistance of Pat Powers, Walt was able to arrange a screening of *Steamboat Willie* on October 19, 1928, for Universal Pictures president Robert Cochran and other executives, and they loved it. They were mesmerized by its perfect synchronization. Walt wrote to Lillian that night, "I have never seen an audience of hard-boiled Film Executives laugh so much."[29]

On the basis of the screening, an appointment was set up for Walt to meet with executives at the Universal offices the next day to discuss a deal. Walt was so elated that he returned to Powers' office to tell him the good news, and then without consulting with Roy, proceeded to sign an agreement by which Powers would serve as the studio's sales agent for two years in return for ten percent of the studio's revenues.

Walt made his way to the Universal offices the next morning eager to hear what they had to offer. According to Walt Disney biographer Neal Gabler:

> Walt met with a Universal executive named Metzger, [and] it turned out that Universal did not want to distribute Mickey Mouse, at least not yet. Instead, without paying any compensation to Walt, they wanted to put *Willie* on the bill with a Universal picture, *Melody of Love*, playing at the lavish Colony Theater, and see how the audience and the reviewers reacted. Then, assuming a positive response, they would contract for twenty-six Mickeys in [1929] and fifty-two the next year. Walt may have been disappointed, but he was receptive, and Universal prepared an option agreement....[30]

That night, Walt reflected on various scenarios and options, and by morning was having second thoughts about dealing with Universal. He had learned from experience to be wary of New York movie executives and their empty promises, and feared what would happen if Universal showed *Steamboat Willie* and then decided not to make a deal. He knew from his prior visit to New York to negotiate the Oswald contract extension that Universal was locked up contractually with Mintz until at least June 1929, and worried that a negative decision by Universal might weaken his bargaining power with other distributers. Walt's reluctance to get caught up in the uncertainty of the situation led him to decline Metzger's offer. He left Metzger's office without signing a contract while agreeing to further considerations.[31]

Based on his experiences doing business with New York film executives, Walt formed an opinion of the caliber and character of those he had to deal with while retaining his optimism, and expressed it in a letter he wrote Lillian that night, October 20, 1928, in which he indicated that he was not going to let Universal "bulldose" him:

> I have certainly learned a lot about this game already. It is the damnedest mixed-up affair I have ever heard of. It sure demands a shrewd and thoroughly trained mind to properly handle it. There are so damned many angles that continually come up that if a person hasn't the experience, etc., it would certainly lick one. They are all a bunch of schemers and just full of tricks that would fool a greenhorn. I am sure glad I got someone to fall back on for advice. I would be like a sheep amongst a pack of wolves. I have utmost confidence and faith in Powers and believe that if we don't try to rush things too fast that we will get a good deal out of this. We will all just have to have patience and confidence. I am very optimistic about everything and want you all to feel the same way. I really think our big chance is here.[32]

Walt maintained communications with Universal, who indicated that they were engaged in further calculations before making Walt another offer. In the meantime, he met with Paramount and Film Booking Office (FBO) to gauge their interest. Like everybody else who had seen *Steamboat Willie*, both were very enthusiastic but were unwilling to pick up the series for distribution.[33]

On Friday, October 26, 1928, after being in New York for seven weeks, Walt's musician-friend and composer Carl Stalling arrived in New York with the finished scores for *Plane Crazy* and *The Gallopin' Gaucho*. The two men stayed up late that night at their hotel talking business and working.

Walt heard back from Universal the next day. While he was hopeful but skeptical that something positive might arise, he was told that because of their distribution agreement with Charles Mintz, they were unable to complete a deal with Walt.[34] Walt was disappointed, but not surprised. His decision not to sign the option agreement originally proposed by Universal was vindicated.

At the same time Walt was in New York, Iwerks was back at the studio animating the next Mickey cartoon, *The Barn Dance*. Walt implored Iwerks to expedite its completion so it could be filmed and shipped to Walt. The print arrived in New York three days after Stalling arrived, and Stalling prepared the score.

Walt fully believed in the viability of his product and was not deterred by his inability to secure a distribution agreement. Everybody who saw *Plane Crazy* agreed it was sensational. Walt was convinced that monetizing the product was now only a matter of time.

Walt was situated in the heart of New York City, in possession of three additional Mickey Mouse cartoons with musical scores completed by Stalling, and in proximity of the recording studio, musicians, and equipment where the task could be completed. Once again he faced what seemed to be his perpetual curse: no cash or access to credit. Roy had already borrowed against everything they owned, including the acquisition of $4,000 by taking out second mortgages on their homes and the sale of Walt's car. Most of that money was already spent. With scoring fees to Stalling, studio recording fees, and living expenses, the cost of his New York venture was already approaching $6,000. Walt estimated a need for another $1,500 to pay for the sound recordings for the other three completed films.[35]

When Pat Powers learned of Walt's predicament, he came to Walt's rescue by offering to pay the cost of the recording sessions. Walt quickly proceeded to record the soundtracks at Pat Powers' studio.[36]

Perhaps the most fortuitous event in Walt's long ordeal of screenings in New York was his good fortune to meet Harry Reichenbach, a well-known and admired public relations specialist who had had an interesting and colorful career as a movie press agent, publicity director, and PR specialist for various motion picture companies. At the time he was working for Carl Laemmle, the founder of Universal pictures and theatres. One of Reichenbach's responsibilities was to increase audiences at Universal's Colony Theatre, on Broadway in midtown Manhattan, with a seating capacity of 1,761.[37]

It was at the Colony that Reichenbach was in attendance at one of Walt's screenings for a prospective distributor. Like others, he was impressed with Walt and his sound cartoon, and immediately recognized an opportunity to capitalize on its novelty to increase attendance at the Colony. Reichenbach provided his informed opinion about movie executives to Walt in the form of a proposition: "Those guys don't know what's good until the public tells them. ... I want to put that cartoon in the Colony."[38]

Walt's first inclination was to reject the idea. He worried that a public showing before he secured a distribution deal would hurt his chances with distributors. But Reichenbach held the opposite view. "You can chase that cartoon all over town and those companies won't buy. Not until the public tells 'em it's good. Let me run it for two weeks so the press can see it. You'll get good reviews, and the people will come in droves." Reichenbach offered Walt $500 per week for two weeks, more than had ever been paid to play a cartoon in a single theatre.[39] Walt had no other current source of income and desperately needed the $1,000 to extend his stay in New York and complete the production of the other three Mickey Mouse cartoons. Without a better idea, he agreed to Reichenbach's terms.

Bob Thomas, in *Walt Disney: An American Original*, describes the historic premiere and industry response to *Steamboat Willie* and Mickey Mouse:

> *Steamboat Willie* opened at the Colony Theater on November 18, 1928, and it was the sensation that Walt had dreamed it would be. The bill featured a talking movie, *Gang War*, starring Olive Borden and Jack Pickford, and a stage show headed by Ben Bernie and his orchestra. But the patrons left the theater talking about *Steamboat Willie*, billed as "the FIRST animated cartoon with SOUND." *Variety* reported: "It's a peach of a synchronization job all the way, bright, snappy, and fitting the situation perfectly. ... With most of the animated cartoons qualifying as a pain in the neck, it's a signal tribute to this particular one. ... Recommended unreservedly for all wired houses." *Weekly Film Review*: "It kept the audience laughing and chuckling from the moment the lead titles came on the screen, and it left them applauding." *Exhibitor Herald*: "It is impossible to describe this riot of mirth, but it knocked me out of my seat."
>
> Even *The New York Times* took note of the first sound cartoon by Walter Disney, described as the creator of Oswald the Rabbit and now of "a new cartoon character henceforth to be known as 'Mickey Mouse.'" The *Times* critic conceded that the film was "an ingenious piece of work with a good deal of fun. It growls, whines, squeaks and makes various other sounds that add to its mirthful quality."
>
> Night after night Walt stood at the back of the theater and listened to the warm, fresh waves of laughter that greeted the cartoon images on the screen. Reichenbach had been right; at last the film companies were calling Walt Disney to come in and discuss a deal.[40]

Disney historian Michael Barrier writes in *The Animated Man: A Life of Walt Disney*, "This Disney cartoon combined sound and pictures with a seeming effortlessness that no other sound film matched. It was no wonder that critics and audiences loved it."[41]

The distributors that approached Walt talked about structuring an arrangement similar in kind to what Mintz had offered to Walt in his failed Oswald negotiations: How much did Walt want per week as a salary to produce Mickey Mouse cartoons? But Walt wasn't looking to be put on the payroll of another studio. He already had his own studio. And he wasn't going to sell the cartoons outright; he was determined to retain ownership of his cartoons. The distributors he was able to talk to post Colony, including Universal, all said they weren't interested in that kind of arrangement.

Finally, once again, Powers came to the table. He recognized that he could leverage the popularity of Mickey Mouse to promote his Cinephone sound recording technology just as the shift to movies with sound was trending. He and Walt agreed that Walt would own the cartoons and remain independent, and Powers would sell rights to the cartoons on a state-by-state basis, pay for the salesmen and all of the expenses, and advance Walt the money he needed, in return for ten percent of the gross revenues. Powers emphasized that his only real interest was in promoting the Cinephone technology.

Walt felt that the offer by Powers was workable and fair, so he accepted. His studio was back in business.

Walt returned to his California studio in December 1928 and presented his contract with Powers to Roy. Roy was furious. Walt had agreed to use Powers' Cinephone sound recording equipment for ten years at a cost of $26,000 a year. "Did you read this? Do you know what you promised?" yelled Roy.[42]

Walt justified the investment by telling Roy he needed the equipment. Rather than having to travel to New York to record the soundtrack for each new cartoon, Walt purchased equipment from Powers, had it shipped to California, and set up his own recording studio.[43] He was no longer comfortable leaving key components of his business process to others.

For each new Mickey Mouse cartoon, Iwerks did most of the drawing with the assistance of some newly hired and experienced animation staff that Walt had recruited while in New York (Ben Sharpsteen, Burt Gillett, and Dick Lundy). Carl Stalling continued to score the music.

Iwerks recalled these as great days, and amongst the best times of his life. "Making films in those days was lots of fun. It really was. We'd hate to go home at night, and we couldn't wait to get to the office in the morning. We had lots of vitality, and we had to work it off. ... We all loved what we were doing and our enthusiasm got onto the screen."[44]

Leveraging Assets for Product Extension, Growth, and Vitality

With the instant overnight success of Mickey Mouse, the studio once again had a potential hit series. Walt worried, however, that his fate was tied to a single character, and it might soon become old and tiresome.

As a way to diversify, Stalling suggested to Walt that he create a new series of cartoons in which the stories would be drawn to fit the music, instead of the music being composed to fit the story. As an example, Stalling described a ghoulish graveyard scene set to the music of Grieg's "March of the Dwarfs," in what would become The Skeleton Dance. Each cartoon would stand alone without repeating characters, and would serve as an experimental testing ground for the studio animators to try out new ideas, techniques, and technologies to further the art of animation. The series would come to be called Silly Symphonies.[45]

The graveyard gags for *The Skeleton Dance* were worked out by Walt and Iwerks prior to Iwerks animating almost all of it himself. When Pat Powers received and screened the completed picture in New York, he wrote back: "They don't want this. MORE MICE."[46]

Walt was convinced Powers was wrong, so he arranged to have *Skeleton Dance* shown at a downtown Los Angeles theatre to test the audience response. The audience was enthusiastic about the film, but the manager said it was too gruesome to recommend.

Never one to concede or give up easily, Walt arranged through an acquaintance for the film to be shown to the owner of the prestigious Carthay Circle Theatre in Hollywood. The owner liked it, booked it, and the response was overwhelmingly positive. Walt sent the reviews to Powers and suggested he contact Samuel L. Rothafel, owner of the 5,920-seat Roxy Theatre in New York. Rothafel also saw the entertainment value of the cartoon and booked it, providing the official launch of the Silly Symphonies series in August 1929.[47]

By this time, Mickey Mouse had been making appearances in movie houses for more than six months, and had become a national sensation. As Walt had done with Alice and Oswald, he pressed his staff for higher quality. Higher quality meant more innovation. This came in two forms: improved organizational design through task specialization, and improved processes. At the same time, the organization had to cope with rising production costs and mounting deadline pressures.

Organizational design changes came about incrementally and informally as better ways were discovered to do the work. The addition of visual and sound synchronization meant that there was a requirement for the animation process to be more structured. On the first few Mickey cartoons Walt assumed the role of director, handled story development, and when sound was added, made decisions about animation timing. Iwerks did almost all of the animation.

Out of necessity, Walt began to see the division of tasks from the perspective of a producer of products requiring the conjoining of artistic creativity with modern production practices. Many animators like Iwerks and others to follow saw this as a constraint on their creative integrity. The issue goes far beyond the question of artistic pride: more fundamentally, in a commercial context, it is a question of whether the artist or the studio owns the work, and who has the authority to make the final call when disagreements arise—the employee or the employer?

Success in business requires clear lines of accountability linked by a hierarchy of capability to a single authority. Effective managerial leadership requires a balancing of interests and a sorting out of conflicts. Leaders of a successful organization cannot tolerate a situation that sanctions or embraces the mis-coordination and mis-alignment of tasks and resources, where each person is free to do one's own thing. As employees, artists work for the studio, not for themselves. They are hired to put forth their best effort to achieve the results that are set out in the work they are assigned. In an employee-employer relationship, it is the judgment of the employer that sets the context and standard for the work to be done and to assess the quality of the output in relation to that standard. Very often artists disagree with the assessment of their work by others. When those assessments are without valid criteria, they tend to be arbitrary and unfair.

Walt saw the value of Iwerks as paramount to the success of the studio, and with pressure mounting to do more, was anxious for Iwerks to make better use of his time by sharing more of his animation obligations with less talented and less proficient animators. The idea was that animators could increase their output by planning out the story and concentrating on drawing key poses (the extremes) and letting less-experienced and less expensive artists do the drawings that fall between the extremes (the in-betweens). Iwerks felt that by drawing the extreme poses and delegating the in-between poses, the quality of the animation would suffer by making it appear more static and less interesting. In contrast to Walt's recommended method, Iwerks preferred to draw every pose himself, relying on assistants to fill in the specific details (for example, the ribs of the skeletons in *The Skeleton Dance*).[48]

Another place where Walt and Iwerks had different perspectives was the timing of animated sequences. Frequently, Iwerks would prepare exposure sheets for the cameraman indicating the timing of sequences, which Walt would later change. Animator Mark Kausler explains in Leslie Iwerks and John Kenworthy's *The Hand Behind the Mouse* how this frustrated Iwerks:

> Walt would be constantly rewriting Ub's exposure sheets to change the timing to something he wanted, and it was different from what Ub imagined when he was animating it. Timing is very sacred to an animator because it's such an integral part. It's not just drawings. It's drawings as applied to film time. The rate of exposure is very important to get the effects across that the animator wants. The fact that somebody was changing it—Walt was fooling around, changing it—probably disturbed him fundamentally because it was breaking that connection between drawing and film timing.[49]

Iwerks and Kenworthy write that at one point Ub Iwerks became furious at Walt's changes and confronted him. "'Don't you ever touch my drawings!' he demanded. 'These are my drawings and this is how I solve the problems, keep your hands off them!' Ub won the immediate battle on *The Skeleton Dance*, but the issue was far from resolved."[50]

As additional skilled and capable animators were hired, Iwerks' role began to change. Walt, Stalling, and Iwerks spent more time working together to develop story ideas set to music, which had now become an integral dimension of all Disney cartoons. Walt had settled in 1929 upon the adoption of a new studio policy "that from now on all the action [in the Mickey Mouse cartoons] will be set to a definite [rhythm] and we will have no more straight action to a mere musical background."[51] As Walt and Stalling matched the story to the music, Walt created the exposure sheet that dictated the timing of the scenes to the artists. Iwerks' primary duty was to sketch the story ideas and show the animators how to stage their scenes, which were assigned to each animator by Walt.[52] Over time and out of necessity, organizational hierarchy, structure, and processes were evolving to meet the needs of the business and ensure its survival.

Walt was busier than ever now that the studio was producing two series simultaneously. In April 1929 he invited animator Burt Gillett to join his staff. Gillett was ten years Walt's senior, and a very experienced and renowned New York animator who had been working for Charles Mintz on his Krazy Kat series at the time of his hiring.[53] Gillett began assisting Walt in preparing story ideas for animation.

In the late summer of 1929, Walt created two distinct work units in which Iwerks served as the director for the Silly Symphonies and Gillett as the director for the Mickey Mouse cartoons.[54] The two directors were given the tasks of working with Stalling to prepare the bar sheets and exposure sheets, and to provide the drawings to stage the scenes of the story for the animators.[55] In recognition of Iwerks' importance to the studio, Walt increased his salary to $150 a week, while Walt continued to earn $75 a week.[56] A full-time background painter was appointed for the first time in 1929.[57]

The addition of synchronized sound created a renewed interest in cartoons among the public. It also created a growing opportunity for expensive errors. It was important to identify animation errors early in the process before costs mounted; otherwise, rework could become prohibitively expensive and consume all of the profits. Greater attention was directed toward finding more efficient and less costly processes, with a pre-emptive eye on quality control.

One such innovation was the creation of the pencil test. Animation historian Michael Barrier reports in *The Animated Man* that around this time, some of Walt's animators discovered that they could film their pencil drawings at the end of the day to review them and see if they turned out as envisioned, before advancing the work forward to the next stages of production. It was prudent to spend some money on quality control up front to preempt more extensive and costly rework later. Pencil tests were also used by animators to check animation cycles for mistakes that if left uncorrected would be seen by the audience over and over again, as aspects of the scene were repeated.

"That Guy's a Crook"

Walt's push for continuous improvement of overall picture quality had led to the addition of new steps to the creative and production process that were pushing up his operating costs. The average cost for each animated cartoon had risen to $5,000, and Walt was counting on his share of box-office receipts from Powers to pay for the added expense.

Mickey Mouse had become a national sensation, appearing on more and more screens, and yet the weeks were passing and no money from box-office receipts had arrived. Roy was suspicious, and suspected that Powers was working with two sets of books. To resolve the problem, Roy agreed to meet with Powers in New York and investigate why the studio wasn't being paid, but Powers refused to share any financial information, leading Roy to the conclusion, "That guy's a crook."[58]

The Disneys hired prominent Yale-educated lawyer Gunther Lessing, who went on to have a successful 35-year career with Disney heading the legal department and in later years being promoted to vice-president and general council of Walt Disney Productions.[59] In part, Lessing was hired for the assignment because of his colorful yet intimidating image as Pancho Villa's lawyer, and his imposing physical appearance.

On January 17, 1930, Walt and Lillian departed for New York to confront Powers. Walt met with Powers on January 21, 1930. Outwardly, Powers was nonchalant about Mickey Mouse, focusing instead on his enthusiasm for promoting Cinephone, but in fact, he was making a lot of money from Mickey Mouse and was desperate to renew Walt's contract when it expired. He was intent on pushing the conversation in that direction. He knew that with the increasing popularity of Mickey Mouse, he was potentially sitting on the proverbial golden egg.

Walt wasn't there to talk about contract renewals and wasn't receptive. He wanted to know why he wasn't being paid according to the current contract. He insisted on being shown an accounting of the receipts for the cartoons, but Powers again refused. Instead, he offered up news that he said would convince Walt to renew the contract. Powers told Walt that he was establishing a new studio to create a new cartoon series to be distributed by MGM, then handed Walt a telegram indicating that he had hired Ub Iwerks to head the studio at a salary of $300 a week, double what Walt was paying Iwerks.

Walt was shocked. He and Iwerks had been working together to build this business since their early days in Kansas City and now that they were starting to reap the rewards, it appeared that Iwerks was leaving to join with the unscrupulous Powers. Not only was Iwerks the highest paid person at the studio, earning double what Walt was earning, he was also a twenty-percent partner and officer of the business, and yet he had mentioned nothing to either Walt or Roy about leaving to start a new studio.

Powers encouraged Walt to phone Roy to confirm that this was true. In a scenario reminiscent of what Charles Mintz had recently pulled by stealing away the bulk of Walt's animation staff, Powers tried to leverage Iwerks' importance to Walt as the animator of Mickey Mouse to induce Walt to join with Powers as a salaried employee. "Don't get upset," Powers told Walt. "You haven't lost Ub Iwerks. You can still have him—if you sign with me." Walt shook his head in disbelief. "No. I wouldn't want him," said Walt. "If he feels that way, I couldn't work with him."[60]

"Look," said Powers, "you and your brother need money. I'll make you a deal that will relieve you of the concern about money matters. I'll pay you a weekly salary. I'm willing to go as high as twenty-five hundred dollars a week."

Walt had no interest in working with a person he considered to be unscrupulous—it went without saying that such a person as a business partner couldn't be trusted—but he remained calm and indicated that he needed to talk to Roy and to think things over.

Upon returning to his hotel he immediately called Roy. According to Bob Thomas, writing in *Walt Disney: An American Original*:

> Ub had come to Roy that day and said he wanted to be released from the partnership. Ub said that artistic differences had developed between him and Walt. He made no mention of the Powers contract.[61]

When Iwerks met with Roy at the studio to announce with no forewarning that he was leaving, Roy too was shocked, and tried to talk him out of it, but Iwerks had made up his mind. Roy had no idea at that time that Iwerks had been lured away by Powers.

Immediately following Iwerks' resignation, Roy sent a telegram to Walt in New York, which read in part:

> Ubbe resigns effective soon as possible. Wants to leave at completion this picture. Will hold him long as possible. Gives his reasons personal differences with you, admits other connections. Declines to say who or what. Will attempt settlement of his interest. Will get full release from all possible claims. Will consult attorney on same. Our talk was limited. He has not given any views on what he expects.[62]

The means by which Iwerks left the Disney organization soon became known. Iwerks had been in secret negotiations for about four months—since

September 1929—with Pat Powers' right-hand man, Charles Giegerich. At the same time Giegerich was working with Walt on behalf of Powers, he was also secretly courting Iwerks to abandon Walt with the promise of financial backing to head up his own studio. Iwerks was promised a doubling of his salary to $300 a week, and in return he was to produce an original cartoon series to be distributed by Metro-Goldwyn-Mayer. In later discussions, Iwerks told Roy that throughout the process, he wasn't aware of who the financial backer of the arrangement was, and only discovered when he was presented with a contract to sign that Giegerich was representing Pat Powers.

After ten years as Walt's top dog, Iwerks felt that he was now ready and capable of stepping out from under Walt's thumb to manage his own studio. He had become one of the best-known animators in the business, because, as Leslie Iwerks notes in her biography of her grandfather, *The Hand Behind the Mouse*, "Disney had always generously granted Ub full drawing credit in the title cards of the cartoons, an honor that most other animation studios did not bestow in any manner."[63]

Iwerks' partnership agreement with the Disneys specified that he had to remain employed by the studio to remain a partner. When his contract was dissolved, so was his interest in the business, and the cumulated contribution of $2,920 he had made toward his one-fifth interest was returned to him.[64]

The day after Iwerks announced his departure, Roy informed staff composer Carl Stalling that Iwerks was leaving, and Stalling proceeded to do the same. Years later Stalling recalled, "When Ub left, I thought something was wrong. When Roy Disney told me that Ub was leaving, I told him, 'Well, I guess I'll be leaving, too.' It was not very pleasant to think about, because we were all good friends. But we were getting worried. Walt paid only half salary for a year or two and I had a home and expenses."[65]

Recognizing the central role Iwerks played at the studio and his oversight of the Silly Symphonies, Stalling feared that Iwerks leaving would be the final nail in the studio's coffin. With the studio running in the red because of its investment in sound and non-payment by Powers, Stalling anticipated the demise of the studio and chose to abandon ship before it sunk. Stalling aggressively demanded his back pay from Roy, who instructed the accounting office to cut him a check for the full amount.[66] As a leader in scoring animation and a stellar professional reputation, it took Stalling just a few days before he signed a contract with Van Beuren's Aesop's Fables,[67] and later joined Iwerks to compose the music for his cartoons.

Stalling too had a partnership agreement with the Disneys. More than a year earlier, Stalling had accepted an offer by Walt of a one-third interest in the Silly Symphonies series, and had been contributing twenty-five dollars a week from his salary since December 31, 1928. As with Iwerks, leaving the studio voided his interest. Stalling had also invested $2,000 in the Disney Film Recording Company in early 1929 when Walt was trying to raise money to pay for Powers' Cinephone equipment. All of Stalling's money was repaid.[68]

Before leaving Disney to start the Ub Iwerks Studio in February 1930, Iwerks tried to recruit Disney animator Ben Sharpsteen, whom Walt hired based on his New York studio experience and was paying $125 a week. Sharpsteen lacked confidence in Iwerks' ability to run a successful studio and turned him down. Sharpsteen would go on to have a successful 33-year career with Disney as a director and producer.[69]

Iwerks also tried to recruit new Disney hire Floyd Gottfredson, who had been at the studio for just four weeks. Gottfredson was offered a substantial raise to $25 a week so he accepted. "I knew by then," said Gottfredson, "that Ub was *the* man in the animation business, and he told me that he would be able to teach me a lot of things that would be beneficial to me."[70] Fellow animators Burt Gillett and Wilfred Jackson confronted Gottfredson when they learned what he had done: "No, you're absolutely wrong about Ub and you shouldn't have done this. While Ub is a great animator, Walt is really the brains and the creative man here—he's the man who's going to build this place into something really big.'"[71]

Confused about what to do, Gottfredson went to Roy, who confronted Iwerks and demanded that he immediately cease his recruitment of Disney staff. Iwerks released Gottfredson from his contract. Gottfredson went on to have a long successful career with Disney as the head of the comic strip department.

As a result of the loss of long-standing loyal friendships with Iwerks and Stalling going back to their days together in Kansas City, Roy and Walt declared that there would be no more partnerships when it comes to studio ownership; that from now on it would be just Walt and Roy.

Future Focus

Back in New York, Walt reflected on his situation. By January 1930, he had delivered a total of twenty-one cartoons to Powers—fifteen Mickey Mouse and six Silly Symphonies. The average cost per film was $5,500 and he estimated that Powers had collected almost $17,000 apiece.[72] As a distributor, Powers was entitled to his 35 percent distributor fee, plus the recovery of costs for prints, processing, advertising, licensing, insurance, music rights, recording fees, print royalties, and foreign dubbing. While the Disneys were certain that Powers was withholding money owed to them, they weren't certain about how much profit there was, but knew the amount owed to them was significant, possibly exceeding $100,000.[73]

Walt maintained cordial discussions with Powers, leaving open the possibility of coming to an agreement, while he decided what to do. When Walt next met with Powers, he told him that Roy had insisted that they were in need of more money to run the studio. Powers offered a check for $5,000, which Walt accepted and immediately mailed to Roy.[74]

At their next meeting, Walt insisted on seeing the film receipts. Powers responded: "Make a deal with me and I'll show you the books."[75] Without a deal, said Powers, they would have to take him to court, which would take considerable time and money that the Disneys didn't have. In discussions with Disney lawyer Gunther Lessing to try and work out a settlement, Powers indicated that he was willing to pay Walt a salary of $2,000 a week if Walt would fulfill the current contract and extend his distribution agreement with Powers for another year.

Walt called Roy to discuss the latest developments. He was not going to work for Powers and give up his studio. The choice that remained was whether to sue Powers for the revenue that was rightfully theirs or to just walk away from a problem that was now in the past. Rather than get bogged down in a long process with a crook, they agreed to walk away and move forward, staying focused on the bigger picture and remaining hopeful about their future prospects.[76]

Still in New York City, Walt immediately began talking to other distributors. Unlike the last time he knocked on their door, he was now welcomed into their offices as the brilliant young cartoon maker of the famous Mickey Mouse. MGM appeared to be interested, but their lawyers quickly decided against it when Powers threatened to sue any company that signed a contract for the Disney cartoons.[77]

Columbia Pictures, on the other hand, was much bolder. They offered Walt a $7,000 advance for each cartoon, and agreed to establish a war fund of $25,000 to combat any potential legal action by Powers.[78]

On February 7, 1930, Walt sent a telegram to Roy:

> HAVE DEFINITELY BROKE WITH POWERS STOP WILL DELIVER NO MORE PICTURES STOP PLAN TO TEMPORARILY SUSPEND PRODUCTION MICKEYS AND CONCENTRATE ON SYMPHONIES WHICH WE WILL DELIVER TO COLUMBIA.[79]

While Walt had good reason to believe that Pat Powers would be his savior when they first met, it turned out not to be so. His relationship with Powers contributed to the phenomenon of Mickey Mouse that was the foundation of all that Walt created thereafter, but it had been a costly beginning.

Walt believed in the value of the films that his studio had created, and agreed to negotiate terms to settle with Powers as the most prudent way out of his current situation, even though he was sure it was Powers who owed him money. In exchange for freedom from his contract and a return of the twenty-one films to Walt, Powers initially suggested a cash settlement in excess of $100,000.[80]

On February 19, 1930, Walt concluded a contract with Columbia Pictures to distribute the Silly Symphonies, which Columbia had been previously distributing under contract with Powers. Columbia had grossed nearly $400,000 on the first thirteen Silly Symphonies, and understood how lucrative a distribution deal would be that also included the much more popular Mickey Mouse. Based on the upside profit potential, the executives at Columbia believed that they could significantly benefit from assisting Walt in removing Powers from the equation.[81] With Columbia now backing his interests and his business in New York concluded for now, Walt headed back to Los Angeles.[82]

With regards to Mickey Mouse, Roy was later sent to New York to participate in a three-sided negotiation between Disney, Powers, and Columbia Pictures, with decisions affecting the studio to be approved by Walt. Michael Barrier, in *The Animated Man*, summarizes the key elements of the settlement reached by the parties after three weeks of bargaining:

> The settlement, signed on April 22, was expensive—the Disneys not only gave up their claims against Powers but had to give him fifty thousand dollars, money they borrowed from Columbia and would have to repay from their films' profits before they saw any profits themselves. But Columbia would advance the Disneys seven thousand dollars upon the delivery of each film—they would actually be able to spend more on each cartoon than they could when they were getting smaller advances from Powers and seeing none of their profits. "I honestly feel elated over everything," Roy wrote to Walt on May 6. "Settlement going to work out good and future very bright."[83]

Now, with Iwerks and Stalling gone, the new hires being assimilated, new cartoons in production and on schedule, and the business matters settled, the future was indeed looking bright for Walt. One of his associates said that it was clearly evident that "a weight of worry" had been lifted off Walt's shoulders, enabling him to sanguinely return to his love for making movies again.[84]

Prior to Iwerks leaving, Walt had relied on him to provide leadership and stability to the animation units. He was the highest paid employee and a partner in the business. When Iwerks announced his resignation and then tried to recruit Walt's staff, Walt learned a valuable lesson: he could never again put himself in the position where he relied so heavily on one person. From the evidence that the studio could successfully survive and continue to thrive without Iwerks, Walt came to the conclusion that nobody at the studio—except his brother and partner Roy—was untouchable.

Walt's ability to continue to overcome adversity through his own leadership led him to the realization that while he needed a strong organization to succeed, many on his staff needed him just as much as—if not more than—he needed any individual on his staff. Walt realized he didn't need stars or heroes. He needed qualified and motivated team players. Many came to learn the lesson that Walt was just learning: that the power of Walt Disney's vision, leadership, and tenacity were the creative driving forces behind the success of the organization. All those who under-estimated this came to appreciate it later, including Charles Mintz, Hugh Harman and Rudy Ising, Pat Powers, Ub Iwerks and Carl Stalling, and a large number of later artists and others critical of Walt's artistic vision and business acumen, who, when given the chance and opportunity, were unable to do successfully what had seemed so simple and obvious when watching Walt do it.

1. Thomas, *Walt Disney*, 88.

2. Thomas, *Walt Disney*, 83–84.

3. Barrier, *The Animated Man*, 75; Steven Watts, *The Magic Kingdom*, 50.

4. Thomas, *Walt Disney*, 89; Iwerks & Kenworthy, *The Hand Behind the Mouse*, 59.

5. Iwerks & Kenworthy, *The Hand Behind the Mouse*, 59.

6. Thomas, *Walt Disney*, 90.

7. Peri, *Working With Walt*, 62-63.

8. Peri, *Working With Walt*, 63.

9. Iwerks & Kenworthy, *The Hand Behind the Mouse*, 61.

10. encyclopedia.jrank.org/articles/pages/2105/The-Talkies-Pro-and-Con.html, accessed November 7, 2016.

11. Peri, *Working with Walt*, 64.

12. Barrier, *The Animated Man*, 60.

13. Iwerks & Kenworthy, *The Hand Behind the Mouse*, 64.

14. Peri, *Working With Walt*, 66.

15. Iwerks & Kenworthy, *The Hand Behind the Mouse*, 65.

16. Thomas, *Walt Disney*, p. 91; Barrier, *The Animated Man*, 61.

17. Thomas, *Walt Disney*, 92.

18. Thomas, *Walt Disney*, 91.

19. Thomas, *Walt Disney*, 92.

20. Thomas, *Walt Disney*, 92.

21. Thomas, *Walt Disney*, 93.

22. Iwerks & Kenworthy, *The Hand Behind the Mouse*, 67.

23. Thomas, *Walt Disney*, 93–94.

24. Barrier, *The Animated Man*, 62.

25. Thomas, *Walt Disney*, 94; Iwerks & Kenworthy, *The Hand Behind the Mouse*, 67.

26. Thomas, *Walt Disney*, 94.

27. Iwerks & Kenworthy, *The Hand Behind the Mouse*, 68.

28. Thomas, *Walt Disney*, 95.

29. Gabler, *Walt Disney*, 124.

30. Gabler, *Walt Disney*, 124.

31. Gabler, *Walt Disney*, 124.

32. Thomas, *Walt Disney*, 95.

33. Gabler, *Walt Disney*, 125.

34. Gabler, *Walt Disney*, 125.

35. Gabler, *Walt Disney*, 125.

36. Gabler, *Walt Disney*, 125.

37. Barrier, "The Animated Man: A Life of Walt Disney: Corrections, Clarifications, and Second Thoughts," at http://www.michaelbarrier.com/Barrier_Books/animated_man_errata.htm, accessed July 22, 2016.

38. Thomas, *Walt Disney*, 95–96.

39. Thomas, *Walt Disney*, 96.

40. Thomas, *Walt Disney*, 96–97.

41. Barrier, *The Animated Man*, 66.

42. Thomas, *Walt Disney*, 98.

43. Barrier, *The Animated Man*, 71; Thomas, *Walt Disney*, 97–98.

44. Iwerks & Kenworthy, *The Hand Behind the Mouse*, 71.

45. Thomas, *Walt Disney*, 99; Iwerks & Kenworthy, *The Hand Behind the Mouse*, 75.

46. Thomas, *Walt Disney*, 100.

47. Thomas, *Walt Disney*, 100.

48. Iwerks & Kenworthy, *The Hand Behind the Mouse*, 76; Barrier, *The Animated Man*, 69, 70.

49. Iwerks & Kenworthy, *The Hand Behind the Mouse*, 78.

50. Iwerks & Kenworthy, *The Hand Behind the Mouse*, 78.

51. Barrier, *The Animated Man*, 70.

52. Barrier, *The Animated Man*, 72.

53. Lenburg, *Who's Who in Animated Cartoons*, 103.

54. Barrier, *The Animated Man*, 74.

55. Barrier, *The Animated Man*, 74.

56 Lenburg, *Who's Who in Animated Cartoons*, 157.

57. Barrier, *The Animated Man*, 72.

58. Thomas, *Walt Disney*, 100; Gabler, *Walt Disney*, 142.

59. http://www.cobbles.com/simpp_archive/gunther_lessing.htm, accessed November 7, 2016.

60. Thomas, *Walt Disney*, 101; Iwerks & Kenworthy, *The Hand Behind the Mouse*, 87.

61. Thomas, *Walt Disney*, 101.

62. Iwerks & Kenworthy, *The Hand Behind the Mouse*, 86.

63. Iwerks & Kenworthy, *The Hand Behind the Mouse*, 80.

64. Thomas, *Walt Disney*, 101.

65. Iwerks & Kenworthy, *The Hand Behind the Mouse*, 87.

66. Gabler, *Walt Disney*, 145.

67. Iwerks, *The Hand Behind the Mouse*, 87.

68. Barrier, *The Animated Man*, 77.

69. "Disney Legends, Ben Sharpsteen," https://d23.com/ben-sharpsteen/, accessed January 19, 2015.

70. Iwerks & Kenworthy, *The Hand Behind the Mouse*, 86.

71. Iwerks & Kenworthy, *The Hand Behind the Mouse*, 88.

72. Thomas, *Walt Disney*, 102.

73. Polsson, *Chronology of the Walt Disney Company*, January 17, 1930.

74. Thomas, *Walt Disney*. 102.

75. Thomas, *Walt Disney*, 102.

76. Thomas, *Walt Disney*, 102.

77. Gabler, *Walt Disney*, 147.

78. Thomas, *Walt Disney*, 103; Barrier, *The Animated Man*, 78.

79. Thomas, *Walt Disney*, 103.

80. Thomas, *Walt Disney*, 103.

81. Gabler, *Walt Disney*, 148.

82. Barrier, *The Animated Man*, 78.

83. Barrier, *The Animated Man*, 79; Gabler, *Walt Disney*, 149.

84. Gabler, *Walt Disney*, 149.

CHAPTER EIGHT

The Merchandising of Mickey Mouse

America's infatuation with Mickey Mouse was almost instantaneous as he began to appear in sound-wired movie houses across America. As a result, the licensing of Mickey Mouse merchandise soon became a valuable source of additional revenue for the studio at a time when cash was desperately needed.

Walt was initially introduced to the possibilities of merchandising his cartoon characters during the Alice Comedies. At the time, picture books and promotional postcards were considered as ancillary promotional products to create greater awareness of the cartoons, but never acted upon.

Universal Pictures took a more proactive approach to merchandise licensing, treating Oswald the Lucky Rabbit in the same manner as it did its other studio stars. Even before the first Oswald cartoon was released in 1927, a "milk chocolate frappe bar" with a likeness of Oswald on the wrapper appeared on the market. According to an August 20, 1927, article in *Universal Weekly*, the promotion of Oswald through chocolate included "an extensive advertising campaign...which includes newspaper space, counter cards, window stickers and banners on all the company's trucks. ... Wherever these bars are sold they form an ideal exhibitor-merchant tie-up which will benefit the theatre and the man selling the candy equally."[1] Other merchandising included novelty buttons featuring Oswald and, in 1928, an Oswald stencil set for children.[2]

As the popularity of Mickey Mouse began to take off in 1929, Walt expressed an interest in using merchandising as a way to enhance Mickey's profile and increase the public awareness of Disney characters. In July he wrote to Powers' associate Charles Gingrich: "I should think that there would be a big market for MICKEY dolls, toys and novelties for the coming season and it may not be a bad idea to feel out the possibilities along these lines as these things are also considered very good publicity."[3]

Walt attributed his first realization of the deeper economic importance of licensing to an event that occurred when he was in New York confronting

Pat Powers in late 1929. One day he received a visit at his hotel by a man who offered him $300 cash for permission to imprint Mickey Mouse on school writing pads. Having need for the money, Walt agreed.[4]

The first signed contract for the licensing of Mickey Mouse was with King Features Syndicate for a Mickey Mouse newspaper comic strip. By Iwerks's recollection, "I got a letter one day from somebody at King Features Syndicate asking me to do a Mickey Mouse comic strip. I turned the letter over to Walt. ... He made the deal, and I did the drawings for a few strips."[5]

Mickey Mouse made his first newspaper comic strip appearance on January 13, 1930, prior to the actual signing of the strip agreement on January 24, 1930, when Walt and his lawyer Gunther Lessing were in New York dealing with Powers.[6]

The strip was originally developed and the drawings for the first eighteen strips roughed out by Iwerks and given to his assistant Win Smith to complete. "Actually, with all the animation work," said Iwerks, "I had no time for comics, I had too much else to do."[7] After six months, Floyd Gottfredson took over its creation and continued with it for his entire career until his retirement in 1975.

For the first year, Iwerks received credit for the strip in a byline, and for the first year-and-a-half Walt reviewed every one until he had enough confidence in Gottfredson that he finally lost interest in overseeing its quality.

Another sign of the rising popularity of Mickey Mouse was the serendipitous proliferation in 1930 of Mickey Mouse Clubs in movie theatres across the country as the Great Depression began to take hold across America, signaled by the stock market crash of October 1929.

The idea for Mickey Mouse Clubs began in September 1929 when a local Los Angeles theatre manager name Harry Woodin was seeking new ways to attract patrons. Woodin approached Walt about starting a weekly children's cinema club based on the growing popularity of Mickey Mouse amongst his customers. Walt was excited by the idea as a way to further promote Mickey Mouse and granted his approval. The club was an immediate success from the very first official club meeting on Saturday, January 11, 1930, filling the Saturday matinee seats for ten or fifteen cents a ticket.[8] Anyone was welcome to attend, but to join the club children were required to fill out a membership application. Other theatre managers took notice of the unique ability of Mickey Mouse to draw audiences, and the idea spread.

Soon Walt was enthusiastic about expanding the club concept across the nation. To help him do so, he hired the man with the original vision, Harry Woodin, to oversee the project, and by the end of 1930, several hundred clubs had been established. Thousands of children were gathering in theatres each week to celebrate Mickey Mouse and engage in activities and games with prizes. Children would leave the theatres with Mickey Mouse masks, pins, banners, candy, and trinkets provided by local sponsors and merchants promoting their wares and looking to build a loyal customer base through association with Mickey Mouse during the depression.[9]

The popularity of Mickey Mouse Clubs grew proportionately with the continued growth in popularity of Mickey Mouse. *McCall's* magazine reported in August 1932, "Mickey Mouse Clubs have been formed in about five hundred American Cities and some 500,000 boys and girls belong to them."[10] By the end of 1932, there were purported to be more than one million children registered, bringing the club on par with membership in the scout movement.[11] Cinema mangers paid a license fee of $25 a year for permission to sponsor a club, which was usually offset through local sponsorships including businesses selling Mickey Mouse merchandise.

By 1935 the studio was finding it difficult to manage the administration of so many clubs, which had now proliferated around the world, and decided to phase out official studio support, thereby allowing theatres to continue on their own. One club in Miami survived into the 1950s.

Roy signed the studio's first Mickey Mouse merchandise licensing contract on February 3, 1930, with the George Borgfeldt Company of New York. Borgfeldt was granted the right to manufacture and sell Mickey and Minnie Mouse figures, toys, novelties, and books, but on renewal toward the end of the year, their representation was restricted to just toys. A sliding royalty scale was agreed upon based on the retail price. The studio would receive two-and-a-half percent on items selling for fifty cents or less, and five percent for more expensive items.[12] Walt understood the profit potential of merchandising and, more importantly, the ability for movies and merchandising to cross-sell and promote one another, but for the most part, merchandising was left to Roy to manage.

As Mickey's popularity increased, merchandising requests began to pour into the studio, and Roy set up an office in New York to manage the merchandising that Borgfeldt wasn't handling.

Within two years, Walt and Roy had become dissatisfied with Borgfeldt. An internal analysis of their performance revealed much: their royalty statement for 1930 indicated that for all of Borgfeldt's activity and talking, the amount paid to the studio was only $63; the time interval from product conception to marketing was too long; they were lazy in identifying new marketing opportunities; and worst of all, the quality of the products featuring Mickey Mouse were often shoddy and inferior, which angered Walt and Roy.[13]

While shopping in Los Angeles one day, Walt was impressed by the department store promotional work of an advertising and promotional professional named Herman "Kay" Kamen. He wired Kamen to see if he was interested in promoting Mickey Mouse. Kamen was very interested and immediately flew from New York to California to meet with Roy.[14]

Neal Gabler describes the meeting in *Walt Disney: The Triumph of the American Imagination*:

> When he arrived at the studio, as Roy remembered it, Kamen walked into Roy's office and said, "I don't know how much business you're doing, but I'll guarantee you that much business and give you fifty percent of everything I do over." It was a sign of both his salesmanship and of the rather offhanded way the company conducted business that they signed a contract with him that July, after the Borgfeldt agreement had expired. Under its terms the studio was to receive 60 percent of the first $100,000 in royalties, with the fifty-fifty split thereafter, and Kamen was to foot all expenses, including his staff, the New York office, and a showroom and hotel suite in Chicago.[15]

Kamen described to Roy how he would merchandise the Disney characters, and emphasized the need to protect the brand by ensuring the quality of the merchandise, which Walt and Roy could appreciate and fully supported. After all, Mickey Mouse was a quality movie star and should be treated as such by being affiliated with the finest manufacturers. Writes Gabler:

> Kamen quickly canceled contracts with less prestigious and aggressive companies and signed up with bigger and better ones—National Dairy Products, Ingersoll watches, General Foods (which would shortly pay a million dollars for the right to put Mickey Mouse and his friends on Post Toasties cereal boxes), and even Cartier jewelers, which was soon marketing a diamond Mickey Mouse bracelet. ... Kamen was a whirlwind. Within a year there were forty licensees for Mickey Mouse products. A year after that, in 1934, Kamen, with a staff numbering fifteen in New York alone, had helped orchestrate $35 million of sales in Disney merchandise in the United States and an equal amount overseas, and he had opened branches across Europe and even in Australia.[16]

By 1935, the phenomenon of Mickey Mouse as a marketing icon was omnipresent. The *New York Times* paid tribute to the marketing of Mickey Mouse in an article on March 10, 1935, noting that the image of Mickey Mouse had become unavoidable. "Shoppers carry Mickey Mouse satchels and briefcases bursting with Mickey Mouse soap, candy, playing cards, bridge favors, hairbrushes, chinaware, alarm clocks and hot water bottles wrapped in Mickey Mouse paper ties with Mickey Mouse ribbon and paid for out of Mickey Mouse purses with savings hoarded in Mickey Mouse banks."[17] Children now lived in a Mickey Mouse world:

> They wear Mickey Mouse caps, waists, socks, shoes, slippers, garters, mittens, aprons, bibs and underthings, and beneath Mickey Mouse rain capes and umbrellas. They go to school where Mickey Mouse desk outfits turn lessons into pleasure.

They play with Mickey Mouse velocipedes, footballs, baseballs, bounce balls, catching gloves, boxing gloves, doll houses, doll dishes, tops, blocks, drums, puzzles, games.

Paint sets, sewing sets, drawing sets, stamp sets, jack sets, bubble sets, pull toys, push toys, animated toys, tents, camp stools, sand pails, masks, blackboards and balloons.[18]

The desire by the public for Mickey Mouse-branded merchandise seemed unquenchable. On more than one occasion, the money received through Mickey Mouse merchandising licenses saved companies from bankruptcy during the depression. Bob Thomas in *Walt Disney: An American Original* recognized two such incidents:

Kamen licensed the Lionel Corporation, pioneer in manufacture of toy electric trains, for the merchandising of a Mickey and Minnie wind-up handcar with a circle of track for the price of $1. Lionel had been hit hard by the depression and had filed for bankruptcy. Within four months, 253,000 of the handcars had been sold, and the association with Disney was credited by a bankruptcy judge as a major factor in returning Lionel to solvency.[19]

The Ingersoll-Waterbury Company, makers of timepieces since 1856, had been pushed close to bankruptcy in the early thirties, when Kamen licensed the firm to manufacture Mickey Mouse watches. Within weeks, demand for the watches caused the company to raise the number of employees at its Waterbury, Connecticut, plant from three hundred to three thousand. Two and a half million Mickey Mouse watches were sold within two years.[20]

Between 1933 and 1939, Ingersoll-Waterbury sold almost five million dollars of Disney-licensed merchandise, contributing almost a quarter-million dollars in royalties to the studio.[21]

There were other examples as well. In 1932, the Norwich Knitting Company of Norwich, New York, closed down several of its textile mills, putting most of the people in the town out of work. It then signed a contract to product Mickey Mouse sweatshirts, putting people back to work, and selling over one million of them a year.[22]

As Gabler notes, "Just as Mickey on film had come to be regarded as a tonic antidote to the depression, so did Mickey's image on merchandise. Round, colorful, appealing Mickey Mouse had become the graphic representation of indomitable happiness even in the face of national despair."[23] Whatever the psychology behind the Mickey Mouse craze, the result of an effectively managed merchandising operation was a cash boon to the studio, as summarized by Gabler:

In his first four years Kamen had increased the licensing 10,000 percent to just under $200,000 in royalties a year, and as early as 1934

Walt was claiming that he made more money from the ancillary rights to Mickey than from Mickey's cartoons. Thus Disney became the first studio to recognize what would become a standard business practice in Hollywood forty years later—that one could harvest enormous profits from film-related toys, games, clothing, and other products.[24]

Kamen would handle the licensing and merchandising of Disney characters for Walt Disney Productions with energy and integrity until his untimely death in an Air France plane crash over the Azores in 1949

1. Merritt & Kaufman, *Walt in Wonderland*, 112.

2. Merritt & Kaufman, *Walt in Wonderland*, 98.

3. Barrier, *The Animated Man*, 83.

4. Holliss, *Walt Disney's Mickey Mouse: His Life and Times*, p. 72; Barrier, *The Animated Man*, 83.

5. Iwerks & Kenworthy, *The Hand Behind the Mouse*, 81.

6. Barrier, *The Animated Man*, 83.

7. Iwerks & Kenworthy, *The Hand Behind the Mouse*, 81.

8. Heide & Gilman, *Mickey Mouse: The Evolution, The Legend, The Phenomenon!*, 22.

9. Heide & Gilman, *Mickey Mouse: The Evolution, The Legend, The Phenomenon!*, 22.

10. Steven Watts, *The Magic Kingdom*, 147.

11. Holliss, *Walt Disney's Mickey Mouse*, 80.

12. Thomas, *Walt Disney*, 107.

13. Gabler, *Walt Disney*, 196.

14. Gabler, *Walt Disney*, 196.

15. Gabler, *Walt Disney*, 197.

16. Gabler, *Walt Disney*, 197.

17. Gabler, *Walt Disney*, 197.

18. Gabler, *Walt Disney*, 197–198.

19. Thomas, *Walt Disney*, 107.

20. Thomas, *Walt Disney*, 108.

21. Holliss, *Walt Disney's Mickey Mouse*, 76.

22. Holliss, *Walt Disney's Mickey Mouse*, 75.

23. Gabler, *Walt Disney*, 198.

24. Gabler, *Walt Disney*, 198.

CHAPTER NINE

Finding a Ratchet to Secure a Stronger Foundation

As devastating as the loss of Ub Iwerks was to Walt in 1930, production at the studio carried on without him. The expanding popularity of both the Mickey Mouse and Silly Symphony series and the distribution deal with Columbia Pictures was bringing more money into the studio than ever before.

One implication of Walt's strategic commitment to sound and quality improvements was the need to follow through with additional investment in studio expansion, which occurred between February and July 1931. An expensive new animation building was built to house the increasing demand for staff, and the advent of sound required that a state-of-the-art soundstage be built to record soundtracks, at a cost of $250,000. The hiring of skilled staff to manage sound work and the complications added by incorporating sound also contributed to an increase in company payroll.[1]

As the Disney reputation for advancing the quality of cartoons grew, the best animators from the leading New York studios wanted to be where the action and opportunities were, and began to seek work with Disney, even though in most cases, Walt was paying lower wages. For many, the thrill of working with Walt Disney and being part of something new and exciting carried intrinsic rewards that exceeded the factory-like drudgery of animation at other studios.

The addition of new and more capable talent prompted Walt to again demand higher quality standards for his cartoons. His animators welcomed the challenge, many having been attracted to Disney precisely because of his serious and thoughtful approach to raising the quality of animation to an art form. Those who signed on to working at Walt's studio were eager to follow his leadership and shared his vision for creating an innovative new art form without traditional boundaries, limited only by the drawing ability of the animators and the boundaries of their imaginations. For many, working at Disney was seen as an unparalleled once-in-a-lifetime opportunity of creative passion and adventure.

Walt's ambitious and ongoing quest for improvement in animation quality, and Roy's desire to constrain Walt's ambition so that he could meet the rapidly expanding weekly payroll and manage the studio within its means, became a cause of ongoing tension between the brothers.

As the Great Depression rolled on, and as Walt invested in operations and infrastructure to support growth, it wasn't long before the studio was again producing films at a loss. As financial pressures mounted, both brothers quickly became dissatisfied with the Columbia Pictures distribution contract. Walt's costs were rising, but the studio wasn't seeing any film revenues above the agreed-upon $7,000 advance per film. By the time legitimate distributor fees and costs were deducted, whatever remained was applied as repayment of the $50,000 advanced by Columbia to buy out the Disney contract with Pat Powers. Walt approached Columbia to ask them to more than double the advance per film to $15,000. Walt argued that the extra money would help keep the company solvent and protect Columbia Pictures' interest in the continued success of Walt Disney Productions. To Walt's disappointment, Columbia declined.[2]

Just eight months after signing with Columbia, Walt entered into discussions with United Artists, an independent film distribution company incorporated as a joint venture in 1919 by leading Hollywood figures Mary Pickford, Charlie Chaplin, Douglas Fairbanks, D.W. Griffith, and lawyer William McAdoo.

UA was supportive of Walt's work as an independent studio and filmmaker, and agreed to the higher advance, but it took until mid-1932 and the delivery of fifty cartoons over two years until Walt was able to work off his obligations to Columbia and for the new agreement with UA to take effect.[3]

---

1. Barrier, *The Animated Man*, 83.
2. Thomas, *Walt Disney*, 113.
3. Barrier, *The Animated Man*, 89.

CHAPTER TEN

Innovation, Training, and Three Precious Pigs

For years Walt had been intrigued with the prospect of adding color to his cartoons, but had been unable to find or develop a process that would work to his satisfaction. Up until this point, color in films had primarily been achieved with stencils and dyes, and didn't look good visualliy. The Technicolor Motion Picture Corporation would change all of that by developing a technology to capture true colors on film that could be reproduced on the movie screen.

In the early 1930s, Technicolor had been experimenting with a way to combine three negatives of primary colors to create a color negative for film. In 1932, after a number of years of R&D trial and error, they developed a process they believed would work for cartoons. By their own estimation their color process was not yet advanced enough to attempt a strategically risky and potentially costly entry into live-action films, but viewed cartoons as an excellent test case, and was supportive of Walt's expression of interest.

Technicolor executives had a test reel prepared for Walt to view. He was impressed and excited about the possibilities, and became convinced of its merits. Walt, along with United Artists, explored the possibility of experimenting with one of the Silly Symphonies.

To proceed in color instead of black and white, however, would, as was the case with the shift from silent movies to synchronized sound, again alter the cost structure of the existing business, requiring a strategic commitment by both the filmmaker and its distributor. For one thing, the cost of color prints was estimated to be $12,000 for 200 prints at a unit cost of $60 each, considerably more than the current cost of producing prints. UA's vice president and general manager for distribution, Al Lichtman, indicated in a letter to Roy that his primary concern was not with the *failure* of a shift to color cartoons, but rather with its *success*. What if color raises the expectations of exhibitors for all future Silly Symphonies? "Could we get enough additional money to pay for the extra cost of colored prints?" he asked.[1]

Rather than fear success and innovation, Walt actively pursued it. He was eager to proceed and push the art of animation forward, and to once again be first with a new technology that would place the Disney name and brand at the leading edge of industry innovation.

Roy had a different opinion. Biographer Bob Thomas writes in *Walt Disney, An American Original*:

> "We'd be crazy to take on the expense of color just after we've made a deal with United Artists," Roy argued. "They won't advance us any more money for color."

> "Yes, but don't you see, Roy?" Walt replied. "Maybe United Artists won't give us any more dough, but the pictures will create so much excitement that we'll get longer play dates and bigger rentals. That'll bring the money back eventually."

> "Eventually! It'll be years before we see that money, with all the advances that are charged against us already. We can't do it."[2]

Going forward with color cartoons wasn't just a matter of using color film. Roy understood that it required the creation of an entirely new, and more complicated, production process. It would require that they lead the disruption of their own business practices with no guarantee of financial success.

Up until now the cels used in animation were painted with black, white, and many gray paints. The formulations of these paints had been perfected. Switching to color meant that new and untested paints would have to be developed and tested, and the animation sequences would have to be coordinated for color. Roy was concerned that the color paints might not adhere to the cels and would chip off. He feared that with no money to spare, the costs of perfecting the process would drive the company into bankruptcy. Walt's answer: "Then we'll develop paints that *will* stick and *won't* chip."[3]

Roy was certain that the move to color was too risky at this time given the existing financial position of the studio, and sought out supporters amongst key studio employees to back his position and try to dissuade Walt from the course he had chosen. But the arguments presented to Walt to postpone moving ahead only persuaded him further of the wisdom to lead the movement to color movies that was inevitable. Walt became convinced that color would raise animation to new levels of creativity that customers were demanding. Why shouldn't Disney be first? The Silly Symphonies lacked a recognizable character to draw audience interest. Presenting them in color would provide a means to establish the series as the leading brand for the artistic and entertainment potential of animated cartoons.[4]

Walt recognized that he and Roy were coming at the opportunity from different perspectives. Where Roy as the business manager focused his imagination on the immediate practical problems that might be encountered and was trying to protect the organization against an over-burden of immediate risks, including bankruptcy, Walt as the creative leader focused his imagination on how the pursuit of new opportunities and progress on a broader and longer-range continuum would expand the reputation and influence of Walt Disney and the Disney studio name.

Walt agreed with Roy that at this point in time he couldn't reopen negotiations with UA to ask for more money to produce color cartoons, given that the additional potential commercial value of color was still unproven. That meant he needed to find another way to overcome this constraint.

With his growing self-confidence and his increasing leverage as an important industry leader brought on by the runaway success of Mickey Mouse, Mickey's prominent influence on popular culture, and Walt's rising celebrity status in the press, Walt went back to Technicolor with a proposal. Writes Thomas:

> Walt used his brother's reluctance to evoke a concession from Technicolor. "Roy says color is going to cost us a lot of money that we'll never get back," Walt argued. "So if we take a chance on it, you've got to assure us that every other cartoon producer isn't going to rush into the theaters with Technicolor." The company agreed to grant Disney two years' exclusive use of the three-color process. Roy grumblingly consented to a contract.[5]

Seeing the Flowers and the Trees—In Technicolor

In June 1932, Disney's twenty-ninth Silly Symphony cartoon—*Flowers and Trees*—had been completed in black and white. Lichtman at UA was impressed and considered it one of the best so far. He decided that it would be the first Silly Symphony released under the new UA contract. But Walt had now decided that this would be his first foray into color. Roy asked Lichtman to delay the release until the completed movie could be re-inked in color and re-photographed in Technicolor.[6]

The cels were washed, repainted in color, and photographed. But there was a problem. It turned out that Roy's fears came to pass: the hot lights needed to illuminate the cels caused the dried paint to chip and fade. Walt instructed his paint laboratory technicians to work day and night to solve the problem and develop a new paint formula that would properly adhere and not fade.[7] Through a considerable amount of trial and error, before long the problem was solved.

Walt was thoroughly impressed by the results. With just a few scenes completed amounting to about one minute of film, Walt approached his friend Bob Wagner, the publisher of a literary magazine, to show him the results, likely with the goal of obtaining some pre-release publicity amongst the artistic community. Wagner was also impressed, and he invited Sid Grauman, owner of Grauman's Chinese Theatre in Hollywood, to see the film.[8]

The true vibrant colors that came from the Technicolor process had never been seen on screen before, and Grauman wanted *Flowers and Trees* to open in his theatre with his next attraction, the Clark Gable movie *Strange Interlude*. Walt had his staff work overtime, and pressed Technicolor to do the same to speed up the processing in order to meet the deadline.

When it was finally reworked into color and completed, *Flowers and Trees* was a sensational success. Writes Thomas:

> When *Flowers and Trees* appeared at the Chinese, in July 1932, it cre-ated the sensation that Walt had hoped for. No longer was the Silly Symphony the neglected half of the Disney product; *Flowers and Trees* got as many bookings as the hottest Mickey Mouse cartoon. Walt decreed that all future Symphonies would be in color.[9]

While audiences and exhibitors were thrilled with *Flowers and Trees*, UA's Lichtman worried that color films would be too expensive for the studio to sustain, and argued with the Disneys for a more cautious and cost-conscious approach. Having seen the grandeur of color cartoons, Walt's mind was already made up, and besides, the two-year exclusivity deal with Technicolor was already signed. As Michael Barrier reports in *The Animated Man,* Roy responded to Lichtman's concerns:

> "I realize that Walt and I do not run our business on a strictly 'business basis,' but honestly we have more concern over re-trenching (sic) our-selves during these difficult times by making our product as desirable to the exhibitor as we possibly can, feeling that if we can only ride out these present times we are really doing well in the final analysis. Then when better times do return, we will still be in the front and be able to take care of the old family sock." Roy, as much as Walt, wanted to go into color, and he was working hard to justify such a move, to himself as well as Lichtman. By November 1932, there was no longer any doubt—it would be wrong, Roy wrote to Lichtman, to do other than make all the Silly Symphonies in Technicolor.[10]

From then on, all the Silly Symphonies were produced in color, with Walt's competitors handcuffed to inferior color products for the remainder of his two-year exclusivity agreement. The success of *Flowers and Trees* vindicated Walt's belief that innovation and a commitment to the highest quality standards was smart business because it creates public interest and drives consumer demand.

In November 1932, Walt Disney was rewarded for his risk-taking by being awarded the first Academy Award for a cartoon—*Flowers and Trees*—as well as a special award for the creation of Mickey Mouse.

In a concession to manage costs, Walt continued to make Mickey Mouse in black and white. And when the transition to color finally came in 1935, not surprisingly, Mickey Mouse saw a spike in both popularity and profits.

Artistic Improvement Through Studio-Funded Professional Training

When Walt started his business, animators like himself, Iwerks, Harman, Ising, and Freleng were all enthusiastic kids who were self-taught and in it for the fun and romance of making movies. But now, with the newfound success and fame of the Walt Disney Studios, Walt was able to select from a much higher caliber of college and art school graduates who were seeking to apply their creativity and artistic training and talent during an economic depression when jobs of any kind were scarce.

From his start in animation, Walt had been pursuing a trajectory to elevate animated cartoons from a string of random visual gags into a new art form. Instead of a bunch of kids trying to draw like professionals, Walt now had a collection of talented artists that he could work with, artists that came to Disney because they were personally motivated by Walt's vision, artistic integrity, leadership, and commitment to excellence. Walt spent a lot of time thinking about what could be done with his new collection of talent and what that might lead to.

In 1931, Walt arranged for his artists to attend studio-funded drawing classes at the nearby Chouinard Art Institute in Los Angeles. While Walt's intentions were good, the classes were not well attended at first and were cancelled after just a few weeks. Soon thereafter, however, the animators realized that Walt was providing lessons with a purpose in mind. With more New York animators being hired, Walt was seeking improved animation of movement in his characters. Staff began to take up the challenge to push the limits of their own drawing skills and creativity in animating scenes.

Then, in the summer of 1932, Art Babbitt, a new hire from the New York animation scene, started to organize drawing classes in his home, using live nude females as models. After a few weeks of increasing popularity, Walt intervened to demand that the classes be moved to the studio sound-stage, not only to improve the access and quality of the lessons, but also because, as Babbitt later described it, Walt was worried that "it wouldn't be very nice if the newspapers ever came out with the story that a group of Disney artists were drawing naked women in a private house...he thought it would look a lot better if these art classes were held on the soundstage."[11]

In November 1932, when Walt had additional funds from the increased advances from United Artists, he hired Chouinard Art Institute teacher Don Graham to conduct classes at the studio two nights a week to help artists learn drawing techniques and the relationship between anatomy and movement. As lessons progressed, there was a marked improvement in the ability of animators to draw more convincing and realistic movement in characters.[12] Studying, utilizing, and perfecting these skills in the short cartoons would pay dividends later when applied to the animating of full-length features like *Snow White* and *Bambi*.

As the abilities of the animators improved and as they came to understand movement and how to draw it convincingly, Walt was able to push animation forward from stiff slapstick gags to a place where the drawn characters possessed the appearance and illusion that they were thinking, acting, and controlling their own destiny based on their own choosing. This shift in style allowed Walt and the animators to raise the humor level of the situational comedy immensely, making the cartoons more challenging to make and much more fun and entertaining to watch.

The key, said Walt, to creating feeling in animation was "psychology." In having a scene involving Minnie Mouse critiqued by Walt, animator Paul Fennell recalled Walt trying to get his ideas across on communicating emotion through animation, telling him: "You've got to really be Minnie, you've got to be pulling for Mickey to beat that big lunkhead. You've got to hit that mat hard, you've got to stretch." Fennell recalled, "I got a good bawling out, but I didn't understand him. Later on, I knew what he was trying to tell me. We learned it: feeling."[13] Walt's vision was to give his characters the illusion of being real actors that would create an empathetic bond between character and audience. It wasn't enough anymore to just have drawn characters move through contrived situations. They had mastered that and Walt was pushing for something better.

The big payoff in hiring and training skilled animators and embracing character animation came with the development and release on May 27, 1933, of the thirty-sixth Silly Symphony, *Three Little Pigs*, which became an international sensation. Walt provided a story sketch to his artists that stressed his desire to accentuate the personality of the four key characters: the big bad wolf and the three pigs. "We should be able to develop quite a bit of personality in them," wrote Walt to his staff.[14]

Responding to Walt's challenge, animators Fred Moore and Norm Ferguson developed characters with distinct personalities that appeared to act their parts rather than simply portray action in the telling of a story. Walt called for a song to tie the elements of the story together, leading to the now famous chorus: "Who's afraid of the big bad wolf?"

"The real genius of the cartoon," notes Disney historian Michael Barrier in *The Animated Man*, "was that all its action took place within the musical framework that Disney described. ... *Three Little Pigs* was the first cartoon to plunge wholeheartedly into the sort of operetta style that had been germinating in the Silly Symphonies almost from the beginning of the United Artists release."[15]

Walt knew immediately that *Three Little Pigs* was a step forward in animation, bringing him closer to his unarticulated vision of the immense entertainment potential of animation. He enthusiastically wrote to Roy in New York: "At last we have achieved true personality in a whole picture!"[16]

As *Three Little Pigs* started to make its way through theatres across the country, the Big Bad Wolf came to symbolize the depression and the chorus of the song became a refrain for optimism. Audiences began to relate to the movie on a personal level, and it soon became a runaway hit.

"No short cartoon had ever been so popular," notes Barrier.[17] "The success of *Three Little Pigs* was unparalleled in cartoon history," writes Thomas. "Theater marquees all over the country billed it above the feature movies. First-run houses changed their feature attractions but kept offering *Three Little Pigs* week after week."[18] The key to the movie's success, opined Walt in 1941, was the ability of his animators to begin "to put real feeling and charm in our characterization."[19]

While the animators drew the charm into the characters, Walt set out the challenge, established his expectations, and provided the overall direction that they worked to. In an addendum to the story outline that he circulated in December 1932 as the story concept was being developed, he wrote:

> These little pig characters look as if they would work up very cute and we should be able to develop quite a bit of personality in them. Use cute little voices that could work into harmony and chorus effects when they talk together and everything that they would say or do in the first part of the story, while they are building their houses, could be in rhythmical manner. Anything that they would say would be handled either in singing or rhyme. The old wolf could be the fourth in a quartette, the bass voice, growling snarling type. When he fools the little pigs, he raises his voice, into a high falsetto. All the wolf dialogue would also carry either in rhyme or song....
>
> Might try to stress the angle of the little pig who worked the hardest, received the reward, or some little moral that would teach a story. Someone might have some angles on how we could bring this moral out in a direct way without having to go into too much detail. The angle might be given some careful consideration, for things of this sort woven into a story give it depth and feeling....
>
> These little pigs will be dressed in clothes. They will also have household impliments (sic), props, etc., to work with and not be kept in the natural state. They will be more like human characters.[20]

"Who's Afraid of the Big Bad Wolf" became the first hit song to emanate from a cartoon. That such a thing would happen never occurred to Walt and Roy, who had not made any publishing arrangements. With a score unavailable, orchestral leaders all over the country were sending their arrangers to theatres to copy the tune and lyrics so the song could be played for audiences. Irving Berlin's music company soon approached Roy seeking permission to publish the song, and permission was granted.[21]

Three Little Pigs demonstrated to Walt the artistic possibilities of character animation. He now felt that he was on an upward trajectory towards uncharted possibilities. He could see that there was new territory to cover, and he was excited, motivated, and confident about bringing his artists and technicians to a higher level of capability under his guidance and leadership.

Of this time period, Barrier writes in *The Animated Man* that Walt's ambitions for animation surpassed that of his staff, and he was demonstrating a maturity of leadership that he appeared to have lacked in the earlier Alice and Oswald days:

> The Disney in charge was once again the enthusiastic, ambitious Disney who had set up his own cartoon studio when he was just twenty years old—but armed now with more than a decade of experience making cartoons and, most important, with an artist's excitement about the possibilities he saw in his medium.
>
> It was this combination, his powerful entrepreneurial drive combined with his new artist's sensibility, that made Disney so inspiring a figure to many of the people who worked for him in the middle 1930s. "Somehow," Wilfred Jackson said, "Walt always made it seem to me that the most important thing in the world was to help him make a picture look the way he wanted it to look. It was a lot of fun to feel I was doing the most important thing in the world, every day."[22]

It was also a common experience around this time for Walt to have his best workers hired away by his competitors. "Let Disney win the awards and train the artists," said one rival; "I'll hire them away and make the money." As Mintz and Powers had already discovered, the secret to creating great cartoons wasn't hiring Ising or Iwerks or the credited director of *Three Little Pigs*, Bert Gillett, away from Walt: the secret ingredient *was* Walt. Try as they might, these shortcuts to fame and fortune were unsuccessful. Competitors were either unable or insufficiently committed to matching Disney quality.[23]

1. Lichtman quoted in Barrier, *The Animated Man*, 89.
2. Thomas, *Walt Disney*, 114.
3. Thomas, *Walt Disney*, 114.
4. Thomas, *Walt Disney*, 114.

5. Thomas, *Walt Disney*, 114–115.

6. Barrier, *The Animated Man*, 89.

7. Thomas, *Walt Disney*, 115.

8. Thomas, *Walt Disney*, 115.

9. Thomas, *Walt Disney*, 115.

10. Barrier, *The Animated Man*, 90.

11. Barrier, *The Animated Man*, 93.

12. Barrier, *The Animated Man*, 93.

13. Barrier, *The Animated Man*, 99.

14. Thomas, *Walt Disney*, 116.

15. Barrier, *The Animated Man*, 95.

16. Thomas, *Walt Disney*, 118.

17. Barrier, *The Animated Man*, 97.

18. Thomas, *Walt Disney*, 118.

19. Barrier, *The Animated Man*, 97.

20. Barrier, *The Animated Man*, 94.

21. Thomas, in *Walt Disney*, 118.

22. Barrier, *The Animated Man*, 99.

23. Thomas, *Walt Disney*, 123.

CHAPTER ELEVEN

Mirror, Mirror on the Wall: Surviving "Disney's Folly"

Both adult and children audiences had come to adore Disney cartoons as enchanting and whimsical bursts of entertainment ahead of the feature presentation. Following the development of high-quality color cartoons via Technicolor and the success of the Academy Award-winning *Flowers and Trees*, Walt's confidence in his vision for the possibilities of cartoons as a unique and highly effective art form was solidified.[1] He realized that cartoons could be used to tell stories in ways that live-action features could not. His ambition now was to develop and push animation to the point where a cartoon consisting of tens of thousands of individual drawings could be visually and artistically pleasing while at the same time presenting characters that could display the same emotional subtleties as live performers. Walt wanted his cartoon characters to be as effective as live-action actors.

It was this thinking that led Walt to seriously contemplate the idea of making a full-length cartoon feature. Having settled into producing Mickey Mouse and Silly Symphonies and seeing the advances in the animation abilities of his staff, Walt was restless for a new intellectual challenge. "After all," write authors Holliss and Sibley in *Walt Disney's Snow White and the Seven Dwarfs*, "a cartoon feature offered practically unlimited possibilities for artistic, dramatic and technical advancement—the opportunity to tell a story that ran for longer than seven minutes, to create real characters and use them not simply to sustain a plot but to move an audience to laughter and tears."[2]

These possibilities excited Walt, but there was another underlying factor pushing him in this direction. Where other animation studio heads feared the idea of a full-length animated feature thinking that such a thing was a practical impossibility, Walt was beginning to see it as an economic necessity.

Walt recognized that cartoons are fun to watch and are an entertaining bonus for audiences, but movie houses don't *need* them. What movie houses *need* are feature-length attractions. That's where the real money is because that's what people are really paying to see. Walt reflected back years later: "If we are going to get anywhere, we had to get beyond the short subject. I knew that if I could crack the feature field, I could really do things. *Snow White* was the answer to that."[3]

In thinking about how to break the constant pressure and stress of living on the financial edge, Walt came to realize that his existing business model wasn't sustainable; that he had to diversify.

Walt recognized that there was a consistent thread through the arc of the Alice Comedies, Oswald the Lucky Rabbit, and now Mickey Mouse and the Silly Symphonies. For Walt to remain ahead of the competition and provide the most appealing product to audiences, he was required to continually push for higher quality, which required ongoing innovation in technique, organization, and technology, which required higher operating expenses, which required higher revenues to sustain the viability of the enterprise. A seven-minute cartoon required fifteen-thousand hand-drawn, inked, and painted pictures, and even though Walt was receiving about fifty-percent more money for Silly Symphonies than was being paid to the competition for their cartoons, they also cost more to make, around $25,000 to $30,000 by the mid 1930s.

Running an animation studio was highly labor-intensive and expensive. With overhead and expenses, each film had to gross around $100,000 to deliver any profits.[4] In 1934, film rental fees plus royalties received on Disney merchandise netted the studio roughly $600,000, which seemed to be just enough to pay salaries and keep the business going.[5]

"By 1934," writes biographer Bob Thomas in *Walt Disney*, "Walt was employing a dozen story and gag men, forty animators, forty-five assistant animators, thirty inkers and painters, and a twenty-four piece orchestra, plus camera operators, electricians, sound men and other technicians. In the six years since the loss of Oswald the Rabbit, the Disney staff had grown from six to 187."[6]

It seemed that no matter how much money Walt was able to negotiate for his films, the final outcome was always too little profit and insufficient funds to keep the studio on a solid financial footing. Walt rejected the idea of forgoing quality as a way to cut costs and increase net income to fund the studio's operations. He believed that such business practices were a form of dishonesty and demonstrated disrespect towards customers, and therefore were, in the longer-term, impractical and detrimental to any business leader trying to do the right thing.

Given the rising costs and razor-thin margins of operating to his vision, Walt concluded that the status quo would lead to a dead end. Having exhausted all other ideas to drive higher profits based on his current business model, and unwilling to just carry on until the money inevitably ran out, Walt began to seriously consider making a feature-length cartoon.

Between 1931 and 1934, Walt carefully thought about a number of possible stories that would be suitable for a cartoon feature, including the science-fiction adventures of Jules Verne, as well as *Cinderella* and *Sleeping Beauty*. In the end, he settled on *Snow White and the Seven Dwarfs*. Not only did Walt have fond and vivid memories of seeing a 1916 silent film version in Kansas City starring Marguerite Clark as Snow White, but also the story was already well known to the public and had all of the characteristics Walt thought necessary to create a captivating cartoon movie-going experience. He later explained why he found *Snow White* so appealing: "[I]t was well known and I knew I could do something with seven 'screwy' dwarfs." Plus, said Walt, "I had the heavy, I had the prince. And the girl. The romance."[7]

The reason *not* to make a full-length animated feature was as obvious to Walt as it was to every other cartoon studio that had rejected the idea. Foremost, because nobody had done it yet the concept was unproven. Almost everybody that had spent time thinking it through was in agreement that moviegoers would not have the patience to sit through a cartoon of such inordinate length. Audiences thought of cartoons as an extravagant and frivolous delight, not as a serious attraction in their own right. To engage an audience of adults in a cartoon for eighty to ninety minutes without the marquee attraction of Hollywood's biggest stars was an idea that was incompatible with the movie-going paradigm of the time.

The second and more important reason why animation studios were not giving serious consideration to a full-length feature was economic: there was a high cost to such a venture both in terms of time and money. A full-length cartoon feature would require hundreds of thousands of hand-drawn and hand-painted cels. Because animation was immensely labor-intensive, the cost of such a venture would be prohibitively expensive and risky. By the conventional standards of the day, the downside risk and perceived high probability of failure was just too great. If audiences didn't go for it, the likely result for the studio that was foolish enough to try it would most assuredly be corporate bankruptcy.

Walt was never one to accept conventional thinking uncritically. He was an independent thinker who insisted on working problems through on his own and coming to his own conclusions before developing a viable plan of action. Putting aside the conventional wisdom of others, he had thought long and hard about how to make a full-length animated feature work. As early as June 1932 Roy Disney had been making inquiries about the availability of the rights to Lewis Carroll's *Alice in Wonderland*.[8]

In April 1933, Walt was approached by, and conferred extensively with, actress and founding partner of UA, Mary Pickford, about creating a combined live action/animation version of *Alice in Wonderland* in which Pickford would play a live-action Alice inside an all-cartoon Wonderland.[9]

Pickford, who was the wife of film star Douglas Fairbanks, was enthusiastic about the project and offered to underwrite the production costs and guarantee a substantial advance. Walt was hesitant and abandoned the opportunity, in part due to Paramount Picture's decision to proceed with its own live-action version of *Alice in Wonderland* around the same time.[10] Pickford was disappointed in Walt's decision not to proceed. She wrote to Walt: "[Y]our apparent lack of enthusiasm on our last meeting, together with the many obstacles you seemed to anticipate, was the crushing blow to my cherished hope."[11]

With the idea of creating a full-length feature circling in his head, Walt began to quietly figure out and carefully plan how to break out of the existing animation-as-shorts paradigm and to slowly move his animation and production capabilities in that direction without anyone's knowledge.

To understand the barriers that Walt was up against, one has to appreciate that up until the release of *Snow White and the Seven Dwarfs* in December 1937, a cartoon was just a series of gags strung together with a vague story line. A cartoon provides five to seven minutes of imaginative escapist fantasy prior to the main attraction that audiences had paid their money to see. Walt concluded that for an animated feature-length cartoon to work, what was needed most of all was a good story with characters that would enchant the audience and draw them into the story and past the sheer spectacle of the animation itself. In addition to the entertainment value of the story, animation quality, scene design, and music would also be necessary ingredients of success.

One of Walt's nagging concerns and fears was whether audiences would be able to make an emotional investment in drawings—an attribute he thought was necessary for them to suspend their disbelief and become truly engaged in the movie.[12] Walt's original thinking in having Mary Pickford play the part of Alice in *Alice in Wonderland* was that it was generally believed that audiences would not accept a fully animated feature, but may be more accepting of a hybrid that combined a live-action Alice in a cartoon world. Walt was weighing the idea that audiences would be more likely to bond emotionally with a human actor.

Another opportunity for a full-length feature was being considered in May 1933. While on a business trip to New York City, Roy became involved in a discussion about the possibility of United Artists financing Disney in transforming the book *Bambi* into a full-length feature for a fall 1934 release.[13] "Would sure like to see you attempt a feature," Roy wrote to Walt. After consideration, Walt set the idea of *Bambi* aside because in his judgment the studio wasn't yet ready to animate such a realistic story.[14]

Toward the end of that same month, May 1933, Walt issued instructions to United Artists to register the title *Snow White and the Seven Dwarfs*. While he may not have yet settled on this as his ultimate choice, it was clear that it was the forerunner in his mind, and may be why he was putting up obstacles to temper Mary Pickford's enthusiasm and financial backing, which the studio desperately needed if it were to undertake a feature project. By the time *Three Little Pigs* opened in May 1933 with its catchy song refrain of "Who's afraid of the big, bad wolf," Walt had made up his mind that *Snow White* was going to be his first animated feature, but he hadn't yet told anyone.[15]

Rather than make a broad announcement of his decision to attempt an animated feature to his staff, Walt would put his storytelling and acting skills to good use by selectively telling his version of the story to others as a way to internalize it, enhance it through retelling, and assess the reaction and receptiveness of others. Most were enthusiastic about the prospect of participating in this new and exciting challenge, if it was to happen.[16]

Roy was in New York in May 1933 where he received a letter from a member of his staff providing an update of happenings at the studio, in which Roy was told:

> We had a business meeting today for no good reason. However, it was very interesting because among other things Walt told us his idea of developing the story, 'Snow White,' and honestly, the way that boy can tell a story is nobody's business. I was practically in tears during some of it, and I've read the story many times, as a child, without being particularly moved. If it should turn out one tenth as good as the way he tells it, it should be a wow.[17]

Walt had hired animator Dick Huemer in April 1933. Huemer reported that later that year while the two of them were sitting in Walt's office, Walt began to excitedly retell the story of Snow White. Huemer recalled: "Walt was such a wonderful actor that my throat started to get tight, and my eyes began to moisten. It was wonderful, the way he was telling it."[18]

It wasn't until July 1933 that Walt first spoke publically to the press of his intention to make a feature-length cartoon, as reported in *Film Daily*: "Disney has plans worked out for a feature-length cartoon picture, but has been unable to find response from United Artists executives, he said."[19]

By November 1933, knowledge of Walt's interest in a feature was spreading. Animator Art Babbitt, a recent Disney hire, wrote to his friend Bill Tytla in New York: "We're definitely going ahead with a feature length cartoon in color—they're planning the building for it now. ... Walt has promised me a big hunk of the picture."[20] Upon receiving this news, Tytla soon packed his bags and moved from New York to California hoping to participate in this groundbreaking venture. Other leading talents in the industry would soon do the same when they learned the exciting news.

It was also around this same time that Walt began to extend his cartoon character franchise with a larger cast of leading characters, including Pluto, Goofy, and Donald Duck. He also began to explore avenues for working animation into mainstream live-action Hollywood features, with some success. In the first half of 1934, Disney characters made cameo appearances in two feature films: Mickey Mouse appeared with Jimmy Durante in the MGM feature film *Hollywood Party*, and Disney characters appeared in a dream sequence with actress Janet Gaynor in the feature film *Servants' Entrance*.[21]

Having settled on the story of Snow White, Walt quietly spent much time researching and studying different versions of the story, making notes, and using his vivid, visual imagination to develop a simple but workable storyline that would tell the tale in an entirely new and innovative way.

As Walt continued his infatuation for converting the story of Snow White into something appropriate for a Disney animated feature and the skills and competencies of his studio, nothing could go forward beyond a state of dreaming without a new source of investment capital. The most fundamental question concerning *Snow White* was: where would the money come from? Earnings were already being reinvested back into the studio as working capital for its current production obligations. There was no savings account into which cash was accumulating for such a venture. In conformity to past practices, Walt asked Roy to take on the challenge of seeking funding by means of a substantial advance.

In November 1933, Roy met with one of America's wealthiest men, Jack "Jock" Whitney, the head of Pioneer Pictures, a motion picture company committed to making color films in the early days of color. Whitney was a major investor in both the Technicolor Corporation (together he and his cousin owned 15%) and the production company of David O. Selznick, for which he was the chairman of the board. Roy also met with Darryl Zanuck, the head of production at Twentieth Century Pictures, and Joseph Schenck who was Twentieth Century's chairman and the former president of United Artists. All were men with money and power in Hollywood.

High-risk investments warrant a high rate of return, and as expected, that's what these high-profile business entrepreneurs and venture capitalists were seeking from a risky investment in Disney's full-length animated feature. Neal Gabler writes in *Walt Disney: The Triumph of the American Imagination*:

> Roy thought they all wanted too large a share of the profits, but he wrote Walt [on November 2, 1933] that "they seemed sold to [*sic*] the idea that the first feature cartoon, at least, would be a big success." Even as the estimated budget kept rising, from $250,000 to $400,000, Schenk, who was one of the few executives the Disneys trusted, yielded and decided to underwrite the entire amount in

exchange for a third of the profits, but when he suffered a sudden financial setback and had to pull out, the Disneys were forced to scrape together whatever they could for the time being and postpone getting the rest of the financing until they started actual production. When naysayers said that Roy was buying himself a sweepstakes ticket by investing so much of the studio's profits in *Snow White*, he said, "We've bought the whole damned sweepstakes."[22]

United Artists, as the Disney distributor for the shorts, was under no obligation to finance or distribute a full-length feature, and knowing that others had elected not to invest after assessing the risk, had no appetite for a tangible showing of support through a substantial advance. This would change by 1935 when they became more supportive of the idea, indicating "foreign countries were yelling for a feature" and estimating that it could easily gross $1.75 million worldwide, an immense sum at the time.[23]

Preparing the Studio for the Arrival of Snow White

Walt had decided to proceed with *Snow White and the Seven Dwarfs* as the studio's first full-length animated feature, but felt the studio wasn't yet ready. Even though his animators had been undergoing art training, he still lacked confidence in their skill to fulfill his vision. Of major concern to Walt was their ability to animate realistic human characters in a manner believable to an audience.

Through the spring of 1934, Walt continued to refine the story and develop the screenplay. A story unit was set up to probe story variations, but Walt's perspective was always the most astute as he guided the process, in many cases following the storyline of the 1916 Paramount silent film version starring Marguerite Clark that Walt recalled seeing in his youth.

To assess the gap between his artists' capabilities and what he felt was needed for audiences to believe Snow White's actions on the screen were appropriately real, Walt put into production the Silly Symphony *The Goddess of Spring* as a preliminary study for *Snow White*, and assigned his top animators to the project.

The Goddess of Spring told the story of the Greek goddess Persephone and her abduction by Hades, the ruler of the Underworld. As Holliss and Sibley write in *Walt Disney's Snow White and the Seven Dwarfs*, "Persephone not only had to move convincingly but also to 'act,' to convey a range of emotion from joy to happiness to sorrow and despair. She was to be the forerunner for Snow White."[24]

While Walt had earlier indicated to the press that he was considering making an animated feature, it wasn't until mid-1934 that he confirmed publically his decision to proceed with the creation of *Snow White and the Seven Dwarfs*. A formal press announcement appeared in the *Los Angeles Times* on July 4, 1934: "Walt Disney will soon be embarking on his first feature picture and won't that be a welcome event on the screen! He'll do a cartoon filmization of the legend of 'Snowhite,' one of the most famous and popular fairy tales...."[25] He referred to it in a letter to a theatre manager as "our first Silly Symphony feature" and optimistically anticipated that the film would be completed "in about a year," toward the summer of 1935.[26]

Walt recognized that he would need to assign his most talented animators to *Snow White*, which meant he would need more skilled artists to replace them in their current roles animating the shorts. He would also need myriad downstream staff—in-betweeners, inkers, painters, etc.—to handle the vast increase in production volume.

In anticipation of a talent shortage, a major studio recruiting drive began in June 1934 through notification to art schools throughout the country that quickly attracted thousands of applications.[27] The studio was able to pick the cream of the crop by using an intensive screening process. Roughly the top five percent of applicants were invited to the studio to partake in a one-week unpaid tryout, of which the top twenty to twenty-five percent would be invited to advance to the next stage of training.[28]

Once they made it past the screening process, the new hires were paid eighteen dollars per week to receive specialized training that would advance the learning curve and bring their skill level closer to Walt's vision for animation that went beyond what his current staff were capable of creating. The new hires spent eight hours every day for about three weeks in drawing classes taught by Don Graham before being assigned to animators as in-betweeners and assistants. At that point, they were still expected to attend additional classes every week, plus an evening class on Wednesday nights.[29]

Graham's classes covered character construction, animation, layout, background, mechanics and direction to establish a standardized base of knowledge and expectations. They provided a consistent introduction to the Disney system for all newly hired artists. By setting incredibly high standards and expectations, and demanding commitment from the very beginning, Walt hoped to avoid the bad habits and poor attitude he encountered among many of the veteran animators he had hired from other studios who, as Walt put it, arrived with their "goddam poor working habits from doing cheap pictures."[30]

In anticipation of the need for more space to house the additional staffing and production volume needed for the animating of *Snow White*, in mid-1934 Walt invested in, and work began on, the construction of a second animation building, adding 11,200 square feet of space on two floors.[31]

Spellbound:
Walt's Unforgettable Solo Performance

By October 1934 Walt was essentially satisfied with the version of the story he created, was convinced he could make it work, and gave careful consideration to the best path forward. Eager to begin, he decided to divide up the story into smaller segments and initially concentrate on those where the plot elements were most solidly established, leaving areas that were "still rather hazy" until a later date.

The first two people to learn that Walt was ready to proceed with *Snow White* were his brother Roy and his wife Lillian. Both reacted skeptically. Roy had already tried to find backers and had come up empty. Without a source of funding for a longer-term capital-intensive project, Roy challenged Walt: "Do you have any idea how much a feature-length film would cost?"[32]

At the time, the average cost to the studio of producing a Technicolor cartoon had risen to $23,500. A feature-length cartoon would be about twelve times as long. The original estimate by Walt for the cost to produce *Snow White and the Seven Dwarfs* was $250,000, which was roughly equivalent to the budget of a first-run film. Roy's experience with Walt's overly optimistic estimates caused him to double the estimate to $500,000.[33]

Stuck in the prevailing paradigm and fearful of the risk, Lillian and Roy tried to talk Walt out of it. Surely it was better to be safe and secure with the status quo than to be wrong and bankrupt?

Walt had done a lot of thinking about this, and not surprisingly, he had a different perspective. Looking to the wider trends in the film industry, he understood that carrying on along the current course was risker, as audiences were tiring of cartoons and theatres were beginning to offer double features to entice cash-strapped movie-goers during the depression. The cost to theatres of having to rent two films for one admission price left them with less money for cartoon rentals, and less time to show them. As the depression dragged on, the short subject had become mostly filler and would soon be squeezed out. With the novelty of cartoons and their perceived value waning along each step in the value chain—from studios, to exhibitors, to audiences—Walt could project forward to a time when the vocation to which he had dedicated himself would be obsolete. The best path forward, in Walt's mind, was to move into feature films, and to diversify.

Walt's mind was made up. Against the predominant thinking and skepticism of the best industry minds at the time, Walt was confident that his vision for *Snow White* and a full-length animated feature film would be brilliant enough to succeed.

Walt had been retelling the story of *Snow White* to others on an individual basis for over a year now. These informal and impromptu small audience performances were Walt's dress rehearsals for what is now an historical and legendary studio event. Up to this point, a considerable amount of work had been done on the story's development by a small circle of writers, It was on October 30, 1934, the evening before Halloween, that a wider circle of Disney artists learned of Walt's specific plans.

Animator Ken Anderson recalled that late in the afternoon Walt approached a group of employees and gave them each 65 cents to go and have dinner at the cafeteria across the street—"which was a sumptuous meal at that time"—and then return to the studio.[34] When they returned, Walt walked them to the empty soundstage and had them take their seats in chairs he had set up. Walt stood in the front, lit by a single white light, "then went through the whole Snow White story for us. From beginning to end, he performed the characters and their voices and we all fell for the story. We sat from eight until nearly midnight, spellbound. He took this simple story and embroidered it."[35] According to Anderson, Walt was "even anticipating the songs and the kind of music, and he so thrilled us with the complete recitation of all the characters that he had created that we were just carried away...we had no concept that we were ever going to do anything else. We wanted to do what he had just told us!"[36]

"We were spellbound," Anderson recalled on another occasion. "He would *become* the Queen. He would *become* the dwarfs. He was an incredible actor, a born mime."[37] It was this extraordinary emotional performance—and other large-scale recitals and story conferences like it that followed—that those who attended would never forget, and that the artists would recall and reflect back on later to inspire and guide their work on *Snow White and the Seven Dwarfs* over the next three years.

At the end of his performance, Walt announced that *Snow White* was going to be the studio's first full-length feature. "It was a shock to all of us," noted Anderson, "because we knew how hard it was to do a cartoon short."[38]

In addition to acting out the story and discussing the story details, Walt began to assign characters to the animators so that they could begin experimenting with their own interpretations of characters and scenes by drawing preliminary sketches to create a visual tableau with an old rustic European feel to capture the story setting.[39] The story department was tasked with writing scenes and dialogue. The music department was given instructions to start composing songs with lyrics integrated to carry the story forward. Everybody was encouraged to submit inspired gags. They were so enthusiastically engaged in the excitement of the project that the story department received boxes full of suggestions.[40]

While there was excitement about the possibilities, there was also deep skepticism in the ranks about whether it was possible. As the idea of adding a full-length feature was being seriously considered, new concerns began to arise, long before production began. For one thing, with Walt's hands already full running the studio and meeting the Mickey Mouse and Silly Symphonies production schedules, where would he find the time to devote to *Snow White*? With Walt's mercurial management style and constant push for new and better ideas, how would the steadiness of production and planning required to complete a feature film be maintained? And with animators and inkers already stretched to meet deadlines, where would the additional staff come from?

The Goddess of Spring Just Ain't Got That Swing

The experimental Silly Symphony *The Goddess of Spring* was released on November 3, 1934.[41] Walt had assigned his best animators to the film as a secret test to see whether the studio was ready for *Snow White and the Seven Dwarfs*. It was clear from Persephone's awkward and stiff movements that his animators hadn't yet mastered the problems of animating humans to the level he needed. Animator Eric Larson commented, "It came out as one of the worst pictures we ever did...because it was one of the first efforts to do a human girl."[42] One commentator indicated that the human figures "were spongy in appearance and movement, the drawing and the animation weak and tentative."[43]

Walt's disappointment with *The Goddess of Spring* had him worrying about the artistic ability of his key animators to achieve the level of realism in human movement he envisioned for the film and as necessary for audiences to accept the illusion. To successfully animate the character of Snow White, who had to be completely believable, the drawing abilities of his most talented artists would have to improve. More training was required.[44] While some may have seen the movie as a failure, for Walt it was a success in fulfilling its purpose. He now had a benchmark from which to measure improvement in the quest for a realistically animated human character.

To help hone the drawing skills of his staff and prepare them mentally to think as artists and not just hired cartoonists, Walt reinstituted mandatory art classes, held every Tuesday night. Doing so was necessary, Walt said, to meet the challenge ahead and to "prepare ourselves now for the future."[45] Animators attended additional classes under the direction of Don Graham two or three times a week on all aspects of their craft, including action analysis, caricature, composition, drawing animals, and theories of color. There were screenings of recent live-action films for analysis, and guest lectures by the likes of writers Alexander Woollcott and H.G. Wells on story, architect Frank Lloyd Wright on the artistic approach, muralist Jean Charlot on composition, and Italian expressionist painter Frederica Lebrun on drawing.[46]

Walt also engaged the participation of his more senior animators in teaching the newer recruits by having them lead their own lectures in areas for which they had expertise, such as timing and achieving particular effects. "In this way," said Walt, "I hope to stir up in this group of men an enthusiasm and a knowledge of how to achieve results that will advance them rapidly."[47]

Over time, field trips were arranged, including monthly excursions to the zoo to observe the actions of animals. Special-effects experiments were undertaken to understand how to realistically draw such things as ripples in water, rain and wind, and breaking glass. Animator Ham Luske was fascinated by, and carefully studied, anticipation.[48]

Much of Walt's time at the studio in October and November 1934 was taken up in marathon meetings with his writers to resolve story issues and refine the Snow White screenplay.[49] Story artist Joe Grant recalled, "Walt would go from room to room and tell that whole damn Snow White story until we were bored stiff. And at each stop, he picked up something new from somebody's reaction. The story was never written; there was never a script; it was in his mind."[50]

Walt's unencumbered excitement about creating Snow White caused him to devote less of his time to the short films and, out of necessity, to delegate more authority to his directors. He still remained highly involved at key milestones and decision points in the animation production process where his approval was required before things could move forward.

By December 26, 1934, Walt had produced a twenty-six-page continuity script in an effort to scale the story back to its simplest elements. However, even with a bare-bones script to guide story sketching, Walt was never satisfied, and continued to refine scenes and make changes right up until the final production deadline, always looking for ways to make improvements to the story, its visual presentation, and its entertainment value to audiences. This was a never-ending process of improvement that Walt called "plussing" in which he always sought ways to enhance and improve the current state.

Entrepreneurship in Motion

The interest and infatuation of Walt and his staff in all forms of the arts carried over into 1935. Walt's staff enthusiastically participated is studying all aspects of art, from analyzing the behaviors of people, to watching movies, to studing staging and editing, to attending the ballet. As artistic abilities rose, so did the desire of the artists to challenge and expand the boundaries of their knowledge and skill. Some studied the movement of breaking glass; others the ripples of rocks being dropped into liquids of different densities. Newly hired animator Marc Davis recalled, "If a film was good we would go see it five times. ... Anything that might produce growth, that might be stimulating—the cutting of scenes, the staging, how a group of scenes was put together. Everybody was studying constantly. ... [It was a] perfect time of many things coming together in one orbit [and] Walt was that lodestone."[51]

There was an organic sense of excitement, discovery, growth, and momentum building at the studio. Those that were involved were sensing that with *Snow White* and Walt Disney they were participating in something groundbreaking, important, special, and historic.

As the studio continued to grow with the ongoing success of Mickey Mouse and Silly Symphonies, the studio's hierarchy and operating structure had also developed. Walt didn't like organization charts because he liked unencumbered access to all aspects of the creative process, though he recognized the importance of hierarchy for managing processes and accountability. By 1935, notes biographer Bob Thomas in *Walt Disney: An American Original*, the organization had taken the following form:

> At the top, of course, was Walt, who supervised the entire process in a total and comprehensive way. Then came the directors, who were responsible for assembling the creative efforts and carrying out Walt's dictates in terms of character and action. The Story Department, with Walt in constant collaboration, provided plots and gags. The animators made the drawings that gave life to the cartoon. They were aided by assistants and in-betweeners, who relieved the animators of the tedium of multiple drawings. Finally came the women who copied the drawings on celluloid with ink and applied the colors.[52]

By now, with the influx of recent hires, the studio had now grown to about 250 employees,[53] but it wasn't going to be enough to carry on with the full schedule of animated shorts plus *Snow White*. The search for skilled artists to be trained as animators continued.

As the story men and artists concentrated on developing their characters and scenes, an inking and painting building was being constructed as well as a building to house apprentice animators. Even so, due to the vast increase in hiring in anticipation of the labor requirements for *Snow White*, the studio was quickly running out of space to expand. Nearby neighborhood apartment buildings and offices were sought and secured for use by artists and the story department, creating a more decentralized and less structured working environment.

Walt's desire to pursue a scientific approach to discovering guiding foundational principles of artistic creativity for his staff wasn't limited to animators and visual representations. In May 1935 he hired Dr. Boris Morkovin, the chairman of the department of cinematography at the University of Southern California, to conduct classes on writing and analyzing story gags, which Morkovin had studied in depth. Morkovin noted,

"Walt's idea is that he has to prepare his young artists just as the U.S.C. football team is prepared."[54] Through the study of art, experimentation, and the provoking, sharing, and testing of new ideas, Walt was trying his best to generate a heightened level of enthusiasm amongst his staff for their craft and to prepare them for achieving excellence. He was succeeding.

In June 1935, Walt, Roy, and their wives traveled to Europe for eleven weeks to celebrate their tenth wedding anniversaries, and for Roy to attend to business matters in their foreign offices (located in London, Paris, and Copenhagen), which handled foreign film distribution and merchandising trademark matters. Before leaving, Walt left written instructions to his senior staff that they were to carry on without him and to make their own decisions about story matters under the leadership of animator and storyman Ted Sears. They were not to let "matters accumulate until my return that will hold up production in any way. … I do not want things to pile up, awaiting my return," Walt wrote. "Keep the ball rolling, and I am counting on you, through your animators and story men, to work out your own problems and make your own decisions." Ted Sears' decisions on production matters were to be considered final, and treated as if Walt himself had given approval.[55]

Their vacation included visits to England, France, Italy, Germany, and Switzerland. Everywhere Walt went he was greeted by adoring fans and received celebrity treatment. When he arrived at Paddington Station in London, hundreds of press and public were on hand to welcome him, requiring the need for police protection. The Disney entourage was immediately shuttled to the BBC where Walt was interviewed on the radio about his work and his future plans.

One day while vacationing in Paris, Walt walked past a cinema advertising that at 11 a.m. every Thursday to Sunday they were showing a selection of seven Mickey Mouse and Silly Symphonies cartoons, plus a live singing and comedy routine. This serendipitous discovery was a revelation to Walt, who felt it boded well for *Snow White* because it demonstrated the interest and desire of moviegoers to accept and sit through an hour of cartoons without getting bored.[56]

The idea of compiling Disney cartoons as a feature of its own began in Stockholm, Sweden, in an attempt by distributor United Artists to boost Disney cartoon revenues in Scandinavia. In the United States, however, Walt did his best to actively discourage theatres from doing the same. Roy wrote to one exhibitor that showing a full program of Disney cartoons "may take the edge off this feature idea and give people the impression that a cartoon feature is merely a hodgepodge of several connected subjects."[57]

Upon returning to the U.S., Walt was more enthusiastic than ever about moving forward on *Snow White*. When they arrived back in New York,

Walt was asked about it at a press conference: "We never tried [a feature] before because we didn't have enough confidence in ourselves. We had to be sure first. You know, it's a big thing. ... We've got it all worked out now. Yes, everything is all ready. We'll start at once."[58]

Unfortunately, getting started "at once" wasn't so easy. Developing and deciding on the story and its design aspects turned out to be more challenging, and the pace of production slower, than Walt had anticipated. Walt oversaw every detail with endless meetings, reviewing every line, gag and story element to be sure that everything was the pinnacle of perfection in his eyes. The smallest details of each sequence of the film were discussed and agreed to long before any animation could begin. "If there was any possibility to a scene," notes Barrier, "he seemed determined not to overlook it. *Snow White* would not be rushed, even if that meant disregarding the original schedule. It would percolate for as long as it took the film to brew."[59]

Two-and-a-half years had now passed since Walt had first started performing *Snow White*, and almost a year had passed since the night of Walt's now-famous soundstage enactment. At last Walt felt that he was ready to move forward beyond story development and to begin animation.

As November 1935 was coming to an end, Walt had scoped out a production plan to move the project toward completion, starting in the middle with the happy and comedic scenes of *Snow White and the Dwarfs*, and then moving to the more emotional scenes of the scary Queen and Witch, and finally the sad scenes. Walt hoped that by following this order, his animators would advance enough in their skill to succeed in building the emotional attachment to the characters that was necessary.

Walt divided the story into thirty-one sequences, each to be produced as if it was a separate short, and in December 1935 he began to assign animation, starting with Snow White's discovery of the dwarfs' cottage. Walt began to cast his animators to specific scenes based on his assessment of their own personalities and their ability to understand the internal motivations of the characters.[60]

To manage and oversee the work, he set up a reporting structure by assigning a supervising director (Dave Hand) to oversee four sequence directors supervising animators responsible for scenes (Ham Luske, Fred Moore, Bill Tytla, Norm Ferguson). Each supervising animator would oversee the work of a team of assigned animators. In the end, the direction of the scenes would be divided up between a number of additional animators and storymen.[61] Walt would oversee the entire process and coordinate the work on the sequences into a single finished product.

By the end of 1935, which was beyond the timeframe that Walt initially anticipated that *Snow White* would be completed, Walt was still working hard at visualizing and capturing the details of the story elements.

The slow pace of advancement continued to put strain on the studio's working capital. Still, Walt was pleased with the progress being made and could see a path to the completion of *Snow White and the Seven Dwarfs* and beyond to other exciting future projects. Walt believed that the investment in training was paying off, and wrote to Don Graham on December 23, 1935, to tell him that as a result of his training classes, "I have noticed a great change in animation."[62] Gabler writes in *Walt Disney: The Triumph of the American Imagination*:

> "I am convinced that there is a scientific approach to this business," Walt wrote Graham in a long memo that December, "and I think we shouldn't give up until we have found out all we can about how to teach these young fellows the business." "A creative structure was being built," remembered I. Klein, who worked at the studio then, "an analytical, educational and artistically functional 'belt line' for producing animated cartoon films to compete with live-action films and to go beyond the limitations of human actors." Animator John Hubley put it more succinctly: The studio was "like a marvelous big Renaissance craft hall."[63]

Walt noted in a correspondence in December that the story of Snow White still hadn't yet been fully worked out but would be completed by the spring of 1936, and the entire film finished by the end of 1936. At that point he anticipated *Bambi* to be his next feature project. (*Bambi* would be Disney's fourth animated feature, released in August 1942, following *Snow White* in December 1937, *Pinocchio* in February 1940, and *Fantasia* in November 1940.)

In February 1936, the preliminary animating of *Snow White* had been set into motion, and Walt was involved in every nuance. The story that he had worked on for years was still being refined week after week. The story department would produce exactly what Walt demanded, and then reconvene the next week in another lengthy meeting where Walt would make additional suggestions in a seemingly never-ending waltz.[64]

As Walt began to ramp up animation, it quickly became apparent that in spite of the hiring campaign of the previous two years, there were still not enough animators to do the labor-intensive in-betweening and cleanup work. Another massive recruiting initiative was rolled-out.

In March 1936 Walt assigned training instructor Don Graham and training supervisor George Duke the task of initiating an extensive talent search to hire 300 artists. Ads were placed in newspapers across the country, and Graham opened an office in New York to interview applicants and assess their portfolios. Walt had recently written to Graham enumerating the very specific qualities he was seeking in a good animator, which, as presented by Bob Thomas in *Walt Disney: An American Original*, included:

- Good draftsmanship.
- Knowledge of caricature, of action as well as features.
- Knowledge and appreciation of acting.
- Ability to think up gags and put over gags.
- Knowledge of story construction and audience values.
- Knowledge and understanding of all the mechanical and detailed routine involved in his work, in order that he may be able to apply his other abilities without becoming tied in a knot by lack of technique along these lines.[65]

Where just a few years earlier Walt was willing to hire anybody who showed an interest in animation and a willingness to learn, now he had set his minimum standards much higher.

Time was ticking, and with all of his new hires and training programs, operating costs were on the upswing. Everything related to the creation of *Snow White* was an overlay upon the existing ongoing commitment to turn out a Mickey Mouse or Silly Symphony cartoon according to schedule, and there was pressure to ensure that it was all done profitably.

The pressure to produce the required footage of animation forced evening work, resulting in a work-life imbalance and signs of burnout. The demand for extra working hours was taking its toll on worker morale and productivity.[66]

From UA To RKO: "I Don't Know What Television Is"

Executives rarely have the luxury of solving one problem at a time in a linear fashion because everything in business is problem solving, and every problem is interconnected to other elements of a larger management system. In the winter of 1936, as Walt and the studio were engaged in expanding and organizing operations to accommodate and begin the production of *Snow White and the Seven Dwarfs*, the studio also ended its distribution deal with United Artists and signed a new contract with the much larger RKO Radio Pictures, Inc.

Dissatisfaction with United Artists had been growing. Walt felt the Disney brand had significant audience pull in the marketplace and provided a high level of audience value for which UA was not adequately compensating Disney, particularly in foreign markets. In addition, when the contract came up for renewal, UA insisted on retention of something called television rights. Walt had learned his lesson many times over about the value of understanding and protecting rights and the risks of relinquishing control over his intellectual property, and refused to grant television rights to his films, even though nobody at the time knew what value, if any, such rights would hold in the future. "I don't know what television is," Walt argued, "and I'm not going sign away anything I don't know about."[67]

RKO, on the other hand, was very interested in distributing *Snow White and the Seven Dwarfs* as well as Disney's shorts and was willing to offer better terms. Walt and Roy were enthusiastic about RKO's support, and in particular, of having the enhanced market power of RKO behind their first full-length release to help ensure its financial success.[68]

By now Walt and Roy had decided to forgo taking on outside partners to finance the production of *Snow White*. Based on the proven economic value of Mickey Mouse and the Silly Symphonies, and with the distribution power of RKO behind them, Roy was able to strike up an important relationship with a major financial institution, the Bank of America. For the first time in its history, Walt Disney Productions was able to establish a revolving line of credit, to be directly offset by revenues received from RKO for film distribution.

Increased operating expenses brought on by work on *Snow White* meant that the studio was once again severely cash starved, with every penny of profits being re-invested back into production capabilities. Having access to Bank of America's line of credit provided a release value of sorts to the constant financial pressure imposed on the studio, and in May 1936, Roy put the line of credit to use by borrowing $630,000.[69]

The New York recruiting office was closed on July 1, 1936, with only twenty-two prospects of more than 2,000 applicants having been referred to the studio, although an unspecified number of promising candidates had been instructed to proceed directly to the studio without vetting in New York.[70]

Sketchy Down the Home Stretch

With RKO as Disney's new distributor, and access to working capital secured through Bank of America, Walt was more committed than ever to completing *Snow White and the Seven Dwarfs* in time for a December 1937 Christmas release. Having officially launched the project in early 1934, by the winter of 1937 full-out animation was underway with only ten months left to meet the revised November 1937 deadline for completion.

Biographer Neal Gabler writes in *Walt Disney*: "[T]hough the animation had begun in 1936, the first cels weren't sent to ink and paint until January 4, 1937, and didn't reach the camera department until March 13. 'Many felt that to have the finished picture ready for showing by Christmas 1937 was impossible,' Dave Hand later confessed, 'but we responsible ones never wavered.'"[71] Completing the picture on time to be in the theatres for the important Christmas season would require everyone's firm commitment.

Even while fully consumed by the challenges of completing *Snow White*, Walt had other important studio business to attend to, and in March 1937, he received an Academy Award for the short cartoon *The Country Cousin*.

Almost a year after borrowing $630,000, Roy returned to Bank of America in March 1937 to ask for an additional $650,000 to complete the movie. By this time the bank was becoming concerned about the rising risk of default on the loans and demanded that the loan be secured against the Disney film inventory. Reflecting back later, Walt said of the need to borrow so much money: "Roy was very brave and manly until the costs passed over a million. He wasn't used to figures over a hundred thousand at that time. The extra cipher threw him. When costs passed the one-and-one-half million mark, Roy didn't even bat an eye. He couldn't; he was paralyzed."[72]

With the bank leaning on Roy, he was doing everything in his power to get the studio budget under control, but Walt resisted, creating tension between the two. In an act of desperation, Roy invited their Bank of America account manager, Joe Rosenberg, to the studio to have a talk with Walt about his concern over the studio's growing debt.

Before arriving, Rosenberg placed some phone calls to the Hollywood establishment. One of the calls was to a producer who had played polo with Walt and who told Rosenberg: "Joe, if Walt does as well on the feature as he has done with everything else he's made, the public will buy it."[73] That endorsement, along with Rosenberg's own experiences with the Disneys, was good enough for him. Nonetheless, it is likely that he gave Walt a stern warning to control costs and get the film completed and released by the end of the year as planned. Rosenberg wanted the loans repaid.[74]

Walt traveled to New York in May 1937, where he spent two weeks with RKO planning the publicity campaign for *Snow White* and encouraging RKO not to take it for granted that the film would sell itself just because of the high level of curiosity in a novelty product. Selling the film to ensure public acceptance would require work and effort. A key to building pre-launch publicity, Walt wrote in a letter to Roy, is "to do a lot of indirect selling to the press" by placing stories in prominent newspapers and magazines.[75] The key to effective marketing was to create curiosity and build anticipation for an unprecedented and spectacular entertainment event.

Walt returned to the studio to make the final push forward on the completion of *Snow White*. Like it or not, Walt did reluctantly heed the warnings from Roy and the bank to control costs, knowing that completing the film was an imperative. Still, Walt continued to focus on all of the ways things could be improved, from elements of the story to imperfections in the animation such as the stiffness in the walking of the Queen or the size of one of Grumpy's fingers.

With the deadline quickly approaching, Walt began cutting out scenes he had previously approved in an effort to tighten up the story. There was no longer enough time available to animate all the possible scenes.[76]

One major scene that was cut in June 1937 involved Snow White teaching the dwarfs etiquette while they are eating soup. Artist Ward Kimball had spent eight months developing the sequence and perfecting the comedic action in the scene.[77] Walt finally decided that as excellent as the scene was, it was interfering with the flow of the film and had to be cut. Kimball was devastated. "It kinda hurt," he recalled decades later, but nonetheless, of the finished film itself, he said, "I still think it's the best thing we ever did."[78]

The budget continued to climb at the rate of about $20,000 a week, and pressure was exerted on the animators to speed up production. Supervising director Dave Hand told the dwarf animators in a story meeting in June 1937 that Walt "is actually tearing out his heart okaying some of the stuff which you know he would like to see better" because of his need to "move the picture as best he can."[79]

Ironically, with everybody at the studio focused on completing their assignments for Snow White, the pace of progress was slower than anticipated and required. Having explicit instructions to speed up production, the work was actually slowing down.

The animators had become so concerned about perfecting the quality of their work to Walt's exacting standards that individual drawings were taking on average more than two hours to complete. Twenty-four drawings were needed to produce one second of completed animation, with productivity measured by number of feet of animation produced. Quality was important, but in the current context, the obsession over quality had to end. It was imperative that work be completed and released for cleanup, inking, and painting. There was an important deadline to meet and the meter was ticking. At one point Roy suggested sub-contracting some of the animation of the shorts to Harman-Ising to create additional studio capacity and free up workers who were engaged in other projects. The studio was already operating 24/7, with animators working three eight-hour shifts and cameramen working two twelve-hour shifts.[80] The studio was operating beyond full capacity.

With the end in sight and production of Snow White plodding forward along its path to completion, Walt began to direct his attention to what he intended to be his next major project. In August, Walt was heavily engaged in story meetings to begin laying out the structure for Bambi. At the same time, he continued to oversee the development of the short subject cartoons. In November he was occupied for many mornings working on the adaptation of a story about a shy bull named Ferdinand. The resulting cartoon, *Ferdinand the Bull*, would win an Oscar Award in the category of Short Subjects, Cartoon, in February 1939.

With so many people on the payroll working on *Snow White*, and with the capital improvements made at the studio to house them, studio costs continued to mount. It had been three years since Walt originally postulated that the movie could be completed in one year. Had he kept to that schedule, he would have already generated revenue and seen a return on his investment. But, as all entrepreneurs and investors know, they carry the burden of paying the bills for all of the related development expenses until the product can be sold in the marketplace, at which point they can begin to recoup their costs. All of those additional salaries brought on by studio expansion and the accompanying operating costs had to be paid for through all of the production delays, until the movie could generate revenue through its theatrical release.

"Disney's Folly" and "Chaplin Prices"

The making of *Snow White and the Seven Dwarfs* was audacious. It was iconoclastic. It was also a huge risk to the studio, the bankers who loaned Walt the money, and by extension, to the animation industry. It was taking so long to complete and the budget had grown so far beyond anyone's expectations at the start that Walt himself began referring to it as "Frankenstein." Rumors began to circulate that the studio was in deep financial trouble and that Bank of America would soon take over the company.[81]

As the effort gained publicity and the extent of production problems and cost over-runs leaked out, *Snow White* was dubbed "Disney's Folly" in anticipation that it would bankrupt the studio. Animator and storyman Bill Peet wrote in his *An Autobiography* that "dire predictions [were] coming from Hollywood bigwigs and movie columnists. They called Snow White Disney's Folly. The picture would be a box office flop! People would never sit through a full-length cartoon feature! Disney was getting too big for his britches! And so on."[82]

Walt ignored the critics and chastised them for their lack of vision and imagination. Because the likes of *Snow White* had yet to exist, critics compared it to what they were already familiar with. They imagined something like ten Disney cartoons joined together into an exhausting sequence of corny gags and ultimately a boring and unsatisfying evening at the movies. But Walt knew enough to know that it had to be something different, something done in grand style, something beyond what anybody had done before, or what was even imagined could be done. If *Snow White* was to succeed at the box office, it had to be a sensational entertainment spectacle and triumph of showmanship. And that was exactly what it would be.

Walt's passion for the project and seeing his vision through to completion meant that he was involved in every aspect of the film. Bob Thomas writes that Walt "insisted on testing each sequence before it was assigned to animation. Storyboards that portrayed the action in sketches weren't enough. He had story sketches filmed on what became known as a 'Leica reel' so they could be viewed in sequence on a movie screen. He also looked at 'pencil tests,' films of rough animation. He auditioned singers for the leading roles."[83]

In the push to complete *Snow White* all studio personnel were required to work an additional three nights per week without additional pay, from 7 to 10 p.m. They also worked their normal Saturday hours from 8 a.m. to 1 p.m. The sheer volume of drawings to be made, cleaned up, inked, and painted made these jobs extremely repetitive and stressful for the workers in those roles, who also earned the least amount of money.

With the completion of *Snow White* and its release fast approaching, Walt faced a new challenge. Having no prior experience with feature-length movies, he and Roy were perplexed about how much to charge exhibitors to rent the film and how much they should demand from RKO as their fair share.

As an independent producer, Walt sought out the expertise of Charlie Chaplin, another independent producer whom he knew and respected. Chaplin helped by providing the accounting records from his 1936 comedy *Modern Times*, which Roy studied very carefully. Relying on Chaplin's experience, Roy pressed RKO to "go out and ask Chaplin prices" and Chaplin terms in both the U.S. and foreign markets.[84] The thinking was that if it was good enough for Chaplin, it was good enough for Disney.

Selling Proof of Concept: Financing on Faith to Make a Pot of Money

As the production of *Snow White and the Seven Dwarfs* was approaching the home stretch, in September of 1937 Walt received news from Roy that the studio was quickly running out of funds and they would have to approach Bank of America's Rosenberg for a third cash injection. Roy set the amount needed at $327,000 and was extremely worried that the bank would refuse.

So far Rosenberg had loaned well over a million dollars to the studio during the hard times of the Great Depression based on the reputation, character, productivity, and business acumen of Walt and Roy Disney. He had seen nothing of the actual projects. This time he insisted on seeing for himself how the money was being spent before making his decision.

The seriousness of the matter required Roy to confront Walt, telling him, "You've got to show Joe what you've done on the picture so far." "I can't do that," said Walt. "All I've got is bits and pieces. You know I never like to show anybody a picture when it's all cut up. It's too dangerous." Even so, Roy insisted: "The only way we're going to get more money is to show them what they're lending money for."[85] Without an alternative path forward, Walt reluctantly conceded.

Because the animation was incomplete, Walt's staff worked overtime piecing together a sequential patchwork of completed animation plus segments of pencil animation and storyboard sketches to demonstrate the collateral for the loan. In Walt's words, they were trying to sell Rosenberg on "a quarter of a million dollars worth of faith."

Rosenberg arrived on the afternoon of September 14, 1937, joining with Walt, studio attorney Gunther Lessing, and some RKO executives in the projection room to watch the first ever rough screening of the still-to-be-completed *Snow White*. Throughout the screening Walt explained how the scenes would be completed and how it would all come together. The soundtrack too was incomplete, and Walt would fill in lines and parts of songs to keep it all flowing, retelling a story he had told at least a hundred times, but none as important as this telling. All the while Rosenberg sat silently, contemplatively, actively watching and listening.

When the screening was over, the RKO executives were ecstatic about the film, but Rosenberg remained reserved. Walt later recalled the incident in a speech almost 30 years later: "He showed not the slightest reaction to what he viewed. After the lights came on he walked out of the projection room, remarked that it was a nice day—and yawned! He was still deadpan as I conducted him to his car. Then he turned to me and said, 'Walt, that picture will make a pot of money.'"[86]

But there was more to it than Walt's dramatic retelling. Before Rosenberg approved the loan that allowed the studio to remain solvent, he instructed Walt not to spend any more money on *Bambi* until *Snow White* was completed.[87]

Later that month, Walt held an evening screening of the completed color animation for the staff so they could get a better perspective on the work they had been doing. After the screening Walt wrote to the head of distributor RKO, "[D]espite the fact that most of the audience have been pretty close to the development of SNOW WHITE for the past two and a half years—their reaction was all that could be hoped for from any audience."[88]

Time was quickly running out to meet the deadline for a Christmas release. Animators were still drawing until November 11, and it looked like the deadline would not be met. The last cels were painted on November 27. Final photography wasn't completed until December 1.

When Walt at last viewed the completed movie, he noticed that something had gone wrong in the filming of the final scene, in which the dwarfs are grieving as the Prince leans over, kisses, and awakens the seemingly dead Snow White. These scenes were animated last because they were the most difficult in the film—they needed to create the proper emotional impact upon the viewing audience. When the Prince leaned down to kiss Snow White, Walt detected a slight "shimmering" of the Prince. Bothered by this flaw in the critical final scene, Walt told Roy that he wanted the film fixed and that it would cost several thousand dollars. "Forget it," said Roy. "Let the Prince shimmy!"[89]

After years of effort, *Snow White and the Seven Dwarfs*—the largest animation project ever yet attempted—was finished. Walt had invested every dime the studio was able to scrape together, coming in at a final cost of around $1.5 million.

Snow White's Top Secret Advanced Showing

The first sneak preview of *Snow White and the Seven Dwarfs* was held on December 7, 1937, in Pomona, California, a small town about thirty miles east of Los Angeles. This was to be the first viewing by a non-studio, non-industry audience for the purpose of gauging the audience reaction and was top secret. Few of the studio staff other than the top personnel was aware of the event. Afterward local newspaper *The Mail* reported, "According to the manager of the cinema, the film had the biggest ovation of any picture ever shown in his theatre."[90]

The studio staff in attendance were elated at the audience reaction, and channeled their enthusiasm about the gala premiere now just a few weeks away by tacking up movie posters all over Los Angeles to generate grass-roots excitement and awareness for this historic event.[91] A movie trailer to publicize *Snow White and the Seven Dwarfs* started to make its appearance at theatres: "From Hollywood, California, motion picture capital of the world, comes exciting news! News of the completion of the most daring adventure in screen entertainment since the birth of the motion picture!"[92]

Describing the creation of *Snow White* as a daring and courageous undertaking wasn't just hyperbole. In fact, the making of *Snow White* was an awesome and audacious technical achievement. In all, more than 750 artists had worked on the film between 1934 and 1937. Together they drew, cleaned up, inked, and painted a quarter of a million drawings in what added up to two hundred years' worth of man-hours.[93]

Snow White was the largest collaborative art project ever undertaken in the United States.[94] It had cost Walt and Roy everything they owned and were able to scrape together to make the film—$1,480,000, more than four times the cost of an average feature film in 1937.[95] Now they hoped the public would show up in movie theatres to see and embrace it so they could earn back their investment.

From Folly to Brilliance:
Snow White's Hollywood Premiere

Snow White and the Seven Dwarfs premiered on December 21, 1937, at the 1500-seat Carthay Circle Theatre in Hollywood, to the astonishment and praise of all who attended. It was a newsworthy, star-studded affair attended by Hollywood dignitaries like Marlene Dietrich, Judy Garland, and Charles Laughton arriving by limousine to walk the red carpet, top executives from the major studios, and the press. All Disney employees and their spouses were invited to see the completed movie for the first time. Searchlights circled the skies, and the Seven Dwarfs appeared in a replica film set built in the parking lot. Walt gave radio interviews on the red carpet and spoke from a podium. When asked if he was going to watch the film he half-jokingly answered, "Yes, and have my wife hold my hand."[96]

As people settled into their seats, Walt was excited but nervous. The audience anticipated that the film would be something special, breathtaking, magical, and unique. They were ready and eager to be dazzled by the creativity of Walt Disney and to witness something new in cinema history. As related by Disney historians Holliss and Sibley in *Walt Disney's Snow White and the Seven Dwarfs*,

> The lights went down and the curtains rose. Frank Churchill's beautiful melody "One Song" swelled through the auditorium. On the screen, the film's opening titles appeared. "A Walt Disney Feature Production—SNOW WHITE AND THE SEVEN DWARFS—Adapted from Grimm's Fairy Tales—Technicolor."
>
> Then came a personal statement by the film's producer: "My sincere thanks to the members of my staff whose loyalty and creative endeavor made possible this production—Walt Disney"; and the list of credits, said, at the time, to be the longest in cinema history. Next, a huge gold-embossed, leather-bound book was seen, opened by invisible hands to a page of illuminated text....[97]

Disney biographer Bob Thomas writes that as the movie played, people sat in awe for "eighty-three minutes of drawings that moved, audiences shuddered at the fearful Witch, delighted in the dwarfs, especially Dopey, and cried when Snow White was awakened by the Prince's kiss."[98]

"As the houselights came up," write Holliss and Sibley, perfectly capturing the poignancy of the event, "the audience—already applauding—rose to its feet, hardened movie moguls and their wives wiping their tear-moistened eyes. For what, only 83 minutes earlier, had been known by all of Hollywood as 'Disney's folly,' was now part of cinema legend."[99]

Disney animator and storyman, Bill Peet, who was in attendance, observed that they didn't have to wait long to know that the audience was going to love what Walt and his artists had created. "I believe everyone in that first Snow White audience could have predicted the enormous success of the film," he wrote in *An Autobiography*. "They were carried away by the picture from the very beginning, and as it went along, everyone was bubbling over with enthusiasm and frequently bursting into spontaneous applause. At the end, the audience exploded into a thunderous ovation—and the voices of doom were silenced for good."[100]

According to Disney animator Ward Kimball, whose soup sequence had been cut from the film, the highlight of the premiere screening for the animators was the bier scene, in which Snow White lies in her glass case after eating the poisoned apple. "As I look back on it," recalled Kimball,

> We knew where they were going to laugh from experience, but we weren't prepared for the crying and sniffing in the audience. That was the thing I started hearing. Clark Gable and Carole Lombard were sitting close, and when Snow White was poisoned, stretched out on that slab, they started blowing their noses. I could hear it—crying—that was the big surprise. We worried about the serious stuff and whether they would feel for this girl, and when they did, I knew it was in the bag. Everybody did."[101]

Shamus Culhane, animator of the famous scene of the dwarfs marching home singing "Heigh-Ho," wrote in *Talking Animals and Other People*:

> It was the most receptive, enthusiastic audience I have ever seen. Every song, every gag, every good piece of acting worked on those people like a bow on a fiddle. There was almost continuous laughter and applause until Frank Thomas' sequence, where the sorrowing dwarfs gather around Snow White's bier. The house fell silent, gripped by the emotional impact of the acting. It was the first time grief had been so dramatically depicted in an animated cartoon. As the picture faded there was a thunderous ovation, which continued long after the houselights flashed on.[102]

Marc Davis, a key animator of the Snow White character, recalled: "People cried when Snow White died and the dwarfs took off their little hats and tears rolled down their faces. People wiped their eyes over these drawings as they appeared on the screen. This is one of the most remarkable things that Walt created. This was the thing that he searched for: to make you believe they were real."[103]

Snow White and the Seven Dwarfs—which the thirty-six year-old Walt created by going more than a million dollars over budget—was an uncontested smash hit and a historic milestone in cinematography, both in the eyes of the critics and the movie-going public.

A *New York Herald Tribune* reviewer wrote in part: "It is one of those rare works of inspired artistry that weaves an irresistible spell around the beholder. ... *Snow White and the Seven Dwarfs* is more than a completely satisfying entertainment, more than a perfect moving picture, in the full sense of that term. It offers one a memorable and deeply enriching experience."[104]

The *New York Times* reviewer was equally enthralled: "Mr. Disney and his amazing technical crew have outdone themselves. The picture more than matches expectations. It is a classic, as important cinematically as *The Birth of a Nation* or the birth of Mickey Mouse."[105]

Movie industry insiders were also ecstatic and grateful for Walt's achievement. Walt's Kansas City colleagues and former employees Harman and Ising wired Walt: "OUR PRIDE IN THE PRODUCTION IS SCARCELY LESS THAN YOURS MUST BE AND WE ARE GRATEFUL TO YOU FOR FULFILLING AN AMBITION WHICH MANY OF US HAVE LONG HELD FOR OUR INDUSTRY."[106]

Cecil B. DeMille also wired Walt: "I WISH I COULD MAKE PICTURES LIKE SNOW WHITE."[107] Even Walt's banker, Joe Rosenberg, wrote to him: "It's probably too soon to talk 'box office' but regardless of the latter I shall always say it's a truly great job which you and your gang have done—and a lot of people will be happier for it."[108]

A broad-scale showing of the film began with limited circulation due to the limited number of prints. As more prints became available, the film gained wider circulation. In New York, *Snow White* opened in early January 1938 at Rockefeller's Radio City Music Hall, then the largest movie theatre in the world with a seating capacity of six thousand, and the premiere showcase theatre for RKO films. Where a one-week run was typical for a major new film, *Snow White* ran for five weeks, grossing $500,000 before Walt and Roy had it removed for fear that a longer run might have a negative impact on regional cinemas if it continued to play there any longer.[109]

In recognition of Walt's achievement, the Academy of Motion Picture Arts and Sciences presented him with a special award on February 23, 1939, consisting of one regular size and seven smaller Oscars, with an inscription that read: "To Walt Disney for *Snow White and the Seven Dwarfs* recognized as a significant screen innovation which has charmed millions and pioneered a great new entertainment field for the motion picture cartoon."[110]

The public also grandly rewarded Walt Disney and the studio for *Snow White*. By May 1939 it had brought in $6.7 million at the box office, becoming the highest grossing film of all time. It would go on to gross $8.5 million on its initial run at a time when an adult ticket cost less than a quarter and children's tickets less than ten cents, surpassing by nearly $2 million the previous record-holder, *The Singing Fool*, which starred Al Jolson.[111]

Snow White had become a worldwide sensation. By the time 1939 drew to a close it had played in forty-nine countries and had been dubbed into ten foreign languages.[112] On the merchandising side, over two thousand different Snow White products were manufactured, and were selling quickly. By May 1938 more than $2 million in Snow White licensed toys had already been sold and another $2 million in handkerchiefs. Even original production cels were made available for sale at a San Francisco art gallery.[113]

New Entrepreneurial Knowledge Changes Everything

Walt was meticulous about proving to the world that an animated feature was viable if it was done right, as he envisioned it, granting full respect to the story, the medium, and the audience. Grim Natwick, one of four animators of the character of Snow White, recalled that "Disney had only one rule: whatever we did had to be better than anybody else could do it, even if you had to animate it nine times, as I once did."[114]

It was Walt's courage, conviction, and commitment to take an entrepreneurial risk by doing something that others had rejected as folly that made him the prime mover in the creation of new knowledge and entrepreneurial information, information that heretofore didn't exist about what is practical and possible in creating economic value and public entertainment. As he had previously done with Mickey Mouse and the Silly Symphonies, Walt again showed his acumen as a paradigm shifter.

As a result of the extraordinarily high quality of the film, writes Martin Goodman in his Animation World article "The Light That Might Have Failed," "*Snow White and the Seven Dwarfs* made a very strong case for animation as an elevated art form rather than simple entertainment. At the same time the animated film became the equal of the live-action feature film in the eyes of critics and paying customers."[115] Walt was of a similar though perhaps not as lofty opinion when he commented to a studio visitor soon after *Snow White* was released that "the days of the animated cartoon, as we had known it, were over."[116]

Reflecting back on the success of *Snow White*, Walt Disney later said:

> The success of the Silly Symphonies gave us the courage for *Snow White*. And you should have heard the howls of warning! It was prophesied that nobody would sit through a cartoon an hour-and-a-half long. But, we had decided there was only one way we could successfully do *Snow White*—and that was to go for broke—shoot the works. There would be no compromise on money, talent or time. We did not know whether the public would go for a cartoon feature; but we were darned sure that audiences would not buy a bad cartoon feature."[117]

Walt's uncompromising standards were not arbitrary or neurotic in nature. They were based on his own high-level integration and rational consideration of the facts, and the objective requirements of what was necessary to succeed in business. Writes David Johnson, "Disney finally unlocked the heretofore hidden potential of a medium whose capability he knew existed for some time."[118]

The resounding success of *Snow White* proved that Walt's assessment of the potential of the medium was right. Instead of listening to skepticism and nay saying of others, Walt relied on his own rationality, unique knowledge, skill, insight, and independent judgment of what was achievable in his field of expertise. By doing so, he was also able to see beyond *Snow White's* success as a singular event and to view it as a fundamental change in his business model and the future of the animation business. That he was already planning future animated features showed that he looked at *Snow White* as a stepping-stone in a process toward a different future with greater possibilities, and not as a single experimental event. Walt remarked: "When Snow White hit, we realized we were in a new business. We knew it within a week after the picture had opened. ... We had been heavily in debt and within six months we had millions in the bank."[119]

Just as the success of Silly Symphonies was the driver and lever of *Snow White and the Seven Dwarfs*, the success of *Snow White* was the catalyst of all that came afterwards.

The Depression and Collective Bargaining: A Shifting Business Environment

There was one other major event in the world of animation in 1937 that was most assuredly on Walt's radar at the time of its occurrence. One aspect of the changing times that would have a major impact on Walt and his staff was action taken under the Roosevelt administration to promote unionization and collective bargaining.

A prominent feature of Franklin Roosevelt's depression-era New Deal was a mechanism for workers to organize and engage in unionization. Two years earlier, in July 1935, President Roosevelt established a new national labor policy and signed the National Labor Relations Act, also known as the Wagner Act, into law. The National Labor Relations Board was put in place to enforce the policy. Workers were given the right to form and join unions, and employers were obliged by law to bargain collectively with unions selected by a majority of employees.

With explicit support by the president of the United States, unionization to organize labor was now on the march. Workers who felt victimized or were seeking better working conditions now had the power and ideology through government sanctioned unions to fight back against perceived wrongs by employers.

Labor unions became increasingly active across the country, organizing workers and exciting their passions through fashionable and emotional Marxist rhetoric of class exploitation of the bourgeoisie by the rich capitalists. As a more practical matter, frustrated animation workers viewed unionization as a defense mechanism against long work hours, unpaid overtime work, and lack of job security that was standard practice at that time in most industries. Union leaders were eager to position themselves as the protectors of jobs and the means to provide power to the powerless.

In 1937, the Commercial Artists and Designers Union (CADU) pushed to unionize the Fleischer animation studio in New York City and demanded a reduction in the work week from forty-four to thirty-five hours, double time for every overtime hour worked, paid vacations and sick leave, and a twelve percent across-the-board raise for all employees.[120] Studio owner and animation legend Max Fleischer refused to negotiate and fired those he considered to be union troublemakers.

As the conflict between workers, unions, and the Fleischer studio owners escalated, the workers became increasingly convinced that management wasn't going to listen to their concerns. On May 7, 1937, the Fleischer Studios employees became the first American animation studio to strike. Most of the animators continued to work, while three hundred lower-paid assistants and ink and painters picketed on Broadway Avenue near Times Square.[121]

The National Labor Relations Board eventually got involved, and finally, in October 1937, after a violent and acrimonious five months in which theatre chains refused to display Fleisher pictures to avoid union boycotts and noisy organized protests in their lobbies, and in which the mayor of New York City, Fiorello La Guardia involved himself personally, the Fleischer Studios formally capitulated and recognized the union and its demands. By doing so, it became the first animation studio to sign an artist's union contract.

To settle the strike the Fleischer's agreed to a twenty percent raise, a forty-hour week, one week of paid vacation, holidays and sick leave, and screen credits to give public recognition and acknowledgement to the work of the artists.

After studying the history of animation unions, author Tom Sito writes in *Drawing the Line*:

> The Fleischer strike was the first major labor strike in animation history. It demonstrated all the tactics and problems that would dominate labor-management conflicts in animation for the next sixty years: employee anger over working conditions but apathy about joining organizations to do anything about the conditions; suspicion of outside labor organizations; artists' denial of basic business

realities; employers trying to stay friends with their staff while acting tough behind the workers' backs; official rhetoric about "free choice" masking strong-arm tactics; intimidation of workers; flouting of government laws and oversight; gestures calculated to pit artists against artists; and stonewalling negotiations while waiting for the artists and their families to starve.[122]

1. See Holliss & Sibley, *Walt Disney's Snow White and the Seven Dwarfs*, 4.

2. Holliss & Sibley, *Walt Disney's Snow White and the Seven Dwarfs*, 5.

3. Walt quoted in Pat Williams, *How to Be Like Walt*, 110.

4. Gabler, *Walt Disney*, 214.

5. Gabler, *Walt Disney*, 214.

6. Thomas, *Walt Disney*, 123.

7. Gabler, *Walt Disney*, 216.

8. Gabler, *Walt Disney*, 215.

9. Kaufman, *Snow White and the Seven Dwarfs: The Art and Creation of Walt Disney's Classic Animated Film*, 16; Williams, *How to Be Like Walt*, 110.

10. Kaufman, *The Fairest One of All*, 31.

11. Gabler, *Walt Disney*, 215–216.

12. Gabler, *Walt Disney*, 219.

13. Gabler, *Walt Disney*, 215.

14. Gabler, *Walt Disney*, 115.

15. Gabler, *Walt Disney*, 216.

16. Kaufman, *The Fairest One of All*, 31.

17. Gabler, *Walt Disney*, 217.

18. Gabler, *Walt Disney*, 217–218.

19. Kaufman, *The Fairest One of All*, 31.

20. Kaufman, *The Fairest One of All*, 31; Barrier, *The Animated Man*, 101.

21. Kaufman, *Snow White and the Seven Dwarfs*, 16.

22. Gabler, *Walt Disney*, 219.

23. Gabler, *Walt Disney*, 219.

24. Holliss & Sibley, *Walt Disney's Snow White and the Seven Dwarfs*, 12.

25. Kaufman, *Snow White and the Seven Dwarfs*, 15.

26. Kaufman, *Snow White and the Seven Dwarfs*, 16.

27. Gabler, *Walt Disney*, 229.

28. Gabler, *Walt Disney*, 229.

29. Thomas, *Walt Disney*, 124.

30. Walt Disney quoted in Gabler, *Walt Disney*, 230.

31. Gabler, *Walt Disney*, 237.

32. Pat Williams, *How to Be Like Walt*, 111.

33. Pat Williams, *How to Be Like Walt*, 111.

34. Anderson in Green & Green, *Remembering Walt*, 108.

35. Ken Anderson in Green & Green, *Remembering Walt*, 108.

36. Anderson in Holliss & Sibley, *Walt Disney's Snow White and the Seven Dwarfs*, 7.

37. Anderson quoted in Kaufman, *The Fairest One of All*, 33.

38. Krause & Witkowski, *Walt Disney's Snow White and the Seven Dwarfs: An Art in Its Making*, 26.

39. Holliss & Sibley, *Walt Disney's Snow White and the Seven Dwarfs*, 9–10.

40. Gabler, *Walt Disney*, 221.

41. YouTube.com/watch?v=5QfeqZkaDQs, accessed July 26, 2016.

42. Holliss & Sibley, *The Disney Studio Story*, 128.

43. The commentator is Barrier, in Barrier, *The Animated Man*, 108.

44. Holliss & Sibley, *Walt Disney's Snow White and the Seven Dwarfs*, 16.

45. Gabler, *Walt Disney*, 230.

46. Gabler, *Walt Disney*, 231; Williams, *How to Be Like Walt*, 113; Shaw, *Animator on Horseback*, 95.

47. Gabler, *Walt Disney*, 231.

48. Gabler, *Walt Disney*, 232–233.

49. Barrier, *Walt Disney*, 220.

50. Joe Grant in Green & Green, *Remembering Walt*, 108.

51. Gabler, *Walt Disney*, 233; also Holliss & Sibley, *Walt Disney's Snow White and the Seven Dwarfs*, 17.

52. Thomas, *Walt Disney*, 126.

53. Barrier, *The Animated Man*, 110.

54. Gabler, *Walt Disney*, 231.

55. Ghez, *Disney's Grand Tour*, 3–4.

56. Ghez, *Disney's Grand Tour*, 58; Thomas, *Walt Disney*, 114.

57. Roy quoted in Gabler, *Walt Disney*, 218–219.

58. Walt quoted in Kaufman, *The Fairest One of All*, 36.

59. Barrier, *The Animated Man*, 222.

60. Gabler, *Walt Disney*, 233.

61. Gabler, *Walt Disney*, 234.

62. Gabler, *Walt Disney*, 231.

63. Gabler, *Walt Disney*, 231.

64. Gabler, *Walt Disney*, 244.

65. Thomas, *Walt Disney*, 124; Holliss & Sibley, *The Disney Studio Story*, 29.

66. Gabler, *Walt Disney*, 242.

67. Holliss & Sibley, *Walt Disney's Snow White and the Seven Dwafts*, 35.

68. Gabler, Walt *Disney*, 260.

69. Gabler, *Walt Disney*, 265.

70. Gabler, *Walt Disney*, 236.

71. Gabler, *Walt Disney*, 260.

72. Gabler, *Walt Disney*, 265.

73. Holliss & Sibley, *Walt Disney's Snow White and the Seven Dwarfs*, 32.

74. Gabler, *Walt Disney*, 266.

75. Gabler, *Walt Disney*, 270.

76. Gabler, *Walt Disney*, 263.

77. Kimball in Greene and Greene, *Inside the Dream*, 51.

78. J.B. Kaufamn, *The Fairest One of All*, 7.

79. Gabler, *Walt Disney*, 269.

80. Gabler, *Walt Disney*, 264.

81. Gabler, *Walt Disney*, 263; Thomas, *Disney's Art of Animation*, 76.

82. Bill Peet, *An Autobiography*, 85.

83. Thomas, *Disney's Art of Animation: From Mickey Mouse to Beauty and the Beast*, 76.

84. Gabler, *Walt Disney*, 271.

85. Holliss & Sibley, *Walt Disney's Snow White and the Seven Dwarfs*, 32.

86. "Walt Disney's Speech accepting the Showman of the World Award," National Association of Theater Owners, October 1, 1966, see Jim Korkis, "Walt In His Own Words," http://jimhillmedia.com/alumni1/b/wade_sampson/archive/2005/04/06/1256.aspx, accessed November 7, 2016.

87. Gabler, *Walt Disney*, 267.

88. Gabler, *Walt Disney*, 266.

89. Holliss & Sibley, *Walt Disney's Snow White and the Seven Dwarfs*, 35.

90. Quote from trove.nia.gov.au/ndp/del/article/54812725, accessed July 7, 2014, now unavailable; see also "December 6, 1937—Pomona Review," http://filmic-light.blogspot.ca/2012/12/december-6-1937-pomona-preview.html.

91. Gabler, *Walt Disney*, 271.

92. Holliss & Sibley, *Walt Disney's Snow White And The Seven Dwarfs*, 35.

93. Gabler, *Walt Disney*, 273.

94. Krause & Witkowski, *Walt Disney's Snow White and the Seven Dwarfs, An Art in Its Making*, 43.

95. Krause & Witkowski, *Walt Disney's Snow White and the Seven Dwarfs, An Art in Its Making*, 47.

96. Gabler, *Walt Disney*, 172.

97. Holliss & Sibley, *Walt Disney's Snow White and the Seven Dwarfs*, 36.

98. Thomas, *Disney's Art of Animation: From Mickey Mouse to Hercules*, 77.

99. Holliss & Sibley, *Walt Disney's Snow White and the Seven Dwarfs*, 65.

100. Peet, *An Autobiography*, 87.

101. Krause & Witkowski, *Walt Disney's Snow White and the Seven Dwarfs: An Art in its Making*, 47

102. Culhane, *Talking Animals and Other People*, 183; also in Holliss & Sibley, *Walt Disney's Snow White And The Seven Dwarfs*, 65.

103. Marc Davis in Green & Green, *Remembering Walt*, 108.

104. Holliss & Sibley, *Walt Disney's Snow White and the Seven Dwarfs*, 65.

105. Holliss & Sibley, *Walt Disney's Snow White and the Seven Dwarfs*, 65.

106. Gabler, *Walt Disney*, 272–273.

107. Gabler, Walt Disney, 273.

108. Gabler, *Walt Disney*, 273.

109. Gabler, *Walt Disney*, 276; Holliss & Sibley, *Walt Disney's Snow White and the Seven Dwarfs*, 66.

110. Holliss & Sibley, *Walt Disney's Snow White And The Seven Dwarfs*, 72.

111. Gabler, *Walt Disney*, 277.

112. Gabler, *Walt Disney*, 277.

113. Gabler, *Walt Disney*, 277.

114. Quoted in Charles Solomon, "The Man Who Was Never a Mouse," at articles.latimes.com/2001/dec/02/entertainment/ca-10570, accessed January 31, 2015.

115. Goodman, "The Light That Might Have Failed" at www.awn.com/animationworld/light-might-have-failed.

116. Gabler, *Walt Disney*, 275.

117. "Walt Disney's Speech accepting the Showman of the World Award," National Association of Theatre Owners, October 1, 1966; Smith, *Walt Disney Famous Quotes*, 87.

118. David Johnson, "The Image—Part One", www.animationartist.com/InsideAnimation/DavidJohnson/ImagePart1.html#DavidJohnson, accessed Jan 31, 2015; also www.animationartist.com/columns/DJohnson/Image01/image01.html, accessed Jan 31, 2015.

119. Smith, *The Quotable Walt Disney*, 123; Smith, *Walt Disney Famous Quotes*, 87.
120. Sito, *Drawing the Line*, 85.
121. Sito, *Drawing the Line*, 89.
122. Sito, *Drawing the Line*, 99–100.

CHAPTER TWELVE

Building a Better Mouse House and Reflecting on Halcyon Days

Walt had risked all that he had on the making of *Snow White and the Seven Dwarfs* based on his own assessment of the competencies of his organization and his ability to lead, manage, and organize the work involved, and his belief that the public would buy it. If he had failed to succeed, the studio would have gone into receivership and its assets sold. Walt's failure would have meant the end of feature-length animation, the attempt at which would have been seen as the downfall of the hubristic Walt Disney, and hundreds of animators, technicians, and support staff would have been looking for another line of work in the midst of the depression.

Instead, *Snow White and the Seven Dwarfs* was a blockbuster hit, grossing an estimated $10 million in foreign and domestic revenues by the end of 1938 and becoming the most successful film to date. For the first time in Walt's career, the studio was flush with money. *Snow White* had proved that audiences were willing and eager to sit through a feature-length cartoon if the quality and entertainment value was high enough, and Walt was equally eager to fulfill that desire.

As Walt reaped payback for his multi-year investment, he began to plan and bring into production new full-length animated features, announcing three more: *Pinocchio*, *Bambi*, and *Alice in Wonderland*. In addition, he was doing research on another three potential features: *Cinderella*, *The Wind in the Willows*, and *Peter Pan*.[1]

Work on *Bambi* was resumed, and *Pinocchio* was set into motion at the increasingly expanding and overcrowded studio. The making of *Fantasia* was not far behind.

Investing Profits for a Better Tomorrow

With the profits from *Snow White*, Walt now had the means at his disposal to make capital improvements to the overcrowded and physically dispersed Hyperion Avenue studio. The existing Disney studio on Hyperion Street had grown from a 1,600 square foot single-story building of just a few rooms when it was purchased in 1926 to an expanded 20,000 square feet by 1931 to accommodate the production of Mickey Mouse and the Silly Symphonies, and now had grown to exceed 70,000 square feet across multiple locations.[2] Disney researcher Michael Bowling writes, "By 1939 there was no more room to grow on the Hyperion Studio lot. By this time, the Disney Studio had 1,500 employees and the layout of the Hyperion Studio was so haphazard there was a feeling among some that the Hyperion Studio could no longer meet the goals of the Disney Studios."[3]

The growing number of simultaneous projects competing for resources was driving the growth of the studio, and there was a feeling that things were getting out of control. The physical constraints imposed by the rag-tag and scattered studio layout contributed to the complexity of coordinating information and action to get work done efficiently. A new studio could help address these operational problems by rationalizing processes in order to control, coordinate, and effectively manage the growing volume of highly technical and specialized work required to ensure the release of a new animated short every three-weeks or so and to make advances on the feature-length projects.

Given Walt's ambitions for further growth in production of animated features, now was the time to re-invest profits in a new custom-designed state-of-the-art studio that would solve these problems. Walt wanted to create an attractive workplace that would set a higher standard for worker accommodations by providing a more comfortable and joyful working environment, and in doing so, put the state of disrepair of all other animation studios to shame. In August 1938, Walt and Roy purchased 51 acres of property on Buena Vista Street in Burbank, California, on which to build a new studio, and hired architect Kem Weber to oversee the design.[4]

With the decision made to move forward with this immense personal challenge, Walt became fully engaged with his hired architects and engineers over every aspect of the new studio's design and how best to create efficiencies in the sequences of the animation process and encourage the creativity of the artists. This was in addition to all his other responsibilities as studio head.

Departments were set up to reflect an efficient flow of work, as described by Walt Disney biographer Neal Gabler:

> The idea was that production would flow smoothly downward from the third floor, where Walt had his office...next to the story department and where the films were initiated; to the second floor, where the directors and layout men divided the feature stories into sequences, devised the staging of the scenes, and eventually screened the roughs in the sweatboxes located there; to the first floor, where some two

to three hundred animators were separated into groups under head animators in each wing to do the actual drawings; to the basement, where the test camera was housed and the roughs were shot. Each wing contained a unit—three devoted to features and one to shorts.[5]

The amount of space now required to operate efficiently greatly exceeded what Walt could have imagined when the Hyperion Avenue studio was completed in January 1926. The new three-story animation building was to be three times as large, as was space allocated to the ink-and-paint department, and the soundstage nearly five times bigger. In total, the new Burbank studio would be four times larger than their current facility.[6]

At the same time Walt was designing the physical space of the new studio and trying to optimize the physical plant flow in 1938, Roy had recognized the need for a documented organization structure that formally identified roles, responsibilities, and reporting relationships instead of the ad-hoc system that was in effect. The business had become large and complex, and the obligations and responsibilities required in roles were too important to be left without a formal structure of accountabilities.

In the early days, when the studio was small, Walt was able to work closely, personally, and informally with all of the staff, and everybody knew what was expected and what needed to be done. But that was no longer possible. As the hierarchical distance between most of the staff and Walt increased, the personal connection between them diminished. In a little over a decade from when he started over with Mickey Mouse and a handful of staff in 1928, Walt had grown to be the CEO of a major Hollywood movie studio with immense responsibilities. Even if he wanted to, he could no longer just be "one of the boys."

The Doors Open on the Swank New Disney Studio

There was a growing cost to creating Walt's high quality cartoons. The economics of the business were such that as a general rule of thumb, domestic U.S. audiences would generate enough revenue to cover the production costs, with profits coming from overseas markets. Forty-five percent of Disney's film revenues were from overseas markets.[7]

World War II started in Europe in the late summer of 1939 with Germany invading Poland on September 1, and Britain's prime minister, Neville Chamberlain, declaring war on Germany two days later. As a result, Disney film releases subsequent to *Snow White* were effectively cut off from generating overseas revenues. The outbreak of war in Europe was making it extremely difficult for the studio to maintain its current cost structure and turn a profit.

The new Disney studio in Burbank officially opened in October 1939 at a cost of $3 million, which was $1 million over the original projected budget.[8] Holliss and Sibley describe the new studio in *The Disney Studio Story*:

Dominating the site was the animation building, three stories high with four wings arranged to provide the maximum available daylight for the artists. Like the rest of the studio, the building was air-conditioned—the name "sweatbox" was used only now through habit....

The building housed everyone involved in the creative process, from Walt (who had a suite of offices and a bed for late nights) and his Production Manager, through the Story Department, the Supervising Animators and their Assistants and In-betweeners, to the "Checkers", responsible for ensuring the accuracy of drawings sent for inking and painting. The building also housed a library and a "morgue" where animation drawings that had been finished with were filed away for future reference. Other buildings nearby were designated to the camera, cutting and ink-and-paint departments, a music soundstage, a dialogue and effects building and a theatre.[9]

Gabler describes the amenities Walt provided for staff at the new studio:

Amid the purported new efficiency Walt had not stinted on the amenities. There was not only an elaborate commissary, where Roy and Walt democratically took their own meals, but also a snack bar on the first floor of the Animation Building and a buffet in the penthouse. Anyone who wanted a sandwich or a milk shake could simply order one, and a traffic boy would deliver it to the office. There was a barbershop for anyone needing a haircut. Walt also provided a gymnasium on the top floor, where a Swedish exercise trainer named Carl Johnson led workouts and a roof deck where animators could and did sunbathe nude. Every noon in the studio's theater there would be a thirty-minute show of animations, newsreels, and scenes from other features. In fact, though the studio had been modeled after a college campus and was still frequently described as one, it had so many frills that Walt himself compared it now to a "swank hotel."[10]

Storyman Homer Brightman described his new workspace in his memoir *Life in the Mouse House* and contrasted it with his workspace at the old studio on Hyperion Avenue: "Our room was spacious, carpeted in dark blue and with two new desks and high, chrome-legged stools with blue naugahyde seats. Our storyboards covered the walls, and several comfortable lounging chairs faced them. We had been accustomed to uncarpeted floors and peeling walls and felt out of place in these new bright rooms."[11]

---

1. Holliss & Sibley, *The Disney Studio Story*, 33.

2. Gennawey, *Walt Disney and the Promise of Progress City*, 69.

3. Michael Bowling, "The Walt Disney Hyperion Studios 1929-1939," DIS Blog, blog.wdwinfo.com/2013/07/28/the-walt-disney-hyperion-studios-1929-1939-the-foundation-of-an-empire/.

4. Holliss & Sibley, *The Disney Studio Story*, p. 34; 51 acre reference from *Time Magazine*, "Walt's Wild Men: LIFE Behind the Scenes at Disney Studios, new.time.com/3614660/walts-wild-men-life-behind-the-scenes-at-disney-studios/; Kem Weber as architect from Gennawey, *Walt Disney and the Promise of Progress City*, 70.

5. Gabler, *Walt Disney*, 323.

6. Gabler, *Walt Disney*, 323.

7. Thomas, *Walt Disney*, 161.

8. Gabler, *Walt Disney*, 330.

9. Holliss & Sibley, *The Disney Studio Story*, 37.

10. Gabler, *Walt Disney*, 323.

11. Brightman, *Life in the Mouse House*, 50.

CHAPTER THIRTEEN

The Crash of 1940: Reality Eats Fantasy for Breakfast

Walt had high hopes for 1940, the year of his next two full-length animated features, *Pinocchio* and *Fantasia*. Even as the studio was undergoing severe financial pressures with the investment in the production of the two feature films, Walt continued to improve the conditions under which his staff worked, provide skills training, and integrate the latest technology into his production processes to advance the art of animation.

Walt was proud to see the building concepts he helped design and work on completed and ready to house production. He was brimming with confidence and exuberance as staff moved in and got settled, and was eager to show it off as the newest artifact of the Disney studio success story.

But at the same time, Walt knew there were problems brewing below the surface. Animation and support staff rivalies had developed and had been operating over the years at Hyperion. At some point the culture amongst animators began to shift from one of sharing, collaboration, and advancing the new art form of animation, to being cliquish, withdrawn, secretive, and competitive. In some quarters, professional camaraderie and the sharing of ideas both within and across project units were being stifled by a lack of trust, teamwork, and the protection of ideas to win the favor of Walt over perceived rivals. Petty jealousies were affecting the ability of staff to get quality work done, which had an adverse effect on productivity and production costs at a time when the studio was suffering from severe financial strain.

One day in early 1940, shortly after moving into the new Burbank studio, Roy summoned Walt to his office to discuss a serious matter. When Walt arrived, Roy instructed him to sit as he closed the door. Disney biographer Bob Thomas in *Walt Disney: An American Original* tells the story:

> Roy took his place behind his desk and said, "This is serious. I've got to talk to you."

> Walt studied his brother's long face and asked, "What's the matter?"

> Roy outlined the financial reversal of the past year: how the profits

on *Snow White* had been eaten up by the costs of *Pinocchio*, *Fantasia*, and *Bambi*; how the European war had caused a sharp decline in theater revenue; how the company now had a thousand employees in a brand-new studio built at a cost of $3,000,000.

"And now, Walt," Roy concluded, "we are in debt to the bank for four and half million dollars!"

Roy expected his brother to be shocked and concerned. Instead, Walt began to grin, and then he burst out laughing.

"What the hell are you laughing at?" Roy demanded.

"I was just thinking back," Walt said between fits of laughter. "Do you remember when we couldn't borrow a thousand dollars?"

Roy too began to laugh. "Yeah, remember how hard it was to get that first twenty-thousand-dollar credit?" he recalled.

They regaled each other with memories of when they had to plead for loans to meet the weekly payroll. "And now we owe four and a half million dollars!" Walt remarked. "I think that's pretty damn good." When their amusement was over, Walt asked his brother, "What are we going to do?"

I'm afraid we're going to need some outside capital," Roy replied. "We'll have to issue a preferred-stock issue."[1]

Both Walt and Roy had misgivings about a public issuance of stock to finance the growth of the company and keep it viable. Together they had built the company from its fragile start when Walt moved to California in the summer of 1923, and neither liked the idea of letting outsiders share in decisions about how the studio would be run.

Walt, in particular, always disliked bankers, outside investors, and accountants for their risk-adverse approach to business in a manner that he felt stifled innovation. Where Walt was driven by a creative passion and thrived on the act of entrepreneurial creation, he viewed bankers, investors, and accountants as being constrained by fear and convention, too often focused on the measurement of expenses and minimizing risk to the detriment of pursuing yet-to-be-proved opportunities. Walt feared that going public would impose an irrational and undue external constraint on his freedom to make his own choices. He feared that a loss of control would tie his hands and tip the balance away from giving customers what they want toward managing short-term returns for short-sighted and narrow-minded shareholders. Nonetheless, with no other funding solution at hand, the decision was made to set in motion the process to take the company public after seventeen years of private ownership.

Rallying the Troops Toward Unity and Away from Danger

As head of the studio, Walt was dealing with a myriad of major issues: *Pinocchio*, the studio's follow-up to *Snow White*, was about to be released; *Bambi* and *Fantasia* were in production, and neither was going well; and discussions had begun with Roy about the need to take on outside investors for the first time and dilute their control of the studio and ability to manage it as they saw fit without outside interference. In addition, and of deep concern to Walt, was an ongoing unionization debate simmering in the background that was quickly becoming a major distraction to his artists in getting their work done. The unions had been successful at organizing animators on the East Coast and were now setting their sights on the biggest prize, Walt Disney Productions.

As a way to try to address some of these issues, on January 30, 1940, one week before *Pinocchio's* premiere, Walt convened a meeting that lasted almost three hours to rally the spirits of his key staff. He had high expectations that *Pinocchio* would echo *Snow White's* box office success, and his message was that they were now finally in a position where anything was possible; that for the Walt Disney Studios, the future of animation held exciting and ground-breaking possibilities.

But to get there, Walt said in an emotional speech, a spirit of collaboration was needed, which he wasn't fully feeling. "I want a group of guys who will get together and discuss their problems and we will take care of their recommendations," he said. "We want to find out what they think...and I want it first-hand from them. ... I want the story groups to get together. I want them to talk over their work. ... I want to get the directors together and layout and the background men. ... We must find the most effective way to unify this plant. I want to unify it in such a way that everybody will be working together."[2]

Walt envisioned that his studio would be a creative artistic community, where people worked together in a spirit of harmony, with pride of workmanship, where each artist participated fruitfully and gained the satisfaction that comes from contributing to their full potential, to the best of their ability, for the benefit of each other, the product, and most importantly, the customer. That spirit which existed during the production of *Snow White* now seemed to be elusive.

As in other things, Walt knew what he wanted. What he didn't know, and was struggling with, was how to achieve the positive working culture he desired for his staff.

Walt told those in attendance that he was thinking about implementing some sort of bonus system so that everybody would have a bigger stake in maintaining the highest quality standards and ensuring the studio's success, but he hadn't yet worked out how it would operate in order to be fair. He was considering a profit-sharing plan linked to an animation rating system where each employee that was part of the plan would be rated based on criteria such as value to the company, tenure, cooperation, and ambition. Bonuses would be established based on corporate profits, and allocated proportionally based on this assessment.

As usual, Walt was thinking about the Disney brand and looking ahead to the future. His desire was for his staff to keep pushing animation forward toward its potential as an unrestricted and unbounded story-telling medium. What he feared most was that if left to their own devices, his artists would get dragged down into pettiness and unproductive work habits, and the studio would lose its leadership status and competitive edge. He was already seeing signs of inappropriate and undisciplined behavior at the new studio, and this meeting was an attempt to signal his intention to do something about it.

In his role as leader, it was proper for Walt to call out the pettiness amongst staff that he was seeing as an impediment to doing work at a level of quality that matched his high performance standards and their capabilities, and asking them to work to a larger vision to ensure that the studio continued to produce great films that they would all be proud of and remain successful. Everybody had a stake in the same outcome, he said. "We've got to fix this thing so the business won't collapse. Maybe I've had too many bad experiences. I know guys, though, who are like that. All they think of is how much money they can get out of a thing."[3] Walt understood that money was important, but in the end it was just a means to an end. It was doing something great with the money that was important and valuable. He also knew that his staff didn't necessarily see things the same way.

Pinocchio Flounders and the Studio Rocks on a Shifting Sea

On February 7, 1940, one week after Walt's meeting with his staff, *Pinocchio* premiered at the 3,500-seat Center Theatre in New York City. It was eighteen months past its scheduled release date and significantly over budget.

The film critics loved the movie, and it opened to great reviews declaring it to be "superior to *Snow White*" and to be the "best cartoon ever made." Walt appreciated the good reviews but was worried that it lacked the heart and emotional impact that made *Snow White* so endearing, and thus wouldn't fare as well at the box office.

It only took a few weeks to observe that attendance for *Pinocchio* significantly lagged *Snow White* and was going to be a disaster in terms of box-office revenues. It appeared to have great appeal to children who packed matinee performances, but adults were less enamored, leaving the movie houses empty at night. Because of the war waging in Europe, the film was only translated into Spanish and Portuguese for South American audiences.

The studio's revenue estimates for *Pinocchio* were quickly revised downward by more than a million dollars, and instead of generating anticipated profits, Roy was now predicting severe losses on the film. When the box office receipts were in, upon its initial theatrical release, the studio posted just $1.2 million in revenues on a total investment of $2.7 million.[4] The effects of the war in Europe were tangible: where *Snow White* had grossed $2 million in England, *Pinocchio* grossed just one-tenth of that, $200,000. Instead of the anticipated millions in profits to fund ongoing operations and underwrite other projects already in the works, the studio was forced to book almost $2 million in losses on the picture.

Along with the disappointment at the mounting cumulative financial losses from feature-length animated films when expectations had been so high, tensions at the new Burbank studio continued to slowly rise. Walt's ability to exert control over expanding operations was diminishing as the number of employees and simultaneous projects pressing for resources continued to increase. The new studio now housed more than one thousand workers employed to keep new products flowing on the expectation that salaries would be paid by healthy profits derived from box-office ticket sales from *Pinocchio* that were not materializing.

The animation unions that had been successful unionizing all of the East Coast animation studios had now set their sights on Disney. They were eagerly and actively exerting their influence in the halls of the studio. A large proportion of staff were young, educated, under-employed, and held no feelings of loyalty to Walt, whom they rarely if ever encountered. Many were ready to air their grievances and take a stand against what they perceived as the studio's autocratic and imperious leadership practices.

Walt had tried to use the enticement of bonuses to raise morale and affect positive improvements in productivity. Had he succeeded, he may have garnered some influence against increasing union activity at the studio. Instead, many interpreted his statement of intention as a promise to deliver, thereby raising expectations that some sort of monetary bonus would be forthcoming based on performance. Now, however, without the expected profits from *Pinocchio* that Walt was counting on, there could be no profit sharing, as there were no profits to share. Circumstances were now such that Walt's inability to deliver bonuses would produce the opposite result of what was intended.

Just as Walt was said to be understandably fickle and moody after the disappointment of *Pinocchio*, perhaps leaving him uncertain about the future prospects of the studio, the charge of fickleness could also be justly attributed to a growing number of his staff.

Without having direct insight into the overall financial situation of the studio, which post-*Pinocchio* was dire, the incorrect perception amongst a large proportion of staff was that the studio was a profit-making machine. And instead of sharing the vast wealth assuredly accumulating in the corporate bank account as a result of the employees working day-in and day-out to create that wealth, many workers felt that Walt and Roy were beginning to cut back on their spending out of a motive of greed to pad their own pockets and those of shareholders at the expense of the workers.

It was a familiar narrative being pushed by the unions actively trying to organize the Disney animators: the capitalist owners were getting rich on the backs of the poor workers struggling for survival. For many of these workers, the time had come to turn the tables on what the union was selling as the exploitative business policies and practices of Walt Disney and the failure of the workers to be treated properly and fairly.

It was true that Walt and Roy, as the two most senior executives and officers of the corporation, were earning the highest salaries paid by the studio. In March 1940, Walt had signed a seven-year contract with the studio to be paid $2,000 per week, with Roy earning $72,000 per year, and lawyer Gunther Lessing earning under $15,000.[5] These salaries were low by Hollywood studio standards, and nobody would deny that the brothers, who built the studio up from nothing starting in 1923, were entitled to them.

The real story, as Walt said at the time, was that the profits earned by the studio were not lining his pockets, but were reinvested in the production of *Pinocchio, Fantasia,* and *Bambi*—almost all of it going to pay the salaries of the staff ahead of any revenues that those films may earn, and thereby keeping staff employed when they would otherwise be without work.

Anticipating and Funding the Future: Walt Disney Productions Goes to Market

In April 1940, with the assistance of investment banking firm Kidder-Peabody, Walt Disney Productions went to market with an IPO of 155,000 shares of six-percent cumulative convertible preferred stock at $25 par value and 600,000 shares of common stock at five dollars. The prospectus listed total assets of Walt Disney Productions at the end of 1939 as just over seven million dollars.[6]

The stock offering sold out quickly based on the success of *Snow White* and investor enthusiasm over the box-office potential of *Pinocchio* and *Fantasia,* and provided the studio with $3,500,000 of much-needed new capital which was used to pay down accumulated and outstanding Bank of America debt.

A short time later, Walt had an encounter with Henry Ford, American industrialist and founder of the Ford Motor Company, at a luncheon sponsored by Ford in Walt's honor. Ford advised Walt that if he was going to sell any of the company, he might as well sell all of it. Walt was worried that by going public, he and Roy had crossed a point of no return with regards to freedom of action in managing their own affairs, values that they had fought so hard for and had agreed never to surrender.[7]

A Division of Passions in Burbank: Creative Haven or "Wretched" Workplace?

Having covered the mounting losses of *Pinocchio* with equity financing, Walt was able to continue investing in the future. He pressed on with work on *Fantasia* and *Bambi* at the new air-conditioned Burbank studio. According to many, the new studio felt more like a college campus than a production factory, and represented the state of the art in film production facilities.

The swank new studio was seen by most as a creative haven, especially when compared to the cramped, over-crowded, and widely dispersed old studio on Hyperion Avenue, and when compared to the other film studios where many had worked prior to joining Disney.

For some, however, there was a perception that the new studio and the way it was being managed made for a more oppressive workplace rather than the creative oasis that Walt intended and desired. A growing number saw it as overly cliquish and unnecessarily stratified, with Walt and his chosen favorites at the top of the hierarchy receiving special treatment and getting rich by paying the less-skilled and over-worked production workers low wages in a depressed recessionary economic environment in which jobs were scarce.

In spite of Walt's best intentions to build a spectacular place for his staff to work that was the envy of the industry, many of those who transferred from the old Hyperion studio to the new Burbank studio were becoming disenchanted with their work and began to form the opinion that the studio was too big, too formal, too structured, too impersonal and lacking in the spirit of camaraderie and excitement that they had experienced at the old studio.[8]

Disney animator and storyman Bill Peet indicated that he wasn't overly impressed by the new studio, writing in his *An Autobiography*: "It would take awhile to get used to the modern building with all-new furniture, especially after feeling so much at home in the old run-down apartment house with faded wallpaper and tattered window shades. Artists need an atmosphere of poverty, a degree of shabbiness to get into a creative mood."[9]

The new building, recalls Peet, had an "intimidating big business atmosphere,"[10] although that didn't appear to interfere with his ability to do his work and enjoy it: "The year and a half I spent on *Dumbo* was a happy time," he noted.[11] So was the time he spent working on *Song of the South*. Working for Walt must have had a number of benefits and intrinsic rewards, for the Burbank studio opened in 1939 and Peet continued to be actively engaged at the studio until 1964.

Storyman Homer Brightman, writing in his memoir *Life in the Mouse House*, took the rhetoric of dissatisfaction one step further, reporting that "by late May [1940, just months after moving to the new studio], a deep dissatisfaction developed among the employees. The new studio was being considered a wretched place to work."[12]

The pace of the work and the constant pushing by Walt for better product, more creativity, and more output from his staff was experienced as both exhilarating and stress-inducing. Even though Walt designed the new studio to provide the best of everything, for a great many of the more junior staff, the day-to-day work of creating animated movies was overly repetitive and mundane, and the formality of the new studio didn't easily accommodate the informal socializing and general playfulness that the veteran animators were used to at the old studio.

The new building, with the new structure, provided greater oversight and transparency of both good and bad work habits. While many artists were thankful to get any work in their chosen field during the Great Depression, they were also dissatisfied with having to do work they may not have valued greatly at wages lower than they felt to be deserved or fair, even though, by virtue of their holding those jobs, their own estimation was that they were the most suitable jobs relative to the available alternatives.

The more Walt did to facilitate improvements, the more a large percentage of his staff cast a cynical eye on his good intentions. It was as if poison had been poured into Snow White's wishing well.

Bonus Anticipation Amongst Growing Discontent

There are a number of explanations for the palpable loss of morale that seems to have occurred among studio employees around the time of the move to the new studio. The disappointment and lack of confidence that resulted from *Pinocchio's* poor box office showing was just one of them. But whatever the multitude of possible reasons, for many of the animation and production workers, their resentment appeared to have had ties back to Walt's failure to provide bonuses to staff years ago for their work on *Snow White*.

Homer Brightman, in *Life in the Mouse House*, tells how he and many of his fellow artists were fixated on receiving these bonuses, and how every event and announcement was turned into a cause for optimistic anticipation that *this* was to be the moment when the studio's presumed vast store of wealth would flow their way.

For example, when *Snow White* premiered on the evening of December 21, 1937, at the Carthay Circle Theatre in Los Angeles, the following acknowledgement by Walt appeared in the event program:

> My sincere appreciation to members of my staff whose loyalty and creative endeavor made possible this production. Walt Disney.[13]

Brightman reflects in hindsight on the state of mind of the studio staff at this time:

> None of us knew the extent of Walt and his brother Roy's financial success, but that little paragraph on the program made us feel we would no longer be laboring for substandard wages. Now we, too, would soon share in the success of *Snow White*.
>
> But months went by and nothing happened. Walt kept us too busy to brood for long. He was starting work on two new features…[*Pinocchio* and *Bambi*]. Walt had also scheduled eleven short subjects for 1938. All talk was about future production, nothing about the past. Just the mention of *Snow White* brought a scowl to his face. *Snow White* was already behind him, and he was charging ahead with new projects. … He dropped the past from his shoulders like an old cloak, a cloak that had our salary increases in the lining."[14]

The Snow White Wrap Party and Bonus Blues

Just when staff were giving up hope that bonuses would be forthcoming, in the summer of 1938 Walt announced that he was holding a 24-hour *Snow White* wrap party for all studio staff and their spouse or guest to celebrate and thank everyone for their hard work in completing *Snow White* in time for its Christmas 1937 release. Walt booked the entire luxurious Lake Narconian resort in the California desert near Palm Springs for the weekend of June 4, 1938.[15] The event was promoted as Walt's Field Day and activities included swimming, tennis, badminton, horseback riding, golf, and Ping-Pong. There was live music, dancing, and plenty of food and alcohol. Overnight accommodation could be purchased at $3.50 a room. Mixed drinks were twenty-five cents, beer fifteen cents.

More than 1,400 people attended. The majority of the staff was single and in their early 20s, and for them it was a spectacular party for drinking and cavorting. But many of the more senior animators and tenured employees were of the expectation that the real reason for the wrap party was for Walt to announce bonuses as further remuneration for the sheer volume of work that the staff contributed to meet the *Snow White* deadline.

At 11 p.m. on the Saturday night, the dancing stopped. After awards were given out for the various recreational events of the day, recalls Brightman, "we waited in happy anticipation, for we knew Walt would make a big announcement this night." He continues:

> Walt was a showman waiting for the perfect moment to step forward and announce the amount of money to compensate each man. What other reason could there be for a big party?
>
> At last he walked onto the stage. Deafening applause greeted him. Here it was! The good news we had waited so long to hear.[16]

Walt stepped in front of the crowd to great applause and proceeded to talk about the importance of the new film projects, the decline in studio productivity, and the need for everyone to dedicate themselves to greater artistic efforts in seizing the challenges that lay ahead. There was no talk of bonuses. Disney historian Paul F. Anderson, in the article "Walt's Field Day—1938" on the Disney History Institute website, notes that to the recently hired, Walt's speech was received positively as a call to action, but for those who were expecting Walt to address the issue of bonuses, "the speech held the bitterness of a small betrayal."[17]

Then, three weeks later, on Tuesday, June 28, 1938, the following news item appeared in the *Los Angeles Examiner*:

DISNEY TO GIVE STAFF 20 PCT OF PROFIT ON SNOW WHITE

Distribution of 20 per cent of the earnings from the motion picture *Snow White and the Seven Dwarfs* to Walt Disney's employees was announced today.

The distribution to employees will be between $800,000 and $1,000,000, with the division being made on a salary basis. It is estimated that the bonus to each employee will represent about 12 to 13 weeks' wages.

About 800 workers will share in the bonus.

According to Brightman, the *Examiner* article improved studio morale "a hundred percent" instantly. "Walt was the greatest guy on earth. Now we definitely would be compensated for those long hours of hard work at sweatshop wages. Walt and his brother Roy were well on the way to becoming millionaires, and we would share in their good fortunes."[18]

Time passed, and nothing happened. There was no mention of bonuses from studio management or commentary on the press announcement. Brightman writes: "Studio management never confirmed the *Examiner* story, but more important to us, they never denied it, either."[19]

Months went by with staff waiting in anticipation, figuring that the bonuses were being delayed because the accounting department was tallying twenty percent of each employee's salary and readying the checks.

Then came another announcement. Walt had purchased a 51-acre lot in Burbank where he intended to build a new, plush, air-conditioned, animation studio. Writes Brightman:

> I think that was the beginning of hard feelings between the staff and Walt, but a lot of the fellows thought the bonus was bound to be paid, otherwise Walt never would have published an account of his intentions in a newspaper.[20]

The rhetoric of dissatisfaction with the vastly improved conditions of the new Burbank studio and complaining about Walt's sometimes grumpy, curt, disrespectful, and seemingly ungrateful attitude, became a preoccupation amongst the creative and artistic staff, although Bill Peet, considered to have been Walt's greatest storyman, notes in his *An Autobiography* that the opinion the artists had about Walt would swing from week to week depending on whether he approved their work at a story session or sent them back to the drawing board.

Artists would work for weeks and sometimes months developing a story idea or animation sequence that Walt was liable to dismiss in an instant for a better idea or to push artistic creativity to higher levels. Peet recalled a two-day story conference to review *Pinocchio* that occurred shortly before the move to the new Burbank studio. Developing the story so it would work as an animated feature had not been going well. The writers were having difficulty trimming the tale down to manageable length and converting Pinocchio as portrayed in the novel by Carlo Collodi into a likeable character that the audience would care about. Walt was needed to make decisions that the other participants were incapable of making. Peet relates the incident:

> As the conference continued through the morning, the jovial Walt who greeted us earlier was getting more and more cantankerous by the minute.
>
> "There's too much stuff here," he kept complaining. Now and then he would step up to a board and rip off a whole row of sketches.
>
> Walt was tough and businesslike as he leaned out on the edge of his chair scowling at the boards. The atmosphere was getting pretty grim until Honest John Foulfellow, a villainous fox, was introduced on the boards. Walt's mood changed in a flash and suddenly he was the sly, debonair fox, overacting the part to perfection.
>
> After seeing the gruff, overbearing Walt it was a refreshing turnabout to see the playful Walt in action. His exaggerated attitudes were truly funny and he had us laughing all the way....
>
> After the fox performance Walt reverted to his bearish ways, grumbling about all the surplus material, all the wasted time and money. Leo [Ellis] didn't make it halfway through his presentation of Bogyland before Walt called a halt.

"We don't need all this stuff," he grumped. "Too much!" So it was goodbye bogies, every last one.

Al [Geise] was the most jittery performer of the lot and nearly lost his voice as he stammered through our seagoing epic to the final great "GULP."

Walt didn't hesitate a minute in dismissing the thing. "That's too scary," he said. "Don't you think we could explain this some other way?"

"Yes, Walt!" was the unanimous verdict, and poor Al was crushed.

Walt must have eliminated more than half the story boards before he called an end to the story conference, and as he was about to leave he turned to us with a satisfied smile and said, 'That was a hell of a good session." It left me wondering what a bad one would be like.

Much later I would appreciate Walt's efforts during that two-day story conference—his uncanny ability to evaluate, to separate the wheat from the chaff.

I also got an idea of how opinions of Walt were formed. Those who had fared well at the conference and came out with their boards intact praised Walt to the skies. He was a great guy! A remarkable man! A great talent! A genius! Meanwhile, the disgruntled losers echoed Al's negative opinions. Of course, those opinions could change from month to month according to their successes or failures.[21]

Storyman Mel Shaw expressed a similar outlook following sweatbox sessions: "One day you could find yourself basking in the sunshine of [Walt's] smile, and the next you could be 'on the outs.'"[22]

Complaining about Walt and his relentless push for something better seemed to have become an ongoing pastime amongst many of his staff. The very nature of creative work is such that anybody and everybody who was good enough to rise to the level where they were presenting ideas and concepts directly to Walt would have a fistful of gripes and hard-done-by stories to tell. Winning in business is a tough game, and somebody has to lead. What many staff failed to understand was that as artists they were invested in creating stories, or scenes, or characters that were all smaller components of a larger production system. It was Walt who was ultimately accountable to his employees, shareholders, and the public for every aspect of creating and delivering movies to theatres that would please audiences and keep the studio in business and his staff employed.

Improvising Dragons and Elephants for Fast Profits

The equity infusion brought about through the April 1940 IPO delivered financial relief to the studio, but Walt knew that this would only be temporary. He needed to bring profitable products to market, and do it quickly. The pressure from the next financial crisis was already building.

The impending release of *Fantasia* was still months away. *Bambi* was in production and Walt was hoping to have it released in the fall of 1941. The scripts for *Peter Pan* and *Alice in Wonderland* were being worked on and it would be years before they would be completed at a cost of millions of dollars each. The studio was under contract to continue to produce short cartoons, but it was felt that they netted very little profit when fully costed, so shifting resources to produce more shorts wasn't the answer. With the excitement and challenge of animated features to occupy Walt's time, he had already delegated most of the responsibility for developing shorts to his staff, although he continued to approve scripts and attend story meetings.[23]

After considering his various options, Walt responded by putting two new short-term feature projects into production.

The first was *The Reluctant Dragon*, an entertaining live-action feature that showed audiences the workings of the new Disney animation studio while also featuring three new animated shorts: *Baby Weems*; Goofy starring in *How to Ride a Horse*; and a twenty-minute telling of the Kenneth Grahame story *The Reluctant Dragon*.

The second new project was *Dumbo*, which Walt conceived as an uncomplicated animated feature that didn't require the subtlety, grace, and life-like drawing skill necessary for *Bambi*, nor the costly and time-consuming special effects required for *Fantasia*. Because it was mostly caricature-style drawing, it could be made at a much quicker pace and for a much lower cost. From start to finish, the story was developed and animated in about eighteen months. Walt was hoping to complete it for $350,000, although it eventually cost a reasonable $800,000. The story itself was so simple and straightforward that Walt was able to tell the complete story to animator Ward Kimball in a studio parking lot conversation in five minutes.[24] The completed movie would clock in at just sixty-four minutes.

Walt's Special Notice: An Emergency Exists

By early June 1940, mere months after the IPO cash infusion, the studio was again under heavy financial strain. Not only were Walt and Roy struggling to keep the studio solvent, they were also contending with brewing employee discontent.

The unions had been successful on the East Coast organizing the Fleischer animation studio in 1938, and now an active campaign was underway to unionize the West Coast studios, especially Disney's animation workers.

By 1940, the Studio had many closed-shop union contracts including musicians, cameramen, and makeup artists, but the number of staff involved amounted to few in number. By contrast, staff at the studio was predominantly engaged in animation and animation-related support roles like animation assistants, inkers, and painters. Having the hundreds of animation-related staff unionize would have a tremendous impact on payroll costs and would restrict Walt's carte blanche management style.

To many of the staff, workplace management at times seemed arbitrary and capricious. Many perceived the salary differentials and long work hours as unfair. Bonuses, when offered, were based on Walt's own judgment rather than a pre-defined and universal methodology. Instead of providing two warnings and two week's notice before firing a worker, as was now the case in unionized studios, Walt continued to operate with the authority to fire anyone at any time, although such occurrences were rare. In fact, it was well known that Walt hated to fire anyone, which was a common complaint from the more productive and responsible staff that carried the burden of pulling the extra weight. If Walt felt a person was making an honest contribution, he would always try to find them more appropriate work.

Another factor in play was the cultural milieu of the age, with the Great Depression ongoing, the Roosevelt administration promoting unionization, and workers seeking a legitimate way to offset their concerns about job security at a period of great economic uncertainty in the cartoon industry and elsewhere. At the same time, the war continued in Europe with uncertainty about America's direct involvement, and talk of conscription to identify and induct men into the armed forces to fight in Europe was under way.

In an attempt to inform and motivate, Walt wrote an inter-office memo to all employees. He wanted them to know that the studio was indeed in crisis and facing severe difficulties that would require understanding, focus, teamwork, and cooperation for the studio to remain operational:

SPECIAL NOTICE TO ALL EMPLOYEES

An emergency exists. Each production hour of everybody in the plant is very valuable and if our time is properly spent and utilized, it may mean that some worthwhile person will be able to retain his job.

I am calling on everybody to help me. We will have to work for the utmost in economy in the use of our time and see to it that every hour of the day is well spent.

I do not want to deny people their privileges. On the contrary, we are trying to design a plan where everyone will be able to continue to enjoy the privileges now in effect. By this I mean the Coffee Shop, the recreational facilities and the noontime showings in the theatre.

However, there has been a terrific loss of time, due to certain people taking uncalled-for advantages. Rather than cut off these things, I feel that if I draw these matters to your attention, you will cooperate with me. First on the list is the business of getting to work on time.

Also, there must be less time spent away from the studio on your own business. Why not let your wife or someone else handle these things for you so that you will be making every working hour count.

All of those people who have been engaged in other pursuits during the lunch period and then eat their lunch on the company's time must take notice.

It has been brought to my attention that there are those who engage in such vigorous games throughout the noon hour that it is necessary for them to take a goodly part of the afternoon to calm and rest themselves before they are able to pick up with their work. In the future it will be necessary that all such violent exercise be taken after hours.

There are those restless people who go through rooms and bore those who are working with their idle, useless chatter. All such visiting must cease.

The wanton waste of supplies must be curtailed. In the future, each and every person in the studio will be held accountable for the supplies given them.

For those of you who, in the past, found it necessary to sleep on company time—due to a lack of sleep the night before—it is strongly recommended that you get the proper amount of rest before coming to work.

I trust that it will not be necessary for me to take the drastic steps that have been suggested to me and I feel confident that once you have been made aware of the existing conditions, I can depend on you to give me your whole-hearted cooperation.

June 8, 1940

WALT[25]

"Walt's special notice was like tossing bullets on a smoldering fire," writes Brightman. "Explosive criticism almost blew the studio apart. Walt was called 'a double-crossing S.O.B.'" The corporate executives were seen by many staff to be Walt's apologists, blaming the studio's difficult situation on the war. Brightman concedes that "the loss of the European markets hurt Walt's pocket book, but that had nothing to do with the *Snow White* bonus promised back in 1938. And that bonus was the root of the resentment."[26]

The perspective amongst Brightman's colleagues was that "Walt had gone out on a limb, financially, and the limb had been chopped off."[27] In other words, staff was angry that Walt had invested *their* money—money to which *they* were entitled—on a new studio that they claimed not to appreciate, and that Walt employed them in the production of new, risky feature-length animation film ventures that turned out to be poor short-term investment decisions. Making things worse in their eyes, Walt refused to take responsibility for the harm he had done to them by failing to succeed.

Summarizing the general sentiment of his studio colleagues at the time, Brightman writes that "[Walt] never blamed himself for failures. He blamed his employees—they worked too slow to meet the emergencies he created."

What this perspective conveniently overlooks and unjustly evades is that were it not for the entrepreneurial initiative of Walt Disney himself, their years of high quality employment from which they and their families benefited during the Great Depression would not have existed at all. Instead of being disappointed but keeping the entire situation in its proper perspective, the result, said Brightman, was that "[t]he new, immaculate fantasy factory in Burbank boiled with turmoil, unheard of in the old Hyperion days. Workers were at odds with each other. Long-time studio friendships broke up. Secretaries took sides."[28]

Returning to the Well

With Walt adding *The Reluctant Dragon* and *Dumbo* to the list of other features and shorts underway, it wasn't long before the studio was again in desperate need for a cash infusion. This time, when approached for additional financial support, Bank of America was reluctant to lend the studio any more money based on their current risk assessment.

To pacify the bankers' concerns, on July 6, 1940, Roy invited Bank of America executive Joe Rosenberg to the studio to screen a reel of *Bambi*. Roy wrote to Walt the day before the visit to remind him that the bank believed in them and supported them and "they rely on everything we tell them to the nth degree, but they are so pessimistic with regard to the outside world that they do not believe they are justified in loaning any money based on expectations involving foreign countries, no matter where they are."[29]

The bank was prepared to loan the studio another $2 million, Roy told Walt, but this time they were demanding conditions. In return they wanted assurances that Walt would put his banker-be-damned attitude aside and that the studio would forcefully impose economic restraint through staff reductions and salary cuts. "I believe strongly," Roy wrote to Walt ahead of the meeting, "that the thing for us to do is not to cross them or even argue with them too much, but to go along with them."[30]

With the studio facing an immediate crisis, Walt heeded Roy's advice. Without Bank of America support, the studio would be forced to shut down, putting the entire staff of over a thousand people out of work. If Walt wanted a shot at saving the company, he would have to abide by the bank's terms.

While there were always creative, production, and financial pressures at the studio, on an overall and day-to-day basis, Walt maintained good relations with his key animators and production staff and was able to inspire them to contribute their best efforts and work the hours needed to meet production deadlines. Walt was also able to earn the respect of his staff and to hold them in awe by his ability to solve any kind of problem.

After twenty years of moviemaking, the scope of Walt's problems was no longer limited to creative and technical aspects as they once were. His responsibilities had become more complicated. They encompassed the entirety of a multi-faceted corporation with global interests. There were now increasing demands on Walt's time to attend to bigger and weightier challenges of sustaining his business empire, forcing him to become further removed from the daily production issues, and more involved in planning and coordinating the higher-level strategic business requirements of the studio.

Walt still enjoyed the creative aspects of story meetings, and was intimately involved on all shorts and features. Now with less time to spend on each project, he was losing his patience for the bickering, office politics, practical jokes, and general loafing of his creative staff that he had once tolerated. Now, more than ever before, there was important work to do, and more pressure on Walt as head of the studio to get films completed and into theatres as quickly as possible. Walt understood that the survival of the studio was at stake, and if staff were to keep their jobs, everybody would have to pitch in and stay focused on the work at hand to help speed up the tempo and increase productivity. There would be no illusions that Walt was in charge and that his staff was working for him, not the other way around.

There and Back Again:
The Safe Return of Ub Iwerks

While Walt may not have thought much of it at the time, the return to the studio of old friend and former business partner Ub Iwerks on September 9, 1940, may have been the best thing that happened to the studio that year.

Iwerks' career since leaving Disney in 1930 to head up his own studio with Pat Powers' financial backing had not been successful. Even though his Flip the Frog and Willie Wopper series of cartoon had broad distribution through MGM for a number of years, they never gained much popularity. By 1936, financial backing for the Iwerks Studio was withdrawn, and it soon folded. From 1937 to 1940, Iwerks held a number of contract jobs as an animation director, before finding his way back to the Disney studio, and coming to terms with his old friend, Walt Disney.

Iwerks assumed a special role at the studio where he applied his vast animation expertise and creativity to technical development, lending a hand in everything from perfecting the multi-plane camera, to developing new and innovative visual special effects, to writing technical scripts, and later, to assisting Walt in the development of many Disneyland and other entertainment attractions.

Iwerks recalled in a 1956 interview: "When I came back in 1940, Walt asked me what I wanted to do. 'Prowl around.' I have been doing it ever since. I'm my own boss."[31]

Planting Seeds in High Places

Around this time, events were such that Walt identified a potential new opportunity for revenues.

In August 1940, President Franklin Delano Roosevelt created a new Office of the Coordinator of Inter-American Affairs (CIAA) at the urging of philanthropist and businessman Nelson Rockefeller. Rockefeller was appointed to head up the CIAA, with the mandate to strengthen cultural ties between the United States and Latin America and counter any German National Socialism ideological sympathies. One platform was to provide American entertainment and educational films through a film division that would harness the talents of the Hollywood film industry to win the hearts and minds south of the border.[32]

Having been put in charge, Rockefeller recruited his friend Hay Whitney to head up a motion picture section. Through Whitney, Disney lawyer Gunther Lessing was appointed chairman of the short subjects committee.

Within just a few months, Walt was engaging in direct meetings with Whitney to discuss the possibility of producing films to support the government's efforts.[33] His argument: what better way to promote the common values of the Americas than through the universally beloved Disney characters?

Walt was planting seeds and keeping them watered, hoping that something positive and beneficial would take root.

Payroll Costs Rise as Profits Fall

Through the late summer and early autumn months, the long awaited and highly promoted third Disney feature, *Fantasia,* was completed and readied for release. At the same time, amidst the ongoing angst at the studio, in late October 1940 the Fair Labor Standards Act of 1938 was revised to standardize the workweek at 40 hours (from 44 hours previously). Amongst other things, the act required employers to keep records of salaried employee hours worked and to pay overtime at one-and-a-half times regular pay. The revision meant an increase in labor costs to the studio for evening and Saturday work. Roy sent out a memo to notify all staff of the changes under the new law that read in part:

> New regulations have made it necessary to reclassify various groups in the studio and those people whose classification has changed will be notified by individual memorandum.

It will be the policy of the studio to conform in every way with the provisions of the Wage Hour Law and overtime will be paid to all those non-exempt employees required to work more than 40 hours per week.

Naturally, the reduction in working hours will add a further burden of overtime payments to the losses already suffered through the curtailment of foreign revenues. May we urge you to consider those facts and to recognize the necessity for maintaining the heavy production schedule upon which we have embarked.[34]

While staff was elated with the prospect of receiving overtime pay, reconfirmation directly from Roy that the studio remained financially strained brought with it rumors of Christmas layoffs, which management denied. Because of the experimental nature of *Fantasia* and its attempt to marry highbrow classical music with animation for a mass audience, combined with a shift in public sentiment and the loss of foreign sales, the studio was preparing for another box-office bloodbath.

Fantasia **Premieres on Broadway**

Fantasia was not only a visual feast with unparalleled animated sequences and unprecedented stunning special effects, it was also designed to be an audio spectacular, introducing in commercial use for the first time multi-tracked symphonic stereo sound developed with RCA, which Walt branded and promoted as Fantasound. Because the multi-speaker sound system had to be custom installed in theatres, the film was released initially in road-show engagements in a series of 13 cities ahead of general distribution.[35]

Disney artist Mel Shaw writes in his autobiography, *Animator on Horseback*:

Fantasia...was recorded in stereo sound, which was not acceptable to the single-sound systems of the day. Most theaters had a single speaker behind the screen, while *Fantasia* required seven speakers to give it a full symphonic effect. That meant it had to be shown via a road show with an expensive array of sound equipment installed at each theater. It was not an economic possibility to show this film.[36]

Fantasia premiered at New York's Broadway Theatre on November 13, 1940. As with the release of *Pinocchio* earlier in the year, moviegoers weren't as responsive at the box office as Walt and his team hoped and expected. With production cost of a whopping $2.3 million, *Fantasia* generated a bigger loss for the studio than did *Pinocchio*, thereby extending the studio's multi-year financial crises. Even so, when *Fantasia* premiered in Britain, Walt donated the opening gross to the British War Relief fund to support the war effort of America's allies overseas.[37]

You Can't Animate with a Broken Arm

Walt's continuing difficulties at the studio translated into a growing opportunity for union organizers. As the Screen Cartoonist Guild learned of the frustrations being voiced by Disney artists, SCG president Bill Littlejohn invited ex-prizefighter and labor organizer Herbert Sorrell to help organize the Disney animation staff. According to Tom Sito in *Drawing the Line*:

> Like teamster Jimmy Hoffa, his contemporary, Sorrell learned his stuff in the violent world of 1930s industrial union organizing. He had the boxer's classic broken nose, thick neck, and cauliflower ears, and roguish smile. When Littlejohn mentioned that one of the animators resisting joining the union at MGM was Jack Zander [one of the most influential and respected MGM animators, and animator of the first *Tom and Jerry* cartoons], Sorrell quipped, "Well, he can't very well animate with a broken arm, can he?" Zander got the message and joined...."[38]

With Sorrell on board, writes Sito, Littlejohn and SCG were ready to take on the task of convincing Disney studio artists that their interests would be best served by joining the independent SCG. One of Walt's leading and most respected animators, Art Babbitt, was leading a secretive unionization effort inside the studio on behalf of the SCG to collect union card signatures.

On December 5, 1940, when they had a majority of employee signatures, a group of union representatives that included Littlejohn, Sorrell, and Babbitt went to Walt's office to demand that he recognize the union as per the requirements of the National Labor Relations Act.[39] Disney lawyer Gunther Lessing informed the group that Walt refused to meet with them, and refused to accept the signatures as valid, demanding that the National Labor Relations Board be given time to verify the authenticity of the voting through a secret ballot. Unable to meet with Walt, Lessing was given a letter from the SCG's attorney announcing their claim and intentions.[40]

While efforts to diminish the financial strain on the studio resulted in a slow but steady stream of isolated layoffs through 1940, the rumored Christmas layoffs did not materialize.

Declining Profits, a Foggy Future, and Diminished Expectations

The ongoing uncertain political and economic situation continued to have an impact on the studio. Hitler was winning territory in Europe, thereby cutting off much-needed profits from foreign markets. There was growing and more serious talk of the need for the United States to throw her muscle behind the allied war effort during a continuing recessionary economy, which meant sending Americans overseas to fight with her allies and defend the principles of political freedom. A concerned American public didn't seem to be in the mood for the kind of entertainment Walt was offering.

The studio's financial situation shifted from a profit of $1.24 million in fiscal year 1939 to a loss of $260,000 in 1940. The share price soon fell from $25 to $3 as both *Pinocchio* and *Fantasia* failed to recover production costs. Without the anticipated profits to fund new ventures, investors were signaling an extreme lack of confidence in the studio's future prospects, of which the studio staff was well aware.

1. Thomas, *Walt Disney*, 164.

2. Gabler, *Walt Disney*, 325.

3. Gabler, *Walt Disney*, 326.

4. Gabler, *Walt Disney*, 327.

5. Gabler, *Walt Disney*, 329.

6. Gabler, *Walt Disney*, 332.

7. Gabler, *Walt Disney*, 332.

8. Gabler, *Walt Disney*, 324.

9. Peet, *An Autobiography*, 110.

10. Peet, *An Autobiography*, 111.

11. Peet, *An Autobiography*, 112.

12. Brightman, *Life in the Mouse House*, 55.

13. Brightman, *Life in the Mouse House*, 45.

14. Brightman, *Life in the Mouse House*, 45.

15. "The Snow White Wrap Party - Part 1," babbittblog.com/2012/04/11/the-snow-white-wrap-party-part-1/, accessed November 7, 2016.

16. Brightman, *Life In The Mouse House*, 46.

17. DisneyHistoryInstitute.com/2013/09/walts-field-day-1938.html, accessed February 4, 2015.

18. Brightman, *Life in the Mouse House*, 47.

19. Brightman, *Life in the Mouse House*, 47.

20. Brightman, *Life in the Mouse House*, 48.

21. Peet, *An Autobiography*, 104–107.

22. Shaw, *Animator on Horseback*, 100.

23. Gabler, *Walt Disney*, 331.

24. Gabler, *Walt Disney*, 333.

25. Brightman, *Life in the Mouse House*, 55–56.

26. Brightman, *Life in the Mouse House*, 56.

27. Brightman, *Life in the Mouse House*, 56.

28. Brightman, *Life in the Mouse House*, 56.

29. Gabler, *Walt Disney*, 338. See also Shaw, *Animator on Horseback*, 102.

30. Gabler, *Walt Disney*, 338.

31. Ghez, *Walt's People: Vol. 10*, 45.

32. Baxter, *Disney During World War II*, 43.

33. Gabler, *Walt Disney*, 372.

34. Brightman, *Life in the Mouse House*, 57.

35. Wikipedia, "Fantasia (1940 film)," https://en.wikipedia.org/wiki/Fantasia_(1940_film).

36. Shaw, *Animator on Horseback*, 102.

37. Lesjak, *Service with Character*, 69.

38. Sito, *Drawing the Line*, 117–118

39. Gabler, *Walt Disney*, 357; Sito, *Drawing the Line*, 118.

40. Sito, *Drawing the Line*, 118.

CHAPTER FOURTEEN

Riding the Perfect Storm and Taming the Wounded Bear: The Studio in Crisis

Walt's ability to drive his business and creative vision forward was now under pressure from political and economic forces outside his control. From Walt's point of view, if staff would spend more time working and less time playing and taking advantage of his generosity, the studio would be more productive, which would reduce the time it takes to get movies completed and into theatres. They would then cost less to make and investments could be recovered more quickly and reinvested to support more work and new sources of profit in an ever-expanding virtuous circle.

From Walt's perspective, the workers were hurting themselves and their prospects for ongoing employment by their casual attitude toward work that needed to get done expeditiously in this time of corporate crisis. The only alternative to significantly increased productivity would be the layoffs the bank was demanding, and which Walt was hoping to avoid.

The Anatomy of Crisis and Burden of Leadership

It bothered Walt that a significant number of employees didn't seem to properly understand or care that most of the money being borrowed from the bank was to pay their salaries upfront with Walt and Roy as major share-holders bearing the personal burden of the financial risk. The investment in films could only be recovered and repaid with box-office revenues upon completion and release to the public. Profits, if any, would be needed to re-invest in the next venture to keep the business going. Staff didn't have to bear the weight of responsibility for funding the payroll and overhead costs of the studio, nor think about where the money for their next pay-check was coming from. That entrepreneurial responsibility was Walt's burden, and he was well aware that without new cash infusion via profits, lenders, or investors to fund ongoing production, every additional delay in getting product to market was like a draining of sustenance, and another nail in the studio's coffin.

Very few employees working for wages are entrepreneurial and as such, they give little thought to what is required to run a sustainable corporation, and to the inherent risks of wealth creation necessary as the bedrock for job creation in modern employment societies. It is from this lack of awareness, experience, and understanding that many staff perceived Walt's overly ambitious nature to drive the studio's growth and success to be the source of both his and their problems. Their thinking was, in effect, that if Walt was less ambitious, less innovative, there would be less pressure on everyone, and they would be better able to make ends meet.

From this perspective, in the eyes of many, Walt's over-sized ambitions were to blame for the studio's financial problems and belt-tightening. Such a viewpoint is completely disassociated from acknowledging that had Walt indeed acted as they desired by taking a safe, middle-of-the-road course and avoided risky investments, Walt Disney Productions would be just like the other struggling studios. Disney cartoons would be of marginal value to theatre owners who were currently buying his products at a premium, and of limited entertainment value to the consuming public. Under these "easier" conditions, Walt would not have had the need to employ most of his staff in the first place. Such a complaint drops the context of why these artists preferred to work for Walt Disney Productions, rather than disembarking to work for Walt's competitors or seeking other employment.

Regardless of the different viewpoints as to the cause of the crisis and whether individuals or economic and geo-political circumstances were primarily to blame, the fact was that the current studio business model and operating structure were misaligned with prevailing customer values and marketplace demands. Financial pressures and studio production were now top-of-mind for Walt and Roy, the board of directors, the Bank of America, and shareholders. There was a balance of powerful interests to be weighed, negotiated, and traversed, and these interests did not always align in favor of Walt and his employees.

If at one time in the not-too-distant past the world was serendipitously aligned with Walt to deliver the unparalleled success of *Snow White* from which he envisioned a golden path to a glorious future of never-ending successes, now with each new animated feature that road was crumbling. He now faced a world that had seemingly turned against him. His ambitions and work in which he had invested so much thought, effort, and money could no longer proceed as planned. His prior mood of elation and optimism was now generally perceived to be sour and melancholy. Once again he was fighting for the studio's survival. Along with the responsibility for making decisions to find and manage a way forward, he felt the weight of a thousand employees and their families that he carried on his shoulders.

Whether the studio staff knew it or wanted to accept it, the only person who could save the studio was Walt Disney, and whether they liked it or not, he was up to the challenge. It was now in Walt's hands to save the company, not by his usual method of moving forward into new territory, but by retrenching; not by creating value for a more distant future, but by shortening the temporal length of his planning horizon and eliminating paths to create value that he could no longer afford. Employees who had benefitted from Walt's tolerance for risk and his desire to invest in their personal artistic services to create new and innovative products, and now wished he had been more prudent about it, were about to have their wish come true.

Walt's need to operate under the new burden of imposed financial constraint began to be observed by others in his visible change in behavior. He now had to do things he didn't want to do, but which he saw as necessary in his role as head of the studio in this time of crisis. Others began to describe his disposition as that of a wounded bear. Burdened by the responsibility of leading what was essentially a corporate turnaround under the pressure of impending corporate and personal bankruptcy for he and Roy, he observed and reacted to the seemingly carefree and unsympathetic attitudes and behaviors of his staff, and he quickly earned a reputation for being moody, fickle, angry, and at times, vengeful.

For Walt, the studio had always been his personal playground, and in trying to save what he and Roy had built with their own entrepreneurial gumption, he was determined to operate within the defined boundaries by his own rules. While he professed his love for a democratic work place and in his eyes tried to live up to it, others would later describe his behavior as more akin to a paternalistic benevolent dictator who could, and would, strike out at dissenters without warning.

Walt was a man of such unique talent and ability—some would say genius—that seeing the world from his unique perspective was something that his employees had never experienced and few could comprehend. The days of Walt and Roy running a small animation studio focused on one or two projects at the same time were long gone. The business had been grown into a multi-faceted and expanding organization that was increasingly international in scope.

To lead successfully required the continuous planning and simultaneous coordinating of dozens of diverse projects and thousands of business elements, continuously trading off one against the other in an attempt to balance a myriad of dynamically complex interrelationships over an extended period of time: revenues, capital investments, operating expenses, talent management, product quality, domestic and foreign partnerships, legal and trade issues, corporate governance, business systems, marketing, sales, licensing, merchandising, brand image, competition, innovation, staff motivation to achieve the best results, and working on solving dynamic problems today that are not anticipated to emerge until sometime in the future.

When an animator, or storyman, or painter, came to work each day, their scope of concern was just a single story, or perhaps more narrowly, one aspect or scene or character in a scene within a story. The director would have to be concerned with coordinating all of the elements of the story and production schedule (story, animation, music, photography, etc.), and manage the various elements of the project for months and sometimes years, but often the accountability of staff was limited in scope to developing a single story in a given time period, or animating a single sequence, or inking and painting cells to the proper standards as part of the established production process. This is neither to diminish the importance of the work nor the value of every employee and the skill, knowledge, and judgment they bring to their work, but rather to identify the reality of completely different dimensions of context, responsibility, and applied capability and problem-solving capacity among different people fulfilling different work functions. At the top of that pyramid of ability stood Walt Disney.

When Walt first started his studio and a small cadre of staff worked together on a single episode of the silent black-and-white *Alice's Wonderland* to meet a production deadline, everybody was working together and operating within a narrow range of weight of responsibility to meet Margaret Winkler's production schedule. In general, the work was shared to complete each film before moving on to the next one. But as the studio grew in numbers, as the work grew in complexity, and as profits were invested in technology and capital improvements were made to win customers and grow sales, a rational division of labor was required to effectively plan, organize, control, and carry out the work.

A structured organizational hierarchy is a natural and necessary requirement of developing and coping with complex systems of organized work, and requires defined decision-making, reporting relationships, and assigned accountabilities for specific work tasks. As in all companies, coordinating and managing work through a hierarchical structure of people can be contentious, especially when many of those people are highly competitive and ego-centric creative artists and writers reporting to other highly ego-centric artists and writers, often dealing with subjective assessments of aesthetic and commercial quality.

Walt was doing his best to lead in difficult circumstances, but he was facing unprecedented challenges, and from the perspective of a large number of the studio's employees he wasn't faring very well.

Walking the High Wire of Union Polls and Declining Payrolls

In early 1941, the struggling Walter Lantz studio in Los Angeles unionized as members of the Screen Cartoonists Guild, Brotherhood of Painters, Decorators, and Paperhangers of America Local 852, a chapter of the Conference of Studio Unions. Lantz was cooperative and contracts were quickly signed. But not all studios and artists were as accommodating.[1]

Tom Sito, in *Drawing the Line*, writes that when the American Federation of Labor union approached the Metro-Goldwyn-Mayer cartoon studio, they were met with stiff resistance in response to what one MGM artist indicated were the hardball roughhouse tactics and "the threatening methods [the unions] used with everyone." MGM animator Gus Arriola recalled that he and other workers "were taken for a walk out in the MGM back lot by one of the tough union guys, and he said if we didn't join the union, we weren't going to walk through that front door to work. So we did. Under protest, we joined. And the funny part of it was that by joining, I doubled my salary. This all happened just when I was transferred out of the animation department to the story board department, and because of the new job classification, story sketchman, I was qualified for a different salary."[2] Ninety percent of MGM animation employees voted to join the union.

The level of union activity and agitation at the Disney studio was rapidly on the rise and had become a major topic of conversation and workplace distraction for staff. For Walt and Roy, there was additional pressure. The studio was within $20,000 of tapping out its $2.8 million borrowing limit with Bank of America.[3] On February 6, 1941, Walt sent the following communication to his staff:

> URGENT!
>
> Statistics prove that the footage output of the plant for the past six weeks has dropped 50%. It is obvious that a great deal of valuable studio time is being consumed in discussing union matters that should be taken care of on free time.
>
> The Company recognizes the right of employees to organize and join in any labor organization of their own choosing, and the Company does not intend to interfere in this right. HOWEVER, the law clearly provides that matters of this sort should be done off the employer's premises and on the employees own time, and in such a matter as not to interfere with production.
>
> Due to world conditions, the studio is facing a crisis about which a lot of you are evidently unaware. It can be solved by your undivided attention to production matters. This is an appeal to your sense of fairness and I trust it will be sufficient to remedy the matter.

Sincerely,

WALT

Disney story artist Homer Brightman summed up the response of his animation colleagues at the studio upon receiving Walt's notice: "This appeal to our 'sense of fairness,' coming from the man who had reneged on his promise to pay us twenty percent of his profits from *Snow White*, created an angry, resentful mood instead of the speed-up in production."[4]

While anger, uncertainty, and confusion may have existed at the studio, the root causes of discontent could not have been as simplistic as pent-up resentment over the expectation of bonuses from years ago. There were additional forces at play involving fairness, respect, worker pride, and a lack of trust in the workplace, driven by fear of unemployment resulting from the possible demise of Walt Disney Productions, unmanaged and unresolved conflict amongst staff and distrust of colleagues, the siren call of unionization, the ongoing economic uncertainty of the Great Depression, the approaching war in Europe, and military conscription in preparation for battles that may be just over the horizon. In September 1940, five months previous, President Roosevelt signed the Selective Training and Services Act, the country's first national conscription in peacetime, requiring all men between twenty-one and forty-five to register and be eligible for selection to one year of military service by the process of lottery.[5]

On February 11, 1941, a few days after issuing his memo, Walt convened two meetings to personally address his staff and try to explain to them why joining the SCG was not a good thing. He read from a prepared speech to avoid any accusations of legal impropriety from the union. He reminded his employees of how he and Roy had built the business, taking immense financial risks and re-investing their profits back into the company, which benefited not only themselves, but also all of the workers and their families. He spoke to the growth of the studio and his inability to get chummy with everybody who joins the organization of over one thousand employees. Still, said Walt, "I know and am well aware of the progress of all the men after they reach a certain spot in this organization. ... And, fellows, I take my hat off to results only." Walt closed by quoting company policy: "The Company recognizes the right of employees to organize and to join in any labor organization of their choosing, and the Company does not intend to interfere with this right."[6]

Ten days later, on February 21, 1941, a major unionization meeting and rally was held at the Hollywood Roosevelt Hotel for Disney studio staff to discuss the situation. In addition to senior animator Art Babbitt, a number of top Disney staff that included animators, story artists, layout artists, and art directors threw their support behind the union.

The drive to unionize continued to disaffect staff and crush employee productivity. Animated films were labor intensive with payroll accounting for 85 to 90 percent of the studio's total costs.[7] Walt was frustrated and angered by the distraction of unionization and its interference in getting the productivity from his staff for which he was paying them, at a time when there was immense pressure from the bankers to make every dollar count.

In fact, on February 24, 1941, Walt and Roy were again called to the Bank of America's San Francisco headquarters to discuss the bank's concern about the rise of the studio's debt from $2 million in 1940 to almost $3 million, and the urgent need for even greater cost-cutting measures.[8]

Roy wrote to Walt in early March 1941, informing him that the bank had reluctantly decided to extend further credit to the studio, but they had been put on notice that they were now on "very thin ice." Roy then proposed a number of cost-cutting measures, acknowledging that they would undermine Walt's vision for the studio.

First and foremost, Roy recommended a cut in expenses of twenty percent, in part by limiting production to projects with less than a one-year time-to-completion, such as *Bambi*, *Dumbo*, and shorts, and identifying and terminating the employment of anyone not needed to complete the immediate work at hand. He also proposed an across-the-board salary cut. Without such drastic action, said Roy, the only path to avoid receivership would be to sell their library of films at a deep discount to raise cash.[9]

At the same time that Walt was struggling to find cash to pay his staff and keep the studio's doors open, a number of unions were coordinating their activities under the leadership of the SCG and filing complaints to the National Labor Relations Board that the Disney studio was refusing to negotiate the terms of unionization in good faith, as the law required. With pressure mounting and staff organizing, a memo from corporate lawyer Gunther Lessing to Walt on April 7, 1941, indicated that they now anticipated that there was no way to avoid a strike at the studio.[10]

Forward Focus: Devising a Wartime Survival Strategy

Walt had faced trying times before, but now the sandbox was bigger and the stakes were larger. In spite of a multitude of internal and external distractions impacting the organization, including the desire of many staff to organize union representation, there was still a business to run. Walt anticipated more hard times ahead and the need to develop a new and different course of action to survive. He set for himself the task of finding other ways to leverage his studio's assets and unique capabilities to keep the studio functioning and his uniquely skilled staff employed.

Perhaps reflecting back on the dental care training film *Tommy Tucker's Tooth* that he created in 1922 for Dr. Thomas McCrum in Kansas City, and linking that experience with knowledge of the decision by the U.S. government agreeing to provide war supplies to its European allies, Walt set up a Disney Defense Films Division to solicit contract training film production work from government and the defense industry as a new source of revenue.[11]

To change perceptions and convince the government in Washington that the studio was just as capable of making training films as creating entertainment, Walt needed a prototype to demonstrate the studio's capability to do the work. Walt acted immediately by approaching airplane manufacturer Lockheed to assess their interest in hiring the studio to produce industrial training films. Walt successfully made the sale and hired one of Lockheed's engineers as an advisor to the creation of an experimental training film about airplane riveting. Out of this came, in April 1941, the highly acclaimed instructional film *Four Methods of Flush Riveting,* which Lockheed used to train new workers. Lockheed was impressed both by the film's quality and its efficacy as a training tool, and proudly showed it around to war industry and government executives.

Walt lost money on the film, but making money wasn't his primary motive. The small project was an investment in knowledge. The Lockheed film was used by Walt to identify the challenges he would encounter in entering the employee training and education market and to test the ability of his organization to make low-cost animated films by cutting corners. It was also used as a sales tool and signal to leading industrialists that in these tough economic times Walt was opening the door to accepting commercial contracts.

In early April 1941, even before the Lockheed film was completed, Walt and Roy hosted a conference at the new Burbank studio to demonstrate their capabilities to produce low-cost training films and to sell their services. The event was arranged after Walt contacted the National Defense Advisory Committee to offer his services in support of the Defense Department's war effort. Additional guests were invited, including representatives from the southern California aircraft industry, aviation experts from California Institute of Technology, officials from the U.S. Office of Education and the U.S. Forest Service, and the head of the National Film Board of Canada.[12]

With the audience assembled at the studio, Walt made a presentation to his guests, using existing and yet-to-be released films and mock-ups to demonstrate different styles and kinds of animation techniques. He showed "The Sorcerer's Apprentice" segment from *Fantasia* to demonstrate animation at its most sophisticated. He showed a rough preview of *The Wind in the Willows* consisting of the filming of storyboard sketches with a test voice track, and the "Baby Weems" segment from *The Reluctant Dragon* to show the effectiveness of the same process in its completed form. He also showed an early test version of *Four Methods of Flush Riveting* to show how these less expensive methods could be applied to actual training films.

Walt indicated to the audience that the studio hadn't yet geared up to make training films, but that everything was in place to immediately move forward. They just needed the orders. "I think we could turn them out as fast as you could cook them up," he said, noting that the rivet film required just six hours with a Lockheed engineer to create the finished storyboards.[13]

The attendees were impressed. With Walt opening up his studio to make available the quality of talent and technology he had assembled, the possibilities were endless. Prior to this, outside access to Disney's talent and proprietary characters for educational purposes was unthinkable. "It never occurred to me that it was possible to happen," said Dr. Hardy Steeholm of the Office of Education.[14]

One of the first to contract with Disney was the Canadian government and its National Film Board, which, in April 1941, commissioned the studio to produce four films to promote and boost sales of war savings bonds, and one military film to train antitank gunners, titled *Stop That Tank!*

Walt set up Animation Unit 2A to produce training films, and put Ub Iwerks in charge. Iwerks was perfect for the role. Not only was he a successful animation innovator and special-effects expert with a passion for mechanical and optical inventions, he had also run his own animation studio from 1930 to 1936, and like Walt, knew every aspect of making animated films. Iwerks also had Walt's full confidence, trust, and respect.

Iwerks was sent for a week to Canada's capital city, Ottawa, to consult with government officials about the film work and later returned with artist renderings of the five films to obtain client approval to proceed. For the most part, the war bond films were a minimal-cost reworking of existing Disney cartoons, using already animated sequences from *Snow White*, *Three Little Pigs*, and a Donald Duck short *Donald's Better Self*. The success of the work done for the Canadians would be leveraged as Walt's calling card for more military training film contracts.

In addition, Walt had been pursuing talks with John Whitney, head of the motion pictures division of Rockefeller's Office of the Coordinator of Inter-American Affairs (CIAA). In May 1941, Walt hosted John Whitney and his assistant at the studio to discuss Walt's interest and participation in making films to assist Rockefeller's Coordinator's Office and the U.S. government in their mission to improve cultural ties between the Americas.

Walt was applying his entrepreneurial focus to identify, create, and bring into existence new forms of value. He was leading the charge for actively trying to win training film contracts and plotting a path forward to reinvent his business and prevent the studio from having to shut down.

As Walt was doing everything in his power to prevent Walt Disney Productions from crashing, the union situation at the studio remained unsettled and was rapidly rising to the boiling point.

Union Hand Rubbing: It's Disney's Time

In May 1941 the Screen Cartoonist Guild had set its sights on organizing Leon Schlesinger's Looney Tunes and Merry Melodies artists. The company responded with a lockout that lasted for six days before Schlesinger became convinced that his interests were best served by giving in. Purportedly, when he signed the union contract with the Screen Cartoonist Guild, he turned to the union leaders with a grin and chuckled, "Now, how about Disney's?"[15]

From the perspective of the SCG, everything done so far to unionize animation employees from New York to California was a testing ground for their eventual assault on Disney's animators. According to animation union historian Tom Sito, in *Drawing the Line*:

> The entire cartoon industry understood that the real decision of whether animation artists could ever function as a union labor force would be made at Disney's. All the SCG successes up to that point brought its membership to just 115. There were more than 800 Disney artists. Those artists felt themselves the aristocracy of their profession, with Uncle Walt the benevolent master over all. Artists were grateful to Walt for plowing profits back into upgrading the studio's working conditions and paying for drawing teachers like Don Graham to show them how to polish their skills. To a profession that was made to feel inferior to fine artists Disney brought new respect. What other cartoon studio would bring in Frank Lloyd Wright to discuss aesthetics with its employees? Walt frequently had his artists and their families up to his Los Feliz house for pool parties. He threw western-style barbecues and picnics. Everyone knew Walt could be counted on to help anyone in trouble. While work in other studios was seasonal or from project to project, Disney employees were rarely laid off. While other studios were housed in dingy industrial spaces with cheap garage-sale furniture, Disney's studio had custom-designed matching furniture, volleyball courts, and a softball field. It wasn't a job; it was like one big family."[16]

The studio was now down about a hundred people from its peak of twelve hundred, and in the drive to remain solvent, more layoffs were expected.[17]

In the midst of these ongoing layoffs, on May 20, 1941, Walt sent a memo to about twenty employees inviting them to a meeting after work. When the meeting was convened, they were informed by Walt that the studio had to let them go, and that it was not based on unsatisfactory performance. Purportedly, at least half of them were sympathetic to the organizing union.[18]

One week later, on Monday, May 26, 1941, with the stalemate between the studio and the union dragging on, the Screen Cartoonist Guild's general membership voted to authorize a strike for the Walt Disney unit unless Walt agreed to meet with the SCG organizing committee. The union wired him a notice to that effect.[19]

The next day, May 27, 1941, many of the studio's corporate backers, including representatives from investment banking firm Kidder-Peabody and the Bank of America, met with Walt to convince him to make a deal with the animator's union and thereby avoid likely strike action.[20] Walt refused to make a deal, but did agree to meet with the union.

Later that same day, a meeting between the negotiating teams from the studio and the Screen Cartoonist Guild was held at the studio.[21] Walt continued to question Sorrell's legal right to speak for the Disney artists. To ensure legitimacy of the vote and that his staff had signed freely and not under duress, Walt insisted that the Labor Department hold a valid secret election. If a majority of workers supported SCG in a legitimate vote, Walt would accept the results.

The SCG again refused the request for a new secret ballot, and sensing that once again they were not getting anywhere after being at this for months, ex-boxer Sorrell, who had now organized a bloc of ten motion picture unions and had become the most powerful union leader in Hollywood[22], exploded on Walt in an aggressive act of intimidation. As Sito tells it,

> To a veteran negotiator like Herb Sorrell it was now time to play hardball. He went right in Walt's face and angrily threatened a walkout. Sorrell yelled at Disney, "I can make a dust bowl of your studio!"... The meeting broke up in an angry impasse.[23]

Walt's recollection of the meeting, as told to and reported by Bob Thomas in *Walt Disney: An American Original*, is that Sorrell demanded a contract with Disney without a vote of employees and threatened, "You sign with me or I'll strike you."

Walt insisted that he wasn't going to accept SCG as their elected union representative without a secret ballot vote by his staff, as required under law by the Labor Board. "Whatever way it comes out," said Walt, "I'll go along with it. Then I'm keeping faith with them. I'm not signing with you on your say-so."

"I'm warning you," Sorrell threatened, "I can make a dust bowl out of your place here, Disney. You don't know what you're doing." With a phone call, Sorrell warned Walt, he could have organizations across the country boycotting Disney products. "I've got friends. I've got connections," he threatened.

That may be so, argued Walt, "But I've got to live with myself. I can't sign these boys to you. I have no right to. ... A vote will prove it."[24]

Walt was so angry and frustrated that when the meeting ended, he immediately fired Art Babbitt and a number of other pro-union artists that had been leading the union cause. They were escorted directly to their cars by studio security while their fellow artists looked on in silent shock.[25]

That night, an impromptu emergency meeting was called for those who supported union strike action, and, after a series of fiery and rousing speeches, a decision was made to strike the studio.

The next morning, May 28, 1941, Walt arrived at the studio to find a picket line blocking the entrance.[26] Animators arriving at work that morning now had to choose whether to side with or against the union, and the decision was not an easy one. All of the top animators whom Walt had dubbed his "Nine Old Men" crossed the line and continued to work. Two of them, Ward Kimball and Fred Moore, argued for over an hour about what to do. As Kimball passed through studio security, one of his assistants yelled out: "Ward! Don't do it! The strike will fail if you go in." Kimball responded: "If I don't go in *Dumbo* won't get made and the *studio* will fail!"[27]

Sorrell had claimed that a majority of staff approved of his union, but only about forty-five percent of staff the union claimed to represent went out on strike. The rest crossed the picket line and remained on the job. At the time of the strike there were 1,079 employees on the payroll. Of these, 294 within the unions' jurisdiction went out on strike while 352 stayed in. Thirty-seven of the strikers returned before the strike ended, while an additional one hundred studio workers honored the striker's picket line.[28]

Disney War Patriotism at Home and Abroad

While workers were picketing outside the studio to put pressure on Walt to capitulate, the majority of staff arrived each day and carried on with their work.

To advance the cause of acquiring outside contract work, Walt entered into discussions with the Navy about producing training films and initiated action to gain the required security clearances to undertake potentially classified assignments. Long before the entry of the U.S. into the European war, Walt was anticipating that some government contract work would come his way, and he was being proactive to ensure that potential roadblocks were removed early to prevent future problems, putting him in the best position to engage in any assignment immediately upon notice.

On June 1, 1941, Walt wrote to his Washington-based sales representative, Chester Feitel: "Check and see that we get the highest priority on Navy Contracts. ... We need highest priority possible if we are to push Navy work with speed requested of us."[29] The response came back: "It looks like we are going to get another contract for a new series of WEFT

[Wings, Engine, Tail, and Fuselage] identification films. This will enable us to keep our studio unit going through 1943."[30] Landing these anticipated government contracts with defined fees at this time must have come as a huge relief to Walt.

Walt's relationship building with Whitney and Rockefeller's Office of the Coordinator of Inter-American Affairs also paid off in June. Roy and Gunther Lessing met with Whitney in New York to discuss a deal in which Disney would be paid $150,000 to produce several South American-themed films. Roy wrote to Walt, "The way he talked to me they are waiting *on us* to give them some definite plan."[31]

As plans and negotiations to produce films progressed, Walt was approached by Rockefeller to participate in something bigger with greater cultural impact: a publicity tour of Latin America to promote goodwill between North America and South America and to generate positive sentiment for the Allied cause of defending democratic freedom against what many feared to be a growing Nazi influence in the region. "Your pictures are popular down there," Rockefeller told Walt, "and there's a Nazi influence you can help offset if you'd go down and meet people."[32]

Walt was reluctant at first, saying that he wasn't good at greeting people and shaking hands, but when it was suggested that he look upon it as a research trip to make South American-themed cartoons, Walt responded positively to the request to be a cultural ambassador to South America. In return for Walt's participation, CIAA would assume the costs of the trip for Walt and a large contingent of his writers and artists to seek out subject matter and gather information and ideas on each county's culture and customs to serve as background to making a series of entertainment and educational films.[33]

Learning of the request for Walt to travel to South America, the Bank of America was concerned that the government would coerce the corporation into making propaganda films that would turn out to be box-office failures. They wanted to know how this initiative would benefit the studio and their interest in Disney loan repayments. In response, the government agreed to underwrite the tour expenses up to $70,000 and to guarantee Walt $50,000 apiece for at least four films. Any profit from theatrical release above the guaranteed amount would be returned to the government until the advance was repaid.[34] The group of studio artists and their wives selected for the trip later became known as El Grupo.

As a patriot, even before the entry of the U.S. into the war in December 1941, Walt had committed his studio to supporting the war effort. As early as June 1939,[35] as a public service, Walt was fulfilling requests for Disney-designed insignia and emblems from military branches of the Armed Forces for the United States and Allied countries including Canada,

Britain, France, and even China. An estimated 1,200 combat insignia would be created and provided by 1945.[36]

In the summer of 1941, Disney voice actors for Donald Duck (Clarence Nash) and Clara Cluck (Florence Gill) toured Canada to promote the sale of Canadian war bonds.[37] A Disney-designed folder for war savings certificates and savings stamps featuring Mickey Mouse and Donald Duck was prepared by Disney artists to promote the marketing effort. The joint national chairman of the War Savings Committee of Canada, W.H. Sommerville, wrote to Walt in July 1941 to thank him for the good work done by he and his staff to serve a noble cause:

> The War Savings Committee has now completed production of a folder application stuffer which will be used as an insert mailing certificates to purchasers. We are enclosing a copy of the stuffer, which in our opinion, is considerably enhanced by the illustration of the cartoon whose reproduction you authorized so generously.
>
> On behalf of the War Savings Committee I would like to assure you of our deep appreciation of the many contributions you are making to the Canadian war effort. It is indeed gratifying to the Committee to have the donations of many talented American artists in various fields and your own efforts are amongst the most valued of these expressions of good will.[38]

The Dust Bowl Strategy in Action: Sorrell vs. Disney and the Non-Striking Workers

The strike that began on May 29, 1941, first went on for weeks and then months. Sorrell and the SCG engaged in well-established and reliable union pressure tactics to impair the business of Walt Disney Productions and the livelihood of its workers—both strikers and non-strikers. According to Bob Thomas,

> Unable to shut down Disney production when other unions refused to honor the picket line, Sorrell organized a secondary boycott of Technicolor, and he successfully stemmed the flow of film into the studio. Sorrell launched a propaganda campaign in union papers and leftist publications across the country, accusing Disney of being anti-union and operating a sweatshop.[39]

Sorrell's efforts were successful and the Disney strikers received tactical support from other unions that further isolated the studio and increased the pressure to settle. In June, the American Federation of Labor called for a nation-wide boycott of all Disney films and merchandise. One union refused to print the Mickey Mouse comic strip in newspapers, even though they were under contract to do so. The refusal by Technicolor Corporation to develop any more Disney film until the strike was settled held up the completion of *Bambi*. It is likely that Disney's very public problems against the coercive tactics of organized labor led to the relatively easy unionization of animators at Screen Gems and Columbia Pictures on June 19, 1941.

At the premiere of *The Reluctant Dragon* at Hollywood's Pantages Theatre on June 20, 1941, strikers formed a ring around the theatre to intimidate moviegoers and demonstrated against Disney with chants of "The Reluctant Disney!"[40] Picketers took similar action when the movie opened at the Palace Theater in New York. The intimidating crowds and bad publicity surely dampened audience enthusiasm about a film purporting to show the positive spirit of the new studio and how animated pictures are made. Even with a much shorter production schedule and lower cost of $600,000, the film in its original showing in 1941 failed to turn a profit,[41] instead delivering a loss of $100,000[42] and putting further pressure on the security of the studio's jobs.

The strike that had gone on for months ended on July 28, 1941, with the arrival of a Department of Labor arbitrator who ordered the studio to immediately reinstate all of the strikers while arbitration took place.

The next day, when most of the strikers returned to the studio, only fifty were assigned work, for most of the production had been shut down during the strike. A few days later *Daily Variety* reported that studio layoffs were in the works as part of the studio's "retrenchment policy" and would be forthcoming when the strike was settled.[43] On the second day of arbitration, August 2, 1941, the studio and union came to agreement on terms to end the strike. Walt did not attend the hearing, leaving the matter to Roy and the studio lawyers.

Needless to say, the strike was acrimonious, pitting staff against staff, and ending long-standing friendships and relationships. Before Walt and his El Grupo entourage left for South America on August 11, 1941, Walt wrote a long letter about the strike to a newspaper columnist in which he expressed his disappointment and disillusionment with the current situation at the studio in the aftermath of the strike, calling it a "catastrophe" and a "God-awful nightmare." Walt wrote:

> The spirit that played such an important part in the building of the cartoon medium has been destroyed. From now on, I get my artists from the hiring hall of the Painters and Paperhangers Union. Out of the 700 artists and assistants coming under this jurisdiction, 293 were on strike and 417 remained at work.

> The union refused to use the ballot to give the people here the right to determine their choice. In turning down the ballot, they said, to use their own words: 'We might lose that way. If we strike, we know we will win.'

It didn't take long to see that there wasn't a fair, honest chance of winning; the cards were all stacked against me, so for the time being I have capitulated.

The lies, the twisted half-truths that were placed in the public prints cannot be easily forgotten. I was called a rat, a yellow-dog employer and an exploiter of labor. ... My plants and methods were compared to a sweatshop, and above all, I was accused of rolling in wealth. That hurt me the most, when the fact is that every damned thing I have is tied up in this business. The thing that worries me is that people only read the headlines and never take enough time to follow through and find out the truth.

I am thoroughly disgusted and would gladly quit and try to establish myself in another business if it were not for the loyal guys who believe in me—so I guess I'm stuck with it.

This South American expedition is a godsend. I am not so hot for it but it gives me a chance to get away from this God-awful nightmare and to bring back some extra work into the plant. I have a case of the D.D.'s—disillusionment and discouragement....[44]

Walt and his artists and writers spent two months in South America gathering material for an anticipated twelve short films. The South American good-will tour was a resounding success for Walt, the studio, and in diplomatic terms, for the improvement of relations between the United States and South America. Two successful feature-length films were produced, *Saludos Amigos* and *The Three Caballeros*. Walt poinetd out that "the government never lost a nickel on them—we paid for our own trip and the pictures, too."[45]

In addition, fourteen educational public service films were created for South American audiences to address pressing problems, such as *The Grain That Built a Hemisphere* about the history of corn and corn-based products in South America and the benefits of good nutritional habits, and *The Winged Scourge*, to teach viewers how to combat malaria-carrying mosquitoes.[46]

On August 12, 1941, the day after Walt and El Grupo left for South America and as the studio tried to get back to work while the union matter was under arbitration and Bank of America exerted pressure to cut costs, Roy submitted a list of 256 layoffs to the union composed of 207 strikers and 49 non-strikers. The union immediately protested on the grounds that it discriminated against the strikers.[47] Within days, on August 15, Roy, with approval from the board of directors, announced that the studio would be shut down for two weeks (except for a small crew working on *Dumbo* and the Mickey Mouse comic strip), until the issue was resolved.

Walt's loyal workers were sent home and told to take their personal belongings with them, raising grave concerns about whether the studio would ever again reopen at all.

Brightman writes in his memoir:

> I drove back home in a state of shock, for I had a wife and child to support. Now I knew how the strikers felt. I consoled myself thinking about my contract. Suppose the studio didn't reopen, where would I find work? ... [W]here would I find another position offering the kind of specialized work I had been engaged in? Cartoon studios were few and far between.[48]

Both parties to the strike were immediately called to Washington for additional arbitration, and the studio remained closed until it was reopened a month later, on September 15.[49]

When the dust from the dispute and arbitration settled, a new formula for layoffs was imposed, wages and hours were standardized, artist credits were to be listed on films, and pay rates were increased retroactively to the first day of the walkout. In some cases, animator pay was increased from $35 a week to $85 a week.

Walt understood that regardless of his own animosity towards the union tactics, he would have to work with both the union and the strikers going forward. Upon hearing of the strike settlement while in South America on the State Department's Good Will Tour, he stated to his staff with regards to the strikers: "For whatever reason they did what they did, they thought they were right. We've had our differences on a lot of things, but we're going to continue making pictures, and we're going to find a way to work together."[50]

Dumbo Takes Flight for Disney

With the strike over, the studio settled back to work as best it could. Work continued on short subjects, government contracted films, and most importantly *Dumbo*, Disney's fourth full-length animated feature, which was being rushed for release. Little more than the rough animation was completed prior to the strike. Getting it completed quickly was a key priority throughout the strike. Work also continued on *Bambi*.

In completed form, *Dumbo* was a mere 64 minutes long. It's short length and simplified form was a major key to its financial success by significantly reducing production time and cost. Its short length, however, created consternation for Disney film distributor RKO Radio Pictures. RKO asked Walt to make it longer, edit it to short-subject length, or issue it as a B-movie—essentially giving it second billing in a double feature. Walt refused to heed their recommendations, and RKO reluctantly issued *Dumbo* in unaltered form.[51]

Released on October 23, 1941, *Dumbo* was instantly a box-office and critical success. Audiences and critics both praised it for its easy style and straight-ahead story about courage, maturity, and self-responsibility in a hostile environment. The *New York Times* review called it the "most genial, the most endearing, the most completely precious cartoon feature film to ever emerge from the magical brushes of Walt Disney's wonder-working artists!" Famed *New Yorker* magazine drama critic Alexander Woollcott wrote Walt to praise the film as the "highest achievement yet reached in the Seven Arts since the first white man landed on the continent." Walt wrote back with the honest truth: "It was just one of those little things that we knocked off between epics."[52]

Dumbo grossed $1.6 million in box office receipts on its initial release, easily paying for production and returning a healthy profit of $850,000, the first feature to do so since *Snow White*.[53]

Also in November 1941, while the studio was still working on Canadian government wartime film projects, the U.S. Navy was actively engaging the studio in discussions to produce similar training films. A series of letters were exchanged between Walt and the head of the Navy film program, with Walt hoping to win more government contract business to keep his staff working and the studio operating.

By mid-November the studio delivered to Canada's National Film Board the first of its anti-Nazi, pro-war-bond cartoons. *The Thrifty Pig*, staring the Three Little Pigs, was released in Canadian theatres mid-December during a "War Savings as Christmas Gifts" promotion.[54] Additional training films, including one titled *Stop That Tank!*, were still in production.

Disillusion in a Workers' Paradise

Over the three-and-a-half months of the strike, the payroll had been pared from around 1,200 when the strike began to fewer than 700 when it was settled. An additional 200 layoffs followed on November 24, including Art Babbitt, bringing the number of staff to 530, less than half the pre-strike number.[55]

With the strike behind him, projects suspended, and the payroll significantly trimmed, Walt's challenge now was to find ways to make the studio productive and profitable again, and to get his staff refocused and working together to make great pictures.

At the same time, Walt remained bitter and unforgiving towards many of the key union "agitators" and "trouble-makers." He eventually came around to accepting Roy's analysis that whatever they personally thought about the union situation, they had to accept the outcome instead of fighting an ongoing battle against a popular social movement that supported collective bargaining and union representation of workers.

In spending millions of dollars building and customizing the Burbank studio, Walt had tried to ensure the best working environment in the world for his staff. It was the envy of the industry. He was personally hurt that a large number of his employees rebuked his efforts. "He suffered disillusion in his plan to make the Disney studio a worker's paradise," writes biographer Bob Thomas. "The noonday volleyball games continued, but the snack shop in the Animation Building was closed. Workers now had to sign in and out on a time clock. Never again would the studio's creative people know the same free, intimate relationship with Walt that had existed in the studio during its formative years."[56]

The strike had ended, but in the words of Disney biographer Neal Gabler, "the studio roiled":

> Longtime friends became longtime enemies. "It used to be, 'Hello, how are you?,' pat you on the back," one employee recalled of the pre-strike days. After the strike the tone of voice and demeanor changed. On the union side, one group of guild members would walk five abreast down the hallways not letting any of the non-strikers pass. On the other side, recalled animator Bill Melendez, who had struck, the nonstrikers "never forgave us for destroying the spirit of the studio." Shamus Culhane believed that both sides harbored a sense of guilt—the nonstrikers over whether they had sided with Walt out of cowardice, the strikers over whether they should have rent the studio as they did. In the end, wrote Culhane, the "esprit de corps that made possible all the brilliant films of the 1930s was dead as a dodo." In the end, Walt Disney's dream of a perfect Haven was dashed.[57]

1. Sito, *Drawing the Line*, p. 104.

2. Sito, *Drawing the Line*, 104.

3. Barrier, *The Animated Man*, 163.

4. Brightman, *Life in the Mouse House*, 58.

5. Wikipedia, "Conscription in the United States," en.wikipedia.org/wiki/Conscription_in_the_United_States, accessed November 7, 2016.

6. Thomas, *Walt Disney*, 168.

7. Barrier, *The Animated Man*, 168.

8. Barrier, *The Animated Man*, 163; see Gabler, *Walt Disney*, p. 330; see Barrier, "Walt Disney's Errors and Ambiguities," at michaelbarrier.com/Commentary/Gabler/GablerErrata.htm, accessed July 8, 2016.

9. Gabler, *Walt Disney*, 350.

10. Sito, *Drawing the Line*, 122.

11. Baxter, *Disney During World War II*, 12.

12. Baxter, *Disney During World War II*, 12–13.

13. Baxter, *Disney During World War II*, 14.

14. Baxter, *Disney During World War II*, 15.

15. Sito, *Drawing the Line*, 106.

16. Sito, *Drawing the Line*, 107–108.

17. Barrier, *The Animated Man*, 168; Sito, *Drawing the Line*, 117.

18. Barrier, *The Animated Man*, 169; Gabler, *Walt Disney*, 364 says all 20 were SGC members.

19. Barrier, *The Animated Man*, 170; Gabler, *Walt Disney*, 364.

20. Sito, *Drawing the Line*, 120.

21. Barrier, *The Animated Man*, 170.

22. Gabler, *Walt Disney*, 35.

23. Sito, *Drawing the Line*, 121.

24. Thomas, *Walt Disney*, 166.

25. Sito, *Drawing the Line*, 121.

26. According to Barrier, press reports confirm the strike began on May 28, as indicated on Walt's desk calendar, so Sito and Gabler's contention it began on the 29th are incorrect. See also Barrier's commentary, "*Walt Disney's* Errors and Ambiguities" at michaelbarrier.com/Commentary/Gabler/GablerErrata.htm. See also Sito, *Drawing the Line*, 121; Thomas, *Walt Disney*, 168.

27. Sito, *Drawing the Line*, 124.

28. Barrier, *The Animated Man*, 170.

29. Lesjak, *Service with Character*, 190.

30. Lesjak, *Service with Character*, 191.

31. Gabler, *Walt Disney*, 372.

32. Lesjak, *Service with Character*, 178.

33. Lesjak, *Service with Character*, 178; Gabler, *Walt Disney*, 372.

34. Thomas, *Walt Disney*, 172.

35. Lesjak, *Service with Character*, 110.

36. Lesjak, *Service with Character*, 110.

37. Lesjak, *Service with Character*, 29.

38. Lesjak, *Service with Character*, 30.

39. Thomas, *Walt Disney*, 169.

40. Sito, *Drawing the Line*, 133.

41. Thomas, *Walt Disney*, 163.

42. Sito, *Drawing the Line*, 135.

43. Barrier, *The Animated Man*, 172.

44. Thomas, *Walt Disney*, 170.

45. Thomas, *Walt Disney*, 174.

46. Lesjak, *Service with Character*, 139; Baxter, *Disney During World War II*, 43.

47. Gabler, *Walt Disney*, 373; Barrier, *The Animated Man*, 173.

48. Brightman, *Life in the Mouse House*, 65.

49. Barrier, *The Animated Man*, 173; Brightman, *Life in the Mouse House*, 67; Gabler, *Walt Disney*, 374 notes that "work finally resumed" on September 16.

50. Thomas, *Walt Disney*, 171.

51. Wikipedia, "Dumbo," en.wikipedia.org/wiki/Dumbo#Box_office.

52. Gabler, *Walt Disney*, 380–381.

53. Wikipedia, "Dumbo," en.wikipedia.org/wiki/Dumbo#Box_office.

54. Lesjak, *Service with Character*, 27.

55. Barrier, *The Animated Man*, 182.

56. Thomas, *Walt Disney*, 171.

57. Neal Gabler, *Walt Disney*, 380.

CHAPTER FIFTEEN

Coping with the World at War

As the war raged across Europe, the important foreign markets of Germany, Italy, Austria, Czechoslovakia, and Poland remained closed. Income generated in England and France was frozen against repatriation. The studio had been anticipating large profits in these overseas markets from the new animated features—*Pinocchio*, *Fantasia*, *Dumbo*, and *Bambi*—to cover the large up-front investments required to create them. Without normal access to, and revenues from, these markets, instead of anticipated profits the studio was now facing huge losses. To cope, the production was scaled back by halting three features being worked on: *Peter Pan*, *Cinderella*, and *Alice in Wonderland*. Disney animator Ward Kimball remarked in 1988: "We had a big market in Europe...we banked on that. That was our profit. The war cuts it off and what are you going to do?"[1]

Walt Disney Productions Gets Drafted

On the morning of Sunday, December 7, 1941, just before 8 a.m., a swarm of three hundred and sixty warplanes from Japan attacked the U.S. Navy station at Pearl Harbor, Hawaii. Shortly thereafter, Walt was at home to answer his phone when it rang. According to Disney biographer Bob Thomas:

> The studio manager told him, "Walt, the studio police just phoned me; the Army is moving in on us."
>
> Still shocked by the news that the Japanese had bombed Pearl Harbor, Walt asked what he meant. "The Army—five hundred soldiers," said the manager. "They told me they're moving in."
>
> "What did you tell them?" Walt asked.
>
> "I said I'd have to call you."
>
> "What did they say to that?"
>
> "They said, 'Go ahead and call him—we're moving in, anyway.'"[2]

Almost immediately, a five-hundred-man Army unit commandeered the studio, placing it under military control, with orders to set up and maintain an anti-aircraft installation to protect the neighboring aircraft factories against the threat of further bombing attacks. Film equipment was removed from the soundstage so it could be used as a truck repair depot. The parking sheds were used to store three million rounds of ammunition. Writes Bob Thomas: "Military police were posted at each gate, and all Disney workers, including Walt and Roy, were fingerprinted and given identification badges to wear at all times. Artists doubled up in rooms of the Animation Building so soldiers would have places to sleep. ... The Disney studio had converted to war."[3]

On the next day, December 8, Walt received a call from the U.S. Navy with a request to produce twenty training films on aircraft identification and another thirty-eight on warship identification, at a fixed cost of $4,500 each.[4]

According to a report in the *Middlesborough Daily News*:

> At eight o'clock in the morning of Dec. 8, 1941, Walt Disney received a call from the Navy's Bureau of Aeronautics asking if he could turn out 20,000 feet of training film. 'I'll turn out anything you want,' said Walt. 'Okay, you can start right away on aircraft identification pictures,' was the reply. 'But who is going to identify the aircraft for me?' asked Walt. 'We'll have a man out there in a couple of hours,' said the Navy. Walt Disney—and his studio—had been drafted.[5]

That same day, the U.S. government formally declared war against Japan, and against Germany and Italy a few days later, on December 11, 1941, almost fifteen months after the British Commonwealth countries had declared war on Germany on September 10, 1939.

Walt had agreed to make the government training films at cost with a contract specifying an amount per foot of film.[6] This was his policy from the start for all government contract production throughout the war. He did this as an act of patriotic duty, stressing that he didn't want to profit from the government's war efforts.

This desire to do work at cost led to a misunderstanding of the pricing agreement because Walt had included his studio overhead as part of the total cost, while the Navy officials argued that the only costs to be included were the direct costs of film production; that the funding of studio overhead was Walt's concern.[7] With Iwerks at the helm, the films were produced on-schedule and on budget, which pleased the Navy and resulted in additional contracts.[8]

The New Spirit of Wartime Taxes

That same week of the Pearl Harbor attack, U.S. Treasury Secretary Henry Morgenthau contacted Walt to request the assistance of the Disney studio in prompting citizens to pay their taxes as a patriotic duty. A revision to the tax code had created millions of new taxpayers and the Treasury Department was worried about a tax revolt. Morgenthau was hoping Disney could lend a helping hand to the government by educating the public on the new tax requirements and by linking the tax increase to the war effort. Morgenthau quipped about Walt: "That man can make even taxes fun."[9]

Reflecting back on this request during an interview in 1956, Walt recalled that he was asked by the Treasury Department to come to Washington D.C. immediately to talk about a very important special project:

> I felt, well, Treasury...war bonds. I was thinking of...things I could to help them sell more war bonds. ... They said, 'We have a problem and maybe you can help us on it. We want to sell people on paying taxes.'
>
> I said, 'That's funny, you're the Treasury speaking. You're the United States government.' I said, 'Sell people on paying taxes? If they don't pay it you put them in jail.' [Commissioner of Internal Revenue, Guy] Helvering [said], 'Well that's my trouble.' He said, 'We've got at least 15 million new taxpayers with this new tax bill. These people have never paid taxes before and I can't prosecute 15 million people. We've got to make them understand what taxes are and the part that taxes play in a war.'
>
> I said, 'Well, I came back all prepared to help you sell bonds.' [Helvering] said, 'That's the point. The people think they buy a bond that's going to help win the war but how are we going to pay off the bond? I don't want to have to prosecute these people. We want them to pay their taxes and be excited about paying their taxes as a patriotic thing.' Morgenthau said, 'You've got the idea now you can work it out.'...
>
> They said [they needed] this in the theatre sometime in February. Now this was the 18th of December. I had to do this...complete cartoon, seven or eight minutes, and it had to not only be finished, it had to be processed through Technicolor, all the prints had to be run out and it had to run in the theatres so that it could get a complete penetration...before March 15.
>
> Before I left Washington, Morgenthau wanted to know what it would cost. I said...I [didn't] know. I said my short subjects were running me about 43-thousand dollars but this [was] liable to cost more.
>
> I got back [to the studio and] got my group of boys in [and] I said '... this is important to the government.' [T]he boys all went with me. We slept on the job. We got beds in...we stayed right there, we worked 18 hours a day [and we] got the film out.[10]

Walt's pro-tax propaganda film featured Donald Duck and was titled *The New Spirit*. In haste, it was completed in four weeks from storyboard approval to finished product, at a time when most shorts took between six to eight months to produce.[11] Animators Ben Sharpsteen and Wilfred

Jackson worked 18-hour days and slept on cots in their offices to meet what Jackson called an "absolutely ridiculous, completely impossible" deadline.[12]

Walt was quick to recognize that releasing a short in which Donald Duck promotes the benefits of paying taxes was publicity-worthy. As Walt told the Treasury Department, casting Donald Duck was the equivalent of MGM offering up Clark Gable.[13] He made sure that the film was highly promoted in popular magazines and newspapers, and in January 1942 wrote a letter to the Treasury Department: "From the look of things at present, we are going to get a lot of swell publicity breaks on the Treasury Film. The response from the newspaper editors, columnists, etc., has been excellent."[14] After the bad publicity surrounding the strike, Walt welcomed the good publicity he was garnering for the studio's war contribution.

Of the $80,000 cost for *The New Spirit*, $40,000 was to cover the cost of production and another $40,000 was needed to produce 1,100 prints of the film so that it could be shown with haste all over the country before March 15.[15] Such government-funded public service films produced for theatrical release were provided to theatres for free as an inducement to create a preference over the regularly scheduled short subject, often a Mickey Mouse or Silly Symphony short.

After requesting the film and the studio going beyond the call of duty to deliver it on time, when Treasury submitted to Congress a request for funds in an appropriations bill, it was met with opposition. An amendment was made to deny funding to reimburse Disney due to an already burgeoning tax burden, which was debated and passed in February 1942.

As a result of the adverse publicity arising from the controversy over payment to the studio for fulfilling its contractual commitment, Walt was the recipient of a considerable amount of hate mail accusing him of being a war profiteer. On the other hand, he also received letters of support and encouragement from citizens who appreciated his efforts that included checks and money to help offset the unpaid costs resulting from the government's legislative decision to renege on its commitment to pay for services rendered from which it profited greatly in incremental tax collection.

Another consequence of the government's underwriting of the cartoon and providing ten thousand free copies to theatres all across the nation was, as Roy foresaw, the cancellation and loss of revenue for the scheduled Donald Duck short that *The New Spirit* replaced. Very few movie houses followed the example of Radio City Music Hall in New York City who submitted a check to the Disney studio anyway, as they would have done under normal circumstances.

As for the film itself, audiences loved it. Theater operators reported that audiences applauded and cheered the cartoon, which showed them how to complete the tax form and encouraged them to mail it in as soon as possible as their patriotic duty to help in the war effort. "By what other means than the theatre screen could 80,000,000 people be reached so effectively?" asked a writer to *The New York Times*.[16]

The War Activities Committee estimated that more than 33 million people had watched *The New Spirit* in the 11,800 theatres in which it played, and a Gallup poll indicated that thirty-seven percent of those responded "Yes" to the question: "Did this picture have any effect on your willingness to pay taxes?"[17]

One of the lessons Walt drew from the success of *The New Spirit* in achieving its objectives was that cartoons would be an effective propaganda medium to educate and influence the ideas and actions of audiences.[18]

While somewhat embarrassed by the reneging of the government on its commitment to fulfill its promise to pay for work rendered, the U.S. Treasury Department eventually paid the money owed to the studio from its own internal budget.

As was the case with *The New Spirit* among U.S. audiences, the War Savings Certificate films for Canada's National Film Board were also able to stir a patriotic response amongst Canadian audiences. Disney writer Bob Carr reported back to the studio that "Canadian audiences stood and cheered at these little pictures, which have been shown in virtually every theater in Canada."[19]

Adapting the Business to the New Normal

The Disney writers and animators were excelling in adapting their craft to serve civil and social causes. The rapid increase in demand and urgency for military training films put considerable strain on the studio as it learned to adjust its production processes to parameters set from outside the studio's control. Walt now had to figure out how to produce to a budget to make a profit on fixed-price contracts, a complete change in policy and protocol from his usual demand for quality over cost. In this new environment, efficiency and economy were critical, and in the transitional learning process, the studio lost money on several films.

Carl Nater, who was Walt's production coordinator for military films, commented that the changeover from movie-house production to military contractual production presented considerable managerial challenges. "It was a mental rather than physical adjustment. Studio personnel accustomed to working two to three years on one picture were suddenly requisitioned to produce a film in four to six months. The financial departments, accustomed to budgeting pictures for three-quarters-of-a-million to one-and-one-half-million dollars found themselves piecing out $12,000 and $15,000 for production budgets."[20]

The change in the structure of work required changes in process to manage the compressed production deadlines effectively. For example, the camera department was required to operate twenty hours a day, six days a week. Units working on black-and-white films began doing their own inking and painting to avoid bottlenecks in the ink-and-paint department and meet tighter deadlines.

The studio had to deal with these and other emerging technical and mechanical issues that arose in combining live action and animated photography. To cope with the challenges of increasing complexity, technical innovation, and resource allocation unique to a particular film, a decentralization of resources began to emerge as the various disciplines came together within each production unit, such as story, direction, layout, animation, background, checking, and inking and painting.[21]

The shift from centralization to decentralization evolved out of necessity, as an unplanned adaptation to growing bottlenecks that were holding up production schedules. One consequence of this decentralization in production methods was that new discoveries and innovations in processes and techniques were created and adopted but not necessarily recorded or shared across production units. Walt recognized that improvements in one area needed to be shared to improve productivity and quality in other areas where appropriate.

After a year of producing military training films, in 1942 Walt authorized the creation of a layout manual as a reference guide detailing the different production methods to be used by staff to reduce production costs on military training films. Walt wrote to his staff in the foreword:

> The technique of our business has changed. Our horizons have rolled back almost to infinity regarding the educational material we handle. [D]uring this transition period, [so] many new methods have been created to solve new problems that there is a danger many of these may become forgotten. Many simple, inexpensive ways have been evolved to achieve effects, which formerly were done by animation. In some instances the newer methods have proved even more effective visually. To preserve these in reference form is the purpose of this manual, for, to be of worthwhile value, a creative man must have at his fingertips every atom of information, past and present, which pertains to his job, and it's impossible for most of us to be that good without something to refer to.
>
> Shrewd, creative men will use these techniques as foundations for newer and more effective methods of creating the animated picture of the future.[22]

A key theme of the layout manual's preface is cost reduction while ensuring quality:

Cost-Per-Foot is a horrible phrase but it's got to be put up with, like hot spells and taxes. The suggestions in this manual should help keep old man CPF where he belongs—and still maintain the Disney quality which is our most vital asset.[23]

The Disney Studio Is Designated a War Plant

As Walt assigned staff resources to fulfill the demand for war-related training films, and as theatrical film revenues for the studio declined precipitously, Walt had to pull back his production of theatrical releases. In May 1942, the *Dunkirk Evening Observer* reported: "After release of the completed 'Bambi,' no more Walt Disney features will reach the screen until at least a year after the war's end. Production of shorts will continue, but 75 percent of Disney's output already is devoted to Army and Navy training films. All the service pictures are being made at cost."[24] Only nine theatrical shorts were completed in 1942 compared to an annual output of 18 to 21 in a typical year.

In June 1942, the studio was formally declared to be a war plant by the U.S. government, and was required to abide by strict government protocol and security measures. A November 1942 *Family Circle* magazine reporter visiting the studio wrote: "Despite Walt's personal invitation to call, it took me 15 minutes to get into the place. There are soldiers at every entrance and in the office at the main gate. After several phone calls, a gent arrived, told the sergeant it was okay, they made a special pass and I was escorted to one of the main buildings."[25]

With the downsizing of staff to about 500, Walt was able to rent available studio space to Lockheed Aircraft Corporation to assemble aircraft components.[26] Profits were still forthcoming from the rental of shorts, comic strips, books, toys, and trademarks.[27]

Motion Pictures Can Solve the Problems Of Peace

The experience of making military training films and the success they were having in educating and entertaining service men had set Walt to thinking about the impact of cartoons as an increasingly important means of education.

Walt revealed a glimpse of his forward-looking optimism and humanism while the world was at war in his introduction to a 38-page informational newsletter. *Dispatch From Disney's* was published by the studio in April 1943 and mailed to all Disney employees serving in military units around the world to boost their morale and keep them informed about the goings-on at the studio. It even included some racy pin-up girl sketches by prominent Disney artists Freddie Moore, Bill Justice, and Milt Kahl.[28]

In the introduction, Walt wrote:

> Animation is proving that it can help with major problems. The lessons learned, you will apply constructively in solving the problems of peace.

> Making training films about torpedo tactics, anti-tank guns, forming methods and others too hush-hush to mention, we are learning techniques for tackling our share of the reconstruction problems ahead. Films for the preservation of health and morale in war lead to comparable films for peace.

> Making films for the development of better understanding between North and South America, we look forward to similar work on a worldwide scale. New and better types of educational motion pictures give cohesion to this torn earth. Light for China and India must reach their millions through the projection machine. Science, Economics, and Industry must be given a voice which all can understand. With these and a thousand other problems, the motion picture can be more helpful than any other force.[29]

The *Dispatch From Disney's* newsletter also contained an essay by war hero and squadron leader Lieutenant Commander James Thach. Thach was stationed at the Disney studio for a year and worked with the Disney artists as a writer, director, narrator, and advisor on a series of top-secret Navy training pictures on fighter combat tactics, referred to collectively as the Jacksonville Project. Ub Iwerks was the series executive producer. The films covered a number of topics including *Use of the Illuminated Gun Sight*, *Don't Kill Your Friends*, *Group Tactics Against Enemy Bombers*, and *Defensive Tactics Against Enemy Fighters*.

Thach's essay reflected and spoke to the importance the armed forces and military personnel attributed to the kinds of high quality animated training films being produced by Walt. He wrote about the significance of animated films in ensuring a consistent and repeatable training regimen for military personal that was heretofore unprecedented:

> The Navy knows that control of the air depends upon the number and quality of the fighters put into the skies. The rapid progress of war makes it necessary to turn out fighter pilots quickly and efficiently. This is a big job for instructors, but it would be an even greater problem without the use of Training Films.

> Our bases are scattered throughout the world, but the use of Training Films brings the same information to each base. This makes it possible to organize teaching facts, so that every pilot will be given the benefit of intelligent instruction.

> These Animated Training Films are not based upon theories of armchair combatants, but contain factual information gained from experience in battle. They convey proper information to the student

flyer through the use of simulated battle action. The enemy is presented to the student just as he will see him in actual combat. The value of this is obvious, for the student sees the conditions he is going to face, gets the feel of battle, but at the same time has the opportunity to study every possible method of combating the most complex problem presented. Training Films break down airplane maneuvers, open up the enemy tactics, so that they can be carefully analyzed. Detail that could not otherwise be detected are brought fully into light.

In the future, animated films will play an important part in our peacetime educational program. But to win this peace we must first send more and better fighter pilots into the sky. Walt Disney Productions' animated training film, "Jacksonville Project," will materially assist fighter pilots to get this job done, quickly and efficiently.[30]

These training films were, in their time, the precursor of the modern flight simulator. Because the work was owned by the Navy and considered confidential, all scripts, artwork, and unused film were returned to the Navy post-production.[31]

Walt also continued to enthusiastically lend the support of his beloved characters to promote the allied victory efforts. The fifth war loan drive of the War Bond Program that President Roosevelt initiated in 1941 was launched on June 6, 1944, the day of the Normandy invasion. To help promote the sale of low denomination bonds, the certificates were printed with the faces of 22 popular Disney characters, including Mickey, Donald, Pluto, Goofy, the Seven Dwarfs, Thumper, and Jose Carioca. The Disney certificates were the center-piece of the Treasury Department's "Bonds For Babies" campaign that would extend into day nurseries, schools, and hospitals, and encourage the purchase of war bonds as a savings and investment vehicle for babies, while at the same time providing parents with a sense of pride knowing they were helping to secure a future of freedom in America for themselves and their children.[32]

The universal appeal of beloved Disney characters was used to promote many other government wartime programs and campaigns beyond treasury-related issues of tax collecting and war bond purchases.

In 1942, the prices of most consumer products were controlled by the Office of Price Administration, which led to forced rationing of such staples as sugar, coffee, processed foods, meat, and dairy products. A booklet for ration stamps was published with Disney artwork featuring Mickey, Minnie, Donald, and Pluto on the front cover.[33]

As with food, fuel was also rationed and drivers were limited to about three gallons of gas per week. Sunoco used Donald and Mickey to promote the message that fuel rationing benefits the armed forces in the war effort, including posters to promote hitch-hiking that read: "Share your car for your country. Planes need gasoline." Illustrations were created by Disney artists at the studio to promote joining the Red Cross, giving blood, and donating to the American Red Cross War Relief Fund for the rescue, feeding, shelter, and medical care of the homeless and orphaned children in war-torn Europe.[34]

Walt also gave his personal support to private organizations, such as the United China Relief Fund, which was created in 1941 to raise $5 million for Chinese citizens who suffered under Japanese occupation. Walt agreed to allow the organization to use the baby mushroom star of the "Nutcracker Suite" in *Fantasia*, Hop Low, in its fundraising promotions. In 1942 the United China Relief fundraising drive raised over $7 million in donations, far exceeding its goal. Walt also donated two iron deer sculptures he had on his front lawn to the country's salvage drive for items useful to the war effort, organized by the War Production Board.[35]

One area impacted immensely by the war was its devastating effect on the supply of fresh and processed foods, and allies in Europe were concerned about the supply of food for basic survival. In 1942, Walt was approached by the Agriculture Department to produce a film to address this concern and reinforce the commitment and determination of the U.S. and its farmers to work hard at increasing food production and to do everything possible to deliver it to those in need. The film *Food Will Win the War* was completed in July 1942, for which the studio was paid $20,000 by the government.[36] The studio also designed carrot characters to be used on posters and recipe booklets to entice Brits to accept carrots as a healthy food staple in their diet.[37]

Disney in "Nutziland"

The CIAA (Office of the Co-coordinator of Inter-American Affairs) headed by Nelson Rockefeller that coordinated and sponsored the South American goodwill trip and funded the South American-themed theatrical features *Saludos Amigos* (1942) and *The Three Caballeros* (1944) also helped finance four anti-Nazi "psychological" short film production in 1943: *Reason and Emotion*, *Chicken Little*, *Education for Death*, and *Der Fuehrer's Face* starring Donald Duck.[38]

The satirical novelty song that accompanied *Der Fuehrer's Face* was released in advance of the film and became a huge nationwide sensation. The film won an Academy Award for the Best Cartoon Short Subject of 1943.[39]

Walt Disney Studios composer Oliver Wallace wrote the song after Walt stopped him in a studio hallway one afternoon. Wallace recalled the event:

> Walt encountered me in the hall and gave me a rush order. "Ollie, I want a serious song, but it's got to be funny." The further information

that it was going to be for a picture telling Donald Duck's adventures in Naziland didn't help very much. "What do you mean?" I asked. "Suppose the Germans are singing it," Walt offered. "To them it's serious, to us it's funny." Walt walked away. I stood in the hall. Once more I was on the spot.

Later that day Wallace came up with the chorus while riding his bike to the store, and completed it within a half hour. Wallace found the tune infectious and was singing it the next day at the studio:

I sang it all over the place. The sound brought Walt out into the hall. "Let's hear it,'" Walt said. I stalled. "Orchestration...there's a funny sound in it...can't be made without an instrument...has to be practiced.'" The truth is, I didn't know what Walt would think of a highly robust Bronx cheer. Could such a sound be used in a Disney picture? "Let's hear it," Walt said. I let loose. Walt laughed. The rest is history.[40]

The song was recorded by then popular satirical bandleader Spike Jones and sung by band member Carl Grayson for inclusion in the film. It was released as the B-side of a 78-rpm record in September 1942 and was an instant nationwide hit, lasting sixteen weeks on the charts and rising as high as the third spot. The song was used in a New York City radio promotion by radio personality Martin Block to sell war bonds. Block offered a free copy of the record to anyone who pledged $50 dollars, thereby raising $60,000 for the war effort.[41] In a short period of time, more than 1.5 million copies were sold, and the title of the film was changed from its original *Donald Duck in Nutziland* to *Der Fuehrer's Face*.

The studio also produced a number of aircraft production training films for the Navy in 1942 and 1943, including *Aircraft Riveting, Bending and Curving, Blanking and Punching, Lofting and Layouts*, and *Template Reproduction*. A film to teach nautical travel rules called *Rules of the Nautical Road* was produced in 1943. The studio also worked on a number of classified military films for which additional layers of security were installed to protect secrets and ensure confidentiality.

A series of eleven Navy films was produced for the Naval Bureau of Aeronautics under the general title Aerology for Navy to help pilots understand and prepare for the different weather conditions they would face. Titles included: *Icing Conditions, The Cold Front, The Warm Front, Fog*, and *Thunderstorms*. These films were based on comprehensive field research by Disney staff, including extensive interviews with prominent civilian, commercial, and military pilots. The *New York Herald Tribune* reported on August 22, 1943: "The lucid and comprehensive style in which these films have been made accounts for the way they have been welcomed so enthusiastically by both Navy trainees and instructors."[42]

Military Mascots and Combat Insignia

Another area in which Disney artists applied their creative talents between 1939 and 1945 was to the development of mascots and combat insignia for military units, government agencies, and contractors involved with war production and home-front activities.[43] Often a donation would be made by the recipient to support the war effort. For example, the McClatchy newspaper and radio chain donated $1,500 to the Army Relief Fund.[44]

For those serving their country, Disney studio insignia for military units were great morale boosters.[45] John Baxter writes in *Disney During World War II*, "It is difficult for us today to fully appreciate how it felt for a serviceman—or woman—to have their unit represented by a Disney-designed insignia. For the generation that fought World War II, Disney character images possessed an iconic heft that has no analog in contemporary animation. A Donald Duck insignia boosted morale, not just because it reminded soldiers of home, but also because it signified that the job they were doing was important enough to be acknowledged by Walt Disney."[46]

As the number of military units grew following the U.S. declaration of war, so did the number of requests by these units to the studio for their own insignia. In early 1942 Walt created a department to handle the rising volume of requests, and assigned former commercial artist and Disney *Snow White and the Seven Dwarfs* animator Henry "Hank" Porter to head-up the work. One day Porter was called up to Walt's office and informed: "Mister, you have yourself a job. Just settle down to it. Make as many insignia as you can. If you get overloaded with work, let me know."[47]

Walt referred to Porter as a "one-man art department" because of the volume of work he handled, even though he often required help from other artists.[48] Requests were received from Army and Navy military units stationed all around the globe.

David Lesjak reports in *Service with Character: The Disney Studio and World War II* that it cost the Disney studio about $30,000 dollars to support its insignia program. "Each design cost an average $25 each to produce. 'Never mind what the job is costing us. That isn't important,' was Walt's attitude. Patriotic words from a man whose studio spent almost the entire war in debt—as high as $1.2 million in 1942."[49]

By using major, minor, and newly invented Disney characters, almost 1,300 insignia requests were fulfilled by the end of the war.

On The Global Stage: Victory Through Filmmaking Power?

The one pro-military full-length feature Walt produced during the war was a film adaptation of Major A. P. de Seversky's *New York Times* best-selling book *Victory Through Air Power.* The book and the film adaptation argue for the importance of a strategic bombing campaign by long-range bombers to help win the war and defeat the Axis powers.

The film was funded by the studio directly without any government support, at a cost of $788,000,[50] with very little chance of recovering its costs at the box office. Nonetheless, Walt decided to take on the project because he believed strongly in the premise of the film and in selling Major de Seversky's vision of how the war could be won in less time and with less loss of life.

Walt was convinced that the film could change the course of the war and the world. He told *The New York Times* in February 1943, "People need to know about it. A lot of them are still bound by traditional ways of thinking and a movie like this can break through a lot of misconceptions."[51] "Walt had made *Victory* for influence and for his own sense of usefulness," writes Disney biographer Neal Gabler. "'Whether it makes money or not,' he wrote radio commentator Upton Close, 'I shall be happy so long as it helps stir up the country and starts people thinking about the importance of real air power,' though just how much it really affected policy was a matter of debate."[52]

Victory Through Airpower premiered in New York City on July 17, 1943, but private screenings were held prior to this for which Walt received high praise from powerful people that held prominent political influence. After attending a screening, famed American newspaper publisher William Randolph Hearst wired Walt to tell him that the movie was a "truly great production" that "rendered a valuable service to the community." Nelson Rockefeller lauded its contribution to the war effort and its demonstration of the limitless possibilities of motion pictures. Film reviewers commended the movie for being "exhilarating," "stimulating," "ingenious." A screening for naval personnel received an enthusiastic response, and in another, air force generals applauded the film and its message.[53]

Eventually, a copy of the film was provided to British Prime Minister Winston Churchill. Churchill was impressed, and asked that a copy be expedited overnight to Quebec City where he was meeting with Canadian Prime Minister William Lyon Mackenzie King and United States President Franklin D. Roosevelt at a highly secret military conference, where discussions for the planning of the invasion of France were to begin. Roosevelt watched the film and then asked for another screening for the Joint Chiefs of Staff.[54]

According to film critic and historian Leonard Maltin, *Victory Through Airpower* "changed FDR's way of thinking—he agreed that Seversky was right" and that "it was only after Roosevelt saw 'Victory Through Air Power' that [the United States] made the commitment to long-range bombing."

The film generated the kind of attention and discussion that Walt was seeking. But it was a failure at the box office, resulting in the studio booking a loss of almost $450,000.[55]

Walt's Wartime Radio Broadcasts

In addition to doing what he could to help the war effort through the work of his studio, Walt was also involved in a series of radio broadcasts aired by the United States Office of War Information to give moral support to the French, Turkish, and Chinese causes. According to a report in *The New York Times*, "Mr. Disney, whose Mickey Mouse and other film cartoons enjoyed great popularity in France before the war, said that Hitler was trembling before the mounting strength of the Allies. 'Yes,' he continued, paraphrasing the feature song of the *Three Little Pigs*, 'Hitler, the Big Bad Wolf, is afraid.'"[56]

Just a few months later, in May 1944, in a pre-recorded broadcast to Turkey, Walt delivered a message of hope and optimism.

> It is a great privilege to speak as a representative of the motion picture industry to the people of Turkey. We like to think of motion pictures as a bond between other nations and ourselves. It is a bond of friendship—because entertainment brings friendship with it.
>
> The adventures and misadventures of Mickey Mouse and Donald Duck, for instance, are enjoyed by audiences in both our countries.
>
> It is very significant that American and Turkish people laugh and cry at the same things. They are moved to pity or stirred to anger by the same things.
>
> There was a time, before the war, when it was popular to talk about different national psychologies. But the longer this war lasts, the clearer it becomes that the people of democratic nations have much the same fundamental ways of thinking.
>
> That is a good omen and assurance that our legitimate hopes for the future have an excellent chance for success.[57]

Studio Wartime Production

By the time the war was over, Disney had produced over 170 films for the armed forces and the U.S. government, and had learned to make them as quickly and cheaply as possible.[58] In addition, many of the Disney characters including Donald Duck, Goofy, and Pluto featured prominently in military-themed short cartoons between 1941 and 1945.[59]

Walt's wartime theatrical movies had mixed success, but there were no blockbusters on the level of *Snow White and the Seven Dwarfs*. *Pinocchio* was released five months after the outbreak of war and suffered from the loss of revenues from overseas markets. *Fantasia* had both its fans and critics, and while it may have helped to further establish the image of Walt Disney as a courageous innovator capable of delivering jaw-dropping animation, audiences didn't find it especially entertaining. *The Reluctant Dragon* (1941) was a low-cost effort to educate and entertain, while showing off the new

Walt Disney Studios.[60] *Dumbo* (1941) was enchanting, entertaining, fun, and profitable. *Bambi* (1942) continued to establish Walt as an innovative storyteller and demonstrated major advancements in the capabilities of his artists to present emotional drama and humor.

Saludos Amigos (1942) and *The Three Caballeros* (1944) consisted of a series of shorter cartoons packaged for the South American market that were inspired by the government-sponsored goodwill visit in 1940. Both films were relatively successful for the studio upon initial release. *Victory Through Air Power* (1943) helped to raise the consciousness of allied leaders and military brass to the potential effectiveness of airpower to provide a strategic tactical advantage on the battlefield to shorten the war.

"Before the war," notes David Lesjak in *Service with Character*, "Disney films had been distributed to 55 countries. By 1944, 81 percent of the studio's box-office revenue was being generated by only three countries," the United States and Canada (56%) and England (25%). Mexico and South America accounted for another 6%; Australia and New Zealand, 6%; and the rest of the world, 7%.[61]

Reflecting On The Lessons Of War

The studio survived the war, but it wasn't easy. In 1945, Walt wrote a short piece for the Princeton University publication *The Public Opinion Quarterly* in which he reflected on how, out of necessity, he had to adapt to circumstances by changing his business practices and reigning in his creative ambitions:

> The pressure of the last four years has forced us all to scrutinize and put on trial the things we do, the way we do them, and the reason we do them. Under the urgency of our national crisis, we have been compelled to reject any move that had no purpose, any method that was cumbersome or slow, and to cast off any means that would not guarantee results. The watchword was to retain whatever was efficient…and to cast off whatever was not effective.[62]

The war had a major effect on the trajectory of Walt's career and the direction he took in filmmaking and entertainment. The economic consequences of not being able to access foreign markets caused a major shift in his business model for almost a decade, mostly away from animated entertainment to educational films and live-action production. Walt was able to envision or imagine how external events would impact his business, and through ongoing active analysis, anticipated the actions necessary to take advantage of a changing operating environment. This strategic approach to business and courage to face reality head-on allowed Walt to take action early in anticipation of changes to his operating environment.

David Lesjak, in *Service with Character,* provides a good summary of Walt's positive, probing, and opportunistic entrepreneurial attitude toward maintaining organizational vitality in the face of external threats:

> The war provided Walt Disney with a chance to experiment, at government cost, with new ways of producing live-action and educational films. And although the profit margin on government sponsored films was small, these contracts kept the Studio in business at a time when there was the threat the Studio would have to close due to the economics of closed markets.[63]

The significance of Walt's contribution to the war effort is debatable. He valued the war effort to fight for freedom and found himself in a position where he could dedicate the service and competence of his business to the allied cause, producing hundreds of thousands of feet of film for the U.S. military to train the troops. John Baxter, in *Disney During World War II,* writes:

> It is impossible to gauge the impact that Disney's training films had on the outcome of the war, but many of the films were lauded at the time by combat veterans and were considered effective enough to remain in use for years after their completion. What Disney brought to the table was not the quality of the content, but the trademark Disney "lucidity" that grabbed the trainees' attention and delivered content in the clearest possible terms. Walt didn't enjoy making training films, and he confessed that he was sick to death of them by war's end, but he still gave each one the Disney treatment. He made no money off them, as he had promised at the outset of the war, despite being nickel-and-dimed by the military along the way, and when the war ended and the studio ended its contract cycle with a surplus, it was paid back and the slate was wiped clean.[64]

One last thought about the impact of Walt's contribution and testament to his wartime effort comes from David Lesjak:

> While Americans on the home front endured tough times, Disney's cast of cartoon characters were on hand to help ease the pain and share in some of the hardship. Disney's involvement in the war prompted one magazine writer to say, "[H]ow fortunate America is to have Walt on the job today. He's a propaganda genius for whom the Axis would gladly give a dozen crack divisions."[65]

---

1. Lesjak, *Service with Character,* 3.

2. Thomas, *Walt Disney,* 175.

3. Thomas, *Walt Disney,* 175.

4. Baxter, *Disney During World War II,* 16; Polsson, *Chronology of the Walt Disney Company.*

5. Lesjak, *Service with Character*, 190.

6. "Walt Disney: Great Teacher," *Fortune Magazine*, August, 1942, afilm.com/blog/Fortune0842_p156.jpg, accessed April 7, 2014.

7. Baxter, *Disney During World War II*, 17.

8. Baxter, *Disney During World War II*, 21.

9. Lesjak, *Service with Character*, 30.

10. Lesjak, *Service with Character*, 31–32; excerpt from Disney interview with Pete Martin in summer of 1956.

11. Lesjak, *Service with Character*, 33.

12. Baxter, *Disney During World War II*, 46.

13. Baxter, *Disney During World War II*, 46.

14. Lesjak, *Service with Character*, 36.

15. Lesjak, *Service with Character*, 36; "Walt Disney: Great Teacher," *Fortune Magazine*, August, 1942, afilm.com/blog/Fortune0842_p94.jpg, accessed April 7, 2014.

16. Lesjak, *Service with Character*, 38.

17. Lesjak, *Service with Character*, 39.

18. See Jackson (ed.), *Walt Disney Conversations*, 36.

19. Baxter, *Disney During World War II*, 42.

20. Lesjak, *Service with Character*, 196.

21. Lesjak, *Service with Character*, 196–197.

22. Lesjak, *Service with Character*, 198.

23. Lesjak, *Service with Character*, 199.

24. Lesjak, *Service with Character*, 2.

25. Lesjak, *Service with Character*, 8.

26. Lesjak, *Service with Character*, 9.

27. "Fortune August 1942 'Walt Disney: Great Teacher,'" A. Film L.A. Blog, May 12, 2008, afilmla.blogspot.ca/2008/05/fortune-august-1942-disney-great.html.

28. Lesjak, *Service with Character*, 18.

29. Lesjak, *Service with Character*, 18–19.

30. Lesjak, *Service with Character*, 200.

31. Lesjak, *Service with Character*, 202.

32. Lesjak, *Service with Character*, 43.

33. Lesjak, *Service with Character*, 53.

34. Lesjak, *Service with Character*, 58.

35. Lesjak, *Service with Character*, 50.

36 Lesjak, *Service with Character*, 68.

37. Lesjak, *Service with Character*, 69.

38. Lesjak, *Service with Character*, 139.

39. Lesjak, *Service with Character*, 182.

40. Lesjak, *Service with Character*, 184.

41. Lesjak, *Service with Character*, 185.

42. Lesjak, *Service with Character*, 193.

43. Lesjak, *Service with Character*, 109.

44. Lesjak, *Service with Character*, 66.

45. Lesjak, *Service with Character*, 18--19.

46. Baxter, *Disney During World War II*, 130–131.

47. Lesjak, *Service with Character*, 113.

48. Baxter, *Disney During World War II*, 122.

49. Lesjak, *Service with Character*, 134.

50. Wikipedia, "Victory Through Air Power," en.wikipedia.org/wiki/Victory_Through_Air_Power_(film).

51. Gabler, *Walt Disney*, 403.

52. Gabler, *Walt Disney*, 405.

53. Gabler, *Walt Disney*, 404.

54. Gabler, *Walt Disney*, 405.

55. Alan Bryman, *Disney and His Worlds*, 9, cites a loss of $436,000. Gabler, 405, indicates a loss of between $400–500,000.

56. Lesjak, *Service with Character*, 70.

57. Lesjak, *Service with Character*, 70.

58. Baxter, *Disney During World War II*, 11; Lesjak, *Service with Character*, 189. Lesjak indicates that 75 were military training films.

59. Lesjak, *Service with Character*, 70–71.

60. Lesjak, *Service with Character*, 207.

61. Lesjak, *Service with Character*, 2.

62. Lesjak, *Service with Character*, 203–204; *The Public Opinion Quarterly*, Princeton University, Summer 1945, "Mickey as Professor.").

63. Lesjak, *Service with Character*, 209.

64. Baxter, *Disney During World War II*, 31.

65. Lesjak, *Service with Character*, 72.

CHAPTER SIXTEEN

Reorienting and Rebuilding Business Capabilities

With the war over and the government contracts at an end, the year 1945 provided Walt with a catalyst for renewal and a new start. Now, more than twenty years after he and Roy began together in 1923, Walt was again looking forward to exerting control over the destiny of his studio. He was eager to return the studio to the renewed production of elaborate animated features that had been taken out of production, including *The Wind in the Willows, Cinderella, Alice in Wonderland*, and *Peter Pan*. He wrote to his sister Ruth in December, "I am now hoping that we can get out two or three features a year now, and are preparing stories for nearly five years ahead."[1]

Walt spelled out his immediate opportunities in a press release titled "The World is our Marketplace." Foreign markets that were once closed were now opening up, and the renewal and expansion of global distribution through RKO and Disney's own foreign offices was underway as a strategic priority. "There is now hardly a spot on the globe, which is not equipped to show pictures, nor where the inhabitants are not hungry to see them. In a condition like this, we have a definite advantage in that our product is universally known and appreciated." Walt's advantage lay in having an inventory of excellent full-length animated features that had yet to see proper foreign distribution, including *Pinocchio, Dumbo, Bambi, Fantasia*, and a number of short subjects. "This backlog of fine product," noted Walt, "available for marketing in many territories yet untouched, is a great reserve of financial strength to help insure [sic] for our company a successful period ahead."[2]

In his message to employees in the 1945 Annual Report for Employees of Walt Disney Productions, Walt spoke to some of his immediate post-war challenges:

> The end of the war has given us the chance to go ahead with plans, which until now we could only think about. It has confronted us with a number of problems.

It's good to walk down the hall and welcome back so many of the fellows who spent years in the service. It's also good to have finished the training film program that absorbed practically all of our energies, and to get busy with the work of making entertainment pictures.

We have many readjustments to make. Our re-conversion job consists of reorganizing our staff to include the experienced men whom we lost and who have now returned, of training others to provide for increased production, and to build up our inventory of stories in preparation and of pictures in work.

This program will take time, work and sound thinking. Our people have the talent and skill to carry it out. I believe it can be done quickly and efficiently in proportion to the enthusiasm and the team work we can apply to it. All these qualities mean good pictures, and good pictures mean that our future is assured.

We have a clear road ahead. Let's get under way.

Walt Disney[3]

In spite of Walt's optimism and the studio coming out of the war in better financial shape than going in, keeping it operational remained a constant struggle.

Over the total period of U.S. involvement in the war from 1941 through 1945, the studio was not profitable, although it did show a profit in the latter years as Walt adapted to the necessities of wartime production. In 1941 and 1942 the studio reported a net loss of around $800,000 and $200,000, respectively. The following three years were profitable, with the studio producing a net gain of $486,000 in 1944 and $351,000 in 1945.[4]

The turn-around in profitability was to a large extent due to the success of the animated compilation features *Saludos Amigos* in 1943, and *The Three Caballeros* in 1944, the latter of which grossed $3.4 million at the box office. The studio was also able to reduce its borrowings to the Bank of America from over a million dollars before the attack on Pearl Harbor to roughly $300,000 at the war's end.[5]

The situation over the previous five years was such that Walt's creativity had been caged by his commitment to put his studio to use serving the allied war effort, which to some extent was also a viable and expedient business survival strategy to keep the studio functioning and his staff employed during a period of economic hardship and the closing of foreign markets to sales.

In spite of Walt's enthusiasm, it was impossible to just carry on from where he left off in 1941 as if nothing had happened. Disney historian Sam Gennawey captures some aspects of the competitive challenges Walt was facing, in *The Disneyland Story*:

> Times were tough at Walt Disney Productions after World War II. ... Walt Disney Productions was no longer the king of the cartoon shorts. Fred Quimby at Metro-Goldwyn-Mayer was winning all of the awards [for Tom and Jerry shorts], and Warner Bros. was winning the box office [with a cast of Looney Tunes characters]. Worse yet, Warner spent half as much to produce their cartoons. Walt had *Cinderella* in production, but he knew that animated feature films took a long time, cost a lot of money, and were risky. The future looked more like films such as *Song of the South* and *So Dear to My Heart*, which combined animation with live-action elements. These films were faster and less expensive to produce.[6]

The social and business environments that Walt and his business colleagues were comfortable working in before the war were undergoing significant turbulence as the world adjusted to a new post-war reality.

For a short period of time following the war, as government contracts ended and the studio reverted back to peacetime commercial operations, private corporations began to approach Walt seeking to utilize freed-up resources.[7] By the end of 1946, the studio had produced eleven industrial training and educational films for leading American businesses, such as *Prevention and Control of Distortion in Arc Welding* (1945) for the Lincoln Electrical Company, *The Dawn of Better Living* (1945) for Westinghouse Electric, *The ABC of Hand Tools* (1946) for General Motors;, *The Building of a Tire* (1946) for Firestone Tire and Rubber, *Bathing Time for Baby* (1946) for Johnson and Johnson, and *The Story of Menstruation* (1946), sponsored by the International Cellu-Cotton Company.

The end of military training contracts meant the studio could also return to the production of theatrical entertainment, which included eighteen short subjects in 1945, up from 14 in 1944, as well as the production of two full-length features—the compilation feature *Make Mine Music*, which combined nine short segments animated to popular music and premiered in April 1946, as well as *Song of the South*, a live-action story in which thirty percent of the movie consisted of the animated tales of Uncle Remus featuring the antics of Br'er Rabbit, Br'er Fox, and Br'er Bear that premiered in November 1946. The renewed investment in production caused indebtedness to Bank of America to double from $528,311 in 1944 to over a million dollars by the end of 1945.[8]

By 1946 Walt was beginning to realize that while he loved animated cartoons and features, the mood of America had changed and the cost to produce top quality animation was becoming too expensive and therefore too risky. Walt began to redefine the way he thought about the core of his business: Disney wasn't just about animation, it was about stories, and Walt always defined his strength as being a great storyman. While the studio's expertise was grounded in animation, stories could also be told with live actors. Looking back at this time period, Walt recalled: "I knew that I must diversify. ... I tried that in the beginning. ... Now I wanted... to go beyond the cartoon. ... I needed to diversify further and that meant live action."[9] Walt had some recent experience with live action with *The Reluctant Dragon* (1941) and *Victory Through Air Power* (1943) and understood that it had the benefits of lower costs and faster production, which reduced both the investment of capital and time required before the film returned box-office cash to his bank account.

Walt also showed his excitement for, and commitment to, continued experimentation in animation by collaborating with surrealist painter Salvador Dali on the film *Destino*. Walt told the press, "I want to give more big artists such opportunities. The thing I resent most is people who try to keep me in well-worn grooves. We have to keep breaking new trails. We were panned for *Fantasia*, yet its audience keeps building each year."[10]

Dali and *Destino*: Return of the Experimental Itch

The studio spent nine months working on *Destino* in which Dali was given near-complete autonomy. For the first eight weeks Dali worked on the third floor of the studio near Walt's office.[11] According to Disney artist John Hench, who worked directly with Dali on the project, "Walt came in and looked at the work from time to time; he saw the storyboard in progress and decided to let Dali go ahead and see what would happen."[12] After eight weeks, Dali departed to a rented studio in Monterey, California, where he worked on other projects and paintings while assuring Walt that he continued to develop concepts for their movie. As assessed by film historian John Canemaker, Walt "was willing to take a significant artistic and financial risk in order to expand the possibilities of the animated film."[13]

Given the financial circumstances of the studio at the time, Walt was devoted to practical business realities and his tolerance to excessive risk was not unlimited. The Destino experiment was eventually abandoned after nine months and an estimated cost of $70,000.[14] A number of reasons were cited: a lack of progress on the story, disagreement about how much of the movie should be animated or live action, financial pressure and difficulty getting credit in the aftermath of the war, and in that total context, the recognition that the film, which was expected to be about six minutes in length, may be ground-breaking but was unlikely to make money.[15]

When Walt pulled the plug, the project had produced a large number of conceptual drawings but only about fifteen seconds of filmed animation. In discussing the film later, Walt said, "It was certainly no fault of Dali's; it was simply a case of policy changes within our distribution plans." In the opinion of retired Disney archivist Dave Smith, *Destino* just got too far out for Walt.[16]

Years later, upon reflection and no longer facing the severe financial constraints of the time, Walt regretted that the film was never completed and that an opportunity to achieve something great was missed. According to Hench, "Years afterward, whenever Walt and I talked about Dali, he always said we should have made that thing anyway. I believe Walt always regretted not making *Destino*, because it was a valuable document."[17] (*Destino* was eventually relaunched and completed under the leadership of Roy E. Disney. It premiered June 2, 2003, at the Annecy International Animation Film Festival in France, and was nominated for an Academy Award in 2004, for Best Short Film [Animated]. It was released to the public in 2010 on the *Fantasia 2000* DVD Blu-ray edition, along with a "making of" documentary, *Dali & Disney: A Date with Destino*.)

By the end of 1946, the studio's indebtedness to Bank of America had ballooned to exceed four million dollars, creating renewed tension between the studio and the bank.[18] The shareholders of the closely held Walt Disney Productions approved a stock-conversion to raise an additional $1,364,200 in cash, which increased the number of shareholders to 1,900.[19]

Stabilizing the Foundation and Rebuilding Competency

In 1947, Walt released his fourth compilation feature, *Fun and Fancy Free*. He felt that the studio had lost the core competency in producing full-length animated features it had held before the war, through downsizing and other factors, and that the production of musically themed compilations would serve as vehicles to hire and train new staff, retrain existing and returning staff, and rebuild the required infrastructure.

With Bank of America refusing to lend any more money, and continuing pressure for an inflow of working capital, Roy negotiated a loan from film distributor RKO in return for an extension of its distribution rights. By the end of 1947, the combined debt to Bank of America and RKO had risen back to almost four million dollars.[20]

One of the studio's greatest saving graces was the merchandising money machine that had been created through the licensing of Disney characters to manufacturers and advertisers, and nurtured since 1932 by Kay Kamen. Kamen provided insight into the scale of the Disney licensing empire in an interview with the *New York Times Magazine*, published September 21, 1947:

> The Disney label, says Mr. Kamen, helps to sell about $100,000,000 worth of goods each year and Mickey is the best salesman of the lot.

Books are the chief item, going at the rate of 10,000,000 a year and ranging in price from kindergarten primers at $1 a copy to a deluxe Deems Taylor edition of *Fantasia* at $3.75. A Walt Disney illustrated *Uncle Remus* ran through a first printing of 150,000 in practically no time and another is on the presses. The Walt Disney Comics, a monthly comic strip magazine, sells to the merry tune of 30,000,000 a year and rates fourth on newsstand sales of all national magazines.

Mickey is a consistent salesman of cereals, soaps, dolls, toys, sweaters, sweatshirts, phonographs and records, radios, hot-water bottles, hairbrushes, caps, robes, slippers, footballs, baseballs, paint sets, porringers and, most notably, the Mickey Mouse watches—600,000 of them sold so far this year. ... A New York department store sold $10,000 worth of Disney-decorated sweaters in a day.

No small-time operator, Mickey has made tie-ups with Standard Oil, General Foods, Standard Brands, National Biscuit Company, Du Pont and National Dairy Products. He has declined bids from liquor companies, cigarette manufacturers, makers of patent medicines.

The net income to Disney from all these sidelines has been, Mr. Kamen estimates, from $500,000 to $800,000 a year. "No doubt of it," says Mr. Kamen, "Mickey Mouse is the greatest thing in the history of merchandising."[21]

The animated compilation feature *Melody Time* was completed and released in 1948, along with fifteen cartoon shorts featuring Mickey, Donald, Goofy, and Pluto.

The studio ended 1948 with a small loss, coming just short of break-even by $39,038.[22]

Busting Foreign Political Constraints

Walt had expected foreign markets to re-open after the war, but post-war opportunities for American studios in the lucrative markets of England and France faced new political challenges. Both countries, as well as others in Europe, imposed restrictive barriers to limit the showing of American films in an attempt to revive their own film industries. To increase the cost to British movie theatres of showing American films, Britain imposed a 75 percent import tax and set a quota that 45 percent of films shown be made in England. In negotiations with the American State Department, France restricted the number of imported American movies to 110, to be provided by the major Hollywood studios, of which Disney was excluded.[23]

In addition to restricting audience access to American films and thereby the potential to sell their products in the British marketplace, the British legislature passed a law prohibiting American film studios from repatriating receipts earned in their country as part of a larger effort to promote the stimulation of its war-torn economy. As a result, what had been earned in Britain was legally bound to remain there.[24]

By the end of 1948, Walt was faced with the difficult challenge of what to do with about $850,000 of blocked funds in foreign countries, including England.[25] This was money that, if it was made available to him, he could put to use to complete current projects and fund new ones.

Walt's first consideration was to set up a cartoon studio, but decided that he already had what he needed in Burbank and would not be able to reproduce the talent and capabilities he already had. Disney film distributor RKO also had funds frozen in England, and suggested to Walt that he invest his frozen funds in creating live-action adventure films, with RKO agreeing to share the production costs of the first effort, *Treasure Island*.[26]

Walt approved the establishment of Walt Disney British Films Ltd., and began making live-action films in England, starting with *Treasure Island* and followed by *The Story of Robin Hood*, *The Sword and the Rose*, and *Rob Roy the Highland Rogue*.[27] The success of *Song of the South* had demonstrated that audiences were accepting of Disney live-action productions, even though it was combined with a number of highly entertaining animated sequences.

Walt was initially directed toward live-action films as a practical strategic solution to the studio's unique financial circumstances. But when he traveled to England to observe the production of *Treasure Island*, he'd thoroughly enjoyed the challenges and the immediacy of live-action filming. When he returned to Burbank, he teased his animators: "Those actors over there in England, they're great. You give 'em the lines, and they rehearse it a couple of times, and you've got it on film—it's finished. You guys take six months to draw a scene."[28]

Walt was only half kidding. The high costs, long production times, and complications in creating feature-length cartoons made them a much riskier class of investments than live-action movies. Such talk made Disney animators nervous that Walt was going to abandon animation altogether.[29] Walt saw it as a way to maintain his core business, which he still considered to be animation. When elite animator Milt Kahl questioned Walt as to why he was spending so much time away from animation, Walt allegedly quipped, "Well, I'll tell you, Milt. I have to make a whore of myself to pay your salary. It's as simple as that."[30]

Roy stated the studio's interest in more business-like terms, noting: "We are not going into these things because we are feeling our oats or getting ambitious. We are doing it for common-sense business reasons, realizing the hazards of our basic cartoon business."[31]

Having completed filming of *Song of the South* and *So Dear to My Heart*, Walt had come to recognize that live-action features could be completed in less time and at lower cost than fully or partially animated features. The quicker a movie could be completed and released, the lower its production cost and the sooner a return on investment could be captured to repay lenders the money borrowed to fund the investment. Quick turnaround and lower costs was the key to improved cash flow and financial viability.

The year 1949 was a busy one for releases. The live-action *So Dear to My Heart* was released along with the first True-Life Adventures documentary, *Seal Island*, and the feature length animation compilation *The Adventures of Ichabod and Mr. Toad*. Of the fifteen shorts released, Donald Duck dominated, along with appearances from Pluto, Minnie, Goofy, and Chip 'n' Dale.

The mostly live-action feature *So Dear to My Heart* had its world premiere in Indianapolis on January 19, 1949. Walt began working with a screenwriter in 1945 with the intention of it being Walt's first fully live-action feature. Production and filming occurred in 1946, but Walt was unhappy with the finished product, and made considerable changes by re-working some scenes in post-production. He was still not satisfied and struggled to improve its overall presentation. More than a year after filming was completed, Walt decided to add some animation sequences to add another dimension of imagination, as he had done previously on *Song of the South*.[32]

Still, as the year drew to a close, the studio showed an increased loss of $93,899.[33] *Cinderella* was now in production, and Walt was envisioning a return to elaborate state-of-the-art feature-length animation.

Bank of America was getting nervous about the continuing trend of increasing debt and the difficulty the studio was having in creating profits. Roy was once again pushing hard for austerity. To appease the bankers, Walt had no choice but to curtail his spendthrift tendencies and adopt a more rigorous disciplinary approach to cost management by defining and sticking to budgets. What he needed was another blockbuster box-office hit to throw off a lot of cash and relieve the financial pressure that was cramping his style.

Launching the Disney Renaissance with a Cinderella Year

As the new decade arrived, 1950 saw the release of *Cinderella*, the first full-length non-compilation feature since the release of *Bambi* in 1942. With *Cinderella*, Walt was finally able to put the burden and uncertainty of the 1940s behind him. As one historian noted, *Cinderella* trumpeted a sort of Disney Renaissance. Roy called 1950 "our Cinderella year" as the movie grossed in excess of four million dollars on its initial release.

The Academy Award winning True-Life Adventures documentary *In Beaver Valley* was also released in 1950, as was Disney's first fully live-action movie,

Treasure Island. On the strength of this line-up, the studio's bottom line was once again in the black, showing a substantial profit of $717,542.[34] The merchandising of *Cinderella* played a significant role in generating income. Walt's vision of diversification of revenue sources and expansion of revenue-generating products beyond just cartoons appeared to be paying off.

The Emerging Threat and Challenge of In-Home Entertainment

An important disruptive force coming into play for Walt and other studio heads in the post-war period was the growing popularity of a new in-home entertainment device called television with the potential to disrupt the movie-going habits of the public.

Recall that Walt was introduced to the potential importance of television during distribution contract renewal negotiations in 1936 with United Artists, who insisted on maintaining all television rights to Disney products. Walt refused to sign over rights to something he said he knew nothing about, and instead signed a distribution agreement with the larger RKO.

Walt began to pay closer attention to this new invention and its implications as early as 1944. In the company's annual report for that year, Walt wrote: "We have been working hard on our postwar plans. We have thought a lot about television...television will need the same basic kind of entertainment the public has always demanded."[35] He told his shareholders that television would have "a tremendous impact on the world of entertainment, motion pictures included."[36]

By 1945, according to a report in *The New York Times*, Walt Disney Productions had "applied to the Federal Communications Commission for a television and FM band in southern California preliminary to the establishment of three to five television stations in various parts of the country. ... Current plans call for the use of the cartoon medium and the 'live' action and cartoon combination in the Disney brand of television entertainment."[37] Fearing the expense involved when the studio had no further access to capital, and concerned that the current technological limitation of black-and-white broadcasting wasn't suitable for the studio's animation products, Roy eventually withdrew the application.[38]

Walt's fascination with television, however, didn't waver, and in 1947 Roy ordered ten-inch television sets for each of the executives so that they could monitor the potential of this emerging entertainment medium.[39]

Walt continued to think about whether and how he could benefit his business by entering the new medium of television to deliver entertainment directly into people's homes. In 1948 he spent a week in New York dedicated to observing and understanding first-hand what was being done in television. Walt wrote back to the studio expressing his conclusion that "television is the coming thing,"[40] and that it was going to be important for him to participate.

Walt was always one to embrace the possibilities of new technologies and the opportunities that they bring for business innovation and industry disruption through first-mover advantage. He was also dismissive of the general consensus of executives from other major film studios that television posed a significant threat to them. Their fear of the negative and destructive impact television would have on the motion picture industry caused them to do everything in their power to erect barriers against technological change. Walt's entrepreneurial curiosity, on the other hand, had him actively investigating its potential to open doors to new business opportunities.

Given the immediacy of television and its different business model in which content was paid for by sponsors and provided for free to consumers, Walt quickly identified the essence of the main challenge television posed. His current business model supported the production of costly hand-crafted animation that required long development times. Television required the exact opposite: low costs and speedy production.[41]

Walt was enthusiastic about the potential of television to create demand for Disney films and to grow box-office receipts. Still, there were many uncertainties about whether or not venturing into the medium was prudent for the studio. Walt hired an independent third party to investigate and received their report in September 1950, which advised the studio to start with a trial run and thereby avoid running headlong into a commitment to develop, produce, and deliver a TV series.

To get things started, Walt needed a television producer to oversee the development of programs. One day, without warning, Walt approached his press agent Bill Walsh to inform him of his new role. "But I don't have any experiences of a producer," Walsh told Walt. Given how new television was, Walt replied: "Who does?"[42]

There was a third factor in play transforming the studio's business direction beyond Walt's new interest in telling stories through live action and documentaries and his anticipation of the impact of television on his future business plans. The business environment pertaining to movie distribution was also changing due to government intervention.

Where movies had traditionally been sold and bought in bundled multi-film packages from the movie studios, the government decreed that this would no longer be allowed. Each movie would have to stand on its own, without the bundling of products to guarantee distribution. As a result of this imposed change in the market structure, major movie studios began to divest themselves of their theatre chains. This created opportunities for independent studios with high quality products and marketing savvy, like Disney, to compete more effectively by creating consumer pull for their films. The Disney brand would give the studio leverage in the marketplace.

1. Gabler, *Walt Disney*, 413.
2. Lesjak, *Service with Character*, Appendix IX, 247.
3. Lesjak, *Service with Character*, Appendix VIII, 245.
4. Lesjak, *Service with Character*, 207.
5. Holliss & Sibley, *The Disney Studio Story*, 53.
6. Sam Gennawey, *The Disneyland Story*, 9.
7. See Lesjac, *Service with Character*, 209–210.
8. Holliss & Sibley, *The Disney Studio Story*, 54.
9. Walt quoted in Holliss & Sibley, *The Disney Studio Story*, 55.
10. Walt Disney quoted in Jordan Young, *Dali, Disney and Destiny*, loc. 102.
11. Young, *Dali, Disney and Destiny*, loc. 227.
12. Hench quoted in Young, *Dali, Disney and Destiny*, loc. 139.
13. Young, *Dali, Disney and Destiny*, loc. 253.
14. Young, *Dali, Disney and Destiny*, loc. 575.
15. Young, *Dali, Disney and Destiny*, loc. 575.
16. Young, *Dali, Disney and Destiny*, loc. 575.
17. Young, *Dali, Disney and Destiny*, loc. 575.
18. Holliss & Sibley, *The Disney Studio Story*, 56.
19. Holliss & Sibley, *The Disney Studio Story*, 56.
20. Holliss & Sibley, *The Disney Studio Story*, 57.
21. Jackson (ed.), *Walt Disney: Conversations*, 32.
22. Holliss & Sibley, *The Disney Studio Story*, 59.
23. Gabler, *Walt Disney*, 470.
24. Gabler, *Walt Disney*, 470.
25. Holliss & Sibley, *The Disney Studio Story*, 60.
26. Barrier, *The Animated Man*, 222.
27. Lesjak, *Service with Character*, 208.
28. Thomas, *Walt Disney*, 212.
29. See Gabler, *Walt Disney*, 470.
30. Gabler, *Walt Disney*, 470.
31. Thomas, *Building a Company*, 172.
32. Gabler, *Walt Disney*, 468–470.

33. Holliss & Sibley, *The Disney Studio Story*, 59.

34. Holliss & Sibley, *The Disney Studio Story*, 60.

35. Lesjak, *Service with Character*, 209.

36. Holliss & Sibley, *The Disney Studio Story*, 60.

37. In Barrier, *The Animated Man*, p. 228; see also Holliss & Sibley, *The Disney Studio Story*, 60.

38. Gabler, *Walt Disney*, 502.

39. Gabler, *Walt Disney*, 503.

40. Walt to nurse Hazel George, in Gabler, *Walt Disney*, 503.

41. See Gabler, *Walt Disney*, 228.

42. Quoted in "The Genesis of Disney Television," The Walt Disney Family Museum, waltdisney.org/blog/genesis-disney-television, accessed November 7, 2016.

CHAPTER SEVENTEEN

Mickey Mouse Park and the Roots of Disneyland

Walt made his mark in animation by applying his natural talent in storytelling and by investing in and capitalizing on the direct development and commercial application of new technological advances within his industry and capitalizing on their benefits. When he started in animation, he was a self-trained outsider living in remote Kansas City, Missouri, competing against the entrenched industry leaders in bustling New York City.

It was a similar story when it came to amusement parks. Walt was an outsider, and it is this outsider's perspective that allowed him to bring new thinking and new solutions to the big problems facing that industry in a way that the insiders were immunized from perceiving.

The amusement park owners and managers of the 1940s operated with a set of shared values codified as conventional wisdom, and had thereby chained themselves to a worldview—or paradigm—that Walt would show to be at odds with the unarticulated values of existing amusement park customers and the general population.

Prior to Walt's entry into the business, amusement park owners were primarily focused on setting low expectations for customers and operating to those low standards by providing customers with the minimum amount of quality and value to profitably maintain their business operations. Walt's key insight was that by doing so, amusement park and midway operators were limiting themselves to serving a small subset of the potential market. They were not customer-focused, and almost without exception, were barely customer-sensitive in the way we understand those terms today and in the way Walt understood them. Walt tried to gauge the happiness of customers as the measurement of business success and untapped business potential, always challenging himself and his staff to stretch the boundaries of their creativity to offer more to customers than a mere business transaction.

Just as Walt had rethought what an animated film could be, and that for a full-length feature to succeed it would have to be fundamentally different from the regular fare of cartoon shorts audiences were familiar with, he had also imagined a different view of what an amusement park could be. He had spent years thinking about how to solve the problem of creating a place where parents could take their children and enjoy themselves sharing experiences and doing things *together*.

Disneyland opened in 1955. It was designed with children in mind, but it was never designed *for* children. It was built for Walt and other adults he imagined were just like him, and wanted the same things he wished for from a park. Walt told biographer Bob Thomas, "Disneyland isn't designed for children. When does a person stop being a child? Can you say that a child is ever entirely eliminated from an adult? I believe that the right kind of entertainment can appeal to all persons, young and old. I want Disneyland to be a place where parents can bring their children—or come by themselves and still have a good time."[1]

The story of the birth of the concept for Disneyland was told many times by Walt:

> Well, it came about when my daughters were very young, and Saturday was always Daddy's day with the two daughters. So we'd start out and try to go someplace, you know, different things, and I'd take them to the merry-go-round, and I took them different places and as I'd sit while they rode the merry-go-round and did all these things—sit on a bench, you know, eating peanuts—I felt that there should be something built, some kind of amusement enterprise where the parents and the children could have fun together. So that's how Disneyland started. It took many years. It was a period of maybe fifteen years developing. I started with many ideas, threw them away, started all over again. And eventually it evolved into what you see today at Disneyland. But it all started from a daddy with two daughters wondering where he could take them where he could have a little fun with them, too.[2]

That's the story from the daddy perspective. But one of Walt's great attributes was his ability to use his imagination to experience something from multiple points of view. Here's another perspective from Walt, the child's perspective:

> I wanted to create a place where a daddy could go and have as much fun as his little girls and boys. Just imagine if you're a little girl, looking forward all week to taking a trip to the park with your dad, and you get on a horse that won't jump. That's awful. Add to this chipped paint, stale popcorn, limp cotton candy and unpleasant employees. What a disappointment.[3]

Walt's idea for a permanent family-friendly amusement park started out to be very conventional, but over the years was refined and expanded into an innovative new concept that was completely different from anything that existed at the time. He honed it over the years and did research during his travels, personally visiting countless parks, state and county fairs, circuses, carnivals, and national parks. He observed the things that made them appealing to visitors while paying special attention to things visitors disliked. Apparently, Coney Island was "so battered and tawdry and the ride operators were so hostile that Walt felt a momentary urge to abandon the idea of an amusement park," wrote Disney biographer Bob Thomas in *Walt Disney: An American Original*. The closest thing Walt could find anywhere in the world to his own vision for a family-friendly park was Tivoli Gardens in Copenhagen, which Walt admired for its cleanliness, variety of family-friendly activities, festive ambiance, and grandeur.[4]

In contrast to the parks he had seen, Walt described what he was trying to achieve at Disneyland: "Physically, Disneyland would be a small world in itself—it would encompass the essence of the things that were good and true in American life. It would reflect the faith and challenge of the future, the entertainment, the interest in intelligently presented facts, the stimulation of the imagination, the standards of health and achievement, and above all, a sense of strength, contentment and well-being."[5] "It will be," said Walt, "a place for the people to find happiness and knowledge."[6]

Walt saw the potential customer base for his park as families, not thrill-seekers, and hence his target audience was far larger than those who were then current customers of amusement parks and midways. From Walt's perspective, most families stayed away from such places because they weren't safe, clean, friendly or fun. In fact, most had reputations for being downright dangerous and magnets for attracting elements of society that engaged in questionable behavior that parents with young children would prefer to avoid.

American carnivals and midways had a long-time reputation for providing exotic entertainment and thrills, while at the same time attracting riff-raff. Chicago University History Professor Neil Harris writes in *Designing Disney's Theme Parks* that in the 1920s, in addition to permanent parks in many large cities, there were more than 150 touring troupes setting up successive temporary residency in smaller towns:

> While the amusement parks and Coney Islands of the world had apparently cleaned themselves up and abandoned the more salacious and dishonest attractions, the travelling carnivals constituted a clear menace to public morals, their girlie shows as dangerous to health as the germ-laden pink lemonade they peddled. Tawdry, violent, dishonest, the carnivals represented the dark side of the recreational dream, excursions into forbidden territory that had to be cleansed or at least monitored. State legislation now mandated periodic inspections, while an association of carnival owners declared itself ready

to police the ranks. The quest for sanitized decency that Walt Disney adopted had a lengthy American pedigree.[7]

Walt's first tentative actions towards realizing the idea of a park occurred during the building of the new Burbank studio in 1939. Walt sent supervising animator Dave Hand to the new studio construction site to find a spot on the lot where a small park could be built.

As the automobile age began to boom in the late 1940s and early 1950s, people were looking for places to go and things to do. Tours of Hollywood studios were becoming very popular with motorists, giving fans a behind-the-scenes peek and, if lucky, the chance to see a movie star. The studios could charge for the tours and sell bagged lunches, refreshments, and studio-lot souvenir maps as a way to create a new stream of revenues.

Walt had received letters at the studio from Disney fans requesting studio tours, but he felt that with animation there wasn't much to see, and fans would leave disappointed. Walt's answer to the studio tour was his 1941 movie *The Reluctant Dragon*, an animated and live-action film to show off the new Burbank studio and educate the curious about how Disney animated films are made.

If fans wanted to come to the studio to get a glimpse of Mickey Mouse, Walt began thinking that he could offer them a park instead of a tour—a park where grown-ups and kids could do things together. Unbeknownst to anybody else, he had been actively planning the park in his head for more than ten years. If people were to come to a park, the park had to contain things to do. The many eclectic hobbies and peculiar interests that Walt indulged himself in over the years—the intricate handcrafted building of miniature model rooms and scenes; his fascination with wind-up toys purchased in Europe and an antique mechanical bird in a cage that would sing and move which he purchased in New Orleans in 1946; the building of scale-sized working steam trains and the installation of a working railroad at his Carolwood Drive home—all played a role in the creation and development of Walt's park. Especially trains.

Building Trains and Laying Track

Leading Disney animators Ward Kimball and Ollie Johnston were train aficionados. Kimball bought his first train, an 1881 narrow-gauge Baldwin locomotive, in 1938. He had it delivered to his San Gabriel home, and constructed 900 feet of track on which it ran. Johnston began building a ride-on steamer in 1946 in his backyard in Santa Monica.

One day in December 1947, Walt was discovered building a model train set on his office desk, and adding trees and other landscape features. He wrote in a letter to his sister, Ruth:

I bought myself a birthday present. Something I've wanted all my life—an electric train. Being a girl, you probably can't understand how much I wanted one when I was a kid, but I've got one now and what fun I'm having. I have it set up in one of the outer rooms adjoining my office so I can play with it in my spare moments.[8]

When Kimball and Johnston heard that Walt was building a train set in his office, they paid him a visit. That's when Walt discovered that Kimball and Johnston had real trains, and he wanted one, too.

With the help of animators Kimball, Johnston, and Roger Broggie, mechanical engineer and head of the studio machine shop, Walt began collecting ideas and researching authentic details for plans to build a working one-eighth-scale model railway of his own.

A big part of the attraction of trains for Walt was nostalgia, as it was for an entire generation that had seen the world progress rapidly and experienced the familiar sights and sounds of their youth disappear forever, to be replaced by modern technological advancements. The hand-crafted buildings and machines that brought America into the twentieth century and now represented the old world were being sold off as scrap or finding their way into the hands of collectors. It wasn't just trains. Whole towns that had been abandoned and forgotten to become "ghost towns" were being bought up, moved, and preserved as historic attractions. The nostalgic era of Walt's childhood was being dismantled at an alarmingly rapid pace and was fading into memory.

The public's nostalgia for railways and the building of model replicas culminated in the creation of the Chicago Railroad Fair in the summer of 1948. The fair was organized to include thirty-eight major American railroads, and to celebrate the 100th anniversary of the first steam engine to enter Chicago.

Walt was keenly interested in attending, and invited senior animator and fellow train enthusiast Kimball to join him. What was for Kimball to be a trip with Walt to celebrate trains was something entirely different for Walt. Yes, Walt was enthusiastic about the nostalgia surrounding trains, as was Kimball, but for Walt, the trip was about more than trains. He was travelling with a secret agenda.

For Walt, attending the Chicago Railroad Fair was more about finding the future than celebrating the past. Having started along the path of designing a family-oriented park, he was just as interested in studying the organizational and attraction elements of the fair as he was in admiring the romanticism of the trains of his youth.

The Chicago Railroad Fair of 1948 would have a significant impact on Walt's conception and development of what would become Disneyland. History professor Karal Ann Marling observes in *Designing Disney's Theme Parks*:

At the fair, as would be the case in Disneyland, a railroad defined the boundaries of the grounds, served as the major artery of internal transportation, and ultimately determined the scale of the buildings adjacent to the tracks. Anxious to promote the railroad as a kind of magic carpet to vacationland, participating lines presented a series of prototypical "lands" or villages, re-creating well-known tourist meccas along their respective routes. The Illinois Central set up a replica of the French Quarter in New Orleans. A consortium of western lines built a dude ranch and slice of a generic national park with a mechanical geyser guaranteed to erupt every fifteen minutes. And the Santa Fe, of course, had Indian villages: pueblos, trading posts, tepees, and all. In each venue, the illusion of being there was sustained by workers in appropriate garb and by restaurants with matching cuisine. As Walt made mental notes about the menus and the outfits, the future Frontierland, Fantasyland, Adventureland, and Tomorrowland of Disneyland were only a daydream away.[9]

There had been many world's fairs and other nostalgic public attractions. What made this exhibit different, notes Marling, "was the coherence and concentration of the experience, the sensation of having taken the train on a whirlwind journey through most of the nation's beauty spots in a single day. What was different, too, was the dramatic unity enforced by the pageant, which gave every exhibit a place in a powerful narrative whole."[10]

On the return train trip to California, Kimball recalled, Walt talked enthusiastically about building a park something like the railroad fair, and in Kimball's words, "Disneyland was already forming in his mind."[11]

Within a few days of returning from Chicago on August 31, 1948, Walt made it known in a memo that he wanted to build a "Mickey Mouse Park" on sixteen acres of vacant land across from the Disney studio on Riverside Drive. The park was to include an old-fashioned town square with a railroad station, town hall, opera house, movie theatre, streetcars, and a stagecoach. The town square would be used to provide guests an opportunity to meet some of the Disney characters. Other areas of the park would feature an old western town, a farm, a riverboat, a circus, and some midway rides. Walt wasted no time in initiating a search for a suitable steam engine to purchase.

Shortly after Walt returned from Chicago, story artist and special effects expert John Hench spotted him pacing-off the lot across the street. "I knew he was measuring space for something...he'd walk a certain direction, then walk another way." When Hench later asked Walt what he was doing "across the street, tramping around in those weeds," he told Hench about his plans for a park. Walt was looking at the empty land and visualizing the imagined park in his mind, mentally constructing many of the types of attractions he would eventually build at Disneyland.[12]

Also after returning from Chicago, Walt soon began machining parts and building his own miniature train with the expert help of Roger Broggie and his staff in the machine shop at the Burbank studio. When blueprints for the train Walt wanted to build were provided in January 1949, Broggie allocated work to the shop's machinists. It wasn't enough for Walt to watch and wait; he wanted to help. Broggie wrote in 1952:

> Walt Disney came into the shop and learned to operate all the machine tools by making some of the parts himself. He made the whistle, flag stands and hand rails on the lathe. He learned sheet metal work by laying out and fabricating the headlamp and smoke stack. Then [he] made numerous parts in the milling machine and learned to silver solder and braze on many small fittings.[13]

Walt would often return to the studio's machine shop in the evenings to work on his train. The train was finished by the end of the year, and on Christmas Eve of 1949 it made its inaugural trial run on a small loop of track built on the studio lawn.

Walt's train would be showcased at the new home he was having built on a five-acre lot purchased on June 1, 1948, on North Carolwood Drive, near Beverly Hills. The idea to build what would become known as Carolwood Pacific Railroad was presented by Walt to his wife, Lillian, and to his daughters, Diane and Sharon, as a whimsical fancy and a happy inspiration of the moment. In reality, and unknown at the time to anyone but Walt, it was a practice run for a much bigger idea—a scale-sized train attraction and surrounding berm for a future Disney park.

Not to be outdone by railroad enthusiasts Kimball and Johnston, when the Carolwood Pacific line was completed in 1950 it consisted of a forty-foot timber trestle, two tunnels, eleven switches, and twenty-six hundred feet of rail. Walt built a steep earth berm around the property to contain the noise and keep peace with his neighbors.

Walt's real pride and joy was the yellow caboose, which he later built on his own in the red barn behind his home that served as his tool shop. "The caboose," writes Marling in *Designing Disney's Theme Parks*, "was a miniaturist's dream. Every detail was correct, down to the acanthus leaves on the legs of the pot-bellied stove and the text of the little newspaper tossed aside by a sleepy switchman whose unseen presence could be deduced from the rumpled little bunk alongside the stove."[14]

Inspiration Through Research and Imagination

When Walt was working on his trains, he was assuredly also thinking about his park, and how old trains would be a central feature and attraction. As Walt's ideas on how to build a park developed, he began to visit and study other parks to identify what was good and bad about them. He would spend countless hours trying to imagine how he could build something better that would improve the customer experience.

Walt was on a vacation in Europe in 1950 when he visited the beautiful Tivoli Gardens in Copenhagen with popular radio and TV personality Art Linkletter. "Unlike the cheap, curbside funlands of Los Angeles," notes Karal Ann Marling in *Designing Disney's Theme Parks*, "the 1843 park in Copenhagen had a beautiful natural setting, fine restaurants, high standards of cleanliness, and plenty of mild amusements for families to enjoy as a group."[15] It was here that Walt found something close to what he was trying to imagine.

"As we walked through it," recalled Linkletter later, "I had my first experience of Walt Disney's childlike delight in the enjoyment of seeing families and in the cleanliness and the orderliness of everything. He was making notes all the time about the lights, the chairs, the seats, and the food." When Linkletter asked Walt what he was doing, he was told, "I'm just making notes about something that I've always dreamed of, a great, great playground for the children and the families of America."[16]

Walt found his visit to Tivoli inspiring, giving him renewed confidence that building a beautiful park had merit in its own right, beyond a rest stop for the studio tour crowd. With Tivoli as his foundation, Walt began to transform the idea of a children's Mickey Mouse park into a uniquely American Tivoli or a permanent American world's fair dedicated to fun, education, and America's heritage.

Keeping his cards close to his chest, he did much of his early research himself, talking to amusement park owners about mundane operational issues like how the rides worked, what people bought at the concession stands, and how people lined up for rides. There was a small family run amusement center in Los Angeles that Walt would frequently visit. The proprietor recalled: "Our park was very tiny. There was a carousel, a little train ride, and another little boat ride for children. ... Walt was out there almost every day, sitting on the end of the bench, watching how children enjoyed the rides. ... He also talked to a lot of the children, which is what he enjoyed the most. He challenged them. 'How was that horse you were riding? What color was it painted? Did you like it?'"[17]

A Christmas Gift: Discovering the Power of Television as a New Path Forward

In the summer of 1950, the Coca-Cola Company approached Walt with an offer to invest $100,000 to sponsor a one-hour television Christmas special. Walt accepted, resulting in Disney's first incursion into television. Roy, too, was extremely enthusiastic about the idea, noting in a memo to

Walt that it would provide the soon-to-be-released *Alice In Wonderland* with a "tremendous send-off" and allow them to "find out a lot about television that we don't know now."[18]

Roy also showed that he had learned to embrace Walt's timeless enthusiasm for respecting the audience and delivering the highest quality product. He wrote a note to Walt that sounded a lot like the notes of optimism and enthusiasm that Walt had written to Roy in their early days: "You think in terms of pouring every dollar they give us into the show...." wrote Roy to Walt. "Give them a socko show that will be the talk of the industry—or even broader than that—the talk of the entertainment world."[19]

The Christmas Day special, *One Hour in Wonderland*, was aired on NBC. It was based around, and primarily served as an advance promotion for, Walt's next animated feature, *Alice in Wonderland*. The show previewed portions of the film in a black-and-white broadcast and included several cartoons and celebrity appearances. Walt made his first on-screen TV appearance to the public as host for the show, and his two daughters, Diane and Sharon, had small cameo appearances.

The public's enthusiasm for the Disney brand and their curiosity for the new medium of television made *One Hour in Wonderland* a spectacular success with both audiences and critics. It attracted an estimated audience of twenty million viewers, which at the time was ninety percent of the total television viewing audience.[20]

Having now participated in the medium, Walt was more fully able to comprehend and envision the power of television as a new distribution channel and promotional device for the studio. The TV special also demonstrated for Walt the heretofore unrecognized power of the Disney brand to create immense economic value within the television ecosystem by drawing a large audience for networks and their sponsors.

Reflecting on his initial TV experience, Walt wrote in the 1950 corporate annual report:

> I regard television as one of our most important channels for the development of a new motion picture audience. Millions of televiewers never go to a picture theatre, and countless others infrequently. ... In these highly competitive days, we must use the television screen along with every other promotion medium, to increase our potential audience.[21]

The Seeds of Breakout Thinking

By 1951, the studio was busier than ever, having returned to feature-length animation with the release of *Cinderella* the previous year and adding live-action features and popular documentaries into the production schedule. Out of necessity, the studio had become a diversified entertainment company. Walt and Roy had established a number of subsidiary companies to manage their many business affairs around the world, including movie production, film distribution, music publishing, and merchandise licensing.

On March 30, 1951, three months after the Christmas airing of *One Hour in Wonderland*, Walt held a meeting with four of his executives to discuss the possibility of producing a half-hour weekly TV show and to engage them in the brainstorming of ideas. Disney executive Harry Tytle's journal notes reflect the purpose of the meeting: "The plan of the program is to boost our theatrical attendance, exploit merchandising, etc., along with the selling of television shows. We mainly discussed various items that would go into the format...."[22]

The format would include black-and-white cartoons (color TVs were not yet commercially available), simplified animation done specifically for television, and live-action subjects. As a follow-up to the meeting, Walt charged his staff with developing three show ideas by the end of the year.[23]

With all of the activity going on at the studio, and a large number of diverse projects being worked on and advanced simultaneously, more than anything else the development of an amusement park had captured Walt's interest. The challenge of converting these ideas from a fuzzy and kaleidoscopic concept into a viable commercial project began to gain momentum.

Walt still had his eyes set on the sixteen-acre plot of studio-owned land across the road from the studio on Riverside Drive. Now, for the first time, he conveyed his idea for a park and its attractions to artists for development. Art director and movie set designer Harper Goff was assigned the task of drawing up concept renderings for the park showing many elements of an old town with a train, riverboats, and a small petting farm. "I don't want to just entertain kids with pony rides and swings," Walt instructed Goff, "I want them to learn something about their heritage."[24]

Moving the project along from a fanciful idea, to a concept, to reality was no easy job for Walt, because to achieve his goal, he first had to convince others to join him and to embrace his vision. Walt Disney Productions had a history of innovation and success, but because it was seemingly always one failed project away from insolvency, Walt found it difficult to convince anybody that building a Mickey Mouse park had business merit and was worthy of serious consideration at this time. This was especially true of Roy, who was burdened with managing the much weightier financial concerns of the studio.

That Roy had little patience for talk of an amusement park shouldn't be surprising given the reputation of amusement parks and fairgrounds, and the generally poor experience of attending one. As with the decision to proceed to make *Snow White and the Seven Dwarfs* fifteen years earlier and the concern that it would distract Walt's attention from what was then the core business of producing cartoon shorts, people thought the idea of Walt spending his time occupied with a Disney park was outlandish when what was needed most was his complete devotion and dedication to creating profitable movies to relieve the pressure of the studio's ever-increasing debt burden.

Knowing Walt's devotion to the success of the studio, Roy found his brother's increasing interest in building a park to be perplexing. In a 1951 correspondence he wrote: "Walt does a lot of talking about an amusement park, but really I don't know how deep his interest really is. I think he's more interested in ideas that would be good in an amusement park than in actually running one himself."[25]

From Roy's perspective, the studio was just getting back on track and finding its groove after years of stagnation brought on by World War II, and he was worried about a number of things: that Walt didn't know anything about the amusement park business; that building and operating an amusement park could put the company under serious financial strain; that shareholders wouldn't go along with such a far-fetched idea; and that Walt's focus would be diverted from where it was needed most—ensuring the success of the film projects already in progress, including the major animated features *Alice in Wonderland*, *Peter Pan*, *Lady and the Tramp*, and *Sleeping Beauty*, plus the live-action films being made in England, and the ongoing production of cartoon shorts and various other projects such as the popular and highly profitable True-Life Adventures documentary series. Perhaps most of all, Roy was worried about the inability of the company to make financial progress and put an end to the revolving door of bank loans needed to remain viable.

What Roy didn't know at the time was that Walt was already furtively engaged in research and planning, and visiting as many tourist attractions as he could fit into his busy schedule, including zoos, fairs, circuses, museums, and many others.

Television and Parks: Islands Without a Bridge

In June 1951, six months after the successful Christmas Day TV special, Walt was invited to a meeting in New York with ABC-Paramount chairman Leonard Goldenson and ABC president Robert Kintner.

At the time ABC was a small broadcasting network struggling to compete and survive against NBC and CBS, the two more established major U.S. television networks. Goldenson was interested in talking to Walt about providing Disney programming content to the ABC network. Walt was intrigued enough to attend the meeting, but not interested enough to commit the resources required to diversify into television. Instead, he kept turning the conversation toward describing his ideas for a studio park—Disneyland—which was occupying a considerable amount of his thought and energy. Donn Tatum, who worked for ABC at the time and was later hired by Walt, was at the meeting between Walt and Goldenson and recalled Walt's perspective: "Well," said Walt, "you want to talk to me about television and I want to talk about Disneyland, so why don't we talk about the two together?"[26]

Tatum later reflected back on the meeting, noting that after a relatively short discussion about producing shows for ABC, Walt "started to talk about Disneyland."

> It was the first time I'd ever heard about it and he talked for a good hour and a half about it: His ideas for it and his ambitions for it. Now that I can finally look back at the arrangement that he made and I can see that he was baiting Mr. Goldenson and Mr. Kintner. He was trying to spark their interest in Disneyland because he probably was at least fondling the thought in his mind then that somehow he could use his desirability as a new television producer as a means of getting some help in developing this idea of his for an amusement park.[27]

With the two sides talking past each other, nothing of substance developed, other than to establish the foundation for a business relationship that would prove to be important in the years to come.

Ideas for TV shows continued to be developed at the studio, and while nothing came of it at this time, seeds for Disney's future in television were being planted and nurtured.

Having now seen how powerful the Disney brand was at drawing TV viewers, Roy had visions of the immense cash value of using television to support the studio's operations through a recycling of the existing Disney film inventory and the attraction of corporate sponsors to underwrite new TV film production. Roy wrote to Walt in September 1951, "We wouldn't have the pressure of putting entertainment product into work unless you really felt good about it, and that would give us a better batting average in the entertainment field and more safety—as well as more peace of mind. The sponsored films would change our business over to almost a new business with unlimited possibilities, in place of the ever-pinching outlook in the strictly theatrical field."[28]

The studio's successful television premiere in 1950 was followed up with *The Walt Disney Christmas Special* which aired on Christmas Day, 1951, this time on CBS, with Johnson & Johnson as the sponsor. Once again the show was an immense success, but with a number of ongoing projects, including Walt's interest in building a park and work on both animated and live-action features, the desire to create a weekly television series remained on hold. Walt understood that he would have to set up a separate infrastructure for

TV production, and perceived it to be a lot of extra work with very little added value or profit to the business at this time.

Walt's decision to proceed cautiously and not just jump into television production had two likely sources. The first was the difficulty Walt was having in finding corporate sponsors willing to make a long-term commitment to fund the development of television movies or series. Talks had been initiated with Ford, Chrysler, and Lever Brothers, but had all stalled, in part because corporate sponsors were hesitant to meet Walt's demand for a three-year sponsorship commitment.[29]

The second reason Walt wanted to proceed cautiously with television was that in spite of the success of *One Hour in Wonderland* in attracting a huge audience and promoting viewer interest in *Alice in Wonderland*, when the film was finally released in July 1951, its box-office performance was weak. The studio had invested almost $4 million in the project, exceeding the cost of *Cinderella* by almost a million dollars.[30] The high cost of creating *Alice in Wonderland* was related to the 50,000 man hours and 700,000 individual drawings required, but there was no other way to make a feature animated film that would satisfy Walt's demand for quality.

The movie premiered in London, England, on July 26, 1951, and in New York City two days later. Most critics at the time panned the movie, especially the British critics. The studio posted a loss for its initial release in excess of a million dollars, and demonstrated that while product promotion on TV could substantially raise consumer awareness, it was no guarantor of box office success.[31]

Walt later attributed the lack of success of *Alice in Wonderland* to the quirkiness of the story and that it was "filled with weird characters you couldn't get with" and had a heroine who "wasn't very sympathetic."[32]

Gross income at the studio fell almost a million dollars in 1951, and while the business was still able to turn a profit, the bottom line dropped almost $300,000 to $429,840 in 1951 from over $700,000 in 1950.[33]

Disneyland's Labored Birth

Walt and Roy headed into 1952 in agreement that doing something more in television was desirable, but felt the need to proceed with caution. Walt knew that he would have to find a way to integrate television into his business model in order to keep up with the impact of changing technology on the growing desire of consumers for in-home entertainment.

If Roy had been initially perplexed about Walt's interest in building a park given how he perceived it to be a distraction from concentrating on more important core business concerns, by early 1952 he appears to have at least recognized the seriousness of Walt's desire to pursue the idea. Roy also knew that the board of directors would not be receptive to allocating resources to such a venture.

Corresponding with Walt from New York in March 1952, Roy indicated that he had given considerable thought to the "Amusement Park matter" and advised Walt to consider approaching the board of directors for approval to alter his business relationship with the company. Roy suggested that Walt propose to the board that they allow him to work on the park and other creative entrepreneurial ventures that the board refused to support and fund, outside of and separate from his work for Walt Disney Productions. "In this way," wrote Roy, "this Amus. Park idea could be the vehicle to straighten out your entire matters."[34]

With this avenue to pursuing the development of a park now open and having Roy's support, Walt, who was chairman of the board, and Roy, who was CEO and vice-chairman, met with and received board approval in March 1952 for Walt to pursue the development of the park and television story concepts free from the studio's oversight, interference, and governance constraints. Walt was granted what he very much desired: full control over the development of the park and TV story ideas without interference or the need to rely on funding approval and oversight from Roy, studio bankers, and the studio's board of directors. Walt's first responsibility would remain as leading the studio and maintaining his authorities, responsibilities, and obligations pursuant to the interests of Walt Disney Productions.

The work Walt sought to do outside the studio's auspices was still directly connected to supporting and enhancing the studio's capabilities and profit potential. As a result, Roy was able to justify and provide a small budgeted amount for research and development of the park concept. Walt, however, would have to take on the challenge of finding ways to fund the park's development on his own should he choose to do so. Walt set up his own entity, Disneyland, Incorporated, for this purpose.[35]

Having now been cleared by the Disney board to pursue opportunities outside of his official studio business duties, Walt moved forward quickly to seek approval to build his park. Within weeks of the board meeting, Walt submitted a six-page prospectus to Burbank city council for approval to build a $1.5 million park on the studio-owned property across the street from the studio. The submission contained references to a canal boat moving past scenes from Disney films, a spaceship, a submarine ride, and a nature preserve on an island that could be viewed from a paddle wheel boat. The prospectus noted that there would be "no roller coasters or other rides in the cheap thrill category."[36]

Walt was quoted about the park in the *Burbank Daily Review* on March 27, 1952: "Disneyland will be something of a fair, an exhibition, a playground, a community center, a museum of living facts and a showplace of beauty and magic." The park would include "various scenes of Americana" and a "zoo of miniature animals." In addition, the park would also become home to a "complete television center."[37]

Walt usually kept his ideas to himself until he was ready to move forward with them, turning them over and chewing on them until they were assessed from every angle. So while he didn't talk about the park and television together, he had now linked the studio's future in television and the creation of Disneyland into a single integrated business concept.

Around this time—spring of 1952—Walt entered into negotiations with Columbia Pictures to re-acquire fifty cartoons they still controlled from their 1930 distribution deal. Almost assuredly this purchase was driven by Walt's emerging plans for television and desire to fully own and control all Disney content. The deal was concluded in June, giving Walt Disney Productions, for the first time, sole ownership of all Disney productions and characters except Oswald the Lucky Rabbit, which was owned by Universal.[38]

Not one to waste time and always looking to move forward, just days after presenting his park proposal to the city on April 3, 1952,[39] Walt arranged a meeting with the principals of a prominent LA-based architectural and engineering firm, Pereira-Luckman, to discuss building a park and to assess their interest and qualifications to provide professional assistance. Walt had known Charles Luckman for years, and Luckman's business partner, William Pereira, had once been an art director and production designer at Paramount Studios and expressed his enthusiasm for working on the project.[40] Luckman later recalled their initial meeting:

> He had a vivid mental image of it all—the streets and stores from other eras, the parade of Disney characters led by Mickey Mouse, the bright lights, the band playing, the variety of restaurants, the scenes and sets of his cartoons to serve as background for the concessions, water rides through enchanted lands, the mechanized people who could speak, the birds who could sing....[41]

Roy was able to authorize $3,000 from the studio for Pereira-Luckman to develop a preliminary concept for the Riverside site.[42]

As Walt was pushing ahead with this early incarnation of Disneyland, he continued to refine his perspective about the future economic value of television to his studio business model. He revealed some elements of his thinking in an interview with a *New York Times* reporter in June 1952. Disney biographer Neal Gabler writes:

> As Walt saw it—and he was largely alone among film executives in this respect—television was not the enemy of the motion picture; it was its ally. It might have the effect of killing off the B-movie, he told *The New York Times*, but it would help advertise movies, he

believed, and he intended to "take full advantage of its potential to create a new motion picture audience and to encourage the fullest box office patronage of our forthcoming pictures."[43]

Walt didn't have to wait very long to hear back from the City of Burbank on the fate of his park. By the end of the summer, in September 1952, he was notified that his proposal was rejected.

While the Burbank Board of Parks and Recreation gave the plan conditional approval if it was linked to a recreational area on adjoining city property, Burbank city council refused to approve it and voted it down.[44] In the words of one lawmaker, "We don't want the carny atmosphere in Burbank. We don't want people falling in the river, or merry-go-rounds squawking all day long."[45]

Walt was disappointed but not deterred by Burbank's refusal. Rather, in the short span of a few months that the city of Burbank had taken to make its decision, Walt's plans had advanced significantly from his original concept for a small studio park where families could have fun together and interact with Disney characters. He now welcomed Burbank's rejection of his idea.

Walt continued to add more ideas for park attractions into his vision while Pereira-Luckman completed their assignment and produced initial conceptual drawings for the now outdated seven-acre park on Riverside Drive. Walt was now convinced that his original thinking for a studio park was too small. He now had an opportunity to find another location without the sixteen-acre limitation of the studio's property. More space would accommodate more imagination, more possibilities, and more "plussing."

Disneyland Park had grown in Walt's mind's eye far beyond being just a meeting place to please fans of Mickey Mouse. To accommodate his new ideas, Walt was now of the opinion that nothing less than thirty acres would be required.

Television and Parks: Two Unresolved Opportunities

In the summer of 1952, from June 23 to September 3, Walt toured Europe with his family and spent some time supervising the production of his third British live-action feature, *The Sword and the Rose*.[46] While overseas, Walt received a letter from Roy revealing Roy's uneasiness with the slow pace of advancing their television prospects. Roy encouraged Walt to pick up the pace. It was important to have a weekly presence on TV, he noted, even if it was only a fifteen-minute show to promote upcoming movies.

As a means to entice quicker action by Walt, Roy articulated an additional benefit tied to Walt's current infatuation with his park: it would "be a wonderful help in the building up of our financial and corporate program for the amusement company, as it would intrigue third parties into coming into it and having a part of it."[47] In other words, a Disney presence on television might serve to advance Walt's interests in funding and building Disneyland. Gabler writes in *Walt Disney: The Triumph of the Imagination*:

> Whether Roy knew it or not at the time, and he probably did, Walt already saw this as the plan. As much as he appreciated television as a promotional tool for the features and as much as he valued the revenue that television could bring to the studio so that the company wouldn't constantly be in financial straits, Walt believed—Walt hoped—that in return for a Walt Disney television program, he could induce a network or a corporate sponsor to invest in Disneyland; that was the reason he had Roy insist on a three-year commitment. He was, in effect, trying to sell his old films and the value of his reputation to finance his park."[48]

Roy was able to accept the virtues of a small park affiliated with the studio to accommodate the burgeoning interest of tourists and their desire for studio tours. But he had little patience for considering a larger amusement park as a viable freestanding commercial entity, and refused to provide significant funds to support Walt. Roy was not prepared to bring forward a proposal for board approval to finance Walt's amusement park, which Roy and other board members would view as money wasted at a time when they had more pressing needs to attend in an already risky and difficult business environment.

With or without the approval and support of Roy and the board, Walt was not prepared to give up on his park. He realized that to continue, he would have to assume the challenge of finding the capital to develop and build it on his own. In many respects, it would be like a return to his youth, investing his money and energy into creating something new that he wholeheartedly believed in.

20,000 Leagues Under the Sea

When Walt began producing offshore live-action films in Great Britain to abide by finance laws against transferring money earned there out of the country, his ambitions were constrained by low budgets and the uncertainty of audience acceptance of Disney-branded live-action-only features. Moving into live-action films presented a whole new challenge and outlet for Walt's creativity, and an excellent opportunity to learn another aspect of the movie business in a low-risk environment.

Having released *Treasure Island* in 1950 and *The Story of Robin Hood* in 1952, and with the pending completion of *The Sword and the Rose* (released in 1953) and *Rob Roy—The Highland Rogue* (1954), Walt Disney Productions was no longer just a cartoon company. The public was accepting of Disney live-action films and documentaries such as the True-Life Adventures series, and it didn't take long for Walt to gain the confidence to create a blockbuster live-action Hollywood-style feature to rival and compete head-to-head with those of the other major Hollywood studios. He chose to make his mark by acquiring the rights to Jules Verne's adventure epic *20,000 Leagues Under the Sea*.[49]

Walt had big ambitions for his first North American live-action production, which meant it would be expensive and risky. The movie would need big Hollywood stars for the leading roles, so he settled on Kirk Douglas, James Mason, Paul Lukas, and Peter Lorre. Scenes would be shot at the Burbank studio and on-location in the Caribbean, primarily Bahamas, Jamaica, and Negril.[50] A new third soundstage with a large water tank costing $250,000 would be constructed to film scenes with the giant squid and other underwater scenes.[51] There would be costly never-done-before special effects, technological innovation in the form of the development and perfection of underwater cameras and filming techniques, the design and construction of the two-hundred foot submarine *Nautilus*, and the creation of a fearsome and massive fifty-foot giant mechanical squid.

Walt's original budget estimate in June 1952, before work began, was $3 to $4 million.[52] Surprisingly to Walt, he had Roy's full approval. Walt later commented on Roy's reaction to the cost:

> I first told him it was going to cost three million with all we had to do. It wasn't contested, and as time went on, I went down to see him and I'd say, "Looks like that thing's going to run three million, three hundred thousand." He'd just nod and smile. And then as I kept going along, we got to where it was three million, eight hundred thousand. He still nodded and smiled. And finally it got to four million, two hundred thousand, and he was still smiling. It was the first time he ever did that on a picture. For some reason, he believed in it from the very start. I got worried then. I thought there was something wrong with him. But he just had faith and confidence in it.[53]

Roy may have had more confidence than did Walt, who once again was putting everything the brothers had built on the line, but this time in a medium he was less familiar with. Set designer and production researcher Harper Goff recalled that Walt's anxiety level was high while making this film, particularly around costs. He was paying Kirk Douglas $175,000 in salary for his twelve weeks of work. When Goff showed Walt his design for the submarine *Nautilus*, Walt was concerned about the amount of detail, asking Goff, "Do you think all of this is necessary? Do you know what all of this is going to cost?"[54] Goff recalls Walt—who was now in his early 50s—remarking to him: "Harper, all the money that my brother and I have made in our lives is tied up in this one stupid picture."[55]

Secrets Behind the Zorro Mask

On December 16, 1952, having recently celebrated his 51st birthday, Walt founded his own personal company, Walt Disney Enterprises,[56] of which he was president and sole shareholder, for the purpose of developing ideas for Disneyland.[57] He bootstrapped the initial capital by selling his beloved and recently built Palm Springs vacation home and borrowing more than $100,000 against his life insurance policy, which was heretofore intended to protect his family in the case of his death. Walt stood as a man alone in this venture, with no support from his family. He quipped to a reporter in 1965 that "my wife raised the dickens with me. She wanted to know what would happen to her if something happened to me."[58]

(The name Walt Disney Enterprises would later be changed to Walt Disney Incorporated in March 1953, and then to WED Enterprises in November 1953, to remove Roy's concern that there might be confusion with the publically traded Walt Disney Productions.[59] Walt's privately owned company, from its inception through its three name iteration, is generally referred to as WED or WED Enterprises, with WED standing for the initials of Walter Elias Disney.)

One of the first people to be put on the payroll of Walt's new company, Walt Disney Enterprises, was his brother-in-law, Bill Cottrell, whom Walt hired as a vice-president to manage the new entity.[60] Cottrell was a long-time Disney employee, originally hired in 1929, and had worked in the story department for a time and then as a director. In 1941 Cottrell married Hazel Sewell, Walt's wife Lillian's sister. As a member of the family, Cottrell was well acquainted with Walt and Roy, and was on good terms with both.

"I don't know why Walt chose me," Cottrell would later say. "I could only assume that he had known me for a period of years and he knew that I was completely honest. Also, I think I knew his philosophy and his policy, and I agreed with most of it."[61] He was also chosen because Walt felt certain he was capable of doing the work and was the best person for the job.

Walt initially housed his new company in a rickety bungalow without air conditioning that had been relocated to Burbank from the old studio on Hyperion. As vice-president accountable to Walt, Cottrell's two main areas of focus were to advance the development of the Disneyland concept and develop a Disney presence in television. Walt didn't want any interference from Roy and the studio telling him how to operate WED, and drew a hard line delineating work across the two corporate entities. He was adamant that WED work was to be done in strict confidence and not be shared with the studio until Walt decided the time was right.

In early February of 1953, Walt's attention continued to be divided across a number of important projects.

Experimental undersea filming in the Pacific Ocean was just beginning for *20,000 Leagues Under the Sea*, using a new process called CinemaScope to enhance the audience viewing experience by bringing a wider image to the silver screen.[62]

On his own, as a personal side project apart from WED and the studio, Walt purchased the television rights to the book *The Mark of Zorro* with the idea of creating a weekly series for one of the TV networks.[63] Walt assigned the task of developing scripts to Cottrell, who hired staff to assist him. The building housing Walt's company became known around the studio as the Zorro building. It was a place where Walt was working on projects of his own for the studio, and was designated off-limits to studio staff.

Walt began hiring people he had previously worked with on the live-action segments of *Victory Through Air Power* and *The Three Caballeros* to work on set designs, putting them on his own personal payroll, one of which was movie art director Richard Irvine.[64]

With the expanding number of projects going on at the studio and Walt's limited amount of time to oversee his wide range of responsibilities, he was too busy to personally manage the development work being done on the park. He assigned to Irvine the task of liaising with architectural firm Pereira-Luckman and to identify and explore alternative site options for Disneyland. "I think the reason that he called me," Irvine reflected years later, "was because I was the first one that built models of a set for him, and he could see immediately the flexibility by rearranging and changing, as to how we could plan the action."[65] Walt recognized that architectural and design planning through the use of models would be critically important in the development and building of Disneyland.

It wasn't long before Irvine needed his own staff to meet Walt's expectations for developing ideas. He was granted authority to hire two respected art directors and set designers he had worked with at 20th Century Fox, Bill Martin and Marvin Davis, and a promotions expert, Nat Winecoff. Together they would develop ideas into concepts, share them with Walt, and then turn them over to the architects for further development.

Cottrell, with some scriptwriters brought over from the studio, continued to develop Zorro into a viable feature film or TV series.[66] Walt's corporate payroll was quickly expanding, but without new cash generated from sales, an accelerated rate of decline of his seed capital set in.

With only a morphing concept of what Disneyland was supposed to be, the new team kept developing various park concepts. Marvin Davis recalls producing "a hundred and thirty-three different drawings and designs, because we had no idea where the park was going to be. ... I just started out putting together the ideas that we had all talked about."[67] Davis' key task was to translate Walt's ideas onto paper and into something more tangible and more objective, so it could be shown to Walt, discussed, worked on, and improved. Given Walt's proclivity for brainstorming and building on existing ideas, it didn't take long, said Davis, before "we were planning something bigger, and we knew it wouldn't fit on the property there [on Riverside Drive]."[68]

As ideas for the park continued to multiply without restriction, so did the size of the property required to accommodate the many features and attractions. When the size of the park reached fifty acres, architect Luckman withdrew the services of his firm. Luckman had concluded that Walt's ambitions and aspirations had far outpaced his reasonable assessment of what it would cost to build a park of that size, which far exceeded the capabilities of Walt to finance its construction and operation. Luckman withdrew based on his conclusion that the park would never be built.[69]

The Leverage of Endurance and Power: Putting the Park in Play

Roy had an interest in the work being done in the Zorro building because it was inextricably linked to the studio, even though entirely funded by Walt. One might think of WED as an arm's length research and development lab, or skunkworks. Roy was more interested in Walt's development of ideas for television than an amusement park, which he thought was an inappropriate use of Walt's time and creative energy. He later commented: "For years...he has been talking about some kind of park where people could enjoy all these creations he dreams up. It sounded crazy. We were in the movie business, not the amusement-park business."[70]

As much as Roy was there to support Walt's creative ambitions and manage the business affairs of the studio, in this case he held his ground against Walt's ambitions, expressing open disapproval of Walt's park infatuation and actively discouraging Walt's efforts. Roy later commented: "We didn't know a thing in the world about amusement parks. None of us around Walt wanted any part of his amusement park. His banker used to hide under the desk when Walt started talking about that park. But you couldn't stop him. He was confident it would be wonderful."[71]

Roy had enough work to do and was happy not to hear anything about Walt's growing obsession with amusement parks. Likewise, Walt was determined to see his vision through to completion without interference from Roy. Still, Roy was astutely aware that Walt had to fund his corporate expenses, including the purchase of the rights to Zorro, and paying his staff. Roy later said in an interview, "I wondered where the money was coming from, but I didn't ask; it was his baby, and he could have it. The next I heard, he had hocked his life insurance. Still I kept quiet."[72]

As Roy slowly began to learn about the extent to which Walt had personally leveraged himself, he began to worry about Walt's financial situation. Almost all the wealth he and Walt had accumulated was invested in the success of the studio through share ownership, and the financial success of the studio had always been precarious. Now Walt was liquidating his assets and investing them in his crazy idea to build and operate a large amusement park. By doing so, he was putting his own financial security and that of his family at risk.

Roy's attempt to disassociate himself from Walt's growing obsession ended one day when he picked up the phone. At the other end was Walt's personal banker at Bank of America making a courtesy call to let Roy know that Walt had just visited the bank to discuss a loan. Roy recalled in an interview, "It's about that park," the banker said. "We went over the plans. You know, Roy, that park is a wonderful idea!" I nearly fell out of my chair. I asked whether Walt had tried to borrow money. The banker said, "Yes, sir, he did. And you know what? I loaned it to him."[73] The bank had loaned Walt $50,000 to help him fund the park's development.[74]

Until this point, Roy supported minimal funding to develop the idea of a park, not because he believed it was beneficial to the business, but because Walt wanted it.

The studio had been extremely prolific in the early 1950s, and Walt's creative energy seemed boundless. *Cinderella, Treasure Island,* the Oscar Award-winning True-Life Adventures documentary *In Beaver Valley,* and 18 short cartoons were released in 1950; *Alice In Wonderland* and the True-Life Adventures documentary *Nature's Half-Acre* and 19 shorts were released in 1951; the live-action *The Story of Robin Hood,* the documentary *Water Birds,* and 19 short cartoons were released in 1952; and *Peter Pan,* the live-action *The Sword and the Rose,* and a spate of documentaries and cartoon shorts—including Mickey's final appearance during Walt's lifetime, *The Simple Things*—were released in 1953.

Unfortunately, even with all of this creative activity, ongoing technological innovation, and more sophisticated product licensing and merchandising, the financial situation of Walt Disney Productions continued to remain tenuous and finding cash to cover working capital needs was always difficult. The biggest concern to Roy was the growing indebtedness of the business due to the high cost structure of manufacturing animated films and revenue disappointments at the box office. While the studio was able to produce a profit most years, it remained heavily indebted to Bank of America, which was increasingly reluctant to continue to lend it money.[75]

Managing the financial and business operations side of Walt Disney Productions and its many subsidiaries was a daunting enough challenge for Roy without the additional distractions and financial burden of adding an amusement park to the mix. It's no wonder Roy had neither patience nor interest in Walt's idea. According to Walt, whenever he approached Roy to discuss the park, Roy didn't want to hear about it: "He'd always suddenly get busy with some figures, so, I mean, I didn't dare bring it up. But I kept working on it and I worked on it with my own money. Not the studio's money, but my own money."[76]

But now with the conservative and cautious Bank of America exuding excitement about Walt's plans to the extent that they were willing to provide $50,000 to support his idea at the same time they were coming down hard on the studio to cut expenses, Roy felt the need to reassess his own resistance. Based on past experience, Roy knew that that there was a good chance he was underestimating Walt and that maybe there was more to this idea than had been willing to admit.[77]

To bring himself up to speed on Walt's intentions, Roy met with Bill Cottrell to gain insight into what was going on secretly behind closed doors at WED and to better understand the specifics of Walt's intentions. Two important things eventually came out of this.

First, Roy had Walt take action on advice Roy had first given to him in 1951 out of concern for Walt's personal financial situation and the protection of his family. When Roy looked into acquiring the rights to L. Frank Baum's Oz books in the summer of 1951, he discovered that Baum's heirs didn't hold those rights. Roy regarded that as a personal tragedy for the Baum family, and wanted to prevent a similar situation affecting Walt's wife and daughters. At the time, and through their own neglect, Walt was currently without a studio contract, his last contract having expired in 1947, leaving his family without suitable protection.[78]

After investigating the legalities of his options, Roy wrote a memo to Walt in September 1951 recommending that he sell his name to the company, thereby serving the best interests of the studio, which, said Roy, used Walt Disney's name "in ways that bring us a lot of revenue." A binding contract would ensure the right of the company to continue using and benefiting from the commercial value of the Walt Disney name "in place of going along as we are now on the basis of indulgence on your part."[79]

Now with Walt severely leveraged and fully invested in his own personal entrepreneurial endeavors, Roy sat down with Walt to discuss the matter again, and suggested that he form a personal holding company and lease his name to Walt Disney Productions on a royalty basis, that he do it with lawyers, and that it be presented to the board of directors at their March annual meeting for approval. Setting up this structure would help to protect Walt's wife and children should something happen to him, by providing them with a considerable source of recurring income.[80]

Second, according to Cottrell, "After viewing the conceptual plans for Disneyland and hearing Walt's dreams, Roy finally became a convert. He realized that nothing could stop Walt from pursuing his desire for a park, and that the best thing to do was what he had always done: lend his support to Walt and protect their shared interests. One of the first things Roy did was object to Walt's plan to locate the park somewhere in Burbank."[81]

If they were to proceed with Walt's dream, said Roy, it needed to be done in a bigger way. Bigger meant more money, and while Bank of America did lend $50,000 to Walt, Roy doubted that given the current indebtedness to the bank and their current skittishness about the studio's financial situation, they would be willing to invest the many millions of dollars that would be required to build the size and kind of amusement park that Walt was developing. Roy recognized immediately that if the park were to be built, an alternative source of funding would have to be found.

Until now, Roy had seen the idea of a Disney amusement park as a risky and tangential distraction from Walt Disney Productions' core business as a film studio. But now he was on board with Walt's larger vision for the park and its purpose. The original concept of a small park opposite the studio to accommodate studio visitors had grown to be something much more important: it could be a vehicle to directly support and promote everything that had come to be associated by the public with Walt Disney and the Disney brand, including Walt's nostalgia for Midwest American values and the exciting possibilities for American ingenuity, innovation, and progress.

Walt had come to understand that Disneyland could become the impetus to change his existing business model, once again. Always thinking bigger and always integrating more knowledge into a larger, more expansive conceptual overview, Walt had reformulated a position consistent with his current personal ambitions. Disney wasn't just in the *film* production business; it was in the *entertainment* business. When seen through a different lens, the park, the movies, and the merchandising could all be self-reinforcing. Walt and his team at WED had advanced their thinking about the park considerably and had produced numerous conceptual drawings and plans to define and concretize his new, larger, vision.

After reviewing the evidence and thinking it through, Roy was now convinced that the park was a valuable commercial concept and could in fact have financial merit and benefit for the shareholders of Walt Disney Productions. The challenge now was to convince and get approval from a board of directors that was cold on the idea, and acquire the funding to build it. What was once a forbidden subject between the brothers had now become Roy's own personal challenge.

Walt was enthused to know that Roy was on his side and that he would have his dedicated support in advancing the interests of the studio. He was also grateful for Roy's financial acumen in identifying a creative way to advance the development of Disneyland and television while simultaneously reducing Walt's personal financial risk in bootstrapping the venture with everything he owned.

Walt followed Roy's financial advice and formed a personal services company to sell the right to use the name Walt Disney and to sell other theme park and television services to Walt Disney Productions. Walt hired his own lawyers to negotiate contract terms with the studio's lawyers as Roy advised.

The negotiations pitted Walt's lawyers against Roy's lawyers, but an agreement was eventually reached. The proposal was then taken to the board for approval in March 1953.

After listening to a complicated series of proposals from Roy and Walt, the board reluctantly and unenthusiastically followed Roy's recommendation to approve support for the continued development of a Disneyland park and adopt an arrangement whereby Walt's company would design and build attractions and sell them to Walt Disney Productions at cost plus overhead.[82]

The Walt Disney name would be licensed for forty years, and WED would receive five to ten percent revenues from the use of the name Walt Disney on anything outside of production, such as product merchandising. Walt would receive a personal services contract in which the studio would pay him a salary of $3,000 per week for seven years on top of his studio salary of $153,000. The agreement also allowed Walt to retain ownership of the Disneyland railroad and later, when it was installed in 1959, the monorail transportation system, both of which were operated by WED under a leasing arrangement.[83] There was still more. He was permitted to make one live-action film per year independent of the studio, and to purchase up to a 25 percent interest in any live-action film by investing proportionally in the film's production cost. He was also granted a guaranteed royalty of $50,000 annually for ten years.[84]

The agreement between WED and Walt Disney Productions provided Walt with a steady stream of revenue to keep WED operating and carry on with the development of Disneyland attractions and television properties without consultation, approval, and interference from Roy or the board of directors.[85]

The accommodation that was finally reached was somewhat controversial. It could be interpreted from the outside that Walt was double dipping in the sense that he was being paid a second time for work he was already being compensated for by the studio. Even more controversial, however, was the decision by Roy and the board to approve the new arrangement without a shareholder vote. Three objecting board members felt strongly enough about the deal's impropriety that they feared a lawsuit by shareholders and subsequently resigned.[86]

In terms of monetary compensation, Disney biographer Bob Thomas notes that based on Hollywood film-studio standards, even with the additional remuneration approved by the board and contained in the new employment contract that Walt signed in April 1953, his total remuneration wasn't excessive. Not only was Walt engaged in hands-on involvement in almost all aspects of the creative and productive work being done at both companies, his total combined pay was certainly less than what other studio heads were earning.[87]

Also, unlike other studio heads who utilized their large salaries to live lavish Hollywood lifestyles, Walt was more interested in reinvesting most of the money paid to WED back into the business. This reinvestment was a direct benefit to shareholders of Walt Disney Productions through the development and execution of television programming concepts and the creation of innovative new attractions and entertainment concepts to drive up park revenues, and ultimately, lay the groundwork for more business expansion.

Not surprisingly, when news of Walt's new arrangement became known, a shareholder lawsuit was soon filed, in June 1953,[88] charging that the agreement was invalid without shareholder approval. Civil lawsuits in California at the time required the plaintiff to post a bond to cover the legal fees of the defense should they fail to prevail. Because the shareholder was unable or unwilling to post the bond, the case was dismissed, and no further challenges to the agreement were ever brought forward.[89]

Within weeks of the March 1953 board meeting, Roy Disney held a press conference to announce that Walt Disney Productions would not become involved in television production and that the studio's focus would remain on theatrical releases because that's where there was real money to be made, not in providing television content. The statement was issued to put aside rumors that the studio was about to sign a deal with one of the major TV networks.[90] Roy's statement was consistent with earlier public statements by the studio, including one Walt provided nine months earlier in June 1952, in an interview with the *Motion Picture Herald*, in which he stated that in spite of the studio's participation in two very successful television specials, "No television deal can equal what we do on theater reissues."[91]

Walt's pursuit of developing content for television broadcasting through his own private company and outside of the control and influence of the studio became the mechanism for this division of labor, and separated the risks inherent in WED's television-related pursuits from the fiduciary security of the studio's shareholders.

Disneyland Finds a Home

WED staff continued to work simultaneously on developing ideas for Disneyland and television scripts for *Zorro*. As the summer of 1953 rolled around, Walt was satisfied with the fourteen Zorro scripts that had been developed. In June, in an attempt to generate much needed income to bolster WED Enterprises' dwindling balance sheet, Walt pitched the idea of producing a Zorro TV series to the West Coast television executives of each network.

NBC, CBS, and ABC each expressed their interest but demanded that Walt produce a pilot. Walt refused, arguing that he had been in the film business for thirty years and surely there was enough evidence to prove he knew how to make a film. Television is different, he was told. Walt wasn't buying it and refused to invest in a pilot without assurance of approval. Discouraged by the resistance of the TV broadcasters, Walt put *Zorro* on hold and refocused his personal efforts on designing Disneyland and moving it forward with bigger and better plans. Meanwhile, Roy made it a priority throughout 1953 to meet with ad agencies and potential corporate sponsors in search of a way to launch a Disney-branded television series under acceptable terms.[92]

In creating ever-changing concepts and plans for the park, Walt would gather his WED staff and discuss his vision and desires in brainstorming meetings he referred to as story sessions. He would spend hours reminiscing about his childhood and Marceline's turn-of-the-century main street, describing his memories as if they were scenes in a movie script.[93]

Marvin Davis, who was both a trained architect and an art-director at 20th Century Fox, was assigned the task of translating Walt's ideas into workable site plans to aid the architects. Davis would make a list of everything Walt mentioned in meetings as the basis for creating his plans. Walt's expectation was that his staff would use the information and input generated to guide the direction of their own work, following Walt's lead in creating a visual story that would integrate the requisite elements to produce the desired psychological effect for park guests. Walt took the approach that he was building a movie set, a stage for an interactive show, with scenes that would change with the passing of time and distance as visitors moved through the park. With a single point of entrance to the park and onto Main Street, every visitor would begin his or her adventure with the same opening scene, but would experience the show unfolding in his or her own unique way.

According to Marvin Davis, the design team was instructed by Walt to build attractions that tied into Disney movies because they were valuable, recognizable, and familiar concepts that also had the benefit of being unique to Disney. Storyboards were used in planning the rides and the layouts to re-create the cinematic narrative, just as they had been used in planning movies. In the later planning stages, scale models and dioramas were produced for study, in order to observe, experience, discuss, learn, and improve the desired result.

Time was marching on, and after years of juggling concepts, Walt was becoming impatient to build his park. He now felt that after years of discovery he had explored enough ideas and concepts to proceed. He needed to make a decision about the size of property required so he could select a location. Walt and his staff had already been scouting the Los Angeles area and south along the Santa Ana Freeway to survey possible sites.

On June 1, 1953, Walt ran into architect Charles Luckman at a house party.[94] Walt asked Luckman if he knew anybody that could help him define the parameters to be considered in choosing a site and to identify viable properties that might be suitable for his park. Without hesitation Luckman recommended a property development consultancy named the Stanford Research Institute (SRI) that specialized in analytical feasibility studies, and whom Luckman had worked with successfully in building a new football stadium in Honolulu, Hawaii.

The next morning, Walt instructed Nat Winecoff to call SRI and find out what they do, and the following day, June 3, SRI's Harrison "Buzz" Price and a Texan named C.V. "Woody" Wood met with Walt, Roy, and Winecoff at the studio in the small Zorro building.

Price recalls in his memoirs that when Walt described what he wanted, it "sounded strange, unlike anything you would expect in an amusement park."

> At a time when most parks were planned in a grid with four side access, he outlined a design concept of a single park entrance passing through a turn-of-the-century main street, which would end in a circular plaza or town square. This area would feed off radially into four thematic activity areas, The World of Tomorrow, Fantasyland, Frontierland and Adventureland. Whereas most amusement parks wanted all the street visibility they could get, Walt's entire park would be hidden from the outside world by a high landscaped berm and an old-fashioned railroad encircling the perimeter on top of the berm, which would provide a view through all the internal areas of the park. He was talking about customized rides, exhibits and attractions instead of the standard off-the-shelf Ferris wheel and tunnel of love. Whereas the typical amusement park offered games and mechanical contraptions (rides), Walt's major investment would be committed to creating a storytelling environment. Rides would be subordinate to story and setting. Most shocking, there were no thrill rides, no roller coaster, no super fast fear of falling rides anywhere. The park would be located in southern California. *He would need a quarter section, 160 acres. He was in a hurry. He wanted to open in 1955.* This was a fast schedule, two years from study to ribbon cutting.[95]

The presentation by Wood and Price included two proposals with a total price tag of $25,000 plus expenses, one for a site location study, and another for a park feasibility study and economic model based on market behavior of other amusement parks and major public attractions.[96]

Based on this meeting and an agreement between the parties that the work was to remain secretive and confidential to protect against the possibility of speculative real estate price increases, Walt hired SRI to find the most suitable location for Disneyland, which Walt had now decided he wanted completed and open to the public in 1955. On behalf of Walt Disney Productions, Roy approved and paid for both studies, at a total cost to the studio of around $32,000.[97]

Before departing, Price pushed Walt for his ideas or biases on a suitable location, and was told: "You tell me," thereby revealing nothing of his own team's opinion on a preferred location.[98]

Six weeks into the project, on July 14, 1953, Price and Wood met with Walt and Roy to present their preliminary site study findings based on an analysis of available data on population growth areas, freeway access, local climate variances, smog trends, available land options, and property prices. The viable area for the park was reduced from four thousand square miles to one hundred and fifty square miles bordering the new Santa Ana Freeway from the Los Angeles county line south to Santa Ana.

SRI searched the target area for all available 160-acre sites with the help of a number of real estate agents.[99] Using a comprehensive methodology of study, Wood and Price presented to Walt and Roy four choices, including what they determined to be their number one location, an existing orange grove in Orange County, one-quarter mile south of the Santa Ana Freeway and Harbor Boulevard, and twenty-seven miles from downtown Los Angeles, placing it in the same general location that Walt's search team had already identified as optimal by speculation and conjecture alone. SRI's confirmation made it easy for Walt and Roy to agree with their assessment, placing the park in essentially the current location of Disneyland.[100]

The next step and major challenge Walt now faced was immediately visible. The preferred site consisted of seventeen individually owned properties, almost all of them family farms.[101]

The good news was that Price had been made aware of this potential site through discussions with a local real estate agent who knew that many of the owners were already talking about coming together and jointly selling to a housing developer, meaning they were already predisposed to selling.[102]

The bad news was that if anybody caught wind that it was the Disney organization that was trying to buy the land to build a major amusement park, real estate prices would skyrocket. For this reason everything about the plans for the park and the purchasing of the land would have to remain a secret until all the land was purchased. Only then could discussions begin with city governments, county governments, and business groups about the need for foundational necessities including appropriate building ordinances and the provision of electricity, water, and sewage infrastructure.[103]

As the week came to an end, Walt, Winecoff, and SRI's Wood drove out to Anaheim together to view the recommended properties on Ball Road in Orange County and strategize about the best way to move forward.[104]

Within weeks of the site visit, Walt concluded that he had enough information to proceed based on the rationale in the preliminary site selection report. Walt was worried about waiting until the end of August for SRI's final report and another few months for their still-to-be-completed economic feasibility study. Eager to begin securing the properties for fear of losing them, on August 8, 1953, Walt engaged a Coldwell Banker real estate agent to start the process of discreetly negotiating to lock-up the land for the Disneyland site before full financing for the land purchase was in place.[105]

As the planning work on Disneyland proceeded and as land acquisition options started to be purchased on the first of the Ball Road properties, financial resources for the project through WED were quickly running out and as usual, financing issues were again a concern.

The studio was already indebted to the banks for around $3 million. It was borrowing heavily to finance the multi-million-dollar live-action film *20,000 Leagues Under the Sea* that required a new large soundstage and water tank to be built on the studio lot. *Lady and the Tramp* was also undergoing production. Both were being filmed in a new wide-screen format called CinemaScope, which required the creation and changeover to new technologies, methods, and processes. With these commitments and other planned film projects, the studio anticipated the need to borrow another $2 million of working capital in the near-term.[106]

A quick solution to the funding conundrum was needed.

---

1. Thomas, *Walt Disney*, 11.

2. Jackson, *Walt Disney: Conversations*, 94, Fletcher Markle interview, CBC, September 1963; Smith, *Walt Disney's Famous Quotes*, 32.

3. Walt quoted in Vance & Deacon, *Break Out of the Box*, 96.

4. See Wikipedia, "Tivoli Gardens Copenhagen," en.wikipedia.org/wiki/Tivoli_Gardens_Copenhagen. To see a picture of Walt at Tivoli go here: http://www.welcome-to-my-copenhagen.com/tivoli_garden.html.

5. Smith, *Walt Disney Famous Quotes*, 30.

6. Smith, *Walt Disney Famous Quotes*, 34.

7. Neil Harris, "Expository Expositions: Preparing for the Theme Parks," in Marling, *Designing Disney's Theme Parks*, 22.

8. Gennawey, *The Disneyland Story*, 10.

9. Marling, *Designing Disney's Theme Parks*, 43–45.

10. Marling, *Designing Disney's Theme Parks*, 45.

11. Marling, *Designing Disney's Theme Parks*, 45.

12. Gennawey, *The Disneyland Story*, 10; Marling, *Designing Disney's Theme Parks*, 52.

13. In Barrier, *The Animated Man*, 213.

14. Marling, *Designing Disney's Theme Parks*, 40.

15. Marling, *Designing Disney's Theme Parks*, 52.

16. Gennawey, *Walt Disney and the Promise of Progress City*, 53.

17. Park proprietor quoted in Gennawey, *Walt Disney and the Promise of Progress City*, 53.

18. Roy Disney quoted in Gabler, *Walt Disney*, 503.

19. Gabler, *Walt Disney*, 503.

20. TV.com, "Disneyland," www.tv.com/shows/disneyland, accessed September 5, 2014.

21. Barrier, *The Animated Man*, 228.

22. Barrier, *The Animated Man*, 228.

23. Gabler, *Walt Disney*, 504.

24. Marling, *Designing Disney's Theme Parks*, 52.

25. Holliss & Sibley, *The Disney Studio Story*, 66.

26. Ghez, *Walt's People: Vol. 10*, 240.

27. Ghez, *Walt's People: Vol. 8*, 107.

28. Gabler, *Walt Disney*, 503.

29. Gabler, *Walt Disney*, 504.

30. Barrier, *The Animated Man*, 230.

31. Barrier, *The Animated Man*, 230.

32. Holliss & Sibley, *The Disney Studio Story*, 62.

33. Holliss & Sibley, *The Disney Studio Story*, 62.

34. Gabler, *Walt Disney*, 502.

35. Bob Thomas, *Building a Company*, 185: "Roy in early 1954 established a new ownership agreement for Disneyland, Incorporated, which Walt had founded in 1951."; Polsson, *Chronology of the Walt Disney Company* indicates that on June 27, 1952, "Walt Disney establishes Disneyland Incorporated, citing Christopher Finch, *The Art of Walt Disney*, 1973, as the source; Holliss & Sibley, *The Disney Studio Story*, 68, indicate 1951; Wikipedia, "Disneyland, Inc.,"

en.m.wikipedia.org/wiki/Disneyland,_inc. indicates incorporation in the State of California on December 16, 1952; Barrier in *The Animated Man*, chapter 8 fn 39, indicates that a request to David Smith of the WD Archives could only confirm "It was in business on August 17, 1953." Original date appears to be unconfirmed.

36. In Marling, *Designing Disney's Theme Parks*, 54.

37. Barrier, *The Animated Man*, 233–234.

38. Polsson, *Chronology of the Walt Disney Company*, June 1952; The Disney Wiki, "Oswald the Lucky Rabbit," disney.wikia.com/wiki/Oswald_the_Lucky_Rabbit, accessed October 6, 2014.

39. Polsson, *Chronology of the Walt Disney Company*.

40. Gabler, *Walt Disney*, 494; Gabler footnote on 767 indicates correspondence from Pereira to Walt dated April 10, 1952, likely from after the meeting.

41. Quoted in Barrier, *The Animated Man*, 235–236, from Luckman's book, *Twice in a Lifetime*.

42. Gabler, *Walt Disney*, 494.

43. Gabler, *Walt Disney*, 503.

44. Gennawey, *The Disneyland Story*, 18.

45. Cited in Marling, *Designing Disney's Theme Parks*, 54.

46. Barrier, *The Animated Man*, 227.

47. Roy quoted in Gabler, *Walt Disney*, 504.

48. Gabler, *Walt Disney*, 504–505.

49. Barrier, *The Animated Man*, 227; also Wikipedia, "20,000 Leagues Under the Sea (1954 film), en.wikipedia.org/wiki/20,000_Leagues_Under_the_Sea_(1954_film); Filming began in spring, 1954.

50. See Wikipedia, "20,000 Leagues Under the Sea (1954 film), en.wikipedia.org/wiki/20,000_Leagues_Under_the_Sea_(1954_film)#Production, accessed 30 May 2016.

51. Barrier, *The Animated Man*, p. 227, indicates the tank size was 60 x 125 feet, 3 to 18 feet in depth; Thomas, *Walt Disney: An American Original* indicates the size was 90 x 165; Gabler provides the cost, p. 583, and concurs with 90 x 165.

52. Barrier, *The Animated Man*, 227.

53. Thomas, *Walt Disney*, 236.

54. Barrier, *The Animated Man*, 241.

55. Barrier, *The Animated Man*, 241.

56. Barrier, *The Animated Man*, 236.

57. Polsson, *Chronology of the Walt Disney Company*, 1952 entries.

58. Walt Disney quoted in Barrier, *The Animated Man*, 239.

59. Barrier, *The Animated Man*, 236.

60. Thomas, *Building a Company*, 180.

61. Cottrell quoted in Thomas, *Building a Company*, 181.

62. Barrier, *The Animated Man*, 227.

63. Barrier, *The Animated Man*, 236.

64. Thomas, *Walt Disney*, 243; Barrier, *The Animated Man*, 237.

65. Irvine quoted in Barrier, *The Animated Man*, 237.

66. Barrier, *The Animated Man*, 237.

67. Davis quoted in Barrier, *The Animated Man*, 238.

68. Davis quoted in Barrier, *The Animated Man*, 238.

69. Barrier, *The Animated Man*, 236.

70. Roy Disney quoted in Jackson, *Walt Disney: Conversations*, 52.

71. Roy Disney quoted in Jackson, *Walt Disney: Conversations*, 52.

72. Roy Disney quoted in Jackson, *Walt Disney: Conversations*, 53; also quoted in Gabler, *Walt Disney*, 502.

73. Roy Disney quoted in Jackson, *Walt Disney: Conversations*, 52; also Thomas, *Walt Disney*, 244. Todd James Pierce in *Three Years in Wonderland* asserts that Roy initiated the call, but provides no footnote for a source different than Roy's own statement.

74. Gabler, *Walt Disney*, 501.

75. Holliss & Sibley, *The Disney Studio Story*, 66.

76. Smith, *The Quotable Walt Disney*, 116.

77. Gabler, *Walt Disney*, 501–502.

78. Gabler, *Walt Disney*, 492.

79. Gabler, *Walt Disney*, 492–493.

80. Thomas, *Building a Company*, 182.

81. Cottrell quoted in Thomas, *Building a Company*, 182.

82. Polsson, *Chronology of the Walt Disney Company*.

83. Thomas, *Building a Company*, 253.

84. Gabler, *Walt Disney*, 493.

85. Thomas, *Building a Company*, 255.

86. Thomas, *Building a Company*, 253–254.

87. Thomas, *Building a Company*, 255.

88. Barrier, *The Animated Man*, 236.

89. Thomas, *Building a Company*, 254.

90. Polsson citing Marc Eliot, *Walt Disney: Hollywood's Dark Prince*, pb edition, 228.

91. Marc Eliot, *Walt Disney: Hollywood's Dark Prince*, pb edition, 228.

92. Gabler, *Walt Disney*, 505.

93. Marling, *Designing Disney's Theme Parks*, 60.

94. Barrier, *The Animated Man*, 239. Price, *Walt's Revolution*, p. 18 sets the date in July, as does Gabler, *Walt Disney*, 500. See Barrier fn as to why those dates must be incorrect—WD out of country.

95. Price, *Walt's Revolution!*, 26–27.

96. Pierce, *Three Years in Wonderland*, 48–49.

97. Barrier, *The Animated Man*, 240. Price indicates the 12-week contract had a price tag of $25,000, "a big fee for 1953," 26. The additional fees were for expenses associated with the project.

98. Price, *Walt's Revolution by the Numbers*, 27.

99. Price, *Walt's Revolution!*, 28; Pierce, *Three Years in Wonderland*, 52.

100. Marling, *Designing Disney's Theme Parks*, 63; Price, *Walt's Revolution*, 28; Barrier, *Walt Disney*, 500, Dick Irvine and Nat Winecoff were sent to survey possible sites along the Santa Ana Freeway.

101. Pierce, *Three Years in Wonderland*, 52.

102. Pierce, *Three Years in Wonderland*, 52.

103. Pierce, *Three Years in Wonderland*, 52, 54.

104. Pierce, *Three Years in Wonderland*, 55.

105. Polsson, *Chronology of the Walt Disney Company*; Gabler, *Walt Disney*, 505; Price, *Walt's Revolution!*, 28.

106. Pierce, *Three Years in Wonderland*, 46.

CHAPTER EIGHTEEN

The Financing and Construction of Disneyland

A challenge that had been buried for future consideration was now at the top of Walt and Roy's list of problems to be overcome. It had dogged Walt since the start of his career, but he had always seemed able to beat it. Where would the money come from? Where would he get the capital to purchase the land and build Disneyland? And how much would he need?

The viability of the very idea of a Disney amusement park on the scale Walt was contemplating was at question given the financial state of the studio. How could they raise the $5–7 million they estimated was needed to build and open a permanent amusement park on 160 acres of land south of Los Angeles that others would surely see as an excessively risky, outrageous, hubristic venture that, like *Snow White* before it, could be the next iteration of "Disney's Folly"? As Walt would later tell it, "Almost everyone warned us that Disneyland would be a Hollywood spectacular—a spectacular failure."[1] Roy was certain that Bank of America and other banks would not even consider the request given the studio's inability to shake their seemingly perpetual debt problems, and if it did lend the money, would demand excessively constraining terms that would make building the park impossible.

Television as the Answer to Park Funding

Walt's desperation for capital and credit to purchase land on which to develop and build his park provided the motivation he needed to weave two distinct problems into one, and solve them together. Walt had a good idea of where he could acquire the money he needed, and it wasn't the banks or the Wall Street venture capitalists.

Walt hoped to find the money in a problem he had been trying to solve on an on-again/off-again basis for the past five years: television. Disney biographer and historian Bob Thomas writes:

> The Disneys had considered television as a medium for their pictures ever since the mid-thirties, when they ended their relationship with

United Artists because the distributor insisted on retaining the television rights. In 1950 and 1951, Walt had produced special programs for NBC [and CBS], and was impressed by the huge audiences they drew. All three networks had urged him to produce a weekly series, but he had declined. Disneyland provided the impetus. He figured a network could help him finance the park. And the series would publicize both Disneyland and the theatrical product.[2]

The time had arrived to leverage the proven power of the Disney brand and the reputation for innovation and success that Walt had built up over the past thirty years, both on the large and small screen. Through two highly acclaimed Christmas specials, Walt had demonstrated his skill at successfully attracting unprecedented television audiences to achieve phenomenal ratings for show sponsors. He would now actively seek to trade a weekly Disney-created television show and its economic value to networks and sponsors for a financial investment in Disneyland.

The Pioneering of New Lands: "There's Nothing Like It in the Entire World"

On September 11, 1953, just two weeks after the August 28 delivery of SRI's final site-selection report titled "Analysis of Location Factors for Disneyland," a meeting of Walt Disney Productions' board of directors was convened to consider the wisdom of the corporation's entry into television and whether to proceed beyond just studying and designing an amusement park to actually building one.

Walt rarely attended board meetings, but on this occasion he relished the opportunity to argue for the need to broaden the vision for the scope of the business from making films to creating family entertainment, that the means to do this was inherent in the idea of Disneyland, and that the estimated $7 million that would be required to convert the plans into a park could be funded through private investment to minimize the risk to the corporation and its shareholders.[3]

The key to funding Disneyland, Walt argued, was to make a network's investment in the park a condition of any television deal. Entering television with a weekly show would require a lot of creative effort and money, Walt told the board, but the goal wasn't to make television production profitable. Rather, television was a small piece of a bigger picture, and would be run as a break-even proposition. The payoff was to use television's power of communication to create immense benefits for the company and its shareholders by promoting the vast Disney film catalogue, attracting bigger audiences to Disney's theatrical films, leveraging merchandising opportunities, and of course, promoting Disneyland itself as a desirable family vacation and tourist destination.[4]

Television was unique in its ability to communicate to a mass audience and bring Disney products and entertainment directly into the homes of millions of people every week. "If I'm going to devote that much talent and energy to a television show, I want something to come out of it," Walt told the board. "I don't want this company to stand still. We have prospered before because we have taken chances and tried new things."[5] Walt was hard-selling the board of directors on the idea that his participation in television and the building of Disneyland was a package deal in which the end (Disneyland) justified the means (television).[6]

In summarizing the board meeting that day, Disney biographer Bob Thomas writes:

> To board members who complained that Disney was not in the amusement-park business, he replied that the company *was* in the entertainment business—"and that's what amusement parks are." He admitted that it was hard for them to envision Disneyland the way he could, but he assured them, "There's nothing like it in the entire world. I know, because I've looked. That's why it can be great: because it will be unique. A new concept in entertainment, and I think—I *know*—it can be a success." When he finished, there were tears in his eyes. The members of the board were persuaded.[7]

There was another reason Walt was so passionate about Disneyland. He was well aware that audience tastes in entertainment had changed over time, and that to remain viable, his business too had to change.

The overall market demand for theatrical cartoon shorts was rapidly declining. Cartoons were now becoming something that people watched on television, and theatres were hardly interested in paying rental fees for shorts anymore, especially when many had moved to a double-feature format to entice the public away from their new television sets as movie theatre attendance plummeted.

As a result, Walt's commitment to cartoon shorts had waned, and as leading animator Ward Kimball noted, short animation was now being used "to keep the animation and story departments afloat between features; if Walt was having a problem with a new feature, you'd mark time by picking up work on a short."[8]

But it was more than just shorts that Walt identified as being problematic. The public's love of Disney-type animation seemed to have run its course. Where animated features used to be an exciting challenge to push the boundaries of innovation and imagination, of late they had become a more stressful and risky proposition. *Cinderella* (1950) was highly acclaimed and did reasonably well at the box office, but the same could not be said for the next two animated feature releases, *Alice in Wonderland* (1951) and *Peter*

Pan (1953). They were both difficult for the studio to create and execute, and the return on investment as measured by first-run box-office receipts was disappointing. In 1953, with Walt's thoughts preoccupied with ideas for Disneyland and television and the continued expansion into live-action films and documentaries, and the ongoing burden of financial debt, Walt told production manager Bill Anderson that he really didn't want to spend his time on animation, but it "has to go on."[9]

According to Disney production supervisor Harry Tytle, the quality of animation at the studio had deteriorated from being the best in the world to the point where he was confident that Walt could have received better quality by outsourcing it.[10] Walt knew it, too, and so did his artists and directors, several of which soon began leaving Disney for other studios that were beginning to shift their focus to the newly burgeoning TV animation market.

The changing public tastes equally impacted the other studios. In 1953, Warner Bros., the producers of Looney Tunes and Merrie Melodies cartoons, temporarily closed their animation studio, and many of UPA's best animators left when its distributor said they only wanted Mr. Magoo cartoons. As part of the same downward trend that Walt was anticipating, animation innovator Paul Terry sold his studio and its library of 1,100 animated shorts to CBS in 1955. With the motivation gone and the low quality of animation that was required to justify any investment in animation products, Walt eventually shut down his shorts unit, the long-standing foundation of his business empire, in 1956.[11] The following year, 1957, MGM would close its animation studio because it was just as profitable to recycle its old inventory on television as it was to invest in creating something new.

But for now Walt was ahead of the pack and seeking to discover and create a new way forward that could link the legacy of the Disney brand and accumulated product capital to the economic opportunities of the future.

Television and Parks: Forging Two Links into a Stronger Chain

Having been given the green light by the board of directors in September 1953 to link a television deal with an investment in Disneyland, Walt moved forward with haste. Roy agreed to go to New York to try to secure financing for the park in return for a weekly Disney television show. He immediately began making phone calls to his high-level contacts at the TV networks and potential investors in New York to expedite meetings, which he scheduled for the week of September 28, 1953, making it clear that funding for the park would be part of any deal.[12]

Walt's WED team had been working on a number of outlines for TV show concepts. These were given to Roy to work into his presentation. But to generate excitement for the park from new backers with fresh capital, what was most needed was something to sell the sizzle, to create excitement for the idea that the project was a worthy investment in its own right, and to put to rest whatever concerns investors might be imagining when they heard the words "amusement park." Instead of thinking "seedy roller-coaster-and-sideshow operation," notes art historian Karal Ann Marling in her book *Designing Disney's Theme Parks*, the Disneys "needed pictures of something so enticing, so convincing and new, that the money boys would fall all over themselves to invest."[13]

Just days before Roy's departure, Walt gathered his Walt Disney Productions management team in his office to enthusiastically share with them, for the first time, his vision for Disneyland.[14] Until this point, the plans were privy only to the small WED development team, which had been working secretively in the Zorro building in isolation from their studio colleagues. Walt told the team that he needed a brochure for prospective investors.

There were a large number of various flat concept drawings of streets, storefronts, and attractions to capture individual elements and ideas for the park, including multiple versions of park schematics drawn by Marvin Davis, but Walt wanted a more visually appealing and exciting birds-eye-view perspective that would capture and convey the uniqueness of Disneyland's architecture and attractions.[15] Walt needed to scramble to create something that Roy could have in hand for his critical New York meetings.

With very little time remaining, and under intense pressure, Walt made an urgent early Saturday morning phone call from the studio to the one person whom he thought could provide what he needed, former employee, set designer, landscape artist, and personal friend, Herb Ryman. Ryman had previously worked for Walt in layout and art direction on *Fantasia*, *Dumbo*, and *The Three Caballeros*, and had traveled to South America with Walt as part of the 1941 Disney goodwill tour. Walt implored Ryman to come to the studio right away and waited at the studio gate for his arrival. Ryman recalled the now famous event:

> I was working at home on a Saturday in 1953, when I received a call from Walt asking me to come over to the studio. I said, "When?" and he said, "Now. How long will it take you to get here?" I told him twenty minutes and I was on my way. When I got to the studio, Walt said, "Hi, Herb. We have a new project. It's sort of an amusement park." I asked Walt what he was going to call it and he said, "Disneyland."
>
> Walt described Disneyland. Then he said, "Roy has to go to New York on Monday to raise money for this. We need a plan to show what it will look like. You know, the bankers don't have any imagination."
>
> I said, "Who's going to do the plan?" and Walt said, "You are, Herb." I said, "I don't even know what it's supposed to be," and Walt said,

"If I stay here with you and tell you what it is, will you make a drawing?" So the first drawing of Disneyland was done over a Saturday
and Sunday.[16]

The two worked straight through the night and long into Sunday, with
Walt providing detailed descriptions and Ryman drawing an extraordinary
39 x 67.5 inch detailed aerial view rendering of the park.[17]

A six page promotional sales brochure had also been created with inspirational text, written to create enthusiasm for the new business concept:
"*Walt Disney* sometime—in 1955—will present for the people of the world—
and to children of all ages—a new experience in entertainment. In these
pages is proffered a glimpse into this great adventure. ... A preview of what
the visitor will find in DISNEYLAND."

In addition, it described Walt's philosophy for Disneyland under the
heading "The Disneyland Story":

> The idea of Disneyland is a simple one. It will be a place for people to
> find happiness and knowledge.
>
> It will be a place for parents and children to share pleasant times in
> one another's company; a place for teachers and pupils to discover
> greater ways of understanding and education. Here the older gener-
> ation can recapture the nostalgia of days gone by, and the younger
> generation can savor the challenge of the future. Here will be the
> wonders of Nature and Man for all to see and understand.
>
> Disneyland will be based upon and dedicated to the ideals, the dreams
> and the hard facts that have created America. And it will be uniquely
> equipped to dramatize these dreams and facts and send them forth
> as a source of courage and inspiration to all the world.
>
> Disneyland will be something of a fair, an exhibition, a playground,
> a community center, a museum of living facts, and a showplace of
> beauty and magic.
>
> It will be filled with the accomplishments, the joys and hopes of the
> world we live in. And it will remind us and show us how to make
> these wonders part of our own lives.[18]

Ryman's map was hand-colored by Marvin Davis and Dick Irvine to
show the highlights of the parks attractions and features, and, along with
the sales material, was prepared for Roy to use in New York.

While in Manhattan, Roy began meeting with TV executives and other
potential investors, including MCA and General Foods. After hearing the
pitch, CBS felt they didn't need a Disney TV show in their line-up and told
Roy they weren't interested.

Roy next approached NBC's parent company RCA, meeting with founder
and chairman of the board, David Sarnoff. Sarnoff appeared to be enthusiastic, and turned the negotiations over to the president of RCA, who

seemed unable to come to terms with the Disneyland investment aspect of the proposal and to make a decision one way or the other. The Disneys were enthusiastic about the prospects, but negotiations with RCA and NBC kept stalling for months, while at the same time the work to design and secure Disneyland continued.

Pioneering a New Paradigm and Facing the Old Guard

Through the fall of 1953, Buzz Price of SRI continued to work on the development of the Disneyland economic model. While it was important in order to understand the cost structure of the park and the management of its operations, Price considered the highlight of the park feasibility study not to be the quantitative findings, but rather a fascinating meeting in November 1953 that occurred at the Sherman Hotel in Chicago at the annual amusement park convention and trade show.

Walt knew that his park was revolutionary, for as he told his board, he had looked everywhere and hadn't found anything like it. Now having decided to proceed, he sent three of his senior WED staff (Dick Irvine, Nat Winecoff, and Bill Cottrell) to the convention to meet the various ride manufacturers in attendance and assess their ability to develop customized rides suitable for Disneyland. While most of the ride manufacturer's provided the typical outdoor amusement rides Walt was trying to avoid, a company called Arrow Development located near San Francisco caught their attention. Arrow Development would come to play an important role in the building and engineering of the customized and unique Disneyland attractions.[19]

Walt also wanted to take advantage of the opportunity to test his ideas with the recognized leaders in amusement park operations and benefit from their wisdom. To this purpose, SRI's C.V. Wood and Buzz Price also attended as part of their park feasibility study. Armed with a copy of Herb Ryman's bird's-eye rendering of Disneyland, Walt's people were able to convene a meeting with the owners of some of the country's top amusement parks to gauge their reaction and gather their feedback.

Former Walt Disney Imagineer Bob Rogers retells the story of this now famous two-hour evening meeting between the old guard and the new disruptive upstarts in a speech he delivered at an amusement park industry trade show in 1997, based on Price's personal recollection of the event.[20]

> The public relations story says that it all started at a merry-go-round in Los Angeles, California, where a father, Walt, had taken his two daughters in a failing attempt to find some family fun...but the real revolution began late one stormy November night in a hotel room in Chicago....

You have entered a classic smoke filled room. There are Cuban cigars, caviar, and entire case of Chivas Regal and seven men. It is [1953], during the annual meeting of the National Association of Parks, Pools and Beaches; the organization that later became the AAPA [and is now the IAAPA—International Association of Amusement Parks and Attractions].

Walt Disney is not here; the three men representing Walt know relatively little about theme parks. They are Buzz Price, Dick Irvine and Nat Weinkoff. The other four men in the room are here to confidently tell the first three why Walt's ideas will fail. They are the giants of our industry in 1953, the most experienced, successful and respected owners and operators of amusement parks. They are William Schmitt, owner of Riverview Park in Chicago, Harry Batt of Pontchartrain Beach Park in New Orleans, Ed Schott of Coney Island [Park in Cincinnati], and George Whitney of Playland at the Beach in San Francisco.

The three from Disney unroll this bird's eye master plan drawn by Herb Ryman and they stick it to the wall with masking tape, and they stand back and invite comments.

It's a massacre! Now I'm going to tell you what they told these guys that night....

1. All the proven money makers are conspicuously missing: no roller coaster, no Ferris wheel, no shoot the chute, no tunnel of love, no hot dog carts, no beer. Worst of all, no carny games like the baseball throw. Without barkers along the midway to sell the sideshows, the marks won't pay to go in. Customers are likely to slip out of your park with money still left in their pockets.

2. Custom rides will never work. They cost too much to buy, they will be constantly breaking down resulting in reduced total ride capacity and angry customers. Only stock, off-the-shelf rides are cheap enough and reliable enough to do the job, and besides, the public doesn't know the difference or care.

3. Most of Disney's proposed park produces no revenue, but it's going to be very expensive to build and maintain. Things like the castle and the pirate ship are cute but they aren't rides, so there isn't any economic reason to build them, is there?

4. Town square is loaded with things that don't produce revenue, like a town hall for the fire department, and of course the town square itself.

5. The horse cars, the horseless carriages, and the western wagon rides have such small capacity and cost so much to run that they will lose money even if they run all the time.

6. You can't operate an amusement park year round; 120 days per year is the best you can do.

7. Walt's design only has one entrance. This is going to create a terrible bottleneck! Traditional wisdom dictates entrances on all sides for closer parking and easier access.

8. You'll lose money providing all those design details and nice finishes. The people are going to destroy the grounds and vandalize the ride vehicles no matter what you do, so you might as well go cheap.

9. Walt's screwy ideas about cleanliness and great landscape maintenance are economic suicide. He'll lose his shirt by overspending on these things which the customers never really notice.

10. Modern mid-twentieth century amusement park management theory dictates: build it cheap and then control your costs. Employment theory is similar. Pay your employees the least you can and then ride them hard and get ready to fire them, because they steal from you.

The bottom line: the customers spend about one dollar per capita when they go to an amusement park and they will never spend more. Mr. Disney's park idea is just too expensive to build and too expensive to operate. Tell your boss to save his money, they said. Tell him to stick to cartoons. Tell him to stick to what he knows and leave the amusement business to professionals.

The establishment of 1953 had spoken!

Marling observes that "the old pros seemed puzzled by Walt's obsession with quality and authenticity. Would the 'marks' notice? And the operators failed to grasp the marquee value of the elevated railroad station atop the entrance to Disneyland.... The old pros in the carnival business thought that nobody would trudge upstairs to get to the railroad tracks...."[21]

"The skepticism was understandable," says Price. It's not as if amusement park owners weren't interested in making their parks better and hadn't tried to do so. But they learned from their experiences and were now constrained by them. Their experience told them that Walt was making a big mistake, that he was vastly over-estimating the sensibilities of the fair-going public.

Walt, on the other hand, was convinced they were wrong, and by now fully invested in their being wrong. In Marling's words, writing in *Designing Disney's Theme Parks*, "Walt's theory was that if the promised goods were good enough, if what was going to be there was clear enough from the environmental cues embedded in the design, the Disneyland guests would go anywhere and relish the trip."[22]

As an entrepreneur, Walt was focused on finding value where it didn't yet exist: the guest experience. As an artist, that led him to adopt a design perspective that traditional amusement park operators lacked. Everything about his park was designed and built with a focus on achieving the desired guest experience, with as little compromise as possible. Walt started the design process by planning the circulation patterns of the customers first, making it a top priority. "He planned every attraction from the perspective of the guest rather than the operator or manager. Walt focused on the people," Rogers noted.[23]

By contrast, the standard industry thinking at the time was just what you would expect: ride operators focused on their own particular problems of operating rides, which mainly pertained to minimizing labor and maintenance costs. These values conflicted with the values and priorities of their customers, who wanted a unique and engaging entertainment experience they could share with their friends and family. As made clear by Walt's success, customers wanted cleanliness, service, adventure, music, surprise, and fun, attributes that were rare in the amusement park business before Walt delivered them at Disneyland. The industry leaders believed that to deliver all of that would *require* magic; Walt believed that if he could deliver all of that his customers would *experience* magic. With the challenge defined, he set out to solve a specific problem: how to create a *magic* kingdom.

"Walt was about to upgrade drastically the nature of what was known as the 'amusement park' business," writes Price. "His revolution was about to be born. The unnamed concept would eventually be known as the 'theme park.'"[24]

When Walt gathered his team to hear about their meeting in Chicago, he was amused when he heard the response of the industry leaders, and brushed aside their criticisms. He took their reaction as further evidence that he was on the right track and confirmation as to why he could succeed where they could not.

This story helps us to appreciate the innovative, forward-looking, and independent thinking Walt adhered to, and his iconoclastic and courageous drive to achieve his desired ends, in contrast to the general malaise of entrenched convention and resistance to change that Walt had to fight against every day, on every front, for years on end, in the creation and building of Disneyland.

For us, today, there have always been theme parks and we take their existence for granted, forgetting that some daring innovator had to invent the concept and prove its worth. In this case, Walt Disney had to overcome resistance to overturn a pre-existing paradigm.

SRI's Financial Analysis and Economic Model for Disneyland

As talks between NBC and Disney continued, on January 25, 1954, SRI delivered to Walt its second report, a feasibility study and financial modeling of Disneyland titled "Disneyland Financial Planning Analysis."[25]

The analysis focused heavily on the nearby San Diego Zoo and Copenhagen's Tivoli as data sources. The SRI team, together with a selection of Walt's seasoned WED staff, had visited major and minor American tourist attractions as well as some foreign destinations, such as Tivoli in Copenhagen, to collect hard data to develop the financial model. Price writes: "We studied attendance peaks and seasonal variations, per capita visitor expenditures, on-site crowd densities, required ride capacity as a function of attendance and investment levels. At the time we did not have names for these things. They had to be invented."[26] This data was then modeled for financial and planning implications, included forecasting peak crowd capacity to plan the size of the park as well as monthly variations in attendance and forecasting of per-capita visitor expenditures. SRI provided a conservative estimate of an annual attendance of between 2.5 million to 3 million, which Walt and Roy found extremely encouraging.[27]

The estimate of total start-up costs by SRI was in the range of $11 million.[28] The cost estimate to construct the park was $5.25 million. In addition to the $150,000 that Walt had already invested, plus money to be raised through the sale of corporate sponsorships and vendor leases for retail space within the park, the biggest source of capital infusion would have to come through the structuring of a television deal.

For the most part, the SRI feasibility study was ignored because by the time it was completed and presented to Walt and Roy, the process to purchase land in Anaheim had already begun, negotiations to acquire financing were underway though incomplete, and work on the park was already proceeding.

Nonetheless, SRI's work provided Walt with an independent third-party assessment of his ideas. The quantitative focus of the SRI study went hand-in-glove with Walt's own qualitative research as a sort of check-and-balance device. For years Walt had been taking excursions to carefully observe parks and fairs, including the Pomona Fair at nearby Long Beach, California, and the Santa Monica Pier. He studied the paths customers would walk, how they lined up at the rides, and the expressions on their faces. He visited nearby Knott's Berry Farm with its relocated western town, rides, shows, and concessions. When he returned to New York from Europe in August 1953, he called up leading Hollywood actor Richard Todd, the star of Disney's *The Sword and the Rose*, and invited him to visit Coney Island. According to Todd, he and Walt "did everything—the switchbacks [rollercoasters], the horses, everything. We ate fluffy stuff [cotton candy]. We had a lovely day, thoroughly enjoyed ourselves."[29]

The SRI report also provided Roy with a reality check to guide the studio's investment.

ABC Sees Strategic Synergy

Walt wanted his park built and open in 1955, less than two years away, yet there was still no decision on a TV deal from NBC. With time running out, Roy became fed up with the lack of progress and flew to New York to meet again with Sarnoff in his office, where both agreed to call an end to negotiations.[30] Angry and disappointed at the time wasted, and still without the financing they needed, Roy immediately called Leonard Goldenson, the chairman of ABC, to assess his interest.

Goldenson was well acquainted with Walt and Roy, having previously been the head of Paramount Pictures' chain of theatres. In 1951 he bought the American Broadcasting Company (ABC) to compete with NBC and CBS. Goldenson had met with Walt that year in an attempt to convince him to produce TV programing for his new network. Now, when Roy got through to Goldenson to ask if he was still interested in doing something together in television, Goldenson jumped at the opportunity: "Roy, where are you," he said, "I'll be right over!"[31]

At that time, ABC was the smallest of the networks with only fourteen affiliates compared to NBC with sixty-three and CBS with thirty.[32] Goldenson was frustrated with the lack of growth at the network and was amenable to Walt's proposition: ABC-Paramount would agree to help finance Disneyland in return for a one-hour weekly program.

As enthusiastic as Goldenson was to acquire a coveted Disney TV deal, he soon discovered what Walt and Roy had already experienced: it was not an easy task to convince board members with a fiduciary responsibility to protect the interests of shareholders that a substantial investment in a multi-million-dollar amusement park would be beneficial or prudent.

Buzz Price provides some insight as to why board members of a struggling TV network were skeptical about supporting Walt Disney's crazy amusement park idea in his book *Walt's Revolution: By the Numbers*:

> At that time (1953) an amusement park was usually a collection of mechanical platforms rides and games that at best could attract an annual attendance of five percent of the available market. The average visitor was good for a stay time of two-and-one-half hours and a $1.50 expenditure in a good park. The environment was generally spare, an asphalt jungle, often manned by a collection of "carnies." The theme was "shill." As for economic results, it was strictly a cash family business. In other words, the income all arrived as cash and very often much of it disappeared before it could be documented. It was a business poorly suited for public ownership. There would be nothing left for the stockholders (or often for the IRS).[33]

ABC's board was fully prepared to support the television side of the deal, but not the amusement park business, and refused to approve funding for what they called "Walt's fairground." As the smallest network, ABC had the fewest number of viewers, which meant it had the lowest advertising fees and lowest revenues, and the board was concerned that it would not be able to secure outside financing to invest in Disneyland.[34] Nor was it inclined to try. "After all, they said," wrote Goldenson in his autobiography, "CBS had turned Disney down. NBC had turned him down. And the banks had said no. More to the point, where were *we* going to get financing?"[35]

Goldenson recognized that if he were to secure the Disney TV series he desperately desired to grow his network, boost his ratings, and increase his profits, he would have to find a different angle to overcome the objections of the board and offset the financial risk to ABC.

The Daring and Courage to Strike a Deal

While Walt had a team working full time on developing Disneyland, he continued to be busy with studio work that included the completion of the live-action big-budget extravaganza *20,000 Leagues Under the Sea*, *Lady and the Tramp*, and various short subject project. Story work on *Sleeping Beauty* and the development of other live-action movies like *The Great Locomotive Chase* and *Westward Ho, The Wagons!* were ongoing. Now, as spring of 1954 approached, a television deal with ABC still had not been finalized.

Executives at ABC were convinced that a Disney-ABC deal was important for their business and their ability to compete effectively against the larger NBC and CBS networks in the upcoming fall season, even if the board was not yet convinced to approve a deal that required an investment in Walt's park. Afraid that Walt or Roy would lose confidence in ABC's interest in going forward together, the ABC executives were taking special care to keep in close touch with the Disney studio about various programming ideas while sorting out their own internal business issues to bring about a deal.

To acquire the financing for Disney that he needed, Goldenson approached a Texas millionaire investor acquaintance, Karl Hoblitzelle, who was also the chairman of the Republic Bank of Dallas, and arranged to have Republic loan $5 million to ABC to finance the Disney deal.[36]

At the same time, optimistic that they could successfully complete a deal with ABC, Walt and Roy began a process of courting executives of the largest American corporations—including Coca-Cola, Pepsi-Cola, Ford Motors, General Electric, B.F. Goodrich, DuPont Chemical, and Kellogg cereals—seeking to lease concessions and attract sponsorship deals to raise working capital for the project even before the final funding deal was signed.[37]

After several days of intense negotiations between Roy and ABC president Robert Kintner in March 1954, an agreement was reached in which ABC would invest $500,000 into Disneyland with the first installment of

$150,000 due upon signing of the contract. In return they would get a weekly TV series to be called *Disneyland*.[38] The ABC executives would get the Disney programming they wanted and felt they needed to compete with the other networks and in return Walt would acquire the funding he desperately needed to build his park. The agreement would require Walt to begin airing shows for the new TV season beginning in October. He would have to start immediately and quickly move up the learning curve with no time to spare.

All of the pieces to consummate a deal seemed to be in place, and arrangements were made for Walt and Roy to meet with the ABC executives in New York on Monday, March 22, to wrap up the final details.[39]

As if Walt didn't already have enough on his plate, he now had to add the creation and operation of a TV production business to his responsibilities. His number one priority was to use his new TV platform to sell Disneyland and the desire to vacation there to his audience. It was imperative to use the unique characteristics of television to demonstrate to potential park visitors that Disneyland was something new and unique that they had to experience first-hand, and to remove the idea that the park was merely another run-of-the-mill fairground or Coney Island.

Having television as a new communication medium and channel for product distribution, Walt was in a position to leverage film footage of the park being built and concept drawings depicting the final creation in all of its architectural glory. The programming was to be designed to create excitement amongst TV viewers for Disneyland as a fun, safe, and magical place they should desire to visit in beautiful southern California. "If I was ever going to have my park," said Walt, "here at last was a way to tell millions of people about it—with TV."[40]

There was no doubt that Walt was fully committed emotionally and financially to making Disneyland a success, and saw the production of high-quality television programming as the means to get him there. At this point, however, he had no format, no plan, and no organization in place.

On Friday, March 19, ahead of their New York meeting, Walt called together fourteen members of his WED staff, plus Roy, to explain what he wanted and discuss how best to proceed.[41] There were two key issues that had to be resolved before going to New York: the format for the series, and how to set up an organization to manage the vast new workload. Walt suggested using the four "lands" at Disneyland to address both challenges. Each installment of the show would be linked to one of Disneyland's themes: Adventureland, Fantasyland, Tomorrowland, and Frontierland. Four corresponding production units would be set up to spread out and manage the work.[42]

By linking the themes of the TV episodes to the park, every weekly show was an overt promotional message to the television viewers for

Disneyland and Disney character merchandise. It was understood that the key leverage offered by television was to develop synergy to connect television, movies, the park, and branded merchandise so that each promotes the other. Walt was quick to remind everyone involved that "the main idea of the program is to sell."[43]

Walt was also deeply aware that he had a responsibility to meet the expectations of the television viewing audience. He emphasized that the Disney brand and the high-quality family entertainment value it stood for had to be respected at all times, while ensuring adherence to the cost structure of each episode under the constraints of the ABC contract. That meant producing new and interesting material for television, and limiting the recycling of old Disney movies and cartoons. Anything less than producing shows that they themselves would be proud of, said Walt, would be cheating.[44]

The agreement to put a weekly Disney-produced show on TV, which included funding for the park, received approval by both the ABC and Disney boards on April 2, 1954, slightly more than six months after Roy first travelled to New York to seek a TV deal.[45] Disney biographer Neal Gabler summarizes the details:

> The deal was complex. ABC agreed to a three-year contract for twenty-six one-hour programs each year, for which it would pay Walt Disney Productions $50,000 per show the first year, $60,000 the second, and $70,000 the third, with $25,000 per repeat the first year, $30,000 the second, and $35,000 the third. Fifteen percent of those funds was then to be funneled from Walt Disney Productions to Disneyland, Inc., a new corporate entity, as a location fee, out of which the latter was to pay off its mortgage bonds. But since Disney estimated that each program would cost the studio roughly $65,000, the real force of the ABC deal was the network's investment in the park. ABC had committed to take $2 million of ten-year bonds, would guarantee loans of up to $4.5 million (Hoblitzelle's crucial contribution to the package), and would put $500,000 directly into the park—in return for a 34.48 percent interest, the same share as that of Walt Disney Productions. Not incidentally, that investment enabled the studio to increase its credit line with the Bank of America to $8 million. As Roy had hoped, the ABC deal also prompted another of the "friendly interests," the Wisconsin-based Western Printing and Lithographing Company, to take $500,000 of ten-year bonds and engineer a $500,000 loan from a local bank secured by Western's Disney royalties, in return for an 13.8% stake. ... Walt was to keep the remaining 16.55 percent as compensation for his contributions to the park.

> With the financing in place, the studio made a public announcement on May 1 [1944]: Walt Disney would be building an amusement park.[46]

Goldenson writes in his autobiography *Beating the Odds*:

The Disneys said they wanted to build an amusement park in a dusty little California town called Anaheim. ... ABC was really Disney's last hope. He'd gone to the banks, and when he tried to explain what he wanted to build, they just couldn't grasp the concept. They kept thinking of a place like Coney Island. Very risky. They turned him down....

I asked Walt how much they thought it would cost to build Disneyland. He said, "About four million dollars, maybe five million at the most."

That wasn't going to be nearly enough, I said. Probably it would take more like $10 million or $15 million. After construction they would have to staff it, train people, and operate at a loss for some time. (As it turned out, it cost $17 million, the first year alone.)

Then I hammered out a deal with the Disneys. We would put in $500,000 and guarantee the loans. In exchange we took 35% of Disneyland, and all profits from the food concessions for ten years. I knew that could be a gold mine.

And of course there was programming. That's what I really wanted from them. We agreed to a seven-year deal, with an option for an eighth, at $5 million a year. At $40 million, it was then the biggest programming package in history.[47]

In retelling the story years later, Walt joked that "ABC needed the television show so damned bad, they bought the amusement park."[48]

A more detailed program format representing a kind of Disney variety show was pitched to ABC shortly after the deal was signed. Walt described a show that would combine segments of made-for-TV cartoons and live-action films, documentary, and behind-the-scenes footage including the progress being made in the building of Disneyland, as well as old cartoons and movie clips. Adventureland programming would highlight the True-Life Adventures documentaries; Fantasyland programming would feature new and classic Disney animation; Tomorrowland would present features about innovations of the future, including man's exploration of space; and Frontierland would feature stories about America's past. Walt himself would be the host of each new episode.[49]

While the announcement that Walt was going to proceed to build a park was significant, the Disney-ABC television deal was even more bold and shocking to the elite of the Hollywood movie studios.

From the first introduction of television sets to the American public, the leaders of the motion picture industry had generally stood firm against television, and refused to allow its contracted actors to participate and to provide content. It was as if a wall existed between movies and television. Disney biographer Neal Gabler writes:

[Walt,] in putting his production company directly in the service of television without any subterfuges, had made what *The New York Times* called the "first move by a leading studio into the home entertainment field," and the *Times* predicted that "if it turns out to be successful, it may very well lead to more such working alliances among the major studios and the networks." The *Times* concluded: "The end result could, indeed, change the complexion of the entertainment business." That was exactly what would happen.[50]

The seemingly benign deal between Disney and ABC was considered both scandalous and revolutionary at the time, and served to further establish Walt's reputation as a reckless and desperate industry maverick. In describing the impact of the ABC-Disney deal, Disney biographer Bob Thomas writes:

> The Disney-ABC deal stunned Hollywood. The movie bosses still considered television the enemy. Stars were forbidden to appear on TV. Even though millions of Americans had TV sets in their living rooms, you never saw one featured in a movie.
>
> Goldenson [owner of ABC and Paramount Theaters], whose Paramount theaters were important buyers of films, remembers being invited to lunch with the top executives of MGM. "You're being a traitor to the motion picture industry," he was told. "You'll take all our directors, producers, and talent over to television, and we won't have anybody to carry on ourselves."
>
> "That's silly," Goldenson replied. "Let me ask you: if I were able to put a trailer of your next picture into every home in the United States, how much would you give me? A million dollars? Well, I rest my case."[51]

Once again Walt proved that he was a more visionary and entrepreneurial thinker and businessman than his value-myopic competitors, be they amusement park owners, television executives, or Hollywood movie-studio moguls.

Where ABC now had the television deal with Disney that Goldenson had desired since meeting with Walt back in the summer of 1951 plus an investment in a park they didn't care for, Walt now had much more. He had synergy, which would soon evolve at the studio into the notion of business integration. It was an ideal win-win situation.

Walt had six months from the signing of the TV contract until the *Disneyland* show was scheduled to begin in October 1954. Meeting that date was important because Walt wanted a full season of television to promote the park ahead of its opening, now scheduled for July 1955. He assigned roles to his staff even though only a few had any TV experience. While the lack of television knowledge was concerning and discomforting to those who were hired and tasked to write and produce the shows, Walt was confident in their ability to do a great job. They may have lacked specific television experience, but Walt knew they had the technical skills of storytelling and film production, which they would need to adapt to the smaller budgets and shorter production deadlines that television work required.

With Walt's team at WED now busy developing television programming for the fall launch, one of Walt's tasks was to ensure the show's success by identifying and meeting with potential major sponsors, trying to convince them to advertise on the program.[52]

At the same time he and his staff were seeking show sponsors, he was doing the same for his park, leading a quest to find and convince major corporations to commit to multi-year sponsorships of park attractions and to secure commitments from park concession operators. Finding early adaptors who were willing to invest upfront in the commercial viability of Walt's vision was a challenge.

Whenever discussions with potential sponsors advanced to the level where genuine interest was being shown, executives were invited to tour the studio in Burbank and sit with Walt and Roy through the pitch. There was overwhelming enthusiasm from those who attended that emanated from directly experiencing Walt's passion and vision. The Disney liaison at the Bank of America, Joe Rosenberg, was told by a Standard Oil vice president that "never in his life had he seen such a wonderful imagination and complete detailed planning," and asked Rosenberg to lobby the Disneys on his behalf to ensure that Standard Oil was a part of it.[53]

Under the Sea

The filming of *20,000 Leagues Under the Sea* began in the spring of 1954, to be completed and released before the end of the year.[54] Anticipating broad interest in the film and looking ahead, Walt assigned a second production team to gather footage on the making of the movie to be called *Operation Undersea*. Walt felt that based on the popularity of his True-Life Adventures documentaries, the showing of a behind-the-scenes documentary on how the movie was made was ideal for television: it was educational, interesting, and provided unprecedented value in promoting Disney products and merchandise right in people's homes.

When the film crew began shooting the giant squid scenes on the new soundstage, the scene was staged on a flat ocean at sunset. After a few days of shooting, Walt put a stop to it. This dramatic confrontational scene in the movie needed to be intense and engaging. Instead it was flat, unexciting, and phony looking. The wires attached to the squid were clearly visible. Director Richard Fleischer was instructed by Walt to postpone this key sequence until later and begin filming the dramatic scenes. Fleisher recalls:

> The fight with the octopus was very difficult, more a mechanical problem than anything else. The first time we tried it, the monster

just didn't work; it got waterlogged, and started to sink. It wasn't engineered properly, and it couldn't do all the things we needed it to do. It looked pretty phony anyway.[55]

To save this important scene, Walt instructed his technicians to build a more convincing squid. This time they built a hydraulically controlled squid that weighed two tons and had eight forty-foot tentacles and two fifty-foot-long feelers. To make it fully operational required twenty-four men. It had large yellow eyes and a snapping beak, and could now act the part of being a real menace to the *Nautilus* and its crew. To make the scene more dramatic, Walt changed the squid attack scene from a calm sunset to a dark, raging storm, utilizing tons of water sprayed down into the tank, and using giant fans to whip up the spray and arc lamps to simulate lightning.

With costs already far exceeding budget, the squid attack scene took eight days to shoot and added more than $250,000 to the budget. Disney biographer Bob Thomas wrote:

> The increased cost strained Roy Disney's warm feelings toward *20,000 Leagues Under the Sea* and tried the bankers' patience with Walt's spending. He was required to show them the early footage from the film before they would agree to lend him more money. The added expense was a worthwhile investment: the squid fight proved to be the visual highlight of the film.[56]

Buena Vista: Forward Integration into Film Marketing and Distribution

Bankers weren't Walt's only problems at this time. For years he had been unhappy with the performance of the studio's film distributor, RKO, and the situation was getting dangerously risky.

The problem began in 1948 when billionaire aviation tycoon and industrialist Howard Hughes acquired RKO and began syphoning off their profit. Due to his interference and managerial neglect, RKO's operations soon descended into turmoil, affecting their relations with the studios.

Walt was particularly distressed when under Hughes' leadership, RKO expressed its reluctance to support the distribution and promotion of the documentary *Seal Island* and the animated feature *The Adventures of Ichabod and Mr. Toad*. Walt and Roy exerted themselves and weathered through, eventually gaining RKO's reluctant cooperation, but the situation at RKO under Hughes continued to deteriorate, making it difficult to do business with them and to obtain the distribution support they needed and expected for the considerable fees being paid.

In 1952, Hughes proposed selling the struggling RKO studio and distribution business to Walt along with an offer of ten million dollars in credit that Walt Disney Productions could badly use, but RKO itself was debt-burdened and unsound. "What do I want that problem for?" said Walt. "I've got my own little thing over here. I don't need another studio on my hands."[57] Hughes eventually sold RKO in 1953, but Walt's troubles with RKO persisted as they continued to put up resistance to the distribution of shorts, insisting that doing so was no longer profitable for them.

Roy decided to renew the RKO distribution contract in 1953, concluding that in spite of his and Walt's concerns, it was the best option for the time being. However, as a result of RKO's resistance to releasing the second True-Life Adventures documentary *The Living Desert*, Roy, in consultation with Walt, elected to establish Disney's own subsidiary film distribution company, the Buena Vista Film Distribution Company, Inc., to handle *The Living Desert's* distribution and allow for first-hand learning of the film distribution business.

Contrary to RKO's assessment of the commercial viability of *The Living Desert*, it was a remarkable box office success, proving once again that Walt understood his audience better than most. With the film costing just a few hundred thousand dollars to make, *The Living Desert* grossed $6.8 million upon its initial release and won the Oscar for Best Feature-Length Documentary of 1953.[58]

Walt and Roy remained dissatisfied with the lack of support and promotion attention Disney films were receiving from RKO under their renewed contract. As a countermeasure, in 1954, Roy recommended the studio hire its own ad agency to promote its films, even though doing so meant assuming an additional cost that should have been borne by RKO.

With RKO in disarray and the confidence of Walt and Roy in their ability to competently promote their films, and with *20,000 Leagues Under the Sea* and *Lady and the Tramp* scheduled for imminent release, Roy went to RKO asking for a $3.5 million advance for those films and pushing RKO to reduce their distribution fee from 22.5 percent to 20 percent of rental revenues to offset the marketing costs the studio would assume. RKO, on the other hand, was asking for an increase in its distribution fee to 25 percent.[59] The need for RKO to increase their fees while providing deteriorating service gave the Disneys little confidence in RKO's ability to effectively distribute their films in an appropriate manner. Walt and Roy decided that the survival of the studio was at stake and entrusting their fate to RKO was too risky.

In September 1954, Roy was facing the uncertainty of RKO's future stability. It was critical that the studio had secure and effective marketing and distribution of its films to maximize revenues. The ability to successfully distribute *The Living Desert* through Buena Vista gave Walt and Roy the confidence that they could eliminate the middleman and thereby capture the benefits of forward integration and an extended supply chain. Controlling their film distribution would provide them with greater control over their destiny. Roy announced that after 18 years, Walt Disney Productions was severing its ties with RKO, and would undertake its own domestic distribution under the Buena Vista banner. "Now, for the first time in its history," notes historian Neal Gabler, "the studio would control the production, the publicity, and the distribution of every one of its films."[60]

Uncle Walt's *Disneyland*

The *Disneyland* TV show premiered on ABC to unanimous acclaim on October 27, 1954, with the premiere episode consisting almost entirely of recycled material including sequences from *Song of the South*, *Plane Crazy*, and the "Sorcerer's Apprentice" segment from *Fantasia* featuring Mickey Mouse. Viewers watched on their black-and-white TV sets. The opening segment presented a brief overview of the studio, followed by Walt himself introducing the Disneyland park and the four "lands" as themes for both the park and the show. There was also an attempt to capture the excitement and mystery of the soon-to-be-released *20,000 Leagues Under the Sea*.

The weekly show was an instant hit with advertisers and audiences, giving ABC its first-ever show to break the top twenty-five in audience viewers.[61] Disney biographer Neal Gabler writes:

> Over the course of the season *Disneyland* consistently attracted over 50 percent of the audience in its time slot [Wednesday nights from 7:30 to 8:30], and its audience kept growing, its ratings climbing, until even its repeats outdrew every program on television save the Lucille Ball situation comedy *I Love Lucy*. ... Disneyland gave ABC an identity that the fledgling company had not had, and astonishingly it accounted for nearly half of the network's advertising billings. By April, with only twenty shows broadcast, *Newsweek* was already calling it "an American institution"—the "first big-budget television show consistently and successfully aimed at the whole family," which was critical. Walt Disney had not only conquered television as he had conquered the screen; he was being credited with using the new medium to bring America together. He was the country's great national uncle, "Uncle Walt," as some took to calling him.[62]

One element that helped solidify the show's popularity was the immense, unanticipated success of three episodes depicting the story of Davy Crockett, which debuted on December 5, 1954, and launched Crockettmania across the country. The opening song, "The Ballad of Davy Crockett," written as an afterthought at Walt's request to lengthen the running time of the episodes due to a shortage of acceptable film footage, became a national hit record. Over seven million copies were sold in six months. An estimated ten million coonskin caps were sold, along with Crockett clothing, toys, books, and other merchandise. Because of the medium of television, Crockett actor Fess Parker became an overnight sensation and was mobbed everywhere he went. Crowds exceeding ten thousand people would show up to greet him on publicity tours to promote the show and cash in on its popularity.[63]

While the story of a national hero certainly resonated with audiences, part of the show's success can be attributed to the story quality and production values, which, Gabler notes, were "vastly superior to that of most television programs and much closer to that of films. (One could call it the first television miniseries.) Children, to whom the program had largely been targeted, had never seen anything on television so grand."[64]

The shows aired in black and white, even though they were filmed in color, at a cost for the three episodes of nearly three-quarters of a million dollars. Walt had the footage edited down into a single color movie, *Davy Crockett, King of the Wild Frontier*, for theatrical release in 1955, which grossed $2.5 million on its initial release, a small sum compared to the estimated $300 million worth of Crockett merchandise sold during the first eight months of the craze.[65] Parker's contractual agreement entitled him to a ten percent royalty on all Crockett merchandise.[66]

The Disney studio earned about $73,000 per *Disneyland* episode, including reruns, with an average production cost of about $100,000. Individual episode costs ranged from $14,500 when mostly pre-existing content was used to more than $250,000 for each Davy Crockett episode.[67]

On December 8, 1954, two weeks prior to the release of *20,000 Leagues Under the Sea*, Walt aired *Operation Undersea*, a one-hour documentary on the making of the movie, as the seventh episode on the *Disneyland* TV series. Millions of people were able to watch from the comfort of their own living rooms what was essentially a one-hour commercial for the upcoming film. Walt was impressed, and it demonstrated the power of television to both entertain audiences and promote Disney products. In this case, the television show, the movie, and the theme park name—Disneyland—were all linked together. It was an early example of Disney brand integration.

Operation Undersea won an Emmy Award in March 1955 for Best Individual Show of the year for 1954, as did the *Disneyland* TV series for Best Variety Series of 1954.

20,000 Leagues Under the Sea was also heavily promoted in print advertisements, radio ads, and theatre trailers, prior to its Christmastime release on December 23, 1954, as a star-studded holiday action-filled blockbuster. The movie was well received, both critically and commercially, earning $6.8 million in gross rentals, but not enough to justify the huge investment and risk given the size of its budget. It won two Academy Awards for Best Art Direction—Color and Best Special Effects, and was nominated for a third, Best Film Editing.

Walt didn't draw a hard line between moviemaking for the theatre and for television. When others told him that television would be different from making movies for the big screen, Walt's reply was, "Well, I know, but I don't think that the audience is any different."[68] On another occasion he said, "There's no appreciable difference. We go through the same motions."[69] In this regard, Walt's presence on TV was another element in his overall business model to reduce the financial risk of moviemaking, or as Walt put it, "[another] medium for exploiting our wares."[70]

Remaining true to his mission, Walt reinvested his TV revenues back into TV production, unconcerned about making TV ventures a stand-alone source of profits. Television for Walt was a means to a longer-term strategic end of promoting the Disneyland park and selling Disney products. It was an amplifier or booster and integrative tool to more deeply infiltrate the Disney brand into the American psyche, as can be measured by the many crazes and fads it created, including the propensity of parents to buy Disney branded merchandise for their children. In addition to Crockettmania, more than two million mouse-ear hats were sold within three months of the introduction of *The Mickey Mouse Club* TV show on October 3, 1955.[71]

Had Walt looked upon TV as a stand-alone profit center, it was unquestionably a loser. Instead, he saw the role it played in the total picture, as one of many components of a total business with its unique ability to contribute to the whole. From this perspective, when seen as a promotional tool and subsidy for the Disneyland park, Disney films, Disney merchandising, and the Disney brand, it was likely Walt's single greatest investment achievement, delivering tens of millions of dollars in profit to the studio in the first five years alone.

Christopher Anderson, in his book *Hollywood TV: The Studio System in the Fifties*, confirms the significance of Walt's strategic vision and ambition:

> In uniting the TV program and the amusement park under a single name, Disney made one of the most influential commercial decisions in postwar American culture. Expanding upon the lucrative character merchandising market that the studio had joined in the early 1930s, Disney now planned to create an all-encompassing consumer environment that he described as "total merchandising." Products aimed at baby boom families and stamped with the Disney imprint—movies, amusement park rides, books, comic books, clothing, toys, TV programs, and more—would weave a vast commercial web, a tangle of advertising and entertainment in which each Disney product, from the movie *Snow White and the Seven Dwarfs* (1937) to a ride on Disneyland's Matterhorn, promoted all Disney products. And television was the beacon that would draw the American public to the domain of Disney. "We wanted to start off running," Walt later recalled. "The investment was going to be too big to wait for

a slow buildup. We needed terrific initial impact, and television seemed the answer."[72]

Walt had incubated his ideas both for creating a new kind of amusement and for leveraging the opportunity of television since the 1930s. Now, twenty years later, he was engaged on the leading edge of a three-pronged thrust to dominate the entertainment industry through films, parks, and television. Walt had a number of advantages in the creation of a new theme park paradigm that current amusement park owners lacked. As a result of his movie and television success, he had an established brand, media access, money, and the ability to create and attract more of each.

More importantly, he had the courage to pursue his ambition and to make his own choices. Personal and business vision, curiosity, commitment, money, and an understanding of how to lead others and get things done to create and deliver value to consumers, employees, and shareholders, congealed to provided Walt with the ability to transform his long-held vision of a place where a family could do fun things together free of fear or worry, into reality. This enabled him to create the self-proclaimed "happiest place on earth" for himself and for all those who derived value from his combination of imagination and engineering-centric creation.

---

1. Walt quoted in in Holliss & Sibley, *The Disney Studio Story*, 66.

2. Thomas, *Building a Company*, 183.

3. Holliss & Sibley, *The Disney Studio Story*, 66.

4. Barrier, *The Animated Man*, 242.

5. Walt quoted in Thomas, *Walt Disney*, 245.

6. See Barrier, *The Animated Man*, 242; Thomas, *Building a Company*, 183; Gabler does not discuss the board meeting, but the timeline falls on 505–506).

7. Thomas, *Walt Disney*, 245; Holliss & Sibley, *The Disney Studio Story*, 66.

8. Kimball quoted in Gabler, *Walt Disney*, 553.

9. Gabler, *Walt Disney*, 553.

10. Gabler, *Walt Disney*, 553.

11. Holliss & Sibley, *The Disney Studio Story*, 65.

12. Watt, *The Magic Kingdom*, 365.

13. Marling, *Designing Disney's Theme Parks*, 69; Thomas, *Building a Company*, 183.

14. Gabler, *Walt Disney*, 506. There are different versions of when Roy left. One is that he left before the map was complete and it had to be shipped to him in New York. Dick Irving, in Jeff Kurti, *Walt Disney's Imagineering Legends*, 21, is quoted as saying "...Herbie did the first birds-eye view of Disneyland by Monday, and I think Tuesday morning Roy took them to New York with him."

15. Holliss & Sibley, *The Disney Studio Story*, 67.

16. Ryman quoted in Green & Green, *Remembering Walt*, 149.

17. Barrier, *The Animated Man*, 243.

18. See "Disneyland's Original Prospectus Revealed", boingboing. net/2014/05/20/disneylandprospectus.html, accessed May 12, 2016; also Smith, *The Quotable Walt Disney*, 55; Marling, *Designing Disney's Theme Parks*, 76.

19. Pierce, *Three Years in Wonderland*, 84.

20. Bob Rogers, "The Coming Revolution in Themed Entertainment," delivered at the IAAPA Tradeshow, Orlando, FL, in 1997, at themedattraction.com/future.htm; see also Price, *Walt's Revolution!*, 29–30; Pierce, *Three Years In Wonderland*, 84–86.

21. Marling, *Designing Disney's Theme Parks*, 66.

22. Marling, *Designing Disney's Theme Parks*, 66.

23. Rogers in "The Coming Revolution In Themed Entertainment."

24. Price, *Walt's Revolution!*, 31.

25. Gabler, *Walt Disney*, 770 fn referencing 508, he cites an SRI report on Financing, "Disneyland Financial Planning Analysis," Jan 25, 1954. I am assuming this the second of the two reports contracted to SRI.

26. Price, *Walt's Revolution!*, 29.

27. Holliss & Sibley, *The Disney Studio Story*, 66.

28. Marling, *Designing Disney's Theme Parks*, 63.

29. Barrier, *The Animated Man*, 242.

30. Donn Tatum, in Ghez, *Walt's People: Vol. 8*, 186.

31. Card Walker in Ghez, *Walt's People: Vol. 10*, 241; Donn Tatum in Ghez, *Walt's People: Vol. 8*, 186.

32. Gabler, *Walt Disney*, 507.

33. Price, *Walt's Revolution!*, 31.

34. Gabler, *Walt Disney*, 507.

35. Goldenson, *Beating the Odds*, 123.

36. Goldenson, *Beating the Odds*, 124; Gabler, *Walt Disney*, 508; Pierce, *Three Years in Wonderland*, 97.

37. Gabler, *Walt Disney*, 526.

38. Pierce, *Three Years in Wonderland*, 98.

39. Date from Gabler, 510 fn on p. 771, "Meeting with Kintner and ABC Executives."

40. Marling, *Designing Disney's Theme Parks*, 71–73.

41. Gabler, *Walt Disney*, 510 and fn.

42. Gabler, *Walt Disney*, 510.

43. Walt Disney quoted in Gabler, *Walt Disney*, 510.

44. Gabler, *Walt Disney*, 510.

45. Gabler, *Walt Disney*, 506–508.

46. Gabler, *Walt Disney*, 508–509.

47. Goldenson, *Beating the Odds*, 122–124; also in Barrier, *The Animated Man*, 244.

48. Walt Disney quoted in Gabler, *Walt Disney*, 508.

49. Walt Disney Family Museum, *The Man, The Magic, The Memories*, 80; Gabler, *Walt Disney*, 510.

50. Gabler, *Walt Disney*, 509.

51. Thomas, *Building a Company*, 185.

52. Gabler, *Walt Disney*, 510.

53. Gabler, *Walt Disney*, 527, July 1954.

54. Wikipedia, "20,000 Leagues Under the Sea (1954 film)," en.wikipedia.org/wiki/20,000_Leagues_Under_the_Sea_(1954_film), accessed August 2, 2016.

55. Leonard Maltin, *The Disney Films, 3rd Edition*, 121.

56. Thomas, *Walt Disney*, 238.

57. Walt Disney quoted in Gabler, *Walt Disney*, 519.

58. Holliss & Sibley, *The Disney Studio Story*, 170.

59. Barrier, *The Animated Man*, 263.

60. Gabler, *Walt Disney*, 520.

61. Gabler, *Walt Disney*, 511.

62. Gabler, *Walt Disney*, 511–512.

63. Gabler, *Walt Disney*, 514–515.

64. Gabler, *Walt Disney*, 516.

65. See amazon.ca description for *Walt Disney Treasures: Davy Crockett—The Complete Televised Series*; also Wikipedia, "Davy Crocket (miniseries)," en.wikipedia.org/wiki/Davy_Crockett_(miniseries), accessed May 24, 2016.

66. Gabler, *Walt Disney*, 515.

67. Gabler, *Walt Disney*, 518.

68. Smith, *The Quotable Walt Disney*, 217.

69. Smith, *The Quotable Walt Disney*, 216.

70. Smith, *The Quotable Walt Disney*, 223.

71. Wikipedia, "The Mickey Mouse Club," en.wikipedia.org/wiki/The_Mickey_Mouse_Club, accessed July 7, 2016.

72. Anderson, *Hollywood TV*, 134.

CHAPTER NINETEEN

From Mickey Mouse to Mickey's House

Walt designed every major aspect of Disneyland after years of careful study, starting with the exact placement of the railway on the property map. He decided on a single entrance to allow for a gate to charge admission, but also to track and control the number of people that came and went. Main Street set the stage, allowing guests to get their bearings in a nostalgic, familiar, and optimistic neutral setting with a message of excitement and future potential. Walt spent a considerable amount of time over a number of years studying circulation patterns at museums and parks, and settled on the spoke-and-hub radial design to provide guests with a sense of orientation and to alleviate tiredness. From the central hub, with a fountain, benches, and floral gardens, the gateway into and back out of each of the "lands" is visible, providing easy identification to guide exploration decisions. Walt imagined and planned Disneyland to be a feast for all the senses while retaining the tranquility, beauty, pace, and serenity that made the world's greatest parks so beloved.

Despite public and private skepticism over Walt's ability to successfully build and operate a large amusement park surrounded by orange groves south of Los Angeles, he was able to find a very small number of backers who either bought into his vision, or at least gave him the benefit of the doubt, such as ABC's Goldenson and Western Printing & Lithographing, both of which provided substantial financial backing.

Western Printing had been the sole publisher of all Disney materials in the U.S. for 22 years. For its $200,000 investment, it received 13.79 percent ownership in Disneyland, Inc., and a bookstore on Main Street.[1] The Hilton hotel chain and Walt's friend Art Linkletter, a radio and TV personality, lacked confidence in Walt's venture and when offered, turned down the opportunity to build a motor hotel across from the park property. Instead, a hotel builder with ties to the entertainment industry, Jack Wrather, immediately jumped at the opportunity when offered.

Walt proceeded to build his park with such haste that planning and execution was somewhat fluid, haphazard, and at times simultaneous. It was as if the park was capitalized, designed, constructed, and marketed by the sheer driving force of Walt's will power. Once the project began, everything was aggressively full-steam ahead. Illustrations and architectural models were made to serve multiple purposes. They were a means to translate ideas into concepts, then into blueprints, and finally into architectural artifacts. They were also used as a marketing tool to generate excitement and drive the desire of potential attraction sponsors and concession lessees to make a financial commitment to the park.

Marling captures this well in *Designing Disney's Theme Parks*:

> The models and the booklets were meant to show the people who sold Wurlitzer organs and Swift meats, Maxwell House coffee, Kodak cameras and Cole of California swimsuits just how their Main Street shopfronts would look, if they took a chance on Disneyland and signed a lease. They were meant to show bankers and network vice presidents that this was no run-of-the-mill fairground, but a collective of evocative, almost-real environments, complete down to the smallest detail of interior design and costume—miniatures enlarged somewhat for ease of use but still model-like in their fussy, highly wrought perfection.

The creation of paintings and models was more than a sales tool; they were an important component of a larger creative process of translating pure concepts of imagination into physical representations of reality for study and further development. Marling continues:

> But the models and the bright, larger-than-life paintings were also practical tools in a frantic, complex, ad-hoc process of turning ideas into architecture. Disney architecture is picture architecture. Everything starts from an illustration, a concept picture, a slice of an animation storyboard showing characters, or settings, or props, or, best of all, their interaction in space and time.
>
> The picture is a marketing tool but it is also a way for the artist to reach beyond an idea or a conversation about a place toward the making of the place itself. The picture that sold a meat packer on Disneyland was also the picture the model maker measured as a guide in building a miniature meat market. And the miniature, nicely painted to look like a full-scale building, became a page in a marketing book or a guide for an artist charged with producing a formal elevation drawing that a contractor could follow when the time came to build the actual Main Street.[2]

The process may have been loose in that it required flexibility to accommodate the stretching of ideas and further integration of architecture and story, but it was a defined and proven process that the Disney story-men had perfected and practiced as a core competency through years of storyboarding. The innovation in methodology that was apparent was the ability to adapt a two-dimensional process into a three-dimensional process, which entailed and had to take into consideration the engineering of direct physical interaction of the audience with the finished product.

Walt and Roy were extremely successful in their personal efforts to sell concession leases and attraction sponsorships from leading American businesses in order to raise funds needed to construct the park, based on the idea of Disneyland and conceptual drawings of the park and its attraction. According to Gabler:

> Prior to the start of construction, $2.3 million in lease payments was collected from concessioners and sponsors, including: $50,000 from the Santa Fe Railroad to sponsor the railway; $45,000 from American Motors to sponsor the Circarama 360-degree movie attraction; $45,000 from Richfield Oil to sponsor Autopia, and $88,000 from the Swift and Company meatpackers for two Main Street concessions.[3]

Tapping into New Capital Sources

With the land deals negotiated and the contracts signed, construction of the park began with the first orange trees on the Anaheim property being removed in August 1954. Walt wanted the park to be completed and open to the public to generate much-needed revenue as soon as possible. He set July 1955 for the park opening, a mere eleven months away.

To ensure that Disneyland was built quickly and properly, Walt and Roy hired Stanford Research Institute president C.V. Wood as executive vice-president of Disneyland, overseeing the building and operation of the park. Wood had been the chief industrial engineer at a young age at the Convair airplane plant in San Diego, and considered himself an expert master planner. In reality, he had not completed his engineering studies at the University of Oklahoma, although he professed to having graduated.[4]

As the man heading up Disneyland for Walt, Wood quickly hired Admiral Joseph Fowler as construction supervisor. Fowler had served for 32 years in the Navy, including the supervision of ship construction during World War II. At one point he supervised twenty-five private shipyards. Wood and Fowler had worked together before, with Wood having previously been a vendor to Fowler on a number of military engagements.

Walt and Roy liked Fowler's no-nonsense, get-the-work-done, military attitude. Walt instructed Fowler to carry on with the work of building the park to the best of his abilities, and that when Walt saw something he didn't approve of, he'd let Fowler know.[5]

The Anaheim property soon became a hub of building activity, with the steady conversion of the flat dry land into a reconfigured topography of rivers, forests, gardens, and a surrounding protective earth berm. As Thomas reports, "Walt made frequent visits to bump over the rough terrain in a Jeep and survey his domain, correcting the sight lines, changing the paint color, attending to a thousand details. Throughout the frantic months, Fowler never expressed doubt that the park would open on time."[6]

With Walt attending to both his studio responsibilities and oversight of the park, Roy dealt with financial matters. ABC's line of credit and the financial leverage provided by concession and sponsor contractual agreements made it possible for the Bank of America to reluctantly extended further credit toward park construction. What was disconcerting to Roy and the bank was that cost estimates were constantly rising. "At ground-breaking, I had a budget of four-and-a-half million dollars," recalled Fowler. "That was before we had any plans at all. Two months later, in September, it went up to seven million dollars. In November, it was up to eleven million. We were still talking eleven million dollars in April [1955]. ... But by the time opening day had arrived, we had spent seventeen million dollars."[7]

With costs rising faster than expected, Walt did his part to ensure the successful funding of Disneyland and the protection of the fiduciary interests of the investors and Walt Disney Productions shareholders.

When *Disneyland* show turned out to be such a big success, ABC exercised its option for a new kind of children's show proposed by Walt—*The Mickey Mouse Club*—which would put more Disney programing on its network, again giving Walt complete creative control.[8] ABC president Robert Kintner stated in correspondence to Walt in December 1954, "I believe in this kid strip, there is the potential for the highest-rated show in the daytime; for the greatest impact on children in the history of communications; and for the creation of a product that not only will have the enthusiastic support of parents, Parent-Teacher Associations, etc., but will bring a new dimension to daytime programming."[9]

Even though Walt Disney Productions and WED were burdened to capacity with important projects, Walt agreed to accept $2.8 million for the first year of the show, even though he expected to take an immediate loss with his costs anticipated to run to around $4 million. What Walt needed, and the key factor in ABC obtaining the additional programming it desired, was the inclusion by ABC of a new line of credit of $2.4 million to support the park[10] at a time when lenders had little confidence in Walt's ability to turn a profit from Disneyland and more funding to build the park was hard to obtain.[11]

Walt provided a summary to an audience of businessmen in early 1956:

> A year ago we were praying that we could have Disneyland open by July, then wondering if we would have enough money to open it.

I reached a point where I needed a few more million dollars, so took on quite a chore and started a new TV show—*The Mickey Mouse Club.* Money from this program was used to help finish Disneyland.[12]

To ensure maximum synergy between *The Mickey Mouse Club* and the Disneyland park, Walt issued clear orders to his staff for the show to feature at least one story about Disneyland each week.[13]

The Drivers of Costs

The nature of the Disneyland park project brought with it a number of major cost drivers. One was Walt's decision early on to develop original one-of-a-kind custom-designed and custom-built rides that were unique to Disneyland instead of buying the standard midway fare. A vast array of vehicles, including trains, boats, surreys, covered wagons, and horse-drawn trams for Main Street were researched, designed, and custom-built by craftsmen to exacting specifications.[14]

The importance of scale and the architectural trick of forced perspective to make the buildings look taller than they were was another cost driver. For example, Walt made the decision to design Main Street to a non-standard scale, with the ground floor generally built to nine-tenths true scale, and the second story to eight-tenths. In Walt's estimation this gave the structures a more toy-like and comforting appearance. Some attractions were also built to a smaller scale for the same reason. The Disneyland railroad and its locomotives as well as the *Mark Twain* Riverboat were constructed to five-eighths scale.

Another big driver of costs was an under-estimation of the expense to move earth and build the park's foundational structure with poured concrete. Walt wasn't building a flimsy and temporary back-lot studio set, but rather a permanent structure that had to conform to proven engineering building and safety standards so as to ensure asset longevity and guest safety.

The biggest cause of expense overruns was the combination of Walt's need for speed in building the park and his insatiable desire for perfection. A general enumeration of the kinds of major events C.V. Wood and Admiral Fowler had to contend with are summarized by Neal Gabler in *Walt Disney*:

> Everyone had to rush. A structural engineer, who had been hired to assist in designing the buildings and coordinating with the WED staff, had to lay out foundations and framing even before the architectural details were finished, which caused problems, especially on Main Street. ... The soil in Anaheim was so sandy and porous that the Rivers of America kept seeping into the ground and clay soil had to be trucked to the site. Unions were aggrieved. A strike at the Orange County plant that was supplying asphalt necessitated hauling asphalt from San Diego. A plumbers' strike limited the number of

water fountains that could be installed before opening. One group of disgruntled machinists "forgot" to bring their tools, while another crew of laborers cut the wires on the Mr. Toad ride because they were angry at being driven so hard. On one occasion union painters at the park sandblasted the locomotive Casey Jr. and repainted it because it had been painted at the studio by members of a rival union. Even nature rebelled: the weather in the spring was the wettest the country had had in twenty years.

And then there was Walt Disney trudging over the site in a straw hat...alternately hurrying [the workers] up and slowing them down, willing the property to conform to his dream. "He walked over every inch of Disneyland," Ward Kimball said, "telling them to move a fence a little more to the left because you couldn't see the boat as it came 'round the corner. I'd be with him out there, and he'd say, 'The lake is too small. Maybe we should make it larger. Let's find out if we can move the train wreck over another fifty feet.' He thought of everything." Morgan "Bill" Evans...recalled, "Walt's approach was to say, 'I need a jungle,' or 'I need a touch of Alpine flavor for the sky ride.' He didn't know which trees would work, but he knew what he wanted." He wanted perfection. He wanted the park as realized to match the park in his mind's eye.[15]

Evans noted that Walt toured the park almost every day from the time construction began, and recalled one incident in which a large pepper tree had been planted beside the Plaza Pavilion restaurant near the entrance to Adventureland. Sam Gennawey in *The Disneyland Story* writes:

> Walt, Fowler, and Evans were walking by the restaurant when Walt turned to Fowler and asked, "Joe, that tree looks a little close to the walkway, doesn't it?" Fowler then turned to Evans and asked, "How about moving that tree, Bill?" Evans did as he was told and "moved all 10 tons of it a little ways back" about 10 feet overnight. The next day, as the men walked past the same spot, Evans said, Walt "didn't say a word. He just smiled."[16]

Walt was excited about building the park, but there were times when he was filled with anxiety about the pace of progress, worried that so much money had been spent on infrastructure with nothing tangible to show for the effort. As the foundation for the train station above the entrance to the park was being poured, Walt quipped to Dick Irvine, "By the time Joe [Fowler] gets through burying all our money underground, we won't have a thing left for the show!"[17]

"By January 1, 1955," write Holliss and Sibley in *The Disney Studio Story*, "building work was so far behind schedule that it was decided to postpone work on Tomorrowland until after the park had opened; but after serious thought, Walt reverted to his original plans, believing that all

Disneyland's themed areas had to be in existence on opening day, which was now set for 17 July."[18]

At the same time the park's infrastructure was being constructed, there were innumerable additional tasks to take care of. Livestock had to be found, transported, and tended to for Frontierland. Rides had to be designed, custom manufactured, and installed. Suppliers from around the world had to be sourced and vetted, merchandise had to ordered and stocked. Contracts had to be drafted and negotiated. Among the things that had to be sourced and shipped to California, repaired, adapted, and installed, were a merry-go-round and carousel horses, arcade games, design elements like railings on Main Street that came from old plantations in Nashville and Memphis[19], and authentic 1850s gaslight lampposts from Baltimore, Boston, and Philadelphia.[20] Trains had to be built and locomotives purchased. Test track had to be developed for the dark rides. Miniature cars for the Autopia attraction were contracted from a firm in Germany. Four hundred thousand dollars worth of greenery had to be bought, delivered, and installed, including 1,200 full-sized trees and 9,000 shrubs. Nurseries were depleted from Santa Barbara to San Diego.[21] There was all of this and so much more.

Expenses continued to rise beyond estimates and additional capital was needed to complete the park, like it was one big money pit. Roy was doing everything possible to find it, including the arrangement of a seven-year loan of almost $2.4 million from Walt Disney Productions to Disneyland, Inc.[22] In addition, according to Disney attorney Luther Marr as reported by Bob Thomas in *Building a Company*:

> [Roy] hocked the pictures, using them as collateral for the Bank of America loan. He hocked the leases at Disneyland; the whole thing had been borrowed on. He used ABC's credit line. He used everything there was to use.
>
> ABC was furious. ... Gunther Lessing and I had a meeting with the executive vice president of ABC-Paramount; he was the head of the whole theater chain...[and he] said, 'Walt Disney is a wild man! We can't control him. It's like a tiger by the tail. We thought it would cost a million seven, and it's just going and going. There's no limit to what it will be, and we're on the line for it. Do something about it!"[23]

Somehow Roy managed to keep the project financed, providing a tour of the construction site to help generate enthusiasm amongst investors.

One day in April 1955, and in desperate need for additional capital, Roy and Fowler walked down an unpaved Main Street with an executive from Bank of America, observing the construction and painting of the buildings. Looking around, the bank executive provided his assessment that it was unlikely that the park could be completed with the funds at hand, even though the budget had already been pushed to eleven million dollars, and suggested that around fifteen million dollars would be needed to complete the park. Roy was instantly relieved to learn that the bank would extend additional credit. Bank of America brought in Bankers Trust Company of New York as a co-investor to share the risk.[24] While committed to the project, by now Roy was beginning to question the wisdom of their ways, having difficulty coming to terms with how something so expensive as Disneyland could ultimately be successful.[25]

The Push to the Opening Gala

With funding once again secured, the push was on to complete the park for its scheduled July 17, 1955, opening. So much had been done in so little time, with so much still left to do.

In June, just six weeks prior to opening, Wood and many of the WED management began to panic as pressure to complete the park increased. Half the attractions still remained to be completed and confidence was waning. When the Orange County plumbers and asphalt workers went on strike, Wood began to test Fowler's receptivity to a six-week postponement of opening day until September. "We might as well postpone until September. We're not going to make it by July," he told Fowler.[26]

Walt wouldn't hear of it. The nation was enthralled in anticipation due to the build-up on the *Disneyland* TV show and through the press, not to mention that further delays meant weeks more of additional costs. Until the park was filled with paying customers, there would be no desperately needed revenues. Disneyland would open on time as scheduled.

When Walt made concerned inquiries, Admiral Fowler reassured him that the park would open as scheduled. "We're gonna make it," he told Walt. His message to Wood was the same: "Woody, we have to make it."[27]

Fowler later commented that he had been indoctrinated during the war: "We had to make dates! There wasn't any two ways about it." Meeting the deadline was important for Fowler not only because he had promised he would do so, but also, "if we had waited until September, when the crowds sloughed off, we might never have gotten it off the ground." The summer crowds were needed to fill the family park while the kids were out of school.[28]

By all accounts, Fowler did an outstanding job managing the plans and the unforeseen contingencies. The plumbers' strike in Orange County almost prevented the installation of toilets and sinks in the park washrooms. To induce the plumbers back to work, Fowler promised that they would be paid the rate they would receive upon settlement of the strike. When the asphalt plants in Orange County went on strike, Fowler was forced to truck in asphalt at a huge premium from San Diego to ensure the job was done and the stage was ready on schedule.[29]

To expedite the construction work to make the opening, the unionized construction crew was tripled in size in the final weeks from about 800 to 2,500 workers, many of whom were working sixteen-hour days at time-and-a-half and double time and taking home a thousand dollars a week.[30]

In the buildup to opening day, staff was being hired to operate the park and concessions. Each had to undergo training and orientation to the Disney Way, a paradigm that work at Disneyland was to be a happiness-creating performance. This led to the creation of some unique nomenclature to reinforce personal behavior as performance, much of it an extension of Disney's show business lineage: guests, not customers; hosts and hostesses, not employees; audiences, not crowds; on stage and offstage; wardrobe; etc.

Perhaps the most important element of the orientation training was the message that Walt's *purpose* for creating Disneyland is to *create happiness*, and that every person on the payroll played an important and equal part in ensuring that outcome for each individual guest. Creating happiness would be the standard against which attractions and performances would be judged. And it was easy to measure by simply observing whether guests were smiling and happy.

Training-program professional Van Arsdale France, who later became the founder of Disney University, developed the initial orientation program. France explained the rationale for the "creating happiness" positioning:

> First...the Disney tradition had been one of entertaining others, and from what I'd read till that time, Walt was concerned about producing a good product, realizing that the profit would follow.
>
> Second...we really didn't know what we were doing. Walt had said that. So, I could say that you might prepare food or park cars or operate attractions or keep things clean, but that is not the end product, the reason for Disneyland was to *bring happiness to other people*.[31]

Up until now, France noted, Disney staff, be they Walt Disney Productions or WED employees, really had no direct contact with audiences. It was up to theatre owners to interact with their customers and create conditions to keep them coming back. Now, "at Disneyland, we represented the entire organization on a person-to-person basis."[32]

France recognized that the essence of Walt's personal philosophy was all about how customers should be treated. To infuse that philosophy into the fabric of Disneyland's operating culture from the very start, employee-guest interactions would have to surpass the conventional transactional approach that was commonplace in other parks, and which gave the amusement park and fairgrounds industry a bad reputation.

Unlike other parks, at Disneyland every interaction between host and guest was to be construed as a Disney *brand* interaction—what later became known in business jargon as a *moment-of-truth*—and the organization would do well to take the behavior of its employees seriously if it was to operationalize Walt's desire for Disneyland to create happiness. France wrote, "In view of these ideas, each of us had a responsibility to look our best... and to represent the entire Disney organization, both within Disneyland and in the surrounding area when we were, as we pointed out, 'off stage.'"[33]

With the opening just weeks away, France's training and orientation program was presented to and approved by a group of Disneyland executives and investors, including Roy Disney and top executives from the Bank of America, Eastman Kodak, and Swift and Company.[34] The unique approach to orienting and training employees engaged in experiential entertainment, and which would later become the foundation for the now famous Disney University training course, was put into place. The hiring and training of park staff could now begin.

Disneyland, Inc. was a separate corporate entity from Walt Disney Productions, and C.V. Wood insisted that there would be no unions in the park. Not surprisingly, the unions had a different idea. The construction union, whose members were working hard to meet the deadline, aggressively assured Wood that if they didn't have union representation the park wouldn't open, that if the park were to be completed and opened on schedule, the unions would have to be on site.[35] According to Disney's labor consultant at the time, "If the construction unions were to walk out for even two days, we'd never get this place opened."[36]

Disneyland management negotiated with the Orange County Central Labor Council and when the dust settled, twenty-nine unions were represented at the park. Where the work didn't correspond to traditional trade unions, such as attraction operators, management agreed to be helpful in directing those workers to the Teamsters.[37]

Not only did the park itself have to be ready for opening day, so too did the surrounding transportation infrastructure of roads to support the park. Anaheim city officials, including Mayor Frank Pearsons, the city manager, the Orange County Roads Department, police and fire departments, California Highway Patrol, and others, were all very supportive in developing and executing plans to accommodate Disneyland's opening date.[38] Not surprisingly, their plans had also fallen significantly behind schedule, and their roles for opening day to manage the volume of automobile and pedestrian traffic, and other contingencies, had to be worked out and coordinated with Disneyland's plans.

Opening day was rapidly approaching, and the imperative to meet the deadline continued to rapidly drive up spending. More spending means more bills to be paid and the cash to pay them. Unfortunately, unpaid bills were becoming a problem. Disney historian Todd James Pierce writes in *Three Years in Wonderland*:

> Milt Albright, a Disneyland accountant, explains that by this point in the park's construction many bills were left unpaid: "We owed everybody in Orange County that had concrete, steel, and anything to sell of consequence." After hearing rumors about the park's financial status, some suppliers refused to deliver additional goods to Disneyland unless they were paid on the spot in cash. Other suppliers considered placing a lien on Disneyland, Inc. for money they were already owed. A series of liens would've been devastating, perhaps even forcing Disneyland, Inc. into bankruptcy. Albright did his best to keep creditors at bay: "Trust us," he told them, "and after we open on July 17, 1955, you will get paid."[39]

To help manage cash flow and deal with the critical problem of late payables, Roy sent a more seasoned studio accountant to Anaheim. Making payroll and paying construction firms and materials providers demanding cash were given top priority. For everyone else, payments were delayed as long as possible. Vendors were invited to visit Roy at the studio for his personal assurances if they had concerns about being paid, and were told that in return for deferring payment they would be granted vendor status "for umpteen years."[40]

Right up until the last minute and late into the evening ahead of the opening, road crews were installing curbing, laying asphalt, and painting lines on the two-lane West Street. Cases of beer and park passes were delivered to city workers as an incentive to keep working to ensure completion by morning. With the help of the California Highway Patrol and the Anaheim police, a crew was installing illegal non-city approved direction signs to help invitees find their way to and from Disneyland with the goal of easing traffic congestion.[41]

"At midnight on 16 July 1955," write Holliss and Sibley in *The Disney Studio Story*, "with a total investment of $17 million now at stake—painters were still at work by the light of arc lamps; and, when opening day dawned, plumbers were still installing washrooms and carpenters were busily at work among the tv crews, who were setting up their equipment to record the event. Tomorrowland was desperately incomplete, and Walt gave instructions to cover up its deficiencies 'with balloons and pennants.'"[42]

All told, it took eleven months to transform the Orange County landscape and build the park and its attractions to reach opening day. More than 3,000 men were employed on construction, utilizing 20,000 feet of lumber, 5,000 cubic yards of concrete, and a million square feet of asphalt.[43]

Disneyland's Opening Gala and Press Preview

Anticipation for Disneyland's opening was heightened by months of promotion and reporting on the park's progress on the *Disneyland* TV show.
ABC was planning a 90-minute live TV special that it promoted heavily
through a $40,000 campaign of full-page newspaper ads. The advertising
was sold out four months prior to the broadcast, and the twenty-nine
camera crews rehearsed every Sunday for two months prior to the event.[44]
This was to be the largest live-broadcast event in television history, with
viewership estimates as high as 90 million.[45]

Sunday, July 17, 1955, was the by-invitation-only opening gala and
"press preview" for the park. Fifteen thousand gold and silver invitations
had been printed and issued to local dignitaries, politicians, celebrities, and
the press, many of whom were expecting VIP treatment. They were also
generously handed out to WED and studio staff and family, construction
crews, and others in return for favors received in order to fill the park to
its 15,000-person capacity.

Some of the nation's carnival owners were invited to the opening day
event, and all but two predicted that Walt's park would fail and be shut
down within six months, citing three reasons: no alcoholic beverages
which meant no revenue from a beer or liquor sponsor; people won't be
willing to pay an admission fee to enter the park; and Walt's insistence on
cleanliness would be too expensive given the proclivity of people to toss
their garbage on the ground.[46]

Walt had a reply for each concern: if people want a drink, they can get
it elsewhere, otherwise the park will attract drunks and trouble-makers;
you'll get a better class of people if you charge them a fee to enter; and
finally, regarding garbage, Walt said, "One of the things I hated most
about carnivals and piers was all the crap that was everywhere. You're
stepping on chewing gum and ice cream cones. I think people want clean
amusement parks."[47]

When the park opened that morning, Walt watched the first guests
enter. Mouseketeer Sharon Baird was there to observe Walt's reaction:

> On the opening day of Disneyland, we [Mouseketeers] were in Walt
> Disney's apartment above the Main Street Fire Station when the
> gates of the park were opened for the first time. I was standing next
> to him at the window, watching the guests come pouring through
> the gates. When I looked up at him, he had his hands behind his
> back, a grin from ear to ear, and I could see a lump in his throat and
> a tear streaming down his cheek. He had realized his dream. I was
> only twelve years old at the time, so it didn't mean as much to me
> then. But as the years go by, that image of him becomes more and
> more endearing.[48]

By noon, it was estimated that 28,000 people had entered the park. As one employee put it, "the members of the press and other dignitaries found themselves in a mob."[49] The public demand to attend was so great that thousands of counterfeit invitations had been printed and distributed. Nobody was prepared for such a huge opening day crowd or anticipated the overwhelming public enthusiasm for Walt's park, which had been hyped on the *Disneyland* TV show for months.

With almost twice the number of people than Walt expected and no trial run to identify and fix problems, the line-ups were long and several rides broke down. There was over-crowding on attractions like the *Mark Twain* Riverboat, which rode so low on its maiden voyage that water was washing across the lower deck.[50]

The concessionaires ran out of food and drinks, and many of the water fountains had not been installed because of the plumber's strike and Walt's decision to give priority to connecting toilets ahead of water fountains. Because of the extreme heat of the day, many women found their heels sinking into the newly laid softened asphalt on Main Street. There was a gas leak in Tomorrowland, which was roped off and closed down on the advice of the fire chief until it was resolved. There was sabotage in Fantasyland, where a disgruntled electrician allegedly cut, or perhaps just unplugged, an electrical cable, forcing some rides to be shut down.[51]

Walt's schedule for the day was too frantic for him to take notice, as he rushed around the park preparing for and taking part in a live 90-minute television special, *Dateline Disneyland*. The TV special was hosted by film actors Ronald Reagan and Bob Cummings, and radio and TV personality Art Linkletter, and was watched by virtually every television household in America, attracting an estimated 70 million viewers, about half the total U.S. population.[52]

The ceremonies opened with a dedication by Walt based on the philosophy for the park that he had used to entice investors a year and a half earlier:

> To all who come to this happy place: welcome. Disneyland is your land. Here age relives fond memories of the past, and here youth may savor the challenge and promise of the future. Disneyland is dedicated to the ideals, the dreams, and the hard facts which have created America, with the hope that it will be a source of joy and inspiration to all the world.[53]

The reviews in the press the next day ranged from descriptions of opening day as a disaster with every shortcoming enumerated, to a report in the *Minneapolis Tribune* informing readers that Disneyland is "the gosh-darndest, most happily-inspired, most carefully-planned, most adventure-filled park ever conceived. No ride or concession in it is like anything in any other amusement park anywhere."[54]

Van Arsdale France, whose role it was to hire and train park employees, recognized and respected the immense risk that Walt and Roy were taking. He wrote a tribute to Walt's entrepreneurial and iconoclastic spirit and determination:

> The Disney brothers had, in the past, gambled heavily on pioneering movie ventures such as *Snow White* and *Fantasia*. But *Snow White*, a major break-through in full-length animation, was only a 5 million dollar gamble.
>
> But along came Disneyland, a 17 million dollar gamble, and a gamble it was—Walt had hocked everything he could, including his life insurance, on this totally new dimension in family entertainment.
>
> [If it] should turn out to be, as the experts predicted, "A Hollywood Spectacular...a spectacular flop," it could lead to bankruptcy and damage to the Disney name and reputation.
>
> One could see why Walt and his brother Roy, who was the financial genius on the brother team, would be concerned.
>
> The preview on Sunday had been for FREE. The thousands of "special guests" came with invitations...gold or silver. The cash flow was flowing in one direction...*out*. There was justifiable concerns that we'd open the gates and nobody would come to PAY.
>
> Twenty years of dreaming, and years, months, days and hours of effort and financing had not, as yet, been proven to be a good investment. To this day, I don't understand how Walt Disney could take the gamble against the advice of bankers, "experts," and many people in his organization.[55]

Post-Opening Plussing for Perfection

After a post-mortem assessment of opening day and a reading of the press reviews, Walt immediately developed and implemented a three-fold plan to address and overcome the worst of the park's shortcomings. Todd James Pierce notes in *Three Years In Wonderland*:

> First, construction crews and maintenance men would work long hours to finish all of the pending rides and ensure that the existing rides stayed operational. Second, the Disneyland public relations staff would launch an energetic campaign to convince media representatives that on opening day Disneyland simply hadn't been ready for its grand premiere. Lastly, though Disneyland remained in substantial debt, Walt would use all available funds in a vigorous reinvestment strategy to expand the park. His long-term goal was to channel 16 percent of Disneyland's income into new attractions—though in that first year, Walt earmarked far more than 16 percent for various improvements.[56]

Because Disneyland was a one-of-a-kind attraction, and Walt assessed every addition through the lens of the quality and authenticity of the experience of his customers, improvements often required creative innovation and imaginative engineering of an unprecedented degree. From the time it opened, Disneyland was in a state of never-ending constant improvement to enhance the experience of guests and entice them to keep returning.

From the beginning, park cleanliness and staff courtesy standards were established, and ways were found to shorten waiting times and improve the experience of standing in line to access attractions. As one example, the Rocket to the Moon attraction in Tomorrowland included a pre-show film to entertain guests as they waited outside to enter. Many guests would walk-by, stop to watch the film, and then continue on their way, mistaking the film for the real attraction. Soon after, the film was hidden from passersby and made part of the attraction itself.[57]

The public was enthralled by the idea of Disneyland, making it an instant hit, in spite of the negative publicity of the opening day spectacle. On the day following the gala opening, Disneyland welcomed more than 26,000 paying guests, with attendance topping 135,000 admissions by the end of the first week.[58] To the relief of all who were invested, the park was finally generating cash.

Years later, Roy spoke of his concerns that while attendance at Disneyland was spectacular for the Sunday premiere gala, those people didn't have to pay. Every dollar the studio could get its hands on was invested in the park, and the question still remained: would the public *pay* to experience Disneyland?

On the morning following the gala opening, Monday, July 18, the first day the park was opened to the paying public, Roy was feeling anxious and decided to visit the park to see how things were going. He recalled that morning in a speech given years later. "Well, on that day I left the studio and headed down the Santa Ana Freeway. I was worried. After getting out of Los Angeles, the traffic began to get heavy. It could have been people going to the beach." Roy took this as a good sign. As he approached Anaheim, cars, pickup trucks, and mobile home campers were lined up, bumper to bumper in a seven-mile traffic jam. "It must have taken more than an hour to finally get to the Disneyland parking lot," he recalled.

Roy drove past the main entrance to the park and followed the roads around the parking lot periphery, which was filling with cars. After parking his Cadillac in his reserved space, far away from the visitor entrance, he later said:

> A young man working there recognized me and came up in a bit of a panic. He wasn't familiar with our first-name policy.

"Mr. Disney," he said, "people have been stalled on the freeway getting into our parking lot. Children are peeing all over the lot."

I looked around at all these people who were coming here to pay to get in. With a great sense of relief, I said: "God bless 'em, let 'em pee!"[59]

After the first month the park was attracting on average over 20,000 visitors per day. Early park attendance exceeded projections by fifty percent.[60] In August almost half the visitors to southern California made it a point to visit the park, and before the end of September, Disneyland welcomed its one-millionth visitor.

What made Disneyland financially successful was Walt's fundamental insight that the key driver of guest spending was stay time—the length of time people spent at the park. Because stay time went up, so did spending on food, retail, and ride tickets. And because the place was an attraction in and of itself, people were willing to pay for admission.

Before Disneyland, the average stay time at an amusement park was less than two hours. Disneyland was no average amusement park, though. It was pleasant and refreshing and fun, and the average stay time was an unprecedented seven hours.

In his 1997 IAAPA speech, Bob Rogers addressed the question of how Walt got people to stay longer:

> Back in the early 1950s, Walt noticed that the atmosphere at most parks was not relaxing. The colors and graphics were garish, the barkers were irritating, and the employees looked dangerous, and the place was noisy and dirty. Stay times were around two hours partly because in that environment, people got tired faster. Walt got those seven-hour stay times by using lush landscaping, a relaxing ambiance, and a balanced blend of big thrills and little discoveries to keep the guests constantly relaxed and refreshed.[61]

With people staying longer, they were spending three times more on attractions, food, and souvenirs than was spent at other parks,[62] and 30% more than had been estimated in the original SRI economic study.

Walt's ability to apply more abstract and integrative higher-level thinking about these connections than his competitors enabled him to identify new ways to unleash hidden and unarticulated human value.

It has been said that a country is more an idea than a place. The same could be said of Disneyland. "Physically, Disneyland would be a small world in itself," Walt reflected, "it would encompass the essence of the things that were good and true in American life. It would reflect the faith and challenge of the future, the entertainment, the interest in intelligently presented facts, the stimulation of the imagination, the standards of health and achievement, and above all, a sense of strength, contentment, and well-being."[63]

With big entrepreneurial risks can come big rewards. Walt's long-standing dream of a park where a father and his daughters could have fun together, and his decision to proceed to build such a park, satisfied an immense latent and unarticulated emotional need within people for just such a thing. Disneyland became the conduit to convert these deeply held personal values and nostalgic emotions into economic value. Walt's entrepreneurial genius was in identifying and understanding that relationship, and in having the vision and courage to build a park that could deliver both sides of the equation: personal value and economic value.

The park completely transformed tourism and traffic patterns in southern California. When Disneyland first opened, there were only sixty motel rooms in the vicinity. The public relations staff that interviewed people in the park reported they received up to 800 requests a day from visitors seeking nearby accommodations. Supply to meet the demand would soon begin, including the construction of the 104-room first phase of the Disneyland Hotel. Peak park employment in the summer of 1955 was about 1,000 people.[64]

It was always Walt's intention to charge an admission fee to keep out the riff-raff and to signal to guests that attending the park had a value unto itself. Prior to the park's opening, talk of admission was fifteen cents for children and twenty-five cents for adults.[65] Because of the huge unanticipated expense of building the park, Walt decided that guests would be charged a general admission fee of $1.00 for adults and fifty-cents for children to enjoy the park and the many free attractions and shows. Admission to individual attractions ranged from ten cents to fifty cents, and each had to be purchased separately. It cost twenty-five cents to park in the twelve-thousand car lot.[66]

The constant need to line up and purchase tickets to access individual attractions left many families with the impression that the park was expensive to visit, and Walt faced criticism in the press. When asked by an Associated Press reporter about the *commercial* nature of the park, Walt responded appropriately: "We have to charge what we do because the park cost a lot to build and maintain. I have no government subsidy. The public is my subsidy. I mortgaged everything I own and put it in jeopardy for this park. Commercial? How have I stayed in business all my life? The critics must know a newspaper exists on advertising. They're crazy." He reminded the reporters who were present: "We have a lot of free things in the park. No other place has as high a quality. I stand here in the park and talk to people. It's a most gratifying thing. All I've got from the public is thank-yous."[67]

To enhance the guest experience by eliminating any potential negative effects of having to continually line up and buy tickets, while at the same time simplifying operations by reducing the handling of coins and balancing out long lines at the most popular attractions like the Jungle Cruise, a decision was made to bundle admission along with a books of tickets for eight attractions in three price categories for $2.50, based on the average of what guests were already spending.[68]

The "Day at Disneyland" ticket book was first offered just months after the opening, in October 1955. Attractions were assigned an A, B, or C designation based on their sophistication, with tickets appropriately marked. Designated D and E tickets were added in 1956 and 1959 respectively for the grandest attractions.

What was once looked upon as Walt's crazy idea was now an astonishing financial success. In the years leading up to the completion of Disneyland, Walt Disney Productions had reported gross income of $8 million in 1953 and $11.6 million in in 1954. In its first year, Disneyland brought in revenues of $10 million to Walt Disney Productions.[69] When added to the revenues from two television shows (*Disneyland* and *The Mickey Mouse Club*), Davy Crockett merchandising, and the release of *Lady and the Tramp* amongst other things, revenues for 1955 more than doubled to $24.6 million, and profits rose to $1.5 million. One year later, in 1956, the company reported a net profit of $2.6 million, the highest ever in its history.[70]

In every way, Disneyland was Walt's park, and with an apartment above the fire station on Main Street, also his part-time home. Disneyland and other theme-park-related projects undertaken by WED and its cadre of uniquely talented Imagineers would now come to occupy the majority of Walt's creative energy and attention. To a great extent, Walt's personal interest in filmed entertainment was waning. His enthusiasm, applied creativity, and commitment to building and continuously improving Disneyland was much more challenging and gratifying. Walt was once again the leading figure in a new business category and entertainment world of his own making.

(The term "Imagineer," which will forever be associated with Walt Disney, comes from the combining of imagination with engineering, and reflects the concept of bringing into reality that which one can imagine, or as Imagineer Marty Sklar described it to Walt, "the blending of creative imagination with technical know-how."[71] Interestingly, the term was first used by Alcoa Aluminum in the early 1940s to describe its ability to engineer innovations in aluminum production in pursuit of the allied war effort. Its application to Walt Disney and WED was uniquely appropriate.)

Walt saw Disneyland not only as an integrating and strategically advanced business venture, it was also his personal playground, a place where he could step into the engineer's seat and ride his beloved train, or drive the fire truck down Main Street before guests arrived in the park, or lead a parade, or entertain world leaders, celebrities, and dignitaries. Most importantly to Walt, it was a place where he could experience the personal joy of bringing happiness to others and sharing with them the things he himself had imagined, created, loved, and valued. It was his own mid-life personal sandbox where he could play, invent, explore, and build. In Walt's words,

> [Disneyland is] something that will never be finished. Something that I can keep developing, keep plussing and adding to. ... A picture is a thing, once you wrap it up and turn it over to Technicolor you're through. ... I wanted something alive, something that could grow, something I could keep plussing with ideas; the park is that. Not only can I add things, but even the trees will keep growing. The things will get more beautiful each year. And as I find out what the public likes...I can change the park, because it's alive. That is why I wanted that park.[72]

With the opening of the park and his weekly appearances on TV, Walt had become a well-recognized celebrity in his own right, and began to see himself as a showman and not just a movie studio executive. He thought about Disneyland as a show—a large coordinated performance. Keeping the show vibrant and energized would require continuous change to prevent stagnation. In Walt's eyes, "Disneyland will never be completed. It will continue to grow as long as there is imagination left in the world." And true to his vision, from opening day the park has been changing and growing, providing something new, imaginative, and exciting for both the workers of the organization and the public whom they are serving.

The continued development of Disneyland maintained its forward momentum from the day it opened. The park itself was the testing-ground for Walt's ideas. Success could be judged by guest enthusiasm as measured by ticket redemption. Attractions that were not accepted by guests or were difficult to maintain and operate could be shut down and replaced. Walt wasn't afraid to learn by experimentation and made experimentation an active part of his methodology of life-long learning for personal and professional growth, and part of the culture of his organizations.

One early Disneyland failure that was a source of learning was the introduction by Walt of the Mickey Mouse Club Circus in November 1955. The one-hour big-top circus show lasted barely two months before the world's largest striped circus tent came down and an important lesson was learned by Walt and summarized by Joe Fowler: "People came to Disneyland to see Disneyland."[73]

In planning and building Disneyland and the operational and organizational structure to support it, there was no existing blueprint, no standards to follow, no model to copy. As Walt himself had said, nothing like Disneyland existed anywhere. Most of it was trial and error based on best judgment. Whatever worked was kept and improved upon; whatever failed to meet the needs of the public was changed and replaced by a better idea.

It is not uncommon for business leaders to operate in conformance with the generally accepted rule that you can succeed by getting about 80% right and ignoring the other 20%. The practice is justified on the basis of expediency, efficiency, and impermanence. Of course the other 20% may just be the little details that really make a difference to the customer relative to competitive offerings, that little something that takes one over the line from good to great. Walt was obsessed with getting everything right, down to the last one percent, which was the secret pixie dust that delivered the magic of his early animation success as well as his success with Disneyland. Customers noticed and customers cared, packing the parks day after day, year after year.

In the end, Walt believed that with the phenomenal success of Disneyland—in the face of ridicule and against all of the skeptics—he had finally demonstrated to his critics and doubters the practicality of his obsession for creating a strong vision and paying close attention to the little details that make all the difference to the experience of customers and the success of his business. He saw it as an issue of integrity, of adherence to his core values. With regards to Disneyland, he said: "Give people everything you can give them. Keep the place as clean as you can keep it. Keep it friendly, you know. Make it a fun place to be."[74]

The practical result of managing to the highest standard of excellence when aligned to consumer values is that you probably won't have many serious competitors. More than half a century after Disneyland opened, Disney is still perceived as the undisputed leading and trusted brand in the category of "family entertainment," and Walt's many paradigm-shifting achievements continue to be studied and copied in an attempt to duplicate the Disney magic.

No Time to Rest When Building on Success

The Mickey Mouse Club television show premiered on October 3, 1955, almost three months after the opening of Disneyland. It aired five days a week for one hour, and was an instant hit, becoming the highest-rated television show ever. Watching the Mouseketeers and singing the show's M-I-C-K-E-Y M-O-U-S-E theme song became a daily ritual for almost every child in America.

While the studio expected to lose over $1 million on the show in its first year of production,[75] Roy was able to reduce the gap in a contract renegotiation at the end of 1956 to around $300,000, and expressed confidence in the 1956 annual report that "the programs will eventually return a good profit from subsequent uses at home and abroad," which of course was true.[76]

Walt's top priority for his Disneyland management team in 1956 was twofold: to fix and enhance anything in the park that could be improved; and to add new attractions as quickly as possible to absorb the growing crowds and keep them occupied and entertained. Walt allocated a budget of $1.5 million to fund park expansion.

A key new addition to the park in 1956 was Tom Sawyer Island, which was personally designed by Walt, and featured, in his words, "all the things I wanted to do as a kid—and couldn't. Including getting into something without a ticket."[77] The original designs for the three-acre narrow island included scale-model reproductions of famous American buildings and replicas of river towns visible from the *Mark Twain* Riverboat. But once the park opened, Walt assessed the need for an area where children could run and play, and freely exercise their imaginations. Tom Sawyer Island was his way to create a safe, controlled environment subject to loose parental supervision.

A quarter-of-a-million dollars was spent to landscape the island to include trails, caves, a suspension bridge, a fort, escape tunnels and secret passages, and to build motorized rafts to transport passengers to the island. There was even a fishing hole stocked with 15,000 catfish, perch and bluegill, where guests could borrow a Huck Finn bamboo pole and a can of worms and try to reel one in.[78]

Another major iconic new attraction at the park was the Skyway to Tomorrowland, a cable-car transportation system that opened in June 1956, in time to enthrall the summer tourists. Before it could open, the attraction had to be designed, sourced, engineered, approved, and built. Sam Gennawey writes in *The Disneyland Story*:

> The Skyway gondola ride was the first of its kind in the United States. The cable drive mechanism came from ski-lift builder Von Roll Company of Berne, Switzerland. The system installed at Disneyland consisted of new components as well as used equipment from the 1955 Rotterdam Fair and the German Federal Garden Show at Karsel, West Germany. The stranded cable extended 1,250 feet to connect Tomorrowland and Fantasyland. It was supported by four cross-braced towers. The tallest tower was 60 feet.[79]

Imagineer Dick Stine designed the forty-two gondolas. Each bucket could seat two guests on patio chairs bolted to the floor for a three-and-a-half minute one-way aerial view of Disneyland.

Perhaps the most ambitious of the new attractions was the Rainbow Caverns Mine Train, a half-a-million dollar attraction that attempted to re-create everything wondrous and wonderful about the Old-West in the form of a thrilling and spectacular train ride on seven acres of land.

A highlight of the train ride was passage through the Rainbow Caverns, which used the relatively new ultraviolet black-light technology to create spectacular underground cave scenes that incorporated water and fountain special effects.[80]

In addition to the mine train ride, the seven-acre western-themed area included pack mule, Conestoga wagon, and stagecoach rides that added to the authenticity of the experience and allowed for alternate ways for guests to enjoy the man-made desert environment.

The design and construction detail of what Walt offered at Disneyland was far beyond anything available at any other popular American amusement park, such as Coney Island.[81]

Each ride and attraction was designed and constructed to Walt's exacting standards. The least complete of the lands at Disneyland's opening was Tomorrowland, which was now given considerable attention. Astro-Jets was the first ride to be added. It was similar to the Dumbo ride but built to go faster and higher, and themed to provide older-guests with "a thrilling spin through space."[82]

The air-conditioned Mickey Mouse Club Theater opened in Fantasyland, as did the Storybook Land Canal Boats, a $200,000 attraction of miniature three-dimensional scenes from the world's great folk tales built on the banks of a man-made canal that held almost half-a-million gallons of water. Scenes included Geppetto's Village, three little houses on Pig Island, Peter Pan's London Park with miniature stunted trees created by containing their roots, and the home of the Seven Dwarfs, amongst others. One scene featured a fifteen-foot tall model of Cinderella's castle designed using forced perspective with spires covered in gold leaf.

Walt was enthralled with minutely detailed miniatures for years. To withstand the outdoor elements, the ones in Disneyland were primarily built of plywood covered in fiberglass on a one-inch to one-foot scale. For an *Alice in Wonderland* scene, Walt wanted a miniature church with an authentic stained glass window, even though he could have simplified and saved money. But for Walt, those details mattered because he knew they mattered to guests. Authenticity was a core value of Walt's way, and it was a non-negotiable element of an operating culture he had built and perpetuated amongst WED's Imagineers. This story about the stained glass window told by Gennawey in *The Disneyland Story* is illustrative:

> Harriet Burns was assigned to the project, and she began work on a window designed by artist Frank Armitage. Burns had been working on the complex project that contained more than 360 pieces of lead when Walt stopped by the model shop as he frequently did. Without thinking, he picked up the window before Burns had a chance to solder it together, and all of the pieces scattered on the floor. Burns did not let it bother her, as she was used to Walt wanting to play with the models.

It would have been simpler to create a window out of celluloid placed behind plexiglass, but Walt expected more. For example, Moley's House had hand-hammered locks and pulls, and the gutters were made of copper. Burns said, "Nobody could really see it, but Walt knew it was there—that was the good part."[83]

For a scene with a windmill, Walt suggested the inclusion of tulips in the landscaping. A horticulturalist was hired to locate and acquire miniature tulips that would fit the scale of the windmills. Tulips from New Zealand were eventually located, but they had long eighteen-inch stems that would have to be buried and hidden. The attempt was made for a short while, but the landscapers had difficulty keeping them alive, and they were eventually removed.

Walt's dedication to detail wasn't limited to this one attraction. It was applied as a matter of course to everything in Disneyland. What makes Walt's dedication to detail on the Storybook Land Canal Boats attraction even more interesting is that in discussing the work to be done with Harriet Burns, he told her, "We can do this little ride, and it will be filler for the moment. Later on we can take it out and put something else there."[84] This intricate, complicated, and expensive attraction was foreseen to be temporary until something better could be devised. Still, he set his mind to creating something unique and beautiful, and challenged his staff to exhibit their creativity and craftsmanship, where others in the business would have simply put in another conventional mechanical ride or retail shop as a temporary plug, with little regard for show quality and integrity to professed values. Walt the showman would have nothing of the sort.

As part of the 1956 park expansion, a New Orleans-themed area opened in Frontierland. Appropriately themed dining areas were added throughout the new area to accommodate hungry guests, as were new shops with uniquely themed merchandise and souvenirs.

Opportunities were also identified for corporate sponsors who were no longer skeptical of the folly of Disneyland, and were now eager to align themselves with Walt's vision of the park's commercial benefits. Corporate sponsorships were a form of advertising, and an important additional source of revenue for the park. Sponsors would have to pay for the privilege and opportunity to reach out to Walt's guests. Disneyland historian Sam Gennawey writes about some of the new sponsored attractions that opened in the park in 1956 in *The Story of Disneyland*:

> On April 5, Crane's "Bathroom of Tomorrow" opened and featured a next generation of bathroom fixtures and a launderette, all done in citrus yellow. The bathroom was equipped with radiant heated floors and a Crane central air-conditioning system. ... The American Dairy Association updated their opening-day exhibit by adding the "Dairy

of the Future," with cows watching color television while milkmen deliver milk with helicopters on their backs. Another new exhibit was the WenMac "Hobbyland," which featured the Thimble Drone Flight Circle, where guests could watch a 20-minute demonstration of model planes in flight and fast-moving model speedboats jetting around a circular fenced enclosure 200 feet in circumference.[85]

By the time the park reached its first anniversary on July 17, 1956, attendance had reached 3.8 million guests,[86] making the park "the largest single private enterprise attraction in the Western Hemisphere." Paid attendance reached five million on October 3. Research indicated that 41 percent of guests travelled to the park from outside California, at a time when trans-continental travel was relatively difficult.[87]

According to a Disneyland press release in July 1956, the ratio of adults to children was a surprising four to one, with an average spending per guest of $2.37 on parking, admission, rides, amusements, and souvenirs, which was considered a substantial amount at the time.[88] According to Buzz Price, "Before Walt came along, the entire industry was getting one dollar per capita. The main things that Walt did was to figure out how to get the per caps up to $4.50 in the very first year. And by the second year they were up to $6. The rest of the industry was astonished."[89] And while the initial launch of Disneyland received considerable negative press, one year later 98% of guests indicated they would recommend the park to their friends and families.[90]

As the park began its second year of operation, the onslaught of enhancements continued. The Autopia attraction in which guests could ride miniature motorized cars around a track was so popular that Walt decided to construct a temporary Junior Autopia on the now-abandoned Mickey Mouse Club Circus site. Junior Autopia was the first park ride in which adults were prohibited from accompanying their children.[91]

In late August the Carnation Plaza Gardens opened at the end of Main Street to serve snacks to guests. Band concerts were help during the day under a large red-and-white canopy, which at night was converted into a dance floor.[92] Walt's primary focus was to continue to enhance the guest experience with the expectation that customers would recognize the uniqueness of Disneyland and acknowledge Walt's efforts in kind by visiting, spending, and sharing their positive experiences through word-of-mouth with their friends and colleagues back home.

In addition to adding seven new rides and doubling the number of free exhibits at Disneyland in 1956, Walt also announced that he would be undertaking a major park expansion to be completed in 1959.[93] He was particularly excited about building a "Hall of Presidents" which he said "will authentically bring to life the America as it was when this nation was founded." Walt imagined life-size figures "like a wax museum" that would recite appropriate speeches. He estimated that it would cost as much as $60 million, but it was important for the youth of America to understand their "God-given heritage." "We'll get the money from somewhere," he said, and was looking for corporate sponsorship "because I want the attraction to be free."[94]

A significant expansion in the number of studio employees also occurred in 1956, largely due to the increase in the amount of television work, rising from 855 in October 1955 to 1,271 in October 1956.[95]

New Attractions and TV Expansion

In early in 1957, Walt decided he wanted to build a haunted house attraction for Disneyland set in the New Orleans section, and work slowly began on the development of ideas and concepts for what would eventually become the Haunted Mansion.[96]

The park continued to need more attractions to absorb the increasing volume of guests and reduce the amount of time spent in attraction lines.

A walk-through exhibit was created in Sleeping Beauty Castle, which opened in April 1957, with actress Shirley Temple as the guest of honor.[97]

The Monsanto Corporation sponsored a House of the Future exhibit that opened in June 1957. It featured an experimental 1,280 square foot house built with plastic as a substitution for conventional building materials, and was placed at the entrance of Tomorrowland. The house had three bedrooms, two baths, a living room, dining room, family room, and kitchen. It was modular in nature to allow for expansion, and was practically indestructible.[98] Walt liked the attraction because it was experiential: people could walk through it, touch it, and interact with a future idea directly, rather than just seeing pictures. For Walt, the House of the Future was an expression of the power of American free enterprise for technological innovation and reflected a sense of optimism about the future.[99]

A half-scale replica of a high-speed train designed to travel at an average speed of 100 mph was also added to Tomorrowland, and dubbed the Train of the Future. Two trains were developed to run between Tomorrowland and Fantasyland on a small loop of track. The attraction was kept for a year before it was removed to create room for new attractions.[100]

With Disneyland performing well financially and Roy's confidence in the ability of the park to continue to generate free cash flow, Roy decided it was time to exercise a buy-back option clause which was included in the Disneyland, Inc. shareholder agreement for all parties except ABC. On June 29, 1957, according to the terms of the agreement, Walt Disney Productions repurchased all shares from Walt Disney, WED enterprises, and Western

Printing and Lithographing, Co., leaving Walt Disney Productions with 65.52% ownership, and ABC with its original share of 34.48%.[101]

Attendance during Disneyland's second year of operation surpassed 4.3 million admissions, a year-over-year increase of 13 percent.[102]

Walt had another television hit on his hands in 1957 when he was finally able to put *Zorro* on the air as a weekly half-hour action-adventure show for ABC. The Zorro series premiered on October 10, 1957, and ran for 78 episodes, achieving record ratings of thirty-five million viewers a week, and leading to a bonanza of Zorro merchandising opportunities and royalties, including hats, masks, capes, swords, and water pistols.[103]

The ongoing success of *The Mickey Mouse Club* TV show meant that the studio was required to continue the stressful task of creating new content every day. It was exhausting for everyone involved, and while each episode was an hour long for the first two seasons, the show was cut to thirty minutes for the third and fourth seasons. The fourth season was made up of re-runs compiled from the first two years.

By the end of 1957, total park attendance since the park's opening in July 1955 had surpassed an astounding ten million guests.[104] It was now a more popular tourist destination than the Grand Canyon, Yellowstone Park, and Yosemite Park.[105] Disneyland had quickly become a bona-fide world-class tourist attraction.

Since opening day in July 1955, Walt had been continuously plussing Disneyland and actively making improvements in infrastructure and attractions to enhance the guest experience that included the addition of many popular new exhibits. The re-investment of profits into the park was paying off.

The Disneyland Public Relations Division put together a report to commemorate the park's third anniversary on July 17, 1958. In just three years, more than twelve million guests had passed through the turnstiles; year-over-year growth was a steady ten percent; park employment increased from 1,280 to 3,400. An additional $6 million had been invested in park improvements since opening day, with the number of attractions doubling from 22 to 44. Guests were spending on average five-and-a-half hours at the park, which was more than double the industry average.[106]

On July 23, 1958, as the park headed into its fourth year, Walt sent a memo to his staff notifying them of his intentions to substantially expand Disneyland in 1959, and outlining their roles and responsibilities. It wasn't until toward the end of 1958, however, that a master plan was developed, at which point, on December 4, 1958, Walt announced to the public that he was undertaking a $5 million expansion of new attractions and improvements in 1959.[107]

The Economic Value of Integration and Diversification

As the decade of the 1950s was drawing to a close and Walt was approaching 60 years of age, Walt Disney Productions was emerging as a powerful entertainment conglomerate. If Walt had been out of phase with the public in the years following World War II and struggling to bring renewal to the studio and to produce profitable entertainment products, that problem was far behind him and he was now moving forward confidently in full stride.

Through design, independent thinking, leadership, courage, and commitment, Walt had undertaken a multi-pronged diversification approach to product creation and delivery via Disneyland, television, movies, and merchandising. It was a business strategy built on developing cross-platform synergies through aggressive marketing, which the business executives referred to as "integration." Prior to 1950, the studio's revenue was predominantly from films. By 1958 the situation had changed dramatically.

In 1952, prior to the studio's TV contract with ABC and Walt's commitment to build Disneyland, Disney stock sold for 35 cents a share on revenues of $7.4 million. Five years later the stock had risen almost seven-fold to $2.44 on revenues of $35 million, and the studio showed a record profit of almost $3.9 million in 1958. This integrative approach helped drive an investor-satisfying cumulative annual growth rate of 29.6 percent from 1952 to 1958.[108] As a result, Walt Disney Productions had become one of the leading corporations in terms of sales and revenue growth, and was becoming a darling of investment advisors.[109]

Roy articulated the corporation's new aggressive value creation approach to a *Wall Street Journal* reporter in 1958: "Integration is the key word around here: we don't do anything in one line without giving a thought to its likely profitability in our other lines." The model is not only replicable for each product, but also replicable across countries. As Roy noted, "Our product is practically eternal." Disney had settled into a formula of re-releasing its animated movies every seven years to a new generation of viewers.[110]

The reporter notes in the WSJ's front-page article celebrating the Disney business model that "Walt's Profit Formula" was to "[w]ring every possible profitable squeal and squeak out of such assets as the Three Little Pigs and Mickey Mouse—first by diversifying into a wide variety of activities, then by dove-tailing them so all work to exploit one another." The key was the ability of the corporation to leverage and coordinate its properties across as many merchandising platforms as possible: "The Disneys and their 1,500 employees are more than movie moguls, of course. They're also television entertainers and educators, comic strip creators, publishers, record makers, master merchandisers and operators of Disneyland...."[111]

By 1958, writes Disney biographer Neal Gabler, "[T]he company, in diversifying, had reduced its income from films to 38 percent of its total revenue, while television accounted for 28 percent, Disneyland for 21 percent, and royalties on merchandise for 13 percent."[112]

1. Pierce, *Three Years in Wonderland*, 100.

2. Marling, *Designing Disney's Theme Parks*, 77.

3. Gabler, *Walt Disney*, 527.

4. Pierce, *Three Years in Wonderland*, 19.

5. Thomas, *Building a Company*, 189.

6. Thomas, *Building a Company*, 189.

7. Quoted in Barrier, *The Animated Man*, 252.

8. Card Walker, in Ghez, *Walt's People: Volume 10*, 226.

9. Gabler, *Walt Disney*, 520.

10. Gabler, *Walt Disney*, 523.

11. Holliss & Sibley, *The Disney Studio Story*, 72.

12. Minutes of the Meeting of Disneyland Merchant's Association Held at the Red Wagon Inn, Disneyland, WED, January 25, 1956, dldhistory.com/disneyland/Articles/2244_001.pdf, accessed July 7, 2016.

13. Gabler, *Walt Disney*, 522.

14. Holliss & Sibley, *The Disney Studio Story*, 69.

15. Gabler, *Walt Disney*, 525.

16. Gennawey, *The Disneyland Story*, 43.

17. Gabler, *Walt Disney*, 526.

18. Holliss & Sibley, *The Disney Studio Story*, 70.

19. Gennawey, *The Disneyland Story*, 56.

20. Gennawey, *The Disneyland Story*, 57.

21. Gennawey, *The Disneyland Story*, 42.

22. Pierce, *Three Years in Wonderland*, 181.

23. Thomas, *Building a Company*, 190.

24. Thomas, *Building a Company*, 191–192.

25 Pierce, *Three Years in Wonderland*, 181; Tatum in Ghez, *Walt's People, Volume. 10*, 242.

26. Thomas, *Walt Disney,* 268.

27. Thomas, *Building a Company*, 192.

28. Thomas, *Building a Company*, 192.

29. Thomas, *Walt Disney*, 268; Thomas, *Building a Company*, 194.

30. France, *Backstage Disneyland*, 45.

31. France, *Backstage Disneyland*, 32.

32. France, *Backstage Disneyland*, 33; see also Lipp, *Disney U*, 46.

33. France, *Backstage Disneyland*, 33.

34. France, *Window on Main Street*, 29.

35. France, *Window on Main Street*, 36–37; France, *Backstage Disneyland*, 44.

36. Ben Nathenson, quoted in France, *Window on Main Street*, 37.

37. France, *Backstage Disneyland*, 44; France, *Window on Main Street*, 37.

38. France, *Backstage Disneyland*, 35; France, *Window on Main Street*, 45.

39. Pierce, *Three Years in Wonderland*, 188.

40. Pierce, *Three Years in Wonderland*, 188.

41. France, *Backstage Disneyland*, 48; France, *Window on Main Street*, 45.

42. Holliss & Sibley, *The Disney Story*, 70.

43. Holliss & Sibley, *The Disney Studio Story*, 69.

44. Gabler, *Walt Disney*, 529.

45. France, *Backstage Disneyland*, 50.

46. Thomas, *Building a Company*, 197.

47. Walt quoted in Thomas, *Building a Company*, 197.

48. Sharon Baird in Green & Green, *Remembering Walt*, 153.

49. France, *Backstage Disneyland*, 50.

50. Holliss & Sibley, *The Disney Studio Story*, 70.

51. Thomas, *Building a Company*, 197.

52. Gabler, *Walt Disney*, 532; YouTube, "1955 Disneyland Opening Day [Complete ABC Broadcast]", youtube.com/watch?v=JuzrZET-3Ew.

53. "Walt Disney's Disneyland Opening Day Dedication," disneylandreport.com/disneyland_dedication_speech.html, accessed July 8, 2016.

54. Holliss & Sibley, *The Disney Studio Story*, 70.

55. France, *Backstage Disney*, 54.

56. Pierce, *Three Years in Wonderland*, 233.

57. Gennawey, *The Disneyland Story*, 106.

58. Pierce, *Three Years in Wonderland*, 231.

59. France, *Window on Main Street*, 50; Thomas, *Building a Company*, 195. Thomas places this story on the Sunday, July 17, 1955. France's recollection of Roy's telling of the story was that it was the Monday, with paying customers, which makes more sense.

60. Barrier, *The Animated Man*, 257.

61. Bob Rogers, "The Coming Revolution in Themed Entertainment," delivered at the IAAPA Tradeshow, Orlando, FL, in 1997, at themedattraction.com/future.htm.

62. Barrier, *The Animated Man*, 257, quoting Price.

63. Smith, *The Quotable Walt Disney*, 48.

64. Gennawey, *The Disneyland Story*, 107–108.

65. France, *Window on Main Street*, 72; France, *Backstage Disney*, 54.

66. Gennawey, *The Disneyland Story*, 101.

67. Walt quoted in Gennawey, *The Disneyland Story*, 106, cited from Randy Bright, *Disneyland: The Inside Story*.

68. Barrier, *The Animated Man*, 257; Gennawey, *The Disneyland Story*, 106; France, *Window on Main Street*, 72.

69. Gennawey, *The Disneyland Story*, 107–108; The Milwaukee Sentinel, "Motion Picture Industry Optimistic for Boom Year," April 8, 1956, news.google.com/newspapers?nid=1368&dat=19560408&id=oG1QAAAAIBAJ&s-jid=jxAEAAAAIBAJ&pg=2864,4204238&hl=en, accessed July 7, 2016.

70. Holliss & Sibley, *The Disney Studio Story*, 70.

71. Marty Sklar in Kurti, *Walt Disney's Imagineering Legends*, v.

72. Smith, *The Quotable Walt Disney*, 58.

73. Gennawey, *The Disneyland Story*, 109. France in *Window on Main Street*, 75, indicates the circus lost $375,000, but according to Pierce, *Three Days in Wonderland*, p. 243, significant capital costs were assumed as an expense by Walt Disney Productions in the production of the circus film *Toby Tyler*.

74. Cited in Naversen, "Contagious Business Philosophy the 'Disney' Way!", .themedattraction.com/disney_way.htm, accessed September 24, 2015.

75. Barrier, *The Animated Man*, 260.

76. Barrier, *The Animated Man*, 261.

77. Walt quoted in Holliss & Sibley, *The Disney Studio Story*, 70.

78. Gennawey, *The Disneyland Story*, 112–113.

79. Gennawey, *The Disneyland Story*, 117–118.

80. Gennawey, *The Disneyland Story*, p. 119.

81. See YouTube, "Luna Park Coney Island, Kiddie Rides, Brooklyn NY, 1956," youtube.com/watch?v=YTf27iSnSLs.

82. Gennawey, *The Disneyland Story*, 111.

83. Gennawey, *The Disneyland Story*, 115.

84. Burns quoted in Gennawey, *The Disneyland Story*, 117.

85. Gennawey, *The Disneyland Story*, 111.

86. Gennawey, *The Disneyland Story*, 126; Gabler, *Walt Disney*, 537.

87. Gennawey, *The Disneyland Story*, 122.

88. Gennawey, *The Disneyland Story*, 126.

89. In Bob Rogers, "The Coming Revolution in Themed Entertainment," delivered at the IAAPA Tradeshow, Orlando, FL, in 1997, at themedattraction.com/future.htm.

90. Gennawey, *The Disneyland Story*, 126.

91. Gennawey, *The Disneyland Story*, 124–125.

92. Gennawey, *The Disneyland Story*, 125.

93. Gennawey, *The Disneyland Story*, 126.

94. Gennawey, *The Disneyland Story*, 127.

95. Barrier, *The Animated Man*, 261.

96. Gennawey, *The Disneyland Story*, 129.

97. Gennawey, *The Disneyland Story*, 134.

98. Gennawey, *The Disneyland Story*, 134.

99. Gennawey, *The Disneyland Story*, 135.

100. Gennawey, *The Disneyland Story*, 138.

101. Gennawey, *The Disneyland Story*, 138–139; Barrier, *The Animated Man*, 278; Wikipedia, "Disneyland, Inc.," wikipedia.org/wiki/Disneyland,_Inc.

102. Gennawey, *The Disneyland Story*, 140; Gabler, *Walt Disney*, 537.

103. Holliss & Sibley, *The Disney Studio Story*, 72.

104. Gennawey, *The Disneyland Story*, 140.

105. Gabler, *Walt Disney*, 537.

106. Gennawey, *The Disneyland Story*, 150.

107. Gennawey, *The Disneyland Story*, 150.

108. Michael Gordon, "Walt's Profit Formula: Dream, Diversify—and Never Miss an Angle," *Wall Street Journal*, Feb. 4, 1958, 1; Holliss & Sibley, *The Disney Studio Story*, 74.

109. Gabler, *Walt Disney*, 563.

110. Roy quoted in front-page WSJ article, cited in Gabler, *Walt Disney*, 563; Michael Gordon, "Walt's Profit Formula: Dream, Diversify—and Never Miss an Angle," *Wall Street Journal*, Feb. 4, 1958, 1.

111. Michael Gordon, "Walt's Profit Formula: Dream, Diversify—and Never Miss an Angle," *Wall Street Journal*, Feb. 4, 1958.

112. Gabler, *Walt Disney*, 563.

CHAPTER TWENTY
Ending the Decade with Gusto

Walt Disney and his animation studio team worked on *Sleeping Beauty* for seven years and by the time of its January 1959 release the film had cost the studio a record-breaking $6 million. While it may have been another Disney masterpiece, it was also initially another financial failure at the box office.

Walt had worked on developing the storyline for years, starting in 1951, but when *Sleeping Beauty* was ready to be put into production in 1956, Walt was fully involved with Disneyland and television production, and delegated most of the responsibility to a team of competent directors and animators.

Many in the animation department saw Walt's absorption by interests other than animation as both a good thing and a bad thing. According to Disney animator Ollie Johnston, for those working on cartoons, the success of Disneyland "took the pressure off. It was a big relief, because before Disneyland we'd always wonder if we would make another film, and that can be a tough way to have to live."[1] Johnston was referring to the perpetual precarious financial viability of the studio.

On the other hand, as Disney historian Michael Barrier notes in *The Animated Man*, the development of the park caused Walt to transfer a lot of top talent from the studio to WED that otherwise would have been available to work on *Sleeping Beauty*. It also diverted his attention from his usual infatuation with every detail of the story. Walt was showing minimal interest in attending meetings where he typically provided his leadership without relinquishing any control. Now, in Walt's absence, the Sleeping Beauty crew were often left to figure out things on their own without Walt's support, having to reluctantly guess at what Walt wanted in order to keep the project moving forward, and finding out later whether Walt liked it or not, causing consternation and delays.[2]

Harry Tytle, often considered to be Walt's "right hand man" at the animation studio, wrote in his diary on August 22, 1957, about a Sleeping Beauty story meeting to walk through the whole picture just prior to Walt leaving for a long vacation in Europe: "[Disney] seems to be tired, has so much on his mind; he didn't give this the treatment he would have in years past, where he'd go in for a couple of days and fine-tooth comb the whole picture. ... He hit more from a broad aspect than from small specifics, like he used to."[3]

Walt had high hopes for *Sleeping Beauty*, talking it up in the press and promising that it would be the studio's biggest and finest animated feature. He applied the latest innovations in film-making to its production, making *Sleeping Beauty* the first cartoon to be filmed in large format wide-screen 70mm, which substantially increased the production costs, in part because new studio processes and equipment had to be developed and adapted for use. Forty-five selected theatres were specially outfitted with stereophonic sound to enhance the audience experience. Even though Walt helped to commercialize stereo sound in movie theatres with *Fantasia* almost twenty years previously, it was still a rarity in films.

Sleeping Beauty premiered in Los Angeles on January 29, 1959. Upon its initial release it grossed just $5.3 million, resulting in a substantial loss for the studio.[4] For audiences, the film lacked overt comedy and charm, reflecting a more classical and somber approach at a time when social mores and generational change were taking hold, and audiences were seeking more irreverence and thrills. This, after all, was the age of the baby boom and the youthful, fun-loving parent.

With *Sleeping Beauty* now behind him, Walt began work on his seventeenth full-length animated feature, *One Hundred and One Dalmatians*.

The number one film at the box office in 1959 was the action-thriller *Ben-Hur*. Disney films in general were not performing as strongly at the box office, which Walt attributed to "a considerable leaning on the part of the public towards pictures involving violence, sex, and other such subjects."[5]

Interestingly, one exception that year to the general trends Walt described was the black and white, low budget, Disney live-action comedy *The Shaggy Dog*, which was originally conceived and proposed to ABC as a pilot for a TV series. Walt was so angered when ABC dismissed the concept that he called a story meeting with his staff thirty minutes after the ABC meeting ended and instructed them to convert the TV concept into a feature picture.[6] The purposefully low-budget film, released in March 1959, had a production cost of under a million dollars, and turned out to be the third highest grossing film of 1959, surpassing $8 million, and earning substantial profits for the studio to offset *Sleeping Beauty's* losses.[7]

Walt was doing so much across so many different media platforms in support of the studio's integration policy that in an interview with Lee Edson published in *Think* in May 1959, he noted, "I can make a flop now and nobody pays attention. We always have two or three things going to save us."[8]

A broadening of business output and scope at a time when consumers showed admiration and support for the Disney brand was a successful strategy to diversify risk, as was noted in the article:

Last year, Walt Disney Productions, which sprawls over fifty-one acres in Burbank, California, proved Disney's point by drawing a gross of nearly $50 million from three TV series and from a veritable tidal wave of recordings, comic books, toys, clothes, and other "character" merchandise. Also included in the figure is revenue from Disneyland, the park. Disney also runs a 16mm film-rental service, and he makes TV commercials for his sponsors. During the year, on top of all this, he released five full-length features.

"We're still doing a bit of everything," he told me when I asked what was coming up.[9]

ABC Contract Renewal Troubles

As Disney's television contract with ABC approached its seven-year renewal, Roy met with ABC in early 1959 to re-negotiate it, offering a three-year renewal for *Walt Disney Presents* (formerly *Disneyland*), *The Mickey Mouse Club*, and *Zorro*. ABC was now flush with cash from expansion and increased advertising revenues built primarily on Disney programming, and, negotiating from a position of greater strength, was only interested in a short-term renewal of a single Disney show, *Walt Disney Presents*. ABC claimed that they had to drop the other two shows due to a lack of advertiser commitment. Walt's take on it was that ABC had made an ill-considered decision to run too many commercials, which resulted in declining public interest.

Along with the economic leverage that comes from having a larger viewing audience for sponsors, ABC was also souring on buying shows from independent producers like Disney. With their newly found financial success, ABC executives felt they could make more money financing their own shows and marketing them around the world, as independent TV production studios like Disney and others were doing. Because of their control over distribution, ABC was able to put the squeeze on independent producers and content providers.

With ABC no longer interested in the very successful *Zorro* and *The Mickey Mouse Club*, Walt wanted to move the shows to another network that would welcome them. ABC refused to allow him to do so, citing the terms of the ABC-Disney contract. Walt offered up a number of new show ideas to ABC to replace the cancelled shows and keep his staff working, but each was turned down, with instructions back from ABC that these new show ideas also could not be sold elsewhere.

Walt was incensed and felt betrayed by what he considered ABC's unreasonable tactics, made worse for Walt by the fact that ABC was their Disneyland investment partner. Walt was of the opinion that partners don't treat partners this way.

Walt decided to pursue legal action to break the ABC contract by threatening them with an antitrust suit and asking for a court injunction that would allow Walt to negotiate with other networks.

Roy recognized that a court fight could be lengthy and costly to both sides, and offered up an alternative. He would use this dispute as an opportunity to buy out ABC's investment in Disneyland on the presumption that the value of Disneyland would continue to rise and that it would cost less to get out of the deal now rather than later. "It seems to us you are not as eager to continue a long-term association with Disney as you once were, " Roy wrote in a letter to Goldenson.[10]

Seeking a New Challenge

At the same time that Walt was working on plans to improve and expand Disneyland, add new television programming, resolve his TV distribution problem, and oversee new feature animated and live-action film projects, he also began to explore ideas about what to do next to challenge himself and his organization. The ideas of themed entertainment had proven to be very lucrative, and Walt had the infrastructure, talent, experience, and reputation to expand in this untapped area.

Walt had made it well known throughout his career that he didn't like to repeat himself, making it a point of pride to learn from his work and apply new knowledge and thinking in innovative ways. "I don't like to make sequels to my pictures," he once said. "I like to take a new thing and develop something, a new concept."[11]

Walt made it an operating philosophy and point of pride to stretch his curiosity, to build on his existing knowledge and capability, to expand and extend his thinking in order to imagine and create something new, innovative, and of practical value to people. He applied the same thinking to his organization, always driving them to a place just out of reach of their current capability, if not their perceived potential. To this end Walt reiterated on a number of occasions that there would never be another Disneyland.

With the master plan for the 1959 expansion of Disneyland completed and construction successfully underway, Walt secretly began to settle in on his next project and challenge, casting his sights on the idea of developing and building a better concept or prototype for the future of urban living, which he referred to as an Experimental Prototype Community of Tomorrow, or EPCOT. He decided that Florida was likely the best location to build it, but, for the time being, was keeping his plans to himself.[12]

Walt needed information to help him formulate a path forward, and once again commissioned Buzz Price to undertake a secret study to help him understand the market and the economic and financial implications of expanding the Disney footprint east of the Mississippi River.[13] By this point, Walt had convinced Price to part ways with SRI and to support him in starting his own business, which Price named Economic Research Associates (ERA).

Disneyland Gets a Major Upgrade

Most of the work for the major Disneyland renewal of 1959 took place during the slower winter season to be in place for the summer crowds.

Walt kicked the year off with a Fantasyland version of the popular Tomorrowland Autopia, in which guests could ride motorized cars around a track. Later that year, in June, a refreshed Tomorrowland Autopia was introduced.

Each of the Fantasyland dark rides—Peter Pan, Mr. Toad, Snow White, and Alice in Wonderland—were also revisited and updated with new paint and improved scenes with modernized effects that enhanced guest enjoyment.

In June, Walt inaugurated the most impressive of what turned out to be $7.3 million of upgrades, which included three major new iconic attractions.

Perhaps the most impressive of the projects was the creation of a 150-foot-high Matterhorn mountain built to a scale one-hundredth of its actual size, planted with pine trees and edelweiss, with two bobsled roller coasters running along the sides and through the interior—the first ever to use tubular steel tracks. It was the tallest structure in Orange County when completed.[14]

The idea came about during a visit to Switzerland by Walt and Lillian while on vacation in Europe in 1958. Walt became infatuated with the natural beauty of the Matterhorn, and was struck by the idea to build a scale model at Disneyland to add more awe-inspiring beauty to the park, while at the same time using it to enhance the attractions. Walt had always found the towers holding up the Skyway ride to be an eyesore, and the mountain could be used to hide them. Skyway passengers would pass through the mountain, adding to the thrill of the attraction.[15] When Walt returned to California, he asked Joe Fowler whether he could build a roller-coaster-type bobsled ride into the mountain, and when Fowler answered in the affirmative, he was instructed by Walt to do so.

The Disneyland/Alweg monorail transportation system was also built and put into operation at this time, thereby becoming the first daily-use monorail system in America. Walt had talked about wanting a monorail in his park for years. While in Europe in 1957, he and Lillian met up with Admiral Fowler and his wife for a few days in Germany. Fowler, recalling Walt's interest, relayed to Walt that he had heard about an experimental monorail being developed in Cologne, Germany, and was going to investigate. In an interview with Bob Thomas, Fowler recalled, "[Walt] said, 'Fine.' I did and I got all the data [I had all the pictures and everything] and I came back to the studio and I told Dick [Irvine], 'Dick, if we show these to Walt, we're sunk. He's going to build it, I'm sure.' And he did."[16]

During Walt and Lillian's visit to Europe the following summer of 1958, Walt drove to Cologne to visit the monorail manufacturer, Alweg Research Corporation, and meet with their executives.

When Walt returned to California, he instructed Imagineer Bob Gurr to draw some renderings. Gurr later recalled the meeting with Walt to show him his drawings: "I made that famous drawing [with two trains crossing in the air] and brought it to a meeting in the animation building. I put the drawing up on the wall, and Walt walked in and just looked at it. His eyes lit up and [he] reached out and tapped it and said, 'Bobby, can you build that?' And I said, "Yeah.' Walt just looked around at everybody and said, 'Okay!' And that was it. End of meeting."[17] Just like that, Bob Gurr and Roger Broggie were assigned the task to begin the development of the monorail project.

Gurr visited Alweg in November 1958 to arrange terms for construction and delivery, but was not satisfied with Alweg's designs. The proposed trains were to be built in Mannheim, Germany, but Gurr found them to be heavy and unattractive. Gurr and Broggie considered another way to get the job done. "Instead," writes Sam Gennawey in *The Disneyland Story*,

> Roger Broggie and Bob Gurr engineered a train based on parts they could purchase in Los Angeles. In the end it was decided to proceed with Gurr's design and to do without the Alweg technology. Although Alweg had very little to do with the final design, it claimed that the trains at Disneyland were its. Construction started at Standard Carriage Works, but they got so far behind schedule that the project was pulled, and the trains were built at the Disney studio.

> Building the monorail trains was not the only challenge. There was also a conflict between "engineering people who wanted to go in a straight line forever with no grades, and the Disney art directors who wanted to draw tight turning radii and plot an interesting ride that climbed the maximum grades in order to thrill the guests," said Broggie.[18]

When the redesigned prototype was built it didn't perform well on steep banked curves. As a result, Gurr re-engineered a new suspension system to prevent the train from leaning.

When it opened on June 14, 1959, a press release declared it "the nation's first practical monorail system—considered a key to future travel." It took just under seven minutes to travel the 0.8 mile loop.[19] Bob Gurr piloted the inaugural run at the grand opening ceremony with Walt Disney, Vice President Richard Nixon, and his family as the first passengers.

While riding in and observing the near-silent monorail transport passengers high above the ground was thrilling and exciting, the monorail station was equally part of the futuristic experience. Writes Gennawey:

> The "ultra-modern station" featured a Speedramp, an inclined moving sidewalk developed by Stephens-Adamson Company that carried guests to the loading platform and back down without their walking a step. For the guests, the monorail was an exciting new ride. For Walt, it was a prototype of a new transportation system that he knew could solve real world problems.
>
> The opening-day press release suggested the monorail was "a practical prototype of high-speed interurban transportation systems, which could well be the answer to the growing problems of metropolitan area congestion."[20]

Another new major attraction was an underwater submarine ocean voyage adventure, with artificial reefs, mechanical creatures, and a mermaid.

The idea for Submarine Voyage was an outgrowth of a more conventional idea to develop a surface-bound glass-bottom boat attraction. Walt significantly upped the ante. "No," Walt said, upon hearing the idea for a glass-bottom boat, "let's do a real submarine ride. Let's take them down and give them ports to look out of. Give 'em a real show."[21]

The submarine attraction cost $2.5 million, which included the building of a crystal-clear nine million-gallon lagoon. The filtration plant had an intake of 1,800 gallons of water per minute. The water was tested three times per day, and was said to be pure enough to safely drink.

Eight air-conditioned submarines were designed and custom-built with three-inch steel hulls and a capacity of 38 passengers each.[22] In addition to encountering fish, eels, crabs and lobsters, guests would also experience a storm, sea serpents, a giant squid, whales, a fight between an octopus and a shark, and the ancient sunken city of Atlantis. Professional swimmers were hired and fitted with mermaid costumes to add an additional element of fantasy, and remained part of the attraction until 1967.[23]

Walt's inspiration for the Submarine Voyage ride came from a series of segments on the *Disneyland* television show that featured the United States Navy's participation in scientific exploration in the Antarctic. Apparently the Navy was interested in sponsoring the attraction, but Walt turned them down because he didn't want to become involved in government bureaucracy. Instead, defense contractor General Dynamics was brought on as the attraction's sponsor.[24]

On Sunday, June 14, 1959, ABC filmed a special 90-minute *Kodak Presents—Disneyland '59* broadcast hosted by Walt and Art Linkletter to celebrate the fourth anniversary of Disneyland and grand opening of the new attractions, including the first three E-Ticket attractions. The show featured a parade of major Hollywood movie and TV stars, and attracted millions of viewers, each eager to get a taste of Walt's improved Disneyland.[25] Approximately 2,000 members of the press were invited to attend, and along with invited celebrities and dignitaries, were given exclusive access to the newly opened attractions.

At the end of the day, Art Linkletter is filmed riding the Skyway. He reintroduces Walt, whom he describes as "the happiest kid in the park," giving Walt the last word:

> Disneyland was made possible by all of you...the millions who have already been here, the people here today...and those we hope to see some day. I think it is appropriate for the occasion to ask these children of the visitors here today to help me officially open Disneyland '59 for its only purpose...the pursuit of happiness for all.[26]

And with that, the Tomorrowland area with the new attractions was opened to the general public.

The *Disneyland '59* footage was edited overnight and aired nationally the following evening, Monday, June 15.

To extend the promotional value of the broadcast and satisfy the general interest of the event, Walt used black-and-white TV footage, combined with color footage and some scenes that were edited out of the original broadcast, to create a 27-minute featurette, *Gala Day at Disneyland*, released in Technicolor to movie theatres across the nation on January 21, 1960.[27]

As usual, Walt was not content to rest and contemplate his prior achievements. He was just getting started with Disneyland. Biographer Neal Gabler summarized some of Walt's major expansion ideas:

> Off of Main Street he had conceived of another street, Liberty Street, and another town square, Edison Square, which would feature buildings in nineteenth-century American architecture housing exhibits on science and technology, and which would be sponsored, Walt hoped, by America's leading technology companies, most prominently General Electric. On the square Walt also envisioned a President's Hall that would house animatronic robots of American presidents. He had thought as well of a New Orleans quarter with a Haunted Mansion, and he had dispatched Herb Ryman and John Hench to the city to take photographs, which later became models for the attraction. In the summer of 1961 he introduced costumed characters to the park as a regular feature, and early the following year he announced a $7 million expansion that would add eight new attractions and improve and expand current attractions. The new construction brought the cumulative investment in the park to $44 million. That amount didn't include Walt's secretive efforts to buy additional parcels of land around the park, on which he planned to build hotels and motels, a bowling alley, a campground, and a swimming pool.[28]

As the chief strategist for the park, Walt set the projects in motion and delegated management authority.

Walt told *The New York Times* that he was able to invest because of the success of the park, and that the banks offered a significantly lower interest rate of 3.75 percent on money borrowed for the park as compared to what they charged to lend into the riskier film business. The continued success of Disneyland demonstrated the wisdom of Walt's idea to treat the park as a living thing that was forever changing to keep pace with what the public likes and to give them new reasons to return.

The park would succeed through the application of the general principles of effective showmanship.

Park Expansion and the City of Tomorrow

Around the time Price was completing his secret study to assess the market potential for an eastern Disneyland in June 1959, Walt attended a meeting with RCA chairman Robert Sarnoff at the NBC studios in Burbank, California. Sarnoff was trying to win Walt's TV business over to RCA's NBC subsidiary now that the ABC contract was coming to an end. As an inducement, Sarnoff indicated that NBC was prepared to partner with Walt in the building of a new theme park in New York City. Sarnoff had initiated his own detailed consultant's report from SRI, Buzz Price's old firm, which put a positive spin on such a venture.

Walt was skeptical of the New York market for numerous reasons, primarily related to economic feasibility. He had reached the conclusion years ago, prior to the opening of Disneyland, that if he was to build in the East, the most viable location was Florida. He had considered other locations east of the Mississippi, but felt Florida offered the best climate to operate year-round and was most conducive to eastern tourism. Unlike the more temperate conditions of Disneyland, however, building in Florida would pose new problems including severe weather and hurricane threats, hot and humid summers, and insects.[29] "You have to have a year-round business to make money from such a large investment," Walt said in an Associated Press article by Bob Thomas in May 1955. "The only other place it would be possible is Florida. In the East, you could get only three or four profitable months."[30]

It was for this reason that Walt questioned the veracity of Sarnoff's SRI study supporting the viability of New York for a Disneyland-type park. He wanted his own study and instructed Price to look into it immediately. Price presented his findings to Walt three days later, coming to the opposite conclusion put forth by RCA and SRI.

In his memoirs, Price indicated that there were four major reasons why New York was not a good place for Walt to build a new theme park:

- In the NYC climate and season, an all-year, 12-month operation was not feasible.
- The short stay and business orientation of available tourism limited the opportunity for an attraction. New York's business-dominated tourism was not as supportive as that of Florida.
- Political climate for construction activity was a problem. When C.V. Wood took charge of building Frontierland in the Bronx for William Zeckendorf a short time later, C.V. sardonically stated to me that he had two working disbursement windows, one for staff payroll and one for building inspectors.
- Major acreages close to the market center would be hard to find.[31]

Walt ultimately rejected the idea of building a park in the New York market saying that if he were to build in the East, he wanted to locate where he could operate year-round, not just 120 days. Only with a year-round operation would he be able to hire and retain a full-time staff capable of operating at service levels he demanded. He also said it was unlikely that he could find the right place in New York City to build a theme park of the scale he had in mind and at a cost that was reasonable. Walt didn't indicate the scale he had in mind.[32]

The larger report Price was commissioned to produce for Walt, "Market for an Eastern Disneyland," was completed and presented to Walt in June 1959. The analysis revealed a number of informative facts about Disneyland's draw for tourists.[33]

Perhaps most revealing was the finding that Disneyland was primarily an attraction for those living in southern California. People in the eastern part of the country were aware of Disneyland and wanted to vacation there, but at the time cross-county travel was difficult and expensive.

Disneyland's market penetration at the time of the study only covered about one-quarter of the U.S. population.[34] Penetration rates east of the Mississippi River were very low: 1.0% penetration in the Atlantic and New England states, 1.7% in the Great Lakes area, and less than 1% in the Southern states.[35] With two-thirds of the U.S. population living east of the Mississippi, the key conclusion from the study was that the only way to significantly grow penetration in the East was to build a second park there.[36]

Price's study helped to reinforce Walt's earlier conclusion that Florida remained the most opportune location for his next project. In August, Walt told a reporter for the *Miami Herald* that in many ways Florida was a better location for a theme park than was California.[37] Even so, Walt remained open to considering other business and entertainment ventures as he more actively considered and explored the opportunities and possibilities for expansion.

It wasn't long before such an opportunity arose when billionaire insurance entrepreneur and Florida real-estate tycoon John D. MacArthur contacted Walt. MacArthur had obtained a large part of his wealth by purchasing and growing a bankrupt insurance company into the hugely successful Bankers Life and Casualty Company, and is perhaps best remembered today as the founder of the philanthropic John D. and Catherine T. MacArthur Foundation. MacArthur had invested his wealth to acquire significant real estate holdings in New York, Chicago, and Florida.

Upon learning that Walt might be seeking new projects outside of California, MacArthur tried to interest him in building a new park on some of the 12,000 acres of property he owned in Palm Beach County, Florida, about 70 miles north of Miami and 160 miles southeast of Orlando, on the north side of the city, inland from Highway 95.[38]

Given that RCA had already approached Walt about investing in a park together, Walt brought in executives from RCA and NBC to meet with MacArthur, spending a weekend together surveying MacArthur's land and exploring the possibilities. In attendance were Walt, Roy, Buzz Price, John West (head of NBC in Los Angeles), Matt Clifford (president of NBC), and John Burns (president of RCA).

While the others were thinking in terms of building an East Coast version of Disneyland, though perhaps bigger and better, Walt was talking about his newfound interest in urban development and the possibility of developing an experimental "City of Tomorrow" for up to 70,000 people.[39]

The weekend ended with a good-will handshake signifying the intentions of the parties to continue to pursue Palm Beach County as a viable location for Walt's ambition to build an East Coast park.

Walt returned to California intrigued about the prospects of building not just a theme park, but a showcase working community. Walt envisioned a collaborative experiment in a controlled urban environment, bringing together American corporations working at the leading edge of applied technologies, with the explicit mission of creating human happiness and a better world. New ideas for urban planning and environmental design would be combined with the latest concepts in building and construction, operating under an experimental community governance model.

Initially, Walt figured the project might cost upwards of $100 million and take fifteen years to complete.[40] To finance such a large-scale long-term project, he would have to convince others of the viability of his dream and spark their imaginations to see the possibilities and the benefits of investing. Putting first things first, Walt would have to find enough land at a reasonable price to build an entire town, and as with Disneyland, it was important to transact the entire acquisition in secrecy. If word leaked that Disney was buying up land, speculators would cause prices to skyrocket.

To gain intelligent business insight about the prospects of building in Florida, Walt instructed Price to perform an economic analysis and to work alongside WED "in determining what kind of interrelated park and city could be developed on that site." According to Price, "Walt wanted to emphasize future development in urban living. The acronym EPCOT was coined, the Experimental Prototype City of Tomorrow. ... The park would take up some 400 acres. A town base of 70,000 people would take up the rest."[41]

Proactively Pursuing Opportunity at the World's Fair

Another development during the summer of 1959 was a growing interest in political circles for holding a world's fair in the United States in 1964 dedicated to "Man's Achievement on a Shrinking Globe in an Expanding Universe" and with the overall theme of "Peace Through Understanding." The fair would be a showcase for American culture and technology.[42]

President Eisenhower appointed a commission to study the feasibility and to solicit and study the plans of interested cities. Delegates from the two leading bids—New York City and Washington, D.C.—were invited to present their bids to the commission on October 22, 1959. One week later, on October 29, 1959, Eisenhower announced that New York was to host the fair, with 1964 corresponding to the 300th anniversary of the founding of New York City.[43] Because the fair was not officially endorsed by the World's Fair sanctioning body, the Bureau International des Expositions (BIE), most European and Asian exhibitors declined to participate.

Walt already had experience with world's fairs. For the 1939 New York World's Fair, he created the short cartoon *Mickey's Surprise Party* for the National Biscuit Company's Nabisco pavilion. It was the first time Walt used his characters in a commercial, with Mickey, Minnie, and the other characters using Nabisco products and referencing them by name. Mickey eventually wins over Minnie's heart with Fig Newtons.[44] Disney also participated at the 1958 World's Fair in Brussels, Belgium, exhibiting what was considered to be the hit of the show, a 19-minute film called *America the Beautiful*, presented in 360-degree Circarama.[45]

Upon hearing news of the 1964 fair, Walt immediately saw an opportunity to develop and stretch the skills of his Imagineers at WED, who were then working diligently on developing new attractions for Disneyland. In Walt's eyes, nobody was better suited than WED for the creation of large-scale public-pleasing attractions.

There were a number of angles from which Walt saw opportunity emanating from the fair: as a research and development program; as a source of revenue; as a way to get others to pay for the development of new competencies and new attractions that might later be moved to Disneyland; as a way to gain long-term sponsorship for Disney attractions beyond the fair; and as a means to develop and expand important executive and board-level contacts at America's leading companies that might be useful at a later date as he crystalized his thinking about EPCOT.

Walt gathered his WED staff to announce his decision to participate in the fair and explain his thinking about the opportunity it afforded. Disneyland executive Donn Tatum was involved in the planning and recalled Walt's words:

> He said, "Look, there's going to be a big fair in New York. And it's going to mean that the big companies in this country are going to be spending a heck of a lot of money building exhibits there. They won't know what they want to do. They won't know why they're doing it other than that they just feel they have to keep up with the Joneses. One company has to do it because the other one's doing it and some of them are going to recognize the need for the kind of service we can offer, because they want to have something that will stand out and capture the attention in competition with the others. It's a great opportunity for us because we're trying to do this kind of thing for Disneyland and we're trying to promote the idea that a place like Disneyland represents an opportunity to do a long-term exhibit where you don't have to spend as much money as you're going to spend at the New York World's Fair, and we go on for five or ten years and get the benefits of it and not just have it fold in a matter of six months or two six-month periods. So let's progressively present ourselves and be very anxious and willing to render our services in trying to build attractions. It will help us. We'll learn a lot of things and it will give us a chance to develop a lot of technology we're working out." He was very far sighted about it. ... About that time the Audio-Animatronics were bursting forth and he was very engrossed in that.[46]

"We won't lose money on the work," Walt said years in 1963 to explain his rationale for pursuing the projects in the context of a viable business model, "but we don't expect to make much, either. We expect these exhibits, or part of them, to end up at the park, where they will add to our free attractions. Or, if the corporations do not decide to exhibit them at Disneyland, they will pay a penalty which will amount to our profit in creating them."[47]

Walt was also curious about two other things that he mostly kept to himself. Would East Coast audiences go for Disneyland-type attractions? And equally important, was his team ready to take on more and bigger challenges while at the same time coping with the expansion of Disneyland?

In the words of Disney financial officer Michael Bagnall, who was hired by Roy in 1962 as assistant treasurer and made his way to become CFO for Walt Disney Productions, "One reason [Walt] went to the New York

World's Fair was to try some ideas for shows on East Coast audiences... most of our attention was local or from the western part of the country. He was concerned whether his attractions would be accepted by the perhaps more sophisticated East Coast."[48] The World's Fair would serve as a testing ground for investing in an East Coast park.

Walt and his staff began reaching out to the leading American corporations to gauge their interest in participating at the fair and to sell WED's creative engineering services. When a positive response was received, a meeting would be set up for Walt to undertake an executive-level sales pitch.

Economic Setting of the City of Tomorrow

Simultaneous to Walt engaging in the very early stages of developing plans to participate in the World's Fair and taking care of his many and mounting business responsibilities, Harrison "Buzz" Price continued to work on his assessment for Walt of the Palm Beach, Florida, site and surrounding area. The final report and recommendations were completed and delivered to Walt in December 1959, bearing the title "Economic Setting of the City of Tomorrow—Palm Beach."[49] This would be the first of many studies undertaken by Price for Walt focused on a secretive Florida expansion that would proceed under the code name Project Future.

"The prospects seemed encouraging," writes Disney historian and author Chad Denver Emerson in *Project Future: The Inside Story Behind the Creation of Disney World*, "so Walt traveled to south Florida to again meet again with John D. MacArthur." Walt booked himself into the Palm Beach Towers under a fictitious name to avoid publicity. Over the next week the two toured MacArthur's property in his Cadillac. Walt eventually settled on several hundred acres he liked and, with a handshake, Walt agreed to purchase a parcel of MacArthur's land.[50]

The year 1959 had been a busy time of expansion for Walt and the studio, and for developing plans for the future. Disneyland had been wildly successful financially, propelling Walt Disney Productions to a level of prosperity it had never seen before. Attendance in 1959 jumped to over five million as Disneyland continued to be a must-see tourist attraction, not just for regular folk, but also for celebrities and dignitaries.[51] While net profits of Walt Disney Productions in 1959 fell by $400,000 from the previous year, Disneyland had undergone a major expansion and rejuvenation, and the organization still showed a very respectable bottom-line profit of $3.4 million.[52]

Apart from the financial stability that Disneyland provided to Walt Disney Productions, Walt discovered that his personal interest in cartoons and movies was waning, and his interest in developing positive environments for human interaction was growing.[53]

1. Barrier, *The Animated Man*, 271.

2. Barrier, *The Animated Man*, 270–271.

3. Barrier, *The Animated Man*, 273; also Gabler, *Walt Disney*, 559.

4. Holliss & Sibley, *The Disney Studio Story*, 74.

5. Holliss & Sibley, *The Disney Studio Story*, 74.

6. Donn Tatum in Ghez, *Walt's People, Volume 10*, 244.

7. Holliss & Sibley, *The Disney Studio Story*, 73; Tranberg, *Walt Disney & Recollections of the Disney Studios: 1955–1980*, vii.

8. Lee Edson, "A Visit With Walt Disney," *Think*, May 1959, 25–27, in Jackson, *Walt Disney: Conversations*, 73.

9. Lee Edson, "A Visit With Walt Disney," *Think*, May 1959, 25–27, in Jackson, *Walt Disney: Conversations*, 73.

10. Gabler, *Walt Disney*, 569.

11. Smith, *The Quotable Walt Disney*, 211.

12. Price, *Walt's Revolution!*, 36.

13. Price, *Walt's Revolution!*, 36.

14. Gennawey, *The Disneyland Story*, 163.

15. Gennawey, *The Disneyland Story*, 148.

16. Jim Korkis, "The Monorail Myth: The Rest of the Story," November 5, 2008, mouseplanet.com/8560/The_Monorail_Myth_The_Rest_of_the_Story, accessed August 5, 2016.

17. Gennawey, *The Disneyland Story*, 149.

18. Gennawey, *The Disneyland Story*, 160.

19. Gennawey, *The Disneyland Story*, 160.

20. Gennawey, *The Disneyland Story*, 161.

21. Gennawey, *The Disneyland Story*, 154.

22. Gennawey, *The Disneyland Story*, 154, 156.

23. Gennawey, *The Disneyland Story*, 157–158.

24. Gennawey, *The Disneyland Story*, 155.

25. Gennawey, *The Disneyland Story*, 161.

26. MousePlanet, Jim Korkis, "Disneyland '59," May 27, 2015: mouseplanet.com/11023/Disneyland_59, accessed September 10, 2015.

27. MousePlanet, Jim Korkis, "Disneyland '59," May 27, 2015: mouseplanet.com/11023/Disneyland_59, accessed September 10, 2015.

28. Gabler, *Walt Disney*, 564-565.

29. Emerson, *Project Future*, 35.

30. Barrier, *The Animated Man*, 301.

31. Price, *Walt's Revolution!*, 38.

32. Price, *Walt's Revolution!*, 38; Emerson, *Project Future*, 21.

33. Price, *Walt's Revolution!*, 68.

34. Thomas, *Building a Company*, 250.

35. Price, *Walt's Revolution!*, 39.

36. Price, *Walt's Revolution!*, 39.

37. Gabler, *Walt Disney*, 604.

38. Price, *Walt's Revolution!*, 39.

39. Emerson, *Project Future*, 21; Mannheim, *Walt Disney and the Quest for Community*, 67; Price, *Walt's Revolution!*, 39–40.

40. Greene & Greene, *Inside the Dream*, 165.

41. Price, *Walt's Revolution!*, 39–40.

42. Wikipedia, "1964 New York World's Fair," en.wikipedia.org/wiki/1964_New_York_World%27s_Fair, accessed September 16, 2015.

43. "Five Men," nywf64.com/building04.shtml, accessed September 15, 2015.

44. Gabler, Walt Disney, 406; Wikipedia, "Mickey's Surprise Party," en.wikipedia.org/wiki/Mickey%27s_Surprise_Party, accessed September 14, 2015; disney.wikia.com/wiki/Mickey's_Surprise_Party, accessed September 14, 2015.

45. Gabler, *Walt Disney*, 574; YouTube, "America The Beautiful Pt. 1," youtube.com/watch?v=8f927DQ6qKw, accessed June 8, 2016.

46. Ghez, *Walt's People, Volume 10*, 251–252; also in edited form in Green & Green, *Remembering Walt*, 169–170.

47. Walt Disney quoted in Barrier, *The Animated Man*, 291.

48. Thomas, *Building a Company*, 251.

49. Price, *Walt's Revolution!*, 39, 68.

50. Emerson, *Project Future*, 22.

51. Gennawey, *The Disneyland Story*, 162.

52. Holliss & Sibley, *The Disney Studio Story*, 74.

53. Thomas, *Building a Company*, 250.

CHAPTER TWENTY-ONE

The Foundations for Building the Future

As the decade of the 1960s was ushered in, Walt was increasingly being criticized for the type of escapist family-friendly movies he was making at a time when Hollywood and audiences were embracing more serious and gritty adult themes. Where at one time the Disney brand stood for path-breaking originality, it had come to represent fun and wholesome family entertainment geared to baby-boomers and their parents. Creatively, Walt found this limiting, but financially, it was a successful formula the studio could bank on. As a result, Walt was spending much more time involved in WED and non-film projects, and less time developing movie scripts and movie sets.

The notion that the studio was creating animation or cinematic art had long since vanished. Walt had spent his career making movies, and with the exception of one unfulfilled story ambition dear to his heart—the children's story *Mary Poppins*—his deep-seated ambition was to figure out how to apply the lessons of Disneyland and multiply them a hundred-fold to lead the way in creating a much-improved social structure to support the capability, ingenuity, and optimism of American capitalism, and to unleash the potential of the human spirit.

Forgoing the Opportune for the Optimum

Discussions to build an East Coast development resumed in Palm Beach in the early months of 1960. As with most of Walt's projects, his vision for Project Future continued to expand with the passage of time, as he integrated seemingly disparate ideas into a larger whole while developing something bold and original.

Not surprisingly, it wasn't long before Walt concluded that the few hundred acres of Palm Beach land he had agreed to purchase was too small to contain his aspirations, and Roy, on behalf of the organization, entered into further discussions with MacArthur to acquire an additional 5,000 to

6,000 acres. Roy then flew to New York to meet with RCA and sell them on the value of investing in a bigger project. The discussions with RCA stalled, and were eventually terminated, in large part because of RCA's reluctance to increase its investment during difficult financial times.[1]

Walt wasn't about to give up on his vision, even if the path remained unclear. MacArthur had originally approached Walt with Palm Beach as an opportunity, but Walt was of the mind that if he was going to expand into Florida, he wanted to ensure his capital was invested in the optimum location, not the most opportune location. Consideration of expansion plans was put on hold.

Coming to Terms with ABC

In June 1960, Walt's dispute with ABC over television rights was finally settled through arbitration in New York City under Roy's leadership.

Roy indicated that he had no idea what ABC's original $500,000 investment for 34% of Disneyland would be worth, but was certain, Walt later recalled, that "if we don't buy 'em out now, we're gonna be payin' a lot more later." Roy phoned Walt for his input prior to the arbitration session, and Walt advised him, "Do what you think is necessary."[2]

Roy had originally offered $3 million to ABC to settle the lawsuit and buy out ABC's investment position in Disneyland. By the time arbitration was over, the amount had ballooned to a final cash payout of $7.5 million. In addition, ABC would receive profits from Disneyland's food concessions for five more years, bringing the total value of the settlement to about $17 million.[3]

Goldenson and the ABC board of directors were elated with the outcome.[4] As part of the settlement, the anti-trust lawsuit was dropped, and Walt was released from his TV contract with ABC. Roy also agreed that they would not pursue another network TV agreement for four months, a stipulation put in place to hinder Disney from competing head-to-head against ABC for the upcoming 1960 fall season.

According to Card Walker, who at the time was vice president of advertising and sales and later became CEO and chairman of the board of Walt Disney Productions, Walt was extremely disappointed in ABC because they had made a lot of money from Disneyland without making any real additional contribution:

> I think the figure [we paid ABC for their share] was 7½ million dollars. I always remember Walt was very unhappy with that. He didn't feel that they made any contribution. They did sign a note and we did go on TV, but when we went on TV, my goodness, we helped build their whole empire. Then to have to pay them seven-and-a-half million

dollars, it just galled him. He said, "What did they do to help me do this?" But in hindsight in evaluating it, it all worked out very good for everybody concerned. I think ABC came off fine. And their network grew after that. They made a lot of money in Disneyland with the food concessions, which lasted for a period of ten years. And we came off fine. We had support when we needed it back at the time when not many people had any confidence at all in what you do with a thing called "Disneyland." So it worked out fine for everybody.[5]

Goldenson had been astute in recognizing the value of acquiring Disney for his network in 1953 when the opportunity presented itself and in leveraging the huge success of Disney programming with audiences to grow the network and close ABC's performance and credibility gap with CBS and NBC. To a great extent, the growth of the network was built through the success of the Disney television shows, especially Walt's idea for *The Mickey Mouse Club*, which invented the concept of children's programming.

After unwinding its successful investment in Disneyland, ABC's Goldenson later complained disingenuously that "the Disneys had turned out to be terrible business partners," and that instead of redistributing Disneyland profits to shareholders, of which ABC-Paramount owned 34%, "Disney kept plowing his profits back into park expansion...[and] I feared that it would be a very long time before we started seeing any return on our original $500,000 investment."[6]

Goldenson and the ABC board did not ascribe to the Disney approach of long-term investing for growth and profit through the creation of value for customers. As Disney biographer Bob Thomas writes: "History questions their judgment. As Disneyland developed into a mammoth success, ABC could have reaped far more if it had continued as an investor."[7]

Walt and Roy took this incident as further confirmation of the importance of retaining ownership to maximize control over one's own destiny.

Prior to the park's opening, friends and others had been sold the rights to operate various concessions within the park mostly as a tactic to fill unoccupied space where the park looked too empty. These rights were also reacquired to consolidate ownership. All of this extra buy-back activity was funded through a $15 million loan that Roy had established with Prudential Insurance and a revolving $5 million line of credit from Bank of America.[8]

Roy merged the two independent legal entities of Disneyland, Inc. and Walt Disney Productions to take advantage of any potential profit and loss offsets. As Gabler reports, Roy also asked Prudential "to revamp their deal to include...$5.5 million that the company owed ABC for Disneyland, raising its total indebtedness to Prudential to $20.5 million—this at a studio that had once scrounged to borrow tens of thousands of dollars to complete

Snow White and that had to suffer economic indignities from the war right up to the opening of Disneyland."[9]

Walt had a reputation for being very stingy in his public praise of others, but when Roy had succeeded in first finding the funds to build Disneyland and then in bringing the parts back together as a wholly owned subsidiary of Walt Disney Productions, Walt publically acknowledged the brilliant job Roy had done:

> That's the thing my brother's been fighting for. He's done a perfect job there. The way I back him up is if I make a good product and the money comes in, then he can do these things. And I think he's really fought there. He fought a long battle to get that thing financed and then freed. Actually, Roy is basically a banker. He's pretty shrewd on the money...I leave all those things to him. I don't question him on those things at all.[10]

Color TV, RCA, and Disney on NBC

Walt was aware of the advancements in television technology and anticipated a not-too-distant future where TV would no longer be seen in black and white. The NBC network was owned by RCA, which was a major manufacturer of television sets, and was currently promoting a marketplace transition from relatively low-cost black-and-white TVs to the latest higher-priced color units. As the developer of the technology and owner of the patents, RCA received a royalty on the sale of every color TV set sold.

Before color TVs were readily available, Walt had the foresight to incur the additional expense of filming his TV shows in color even though at the time ABC could only transmit them in black and white. This gave him a library of color content that could be re-broadcast when black and white was surpassed by advancing color broadcasting technology. Walt had seen this kind of disruption play out before in his career, recalling the introduction of *Flowers and Trees*, the first Silly Symphony to be released in Technicolor more than twenty-five years earlier. Walt was aware that what happened in film would repeat itself in television.

NBC's push to color broadcasting made them the leading candidate toward which to pitch a new show. Without color content to broadcast, there was no incentive for consumers to purchase expensive color TV sets, and the uptake was lackluster. At the time, according to Card Walker, "CBS and NBC-RCA were in a fierce competition over their color systems. The CBS system was like tying a washing machine down in the den because the picture would shake, rattle, and roll. We thought the RCA system was better."[11]

Walt's strategic foresight to invest in color programming ahead of the technology curve gave him the credentials, and more importantly, the beloved color content NBC so desired. The basis for a deal was in place.

Before the four-month moratorium from pursuing an alternative deal with other television networks expired, as agreed to with ABC, Walt, Roy, and Disney executives Card Walker and Donn Tatum went to New York to meet with RCA chairman Robert Sarnoff and other RCA and NBC executives to make their sales pitch. According to biographer Bob Thomas, "it was a virtuoso performance, and the television executives were overwhelmed."[12] In a 1973 interview with Thomas, Tatum recalled that shortly after the ABC settlement:

> Walt called me up and said, "Now we want to go to NBC and talk about color." I called Bob Kintner [Kintner had been president of ABC at the time the Disney deal was struck, then moved to become president of NBC in 1958[13]] and said, "Bob would you be interested in talking to us about a series on NBC in color?" He said, "How fast can you get here."... We had about fifty...possible programs, all beautifully illustrated in color [on these beautiful cards]. Walt came with us and we went to New York and had a big meeting up in the RCA boardroom. Everybody was there. Card [Walker] and I got in ahead of time and we had these cards all around the boardroom. Everyplace you looked, the place was just alive with these marvelous-looking subjects, in color. Walt made the presentation himself upon what he saw as a program and how he felt that it would really bring color to the screen and how it would stimulate the interest of the public in the color medium, which was kind of lagging at that time.[14]

The RCA and NBC executives were impressed with Walt's presentation,[15] but didn't jump at the offer right away, indicating they had to evaluate the implications of a long-term association with Disney. Walt had to leave New York but left Tatum and Walker behind to advance the proposal. Tatum recalled that when they were dropped at their hotel, Walt told them in earnest, "Fellas, I want this deal. If necessary I'll stand on my head in Macy's window."[16]

It took Disney and NBC about eight weeks to conclude a deal. NBC offered Disney what ABC's Goldenson called "a phenomenal sum" and "an amount that just would have been too much money for us."[17] At the end of negotiations, NBC agreed to a three-year deal to pay $5 million per year in return for twenty-five installments per season of *Walt Disney's Wonderful World of Color*.[18] They also offered Walt what he felt was the ideal time slot: early Sunday evenings when families are able to enjoy the show together.[19]

NBC granted complete control over the show to Walt, allowing him to produce and air whatever he wanted, in color, which renewed his excitement and creativity for producing entertainment and educational content for television. He didn't have that freedom at ABC, who kept after him to produce westerns to compete with popular shows like *Gunsmoke* on CBS and *Wagon Train* on NBC. *TV Guide* quoted an unnamed friend of Walt's as saying "I never saw such an overnight change in a man. Where he had been preparing the ABC programs almost automatically like a man in a dream, all of his old enthusiasms returned. ... He began to think in terms of color... and one new idea after another came tumbling out of him. He kept saying over and over again, 'Oh, boy! Color—and no westerns. I can do whatever I want. Do you hear me? I can do whatever I want.'"[20]

WED Chases Pay-for-Service

Walt continued to enhance Disneyland with new upgrades and attractions. In 1960 he added a mine train ride through Nature's Wonderland and the 360-degree Circarama film America the Beautiful.[21]

In addition to building new attractions for his own use at Disneyland in 1960, Walt was occupied with the prospect of using the unique entertainment design and engineering knowledge and competencies at WED to design mass-audience attractions for third-party sponsors.

Two of the strengths that helped New York City win the 1959 bid to host the 1964 World's Fair were that it would be built on the same New York City site as the successful 1939–1940 World's Fair, in Flushing Meadows, Queens, and that Robert Moses, an influential and well respected urban planner and "master builder" of mid-20th century New York City and the surrounding area, was appointed president of the organization leading the project.

As Moses settled into this job of designing the fair, which included the controversial decision to forgo midway rides of any kind, he wanted to include an eight-acre children's village that would later be converted into a permanent park. He approached Walt to design and run the park. Walt considered it, but having already completed an assessment of the New York market as a viable location for a park, was skeptical that such a park could be run profitably, and quickly declined.

Even so, Moses was enthusiastic about having Walt's participation and the accompanying value of the Disney brand to draw crowds, and asked him if he would be interested in participating as a pay-for-service pavilion designer for other exhibitors at the fair. Walt was way ahead of him, having already spent months actively contacting America's leading corporations to offer Disney's services. On the same August 1960 trip to New York in which Moses asked Walt about designing pavilions for others, Walt had meetings scheduled with a number of executives at leading corporations to discuss exactly that, including RCA, American Machine and Foundry, IBM, AT&T, General Dynamics, and General Electric.[22]

As 1960 came to an end, the studio showed a net loss of $1.3 million after a write-down of $6 million. There were no major animated releases that year. Instead, audiences were given three live-action features: *Kidnapped*, *Pollyanna*, and *Swiss Family Robinson*.

According to Disney historian Michael Barrier, "Gross income, which had shot up since the opening of Disneyland, fell to around $46.4 million from $58.4 million the previous year. Film revenue fell by more than $7 million, largely a reflection of *Sleeping Beauty's* performance, and television revenue by $4.6 million, thanks to ABC's cancellation of *Zorro* and *Mickey Mouse Club*. Only Disneyland's revenue was up."[23] The irony of the income statement, as Disney historians Holliss and Sibley point out, is that "the only increasingly prosperous venture was Disneyland, the one so many critics had predicted would end in failure."[24]

Animation Fades from the Limelight

Walt had high hopes for *Sleeping Beauty*, but after experiencing disappointment at the box office, he no longer had the same fire-in-the-belly exuberance for the possibilities and prospects of commercial animated features that he once had. Walt still loved stories and animation, but given his current interests and priorities, he had less time for it. For one thing, a feature-length animation project took years to complete, and Walt's responsibilities no longer allowed him to spend years completely immersed in every detail of a single project as was the case with *Snow White and the Seven Dwarfs*, *Pinocchio*, and *Fantasia*. There was now an experienced organization, master animators and directors, and proven processes in place to provide effective oversight.

As Walt continued to shift his focus away from animation, there was less need for developing animation artists and keeping them employed. By 1961 it was clear to all that the animation studio lacked the depth of talent it was once famous for. With rising costs to produce quality animation and his unwillingness to spend more time on animation than was absolutely required to ensure a good story, Walt's ethic when it came to animation became one of simpler and cheaper. He was now devoting his attention to bigger and more complex social challenges, including the creation of an integrated school of the arts (CalArts), entertainment and recreational complexes, and city planning.

In terms of sheer output and variety, Walt's decision to get into live-action production and compete with other Hollywood studios allowed him to produce a half-dozen live-action features in the same amount of time as a single animated feature because they didn't require as much of his attention. Once the story and casting were completed, the director was sent on his way. Walt was still involved, and reviewed the daily rushes to ensure projects were on track, looking for any signs of problems, and providing his input and direction for course correction when asked or when he decided it was needed. For the most part, however, he was uninvolved until editing, leaving the directors in charge of their own production operations.

Having multiple projects in play at the same time and having the ability to produce more live-action films in less time and at a reasonable cost for baby boomer parents that appreciated the output proved to be good for business. It was also smart from the point of view of the speed at which revenues could be collected at the box office, diversifying financial risk, and building long-term shareholder value.

The big kick-off of 1961 for the studio was the February release of *One Hundred and One Dalmatians*, which cost $3.6 million.[25] It became an instant major box-office hit. Following the highly stylized design of *Sleeping Beauty*, *Time* magazine called *Dalmatians* "the wittiest, most charming, least pretentious cartoon feature Walt Disney has ever made."[26]

The movie introduced a new and less costly technical advancement in animation that Ub Iwerks had worked on for years, in which artist drawings were copied onto cels mechanically using a Xerox process instead of each drawing being carefully traced by hand onto a cel from the animators' original drawings.

After striving for decades to perfect animation, Walt wasn't convinced that the innovation was an artistic advancement. The new process resulted in heavy black outlines around all shapes and characters, where previously animator drawings were exactingly copied using the appropriate color inks, which was time consuming and expensive, but resulted in a more realistic portrayal of characters and scenes.[27]

What Walt did like and appreciated after the significant losses on *Sleeping Beauty* was that by eliminating a complete step in the animation process, the Xerox process had the potential to speed up production time, significantly lower costs, and allow for a more accurate rendering of the artists' original drawings.[28]

That year also saw the release of *The Absent-Minded Professor*, *The Parent Trap*, and *Babes in Toyland*, amongst other less notable live-action features, and just a couple of animated shorts, for which there was really no longer any theatrical demand.[29]

Walt recognized the lack of seriousness of many of his movies, which were, by his own estimation, "corny." He was unapologetic for his approach to creating product, and is quoted in a 1962 *Newsweek* article: "Our part in things is to build along the lines we are known for, with happy family stories and comedies. I've never thought of this as art. It's part of show business."[30]

Seeking a Florida Home for Project Future

In addition to his other responsibilities, including films, television, and improving Disneyland, and pursuing the development of exhibits for the World's Fair, Walt was again ready to pursue the idea of an East Coast venture.

Roy visited MacArthur in 1961 to continue discussions and land negotiations. MacArthur was put off by Roy's insistence that Walt's plans had now changed, and the previously discussed purchase of Palm Beach property wasn't going to be nearly enough land. Typical of Walt, in exploring his imagination for ideas of what was possible, the wealth of opportunities expanded. Walt had concluded that a lot more land would be needed.

Walt still envisioned the need for 400 acres to build a bigger and better East Coast version of Disneyland. But what he was really interested in was enough additional land to build a town to house and employ up to 70,000 people. MacArthur suggested an area near Orlando where he also owned land, much of which he would eventually sell to Disney as part of an overall purchase of nearly 30,000 acres to build Walt Disney World.[31]

Soon after Palm Beach was abandoned as a viable location for his new project, Walt instructed Buzz Price to initiate a new study to find the optimum place in Florida to build Project Future. Almost every region of the state was studied to determine key factors such as weather, infrastructure, and vacation trends.[32] By the spring of 1961, Price had begun identifying and informing Walt of potential sites.[33] Almost immediately thereafter, in May, Donn Tatum, vice president of Administration at the studio, was sent to Florida to identify potentially suitable large tracts of land in the central parts of the state. Tatum reported to Walt that he was enthusiastic about the prospects of acquiring the amount of land Walt was seeking.[34]

Walt Disney's Wonderful World of Color

In September 1961, *Walt Disney's Wonderful World of Color* made its television debut. Critics and audiences loved the show, which became the first "killer app" to drive sales of color TV sets. Walt aggressively pushed his competitive advantage by reminding his tens of millions of viewers each week that his show was in color at a time when ABC and CBS lacked the capability. ABC delayed its first color series until 1962 and CBS didn't offer regular scheduled programming in color until the fall of 1965.[35]

To create content and leverage his existing film inventory assets, many of Disney's live-action theatrical releases like *Pollyanna*, *Summer Magic*, and *Toby Tyler* were edited into multi-part stories for the TV show. With television as a second distribution channel, a failure at the box office could now be recycled as valuable television content. The opposite was also true. Walt had made it a practice of taking many of his multi-part serials that were produced for

TV and re-editing them for theatrical release in North America and Europe. He first did this with his Davey Crockett episodes in 1955, releasing *Davy Crocket: King of the Wild Frontier*, and in 1956, *Davy Crockett and the River Pirates*. He did it again in 1958 when he combined eight Zorro TV episodes into the movie *The Sign of Zorro* for international theatrical release in 1958 and U.S. release the following year.[36] As he did at ABC, Walt continued to use *Walt Disney's Wonderful World of Color* to entertain and educate the public, and to promote Disneyland and his other commercial endeavors.[37]

The Growth of WED and Imagineering

As the role of WED and the work of the Imagineers expanded to support the expansion of Disneyland and television production, it wasn't long before the WED payroll grew from just a handful of staff in 1953 to 300 employees, with all of the organizational and managerial requirements of any business that size. WED Enterprises had outgrown the space available at the Burbank studio and in 1961 relocated to an industrial park in Glendale, California.

The best thing about WED for Walt, said Bill Cottrell, president of WED from 1952 to 1964,[38] was its complete independence from the studio's bureaucracy, which included the inevitable considerations about what the bankers and shareholders would approve. "Nobody had to ask anyone at the studio for permission," said Cottrell. "If you wanted to start developing a thing like Audio-Animatronics, you'd do it as long as you had the money to do it. And by this time, Walt had the money."[39]

Walt always had to be careful to balance his enthusiasm for WED projects with his regular studio duties. As a coping mechanism, he tried to delegate as much authority at the studio as he could to free up time for the development of more creative WED projects. Walt was always pushing the boundaries of conventional thinking, so WED was always engaged in solving difficult engineering and creative problems. Walt would sometimes describe WED as his "sandbox" and others would observe that his work at WED gave him the most enjoyment.[40]

The main source of funding for WED remained the licensing agreement with the studio to pay a royalty for the use of the Walt Disney name and from the merchandising of Disney products. Walt mostly ran WED as a research and idea development lab for his Disneyland projects. He didn't run WED with an eye to profit, per se. According to early WED executive Mickey Clark, who managed the start-up financing and accounting at WED,[41] "[Walt] charged labor costs plus his out-of-pocket expenses" back to the studio. "He just wanted to get the job done."[42] Walt also continued to receive substantial financial benefit from the personal services contract he had arranged with the studio. In 1960 he received personal fees of

$156,000 from Walt Disney Productions, with a further $188,835 paid to WED for services rendered.[43]

Walt and his team of Imagineers at WED had been working on ideas and concepts for World's Fair attractions with interested corporate sponsors starting in 1960, including General Motors, Coca-Cola, and AT&T,[44] but it wasn't until September 1961 that Walt signed on his first client, the Ford Motor Company. Ford was already a sponsor of Ford's Magic Skyway at Disneyland. WED would design a pavilion for the fair in which people rode through a presentation of history, from the caveman to the spaceman, in the newest Ford convertible cars, including the newly introduced Mustang.

General Electric also acquired WED's services after Walt made a presentation using ideas for an undeveloped Disneyland concept to celebrate the achievements of Thomas Edison in a proposed Edison Square, out of which came the Carousel of Progress.

In addition to paying material costs plus a significant retainer fee to WED (GE paid a fee of $850,000), both companies agreed to an additional sponsorship fee of $1 million for the promotional use of Walt Disney's name on the exhibit.[45] Another important aspect of the sponsorship deals was that all equipment brought to the World's Fair by WED would remain the property of WED after the fair, providing Walt with the option of moving whatever he thought would be useful to him back to Disneyland when the fair ended in October 1965, and discarding the rest.

The Future Is Sunny as Walt Turns 60

Toward the end of the year, in November 1961, Price submitted to Walt his study "Site Location Project Future." The report recommended Ocala as the prime location after mistakenly identifying plans for the Florida Turnpike and Interstate 4 to intersect near Ocala, north of Orlando, rather than Orlando. The error was quickly discovered, and Orlando in central Florida was touted as the ideal spot. When the highway system was completed, the small town of Orlando would be the hub of Florida tourism and the most centrally located of the best options.[46]

Walt had plenty of reasons to celebrate when he turned 60 on December 5, 1961.

The year had been full of uncertainty for Walt in many ways, but it was clear that he, WED, and the studio had forward momentum, building on their core skills and expanding in new directions. *One Hundred and One Dalmatians* laid the foundation for a banner turn-around year that also included the release of a number of other major and minor full-length features. The studio was able to post $70 million in revenues and convert 1960's $1.3 million loss into a $4.5 million profit for 1961.

An additional cause for celebration came with the retirement of the studio's 22-year-old liability to the Bank of America, prompting Walt to joke to newspaper columnist Art Buchwald, "For the first time the banks owe me money."[47]

By following his dreams, determinedly pursuing his values, and pressing his bets with long odds, Walt had slowly and organically built a corporate empire. He was also solidifying his reputation as an iconoclastic business leader and cultural visionary.

Newsweek featured Walt Disney as its cover story in its December 31, 1962, issue, noting that Walt "has produced 550 motion pictures, lent his name to 2,500 books, turned out more than 600 television shows, raked in royalties on countless millions of dolls, sweatshirts, and wrist watches. But the Disney imagination, tireless as his own frenetic Donald Duck, churns on."[48] The article reminded readers of the phenomenal achievements of Walt and Roy, and enumerated the ways in which the studio makes money and the integrated nature of its global business model:

> The dollars come from the forty-year-old business empire known as Walt Disney Productions. In addition to the theatrical films, TV shows, and Disneyland, Disney licenses a monthly circulation of fifty-million in magazines distributed in fifty countries and fifteen languages, makes television commercials and business and educational films, runs art shops, distributes songs and comic strips, and licenses hundreds of manufacturers to use the names of Disney characters in promoting their merchandise. (The usual license take: 5 percent of the wholesale price, with a guaranteed minimum of $5,000.)
>
> The Tie-in: All these activities are firmly linked in the Disney concept of "total merchandising." As Roy Disney, Walt's sixty-nine-year-old brother and self-effacing president of the company, puts it: "Everything we do helps something else." A television show plugs a Disney movie; the movie characters can move into Disneyland or be used as the basis for more television, comics, songs, and toys. In a circle of mathematical perfection, the secondary promotions build up new interest in the movie, which can be released again. *Pinocchio*, for instance, brought the studio only $1.5 million of its $2 million production cost when first released in 1940—but two later distributions brought in $2.7 million, and a third, now in process, will return about $4 million in purest gravy.[49]

---

1. Emerson, *Project Future*, 23; Gabler, *Walt Disney*, 604.

2. Gabler, *Walt Disney*, 569.

3. Goldenson, *Beating the Odds*, 124.

4. Card Walker in Ghez, *Walt's People, Volume 10*, 227; Gabler, *Walt Disney*, 569.

5. Ghez, *Walt's People, Volume 10*, 227.

6. Goldenson, *Beating The Odds*, 124; also in J.A. Aberdeen, "Walt Disney: The SIMPP Years," at cobbles.com/simpp_archive/walt-disney_post-simpp.htm, accessed November 8, 2016.

7. Thomas, *Building a Company*, 208.

8. Thomas, *Building a Company*, 207.

9. Gabler, *Walt Disney*, 563.

10. Walt Disney quoted in Thomas, *Building a Company*, 207.

11. Greene & Greene, *Inside the Dream*, 118.

12. Thomas, *Walt Disney*, 287.

13. Wikipedia, "Robert E. Kintner," en.wikipedia.org/wiki/Robert_E._Kintner, accessed November 8, 2016.

14. Ghez, *Walt's People, Volume 10*, 247–248.

15. Tatum in Ghez, *Walt's People, Volume 10*, 248.

16. Tatum in Ghez, *Walt's People, Volume 10*, 248.

17. Goldenson, *Beating the Odds*, 251; *Los Angeles Times*, February 3, 1991, Leonard Goldenson, "TELEVISION: How ABC Changed Hollywood's Mind About TV," articles.latimes.com/1991-02-03/entertainment/ca-693_1_color-television, accessed November 8, 2016.

18. Gabler, *Walt Disney*, 570.

19. Tatum, in Ghez, *Walt's People, Volume 10*, 248.

20. *TV Guide*, 1961, "The Latter Day Aesop," at Jerry Beck, Cartoon Brew, cartoonbrew.com/disney/disney-interview-in-tv-guide-1961-26537.html, accessed November 8, 2016; also Gabler, *Walt Disney*, 570.

21. Holliss & Sibley, *The Disney Studio Story*, 790.

22. Gabler, *Walt Disney*, 575.

23. Barrier, *The Animated Man*, 270–271.

24. Holliss & Sibley, *The Disney Studio Story*, 74.

25. Holliss & Sibley, *The Disney Studio Story*, 76.

26. Holliss & Sibley, *The Disney Studio Story*, 76.

27. Holliss & Sibley, *The Disney Studio Story*, 75.

28. Holliss & Sibley, *The Disney Studio Story*, 75.

29. Holliss & Sibley, *The Disney Studio Story*, 187–190.

30. Gabler, *Walt Disney*, 586–587.

31. "County Wasn't Big Enough for Both Walt Disney, John D. MacArthur," *Palm Beach Post*, 18 Nov. 2011, palmbeachpost.com/news/travel/county-wasnt-big-enough-for-both-walt-disney-joh-1/nLzpQ/, accessed October 2, 2015,

no longer available at November 8, 2016; see also *Orlando Weekly*, "Disney World could have been in Palm Beach County," orlandoweekly.com/Blogs/archives/2013/03/07/disney-world-could-have-been-in-palm-beach-county#, accessed November 8, 2016.

32. Emerson, *Project Future*, 24.

33. Gabler, *Walt Disney*, 604.

34. Gabler, *Walt Disney*, 605.

35. Wikipedia, "Color television," en.m.wikipedia.org/wiki/Color_television, accessed November 26, 2014.

36. The Disney Wiki, "The Sign of Zorro," disney.wikia.com/wiki/The_Sign_of_Zorro, accessed June 13, 2016.

37. Holliss & Sibley, *The Disney Studio Story*, 79.

38. Wikipedia, "Walt Disney Imagineering," en.wikipedia.org/wiki/Walt_Disney_Imagineering, accessed September 21, 2015.

39. Cottrell quoted in Greene & Greene, *Inside the Dream*, 131; also Gabler, *Walt Disney*, 588.

40. Greene & Greene, *Inside the Dream*, 130.

41. "Rest in Peace, Royal 'Mickey' Clark," retlawyensid.com/2014/09/rest-in-peace-royal-clark.html, accessed September 21, 2015.

42. Greene & Greene, *Inside the Dream*, 130.

43. Gabler, *Walt Disney*, 589.

44. Tatum in Ghez, *Walt's People, Volume 10*, 252–253.

45. Holliss & Sibley, *The Disney Studio Story*, 80; Gabler, *Walt Disney*, 576.

46. Price, *Walt's Revolution*, p. 68; Emerson, *Project Future*, 24.

47. Holliss & Sibley, *The Disney Studio Story*, 76; Gabler, *Walt Disney*, 563.

48. *Newsweek*, "The Wide World of Walt Disney," December 31, 1962, in Jackson, *Walt Disney Conversations*, 82.

49. *Newsweek*, Dec. 31, 1962, in Jackson, *Walt Disney, Conversations*, 84.

CHAPTER TWENTY-TWO

The Wide World of Disney

As 1963 progressed, Walt began spending less time occupied with developmental work and planning for the delivery and installation of exhibits for the fair. He began to shift his attention back to improving Disneyland and how to use recent technology advancements in Audio-Animatronics to improve the attractions and refresh and heighten the guest experience.[1]

For example, incremental improvements that leveraged advances in Audio-Animatronics were made to the Jungle Cruise and other attractions to enhance visual humor and corny fun throughout the park. A giant step forward and the biggest proof-of-concept of audio-animatronics entertainment was the development of the successful Enchanted Tiki Room attraction that opened in June 1963. The show featured 225 computer-controlled animated birds with synchronized sound and movement engaged in a raucous sixteen-minute live-action show.

Walt was prolific in developing new ideas and uses for Audio-Animatronics in the park through the creation of fully automated character performances. Perhaps the most ambitious was his idea for a major new pirates-themed attraction that would evolve into Pirates of the Caribbean. When it opened in 1967, the attraction featured sixty-five animated figures consisting of pirates, townspeople, and animals, and a dazzling array of special effects.

Moses Meets Mr. Lincoln

When New York World's Fair President Robert Moses visited WED in 1963, Walt took him on a tour of the studio and talked about some of his plans for the future. He showed Moses designs for the Hall of Presidents exhibit he was planning to build at Disneyland and an early prototype of an Abraham Lincoln Audio-Animatronic figure.

Moses was excited about the robotic Lincoln and pushed hard for Walt to finish the prototype in time to make it a must-see attraction at the fair. To his credit, Moses took it upon himself to find a sponsor and after months of searching, was eventually able to entice the State of Illinois, the home of Lincoln's birth, to utilize Disney's robotic Lincoln in their state exhibit, and thereby underwrite a quickened pace of research and development.[2] Walt later reflected in an interview on the advancements brought to the development of robotic entertainment through the State of Illinois' sponsorship:

> I figured it would take me ten years to get Mr. Lincoln going. Well, I had him in what we called Mark I and I had him under manual control. We could make him stand up and put his hand out. Robert Moses was getting the World's Fair going, and he came out. He came and visited Disneyland. He wanted to visit the studio. He was trying to get ideas on what could be done. So I had him meet Abraham Lincoln. I said, 'Would you like to meet Mr. Lincoln?' He gave me a funny look. I said, 'Well, come on in—meet him.' So when he walked in the door, I said, 'Mr. Lincoln, meet Mr. Moses.' and Lincoln stood up and put his hand out and Moses went over and shook hands with him. Well, Moses is quite a showman and he said, 'I've got to have Lincoln in the fair.' But I said, 'This is five years away, anyway.' But Moses wouldn't take no for an answer. The next thing I knew he had gotten with the State of Illinois and was trying to sell them on a pavilion. And before I knew it, I had my arm twisted and I said, 'Yes.' We now had to get Mr. Lincoln on the road, I think, in about thirteen months.[3]

The first three pavilions that Walt and WED had contracted to design for the World's Fair were the Magic Skyway (Ford), Carousel of Progress (GE), and Great Moments with Mr. Lincoln (State of Illinois). They all had one thing in common, and it wasn't by accident. Each utilized the application of Audio-Animatronics, which allowed Walt to engage in R&D of the technology for automated, computerized, and synchronized show-like attractions, financed with other people's money, i.e., the sponsors of the fair's attractions.

Making Time for a Little Boat Ride

Late in the summer of 1963, and with just nine months to go until the opening of the fair, Walt agreed to take on the development of a fourth exhibit. Pepsi-Cola approached the studio to commission a pavilion for the United Nations International Children's Education Fund (UNICEF), from which the idea for It's a Small World was developed.

At the time, WED staff was overwhelmed with the work they had to do for Disneyland and the World's Fair. Then one day Walt called an emergency meeting. Imagineer Rolly Crump was in attendance and recalls:

> Walt came in and he said to us, "Well, there is one more piece of real estate left at the World's Fair. I'd like for us to get it." We all looked around at each other in disbelief. ... Apparently, Pepsi-Cola wanted to be the sponsor, and it would be a salute to UNICEF.

"I'd like us to do a little boat ride," he continued. Well, we all kind of thought to ourselves, 'Oh my God, he's lost it.' Our plates were already full. We had to perfect the show for Mr. Lincoln, the first time in history that an animatronic figure was going to stand up. We were working on Carousel of Progress for General Electric's Progressland, with all the Animatronics that were going in there. We had to make sure the conveyance system worked for the Ford pavilion. And here he was, wanting to do a little boat ride, too!

[W]e didn't know how to react. But Walt wanted it, so Walt was going to get it! So, of course, what everyone actually said was, "Sure, Walt, sure!" That was the beginning of It's a Small World.[4]

Crump, who had about 30 people reporting to him, was amazed by the team's ability to complete the project from a standing start in a mere nine months with everything else that they were already doing. With a hard deadline in place, work began. Design concept sketches of the ride were created. Two hundred toy props had to be built from scratch out of Styrofoam and papier-mâché. Sketches had to be converted into three-dimensional models. Sets had to be built. Costumes for the dolls had to be designed, materials sourced, and sewn. The mechanical aspects of the ride had be developed and built. Music had to be written, scored, and recorded.

"When you stop and think about it," Crump reflects in his memoir, "it was quite a laborious process. We had to set it up, get it all running for Walt to see, take it down, ship it to New York, and then set it up all over again. It was absolutely marvelous. What was really interesting, to me at least, was that we designed it, built it, and then installed it in only nine months."[5]

The Joy and Pain of Mary Poppins

The one exception to Walt's relative lack of interest in film projects during the 1960s was *Mary Poppins*. Walt had first read the P.L. Travers book in 1943 and soon after sought to acquire the film rights. At the time, during World War II, Travers was living in New York with her son. It wasn't until 1946 that Roy met with Travers in New York and an agreement was reached under which the studio would acquire the rights for $10,000. The deal fell apart, however, when Travers insisted that she be given final approval of the script. Walt refused.[6]

Thirteen years later, after the creation of Disneyland, Walt tried again. This time Travers' agent set the price at $750,000. Walt flew to London to meet Travers with the hopes of reaching an agreement, but again Travers shifted the basis for a deal. She was now asking for five percent of the profits with a guarantee of $100,000 and one thousand British pounds to do the treatment.[7] Walt and Travers negotiated aspects of the film for more than two years before Travers, in 1960, finally agreed to sign a contract. According to the Disney studio songwriting team of Richard and Robert Sherman, "Travers had hated everything we had done. Disliked it with a passion!"[8] A full year later, after working directly with the Disney writers, Travers was still critiquing the script.[9]

When casting for the movie began in 1961, Walt was initially keen on Mary Martin, whom he had seen perform in *The Sound of Music*, but in August he attended the musical *Camelot* in New York and was immediately convinced that Julie Andrews, who played the lead actress next to Richard Burton, should be Mary Poppins.[10]

It took Walt almost a year to convince Julie Andrews to accept the lead role. Andrews had since moved on to play the role Eliza Doolittle in *My Fair Lady* on Broadway and her heart was set on winning the lead role in the film version of *My Fair Lady*. Instead, Warner Bros. head Jack Warner selected proven screen star Audrey Hepburn to play the lead on the basis that nobody had ever heard of Julie Andrews. With that opportunity now behind her, Andrews reluctantly agreed to join Walt's cast. Walt invited her and her husband to the studio in June 1962. Travers was not happy with Andrews as Mary Poppins. She was also unhappy with Walt's attempt to get Cary Grant for the male lead, as well as with his eventual choice of television comedian Dick Van Dyke.[11]

Van Dyke later reflected on his casting meeting with Walt:

> Walt had rooms of storyboards that he showed me, and his enthusiasm for the film grew as he spoke. He was like a kid, getting so excited about it that by the time I left him I was excited about it, too. He had me sold. I wanted to be a part of that movie so much.[12]

With all the pieces now in place—the casting, the story, the script, the musical score, the sets—Walt was ready to produce his most elaborate and expensive live-action film since *20,000 Leagues Under the Sea*. Disney historian and entertainment commentator Neal Gabler writes in *Walt Disney: The Triumph of the American Imagination*:

> "There wasn't a sad face around the entire studio," Walt said, and admitted he became concerned when, as the budget swelled, not even Roy attempted to interfere or request that he show the "dailies" to the bankers. It had been years since Walt was so personally invested in a film. On just about every picture now, no matter how much he might labor over the script or the casting, he would fix, approve and then disappear. On Mary Poppins, which was shot entirely on the Burbank lot, he visited the set almost every day with the objective—in the words of Karen Dotrice, who played the little girl under Poppins' authority—of "making sure that everybody was happy. That was the thing—he wanted everybody to enjoy the experience." Later, Dotrice, echoing Van Dyke, said he was "like a big kid."[13]

The principal photography for the film was completed at the end of the summer of 1963, with the animation, special effects, and editing to follow.

The Secretive Florida Project Fellowship

With development work for the New York World's Fair and Mary Poppins seemingly in hand, Walt once again turned his focus to Florida and Project Future.

Sometime in the summer of 1963, Walt discreetly convened a small, handpicked team of trusted executives and board members to set in motion a secretive process of purchasing land in Florida to serve as Walt's new sandbox. The project was considered so sensitive that when it was launched, only Walt, Roy, and seven other Disney executives knew about it—Card Walker, Donn Tatum, Jack Sayers, Larry Tyron, Mel Melton, Joe Fowler, and attorney Bob Foster.[14]

The challenge he put before the group was to devise a methodology to secretly find five to ten thousand acres in Florida to build a new park.[15] With considerable time having passed since Price's original 1961 Florida study, Walt instructed him to conduct a new detailed study to identify the best Florida development sites. It was important to Walt to base his decisions on the best available current information.

In September 1963, an early plan on how to proceed in secrecy to prevent the potential problem of soaring property prices was submitted to Walt and Roy by Card Walker, VP of Advertising and Sales and a board member, on behalf of the Project Future team:

> We would carefully select a third party (like Governor Arnell) who would be our front. He would actually be seeking the land for another carefully selected company or person. In turn, this third party would select a real estate man or lawyer knowledgeable in real estate who, on a pre-determined plan, would assemble the land. The real estate man would *never* know we are involved. We would have a "team" to follow and call every move as it develops. The land, for example, might be a "retirement village" for senior citizens, as it would be similar to our project.[16]

Price completed his new Florida site location study in December 1963. "The key conclusion," writes Price in *Walt's Revolution*, "was that central Florida (not Miami as most people expected it would be) was the point of maximum interception of Florida tourism, and that Orlando, centrally located, was the point of maximum access to the southerly flows of Florida tourism from both the east and the west shores of the state."[17]

One of the reasons Walt sought so much land was his desire and determination to control the external environment around his property and ensure that the corporation could secure the maximum benefit from the economic value it was creating. One of Walt's constant complaints about Disneyland was that its success had attracted a neon-lit perimeter of seedy hotels and shabby tourist retail shops, giving it a cheap Las Vegas feel. It bothered him that when he initially bought land in Anaheim he lacked the funds needed to control the environment surrounding the park to protect and enhance the experience of his guests. It also bothered him that Disneyland was the central attraction drawing tourists to the area, yet operators outside the park often earned more money than he did from park guests.

If Walt was to build in Florida, he wanted to exert greater control over the entire guest experience, from arrival to departure, which included an expanded selection of recreational facilities, accommodations, and restaurants on Disney property and under Disney control.

Walt celebrated his 62nd birthday in December 1963. He was so busy creating and managing the development of new ideas that year that he resigned all his official titles and simply called himself the studio's "executive producer." "I'm the boss of everything that's produced here," he told one journalist.[18]

Animatronic Lincoln Is A-Number-One, Top of the List

The opening day of the New York World's Fair, April 22, 1964, was fast approaching, but things were not going well for those working on the Lincoln Audio-Animatronic, which had been developed and built in a secretive locked room in the animation building at the studio in Burbank[19] and then shipped to New York the week prior to the fair's opening. According to Holliss and Sibley in *The Disney Studio Story*:

> The show was titled "Great Moments with Mr. Lincoln," but, for a while, it seemed as if there were not actually going to be any. First, there was trouble with the wiring; then there were problems with the power supply. On 20 April, when 200 invited guests arrived for the premiere of Lincoln's performance, the president—who was capable of 48 separate body actions and 15 facial movements—was still not functioning properly, and Walt refused to let the show go ahead. There was a tense week of long hours and frustrating attempts to make the Audio-Animatronics figure work before the problems were solved and Lincoln could rise from his chair and speak of mankind as having been "made for immortality."[20]

Journalist and author Chuck Schmidt recalls his personal memories of visiting the attraction as a teenager in his book *Disney's Dream Weavers*:

> The fair was an exciting experience, if a bit overwhelming; there was just too much to see in one day. ... [F]or me, by far the most

stunning attraction was Great Moments with Mr. Lincoln. ... First he stood up from his chair and then—incredibly—he began to talk to the audience, reciting verses from many of his famous speeches. He even moved his arms as he put extra emphasis on his words. And as he spoke, we in the audience became speechless; it was truly a breathtaking presentation.[21]

A general audience had never seen the likes of the Audio-Animatronic Lincoln before, making the show a sensational hit and major attraction of the fair. Lincoln's performance was so life-like, entrancing, and stirring to audiences that *National Geographic* magazine proclaimed the figure "alarming" in its realism.[22]

Magical, Joyous, Complete, Corny...Mary Poppins

With crowds packing Disneyland on the West Coast and lining up for Disney's exhibits at the World's Fair on the East Coast, *Mary Poppins* premiered at Grauman's Chinese Theatre in Hollywood on August 27, 1964, to a rousing standing ovation. Movie producer Sam Goldwyn wrote a letter to Walt after seeing the picture: "You have made a great many pictures, Walt, that have touched the hearts of the world, but you have never made one so wonderful, so magical, so joyous, so completely the fulfillment of everything a great motion picture should be as MARY POPPINS."[23]

Mary Poppins was Disney's most expensive live-action movie at the time, costing $5.2 million, and it was hugely successful upon its initial release, grossing $30 million in the U.S. and nearly $45 million worldwide.[24] The success of *Mary Poppins* boosted corporate revenues in 1964 above $100 million. It was nominated for thirteen Oscars, including Best Picture, which it lost to *My Fair Lady*. It did win in five categories: Best Special Visual Effects, Best Score, Best Song ("Chim Chim Cher-ee"), Best Editing, and Best Actress (Julie Andrews).[25]

While *Mary Poppins* was a box office success, for many it was a magnet for further criticism of Disney. Walt responded to his critics in a November 1964 interview published in *Los Angeles Magazine* and reported by Michael Barrier in *The Animated Man*:

> "I like perfection, but I also like corn," he said. "I don't make pictures for sophisticates. Styles may change on the surface, but at bottom the big audience taste doesn't change. They like sympathetic characters and life-like action. And that's what I like, too, whether it's cartoon, live action or all those creatures at Disneyland."[26]

In a press interview earlier that year, Walt openly defended his populist style and what some saw as his corny and sappy optimism and romanticism:

I am not a literary person. As far as realism is concerned, you can find dirt anyplace you look for it. I'm one of those optimists. There's always a rainbow. The great masses like happy endings. If you can pull a tear out of them, they'll remember your picture. That little bit of pathos was Chaplin's secret. Some directors in Hollywood are embarrassed by sentimentality. As for me, I like a good cry.[27]

Some think that success relieves the performance pressure felt by executives, but Walt didn't see it that way. Walt always viewed success as verification of the efficacy of knowledge and action, and of setting a new higher-level foundation from which to raise the bar for what comes next. Each rise of the bar creates higher expectations among the public and the critics. "I'm on the spot," Walt said in another interview. "I have to keep trying to keep up to that same level. And the way to do it is *not* to worry, *not* to get tense, *not* to think, 'I got to beat *Mary Poppins*, I got to beat *Mary Poppins*.'... The way to do it is just to go off and get interested in some little thing, some little idea that interests me, some little idea that looks like fun."[28]

In recognition of his unique achievements and his continued rising status as a celebrity, business tycoon, and cultural icon, Walt was invited to the White House to receive the Medal of Freedom, the highest honor that can be bestowed upon a civilian by a president. At a ceremony in the East Room on September 14, 1964, President Lyndon Johnson presented the award to Walt and 25 other Americans. "On the talents of such citizens," said the president, "rests the future of our American civilization, for it is from the genius of the few that we enrich the greatness of the many."[29]

---

1. Barrier, *The Animated Man*, 293.

2. Gabler, *Walt Disney*, 580–581.

3. Smith, *The Quotable Walt Disney*, 206.

4. Crump, *It's Kind of a Cute Story*, 67–69.

5. Crump, *It's Kind of a Cute Story*, 71.

6. Gabler, *Walt Disney*, 596.

7. Gabler, *Walt Disney*, 596.

8. Gabler, *Walt Disney*, 597.

9. See *Saving Mr. Banks*, starring Emma Thompson and Tom Hanks.

10. Gabler, *Walt Disney*, 597.

11. Gabler, *Walt Disney*, 598.

12. Gabler, *Walt Disney*, 598.

13. Gabler, *Walt Disney*, 598–599.

14. Gennawey, *Walt Disney and the Promise of Progress City*, 135.

15. Gabler, *Walt Disney*, 605.

16. Gabler, *Walt Disney*, 605.

17. Price, *Walt's Revolution!*, 41, 68; Emerson, *Project Future*, 174 gives the report date of January 1964. It's possible that it was completed and dated 1963 but not presented or submitted until the New Year, 1964.

18. Gabler, *Walt Disney*, 584.

19. Gabler, *Walt Disney*, 580.

20. Holliss & Sibley, *The Disney Studio Story*, 80.

21. Chuck Schmidt, *Disney's Dream Weavers*, 4–5.

22. "The Disneyland Story presenting Great Moments with Mr. Lincoln," disneyland.disney.go.com/attractions/disneyland/disneyland-story/, accessed 20 Oct. 2014.

23. Gabler, *Walt Disney*, 600.

24. $44 million gross, says Barrier, *The Animated Man*, 282.

25. Barrier, *The Animated Man*, 282.

26. Barrier, *The Animated Man*, 284.

27. Barrier, *The Animated Man*, 284.

28. Walt quoted in Gabler, *Walt Disney*, 601.

29. Lyndon B. Johnson, "Remarks at the Presentation of the 1964 Presidential Medal of Freedom Awards," presidency.ucsb.edu/ws/?pid=26496, accessed June 18, 2016; Barrier, *The Animated Man*, 307.

CHAPTER TWENTY-THREE

Designing a Prototype City of Tomorrow

Walt kicked off 1965 with a special episode of *Walt Disney's Wonderful World of Color* to celebrate the park's 10th anniversary showing the progress of the park over the previous decade as well as a fascinating but brief behind-the-scenes tour of WED and a glimpse of future attractions that were being worked on. In the ten years since its grand opening, park attendance had surpassed 52 million visitors.[1]

While work on developing Disneyland continued, Walt's main interest remained what now was called the Florida Project. A key initiative in 1965 was the creation of an economic master plan to stake out Walt's vision for his planned Orlando-area development and assess the best use of the land. According to an assessment by Buzz Price, first-year attendance was projected to be 8.5 million visitors.[2]

As planning for a Florida theme park and the EPCOT project proceeded under a shroud of secrecy, Walt pursued his seemingly insatiable interest in urban planning and the principles of building people-friendly communities and cities. He experienced directly the positive effect that Disneyland had on the psyche of park visitors, and was curious about trying his hand at expanding the success he had in creating a sense of optimism and overall well-being beyond the berm, in a bigger and more impactful way.

To facilitate his own learning and test his ideas, Walt made the time in his busy schedule to devote a week in 1965 to meet with pioneering urban planner and real estate developer James Rouse to share ideas and to tour the leading-edge planned communities of Columbia, Maryland, and Reston, Virginia. By this time, Walt had already spent years developing concept drawings for his futuristic city, applying existing technologies in new and innovative ways.

Studying the Planned Communities of Today for Tomorrow

James Rouse had made an important contribution to suburban living as the first person to develop an indoor shopping center for which he coined the term "mall." The idea was that the mall would serve as a surrogate town center for suburban developments, which lacked their own sense of a downtown as a centralized meeting place.

What attracted Walt to Rouse's Columbia, Maryland, development was the similarities in their philosophy of using urban planning to develop people-centric communities. Rouse approached his design of Columbia with four goals in mind: respect the land, build a real city as distinct from a suburban bedroom community, promote growth of the individual and family, and finally, as a land developer, to make a profit.[3]

Walt's approach for EPCOT included two additional tenets beyond those of Rouse: partner with American industry to test new technologies beneficial to the public, and contribute through principles of urban design to the creation of happy and life-affirming communities.

Rouse's first planned residential community was the Village of Cross Keys, built in Baltimore on sixty-eight acres of land he bought in 1961. It was his stated intention to bring to the residential field "some of the fresh thinking, good taste and high standards which we believe have marked our shopping center developments. ... There is a real need for residential development in which there is a strong sense of community; a need to feed into the city some of the atmosphere and pace of the small town and village; a need to create a community which can meet as many as possible of the needs of the people who live there; which can bring these people into natural contact with one another; which can produce out of these relationships a spirit and feeling of neighborliness and a rich sense of belonging to a community."[4]

While the Village of Cross Keys was still under development, Rouse proceeded with a much more ambitious project: the building of an entire city, Columbia, Maryland, on 14,000 acres of farmland. Rouse wanted to use Columbia to show that a city could simultaneously serve human and economic values to enhance the quality of life of its residents.

Rouse brought together a wide assortment of thinkers and scholars to contribute their expertise in the areas of health, family life, education, recreation, government, transportation, and employment. Not surprisingly, the conclusion was reached that what was needed was a multi-faceted city which could provide its residents access to jobs, education, health care, and other necessities, and not another bedroom suburb.

To achieve the desired living experience, the city was divided into twelve subdivisions of "villages" of 10,000 to 15,000 people, which was thought to enhance and foster a closer sense of community connection. Each village would have its own central core where people of different income levels and housing types would cross paths and interact. Each village would have its own schools that all children in the neighborhood would attend together and receive the same high-quality education, participate at common community centers and recreational facilities, and interact at a supermarket, a library, a hospital, an auditorium, offices, restaurants, specialty shops, and an interfaith non-denominational house of worship.[5]

The city of Columbia itself would have a central downtown core that would include retail stores arranged as a mall, a hotel and conference center, a hospital, a community college, and a number of recreation and entertainment facilities, including a main entertainment area to be known as Tivoli, named after the famous park in Copenhagen.[6] The downtown mall would be connected to a man-made lake to form the town's centerpiece.

As Walt admired the building principles and community philosophy inherent in Rouse's work, so too did Rouse admire similar values he observed in Walt's work at Disneyland. In a speech at an urban design conference held at the Harvard Graduate School of Design in 1963,[7] Rouse told his audience:

> I hold a view that may be somewhat shocking to an audience as sophisticated as this: that the greatest piece of urban design in the United States today is Disneyland. If you think about Disneyland and think of its performance in relationship to its purpose, its meaning to people—more than that, its meaning to the process of development—you will find it the outstanding piece of urban design in the United States.
>
> It took an area of activity—the amusement park—and lifted it to a standard so high in its performance, in its respect for people, in its functioning for people, that it really does become a brand-new thing. It fulfills all its functions it set out to accomplish, un-self-consciously, usefully, and profitably to its owners and developers.
>
> I find more to learn in the standards that have been set and in the goals that have been achieved in the development of Disneyland than in any other piece of physical development in the country.[8]

The city of Columbia opened in 1967, and in recent times, has consistently ranked in CNN Money's top ten Best Places to Live in America.[9]

As part of his weeklong excursion to study city planning, Walt also toured the city of Reston, Virginia, which was conceived and planned by developer Robert E. Simon, and founded in 1964. It was the first modern, post-war planned community in America, sparking a revival of planned communities.

Simon's family had owned Carnegie Hall, which was sold and the money used to create Reston. In 1962, Simon articulated the principles by which Reston was to be planned and built, principles that resonated with Walt:

- That the widest choice of opportunities be made available for the full use of leisure time. This means that the new town should provide a wide range of cultural and recreational facilities as well as an environment for privacy.

- That it be possible for anyone to remain in a single neighborhood throughout his life, uprooting being neither inevitable nor always desirable. By providing the fullest range of housing styles and prices—from high-rise efficiencies to 6-bedroom town houses and detached houses—housing needs can be met at a variety of income levels and at different stages of family life. This kind of mixture permits residents to remain rooted in the community if they so choose—as their particular housing needs change. As a by-product, this also results in the heterogeneity that spells a lively and varied community.

- That the importance and dignity of each individual be the focal point for all planning, and take precedence for large-scale concepts.

- That the people be able to live and work in the same community.

- That commercial, cultural, and recreational facilities be made available to the residents from the outset of the development—not years later.

- That beauty—structural and natural—is a necessity of the good life and should be fostered.

- Since Reston is being developed from private enterprise, in order to be completed as conceived it must also, of course, be a financial success.[10]

Through careful planning and zoning, Reston provides "common grounds, several parks, large swaths of wooded areas with picturesque runs (streams), wildflower meadows, two golf courses, nearly 20 public swimming pools, bridle paths, a bike path, four lakes, tennis courts, and extensive foot pathways. These pathways, combined with footbridges and tunnels, help to separate pedestrians from vehicular traffic and increase safety at certain street crossings. Reston was built in wooded areas of oak, maple, sycamore, and Virginia pine."[11]

Reston was designed to increase housing density and to conserve open space, with the utilization of mixed areas for industry, business, recreation, education, and housing.

How to do this effectively was foremost in Walt's mind as he developed ideas for EPCOT. Walt was looking at the work in urban design concepts of Rouse and Simon, of Reston and Columbia, along with his experience in building a studio and operating Disneyland as a new baseline and starting point upon which to overlay his own creative intent.

Where Rouse and Reston sought ways to reconfigure the conventional idea of a city, Walt's plans were much more radical and unconventional, building on existing technological innovations and methods used in the most advanced labs and industrial factories of America's most respected companies. According to one source:

> [I]n 1966, Epcot and Columbia were uniquely ambitious, striving to push the limits of urban planning. However, the original EPCOT plan was light years ahead of Columbia in terms of strikingly original features. Its original layout was straight out of science fiction: an impossibly elaborate transportation system with a high-speed monorail and a light duty circulator system, and an underground road network for cars, trucks and service vehicles. The urban hub featured a high-rise hotel and office complex surrounded by high-density multifamily, then a green belt with churches, schools and parks, and beyond that, a low-density green space with plenty of single-family detached homes. It was a picture-perfect mix of commercial, residential, and entertainment, not to mention an idyllic 1,000 acre industrial park nearby promising jobs for everyone. From the outset, it was designed to serve a very corporate America in a pristine, climate-controlled protective bubble. Pedestrians would be king, served by a friendly local circulator, rapid transit to destinations outside the city, with cars and trucks relegated to second-class status in underground tunnels and parking. It would also require a whole new concept of people mover: the WEDway, modeled after the people mover already used at Disneyland in Anaheim, California.

This was to be a truly new type of city, a showcase of industry and futurism where 20,000 people lived, worked, and played. Schools would welcome new ideas and people would have little need for their cars except on weekends. And there would be full employment. This truly was an exciting blueprint of the future, full of wild-eyed optimism like so many projections of the future made in the early and mid-20th century (think Jetsons).[12]

Disney Attractions Win Over New York Audiences

By the time the New York World's Fair ran its course and came to a close in October 1965, it had attracted 51 million visitors, with almost all having visited the Disney attractions. A Gallup poll indicated that three of the top-four-rated-attractions among visitors were Disney developed exhibits, with It's a Small World scoring lower.[13]

In spite of the impressive attendance numbers, by the time it had drawn to a close, the fair itself was considered a commercial failure. The financial projections for break-even were based on a much larger attendance of 70 million. Author and futurist Ray Bradbury offered his assessment that the fair under-performed because "Walt did not design the whole thing.

There were not enough benches, not enough trees, not enough restrooms... all the things that developers think are not necessary Walt would have provided."[14] Walt's creation of Disneyland had raised the standard by which people now judged fairs and outdoor public spaces. Disneyland *was* the new standard of comparison.

Walt's decision to participate as a designer rather than an exhibitor worked out well for him. He was able to entice others to pay for new research and development into Audio-Animatronics and new high-capacity ride-systems and to test them under extreme conditions so that they could be improved upon when moved to Disneyland, and later to other Disney parks. When the fair was over, General Electric's Carousel of Progress was dismantled and shipped back to Disneyland to take its place as a new attraction, as were the prehistoric panorama and an Audio-Animatronic Stegosaurus and T. Rex locked in combat from the Ford exhibit. A brand-new and larger It's a Small World was built. A third-generation Audio-Animatronic Abe Lincoln had already been developed and installed to become the centerpiece of Disneyland's Great Moments with Mr. Lincoln attraction, which opened in the park before the fair closed.

Perhaps most importantly, Walt was now fully confident that sophisticated and industrious East Coast audiences would be just as receptive to Disneyland-type entertainment as the more laid-back West Coast crowd.

1. Holliss & Sibley, *The Disney Studio Story*, 79; YouTube, "Disneyland's 10th Anniversary (1965)," youtube.com/watch?v=U3BIWJ9QmZs, accessed June 30, 2016; aired January 3, 1965, IMDb, imdb.com/title/tt0768379/, accessed July 1, 2016.

2. Price, *Walt's Revolution!*, 42.

3. Mannheim, *Walt Disney and the Quest for Community*, 24.

4. Wikipedia, "James Rouse," en.m.wikipedia.org/wiki/James_Rouse, accessed October 14, 2014.

5. Wikipedia, "James Rouse," en.m.wikipedia.org/wiki/James_Rouse.

6. Wikipedia entry for James Rouse, en.m.wikipedia.org/wiki/James_Rouse.

7. Barrier, *The Animated Man*, 302.

8. Quoted in Walt Disney's film outlining the plans for his Florida property, a transcript of which is available at: sites.google.com/site/theoriginalepcot/film-transcript, accessed November 8, 2016.

9. Wikipedia, "Columbia Maryland," en.m.wikipedia.org/wiki/Columbia_Maryland, accessed 16 Oct. 2014.

10. Wikipedia, "Reston, Virginia," en.m.wikipedia.org/wiki/Reston,_Virginia, accessed October 16, 2014.

11. Wikipedia, "Reston, Virginia," en.m.wikipedia.org/wiki/Reston,_Virginia, accessed 16 Oct. 2014.

12. "James Rouse, Planning Visionary," bridgecolumbia.org/2011/08/ james-rouse-planning-visionary, accessed October 19, 2015. This article is no longer available, having been replaced with a rewritten essay by Peter Tocco, "History Of Columbia," bridgecolumbia.org/#!history-of-columbia/orr5c, accessed, August 7, 2016.

13. Gennawey, *Walt Disney and the Promise of Progress City*, 110.

14. Bradbury quoted in Gennawey, *Walt Disney and the Promise of Progress City*, 119.

CHAPTER TWENTY-FOUR

EPCOT as Walt's Biggest Dream and Final Frontier

Having conquered parks through an intuitive sense and application of principles of urban design to create what Imagineer John Hench described retrospectively as an "architecture of reassurance," Walt was now setting his sights on reinvigorating cities through urban planning.[1] The new challenge and act of visionary leadership Walt set for himself was to integrate and apply all that he had learned so far about building positive interactive spaces with the unique set of creative talent and engineering skills he had assembled at WED and the studio, to pursue the audacious task of improving human happiness and making a positive contribution to change in society.

From his humble teenage beginnings creating primitive cartoons in his father's garage, Walt had become a self-taught expert in such things as entertaining, education, technological innovation, industrial and commercial design, crowd control, security, television production, transportation systems, business operations, and facilities management for a park infrastructure and property serving millions of visitors annually. Walt would later say, "I don't believe there's a challenge anywhere in the world that's more important to people everywhere than finding solutions to the problems of our cities."[2]

According to WED planner and architect Marvin Davis, who worked on the project design with Walt, "It was his philosophy not to build a city that would solve all the urban problems all over the world, but to give a chance to American industry to experiment and show to the world just how the problems of traffic and housing could be solved. ... It would be a place not only for testing physical things, but educational developments and all forms of communication. He was greatly interested in solving the young adult problem that faces everybody. ... So the amusement park was really a secondary thing. He was interested in solving the urban problem. It's a big scope, but that's exactly what he was thinking."[3]

"He wanted to try going beyond the park experience," noted Walt's research confidant, Buzz Price. "He wanted to try to improve the environment, the urban setting. He was full of ideas about what that place would be like. Epcot would not be just a park, but an urban experiment where you could try to improve the way people live, creating alternatives to our frantic, automobile existence."[4]

As with most of Walt's major projects, which he thought about for years before taking decisive action, Walt's interest in urban planning wasn't a sudden inspirational whim. As early as 1959, as he was just learning of the New York World's Fair and rejecting the idea of building a park in New York City, Walt had started to become a student of modern urban planning, and began to think about applying what he had learned through the building and operations of Disneyland to communities at large.[5] This was around the time that Walt began investigating the purchase of land in Florida with the idea of developing some sort of showcase planned community or city.

In his desire to learn more about how to address the growing social problems brought about by the urbanization of cities, Walt sought out other like-minded planners and studied their work as a source of inspiration and a way to test his own ideas, in particular James Rouse and Robert E. Simon. He was influenced to a great degree in his approach by Victor Gruen's plan for Washington, D.C.'s 1964 World's Fair proposal, outlined in Ada Louise Huxtable's 1960 article, "Out of a Fair, a City."[6]

His primary influence is said to be from two books that he kept in his office or carried around, and to which he frequently referred: Victor Gruen's *The Heart of Our Cities*, published in 1964, which focused on overcoming the problem of auto-centric developments in favor of a people-centric planned approach, and a 1965 reissue of Ebenezer Howard's 1902 book *Garden Cities of To-morrow*.[7]

As he applied himself to the practical problems of city building, Walt commissioned Buzz Price's Economics Research Associates to undertake a study on the history of planned cities. From what he had seen and studied, Walt considered most modern planned cities to be problematic and sub-optimal, and tried to identify why they did not succeed. He looked upon their shortcomings and failures as a gift to guide a path to improvement, and recognized that there were many obstacles to positive change that he would have to overcome. Urban planner Sam Gennawey observes that "[Walt] wanted to change the public's expectations of what a city—and happiness—could be" by building an entire planned community based on the premise that out of behavior comes happiness.[8] Walt's thinking was that new technologies could underpin new design techniques to create living environments, communities, and cities that are better aligned to desired human values. Values would drive behavior in the direction of happiness.

Walt's approach to the development of EPCOT was also significantly influenced by the cautionary story of a major developer that had invested tens of millions of dollars developing plans to build ten model cities that in the end came to nothing, having been defeated by archaic building codes, protective labor unions, and shortsighted politicians that, when taken together, made progressive change impossible.[9]

Disney Scripting of a "Cloak-and-Dagger" Operation

Early in 1964, vice-president of legal affairs for Disneyland, lawyer Bob Foster, was assigned the task of leading the charge on the ground in Florida to secretly identify and buy viable parcels of land in a manner that would keep the costs down. Walt was aware of, and feared, that property prices would soar if it became known that Disney was seeking large amounts of predominantly swampland for a major new development in central Florida. To help ensure that the project and the purchase of land remained inconspicuous, Disney executives travelling to Florida were forbidden to fly direct from California, instead having to transfer through another city.

Roy laid down one other condition: the land must be such that it could be justified to shareholders as "a sound real estate investment for a public company" in case it had to be sold at a later date.

Foster studied maps and real estate ads in Florida newspapers to identify potential sites. To hide any trail that would lead back to of Disney as the buyer, a number of corporations were set up in Florida to surreptitiously purchase land under the names Tomahawk Properties, Reedy Creek Ranch, Latin American Development and Management Corporation, Bay Lake Properties, and AyeFour Corporation.[10] The five companies were owned by a Disney-controlled Delaware corporation registered as Compass East.[11]

One of Disney's lawyers in New York recommended Miami attorney Paul Helliwell to handle the local affairs. In a cloak-and-dagger manner, Foster was sent to Florida to meet Helliwell and check out the suitability of his firm to take on the assignment. Writes Bob Thomas in *Building a Company*:

> The plane reservation [from New York to Florida] bore his first two names, Robert Price, which would be his nom de guerre in the coming year in Florida. Meeting with Helliwell in his Miami office, Foster revealed his true name but not his employer. After determining that Helliwell had no conflict of interest and a staff capable of handling a complex matter, Foster explained that his client was a large corporate client, listed on the New York Stock Exchange, seeking as much as 10,000 acres in the middle of the state. The parcel would be large enough for recreational use and for land use as well.[12]

Helliwell recommended a real-estate agent, who spent a month with Foster seeking and inspecting potential sites.

In late May Foster returned to California to report his findings to Walt, Roy, and the Florida Project committee. Foster provided three recommendations of sites where he was able to identify appropriate land: near Daytona Beach, near Orlando, and near Osceola City. Showing the locations on a large map, Foster indicated his preference for the most northern location near Daytona Beach, to which Walt commented: "What the hell are you doing way up there?"[13] Based on his own sentiments and Price's prior study, Walt and the committee had already determined that the area around Orlando was the most appropriate climate and location.

The preferred site consisted of 27,000 acres located fifteen miles southwest of downtown Orlando, but was in escrow and therefore not available. A decision was made to be patient and keep watch on the preferred escrow property closer to Orlando rather than pursue a hasty purchase that was considered to be less than optimal.[14] Fortunately, before a decision was made, the preferred site came out of escrow unsold.

An acquisition team was established, and Roy approved an option on the purchase of the first parcel of land, 12,400 acres owned by a syndicate of Orlando homebuilders. The owners had paid $100 per acre in 1961, and were now asking $165. The price was eventually negotiated down to $145 an acre.

By August 1964, two more important properties were locked down, adding almost ten thousand more acres, and bringing the total to 22,000 acres. About fifty smaller parcels of land remained,[15] mostly owned by relatives of the original owners, who lived all over the country. Slowly, over the following months, property owners were identified, tracked down, and contacted. Piece-by-piece options to purchase the properties were acquired, but still, there remained some holdouts.

By April 1965, Walt had acquired actual title or options to 27,400 acres of land, totaling more than 43 square miles of central Florida[16]—an area twice the size of New York's Manhattan Island—for about $5 million,[17] and negotiations were underway with the few remaining owners.

Importance of Maximizing Political Autonomy to Minimize Interference

An experimental city required a new approach and perhaps a new way to govern that could be explored without the rigid limits imposed by existing governmental bureaucracies. For this reason, upon the acquisition of the land, Walt's focus shifted to legal matters related to the building of EPCOT.[18]

To have any chance of success at building a privately owned city with futuristic prototype products and technology, Walt knew he would first have to overcome the myriad legal and regulatory challenges. He would have to ensure that the right conditions were in place to guarantee his freedom to create the outcome he desired. Without these conditions in place and guaranteed, he would have nothing unique to entice the participation of industry and obtain their financial support. He would also need to develop a governance structure that would protect and ensure the safety of citizens and provide for public services like water, sewers, power, roads, garbage collection, zoning, fire protection, and postal service. Arbitrary political interference of the kind typical of politicians and bureaucrats eager to enforce archaic regulations could lead to an economic disaster for the studio and EPCOT partners, sponsors, and investors.

During the week of June 14, 1965, and prior to Walt's plans for Florida becoming public, a secret four-day strategic implementation meeting was convened to discuss practical foundational matters pertaining to building in Florida and how they could best be approached in order to retain as much control as possible in managing the property effectively.[19] It was attended by Disney officials working on Project Future plus the company's outside board members whom Roy invited. Walt attended the opening and closing sessions, and had daily access to the meeting transcripts, but otherwise did not participate directly.[20]

According to Chad Emerson, author of *Project Future*, the agenda items included technical and legal matters of significant importance, such as the protection of Disney trademarks within Florida, the possibility of an involuntary annexation of the project by the City of Orlando, the liability or tax benefits of Disney establishing its own drainage district, the applicability of existing building codes and local planning and zoning ordinances to the site, and the issue of control of the waterways within the property.[21]

The way to maximize control and minimize interference, argued Disney's Florida legal counsel, Paul Helliwell, was to create a municipality to oversee "everything from permits for a parade to a license to sell popcorn or balloons on the street."[22] They discussed the problem of providing utilities to the property. There was a concern that Florida Telephone Company and Florida Power Company would not be able to meet the financial and technical requirements necessary for the project nor be flexible enough in their regulations to allow the type of innovation Walt aspired to. Creating and operating under a municipality would likely provide the increased amount of control and kind of protection from political interference that the team was looking for. It was noted in the meeting that "[i]f a municipality is not formed the controls which would otherwise be granted to it would be vested in the county (over which we would have no control)."[23]

Walt had already been investigating these issues on his own, including discussions with Jules Stein, his friend and chairman of the board of MCA. In a 1952 buy-out, MCA had acquired Universal Pictures, and with it came ownership of Universal City, approximately 415 acres within the City of Los Angeles, which had been set up as a municipality.[24] Since then, Stein told Walt, he had nothing but headaches dealing with Los Angeles city and county politicians. They were exactly the kind of meddlesome and costly interference Walt wanted desperately to avoid, and on that basis Walt rejected operating in Florida as a municipality. "Jules Stein said it was a bad idea, and that's good enough for me," was Walt's position.[25]

Through further investigation, it was discovered that Florida had a special law to facilitate the creation of an "improvement district." Florida had created the designation of improvement districts in 1822 to help finance wetland reclamation to build roads through swampy areas. The idea being put forward now was to expand this concept to embrace a broader array of issues beyond drainage, such as those pertaining to more conventional municipal government structures.

At a later meeting in which the various governance options were presented and discussed, Walt concluded that the best framework to organize the development of the property was the creation of what would become the Reedy Creek Improvement District. The improvement district would oversee regulatory requirements of the property, with municipal functions residing in two municipalities, the cities of Bay Lake and Reedy Creek (later renamed Lake Buena Vista).[26]

Florida Extends an Invitation

Even though it was unknown to Florida state officials that Disney was behind the massive Orlando-area land purchases, the idea that a Disney park would be a good thing to have in Florida was on the mind of Florida governor Haydon Burns.

In the early days of August 1965, before Disney's intentions to build in Florida had been made public, Roy received a call from a retired acquaintance of his who had become chairman of the Florida Development Commission. Governor Burns was on his way back from Hong Kong, and wanted to know if Walt and Roy were available to meet with him to discuss "the idea of your possibly building an entertainment plant in Florida." While Roy declined the offer to meet with the governor on the false grounds that neither he nor Walt was available, they were now confident that when the time came to announce their Florida intentions, they could almost certainly count on the governor for his support.[27]

General Joe Potter,
Vice President of Florida Planning

While participating at the New York's World Fair, Walt had the fortune of meeting and working with the man Robert Moses had hired as his executive vice president, retired General William Everest "Joe" Potter. General Potter had a distinguished army career utilizing his engineering and logistical planning capabilities. Walt met him in his capacity as the man responsible for overseeing the construction of twenty-six state pavilions and the $17 million United States federal pavilion.[28]

Walt admired Potter not only for his ability to get things done in building the fair, but also because he had served President Dwight D. Eisenhower as governor of the Panama Canal Zone from 1956 until his retirement in 1960. In his role as governor, Potter was responsible for governing a community of 40,000 people, and ensuring civil services including education, public health, medical care, and fire and police protection.[29]

Having purchased more than 27,000 acres of land upon which to build, Walt recognized that he needed a man on his team with the knowledge, skill, and experience Potter possessed to build and govern EPCOT in Florida. When the first year of the New York Fair concluded toward the end of October 1964, Walt began to entice Potter to work for him.

Just three weeks before the World's Fair's two-year run came to an end, and with the permission of Robert Moses, General Potter left his job as executive vice president of the New York World's Fair to begin work as Walt's vice-president of Florida Planning on September 27, 1965.[30] Within weeks he was in Florida with Walt, Bob Foster, and others to see the land they had purchased.

Bob Thomas writes:

> [Walt] flew off to Florida in the company plane with a few of his executives [where he] viewed the proposed site from the air. The land was a broad vista of cypress groves and black-watered swamps, and it seemed a forbidding task to raise a theme park and a city of the future from the wilderness. But Walt was immensely pleased. "Yeah, it's going to be fine," he said.[31]

By this time, October 1965, less than three hundred acres of land in the desired location still remained to be acquired.[32]

The Florida property was purchased at an average cost of $180 an acre, about one-tenth the cost paid to acquire the Disneyland property ten years earlier.[33] The purchase of such a massive amount of property did not go unnoticed. There was immense speculation in the area and in the newspapers as to who the buyer may be. The leading contenders included Ford, Hughes Aircraft, Martin-Marietta, McDonnell-Douglas, General

Dynamics, and Disney. There were rumors, but so far Walt had been successful in keeping his activity and intentions secret.

The Mystery Industry Is Disney

On Sunday, October 17, 1965, the *Orlando Sentinel* published a front-page headline based on their investigative reporting: WE SAY: 'MYSTERY' INDUSTRY IS DISNEY. The front-page sub-headings speculated on the scope of the project: "City To Become Hub for Millions Of Tourists, Billions Of Dollars," "Disneyland Produces Fantastic Prosperity," and "City Housing 10,000 People Will Be Built."[34] Just as Walt had feared, because of the story the price on the remaining few hundred acres of land not yet acquired immediately jumped from $183 per acre to $1,000.[35]

With Disney now identified as the buyer of vast amounts of property near Orlando, Governor Burns' office was quickly on the phone to the studio asking for confirmation, noting that if Disney was indeed coming to Florida, the governor and his administration needed to know about it.

Walt decided that with most of the land he desired now under his control, it was best for him to go public. Foster and Potter were dispatched to Miami to brief the governor in preparation for an official announcement. Walt agreed to allow the governor to make the announcement at the Florida League of Municipalities Convention on Monday, October 25, 1965, at which Governor Burns was already a scheduled speaker. Walt did not attend, but a number of Disney executives were present when the governor announced to an exuberant audience that Walt Disney Productions would be coming to Florida.[36]

With the news now out, the cloak-and-dagger secrecy was no longer required. The time had come to explain the plan to the politicians and residents of Florida and gain their approval. The Disney organization could now work openly and directly with state officials and leaders. Most, including Governor Burns, who was running for re-election, were enthusiastic about the prospects of Disney investing in the development of a Disney-quality central Florida tourist attraction.

To capitalize on the enthusiasm for the Florida projects, two press conferences with Walt and key WED staff were held at the Cherry Plaza Hotel in Orlando on November 15, 1965, attended by almost 500 reporters. Governor Burns praised Walt as "the man of the decade, who will bring a new world of entertainment, pleasure and economic development to the State of Florida."[37]

Walt in turn explained to the press and the public his plans and the concept of EPCOT in rather vague terms. The reality was that there really weren't any specific development plans beyond broad conceptual aspirations at this point. "We've still got a lot of work to do before we can even begin to think about starting construction," Walt said. "You can't just go out and build a whole new world of entertainment without lots of studies and before our people solve a lot of problems."

Walt optimistically anticipated that the park wouldn't open until 1969 and would cost $100 million just to get started. "This is a tremendous challenge to us," he confessed. "We are terrified by the project. Just think! We need one hundred million dollars just to get the show on the road!"[38]

To generate enthusiasm and political support, Walt stressed that Disneyland had attracted nearly $1 billion in tourism revenues to southern California, and Governor Burns predicted Disney's new park would result in a fifty percent increase in Florida tourism and tax revenues. Walt made it clear that the corporation expected to make money in Florida, but that "making money is the furthest thing from our thoughts in this new enterprise. I mean it. We want it to be a labor of love."[39]

Walt also paid tribute to his brother Roy in his opening remarks to the press:

> This is the biggest thing we've ever tackled. I might for the benefit of the press, explain that my brother and I have been together in our business for forty-two years now. He's my big brother, and he's the one that when I was a little fellow I used to go to with some of my wild ideas, and he'd either straighten me out and put me on the right path—or if he didn't agree with me, I'd work on it for years until I got him to agree with me. But I must say that we've had our problems that way, and that's been the proper balance that we've been needing in our organization. ... In this project, though, I'd just say that I didn't have to work very hard on him. He was with me from the start."[40]

Up until this point, all the talk was about building a new park, as if Walt had bought property twice the size of Manhattan Island to build a bigger and better Disneyland. Walt now revealed publically for the first time that his Florida plans went beyond building another theme park, and that his true desire was to build a prototype city unprecedented in its purpose, functionality, and design:

> I would like to be part of building a model community, a City of Tomorrow, you might say, because I don't believe in going out to this extreme blue-sky stuff that some architects do. I believe that people still want to live like human beings. There's a lot of things that could be done. I'm not against the automobile, but I just feel that the automobile has moved into communities too much. I feel that you can design so that the automobile is there, but still put people back as pedestrians again, you see. I'd love to work on a project like that. Also, I mean, in the way of schools, facilities for the community,

community entertainment and life. I'd love to be part of building up a school of tomorrow.[41]

The immediate take-away by the press was the exciting news that Walt Disney was going to build another Disneyland in central Florida, to be called Disney World. Walt, however, had very little interest in participating in the building of another Disneyland.

After returning from Florida to the studio, said Joe Potter in a 1973 interview, "Walt paid no attention to the park. He said, 'We know how to do those. It's no different from Disneyland except for more water.'"[42] Walt decided that he could leave the building of a bigger and better Disneyland to his experienced park designers, and asked to be *excluded* from the central committee formed by Roy to set park strategy. He would rather concentrate his efforts on envisioning and designing his City of Tomorrow. Roy told one journalist, "Walt instinctively resists doing the same thing twice. He likes to try something fresh."[43]

What was fresh and exciting to Walt now was the real opportunity to fulfill his dream of building an entire experimental urban city, of transforming ideas on how to improve human well-being into reality.

By this point, as with Disneyland before it, Walt had spent years thinking about and researching ways to enhance the lives of people through improved people-centric urban environments. EPCOT would be a city designed not just as a place to live, but to address contemporary social problems inherent in urban living and the generational unrest being experienced at the time in urban centers and crumbling inner cities across America. EPCOT, as Walt imagined it, was to be a social experiment on a grand scale. It would surely be the boldest and most original commercial venture in the career of the world's leading and most trusted entrepreneurial maverick.

Now with the press conferences and announcements out of the way, it was time for the real work to begin. Walt established a small planning group consisting of himself, Marvin Davis, and Joe Potter, and designated a room at WED in Glendale, known as the Florida Room, as the top-secret design center for the Florida Project to which few people were granted admission. There were just three keys to the room—one for each of them.[44]

Walt's Vision for an Experimental Prototype City of Tomorrow

Because of Walt's untimely death just thirteen months after his initial Florida press conference in November 1965, the details of Walt's EPCOT vision aren't entirely clear. But through Walt's own work and interviews with those he was working with at WED, many of the pieces surrounding Walt's thinking are known.

Marvin Davis, who worked closely with Walt on the master plan for Disney World, recalled in a 1968 interview:

> Walt said: "Now, we will do [the theme park] as a weenie, as an attraction." And he just kind of relegated that to "we'll do it up in this area here."

> "Now," he said, "in addition to that I want to think about this city." And at the time no size was given to it. It varied from 120,000 down to a maximum of 20,000 people living in EPCOT. Walt was intrigued with solving the problem of having a central commercial area and a residential area, and making the whole thing work for the moving of people and traffic in and out. Also, in the back of his mind was the showmanship that he used on everything to make this thing not only a place to live comfortably, but an exciting and entertaining place to live.

> [I]t was his philosophy actually not to build a city that would solve all the problems or the urban difficulties that are all over the world now, but to do something where there would be a chance for American industry to experiment and show to the world just how problems could be solved, problems of housing and problems of traffic. He figured that if we could create a community in which people living there could be a constant source of testing out material ideas, and philosophies, not only just physical things but educational developments and all forms of communications, as well as the governmental things, that could be solved, too.[45]

Disney historian Paul Anderson describes the city itself to the extent that it had been developed:

> Walt developed a plan for Epcot that was based on radial design. ... At the very center of the radial was a 50-acre domed-in city, the dynamic center of the city. Here's where we'd find the restaurants, the entertainment, the shops, and a 30-story, futuristic, cosmopolitan hotel.

> At the very heart of the central city we find the transportation lobby. This is where the two forms of transportation within Epcot would meet. You had the people-mover, which was a continuing service of vehicles transporting people from the city center out to the low- and high-density residential areas. And you also had the monorail, the high-speed transportation system, that took people to the entrance complex, to the airport, to the theme park. Walt once said that in Epcot the pedestrian would be king, so the plans indicate that the transportation, like the monorail or the people-mover, would be elevated one level above the walkways.

> Surrounding the dynamic city center you have the high-occupancy residential area of apartment buildings. Circling this area is a broad, expansive greenbelt, where you would find parks, churches, schools.

And then radiating out from that, almost like spokes on a wheel, are the low-occupancy residential areas, the houses. These houses faced inward to a greenbelt that contained walkways, rivers, and lakes, and an elevated people-mover station to take residents into the city center. It was really a brilliant design.[46]

Walt saw the people living in EPCOT as mostly the workers of Disney World and the corporations and businesses that set up residence in EPCOT's industrial park and downtown core. They would be the recipients of, and a test market for, the new ideas of American industry. According to Imagineer and Disney architectural designer Marvin Davis,

> [Walt] really wanted to open this thing up to American industry to the degree that would allow them to expand and use all the things they have in their research and development programs, but can't use on the public because of archaic ordinances and rules and various restrictions which we figured we wouldn't have in this area. And he was successful in getting legislation through the Florida legislature that gave us exactly that privilege of writing our own building and zoning codes and ordinances. In fact, we have all the powers and authorities which are granted to counties. So, as a consequence we have written our own building code and building and safety codes and zoning ordinances. And that is the attraction that the American industry is fascinated with, because there is no place in the country where they can go and build things without ordinances and restrictions, some of which are 50 years old.[47]

Walt was seeking the practical application of leading-edge technologies to improve human welfare and fulfill consumer aspirations. Admiral Joe Fowler, who supervised the construction of both Disneyland and Walt Disney World, said of Walt:

> He expected things that people have been hoping for twenty-five and thirty years in the future. He expected a house that would be completely self-sufficient. It will have its own power plant, its own electricity. There will be no garbage or trash collection. It will all be automatically taken care of with pipes that belong to the place. Now the obvious answer is the fuel cell that we are working on at the moment. You have your power plant that supplies all your needs, and once a week put in a couple of gallons of fuel and that's it. That's what he expected.
>
> Then he was going to expand urban transportation in all of its modern forms, without automobiles in the streets.
>
> He was going to expect education facilities that are twenty years ahead, and communications, and the things that people want to live. It's going to take time.[48]

Educating for Political and Governance Control

Walt had laid out a foundational vision for EPCOT, but for Walt and Roy, the greatest barrier to getting started was acquiring assurances from the State of Florida that they would be allowed to operate with a wide degree of political freedom and governance control. A public relations and marketing offensive was initiated to proactively reach out, inform, and win the confidence and support of those who would be influential in helping Walt remove the roadblocks to achieving his Project Future objectives in Florida.

A number of state official were quickly invited to visit Disney's operations in California, and in December 1965, just weeks after the announcement of Disney's Florida plans, the state comptroller and ten Florida officials were flown out to California for a three-day fact-finding trip to experience the uniqueness of Disneyland first-hand. Walt's primary purpose for arranging the trip was to showcase Disneyland's uniqueness, and thereby, to demonstrate that Florida's existing regulations and building codes were not appropriate for what Walt was trying to create. It was important from the start to make it very clear that flexibility on the part of the State of Florida would be required if the project was to proceed.[49]

Other Florida politicians and business leaders were also generously provided with complimentary admissions and executive guided tours of Disneyland so they too could experience first-hand the quality and integrity of Disneyland, its operations, and the organization behind it. The key message was that Walt and the Disney organization could be trusted to adhere to the highest standards of excellence in engineering and maintenance, even without strict government oversight.

Delegating the Past to Build the Future

As Walt headed into 1966, he was so enthusiastic about the prospect of building a city with the latest scientific and engineering advances as a showcase to the world that he was openly talking about delegating much of the studio's operational decisions to his highly professional and capable management team. Walt had many conversations about this with his son-in-law, Ron Miller, who was a film producer at the studio at the time and eventually rose to be CEO of Walt Disney Productions in 1983.[50]

"He was so excited about EPCOT," recalled Miller. "Walt always looked for new challenges, and EPCOT was his new and fresh challenge. He knew how huge the project was. And he once said to me, 'You know, I think I need 15 years to conclude this project. I think we're in a position now where I can turn over the films to Bill Anderson, Jim Algar, Winston Hibler, Bill Walsh, and you. ... I have to concentrate on Epcot.'"[51]

Petitioning for Legislative Approval

By the early months of 1966, Disney officials settled on a general strategy and desired plan of action for building in Florida that met Walt's approval. Work began to prepare a formal proposal for the Florida legislature to review and approve. Numerous meetings were held with Florida officials to identify and resolve legal and technical issues, including the building of roads and infrastructure. At all times the Disney team remained vigilant to ensure they retained effective control over their property and plans.[52]

In March 1966, Walt Disney Productions officially petitioned the Florida courts for the creation of the Reedy Creek Drainage District. The following month, General Potter called for a meeting with Osceola and Orange County commissioners and flood-control officials, where he made it clear to them that without state approval of the Disney-controlled drainage district the project could not go forward. He also made them aware that the current estimate of the capital investment for the project was no longer the $100 million that Walt had cited in the press conference. The latest estimate put the number at $500 million.[53]

To accentuate the importance to the project of the granting of the drainage district request, Roy Disney accompanied lawyer Bob Foster in attending the Florida court hearing. To their delight, the establishment of the Reedy Creek Drainage District was approved and incorporated on May 13, 1966. Now, with approval in hand, they could begin the draining and land reclamation that was needed before construction was possible. It also allowed the corporation to issue tax-exempt bonds to fund construction.[54] An important hurdle had been cleared.

Seeking EPCOT Partners and Sponsors: "Tell Them I Sent You"

With the Florida property secured and in place and enthusiastic local and state political support, Walt devoted a considerable amount of time in 1966 to knocking on corporate doors seeking the partners and sponsorships needed to move the Florida Project forward. In addition to financial support, what he needed was a contribution of intellectual capital and R&D innovation from the laboratories of great corporations to fund his idea bank and put those accounts to good use.

Walt assigned to General Joe Potter the task of finding out what was going on in the leading R&D labs and think tanks and to finding ways to include this know-how so it could be put to use in their own planning. Potter recalled: "During the planning process Walt told me to find out what the industry was thinking about the future. He asked, 'What's going on in the labs?'"[55] Potter recalled the conversation: "I said, Walt, how am I going to get in? And he said—Tell them I sent you! And I wrote to all these industries saying what we were going to do, and I would like to come and talk to them...and I never got turned down once."[56]

Letters were sent to the 500 biggest corporations, with Potter and Jack Sayers (head of Disneyland lessee relations) following up and meeting with senior representatives of more than 65 American industries in 1966 to inform them of the benefits of participation.[57] Within months, Walt was meeting with executives at America's top research companies, including Westinghouse, General Electric, IBM, and the Sarnoff labs at RCA to share his vision and pitch the advantages of setting up residence at EPCOT.[58]

What Walt could uniquely offer to industry and think tanks was a live laboratory to test new technologies, concepts, and ideas, which would speed up the cycle of innovation and product development. In return, by doing so, they would help make EPCOT a world showcase for the products and brands of sponsors, and a model for modern leading-edge living.

Walt and other Disney staff were given tours of the labs. When Walt asked executives when he would be able to buy the technology they were developing, many admitted to not knowing if the public would be interested. According to Marty Sklar, this was further verification for Walt that EPCOT was an important and viable solution. "Walt wanted to be a middleman between the public and these big corporations, introducing technologies in a way that demonstrated how the innovations could be part of people's lives."[59]

Developing the Florida Master Plan

By June 1966, Walt began to convert the ideas in his head into a master plan for the property. He assigned to Marvin Davis the task of bringing the various ideas that had been discussed into an overall site plan for EPCOT and a new park. Before long, the 16-foot walls of the Florida Room were covered with concept drawings and plans for the project site. The Florida Room became the birthplace of Walt's famous EPCOT promotional film, although the film itself was shot on a soundstage.[60] Walt would visit WED three or four times a week to discuss ideas and develop plans. He would "sketch away with a big pencil while the rest of us were sitting around, ideas going back and forth, right and left," recalled Imagineer Bob Gurr.[61]

Just as Walt had called upon Herb Ryman in September 1953 to prepare an aerial map of Disneyland for Roy to use in his sales pitch to fund the park, he followed the same process to create a map of EPCOT, describing to Ryman and Marvin Davis what he envisioned while the two artists drew renderings. With EPCOT, however, Walt went one step further.

Walt liked to have models built to help him better understand and comprehend ideas visually, and to identify contradictions and incongruities, and then use these to generate better solutions in the development phase. Around this time, Walt instructed his team to begin to create a massive and intricate one-eighth-scale model of EPCOT called Progress City largely out of the concept drawings of Ryman and Davis. The model was intended to generate enthusiasm for the project by showing how leading-edge designs, materials, and technologies could be used to build a better city. Walt approved and set the model's development in motion, but it was not fully completed and displayed in public until after Walt's death.

According to Imagineer John Hench, Walt was not overly particular about the exact details of the model in terms of his own thinking. What he wanted was something to capture the essence to spark people's imaginations. Walt thought that what was needed was "a simple statement for people and that would be enough. And so the other things were still in his head and still crystallizing."[62] Imagineer Marty Sklar noted, "the model almost exactly matched all our planning for EPCOT. I think Walt got a kick out of doing that model."[63]

When the Progress City model was completed after Walt's death, it was displayed on the upper floor of General Electric's Carousel of Progress from July 1967 to 1973.[64] It was immense, measuring 115 x 60 feet, totaling 6,900 square feet. It contained more than 20,000 miniature hand-planted shrubs and trees, 4,500 buildings and structures, many with internal lighting, 1,400 working streetlights and a complete functioning miniature amusement park. The model included a city-center with skyscrapers and retail shopping, residential housing, a green belt, industrial park, sports stadiums, recreational facilities, an airport, a nuclear power plant, monorails, electric sidewalks, playgrounds, schools, churches, electric trains, and electric carts. It was fully animated with 2,450 vehicles—monorail, automobiles, WEDway PeopleMovers—in constant motion. Everything was electric, in part, because the exhibit resided in a building sponsored by General Electric, but it was also the preferred way to eliminate pollution and noise.[65]

By mid 1966, according to Roy, Disneyland was bringing in about $1.5 million per week in revenue, and the re-release of *Bambi* in the U.S. and Canada was approaching $5 million in gross box office receipts.[66]

Family and Fishing in Alaska

In July, Walt indulged in a two-week vacation with the entire family, including his grandchildren, on a rented 140-foot yacht visiting the west coast of British Columbia and Alaska. In the evenings he would sit on the upper deck reading scripts, books on city planning, and one on how to select a college president to guide his interest in CalArts.[67] By the end of the trip,

Walt appeared to be less vibrant, more sluggish, had stiffness in his leg, and was increasingly in pain. He was eager to return to the studio so he could get back to work.

Upon his return he visited a doctor and agreed to see a specialist about his neck and hip pain. He did so and reluctantly agreed to undergo what was considered a routine procedure to relieve pressure on the nerves in his neck, but didn't follow through at the time. His attention was focused instead on pressing forward with the Florida Project.

The Engine That Couldn't Slow Down

For years Walt had been living in daily pain from a cracked vertebra in his neck, received when he fell off a polo pony back in 1938. According to Disney historian Jim Korkis,

> One of the players hit the ball just as Walt, who was on his horse, was turning around and the ball hit Walt hard enough to knock him from the saddle.
>
> Walt had four of his cervical vertebrae crushed and was in tremendous pain. Instead of seeing a doctor, he went to a chiropractor, who manipulated Walt's back. Sadly, the injury might have healed if Walt had been placed in a cast. Instead, it resulted in a calcium deposit building up in the back of his neck that resulted in a painful form of arthritis that plagued Walt for the rest of his life.[68]

In his later years, Walt's calcified vertebrae would flare up, causing him excruciating pain that would often keep him up at night. At the studio, he had settled into a routine in which he would return to his office at the end of each day to relax with one or two watered-down scotch mists and a therapeutic neck massage and application of compresses from the studio nurse, Hazel George, before driving home each night.

By 1966 Walt was finding it difficult to walk without dragging his right leg due to pain in his hip, and took to riding a golf cart around the studio. He had sinus problems that required him to apply hot compresses to his face at night, and had developed a kidney ailment.[69]

While he was trying to function as normally as possible, many who observed him suspected that he was not well, ascribing his ill health to the pressure of the job. Walt too seemed to have a sense that his health was failing him. He was frequently functioning in acute pain and was extremely impatient to get things done as quickly as possible, looking upon every passing hour as a measure of lost time.

Even with his mounting health problems, or perhaps because of them, Walt refused to slow down, and 1966 was a busy year for Walt. "Despite his slackening energies," writes Disney biographer Bob Thomas in *Walt Disney:*

An American Original, "Walt seemed to accomplish more than ever before. He visited WED daily, overseeing the planning for the Florida Project, as well as new developments for Disneyland. He prepared *The Happiest Millionaire* and viewed rushes on films in production. He continued planning CalArts. He appeared in television lead-ins, and he found time for a variety of charities and to serve on the boards of the Performing Arts Council of the Los Angeles Music Center and the California Angels baseball team."[70] With work having been started on *The Jungle Book,* Disney's nineteenth animated feature, Walt found a renewed interest in animation and participation in the storyboard sessions, enjoying camaraderie with his long-time associates and top animators.[71]

Walt spent three days in Pittsburgh at the Westinghouse Research Center learning about rapid transit systems and other emerging technologies and innovations. He visited shopping centers in a number of cities to study them and observe the shoppers and the traffic flow. He was disappointed in most of them, finding them functional yet cheerless. The one exception was a mall in Dallas with a glass ceiling to admit natural light. Walt visited Florida to observe a new composting system with EPCOT in mind, and to visit the Disney property from a helicopter. He quipped to Dick Nunis: "It's like standing on the top of the Matterhorn and looking seven miles in one direction and eleven miles in another. It's all ours. Why, we could not only have our own Disneyland, but our own Sea World, our own Knott's Berry Farm, as well as a couple of cities. And we'll run it all the way it should be run."[72]

Those who worked with Walt on a regular basis were well aware of his grueling schedule and ambition, and were able to observe his deteriorating health. Most were unaware of his underlying health problems, and attributed his visible decline to stress resulting from Walt's unrelenting work habits. Quietly amongst themselves they would talk about their concern. In later years, Disney animator and friend Ward Kimball commented in an interview:

> Here is the same man who had just built the park, then been in on every phase, who was sitting in his office okaying and reading scripts far into the night, going to people's rooms and looking over their story work, making decisions on films, making decisions on [the] corporate level, laying out the new Florida complex, plus the decisions on the Lake Buena Vista EPCOT city of tomorrow, making personal appearances, greeting visitors, going down on sets, choosing.... [H]e wouldn't admit that, physically and mentally, he couldn't handle this...his body just gave up."[73]

Preparing and Filming Walt's Biggest Pitch: *Project Florida*

In the final week of October 1966, Walt prepared a filmed sales pitch for Disney World and EPCOT titled *Project Florida*, appearing before the camera to explain the scope of the project and his vision to generate excitement and commitment from legislators, business leaders, and potential corporate partners, and the public at large. Walt was extremely ill at the time and didn't yet know that he had a cancerous tumor in his lung. It is alleged that during the filming Walt became so fatigued and short of breath that he had to be administered oxygen.[74]

The mission of EPCOT, Walt said in *Project Florida*, was to "always be a showcase to the world of the ingenuity and imagination of American free enterprise." He said the project "will take its cue from the new ideas and new technologies that are emerging from the forefront of American industry. It will be a community of tomorrow that will never be completed. It will always be showcasing and testing and demonstrating new materials and new systems. ... There's enough land here to hold all the ideas and plans we can possibly imagine."[75]

This would be Walt's second-to-last filmed performance, but perhaps his most important.[76] As Chad Emerson notes in *Project Future*, in Walt's absence it would have to be inspiring enough to convince Florida officials "that the state should approve a creative, new legislative package for this unique effort."[77]

Using maps, drawings, models, and film as backdrops, the *Project Florida* film described Walt's vision for a city of 20,000 people in the heart of Florida, with an ultra-modern transportation system of monorails, trains, people-movers, and electric vehicles, all contained under a temperature-controlled glass dome. Among the major features of EPCOT were to be "a cosmopolitan hotel and convention center towering thirty or more stories. Shopping areas where stores and whole streets re-create the character and adventure of places around the world...theaters for dramatic and musical productions...restaurants and a variety of nightlife attractions. And a wide range of office buildings, some containing services required by EPCOT's residents, but most of them designed especially to suit the local and regional needs of major corporations."

But there were also more unconventional visionary aspects of EPCOT: "The entire fifty acres of city streets and buildings will be completely enclosed. In this climate-controlled environment, shoppers, theatergoers, and people just out for a stroll will enjoy ideal weather conditions, protected day and night from rain, heat and cold, and humidity. ... Only electric-powered vehicles will travel above the streets of EPCOT's central city."[78]

Standing in front of a giant map of the Florida property with an illustration of EPCOT and the Magic Kingdom, Walt held a long pointer in hand as he described his vision directly to the viewing audience:

> But the most exciting and by far the most important part of our Florida project...in fact, the heart of everything we'll be doing in Disney World... will be our Experimental Prototype Community of Tomorrow! We call it EPCOT. EPCOT...will take its cue from the new ideas and new technologies that are now emerging from the creative centers of American industry. It will be a community of tomorrow that will never be completed, but will always be introducing and testing and demonstrating new materials and systems. And EPCOT will always be a showcase to the world for the ingenuity and imagination of American free enterprise. I don't believe there's a challenge anywhere in the world that's more important to people everywhere than finding solutions to the problems of our cities. But where do we begin...how do we start answering this great challenge? Well, we're convinced we must start with the public need. And the need is for starting from scratch on virgin land and building a special kind of new community. ... Everything in EPCOT will be dedicated to the happiness of the people who live, work, and play here...and to those who come here from all around the world to visit our living showcase. We don't presume to know all the answers. In fact, we're counting on the cooperation of American industry to provide their best thinking during the planning and creation of our Experimental Prototype Community of Tomorrow. And most important of all, when EPCOT has become a reality and we find the need for technologies that don't even exist today, it's our hope that EPCOT will stimulate American industry to develop new solutions that will meet the needs of people expressed right in this experimental community.[79]

December 15, 1966

With his participation in the filming of *Project Florida* complete, Walt flew to Williamsburg, Pennsylvania, in the last days of October to receive the American Forestry Association award for "outstanding service in conservation of American resources." Upon returning to California, his shortness of breath and severe pain when he walked convinced him to proceed with the recommended surgery.

Walt entered St. Joseph's Hospital on November 2 for more tests. The hospital had been built right across the street, facing his Burbank studio, on the land Walt had once considered for Mickey Mouse Park. The X-rays revealed a walnut-sized spot on Walt's left lung. He was immediately scheduled for surgery on Monday, November 7.[80]

"Walt didn't want any fuss made over him," writes Bob Thomas in *Walt Disney: An American Original*, "and he told Lilly not to come to the hospital.

But Diane insisted that the family should be there, and she and Sharon and their mother sat in the hospital room to await the outcome of the operation."[81] The surgeons had found cancer in his left lung, and the lung was removed. The lymph nodes were oversized. The prognosis was poor, and the doctor projected that he only had another six months to two years to live.[82]

As Walt convalesced in the hospital, he began to feel stronger and more cheerful. After two weeks, the doctors cleared him to leave. Even though he was weak and drawn, he insisted on going across the street to his office at the studio to receive project updates and, in the estimation of some of the people he met with, to say his final goodbyes.

Walt met with friend, writer, narrator, and director Winston Hibler, who had worked for Walt for more than 20 years and was involved in many of Disney's Academy Award winning pictures. Hibler was seeking Walt's advice on the script of *The Horse in the Gray Flannel Suit*, which he was working on. Bob Thomas writes of their meeting:

> "I had a scare, Hib," Walt said. "I never had this sort of thing before. But I'm going to be okay—just off my feet for a little while. You guys will have to carry on with the motion-picture product. I'll be around to help you; when you get stuck on something, I'll be here."

Walt made a number of suggestions to improve the script and adding some words of advice: "Get the story. The story's the most important thing. Once you've got the story, then everything else'll fall into place."[83]

Walt had lunch in the studio dining room joining his friends at the WED table. He did not look well, informing those at his table that part of his left lung had been removed. He quickly moved the subject back to the WED projects that were being worked on, and after lunch returned with this staff to the WED building, a few miles away, to review their work.

He inquired of his original Imagineer, Roger Broggie—who more than a dozen years earlier set Walt up in the studio machine shop and taught him how to use the tools to build his one-eighth-scale miniature steam engine—as to the progress on the new Pirates of the Caribbean ride that was currently being built at WED. It had been shipped to the park to be installed, said Broggie, and more tests were needed before opening it to the public. There was pressure by the business side of the studio to have the attraction opened before Christmas, but Walt was emphatic: "Broggie, don't you tell them you can do it; that show isn't ready." Broggie held fast until it was properly completed and opened in mid-March 1967.[84]

Walt then met with Marc Davis, his long-time associate who had joined Walt at the studio in 1935, and, like many others at WED, had dedicated his career to helping Walt realize his dreams. Bob Thomas picks up the story:

Walt sat down to talk with Marc Davis, who had been with him from the creative years of the early features through the Imagineering of Disneyland and Disney World. Mel Melton, whom Walt had made president of WED, came by, anticipating that Walt might have some business matters to discuss, as he usually did on his visits. "I'm not working now," Walt said, giving Melton a pat on the stomach. "I just want to sit here and talk to Marc."

Walt laughed heartily at sketches Marc had drawn for an Audio-Animatronics bear-band show at Mineral King. Walt kidded Marc about losing weight, and Marc replied, "Well, one thing—they sure knocked a lot of weight off you." He regretted saying it and quickly mentioned that a mock-up of a moon-ride show was ready for viewing. Walt and Davis, along with Dick Irvine, John Hench and other WED engineers, inspected the mock-up, and Walt made suggestions for improvements. Then he turned to Irvine and said, "I'm getting kinda tired; do you want to take me back to the studio?" Walt walked to the door and turned to say to Davis, "Goodbye, Marc." Davis had never heard Walt say goodbye before.[85]

Walt spent a few more days at the studio and spent some time with his children and grandchildren before he and Lillian flew to Palm Springs where Walt could rest and recuperate. After just one night, the pain became severe, and feeling himself weakening, he flew home the next day, November 30, and went straight to St. Joseph's Hospital.

Walt spent December 5, his 65th birthday, in room 529 of St. Joseph's Hospital.[86] Ten days later, at 9:35 a.m. on December 15, 1966, he died in his hospital bed of cardiac arrest due to bronchogenic carcinoma.[87]

Final Approval: The Creation of the Reedy Creek Improvement District

In the final fifteen-year period of Walt's career, from 1952 through 1966, the cumulative annual profitability growth rate of Walt Disney Productions under Walt and Roy's leadership was a very impressive 24.7 percent, rising from $452,000 to $12.4 million. It was this success and the immense respect for Walt and Roy's achievement and status as elite entrepreneurs that enabled Walt's future plans for Florida to go forward.[88]

To help Roy prepare for a critically important presentation to the Florida legislature scheduled for February, research was commissioned early in January 1967 to assess and project the economic impact Disney World would have on Florida. The key findings of Buzz Price's research are summarized by *Project Future* author Chad Emerson:

> The report concluded that, from the start of construction through the first decade of operation, the project would generate more than $6.6

billion in "new wealth." In particular, the report estimated new visitor expenditures exceeding $3.9 billion, new payrolls reaching $2.2 billion, and more than $400 million in construction-related expenditures.

The study also estimated that the state government would realize $243 million in sales tax receipts from new visitors and new residents resulting from the project, while local governments would obtain more than $100 million in additional tax revenues. Ultimately, the report concluded that the estimated 19.5 million additional visitors coming to the Disney project in the first ten years would make a significant impact on the entire state.

The clear result was that ERA anticipated a major net gain for both the state and local governments and an opportunity for Florida to define itself broadly in terms of tourist attractions.[89]

On February 2, 1967, just six weeks after the shock of Walt Disney's death, Roy Disney and the Orange County and Osceola County delegations to the Florida legislature, the two counties in which Disney's Florida properties were situated, convened an event in Winter Park, Florida, with over 900 business leaders, government officials, and members of the press in attendance. It was here that the *Project Florida* film with Walt explaining his vision for EPCOT was exhibited for the first time, followed by Roy's address to the audience, which is described by Sam Gennawey in *Walt Disney and the Promise of Progress City*:

> When the film ended, the audience learned the reason why they had been invited. Waiting for the audience to catch its breath, Roy stood before the crowd; then he began, "Wasn't that a dream? Doesn't that stagger you?" He continued, "Our Corporation is dedicated to making Walt Disney's dream a reality, but it cannot be done without the help of you people here in Florida." Roy laid down his challenge: "We must have a solid legal foundation before we can proceed with Disney World. This foundation can be assured by the legislative proposals we are presenting in the next session of the Florida legislature." He added, "If these requests are granted, I believe that we can make the new theme park a reality by 1971."[90]

Of utmost importance to Roy was to convey the critical importance for the State of Florida to approve the proposed Reedy Creek Improvement District (RCID) to act as the overall governing body and administrator of the entire Disney property before they could proceed.

Roy provided additional details of the project and outlined the tourism benefits that would accrue to Florida. He estimated the park would attract 50,000 guests per day in the first year, which would require road infrastructure and parking to accommodate more than 12,000 cars per day. If Florida could provide adequate traffic infrastructure from the new

Interstate Highway I-4 to the park, Disney would build and maintain all the roads on the property.[91]

The sooner Disney could proceed, the sooner Florida could reap the economic benefits, both in terms of employment opportunities and economic development through tourism. As Gennawey aptly summarizes: "Disney was not seeking public funds for a private enterprise. They were seeking unprecedented control over their property. They wanted flexibility, not red tape."[92] Roy let the audience know that the Disney project was now projected at $600 million of invested capital.[93]

When the meeting ended, Roy and new Florida governor Claude Kirk flew to Jacksonville, Florida, to tape a television special to air throughout the state that night promoting the virtues of the Disney venture and to show Walt's sales pitch by means of the EPCOT film. As Chad Emerson observes in *Project Future*, "The company was doing everything it could to inform and to persuade Floridians that Project Future would benefit everybody."[94] The Disney strategy was to generate as much upside enthusiasm as possible amongst Floridians for fulfilling Walt's final project, thereby making it very difficult politically for the State of Florida to say no to a Disney initiative that could turn Florida into a tourism mecca.

On April 17, 1967, both the Florida House and Senate officially introduced the Disney legislative package to approve the recommended governing structures. The EPCOT film was shown in both chambers, and Governor Kirk explained in a joint gathering why these unique governing structures were needed and approval required.[95] As summarized by Emerson, "The improvement district would serve as the primary regulatory tool, one that would govern many of the typical responsibilities of land use regulation, building codes, utility service, and the like. For regulatory areas that the improvement district could not govern, the two municipalities would step in and control."[96] At the time, RCID was more than sixteen miles from the closest urban development.[97]

Just weeks later, on May 12, 1967, Florida's governor signed the 481-page bill in a garden ceremony at the governor's mansion[98] to create the RCID and the cities of Lake Buena Vista and Bay Lake within the district. In so doing, Roy was able to acquire the governance powers Walt had desired, as a precondition to begin developing 27,000 acres of what was predominantly Florida swamp.

From EPCOT to Epcot

Walt Disney's presentation of EPCOT to the public was filmed one month before he died, but not shown until after his death. He knew he wouldn't live to see the start of EPCOT and Walt Disney World, and so it's hard to tell how much of his vision was unconstrained by the practical realities of building it profitably in the late 1960s and early 1970s.

All aspects of an experimental city as Walt envisioned it were absent from EPCOT at its eventual opening in 1982, indicating that Walt's vision was not widely and enthusiastically shared by those leading the company at that time. EPCOT was Walt's vision, and without his superior leadership capability and the immense respect he garnered from politicians, industry leaders, and the public, it shouldn't be surprising that those without his iconoclastic status felt that completing Walt's dream was too difficult, if not an impossible task.

The work to build EPCOT was immense, and without Walt's demonstrated capabilities and the assurance and enthusiasm he conveyed to other interested partners, the risks to the corporation were extremely high. Instead, the board of directors and corporate executives played to the organization's strengths and what they knew best: building best-in-class parks and themed attractions.[99]

This was not the first time that the corporate interests did not see eye-to-eye with Walt's vision. Recall, for example, that Walt had to form his own corporation, WED Enterprises, to pursue his dream of creating Disneyland.

Marty Sklar, who Walt brought into WED from Disneyland in 1961, and who was the vice president of Concepts/Planning in 1974 in charge of guiding the creative development of what became known as EPCOT Center at Florida's Walt Disney World Resort, spoke to the issue of completing EPCOT without Walt:

> It was a great idea, but it was Walt's vision...and only Walt Disney could have convinced industry to support it. What we were left with was 27,000 acres of land in Florida, and a corporate management that didn't know the talent at WED. ... It was clear pretty early that no one in the company knew how to get hold of the EPCOT idea. But everybody knew how to do...another Disneyland in Florida with hotels where people could stay.[100]

And yet perhaps there is considerable hidden economic value in the creation of a fully controlled experimental prototype community of tomorrow that also serves as a tourist attraction, hidden value that Walt implicitly understood but was not able to articulate in the form of a rational argument or fully developed quantitative business case to support his intuition and convince financial backers that the upside potential far outweighed the downside risks. Even so, given the high cost and vast number of variables involved, surely nobody but an iconoclastic visionary and maverick thought-leader like Walt Disney himself would be willing to bet the whole company on such a high-risk endeavor—perhaps to be the last in a succession of Walt's Follies.

Without Walt's driving passion and dedication to his vision to contend with, it was easy for the board of directors, management, bankers, and lawyers to mitigate the risk and say no to Walt's imagination and final dream.

1. See Hench, *Designing Disney*.

2. Smith, *The Quotable Walt Disney*, 70.

3. Thomas, *Building a Company*, 275.

4. Price quoted in Greene & Greene, *Inside the Dream*, 164.

5. Marty Sklar in Green & Green, *Remembering Walt*, 175.

6. See Marty Sklar in Green & Green, *Remembering Walt*, 175.

7. Barrier, *The Animated Man*, 308; Gabler, *Walt Disney*, 608; also Sam Gennawey, "E.P.C.O.T. and the heart of our cities," sites.google.com/site/theoriginalepcot/epcot-and-the-heart-of-our-cities, accessed October 23, 2015.

8. Gennawey, *Walt Disney and the Promise of Progress City*, 10.

9. Thomas, *Walt Disney*, 339.

10. Gennawey, *Walt Disney and the Promise of Progress City*, 134.

11. Emerson, *Project Future*, 63.

12. Thomas, *Building a Company*, 279–280.

13. Thomas, *Building a Company*, 280.

14. Price, *Walt's Revolution!*, 41.

15. Price, *Walt's Revolution!*, 41.

16. Emerson, *Project Future*, 63; Gennawey, *Walt Disney and the Promise of Progress City*, 137.

17. Memo from Foster cited in Gabler, *Walt Disney*, 606; Emerson, *Project Future*, 63.

18. Emerson, *Project Future*, 63.

19. Emerson, *Project Future*, 74.

20. Emerson, *Project Future*, 67.

21. Emerson, *Project Future*, 69.

22. Helliwell quoted in Emerson, *Project Future*, 71.

23. Emerson, *Project Future*, 72.

24. Wikipedia, "Universal City, California," en.wikipedia.org/wiki/Universal_City,_California, accessed October 9, 2015.

25. Thomas, *Building a Company*, 286.

26. Emerson, *Project Future*, 76–77.

27. Gabler, *Walt Disney*, 606–607.

28. Ghez, *Walt's People: Volume 10*, 264–265.

29. Ghez, *Walt's People: Volume 10*, 264–265.

30. Ghez, *Walt's People: Volume 10*, 265.

31. Thomas, *Walt Disney*, 336.

32. Thomas, *Walt Disney*, 337.

33. Gabler, *Walt Disney*, 606.

34. Orlando Sentinel, "Our headline from 1965: 'Mystery' Industry Is Disney," orlandosentinel.com/travel/attractions/theme-park-rangers-blog/os-orlando-sentinel-headline-disney-1965-20141024-post.html, accessed October 9, 2015.

35. Thomas, *Walt Disney*, p. 337; Potter in Ghez, *Walt's People, Volume 10*, 266.

36. Emerson, *Project Future*, 84.

37. Thomas, *Walt Disney*, 337.

38. Emerson, *Project Future*, 87.

39. Gabler, *Walt Disney*, 607.

40. Thomas, *Walt Disney*, 337–338.

41. Thomas, *Walt Disney*, 338.

42. Potter in Ghez, *Walt's People: Volume 10*, 266.

43. Thomas, *Walt Disney*, 338.

44. Potter in Ghez, *Walt's People: Volume 10*, 266. Potter says the Florida Room was at WED, in Glendale; Emerson, *Project Future*, 93 says the Florida Room was in Burbank.

45. Ghez, *Walt's People: Volume 6*, 205.

46. Greene & Greene, *Inside the Dream*, 165–166.

47. Davis in Ghez, *Walt's People: Volume 6*, 205–206.

48. Ghez, *Walt's People, Volume 6*, 210.

49. Emerson, *Project Future*, 84.

50. Wikipedia, "Ron W. Miller," en.wikipedia.org/wiki/Ron_W._Miller, accessed October 9, 2015.

51. Miller quoting Walt in Greene & Greene, *Inside the Dream*, 165.

52. Emerson, *Project Future*, 92.

53. Emerson, *Project Future*, 98.

54. Emerson, *Project Future*, 98; AllEars.net, "Reedy Creek Improvement District," land.allears.net/blogs/jackspence/2009/12/reedy_creek_improvement_distri_1.html, accessed June 27, 2016.

55. Potter in Ghez, *Walt's People: Volume 10*, 266; Thomas, *Walt Disney*, 338.

56. Anthony Haden-Guest, *The Paradise Program*, 297, quoted also in Barrier, *The Animated Man*, 308, quoting Potter from *The Paradise Program*.

57. Mannheim, *Walt Disney and the Quest for Community*, 94.

58. Barrier, *The Animated Man*, 307; Gabler, 610; Greene & Greene, *Inside the Dream*, 166.

59. Sklar in Greene & Greene, *Inside the Dream*, 167.

60. Emerson, *Project Future*, 93.

61. Greene & Greene, *Inside the Dream*, 169.

62. Hench in Mannheim, *Walt Disney and the Quest for Community*, 13.

63. Sklar in Mannheim, *Walt Disney and the Quest for Community*, 12.

64. Mannheim, *Walt Disney and the Quest for Community*, 12.

65. See YouTube, "Progress City," youtube.com/watch?v=N8OfPzmnU6Q, accessed 20 December, 2014; YouTube, "Walt Disney's Original E.P.C.O.T./ Model Show," youtube.com/watch?v=BG_rPMxICug, accessed 29 June 2016; Mannheim, *Walt Disney and the Quest for Community*, 12; Gennawey, *Walt Disney and the Promise of Progress City*, 151–152; On the Model of EPCOT and its history, see Marty Sklar & Jeff Williams, "Model History," sites.google.com/ site/theoriginalepcot/model-overview, accessed July 1, 2016. Sam Gennawey provides excellent insight into Walt's EPCOT intentions at his website *The Original EPCOT Project*, sites.google.com/site/theoriginalepcot/.

66. Thomas, *Building a Company*, 289.

67. Thomas, *Walt Disney*, 345.

68. Jim Korkis, "Horsing Around With Walt and Polo," mouseplanet. com/8203/Horsing_Around_With_Walt_and_Polo, accessed October 11, 2015.

69. Thomas, *Walt Disney*, 340.

70. Thomas, *Walt Disney*, 343.

71. Wikipedia, "The Jungle Book (1967 film)," en.wikipedia.org/wiki/The_ Jungle_Book_(1967_film), accessed June 26, 2016.

72. Thomas, *Walt Disney*, 345.

73. Kimball in Gabler, *Walt Disney*, 622–623.

74. Gabler, *Walt Disney*, 625.

75. Gennawey, *Walt Disney and the Promise of Progress City*, pp. 142; You-Tube, "1966 EPCOT Film—The Florida Project—Restored," youtube.com/ watch?v=UEm-09B0px8, accessed June 29, 2016.

76. Walt's final recording was on 27 October 1966, in which Walt talks about *The Happiest Millionaire* and an introduction to the film *Follow Me, Boys!* See D23 Armchair Archivist, "Walt Disney's last filmed appearance (1966)," you-tube.com/watch?v=vp4VrjvSW_k, accessed 29 June 2016.

77. Emerson, *Project Future*, 93.

78. From the transcript of Disney's EPCOT film, Florida Project, at sites. google.com/site/theoriginalepcot/film-transcript, accessed November 8, 2016.

79. Smith, *Walt Disney's Famous Quotes*, 53.

80. Barrier, *The Animated Man*, 315.

81. Thomas, *Walt Disney*, 350.

82. Thomas, *Walt Disney*, 350.

83. Thomas, *Walt Disney*, 351.

84. Thomas, *Walt Disney*, 351.

85. Thomas, *Walt Disney*, 352.

86. Barrier, *The Animated Man*, 315.

87. Barrier, *The Animated Man*, 317.

88. Mannheim, *Walt Disney and the Quest for Community*, 97.

89. Emerson, *Project Future*, 148–149.

90. Gennawey, *Walt Disney and the Promise of Progress City*, 142.

91. Gennawey, *Walt Disney and the Promise of Progress City*, 142.

92. Gennawey, *Walt Disney and the Promise of Progress City*, 143.

93. Emerson, *Project Future*, 103.

94. Emerson, *Project Future*, 107.

95. Emerson, *Project Future*, 111.

96. Emerson, *Project Future*, 115.

97. Gennawey, *Walt Disney and the Promise of Progress City*, 146.

98. Emerson, *Project Future*, 113.

99. See also Gennawey, *Walt Disney and the Promise of Progress City*, 10.

100. Barrier, *The Animated Man*, 320.

PART TWO

The Nine Principles of
Walt Disney's Success

Know What You Value and Why

Walt Disney once said, "I am interested in entertaining people, in bringing pleasure, particularly laughter, to others...."[1] This is what Walt valued passionately, pursued vigorously, and devoted his life to. This was Walt's personal statement of purpose.

Walt and Roy took values seriously as guiding principles necessary for successfully achieving long-term goals. The two brothers weren't fly-by-the-seat-of-your-pants business pragmatists. They started in business with a core set of conservative middle-American Judeo-Christian moral values and principles and continually integrated their new business experiences into this framework to guide their decisions. Those values became reflected in the operating culture of the company, and were eventually informally codified based on established studio traditions as the "Disney Way."

Walt's foundational values were what he called traditional American values, and included "liberty and justice for the individual" and other ideals and values "our forefathers...shed their blood for...." He identified more tangible moral values that included honesty, truth, respect for people, and fellowship.

Walt's primary orientation was to face each day with optimism and a belief in the heroic capabilities of mankind. "Faith I have, in myself, in humanity, in the worthwhileness of the pursuits in entertainment for the masses. But wide-awake, not blind faith, moves me. My operations are based on experience, thoughtful observations and warm fellowship with my neighbors at home and around the world."[2] These were the values that formed the bedrock of his business culture and guided his commercial interests and operating philosophies. "My business," he once said, "is making people, especially children, happy."[3]

For Walt, purpose and values were to be taken seriously as practical and proper guides to action, providing rational guidance for how best to conduct himself in pursuit of his goals. They weren't vague and abstract notions that could be ignored with impunity. With his active imagination, he could visualize the results he desired and the actions required to achieve them while taking into consideration his intuitive sense of the moral values necessary to lead a purposeful, happy, and successful life. Over time, Walt's integrity to common-sense decent values even in the depths of adversity was recognized and respected by others.

Walt once ascribed to himself a personal motto. At the time, he was involved in the creation of films, but it served him just as well as his horizons expanded.

> The inclination of my life—the motto, you might call it—has been to do things and make things which will give pleasure to people in new and amusing ways. By doing that I please and satisfy myself. It is my wish to delight all members of the family, young and old, parent and child, in the kind of entertainment my associates and I turn out of our studio in Burbank, California. I think all artists—whether they paint, write, sing or play music, write for the theater or movies, make poetry or sculpture—all of these are first of all pleasure-givers. People who like to bring delight to other people, and hereby gain pleasure and satisfaction for themselves.[4]

Purpose and values, when articulated, serve to attract the same in kind. As Walt's reputation grew he was able to attract the best and brightest in the business to work for him, learn from him, and contribute to sustaining the fruits of those values under his leadership.

It was Walt's perspective from early in his life that adherence to a single set of core values was necessary to be successful; that there weren't two sets of conflicting values, one for living a successful personal life and a different set for success in business.

Both he and Roy were in agreement that a compromise in core values to achieve one's stated purpose or to increase profits was illusionary, although they sometimes disagreed with each other when approaching situations based on conflicting contexts. For example, profit was a core business value for both, but how to best achieve profit and the most opportune time to invest was often at the core of their disagreements. Because Walt didn't live day-in and day-out with the daily pressures of managing the financial aspects of the company, he often had a longer-term perspective on investing for profitability in contrast to Roy's more immediate concerns about cash flow. Walt was usually successful in convincing Roy of the soundness of his thinking, even when cash flow concerns won out.

Walt's drive to create new value made him more comfortable accepting risk than was Roy, who often served as a counter-force in preventing Walt from over-reaching and over-extending to protect the more immediate financial interests and concerns of lenders and shareholders. In contrast, Walt had a more integrated approach to identifying opportunity and measuring the profitability of value creation over the longer term. This provided him with a less constrained perspective of what it was possible to achieve. He refused to limit his options because of pressure to measure success or investment returns within arbitrarily short time periods.

Anticipate and Adapt to Changing Circumstances

The single characteristic that most separated Walt from his competition in animation and other business matters was his vision and passion. His visionary and imaginative powers never waned even as his business focus and commercial interests changed many times throughout his career. He always seemed capable of identifying, creating, and capitalizing on new opportunities. Where others sought to make a quick buck on a passing fad, Walt enjoyed panoramic visualizing both in scope and depth, taking into account second- and third-order effects and implications. He was constantly reassessing, questioning, and seeking answers to his business problems in an effort to learn, improve, and survive.

The kind of thinking he engaged in and brought to bear on his early troubles in animation is instructive for revealing the general pattern of Walt's ongoing strategic reassessment.

Walt entered the industry with the conviction that animation was a creative art form limited only by imagination and technical skill. He was excited by the prospect that if an artist can imagine it, animation can create it. "Animation can explain whatever the mind of man can conceive," said Walt. "This facility makes it the most versatile and explicit means of communication yet devised for quick mass appreciation."[5]

Walt later elaborated on this theme:

> The screen has too long been confined to what we can see and hear, what the camera can show...things which reveal not the half of a man's life and his most intense interests, with live actors attempting to interpret the unseen—the emotions, the impulses of the mind. And doing it, we must admit, rather clumsily most of the time. Relying largely on words often almost meaningless. Now, with the animated cartoon, we have another perfected tool—another scope—for getting at the inner nature of things and projecting them for the eye and the ear.[6]

Walt's deepest desire was to enhance the spirit of man through the ability of movies to educate, inspire, and motivate. Walt described motion pictures as "one of the marvels of all time," as "a true Wonder of the World in its magic power." "Itself a marvel of science," he noted, "it can and will serve with equal facility the space enthusiast looking beyond the sun, and the homebody content with the warm familiar earth and all its bounties when he goes with his family seeking entertainment and inspiration."[7]

Prior to Mickey Mouse, people viewed Walt and his studio as just another movie production house supplying novelty cartoons. But he was able to sustain his success because he was motivated by a deep sense of purpose and personal aspiration beyond merely working for profit. Walt didn't define his aspirations in monetary terms, and focused instead on creating a meaningful new form of creative communication and using the medium of film to do so much more.

With each new film, Walt was intent on pushing the boundaries and expanding the possibilities of his craft. He constantly focused on improving his product by adding something new or experimenting with a different approach through applied creativity and innovation—what he called "plussing." His indefatigable dedication to constant exploration kept Walt's films at the forefront with audiences, critics, and competitors. Through continuous improvement and breakthrough innovations, he advanced cartoons from being amusing pre-feature-film diversions to becoming attractions in their own right as a new art form in the realm of entertainment, education, and even propaganda.

When everybody in the industry was convinced by the mid-1920s that the demise of cartoon films was inevitable and had all but given up any pretense at forward momentum, Walt had the gumption and tenacity to persevere with Mickey Mouse, thereby single-handedly leading a cartoon revival. He established a new standard for cartoons by creating characters with personalities that could think and act convincingly within derived situations and stories. Audiences saw this as a huge improvement over meaningless and repetitive slapstick gags that had run their course.

Cartoons had again become so popular amongst movie-going audiences that in 1932 the Academy of Motion Picture Arts and Sciences created a new award category, Short Subject: Cartoon, for which the Disney movie *Flowers and Trees* was the first recipient. Walt was also presented with a special Academy Award to recognize the importance to the motion picture industry of his four-year-old creation of Mickey Mouse.[8] Disney cartoons were the recipients of the Oscar for best cartoon each year throughout the 1930s.

Disney historian Don Peri notes that from 1932 to 1937, almost every significant advance in animation came from the Disney studio and that Walt had "almost single-handedly raised the quality of cartoons from a novelty to an art form."[9] Famous Warner Bros. cartoon director Chuck Jones acknowledged Walt's ascent to lead the industry, noting "Everybody stole from Disney then."[10] Jones recalled in a 1980 interview,

> As far as general-audience entertainment is concerned, Disney probably had the best touch of anybody in the whole world. Walt was a strange kind of guy, but he's still by all odds the most important person that animation has ever known. Anybody who knows anything

about animation knows that the things that happened at the Disney Studio were the backbone that upheld everything else. Disney created a climate that enabled all of us to exist.[11]

Walt's strategic commitment to leveraging technological and artistic innovation to secure first-mover advantages was costly, making it immensely difficult to convert popularity into profit. The inclusion of sound, color, music, and other elements of technical innovation to win over audiences and meet their rising expectations created a huge cost burden to a labor-intensive production process. Walt was reinvesting all of the studio's profits plus every penny he could borrow to pursue his vision for improved quality and fantasy-realism in characterization. Seen in this way, every "plus" was also a minus. Being the industry leader was proving to be prohibitively expensive, with production costs rapidly rising beyond what customers were willing to pay.

In spite of the glory being heaped on Walt at the time for his creative brilliance, he was astute enough to realize that it was feature films that filled theatre seats; that the business model of creating and renting short-subject cartoons was dead; that the Disney studio was slowly going out of business with each new cartoon short they produced.

Walt had the wherewithal to understand that a change in his business model required an evolution in his vision. If he was to remain in the cartoon business, he had to pursue a bold new path consistent with his vision and purpose, a path that had been feared by all others in the business: the creation of a full-length cartoon feature that could in itself be attractive and entertaining enough to fill theatre seats.

Business as a Value Exchange

Walt was decades ahead of his competitors and other business leaders in recognizing that quality as perceived by customers is critical to business success. Walt's thinking about quality was premised on his belief that commerce begins with respect for people and *their* values, which, if fulfilled by an entrepreneur, results in a fair exchange and a successful business. Walt accepted the customer as king, and acted accordingly.

Even in his youth—from his paper-route days, through his work for the post office, to his start at Pesmen-Rubin Commercial Art Studios—Walt was eager to work hard and do his best, and expected the same mindful and respectful approach from others. He looked at it primarily as an obligation that arises from a promise to one's employer and by extension to customers, but also as a matter relevant to moral character and personal reputation.

Over his career, Walt never lost his love for doing the things that most interested him. This was always of greater value to Walt than the size of the prize. In this respect, Walt was different from the traditional risk-averse bean-counter businessman focused primarily on seeking to optimize business results by finding the point on some chart where the minimum cost and maximum profit lines cross, while at the same time ignoring the needs and values of customers in the equation.

Walt was generous with friends and contributed to causes he felt strongly about, even when he could have put forward a case that he lacked the means to do so. Both he and Roy were extremely patriotic, both having served their country during and immediately following World War I.

When troops were risking their lives and dying in defense of liberty in the 1940s, Walt once again saw it as his patriotic duty to support the war effort. One small way to help was through the creation of insignia in response to direct requests from military units. Walt reflected, "They'd sometimes send in telling us what they wanted, they didn't know where to get it...we did it for them for nothing...we took care of them...because you can hardly turn them down, how can you?"[12] "[The insignia] meant a lot to the men who were fighting," he said, "and they didn't know who else to go to. I had to do it. Those kids grew up on Mickey Mouse. I owed it to them."[13]

In those times of hardship and daring courage, Disney insignia provided a focus for camaraderie and pride among the troops. Lieutenant John Bulkeley, commander of the Motor Torpedo Boat Squadron of the Mosquito Fleet operating in the Philippines war theatre wrote to Walt: "This squadron carried an insignia designed and painted by you of a mosquito riding a torpedo symbolizing the Mosquito Fleet. The officers and men of the squadron all feel that your insignia contributed materially to the spirit and morale of the Squadron. I feel that you have had a definite part in the successful operations of the Squadron...and General MacArthur's successful withdrawal from Bataan. Well done!"[14]

Walt's approach to business always started by asking the most important question: what would people want? The answer for Walt always included *happiness* and *authenticity*. By making this his mission and purpose and delivering it, he was always able to stay close to what people wanted. Walt valued uncompromised quality in all of his business endeavors because he believed that people valued quality, could recognize it, and would reward businesses that were able to produce to higher standards. Walt explicitly understood the notion of consumer sovereignty and made it an important tenet of the Disney corporate culture as a standard for assessing creative work.

This driving focus by Walt on what consumers value is the central theme of entrepreneurship and the discipline of marketing, and is commonly known today as being market-driven or market-focused. Walt intuitively practiced what would later be referred to in academic circles and amongst marketing professionals as the "marketing concept."[15]

Peter Drucker put forward the modern formulation of the marketing concept in 1954 as the basis for a customer-centric business philosophy: "The purpose of a business is to create (and keep) a customer." Drucker was the foremost advocate of market-based management. For Drucker, marketing is more than a functional business unit; rather, "it encompasses the entire business. It is the whole business seen from the point of view of its final result, that is, from the customer's point of view. Concern and responsibility for marketing must therefore permeate all areas of the enterprise."[16]

As we have seen, this idea was at the core of Walt's business philosophy throughout his career, which he expressed simply as "give the customer what he wants." He lived by this maxim everyday, and took its application as a form of serious business guidance. He implored his staff to always do the same. The self-interested values that guide consumer choices are part of the business reality, and Walt was always sure to figure it heavily into his decision-making.

Over time, as the studio diversified and grew, so too did the degree of risk inherent in many strategic decisions. One method Walt adapted to mitigate financial risk was to engage in product testing and concept research, both formal and informal, to help identify consumer preferences.

The following anecdote about an incident during the building of Disneyland speaks to Walt's immense passion and commitment to his pursuit of vision, purpose, values, and respect for customers.

John Hench, who was working for WED at the time, recalls an incident that occurred prior to the park's opening, in which he was trying to talk Walt out of putting what he thought was excessive detail on a stagecoach, to simplify the building process and reduce costs. Given the immense cost overruns and pressure to complete everything on time for the grand opening, Hench thought he was being reasonable. Walt had a different opinion. Hench writes in his book *Designing Disney*:

> Walt had the idea that guests could feel perfection. I once complained to him about the construction of some stagecoaches. Walt had asked that the cab be suspended by leather straps as early western stagecoaches had been. I thought that this was too much and told Walt, "People aren't going to get this, it is too much perfection." "Yes, they will," he responded. "They will feel good about it. And they will understand that it's all done for them." He went on to lecture me, "If they don't understand it, if you do something and people don't respond to it, it's because you are a poor communicator. But if you really reach them and touch them, they will respond because people are okay." He then insisted that there were "no bad people; some act badly because of incorrect information." I knew then that he expected us to give

our guests good information in both design and story.[17]

Hench noted, "Walt genuinely liked people. ... There was nothing cynical about him. Perhaps that is why he wanted so badly to communicate his stories to them. He just wanted to make them happy. We put the best darned leather straps on that stagecoach you've ever seen."[18]

The Value of Self-Confidence

Relying on practical moral values consistent with the pursuit of his own well-being and business success provided Walt with two key benefits.

First, it allowed him to make independent decisions that he believed in and could defend, consistent with his longer-term goals. This gave him confidence and assurance even when he was inexperienced and struggling with adversity. By adhering to his values, Walt protected himself by ensuring he didn't act in self-destructive ways that might later undermine his self-confidence and reputation, and that of his colleagues.

Second, as a by-product of his efforts to create alignment between his values and actions, he was perceived by others as a man of high personal integrity, a necessary component of leadership and effective partnership that many other studio heads and players in the industry seemed to lack.

In the early years of his career, Walt's vision, integrity, intellectual acumen, and genuine good nature, natural optimism, curiosity, and respect for people must have made him a very attractive leader to others who shared his values but perhaps were of lesser ambition, vision, drive, resourcefulness, and had a lower entrepreneurial tolerance for risk. Animation historian David Johnson writes of Walt's early years in Kansas City:

> Walt was not only ambitious. He was likable and must have been an extremely hard sell. After moving to larger quarters (he had been working in a small garage), he began recruiting anyone he could find and with typical enthusiasm and optimism, persuaded his young flock to work for nothing (like himself), in return for a chance to learn a new profession in a newly formed company. Within a short time, Walt somehow managed to find not only a New York distributor but backing for his new studio at the not inconsiderable sum of $15,000, quite a feat for a man only just past twenty. Called "Laugh-O-Gram Corporation" (after his earlier efforts made for the local Newman theaters), Walt and crew produced updated versions of popular fairy tales like *Puss-in-Boots* and Grimm's *Four Musicians of Bremen*. For a time, a success of sorts seemed to be materializing as Walt's crew began to savor their first pay checks and Walt himself his new position of president of Laugh-O-Gram Corporation.[19]

Some thirty years later, Walt remained just as ambitious and an equally hard sell. Journalist Don Eddy wrote of Walt in 1955: "He is a dreamer, but he also an intensely earnest driver and a tireless doer, an unbending perfectionist who tolerates no compromises with himself or with any other person or thing. He knows exactly what he wants, and will work himself and his colleagues to the bone to get it."[20]

Management by Values

Walt understood that anything worth doing was worth doing right, and that the standard of "right" in business has to include respect for other people and *their* values.

Walt's ongoing personal challenge as a businessman was to figure out the point of intersection between what he enjoyed doing and excelled at, with what he could sell in the marketplace to fund his endeavors and pursuits. He had immense respect for the hopes, wishes, and desires of his audiences, which he considered to be regular, hard-working, and life-loving people like himself. His success was best guaranteed, he believed, by making people happy, and because it would take time to learn and develop the things he wanted to do, he was focused on managing for longer-term value creation.

Following Walt's death, Roy Disney was asked to comment on the secret of the company's incredible success. Roy answered:

> It's no secret. We've always tried to manage by our values because when you know what your values are, decision-making is easier. We believe that top-line thinking is the cause which produces good bottom-line results, or the effect. You've got to have your values in synch with your goals; then people are self-motivated. They don't require a shot in the arm or motivational hype, although it doesn't hurt to perk things up once in a while. Most people have ability. You've got to encourage them by setting lofty standards and then help them master their skills. This is why we put so much emphasis on training and education.[21]

Roy was also asked to comment on how he made difficult decisions:

> When your values are clear to you, making decisions becomes easier. It is never really easy, but I think when your values are in order, the process is easier. Management consists of making decision after decision, all day long, and if your values are destructive, I found that ultimately, your decisions tend to be bad, fuzzy. But on the other hand, if your values are constructive, I find that your decisions tend to be good. Management is all a matter of values in the final analysis.[22]

Walt would have agreed wholeheartedly. Management by values was, in the end, the secret ingredient of the Disney Way.

Bob Thomas in *Building a Company* provides some context to Roy's advice about the positive benefits of managing with a values-based approach:

To the Europeans, Roy seemed to be a different kind of American. Many of the American entrepreneurs who came to Europe following the war appeared intent on making deals that would take advantage of the financially strapped countries. Roy insisted on contracts that were fair to both sides. As in Wall Street, his folksy manner was sometimes mistaken for weakness. He could be ruthless with anyone who failed to honor a contract. If an employee was found guilty of dishonesty, he would be fired summarily, often with a blistering sendoff."[23]

Roy had an opportunity a few years after Walt's death to reflect on how Walt was perceived by others, writing,

Walt was a complex man. To the writers, producers and animators who worked with him, he was a genius who had an uncanny ability to add an extra fillip of imagination to any story or idea. To the millions of people who watched his TV show, he was a warm, kindly personality, bringing fun and pleasure into their homes. To the bankers who financed us, I'm sure he seemed like a wild man, hell-bent for bankruptcy. To me, he was my amazing kid brother, full of impractical dreams that he made come true.[24]

Lessons We Can Learn from Walt Disney's Business Success

- Take values seriously as guiding principles for successfully achieving long-term goals.
- Define your core values and reflect them in everything you do.
- Define the purpose of your work and the pursuit of your goals in terms of the value you create for yourself and others.
- Recognize the importance of integrity—loyalty to one's convictions and values—as a critical pillar of success. (Don't betray your core moral values or your purpose for momentary convenience.)
- Embrace your vision and passion for what you believe in—educate, inspire, and motivate.
- Anticipate and adapt to changing circumstances. Probe, assess, question, and research in order to learn, improve, and survive.
- When you achieve your goals, set that as your new starting point and look for ways to "plus" it.
- Business is a value exchange. Do good and do well by trading value for value.
- Self-esteem, moral confidence, and reputation are more valuable than money.

- Never forget the customer's desire for happiness and authenticity, and trust customers to respect and reward you for it.
- Anything worth doing is worth doing right.
- Manage by your values and synchronize your values to your goals because when you know what your values are, decision-making is easier.

---

1. Smith, *The Quotable Walt Disney*, 232.

2. Smith, *Walt Disney Famous Quotes*, 57.

3. Smith, *The Quotable Walt Disney*, 133.

4. Walt Disney, quoted in Smith, *The Quotable Walt Disney*, 259.

5. Smith, *The Quotable Walt Disney*, 10.

6. Smith, *The Quotable Walt Disney*, 28.

7. Smith, *The Quotable Walt Disney*, 27.

8. See http://www.filmsite.org/aa31.html.

9. Peri, *Working with Walt*, xix.

10. Peri, *Working with Walt*, xiv.

11. Jim Korkis, "Chuck Jones: Four Months At Disney," mouseplanet.com/8944/Chuck_Jones__Four_Months_At_Disney, accessed November 10, 2016.

12. Lesjak, *Service with Character*, 135.

13. Lesjak, *Service with Character*, 148.

14. Lesjak, *Service with Character*, 112–113.

15. See for example, "How To Understand The Marketing Concept," process-excellencenetwork.com/lean-six-sigma-business-transformation/columns/how-to-understand-the-marketing-concep, accessed November 10, 2016.

16. Drucker, *The Practice of Management*, 39.

17. Hench, *Designing Disney*, 22.

18. *Walt Disney Imagineering*, Hyperion, New York, 1996, 158.

19. David Johnson, "The Image—Part Two 'The Man,'" at animationartist.com/columns/DJohnson/Image02/image02.html.

20. Jackson, *Walt Disney: Conversations*, 44.

21. Vance & Deacon, *Think Out of the Box*, 180.

22. Quoted in Mike Vance, "Management By Values," Tape 1, Side A.

23. Thomas, *Building a Company*, 212.

24. Roy O. Disney, "Unforgettable Walt Disney," *Readers Digest*, Feb. 1969, 213, dix-project.net/item/2307/reader-s-digest-unforgettable-walt-disney, accessed August 11, 2016.

PRINCIPLE TWO

Demonstrate the Courage of Leadership

From very early on in life, Walt demonstrated exceptional leadership abilities. He held definite ideas and values and pursued them vigorously by defining goals and taking action. He was a confident and independent thinker who acted on his own conclusions. He was able to create aligned interests and shared ambitions with others, and to inspire them to participate in the achievement of shared visions and goals.

When asked to provide his perspective on leadership, Walt responded, "Leadership implies a strong belief in something. It may be a cause, an institution, a political or business operation in which a man takes active direction by virtue of his faith and self-assurance. And, of course, leadership means a group, large or small, which is willing to entrust such authority to a man—or a woman—in judgment, wisdom, personal appeal and proven competence."[1]

Walt exhibited leadership early in his career when he decided at great personal risk to rework and add synchronized sound to an already completed silent, *Steamboat Willie* (1928). Paul Hollister, writing in the *Atlantic Monthly* in 1940, wrote about Walt's insistence on accepting the challenge:

> Overnight, when the first raw sound began to bark at you from your favorite movie screen, it became evident that you wouldn't long be interested in watching a silent movie. ... [A] third [Mickey Mouse] film, *Steamboat Willie*, as mute as the other two, was ready to go—when sound "arrived." *Steamboat Willie* was yanked back into the plant, its story torn apart, new sequences and new "gags" were drawn in to show musical instruments, actual music to fit the instruments was recorded and patched into the film by a strange new device called a 'sound track'—and *Steamboat Willie*, delivered to the exhibitors on July 29, 1928, served notice that Walt thenceforth aimed to please not only the eye but the ear.[2]

Walt acted quickly and incurred real costs to launch the career of Mickey Mouse, which he saw as an investment in his future success. To do so, he had to go against Roy's counsel not to spend money unnecessarily. Because of his confidence and determination, Walt was able to establish himself as the industry leader and enhance his personal status and reputation immeasurably. He signed contracts with Pat Powers that were expensive, and he took heat for it from Roy, but in hindsight, those leadership decisions were critical to the re-launch of his studio and the subsequent decades of growth. That's why Walt famously said, "It all started with a mouse."

Walt is described as "the spark-plug of production" in his role as leader at his new studio in Burbank by Paul Hollister in his 1940 *Atlantic Monthly* article: "No story starts toward a picture until Walt has bought it or invented it, shaped it, tried it out, and given it a push." While the "central casting bureau" is responsible for assigning talent to the pictures (Disney employed 650 artists at this time), Hollister notes, "Through the production pattern of every picture Walt threads in and out like a guiding outline. Having done single-handed at one time or another, nearly everything that is being done in the studio, and having designed every functional fraction of the plant, Walt knifes into the most minute step of the most microscopic element in an effort to help, help, help. 'He knows every detail of every process in the place,' they say. 'Don't look to me for the answers,' he warns; 'all I want you to use me for is approval.'"[3]

Late in his career, when asked by a child what he did at the studio given that he himself hadn't drawn any sketches for animation since about 1926, Walt replied: "Well...sometimes I think of myself as a little bee. I go from one area of the studio to another and gather pollen and sort of stimulate everybody. I guess that's the job I do."[4]

"Walt valued the opinions of those working with him," wrote Roy, "but the final judgment was always unquestionably his."[5]

Curiosity, Confidence, and Courage

In an August 1955 article for *Woman's Day* to coincide with the opening of Disneyland, writer Don Eddy provided his take on Walt's secret of success in making dreams come true:

> This special secret, it seems to me, can be summarized in four C's. They are Curiosity, Confidence, Courage, and Constancy, and the greatest of these is confidence. Without his confidence, Disney would not be where he is. When he believes a thing, he believes it all over.
>
> From his insatiable curiosity, as persistent and all-embracing as a child's, he gets his ideas. When he settles on one idea, his confidence takes supreme command; nothing can shake it. His courage keeps it alive and active against all obstacles, and he has plenty of obstacles. And he is constant to it until it becomes reality. Then he drops it abruptly and rarely mentions it again.[6]

Walt attributed his restless, never-ending quest for knowledge to his unending curiosity. For Walt, curiosity was the first step to discovery along the road to action. "When you're curious," he said, "you find lots of interesting things to do. And one thing it takes to accomplish something is courage."[7] Walt was always investigating, learning, and reassessing, trying to connect things to projects he was working on, or to discover new, interesting endeavors.

Walt believed that between curiosity and action resides courage and confidence. Confidence is the recognition that one is capable of knowing reality and dealing with it effectively and honestly. When reality is knowable, when cause and effect are absolute, one is able to assess opportunities and risks in terms of confidence.

An integral component of successful leadership is courage. To make dreams come true, said Walt, "What is needed, in addition to the creative ability is courage—courage to try new things, to satisfy the endless curiosity of people for information about the world around them."[8] Walt noted, "Courage is the main quality of leadership, in my opinion, no matter where exercised. Usually it implies some risk—especially in new undertakings. Courage to initiate something and to keep it going." Courage, he said, was foundational to having a "pioneering and adventurous spirit to blaze new ways."[9]

"Courage and confidence," philosopher Ayn Rand wrote in *Atlas Shrugged* in 1957, "are practical necessities, that courage is the practical form of being true to existence, of being true to truth, and confidence is the practical form of being true to one's own consciousness."[10]

Disney Imagineer Bob Gurr recalled, "Walt never wavered in his courage. He was always interested in what could be…always curious and optimistic." Gurr was asked what he learned from Walt: "Always know you're going to figure things out. He always had upbeat ideas for something new and he always followed each project almost daily."[11] Walt's message was that to be courageous, you must know what you value and have confidence in your ability to attain the outcome you desire.

It is true for all values that action must be taken to make them efficacious. For example, if a person values honesty, they must *be* honest and act in ways consistent with their convictions. If a CEO values the work of their employees, they must *act* in ways that demonstrate those values. To profess a value for which there is no corresponding action demonstrates a breach in integrity, integrity being loyalty to one's values. A professed value cannot be held or achieved without appropriate action being taken. Action and effort in pursuit of a value is what distinguishes a value from a mere wish. You can discern what a person values by the seriousness they give to pursuing it. It was through curiosity, confidence, courage, and commitment that Walt was able to make wishes and dreams come true. He could not have succeeded by merely wishing upon a star.

Many executives and managers fail to stand up for their professed values when faced with resistance. To stand one's ground requires a clear understanding of the importance of the values one holds in relation to one's larger purposes, and the courage of one's convictions to act to gain and keep one's values. The larger the vision, the greater the courage required, because it requires a wider integration of diverse values into a comprehensive value-web or world-view that forms the basis for an organization's purpose, strategic aspirations, corporate culture, and effective managerial leadership practices.

We have seen many examples where Walt demonstrates his independent judgment and courage of his convictions, such as the creation of *Snow White* and Disneyland. In the eyes of many, such fiercely independent and bold initiatives were admirable and inspirational because they portrayed real-life examples of heroic confidence, courage, commitment, and success against the opinions of influential entrenched experts and establishment naysayers.

On balance, those who worked with Walt found him to be an effective and inspirational leader. When asked what they most admired about him, they often spoke in heroic terms, as did Imagineer and executive John Hench when he said, "Disneyland was very courageous on Walt's part, and Florida shows the most guts of anything...to take a kind of civilization, make it ideal, and then to make it practical."[12]

We have seen repeatedly how throughout the many events of his life, Walt operated on the premise of exchanging value for value by appealing to the practical interests of myriad parties. He abhorred the kind of devious high-pressure underhanded tactics that he encountered in the likes of Mintz and Powers. Walt could see that in the end their devious and dishonest methods failed to create a proper alignment of personal and business interests, and thereby would necessarily fail to achieve the desired results. Walt believed it was important and practical to do the right thing, to stick to his principles and values, and not to sanction or align his interests with others who stood against them.

When fundamental values became misaligned, Walt walked away and established new circumstances suited to his needs while conforming to his moral principles and values. He sought others who could benefit equally through cooperation on mutually agreeable terms. When others crossed the line, Walt terminated relationships and found other paths forward.

Over time, others recognized Walt's integrity and character, and it worked to his advantage. Recall that many times Bank of America reluctantly loaned additional funds to Walt based on their assessment of his character and judgment. For example, Walt was able to attract capital and sponsors needed to finance Disneyland precisely because he was trusted and recognized based on his past performance as a man of honor by those who knew him, even though they may have been highly skeptical of the project itself.

Constancy, Commitment, and Determination

Walt demonstrated his unwavering commitment to the achievement of his goals through his words and actions. When he made up his mind to proceed and set himself to a task, he was fiercely determined to do everything in his power to bring it to a successful end.

Art historian Christopher Finch notes that Walt moved to California when he was 21 and by the time he was 30 he had become a very public figure:

> What distinguished him from the rest and made his face memorable, was a sense of determination and purpose which was apparent even in his most relaxed poses. ... In later years he entered our living rooms and addressed us from the television screen. By that time his face and frame had broadened. ... The mustache and the smile remained, however, as did the evident purpose and determination."[13]

Walt's commitment and determination was evident in his passion to invent a new kind of amusement park experience that became Disneyland. Through all of the trials and tribulations of traversing from the original idea to its eventual creation, he never wavered in his enthusiastic commitment to succeed. His devotion to the Florida Project is just as impressive.

After more than thirty years of continuous struggle to harness creative and technical innovation in money-making films and related supporting commercial enterprises, Walt's commitment to bring it all together in an integrating physical place and enveloping human experience was an extreme act of audacious brilliance. Disneyland was Walt's way to keep Walt Disney Productions vibrant, competitive, and meaningful to the paying public and to bring new economic value to the studio's historic movie and character assets.

Against the snickering skepticism of naysayers and disbelievers, including his wife, brother, friends, staff, bankers, and industry insiders, Walt risked everything he had created and built throughout his career on his vision for a new kind of entertainment. Walt's dedication speech at Disneyland was also a tribute to his own idealism and the values he held in such high regard: happiness, nostalgia, dreams, hope, joy, and the ability of each individual to overcome the obstacles in life and meet the promises and challenges of a better future. Completing the park and opening on schedule was itself a tribute to his courage and leadership.[14]

John Hench recalled, "While we were planning Disneyland, every amusement park operator we talked to said it would fail. And Walt would come out of those meeting even happier than if they'd been optimistic."[15]

Where many would be inundated with self-doubt, Walt had impeccable self-esteem, giving him the confidence to face and solve problems. Walt saw criticism not as shortcomings of his plans, but as benefits of his business model and confirmation of how special Disneyland would be if he could operationalize his vision of the guest experience, thereby assuring its acceptance by the public and financial success.

Walt did hire a couple of major amusement park operators as advisors, but he refused to hire anyone with previous amusement park experience to build the park because Disneyland wouldn't be an amusement park. Walt knew he was building something that didn't yet exist and he didn't want to start from the constraining mindset of the existing amusement park business paradigm. Walt didn't want amusement park experts working for him who thought they already knew all the answers about how things should be done. He wanted people who were willing to understand and share his vision, learn new ways of working that would always put the customer experience first in delivering a great show and creating happiness, and make mistakes as they discovered new and unique solutions rather than rely on the dogmatism of old and tired industry rules and accepted wisdom.

Independent Judgment

Walt made it his policy to think independently about the goals he wanted to achieve and the problems he needed to overcome. At the appropriate times, he would actively engage and seek input from others to optimize his decisions based on the information available, and then move forward with full confidence in his ability to deal with problems that might arise.

From his earliest days in animation, Walt embraced market research by paying careful attention to audience reactions of his films. He would often arrange secret pre-screenings to gauge audience reactions. Later, he engaged SRI and other research experts to more formally gather intelligence through independent research and economic analysis, relying on their research and recommendations to assess situations, solve problems, and incorporate into the studio and WED's business plans. Price, in his book *Walt's Revolution! By the Numbers*, quotes Walt as saying, "It is good to sort out these projects this way, but when that is done you still have to make up your own mind on what you want to do."

Walt recognized that you could do all the research you want and gather as many opinions as you think necessary, but in the end someone has to make a decision. What is too often overlooked is how difficult it is to make such important and weighty decisions when so much is at stake for so many people.

Trust and Respect

In 1929, Walt recruited experienced animator Ben Sharpsteen from Max Fleischer Studios in New York at a salary of $125 a week. At the time he was paying Iwerks $75 and himself just $50. Sharpsteen had worked for a number of studio owners and immediately recognized something different about Walt. Compared to the others, Walt possessed a unique sense of purpose, confidence, and certainty. Reflecting back to 1929, Sharpsteen noted, "Walt struck me as being absolutely sure of himself. There was nothing in his attitude that suggested the approach, 'We'll try this to see how it works.' He was positive about what he was going to do."[16] Perhaps it was this combination of vision and certainty that led Sharpsteen to observe of the first Mickey Mouse cartoons that "[my] first reaction was that they were excellent, compared to animation I knew."[17]

It was this combination of vision, certainty, and seriousness from the leader of the business that made the Disney studio different from the rest. The difference was not to be found in the technical expertise of the animators or production staff, but in the quality of Walt's leadership and his ability to generate enthusiasm amongst his people. It was leadership that enabled Walt to succeed when key staff was hired away from him on more than one occasion, leading others to conclude that the failure of his studio was imminent.

What made Walt an effective leader was the respect he was afforded by others who felt they understood his aspirations and wanted to participate with him. They recognized Walt's role as business owner and boss, trusted him for his honesty, good will, and integrity, and were inspired by his skill, knowledge, capabilities, and determination to provide them something they could benefit from in the context of their own pursuits and interests.

As a determined and conscientious leader, Walt could be difficult to work for at times in his ongoing push for greater animation realism and an improved audience experience through innovations like synchronized sound, Technicolor, and musical narration. While it was common for his staff and industry colleagues to described him as unpretentious and generous, when it came to work, his primary focus was always to place results ahead of people's feelings.

At times he could be very harsh in his criticism, which could lead to morale and productivity problems. But Walt's criticism was rarely personal, and he was almost always enthusiastic about providing improvement ideas and making himself available to offer suggestions and recommendations. Walt could become very agitated and curt when under severe stress or suffering from the pain in his neck and back from his polo injury. At such times the animators and directors who worked closest to him would describe him as having the disposition of a wounded bear, and knew it was prudent to avoid him if possible.

Still, these same colleagues trusted and respected him for his earned authority and proven capability to keep them working together effectively and to present them with unique and exciting personal and career challenges. They may have preferred a more congenial management style than they received from Walt, and perhaps a different style may have been more effective, but there is no dispute that Walt's leadership from an early age and throughout his career was appropriate, effective, and successful. As gruff and unsophisticated as he could be at times, even those who complained bitterly about the worst of his traits seemed to love him dearly.

On the other hand, there are many who knew Walt and reported directly to him who say they were never treated disrespectfully.

Executive and Managerial Leadership

The observation by Walt that leadership involves initiating something and keeping it going is very astute because it combines leadership with management. It is not surprising, then, that he also said: "Of all the things I've done, the most vital is coordinating those who work with me and aiming their efforts at a certain goal."[18] In a 1962 *Newsweek* article he is quoted: "I saw very early in this business one thing—that organization was where you had to put the emphasis. You have to break things down, specialize."[19]

In speaking about the important role leadership plays in organizing people and coordinating work and resources, Walt seems to be talking about managerial leadership in ways strikingly similar to what is discussed by management theorists Elliott Jaques and Stephen Clement in their groundbreaking book *Executive Leadership*.[20]

As we have seen, Walt was most effective when he and his staff moved together along the same path toward a shared goal. In discussing the ideas of managerial leadership, Jaques and Clement write:

> It is interesting that leading and following have only recently come to take on the meaning of the "leader" in front and the "followers" trailing behind. Such a meaning is a decided handicap for anyone in the managerial leadership hot seat. Managers need their people to be up with them, and with one another, all going in the same direction, working together when necessary, in pursuit of the common goal that has been set. ... Each person should be free and able to use his or her own initiative within his or her manager's framework. The managers too are then free to get on with what they have to do, safe in the knowledge that, unless they hear otherwise, all is going well and that things will come together as they want them to. ... In short, leading and following are about going along together.[21]

Jaques and Clement define leadership as "that process in which one person sets the purpose of direction for one or more other persons, and gets them to move along together with him or her and with each other in that direction with competence and full commitment."[22] Walt appears to have taken these responsibilities seriously throughout the many phases of his career.

An important component of leadership is taking responsibility for identifying a problem or constraint, finding a solution, and bringing others along in a cooperative and collaborative effort to achieve the desired result. Walt typically looked to collaboration and input from others as a way to begin and sustain projects. The re-occurring pattern is that Walt would begin with an idea then follow-up with collaboration through brainstorming and other techniques as a means to discovery. As he focused in on the best ideas—as his vision for a picture, story, scene, or idea formed and crystallized to the point where it worked—he would lock in his decisions and move to the next stage while remaining open to adaptations and refinements if the situation changed or he could be swayed by a better idea.

Once he knew *what* he wanted, he became single-mindedly focused on the *how*, usually engaging others in collaboration and using his earned and role-vested authority as boss to ensure work was done to his satisfaction.

When it came to leading the business itself, as distinct from the various film and other projects in which the business was engaged, here too Walt was open to considering advice from others while insisting on reaching his own conclusions in exercising authoritative control. We see that throughout his career he sought out and relied on the advice of experts—from trade journalists, to corporate R&D labs, to small amusement park operators, to specialized artisans, to world-renowned architects and engineering firms.

Walt's tolerance for advice evolved with changing circumstances and his own personal growth and development. For example, when he first started out with Winkler and Mintz, he was very open to their recommendations of how to improve his cartoons. As Walt gained experience, he discovered that his own conclusions about what audiences wanted was equal to or better than the advice he was receiving from his distribution partners. He remained open to receiving their knowledgeable advice, but began using it as a data point with which to assess the validity of his own thinking and conclusions in controlling his own destiny.

Over time, Walt's capability and confidence in assessing an opportunity from multiple angles grew, and the perspective from which others gave advice became more narrow and limiting, no longer holding the value for Walt that it once did. He never lost sight of the customer as the proper standard by which to judge business performance.

In addition to Walt's own authority and responsibility to lead, he understood that to build a successful organization with appropriate division of tasks and responsibilities, his subordinates in the hierarchical chain were also required to understand their own responsibilities and accountabilities for work assigned and under their control, and to lead their staffs appropriately. They too had to act as effective managerial leaders among their peers.

Walt always had legitimate vested-authority in his role as CEO, but at times he lacked earned-authority amongst some sub-sets of staff, resulting in their lack of emotional commitment and enthusiasm to be engaged and fully contribute. The time leading up to and during the 1941 strike is one such example. This can be seen in contrast to the excitement and commitment of studio staff to working on *Snow White and the Seven Dwarfs*, *Pinocchio*, and *Fantasia*. Walt didn't seem to have issues with earned-authority in his leadership of WED from the early 1950s.

Walt did not always achieve togetherness and alignment in organizing and managing his staff, but for the most part, over his career, Jaques and Clement's general description of effective executive leadership could have been written to describe Walt's approach. There are innumerable examples across Walt's career of his leadership acumen, from his late night storytelling of *Snow White* to gain the enthusiastic support of his staff, to the freedom he gave them to develop and present their own ideas, to finding sponsors and developing attractions for the 1964 New York World's Fair, etc., and on a thousand smaller projects and lesser tasks in between.

There were many times over the years when staff felt deflated by their perceived inability to live up to Walt's ambitious demands. Still, in such situations, Walt expended effort to bolster morale and maintain alignment, recognizing that it was critically important.

Neal Gabler in his biography *Walt Disney* indicates that the confidence and motivation of Walt's artists became factors at many times during the four years *Snow White and the Seven Dwarfs* was in production. For months on end in 1936 animators would draw scenes and review the rough pencil drawings with Walt and other animators in a search for ever-greater perfection. The message was clear: make a perfect animated cartoon for the ages that could compete with, and hopefully surpass, anything done in live action.

Trying to reach a lofty goal can be a lot of fun during practice, but when game time arrives, nervousness and doubts begin to set in. That's exactly what happened.

The animators carried out their work with confidence until it came time for cleanup and the release of scenes for Walt to review. For many there was an unsettling feeling of loss of control and the nagging question of whether their work was really good enough—after all, they were doing something that had never been done before, tempting fate by engaging in the impossible, and trying to make a success of "Disney's Folly." Gabler writes: "Many of the animators were now despairing of ever completing the project satisfactorily, and Walt complained that once scenes were finished and ready for cleanup, the animators seemed to lose the initiative in assuring that everything was ready for the camera."[23]

At one point Hal Adelquist, who had been appointed head assistant director on the project in February 1936, was instructed by Walt to deliver a message to the assistant directors for their benefit and that of their staff. "'This picture is a tremendous thing,' Adelquist told the assistant directors, delivering instructions from Walt. 'You think you will never be finished. There seems to be twice as much work on your desk at night when you leave, but if you will just keep plugging and checking I am sure you will find that things will work out all right.'"[24] The message from the studio's leader through Adelquist was to stay focused, stay motivated, stay productive, keep the faith, and we can all get through this successfully and make ourselves proud.

Leaders Know How to Dream, Aspire, and Take Risks to Improve Happiness

For many business leaders, avoiding risk is seen as a way to stay out of trouble and reduce stress. This is often the position of those with financial oversight who attempt to reign in *any* exuberance in the boardroom for risky investments, be it rational or irrational, to protect shareholder interests, profits, and ROI.

In fact, paradoxically, in today's fast-paced, highly competitive world, the biggest risk is to fail to take a risk. Great entrepreneurial leaders operate with a high level of abstraction and integration, allowing them to navigate more clearly through the fog of complexity. This provides them with a seemingly uncanny and opaque intuitive means to successfully identify unseen opportunities, manage risk, and create order out of what others see as apparent chaos. In a competitive marketplace, maintaining the status quo is never an option, and never a fruitful road to the satisfaction of consumers and the enhancement of shareholder value. Consumer values and expectations are continually shifting and evolving, as is technological innovation to deliver better products and services. When it comes to keeping customers happy, if you aren't keeping up—pushing forward to be the leader or compete with the leaders—you're falling behind.

Walt was unquestionably a force of forward momentum in pursuit of his vision to bring joy, happiness, entertainment, and a positive and thoroughly American sense of life to the masses, and that often created business friction and opposing forces seeking inertia.

It takes a person with curiosity, courage, commitment, independent thought, and strength of character to be a leader capable of stepping forward and walking an uncharted path based on his or her own assessment of the situation. And it takes people with similar characteristics to materially and spiritually support such innovators and prime movers.

It was Walt's persistence, enthusiasm, reliance on the talents of others, demonstrated integrity (willingness to stand up for his own values and beliefs), and ability to demonstrate the validity and viability of his ideas in a real-world business context that allowed him to raise the capital and create the partnerships he needed for each of his projects.

Leaders Improve Their Alignment with Reality Through Failure

Walt wasn't always right and his ideas weren't always successful. But he was curious and honest, and therefore also committed to recognizing and assessing his own failures and learning from his mistakes. "All the adversity I've had in my life, all my troubles and obstacles have strengthened me," he said.[25] Adversity isn't an advantage unless one can reflect on the causes of failures and learn from them.

Walt saw his early failures as humbling, character-building lessons. He liked to reminisce and to remind people that his business kingdom had all started with a mouse. But Walt's business career as a maker of silent films started long before the 1928 creation of Mickey Mouse, by which time he had already created over one hundred movies. His most notable early failure was the 1923 bankruptcy of Laugh-O-gram Films, Inc., in Kansas City, Missouri, where he was president and chairman.

Walt didn't fail and then move on. He took personal responsibility for his failures, contemplating why they occurred and how to prevent their reoccurrence. He was a problem-solver, not a finger-pointer. He looked upon failure as a natural ingredient of a lifelong learning process, as a valuable way to gain real-life experience and wisdom. Discovery through failure allowed Walt to be better prepared to boldly move forward in the setting of new goals and pursuit of new dreams. As an admirer of Thomas Edison, perhaps he was following his dictum that "failure is the most important ingredient for success."[26]

Those early years of Walt's silent filmmaking career in Kansas City and Hollywood served as the training ground to support his entrepreneurial education and later breakthroughs and refinement of his management talents and no-holds-barred creative capabilities. The trajectory of his career advanced as he built on his previous experience and knowledge.

It was common for Walt to structure work assignments or specific courses of action as an experiment or test, in order to learn through failure. Walt would frequently initiate a plan of action to try something so he could learn from the results, advance his thinking, and then try again, taking corrective action based on his new knowledge. One example is the animating of Persephone in *Flowers and Trees* by the studio's best animators to determine whether they were sufficiently skilled to take on the challenges of animating *Snow White and the Seven Dwarfs*.

Walt was also known to assign the same development task to multiple people or groups in isolation and send them off to solve a problem or develop a storyline as a way to gather diverse ideas for comparison, knowing that he would dispose of most of the work in the process of discovery. When workers later found out, they were often angry, feeling that their time was wasted. But from Walt's perspective, it was time and money well spent.

Leaders Make Aspirational Strategic Decisions

There were reasons why Walt's studio was recognized as the industry leader, and a reason why the best wanted to work for him, often at a lower salary than they could earn elsewhere while being thankful for the opportunity. For these types of career-oriented conscientious workers, the challenge of working for a visionary leader in relentless pursuit of innovation was exhilarating.

For those who didn't value the challenge the same way, a day working at the studio was just another day on the job. As in any large organization, not everyone is up to the task of pushing himself or herself—or being pushed—beyond the ordinary toward the extraordinary. Setting a standard of excellence is a difficult place to live, and often creates disillusionment and resentment when the work falls short and it seems that the effort was wasted.

The reality was that the artists would always have to defer to Walt's final judgment. Successful studio staff fully understood that this was a normal condition of employment and learned to cope with it. Like it or not, without a division of labor and hierarchy of accountability, it would be impossible for any complex work to be done effectively, including movie production.

Some artists thrived on the challenge of working for Walt, while for others it was a love-hate relationship. For some, those least confident or secure in their abilities, or less mature, fear of failure shaped their outlook.

Robert Sherman, who with his brother Richard wrote film scores for Walt in the 1960s, gives us some idea of what working for Walt must have been like. He writes in his memoir *Moose*,

> At one point, maybe a year after we began working at the studio, one producer put in a request for our songwriting talents. It was a heavy project. But when [Walt] asked us, we felt that we were in over our heads with the four other films. We complained trepidantly. Walt chuckled and took a bite out of an apple.
>
> "Listen fellas, you're not really working hard until you're juggling seven or eight balls in the air. It's good for you. Keeps you fresh. You want to keep fresh, don't you?"
>
> At that time Walt had probably twenty-eight balls in the air.[27]

Walt was not always a good personal communicator, and often kept the full scope of his ideas and plans to himself until they were more fully developed and he was ready to reveal them. From Walt's vantage point, what was good for him and the studio was also a benefit for his staff because it provided for their livelihood, although others at times saw his behavior as patronizing. In Walt's eyes, staff hired by the studio always had the option to work elsewhere if the opportunities and conditions provided weren't to their liking. He would have expected nothing less from them: if they weren't happy working at Disney, they should find more suitable employment elsewhere.

Walt spent the majority of his working time obsessed with the challenge of applying human ingenuity and energy to transform his ideas into commercial reality. He assumed personal responsibility and oversight for managing the final presentation to the public to ensure that his own high standards were never compromised. One Disney scholar wrote of Walt:

> Improving the product seems to have occupied his mind night and day. After hours and on weekends he would prowl the studio—familiarizing himself with the development of every project. He subjected each decision to intensive discussion, drawing upon every available source of expertise, and there is ample evidence to suggest that he sometimes mulled over ideas for years before they were permitted to reach this stage.[28]

There was rarely a moment in Walt's career where he did not demonstrate the qualities of leadership as a major component of his entrepreneurial and managerial accountabilities.

Lessons We Can Learn from Walt Disney's Business Success

- Believe strongly and sincerely in your cause.
- Vigorously define your goals and take action to meet the challenge.
- Create aligned interests and shared ambitions through commonly held underlying values.
- Earn the trust and respect of others through sound judgment, wisdom, personal appeal, and proven competencies.
- Encourage and embrace alternative ideas and input, but don't delegate decisions for which you are responsible.
- Pursue your mission and purpose boldly with a spirit of adventure.
- Be optimistic about overcoming challenges through appropriate action.
- Think for yourself then make your own decisions. Don't uncritically follow entrenched experts and established naysayers.

- Leadership authority must be earned to be effective.
- Be aware of the capabilities of workers and challenge them with new task assignments to encourage their personal and professional growth.
- Stay focused and flexible in the face of new information and ideas.
- Embrace technological advances and adapt quickly.
- Learn from your own and others' mistakes and failures to prepare yourself for the future. Be a problem-solver, not a finger-pointer.

---

1. Smith, *Walt Disney Famous Quotes*, p. 66.

2. Paul Hollister, "Genius At Work: Walt Disney," *Atlantic Monthly*, December 1940.

3. "Walt Disney," in *The Atlantic*, Dec. 1940.

4. Smith, *Walt Disney: Famous Quotes*, 84.

5. Roy O. Disney, "Unforgettable Walt Disney," *Reader's Digest*, 216.

6. Don Eddy in Jackson, *Walt Disney: Conversations*, 55–56.

7. Smith, *The Quotable Walt Disney*, 246.

8. Smith, *The Quotable Walt Disney*, 239.

9. Smith, *Walt Disney Famous Quotes*, 66; Smith, *The Quotable Walt Disney*, 237.

10. Ayn Rand, "Galt's Speech," *For the New Intellectual*, 129.

11. Bob Gurr interviewed by Jim Korkis, in "Disney Legend Bob Gurr: Filling the Gaps," at mouseplanet.com/9361/Disney_Legend_Bob_Gurr_Filling_in_the_Gaps, accessed October 20, 2014.

12. Hench quoted in Gennawey, *Walt Disney and the Promise of Progress City*, 128).

13. Christopher Finch, *The Art of Walt Disney: From Mickey Mouse to The Magic Kingdom*, 1975, 11.

14. Walt Disney's Dedication to Disneyland: "To all who come to this happy place: Welcome. Disneyland is your land. Here age revives fond memories of the past, and here youth may savor the challenge and promise of the future. Disneyland is dedicated to the ideals, the dreams, and the hard facts that have created America, with the hope that it will be a source of joy and inspiration to all the world." Walter E. Disney, July 17, 1955.

15. Gabler, *Walt Disney*, 524.

16. In Peri, *Working With Walt*, 5–6.

17. D23, Ben Sharpsteen, d23.com/walt-disney-legend/ben-sharpsteen/, accessed August 10, 2016.

18. Smith, *Walt Disney Famous Quotes*, 80.

19. Walt quoted in Jim Korkis, "In Walt's Words," Sept. 27, 2006, at mouseplanet.com/articles.php? art=ww060927ws, accessed November 8, 2016.

20. Jaques and Clement, *Executive Leadership: A Practical Guide to Managing Complexity*, Blackwell Publishers, 1994.

21. Jaques and Clement, *Executive Leadership*, 12–13.

22. Jaques and Clement, *Executive Leadership*, 4.

23. Gabler, *Walt Disney*, 261.

24. Gabler, *Walt Disney*, 261.

25. Smith, *Walt Disney Famous Quotes,* 55.

26. Manuel London (ed.), *The Oxford Handbook of Lifelong Learning*, 83.

27. Sherman, *Moose: Chapters from my Life*, 280.

28. Christopher Finch, *The Art of Walt Disney, From Mickey Mouse to the Magic Kingdom*, New Concise Edition; Abrams, New York, 1975: 12.

PRINCIPLE THREE

Money Is a Means, Not an End

From the start of his career, Walt Disney was somewhat philosophical about money and understood its importance to business success. Walt was responsible for meeting payroll and accountable to shareholders as CEO of Laugh-O-grams when he was twenty years old. Walt did everything within his power to keep the business alive and save shareholders from losing their investment, including tolerating homelessness, scavenging for food, and bathing once a week in the public showers at the Kansas City train station.

Bob Thomas, in *Building a Company*, quotes Walt explaining his attitude toward money:

> People look at me in many ways. They've said, "The guy has no regard for money." That is not true. I have had regard for money. It depends on who's saying that. Some people worship money as something you've got to have piled up in a big pile somewhere. I've only thought about money in one way, and that is to do something with it. I don't think there's a thing I own that I will ever get the benefit of except through doing things with it. I don't even want the dividends from the stock in the studio, because the government's going to take it anyway. I'd rather have that in [the company] working.[1]

For Walt, money was first and foremost a means to achieve bigger and more meaningful ends. He once said, "I have little respect for money as such; I regard it merely as a medium for financing new ideas. I neither wish nor intend to amass a personal fortune. Money—or, rather the lack of it to carry out my ideas—may worry me, but it does not excite me. Ideas excite me."[2]

Ideas and money went hand-in-hand for Walt. It took $17 million to open Disneyland, far in excess of the original estimate, and year after year Walt continued to invest more money into new ideas and attractions. In an interview on NBC in 1966, Walt said, "[L]ike the old farmer, you have to pour it back into the ground if you want it to grow. That's my brother's philosophy and mine, too."[3] By the time Walt died in 1966, the Disneyland theme park represented a total investment of around $92 million.[4]

Sustained investment for continued growth was not as common amongst executives Walt encountered as one might expect. Recall ABC's Goldenson's criticism of Disney for reinvesting in growth rather than distributing profits as dividends. Goldenson's criticism in part demonstrates what set the visionary and forward-thinking Disney brothers apart from the short-term conventional business thinking of their competition. In response to ABC's criticism, Roy complained: "They're just a dollar-minded bunch. They run the business for money first."[5] The Disneys often encountered this difference in perspective about investing in quality and growth for future success, making it difficult at times for them to find or sustain effective business partnerships.

Walt and Roy demonstrated their growing confidence in their own capabilities and their desire for adventure by reinvesting in their enterprises. Walt commented in an interview published in the January 1964 issue of *Look Magazine*:

> WALT: It's been our policy here to reinvest. And everything that is earned here by pictures, or in any other way, always goes back into the business, goes back to improve our studio facilities, to improve the operations of any one of these things, like Disneyland. It's always going back into the business.
>
> I know different ways of looking at things. I have my stockholders, and I feel a very keen responsibility to the stockholders, but I feel that the main responsibility I have to them is to have the stock appreciate. And you only have it appreciate by reinvesting as much as you can back in the business. And that's what we've done.
>
> FOWLER: Their dividends this year should have been satisfactory.
>
> WALT: Well, this year we gave them stock dividends. And stock dividends to a lot of people who own stock is preferable to cash because you don't have to pay your income tax on a stock dividend until you finally sell the stock. And the stock can appreciate. And by giving them a stock dividend, we retain the money in the business, to keep building the business. And that has been my philosophy on running the business.[6]

One thing Walt resented when it came to money was other people using money as a limitation or constraint against applying their own creativity and imagination. Walt expected his staff, regardless of their role, to identify and bring forward the best solutions they could imagine, and to contribute their most authentic work. It was Walt's responsibility as managerial leader to define the work parameters (context, quality, quantity, time, and resources), and not for others to infer how much something should cost as an excuse for opposing Walt's role-vested authority and frustrating his legitimate expectations.

As a strategic thinker and business leader, Walt often thought about his endeavors holistically and synergistically, especially in the years of rebuilding the studio's capabilities following World War II. He was able to look beyond the immediate value and return on investment of any single idea in isolation, to how it could support and contribute to the larger business system.

An incident related by Imagineer Marty Sklar (later president of Walt Disney Imagineering) provides insight into Walt's integrative approach to thinking:

> [I]n the late 1950s, it cost 24 cents to purchase and merchandise the Disneyland souvenir guide, which sold for 25 cents. The company was only making a penny on it and the merchandising people wanted to raise the price. So they went to Walt and made their pitch and he said, no. They were in shock.

> "Look," he said. "You don't get it. I don't care about making money on this. What I want is as many of these souvenir guides as possible on people's coffee tables. I want others to see what Disneyland is all about and come for a visit. We'll make money when they actually come to Disneyland and buy tickets and souvenirs. I don't care about making money on every single item. I want people to visit Disneyland!" Walt was looking at the big picture all the time.[7]

At times when cash flow was problematic, Walt and Roy would come at issues from different contexts with Roy protecting the more immediate financial needs of the business and Walt focusing on creating value for the future. Because both shared the same high-level values and goals, they were always able to find an agreeable solution. Both recognized that it was only by doing what was best for the customer that they could at the same time do what was best for the business. The key for Walt was to prevent the more seductive ease of short-term convenience from slamming the door on more promising longer-term opportunities. A good early example was his refusal to sign away television rights in 1936 during contract negotiations with film distributor United Artists, precisely because he didn't understand their importance.

A widely accepted practice today is for business leaders to focus on immediate short-term results, leading them to micro-manage most aspects of the business as isolated profit centers, with extreme lack of regard for the fact that a business is an integrated production system that converts inputs into outputs to profitably produce something customers value. Without profits to fund its ongoing and future operations, a business will eventually run out of cash and be forced to cease functioning. When that happens, unproductive resources and inventories are freed up for reallocation to producers and consumers.

It is via the pricing mechanism, the profit motive, and consumer sovereignty in acquiring and exchanging values that consumers and producers decide over an appropriate time frame what will be produced and who will earn and benefit from profits. Profits are an outcome of effective economic and commercial activity, and are a guide to business leaders to adjust their efforts at satisfying consumers.

Peter Drucker, whom the *Los Angeles Times* designated the "founding father of the science of management," was one of the early management thinkers and educators to apply his knowledge of economics and finance to the understanding and teaching of business management and organizational effectiveness. Having no knowledge as to whether Drucker and Walt Disney ever met, many of Drucker's key observations about business purpose and customer alignment are such that they could have emanated from the study of Walt's business philosophy and practices.

Drucker warned organizational leaders that if they ignore the important role customers play in their business success, they do so at their own peril. He articulated more fully what Walt understood more simply and directly, writing in his 1986 book *The Practice of Management*:

> It is the customer who determines what a business is. For it is the customer, and he alone, who through being willing to pay for a good or for a service, converts economic resources into wealth, things into goods. What the business thinks it produces is not of the first importance—especially not to the future of the business and to its success. What the customer thinks he is buying, what he considers "value," is decisive—it determines what a business is, what it produces and whether it will prosper.[8]

Drucker wrote elsewhere, "To satisfy the customer is the mission and purpose of every business...[and] any serious attempt to state 'what our business is' must start with the customer, his realities, his situation, his behavior, his expectations, and his values."[9] Harvard University marketing professor Theodore Levitt succinctly summarized Drucker's insight by stating: "The first business of every business is to get and keep customers."[10]

While this seems to be an obvious truth, many of Walt's partners and competitors through the years rejected this customer-centric approach to doing business.

Walt lived by this knowledge.

You Can Use Money to Do Stuff and Bring Pleasure

Walt Disney made money by being a perfectionist at delivering what he thought consumers wanted. "We're not out to make a fast dollar with gimmicks," he said. "We're interested in doing things that are fun—in bringing pleasure and especially laughter to people...it's proven it's a good business policy. Give the public everything you can give them."[11]

In discussing the attributes that made Walt successful in business, Disney animator Ward Kimball observed:

> If you want to know the real secret of Walt's success, it's that he never tried to make money. He was always trying to make something that he could have fun with or be proud of. He told me once, "I plow back everything I make into the company. I look at it this way: if I can't use the money now, if I can't have fun with it, I'm not going to be able to take it with me." That's the way he talked. That's the way he felt. Walt was really more concerned with the end result than the money. If it made money, fine. He felt that if you put your heart into a project and if you were a perfectionist, people would automatically like it.[12]

Walt seemed to associate money with work and work with fun, as indicated in his statement, "Disneyland is not just another amusement park. It's unique, and I want it kept that way. Besides, you don't work for a dollar—you work to create and have fun."[13]

Marc Davis, one of Disney's key animators of feature films, reflected on Walt's perspective on money:

> I was in Walt's office around the time he was starting Disneyland, and he was a little embarrassed, because he'd borrowed on his life. He looked out the window, turned to me and said, "I'd like to sell the property underneath the studio: We own all the improvements on it—we could lease them back. Do you realize the wonderful things we could do with all that money?" "What we could do with all that money," not "I would be rich." I don't think Walt ever cared about that; he was interested in what you could do.[14]

Walt Disney's nephew and former Walt Disney company executive and vice-chairman of the board, Roy E. Disney, commented on what his father, Roy O. Disney, said about Walt:

> He said, "Walt isn't interested in money. He doesn't care about money, except that he can use it to do stuff. And that's how Walt sees the value of money." And I thought, you know that's a really smart way to think about it, even though you probably have to sidestep that problem every now and then. But It really makes you stop and think about what you're doing and why. Because a lot of movie companies just make a bunch of movies, and they do it because they have to, because there's some production schedule set up and there's some money that has to be spent before they lose it—you know, all of those pressures that are false in terms of the art.[15]

Todays Profits Are Tomorrow's Expenses

Rich or poor, a man can dream all he wants to. But it takes an entrepreneur to convert dreams into plans, and plans into economic wealth. As Merlin Jones writes in his essay "The Spirit of Youth," Walt's ability to realize his dreams and promote them had a way of "mesmerizing audiences" and capturing their imaginations, allowing him to make a fortune and build an entertainment empire. Jones writes: "Historically, the more Walt horrified his bankers by reinvesting profits into seemingly impossible dreams, the more wealthy and powerful he became, the more the company grew and prospered, the greater the value came to the name 'Walt Disney.'"[16]

Peter Drucker pointed out that it is through reinvestment that today's profits become tomorrow's expenses, meaning that business profits are required to fund the ongoing sustainment and expansion of any business. In this way profits benefit owners not primarily by putting money in their pockets, but rather by increasing the value of their investment and ensuring the future viability of the business to provide customers with something they value. Ongoing business success requires ongoing investment in business innovation, enhancements, and improvements that customers desire enough to purchase at a price that motivates the seller.

Whatever idea Walt deemed viable, he and his staff first imagined what was possible, then how to make it possible, and finally, what concessions to the possible had to be made for the sake of practicality. Walt was not good at accepting concessions, and was famous for spending much more time and money than the accountants and bankers thought prudent or rational. Through it all, his confidence that he could and would succeed was usually unshakeable when it was clear in his mind how to do things right, even under the most adverse conditions. Roy wrote in a 1969 article for *Readers' Digest*:

> Walt thrived on adversity. Even with Mickey a hit, we were constantly in hock to the banks. When he made his first real financial bonanza, with *Snow White*, he could scarcely believe it. Sure enough, the good fortune was too good to last. *Snow White* made several million dollars when it came out. But Walt soon spent that and then some by plunging into a series of full-length cartoon features and building our present studio. To keep the studio afloat, we sold stock to the public—and it sank immediately from $25 a share to $3. Troubles piled up. The studio was hit by a strike. Then World War II cut off our European market. More than once I would have given up had it not been for Walt's ornery faith that we would eventually succeed."[17]

For Walt, spending money to ensure products of the highest quality was a long-term investment in the Disney brand and its reputation for unsurpassed excellence that Walt hoped would pay dividends far into the future.

To not invest this way was perceived by Walt as accepting a standard that abused the trust of the loyal Disney customer, and was a sure path to failure.

Time and time again business results demonstrated the wisdom of Walt's integrity to his values and his obsession for what we now refer to as a market-driven total quality philosophy.

Focus on Creating, Not Constraining

Walt was the studio's visionary and dreamer. He also understood and was involved in the financial aspects of the business, while leaving most of the operational business matters to Roy. Walt once said of Roy, "We started the business here in 1923, and if it hadn't been for my big brother, I swear I'd have been in jail several times for check bouncing. I never knew what was in the bank. He kept me on the straight and narrow." The role Roy played in Walt's success and achievements is summarized nicely, if somewhat understated, by Merlin Jones: "Roy's wisdom was to create a well-protected playpen for his younger brother—and then to stand back and watch him create."[18]

Roy was often frustrated by Walt's dismissiveness about finances and his tendency to put the challenge to Roy to find the necessary funds. Walt just wanted to get things done based on his assessment that doing them would be worthwhile, and that somehow and at some point he would figure out a commercial angle, even if it couldn't be seen right away.

In 1955, Disneyland was in the midst of construction, and Bank of America and ABC-Paramount were bearing down on Roy because of huge budget overruns and a growing lack of confidence in the project. Walt was well aware of the cost overruns, but he was determined to build the park the way he wanted it built. One day, designer Herb Ryman was driving with Walt from the studio to visit the park. Walt had asked Ryman to design a restaurant to be built at the end of Main Street, and Ryman was apologizing that after having worked on it for three weeks, he wasn't getting anywhere. Walt seemed unconcerned. "Herb...you know the worst thing that can happen to you? You could go broke. I look at it this way. I've been broke five times in my life. One more time won't hurt."[19]

Almost two months after Disneyland opened, Bruce McNeill, the general contractor for Disneyland, arrived in Roy's office to announce the discovery of a drawer full of unpaid bills that totaled almost two million dollars. Roy was furious, and after an investigation, it was determined that the culprit was Walt, who had been going around ordering aesthetic changes to be made at the last minute without considering the costs. "Walt didn't care about the cost at all," said attorney Luther Marr. "It was a matter of what it looked like, the result. So Roy had to dig up some more money. I don't know where he got it, because he had used up all the credit he could come by."[20]

By 1958 the financial situation was better than it had ever been. Roy was eager to see the company free and clear of debt, and informed staff that the studio was now "getting out of the hole" and further expansion plans would have to wait two to three years. He then left for Europe. According to Jack Lindquist, who was the advertising manager at Disneyland and would later become president of the park, Walt met with WED staff to announce his decision and discuss plans to build a 150-foot-high replica of the Matterhorn with a bobsled ride inspired by their recent climbing adventure *Third Man on the Mountain*, a submarine underwater adventure ride inspired by *20,000 Leagues Under the Sea*, and a futuristic monorail transportation system. When Walt was told of Roy's instructions to steer away from debt, Walt responded, "Well, we're going to build them. Roy can figure out how to pay for it when he gets back."[21]

The attractions were built at a cost of $5.5 million. They opened in June 1959 with the fanfare of an hour-and-a-half nationally televised special featuring Vice President Richard Nixon taking the inaugural monorail ride with Walt.

On one occasion during a staff meeting with Walt in attendance, Marc Davis presented the plans for a new attraction called Nature's Wonderland. As told by Gabler in *Walt Disney*,

> Davis opened by saying that there were two ways of executing the project—an inexpensive one and an expensive one. "And Walt got all the way up from his seat and walked around to the front of the room where I was," Davis remembered, "and put his hand on my shoulder and he said, 'Marc,' he said, 'you and I do not worry about whether anything is cheap or expensive. We only worry about if it's good.'"[22]

On another occasion, Walt was asked and accepted the honor of staging the ceremonies at the Winter Olympics in Squaw Valley, California, in 1960. The plans included a thousand-piece band for the grand opening and entertainment every night. When the Olympic organizers began to complain about the proposed costs, Walt declared: "Either we're going to do it the right way, or Disney will pull out."[23]

Charles Shows was creating a film about the African lion, but was unable to locate the footage he wanted for the opening scene, a close-up looking down on the lion's open mouth. Shows writes:

> I told Walt that I hadn't found the opening shot I wanted, but that I had thought of a way of getting it—easily. And I was sure he'd like the idea when he heard how little it would cost. "I'll take a camera crew up to Griffith Park Zoo," I told him, "back up a big lion against some bushes, move in tight, and get a close-up shot of the old boy's tonsils."
>
> But Disney didn't react as I had expected. "You do," he growled, "and you won't be here tomorrow."

I thought he was kidding, but the stern look on his face told me he was not.

"We tell moviegoers that these nature films are shot in Africa," Walt made clear, "and by God, not one foot of phony film is going into my nature pictures."

I got the picture!—and I didn't get the zoo lion's picture.

Once more, I realized that it was honesty like this that makes Disney films worldwide favorites.[24]

Walt clearly understood and appreciated the role of money and the need for business discipline and responsibility over time periods spanning decades to create value. What he loathed to do was accept the knee-jerk assessment of others, particularly of risk-averse accountants and bankers, as to where the lines should be drawn. Joe Potter recalled a meeting he attended to discuss the acquisition of corporate sponsors for EPCOT: "Once in a planning meeting Walt was mad because a finance guy was present. Walt said to the finance man, 'What the hell are you doing here?' He made him leave. He wanted creative people there only."[25]

Roy noted that Walt had good reason for his animosity toward finance guys:

Bankers, bookkeepers and lawyers frequently tried to put the brakes on his free-wheeling imagination and were the bane of Walt's existence. As his business manager, I was no exception. "When I see you happy, that's when I get nervous," he used to say. Since Walt would spare no expense to make his pictures better, we used to have our battles. But he was always quick to shake hands and make up.[26]

It wasn't that Walt didn't value financial insight but rather that there was a proper time and a place for it. Disney researcher Harrison "Buzz" Price, who began working with Walt and Roy in 1953, noted: "It is a fiction that Roy was only the numbers man and Walt was the artist. They were both bird dogs analytically. 'Why?' 'Why?' 'What?' 'How much?' Walt was just tenaciously interested in that stuff, along with Roy. Both of them were smart as hell."[27]

Roy's son, Roy E. Disney, verified that his father and uncle had a different perspective on business matters when it came to money. His father's attitude was that "if you don't have the money, you can't make the thing in the first place. Walt's attitude about it," he said, "which was very astute, was 'if I make something that people want to see, we're going to do fine.' So his business sense was centered on creating, while Dad was sort of the flip side of that, which was one reason why the partnership worked so well."[28]

The real difference in approach was that Walt was focused on creating something unique and outstanding that people would want to experience and be a part of, which would draw revenue to pay back the investment in the creation and launch of the product. Roy's more traditional approach was to create a budget from prior earnings and develop to the pre-established constraints established for the project, and hope for the best.

Innovation, Disruption, and Creative Destruction

It is well documented that business success breeds financial conservatism. Continuous innovation is difficult and taxing on workers. People enjoy the exhilaration of the creative process, of building something new in the world or improving on the old ways of doing things, of imagining an alternative and creating it in reality, of doing what others have said to be impossible. In today's world, innovation is usually the result of hard work intellectually, not physically, although the amount of work and dedication required can take its physical toll. When the work is done, personal success is measured by one's contribution to achieving the goal, and business success is measured in the form of sales, market share, increased revenues, and ultimately increased profits and return on investment.

At some point, those who were part of the winning team want to celebrate, rest, stand still, and bask in the sunshine. But the marketplace wants to move on. Consumers never cease wanting better, cheaper, faster. In a world of competition and insatiable consumer demand for value satisfiers and value fulfillment, no organization can stand still for very long. No matter how brilliant or small an innovation, other entrepreneurs stand ready to copy and improve upon it to win consumers and profits, thereby diluting the market value of previous innovations.

Economist and political scientist Joseph A. Schumpeter (1883–1950) coined the phrase "creative destruction" for this ongoing process of endless change. Creative destruction is the simple concept that when we are free to solve problems in the pursuit of new opportunities for our own well-being, we necessarily destroy the old way of doing things. Continuous innovation entails continuous change, and in the process new wealth is created and old wealth is destroyed. In a key passage from his 1942 book *Capitalism, Socialism and Democracy*, Schumpeter describes the disruptive process of transformation that follows the adoption of new ideas and commercialization of innovation:

> Capitalism, then, is by nature a form or method of economic change and not only never is but never can be stationary. ... The fundamental impulse that sets and keeps the capitalist engine in motion comes from the new consumers' goods, the new methods of production and transportation, the new markets, the new forms of industrial organization that capitalist enterprise creates. ... The opening up of new markets, foreign or domestic, and the organizational development from the craft shop and factory to such concerns as U.S. Steel illustrate the same process of industry mutation—if I may use

that biological term—that incessantly revolutionizes the economic structure *from within*, incessantly destroying the old one, incessantly creating the new one. This process of Creative Destruction is the essential fact about capitalism. It is what capitalism consists in and what every capitalist concern has got to live in.[29]

The marketplace rewards with wealth the innovations it approves. Buyers are willing and eager to trade something they have for something they perceive to be of greater value. Sellers are willing and eager to do the same. The result is voluntary value exchange, with both parties of the immediate transaction benefiting, as well as all parties in the long tail of economic production and work that was required to enable the final consumer purchase.

Walt's career growth was similar in kind to most entrepreneurs, beginning with very modest means and creating something new that others find valuable and are willing to pay for. When demand is high and the product can be delivered profitably, entrepreneurs can become wealthy very quickly. Walt and the studio struggled for years to be financially successful, from his early start in Kansas City in the 1920s through the creation of the characters of Oswald and Mickey, always struggling to innovate in one way or another with new ideas to create a more highly valued product and to take away the pressure of meeting payroll from week to week. With each new innovation, new ways of creating and doing things replaced the old in a process of evolutionary improvements and creative destruction.

Each stage of Walt's success was the result of creating and delivering something new that was valued highly, not by Walt and Roy, but by movie houses and movie-going consumers. At first it was Laugh-O-gram fairy tales, followed by the Alice Comedies, then by Oswald the Lucky Rabbit, leading to the huge success and phenomenon of Mickey Mouse, and later other characters, particularly Donald Duck. Unlike many others in the cartoon business who flogged the same old products in multiple variations to an increasingly disinterested consumer, Walt continued to innovate in quality, sound, and color, as new technologies became available and public tastes evolved. But it wasn't until Walt created, and the public accepted, the brilliance of something brand new and at the time astonishing—an emotionally and visually engaging full-length animated feature film—that Walt Disney Productions received a drastic increase in the in-flow of money from ticket purchases. Since starting the Disney Brothers Studio in Uncle Robert's garage in 1923, it wasn't until 1938 that Walt and Roy could finally put their money worries behind them (at least for a little while).

Consumers embraced the innovation and in the process of choosing to buy tickets to see *Snow White and the Seven Dwarfs*, inadvertently made the creators of that product wealthy; *inadvertently* because movie-goers neither think about nor care who they are making rich or poor when they make consumer choices. They could have just as easily decided to avoid an animated film, as most studios and experts in the industry expected. Had that been the case, *Snow White* would have bankrupted the Disney studio. Instead, Walt was richly rewarded for his risk-taking. His employees, suppliers, investors, and distribution channel partners were also rewarded by Walt's vision, courage, and entrepreneurial risk-taking.

It is in this way that a harmony of interests exists in the voluntary pursuit of values both within organizations and across society. Entrepreneurs and capitalists invest in production infrastructure and pay wages to those who contribute as employees, each in pursuit of their own economic and personal interests and values. Economist George Reisman identifies the essential element of such prime movers and business titans as providers of "guiding and directing intelligence at the highest level in the productive process" to achieve the goal of producing a product, creating customers, and achieving profits.[30]

Lessons We Can Learn from Walt Disney's Business Success

- Money is a means for financing new ideas. Put it to work.
- Don't let a lack of money limit your creativity and imagination.
- Look at the big picture. Give priority to longer-term strategic spending, not narrow and more immediate ROI at the project or task level.
- The customer controls the success of your business because the customer is king. Give the public everything you can give them.
- Make earning money a by-product, not a goal. Don't work for a dollar, work to create and have fun.
- Do things the right way or not at all.
- Understand the numbers. Become an analytical bird dog.
- Embrace creative destruction. Constantly seek ways to adapt to changing circumstances that will affect consumer expectations and perceptions.

---

1. Thomas, *Building a Company*, 240.

2. *Walt Disney: Famous Quotes*, 70.

3. *Walt Disney: Famous Quotes*, 71.

4. Mannheim, *Walt Disney and the Quest for Community*, 97. J.A. Aberdeen reports the investment at this time to be in excess of $125 million, "Walt Disney: The SIMPP Years", at cobbles.com/simpp_archive/walt-disney_post-simpp.htm.

5. J.A. Aberdeen, "Walt Disney: The SIMPP Years," at cobbles.com/simpp_archive/walt-disney_post-simpp.htm, accessed October 6, 2014.

6. Hooper Fowler interview with Walt Disney for *LOOK* magazine, January 1964, in Jackson, *Walt Disney: Conversations*, 107.

7. Marty Sklar in Green & Green, *Remembering Walt*, 163.

8. Drucker, *The Practice of Management*, Perennial Library, 1986, 37.

9. Drucker, *Management*, Harper & Row, 1973, 79–80.

10. Levitt, *Innovation in Marketing*, McGraw-Hill, 1962, 243.

11. Quoted in "Foundations for the Disney Business," imagineerebirth.blogspot.ca/2007/01/foundations-for-disney-business.html.

12. Quoted in Merlin Jones, "The Spirit of Youth,"songofthesouth.net/news/archives/savedisney-spiritofyouth.html.

13. Smith, *The Quotable Walt Disney*, 59.

14. Quoted in Charles Solomon, "The Man Who Was Never a Mouse," articles.latimes.com/2001/dec/02/entertainment/ca-10570.

15. Roy E. Disney, quoted from the 2009 documentary film, *Waking Sleeping Beauty*, commentary track during the end credits.

16. Jones, "The Spirit of Youth," songofthesouth.net/news/archives/savedisney-spiritofyouth.html, accessed October 13, 2016.

17. Roy O. Disney, "Unforgettable Walt Disney," *Reader's Digest*, 1969, 216.

18. Quoted in Merlin Jones, "The Spirit of Youth," songofthesouth.net/news/archives/savedisney-spiritofyouth.html.

19. Thomas, *Building a Company*, 190.

20. Thomas, *Building a Company*, 200.

21. Walt quoted in Gabler, *Walt Disney*, 564.

22. Gabler, *Walt Disney*, 564, citing Marc Davis interview with Bob Thomas.

23. Thomas, *Walt Disney*, 346.

24. Shows, *Walt: Backstage Adventures with Walt Disney*, 182.

25. Ghez, *Walt's People: Volume 10*, 266, Interview with Joe Potter in regard to finding corporate sponsors for EPCOT.

26. Roy O. Disney, "Unforgettable Walt Disney" in *Reader's Digest*, 1969, 216.

27. Price in Thomas, *Building a Company*, 186.

28. Roy E. Disney quoted in Green and Green, *Remembering Walt*, 100.

29. Joseph A. Schumpeter, *Capitalism, Socialism and Democracy*, 82–83. Also Wikipedia, en.wikipedia.org/wiki/Creative-destruction, accessed January 15, 2014.

30. See Reisman, "Classical Economics vs. The Exploitation Theory," mises.org/library/classical-economics-vs-exploitation-theory, accessed November 8, 2016; see also Reisman, *Capitalism*, 482–483.

Strive for Perfection and Don't Compromise Quality

Walt Disney was a perfectionist in the best sense of the word. He set a high standard for quality because he knew that high standards are achievable and a demonstration of moral virtue. Unlike the heads of other studios, he didn't just leave matters to chance or the whimsical discretion of others. He defined the attributes of the standards he demanded, taking into account both the cost of achieving them and the cost of failing to achieve them.

Walt's devotion to quality and value creation in service to his customers was applied to everything he did. It was more akin to a moral principle than a business policy. Consider his perspective on park maintenance at Disneyland.

"Disneyland is a work of love. We didn't go into Disneyland with the idea of making money...even trying to keep that park clean is a tremendous expense. And those sharp pencil guys tell you, 'Walt, if we cut down on maintenance, we'd save a lot of money.' But I don't believe in that—it's like any other show on the road. It must be kept fresh and clean."[1]

Nate Naversen writes: "When Disneyland closes, the maintenance starts. At the beginning of every day the park is to look like it looked on opening day July 17, 1955. Not only does this make the guest experience better, but it also creates a better atmosphere for the cast members. At night, everything is repaired to look like new. Instead of having one or two people maintaining the park, Disney hires hundreds. Do those workers pay for themselves? I guarantee they do."

The notion of striving for perfection implies a belief that high standards can be objectively defined and achieved. It requires a "can-do" mindset and an inherent ambition to succeed through productive thinking and action. It implies a particular worldview that as humans we can apply ourselves to overcome the barriers to success we find before us. The ability to achieve the results we seek gives meaning to the work we do by providing self-esteem and pride in achievement.

From the beginning of his career as a filmmaker, Walt tried to ensure that each film had some element of improvement in the direction of pleasing the public so that over time, many small steps would amount to a giant leap over his competitors. Not only were improvements required in the capabilities of staff to maintain this upward slope, but there was also a need to embed within the corporate culture ongoing improvements in technical and operating processes.

For Walt, doing one's best in pursuit of quality was the right standard for all personal endeavors, which by extension meant it was good for business because it promoted the creation of long-term value. He was surprised to learn that what he thought should be common sense seemed to be a rare trait amongst businessmen he encountered. Very few of his film, television, and amusement park competitors were willing to set the quality bar as high and dare to achieve it, and were instead content to settle for much less. Walt had learned through observation in his formative years, primarily in New York City, that for most business leaders in his industry, the quality of the product and the personal integrity of the players was less important than the budget and production schedule.

To the extent that it was possible, neither Walt nor Roy separated their personal code of conduct and value-centric action from their professional conduct and business values. As an example of Walt's integrity and moral commitment to keeping his word and maintaining the highest standards of quality, consider his attitude toward the completion of the Alice series before transitioning to Oswald the Lucky Rabbit.

Walt knew in January 1927 that the Alice series would be coming to an end, and he would be moving on to the fully animated escapades of Oswald the Rabbit. With only a few more Alices to complete, Walt could have elected to lower his standards and let the quality slip. Yet even though he was eager to move on to something new, Merritt and Kaufman note, "the final entries showed no flagging of inspiration or effort. The look of the pictures was more lavish than ever, and the gags were increasingly plentiful and imaginative. All in all, Disney could well afford to be proud of the Alice films. During the course of their production he had proven himself as a producer, and had built up an animation studio that was the equal of any in the business."[2]

Similarly, when Walt already knew that Mintz had raided his studio for the talent of the "renegades" he continued to send encouragement and instructions to his animation staff to involve as many gags as possible in *The Fox Chase* and bring Oswald into the story more to ensure he maintained the high quality standards of the Oswald films that bore his name.

Walt was known to perpetually push his staff to embrace experimentation and skill upgrading so that he could expand the possibilities of animation and maintain his brand-leadership position. Walt's excitement for new ideas was contagious among his best staff, who were often competitive with each other to win Walt's favor and contribute in significant ways.

Experimentation was costly because it required the investment of time and resources beyond what was needed to simply maintain the status quo, but Walt believed it was also the key to serendipitous discovery and the inclusion of small details to enhance audience enjoyment and appreciation. Consider as just one example that after parts of *Snow White and the Seven Dwarfs* had been animated, one of the animators created a special Dopey walk that exuded happiness and was always slightly out of step with the other dwarfs. "After realizing that this is exactly how Dopey should be animated," writes one commentator, "Disney required each scene with Dopey to be re-animated using this walk even though the picture was already running far over its projected budget."[3]

It was this kind of dedication to detail and Walt's belief that people feel good about perfection and appreciate it because they understand that it is done for them, that helped a cartoon everyone thought would fail miserably as "'Walt's Folly'" when instead it became the top-grossing film at that time. It helped Walt promote the discipline of building a high-performance business culture that would contribute to his future success.

Throughout his career, Walt had to fight against his accountants, bankers, co-workers, family, and friends to maintain the integrity of his high standards. Quality and integrity to his own values and those of his customers—"the public"—served as his guiding compass throughout his career. Walt held that a conscious decision to produce less than what was possible for short-term gain was inherently more risky in the long run than striving for, and investing in, excellence.

Walt had proved that his devotion to uncompromised standards of excellence was a viable, value-enhancing business strategy. He succeeded in creating a culture that proudly shared his values of excellence, although this commitment to "management by values" was always a struggle. "I'm not the perfectionist anymore," Walt noted later in his career. "It's my staff. They're the ones always insisting on doing something better and better. I'm the fellow trying to hurry them to finish before they spoil the job. You can over-work drawing or writing and lose the spontaneity."[4]

Walt's unequivocal passion and commitment to excellence is one of the keys to his heroic stature in the annals of 20th century business history.

Creative Innovation Through "Plussing"

When long-time Disney animator Ollie Johnston was asked about Walt by Disney biographer Bob Thomas, he replied, "He was a fair man, but he had little patience for anything weak."[5]

Walt was constantly curious about how and why things worked, and then, if he was so inclined, sought solutions on how to improve what seemed to him to be merely conventional. He called it "plussing," which was his name for the process of adding something more to lift an idea higher and make it better. Walt made "plussing" a natural part of his thinking, a standing order in his conceptual process.

It was by first understanding how things worked and then applying imagination that Walt was able to envision how things might be improved. He engaged in a process with his staff that intertwined the elements of critical thinking, creativity, and innovation to figure out a better way to do something and perhaps to create something completely new.

Problem solving is at the core of all work. In Walt's eyes, when employees weren't problem solving they weren't really doing value-adding work—work that he was confident they were capable of doing. Walt understood well the lessons that Charles Mintz learned the hard way when he hired away almost all of Walt's animating staff in 1928: that the real work that differentiates greatness from mediocrity is the ability to create through problem solving something new and unique, something innovative, something that delivers to the public elevated levels of perceived value that people will want and pay for. Mindlessly repeating what has already been done will inevitably lead to decline as a bored public seeks new forms of entertainment.

Audiences want something new and fresh. That's why Walt was fixated on moving-forward, experimenting, trying new things, and constantly plussing. It's why he didn't like sequels. It often took him years, and in some cases decades, to figure out how to apply many of his ideas. When he wasn't making progress, ideas were put on the shelf and when the time was right, brought out again for further development, experimentation, or application.

You Can Lick 'em with Product

From his earliest years in business, Walt had a passion for quality, perhaps instilled into him by his father who demanded of his sons that when newspapers were delivered, they must be placed inside the screen door, not just tossed on the stoop. One of his observations from his first job as a commercial artist at Pesmen-Rubin Commercial Art Studio was that sometimes quality has to take a back seat to practicality through the cutting of corners. But he also learned at his next employer, the Kansas City Film Ad Company, that their processes could be improved upon, particularly the way they did animation, to win business away from competitors, and that when business leaders and managers feel comfortable, they become intellectually lazy and resist learning and adapting to new innovations and the changing needs and wants of their customers. For Walt, this was all tied together with producing and delivering quality products and service to customers to compete effectively and succeed in business.

Walt encompassed what he had learned in his early business years about quality, innovation, and competitiveness into a general principle. After struggling in 1928 with the loss of Oswald and almost his entire studio of animators, Walt decided that in spite of being cheated twice by distributors, he would succeed by producing a product so good that the public would demand to see it, which would force the hand of distributors to come to him and not he to them. He put it this way to animator Ben Sharpsteen in 1929: "You can lick 'em with product." It was Walt's fundamental belief that audiences had discerning tastes and could be relied upon to discern and choose quality over what they deemed to be lesser efforts and products.

Pushing Back Against the Total Quality Pushback

Disney biographer Bob Thomas writes in *Building a Company*, "Walt presided over the creative side, and he ruled with a firm hand. Discontent was common, since he goaded his artists to achieve what they thought was impossible for them. He expected perfection and was frustrated when they didn't achieve it.... Walt's boys were motivated not by being stroked, but by the sheer power of his genius."[6]

Walt's optimism and tenacity to constantly seek improvements would often create conflict or tension when an artist was convinced that his or her work was good enough and was looking for the green light to move ahead, but found Walt prepared to hold up production to search for something better, something more perfectly aligned with what he envisioned in his mind's eye. Instead of moving on to a new scene or task, an artist would begrudgingly engage in rework that Walt perceived to be important and valuable.

There were many examples where staff pushed back, arguing or implying that quality improvements were not required because nobody would notice the difference. Resistance to maintain the status quo and the conventional usually raised Walt's ire, and rarely succeeded.

When cash flow was tight, resistance against Walt's seemingly spendthrift ways was often led by Roy, who would argue that given the choices of how to use cash on hand, rework wasn't necessary in most cases because it resulted in the extension of the production schedule, costing the company money that could never be recovered. Roy and Walt were very much on the same page when it came to the value of quality and Walt's ability to produce results. Their disagreement in these types of matters was more often about timing than principle given the constant financial pressures and struggle to keep the studio solvent. Recall that Roy initially resisted the timing of the addition of sound to Mickey Mouse because of a lack of working capital.

He resisted adding color to *Flowers and Trees* for the same reason—Roy felt at the time that it was likely to create problems for which they lacked the resources to resolve. When Walt wanted to fix a technical problem with the Prince in *Snow White*, Roy responded, "Let the Prince shimmy."

Walt had a different perspective. For him, rework was based in a more fundamental work ethic and adherence to operating principles tied to integrity and creative purpose. It was about creating the best work possible, which was an investment in success through quality and excellence in entertainment that would be recognized and appreciated by the public, and not about additional costs that diminished profits. We must remember, of course, that it was Roy, not Walt, who was tasked with the difficult job of finding and managing the cash to support Walt's intransigent vision.

Walt also displayed an optimism and respect for the capabilities of all people. He recognized when effort was lacking and staff was coasting on their skill, knowledge, and talents. He was constantly pushing and motivating them toward self-improvement and lifetime learning, believing this would translate into more highly skilled and motivated employees. The most well-known example is the creation of company-paid art classes at the nearby Chouinard Art Institute in preparation for *Snow White*, which he later brought in-house to both improve the scope of the program and expand the opportunity for artists to attend. An important part of the program involved peer-to-peer teaching.

Roy once commented on Walt's passion for self-improvement and his expectation that others who worked for him embrace it:

> Walt could never tolerate a guy who was self-satisfied with his art. I heard him again and again say to fellows, "Look, you're capable of a hell of a lot better work. You can't just get a certain degree of proficiency and sit there all your life. You have to keep at it all the time!"
>
> He'd compel them to go to Chouinard Art School. The guys who would revolt or rebel, they didn't last very long. They left with chips on their shoulders, as though Walt were some kind of ogre.
>
> Walt was obsessed with the idea that, in life, you continually go to school. You never reach any plateau of finished perfection. And he preached that, too, in everything he did. But there were a lot of people who looked for alibis for their own inefficiencies or laziness and they were the ones who grumbled and fell out with Walt.[7]

Disney film and television writer Jack Speirs tells a story of Roy coming to Walt to inform him that some of the artists were taking supplies home to do drawings and paintings. Roy wanted to put a stop to it and Walt objected. "But Walt," Roy said, "you know they're selling their art." Walt responded, "Don't worry about it. We get the benefit. They're practicing. So let them go home and practice."[8]

Attitude, Thoughtfulness, and Vigilance Create Quality

Walt learned rudimentary and primitive animation techniques at his job for the Kansas City Film Advertising Company, but pursued more advanced techniques of animation after acquiring from the library a book written by E.G. Lutz in 1920, *Animated Cartoons: How They Are Made, Their Origin and Development*. The book explained the methods and techniques required to produce commercial quality animated cartoons quickly and efficiently. Because animation was extremely labor-intensive, the key to efficiency was to acquire the skill of careful and thoughtful planning, a lesson Walt learned well: "Of all the talents required by any one going into this branch of art," wrote Lutz, "none is so important as that of the skill to plan the work so that the lowest possible number of drawings need to be made for any particular scenario." How to do this effectively really constituted the tricks of the trade—how to create cycles, use cutouts, and reuse drawings.

As Merritt and Kaufman write in their book about Walt's silent film years, *Walt in Wonderland: The Silent Films of Walt Disney*,

> Disney unhesitatingly accepted [these] principles, eagerly embrac-
> ing the use of time-saving tricks. ... But Disney added a twist: he
> strove from the first for an ever-higher standard of quality on the
> screen—better drawings, more and better gags, abundant detail.
> By the mid-thirties he had refined and synthesized [these concepts
> that had become standard in the industry]. The Disney studio was
> by then a "factory" like the others, one which could release films on
> a regular schedule. But this "factory" was built to support a great
> number of individual artists, and designed to promote the develop-
> ment and growth of each one. Disney's approach was vindicated, if
> need be, by his results.[9]

Without these principles and their ongoing refinement and improvement, note Merritt and Kaufman, spectacular and intricate animated films like *Fantasia* could never have been produced.

Walt had become a fiend for quality from start to finish. Animator Ben Sharpsteen experienced this first hand. Sharpsteen recalled how impressed he was on his first day working at the Disney studio in 1929 after years of working for the leading New York animation studios. Most impressive was the attitude of his new boss, who was six years his junior: "He was not concerned with speed, with the time it took to animate a scene; of paramount importance was the quality of the finished product. As I joined his staff of about ten people, I felt somewhat confused, but I simply went ahead and did the best that I could."[10]

Sharpsteen was quick to learn that Walt held every moment of every scene as being important. Walt asked him to work on a scene "that I would have considered to be of run-of-the-mill importance, but I could see that he did not hold it that way. In Walt's estimation, everything that was to be done had to be executed with a great deal of thought toward finesse in order to make it better."[11] Sharpsteen surely communicated his experiences working with Walt to his colleagues in New York, setting expectations should any decide to make the move to California.

Quality Begets Quality

Many of New York City's top animators were dissatisfied with their current work assignments, which they found to be overly repetitive. Walt's reputation for quality made his studio a major attraction for qualified animators, giving him a competitive advantage when it came to recruitment for expansion. The best talent wants to work for the best employer, and the Disney studio was the recognized leader in the animation field.

Working for Disney provided greater challenges, and many with the passion and motivation to expand their horizons were willing to take substantial cuts in pay in exchange for the personal and artistic growth Disney offered, plus the opportunity to work directly with Walt himself.

Carman Maxwell was working for Harman-Ising when he wrote to Walt seeking re-employment. "Believe it or not," he wrote, "I'd prefer to work harder and make less money, if I knew my efforts were going into pictures that were carefully planned and properly made." Maxwell was associated with the "renegades" and had been fired by Roy. He wasn't rehired.[12]

Art Babbitt was working at the Paul Terry animation studio in New York City when he saw Ub Iwerks' *The Skeleton Dance*. "I knew that was the place I wanted to work," he said, and traveled across the country in 1932 to apply for a job with Disney.

Dick Huemer was working for Charles Mintz when pay cuts were announced in 1933. He quit, headed to California, and joined Disney earning about half of his New York salary.

Grim Natwick invented and was drawing Betty Boop for the Fleischers when he was invited by Walt to join him. Natwick had heard that Iwerks was the real genius behind Walt's animation, so he joined Iwerks' Celebrity Pictures instead. After three years he had realized his mistake and reapplied to Walt, where he took up residence in 1934.

Bill Tytla also left New York to join Disney in 1934 because of his desire to have the opportunity to do better work.[13]

These are some early examples specific to animators, but the attractiveness of working for a forward-looking studio with challenging and interesting assignments extended to other studio-related trades as well. Walt's reputation for artistic creativity and innovation helped attract great artists like Salvador Dali, Marc Davis, and Herbert Ryman, experienced engineers like Roger Broggie, General Joe Potter, and Admiral Joe Fowler, as well as movie actors, film directors, music composers, and other top-caliber technicians and professionals.

Many top people who left Disney to pursue higher-paying opportunities at other studios later expressed their regret at missing out on participating in Walt's grand adventures.

Competing More Effectively Through Quality Control Innovation

Almost all leading animation studios in the 1930s were focused on the *quantity* of animation produced each day and extremely lax about *quality*. Walt was different. He initiated, encouraged, supported, and invested in a large number of process and technological innovations to improve overall quality. Many of these improvements were suggested and developed by his staff.

In the early years of animation, it was impossible to really assess the effectiveness of the immense amount of work put into the creation of a scene until the end of the production process when the animation could be reviewed on the screen. The costliest thing you could do was complete the film and then find out that it lacked the required content and quality. By then all of your production costs were already sunk and you either had to release a quality-impaired film to the public and risk damaging your brand reputation through poor reviews, or reanimate, which would increase costs and wipe out your profits. To deal with this problem, Walt devised ways to review the work quickly and in the early stages of the animation process, before large sums of money were invested.

In the early 1930s, Walt's animators discovered that they could better observe their work and make improvements by making a low-cost film of their drawings for review instead of the traditional way of flipping the pages to simulate movement, like a flip book. Biographer Bob Thomas describes it this way:

> One technique was the practice of photographing the animator's pencil sketches for a scene at the end of the day and slicing the short film into a loop. The films were projected in a small closet to provide a visual impression of how the action would move so it could be assessed. This small closet review became known as "the sweatbox."[14]

Michael Barrier writes in *The Animated Man*:

> Around the beginning of 1932, in a step that speaks of Disney's new confidence in his role as coordinator, he ordered his animators to

start making their animation drawings as rough sketches, rather than finished drawings, and to make pencil tests of the roughs. Until then, pencil tests were shot only after the animation was in finished form, ready to be inked on cels. In Wilfred Jackson's recollection, it was seeing some of Norm Ferguson's very rough animation in pencil test—animation that "read" clearly despite the sketchiness of the drawing—that spurred Disney to make the change.

"By encouraging Fergy to concentrate on the actions with rough drawings and assigning to him an excellent draftsman to clean up his animation drawings," Jackson wrote, "Walt felt Fergy was able to produce better quality as well as great quantity of outstanding animation. Walt felt, also, that it should work this same way for his other animators and let them know he expected them to do their animation in the same way too."[15]

By holding up Ferguson's work and the work of his cleanup assistant as the preferred way of working going forward, Walt and his animators were now better able to assess the suitability of their scenes before it was too late or became too expensive to make major changes.

At the beginning, Walt would review pencil tests with each animator, but soon realized that he was losing an opportunity for his artists to learn and share together. According to Wilfred Jackson, Walt adopted the sweatbox process of a more collective and participatory end-of-the-day review in large part so that the animators could observe and learn from each other and from Walt's scrutiny what was admirable and desirable as well as what was questionable.[16]

The animators soon moved from daily reviews to filming their complete scenes of pencil drawings so that Walt, directors, and animators could assess the quality and effectiveness of the overall scene, and identify areas for improvement before moving on to the rest of the animation process.[17]

Walt's change in process was directed toward changing the way his animators were thinking about the work they were doing; it was directly driven by Walt's vision of a better final product rooted in the standardization of process. Walt understood that realism and believability in animation—of having the audience believe that the drawings they are watching on the screen are real characters—required a break from rigidity. As Michael Barrier identifies in *The Animated Man*:

By insisting that they draw their animation roughly, Disney was encouraging his animators to think in terms of movement, rather than individual drawings. "The hardest job," he said in 1956, "was to get the guys to quit fooling around with these individual drawings and to think of the group of drawings in action. They couldn't resist when they had a drawing in front of them that they had to keep noodling."[18]

Another effective quality control tool used extensively at the studio was the storyboard. The storyboard wasn't invented at the Disney studio, but Walt put it to use as a way to perfect the complete telling and visual showing of the story prior to the more expensive process of actual animation.

The storyboard was a large four-feet by eight-feet board on which artist sketches were sequentially pinned as the development of the story progressed, like a comic strip. This made it easy for the story team to discuss changes and for Walt to visualize the film in its entirety. Sections could be unpinned and shifted around in story meetings to assess the impact of adding, moving, or eliminating scenes. When the boards were finally approved, they provided a blueprint to guide film production. The first storyboard simply involved taking various story and gag sketches and pinning them to the wall in their proper sequence to make the story easier to follow and talk about. Eventually, the sketches were pinned to multiple large corkboards that could be moved from room to room to tell the complete story from start to finish.[19]

Seen in isolation, the story board process added time and cost to the total production schedule, but in return it enhanced the quality of the story and ensured that everybody involved was on the same page regarding what needed to be done. It also served as a quality control device by preventing a project from proceeding to animation before it was ready, as was the case at many other studios where the artists took their ideas and ran with them, only to find out later that there were gaps in the story or that the film fell flat.

On the face of it, if seen through the eyes of the finance guys or from a pure cost perspective, one could look upon these innovations as adding unnecessary time and costs to production. It's easy to ignore the cost-savings and quality-improvement benefits of pre-production planning when cost savings and quality can't be seen and calculated directly.

That's not how Walt saw it. For him, these process innovations were a means to achieving a higher quality product at a lower cost than would otherwise be the case if one went back after the mistakes were made to fix problems and improve quality. The effort to build quality into the production process played to the Disney strategy that audiences appreciated quality and would notice and reward the extra effort. Walt focused on the larger value of the Disney brand standing for high-quality family entertainment, rather than having a micro lens focused on minimizing the cost per foot of each project, as was the case at other studios.

Other studios that competed with Disney didn't like Walt's innovations, but were forced to follow his lead because the quality of their work was being judged by the benchmark standard set by Disney films. For most, their failure to keep up placed them at a distinct competitive disadvantage when it came time for theatre owners to do their buying. Mickey Mouse and the Disney name on the marquee helped to draw audiences, sell tickets, and please patrons because they provided dependable entertainment value. The result: top film houses paid higher rents on Disney films than they were willing to pay Walt's competition.

Learning to Embrace the Lessons of Failure

Walt also understood and embraced the notion that skill, knowledge, and wisdom come from doing, and doing often results in failure. He knew that from failure could arise valuable lessons and insights that can lead to more valuable discoveries and engender more successful outcomes through a form of spiral learning. As an optimist, Walt saw mankind's creative and innovative abilities as the engine for continuing human advancement.

Many examples of Walt's ability to take action, check results, and learn from failure can be found in the building and operating of Disneyland. Walt had to learn as he went along, solving each new challenge in a manner consistent with his vision for creating a great guest experience in real time, every time, and when he failed, to ensure he had in place an effective service recovery program.

At the time of the park's opening, Walt had hired third-party vendors for custodial services to keep the park clean. Once on the job, they applied conventional standards of cleanliness that were suited to their existing commercial clientele. As might be expected, Walt found these conventional standards to be unacceptable. A similar situation emerged with park security. Third-party security personnel had been taught and trained by their employers to operate with a mindset that all customers were potential threats to be treated with suspicion. As a result they brought to their work at Disneyland a conventional aura of distrust, intimidation, and disrespect toward everyone who came through the gate.

Both companies failed to adapt to Disneyland's mission and Walt's vision for creating happiness, and their contracts were soon terminated. Walt quickly concluded that to control his environment and produce the desired guest response, Disneyland had to have direct operational control over staff anywhere on the property, not just inside the berm. Walt was adamant that the number-one attribute of a good employee was to be customer-friendly, for which standards had to be set and employees trained and held accountable. All it took was one surly encounter with a park worker to introduce the disharmony that he was striving to eliminate.

Walt was dedicated to finding people who could relate to his vision and help him create a new standard of excellence that surpassed the expectations of park guests. He was committed to delivering a level of experiential service quality second to none, something he believed customers deeply desired but were unable to articulate precisely because they had never experienced it before and had given up expecting to be treated with the respect and personal dignity they were entitled to as Disney customers.

As if to confirm Walt's intuition about what would win the hearts of customers at Disneyland, *respect* was identified in contemporary research by Texas A&M University professor Leonard Berry as one of seven core "success-sustaining" values of great service companies, along with excellence, innovation, joy, teamwork, integrity, and social value (the idea that good works produce economic profit). Many of these values in the context of the mid-1950s could have easily emanated directly from Walt's creation of a unique service quality environment at Disneyland.

In studying the most common service *complaints*, Berry's research identified the underlying common denominator to be *disrespect*. Writes Berry: "On the surface, respect seems too elementary and nebulous to forge competitive advantage. But it is a powerful influence. Respectfulness dignifies transactions for both customer and server; it invests esteem into the proceedings of business; it underscores worthwhileness."[20]

Walt was a leader in recognizing customer respect as a core operating value and converting it into a tangible and measurable deliverable.

The Quality Quest Means Never Being Satisfied

The one advantage of an ongoing quest for customer-driven quality is that organizational complacency is never a threat. Such an ethos and course of action can keep an organization on the leading edge of innovation, which is motivating and rewarding. On the other hand, it can also be risky, expensive, and exhausting if not managed smartly and effectively. Walt had to lead by example, and spend considerable time challenging and motivating his staff to understand and buy into his evolving vision and plans, believe in the importance of the work they were doing, and accept their assignments enthusiastically.

There were times when staff resented Walt's imperious methods, but without his determination to control production processes, create a workable division of labor, and assign tasks based on matching talent to the work required, he would likely not have been able to lead the studio through its many crises and changes to reach the heights of success attained.

Walt had fantastic ideas, vision, and imagination, but was well aware that he lacked the drawing skills needed to render his own visions and ideas; that to attain the end result he desired, he had to rely on the artistic and engineering knowledge and skills of others whose task it was to create what he envisioned. This process of translating ideas into drawings into renderings into designs into final products was an ongoing challenge for Walt's artists as they struggled together to capture the essence of what Walt was seeking. It was the reason why there was often so much pushing, pulling, and experimentation in the early story meeting and development stages of projects and why in the later stages of projects there could be so much costly and frustrating rework and enhancements.

According to those who worked closely with him over decades, Walt experienced frustration and dissatisfaction with almost all his major endeavors. His imagination was so vivid and his expectations so high that in the end there was necessarily and inevitably disappointment. There were always gaps and shortcomings arising from the nature of the creative process itself, so that by the time a project came to its conclusion, Walt was often pleased, but never satisfied. Reality always entailed a compromise of quality in relation to the ideal and could never live up to the dream.

If any single project should have satisfied Walt based on the effort, cost, and resounding public acceptance, it should have been *Snow White and the Seven Dwarfs*, which Walt spent almost four years creating. Yet, as is often the case with visionaries, Walt's ability to communicate his vision and manage the work of other artisans failed to live up to the expectations of his imagination. Gabler eloquently captures this pathos of Walt's existence in writing of Walt and *Snow White*:

> In the end, even after all the final touches had been applied, Walt, ever the perfectionist, was disappointed. "We've worked hard and spent a lot of money, and by this time we're a little tired of it," he confessed to one journalist shortly after its completion. "I've seen so much of *Snow White* that I am conscious only of the places where it could be improved. You see, we've learned such a lot since we started this thing! I wish I could yank it back and do it all over again." Even more than a decade later Walt was sighing over the film's flaws. "There were some things in *Snow White* that make me crawl when I see them now," he said. "The bridge on her nose floats all over her face. And the Prince jitters like he's got palsy."[21]

Good Enough May Be the Best It Can Be

Walt was not prone to compliment the exceptional work of his staff, which is unfortunate, because he likely could have achieved the same quality results under conditions of higher employee morale and less stress. Nonetheless, his reason for reserving compliments was that he expected work of the highest quality from his staff as a condition of their employment. Walt was aware that his animators were hyper-competitive at times, and believed rightly or wrongly that complimenting staff would lead to perceived favoritism, unnecessary conflict, and professional complacency. Walt set exceedingly high standards, and he had no time for coddling artists who lacked the confidence to contribute at the level required to be Disney-worthy.

In displaying their work to Walt for his assessment, artists were often looking for a strong confirmation that they had successfully carried out their assignment. But in many cases, Walt himself didn't know what he wanted until he had something in front of him to consider and critique. Only after seeing something tangible was Walt able to provide more concrete guidance.

His methodology was to rely on his staff to think carefully about the practical elements of creative design and problem solving to create something that would work. Walt would then gather his staff, and together they would look at what was created and consider whether it was appropriate, then investigate more ways to improve it. Walt was constantly pushing for more creativity and deeper thinking. If the work or solution came too easily, Walt was always of the mind that a better solution could be found.

Identifying improvements was the purpose of Walt's story meetings, gag meetings, and sweatbox sessions. Walt felt that providing a compliment was to indicate his satisfaction with the work done, and Walt was rarely satisfied. When he saw something close enough to what he liked, he would typically comment, "That will work" or "That will do," meaning that the solution presented was sufficient, for now, and it was time to move on to the next task.

It was common for Walt to work on something for an extended period of time, drop it, and come back to it years later, as he did in developing *Alice in Wonderland* and a number of other story ideas. It was common for Walt to assign the same challenge to multiple staff so he could weigh their different approaches and spark his own thinking and decision-making process. Walt wasn't looking for people to like him or to enhance his popularity with the boys. He was trying to motivate his staff to go beyond the conventional easy approach and into a zone of discomfort.

This push for out-of-the-box thinking requires of people that they concentrate on something for which they typically feel insecure or even find distasteful. It is often effective to assign challenges to capable people with perceived weaknesses to stimulate new approaches to seeking better results.

With Walt as the arbiter and final judge of what was acceptable, artists could never be sure of what he would approve, and therefore what was required of them to attain his approval. It was a policy of Walt's to make sure his staff was never overly comfortable in their work, and kept slightly off-balance. An artist may have worked relentlessly and have exhausted their worthy ideas only to have Walt cast a seemingly capricious and unwarranted judgment on their work, or, what they took to be just as devastating, a seemingly dismissive comment from Walt such as, "Does anybody else have any ideas."

Walt felt his method was sound but his interpersonal technique, by his own admission, was often brusque, cold, and insensitive. Nonetheless, Walt's best artists and closest colleagues understood his intentions and didn't let his withholding of compliments affect the quality of their work. The best of them rose to the challenge time and time again by literally going back to the drawing board and creating something they themselves would later admit was a better final product because of Walt's refusal to accept their earlier submission.

Even Ward Kimball, after spending months developing a comedic soup-slurping scene for *Snow White*, admitted that as great as the scene was, when seen from the proper perspective of what was the best thing to do for the movie and the audience, Walt did the right thing by cutting it out of the movie.

The Secret to Brand Quality Is Hidden in the Smallest Details

Imagineer and Disneyland designer John Hench worked closely with Walt in the creation of Disneyland, and notes that a major reason for Disneyland's appeal to the public was "attention to infinite detail, the little things, the minor picky points that other companies just don't want to take the time, the money, the effort, to do right."[22]

Walt was obsessed with detail, says Hench, because "Walt knew that if details are missing or incorrect, guests won't believe in the story, and that if one detail contradicts another, guests will feel let down or even deceived. This is why he insisted that even details that some designers thought no guest would notice—such as replicated period doorknobs on Main Street, U.S.A.—were important. Inappropriate details confuse a story's meaning."[23]

The designers of Disneyland had spent their careers in film, and were conditioned by their profession to think in visual movie terms of framing a wide shot of the scene to establish a sense of place, and then zooming in on the detail of the action. Hench notes that every visual element that appears on the screen is carefully designed and placed to tell the story:

> Film directors and cinematographers are careful to choose details for close-ups that support what they want to say, and that validate the space in which action takes place. Choosing appropriate details keeps contradictions from creeping into the film. Similarly, in the theme parks, the details guests see close up must confirm the understanding they have of place upon first glimpsing it at a distance. If, when they walk into a place, the details guests see agree with their expectations, they will believe in it; if not, a single out-of-place element can shatter an artfully constructed story environment.[24]

When elements of a story being told are out of place, or the details are inconsistent with the stated outcome or customer expectations, however those expectations are formed, audiences experience clutter and confusion. They sense that something is not right. "Mixed messages set up conflicts, create tension, and may feel threatening," writes Hench.[25]

One of the ways to avoid contradictions in storytelling at Disneyland, says Hench, was to write "rules of the land," which are "guidelines that we develop as we create a land, build new attractions, or use when refurbishing older attractions. The rules of the land detail the background narrative, geography, and historical time period appropriate to each project. Such guidelines prevent us from creating obvious contradictions, like installing a modern computerized cash register in a turn-of-the-twentieth-century Main Street shop."[26]

Walt would scour his scripts, movies, and Disneyland itself for hours on end seeking contradictions in story-telling and ways to improve authenticity in his products to enhance the creation of value for customers on terms they were seeking, even if customers weren't consciously aware of it.

Hench's observations don't just apply to theme parks. When he speaks of the need to meet customer expectations, he is speaking about a universal principle applicable to all businesses and organizations and their key elements and value-driving components, from product quality to service quality, from tangible elements of interaction to intangible perceptions at each point of interaction or moment of truth.

The totality of customer perceptions about a product or business is contained in the concept of *brand*. In its most fundamental meaning, brand *is* the customer experience; it is the judgmental *perception* of a company or an identifiable product or service as measured against a consumer's expectations. *Branding*, on the other hand, pertains to the actions taken by the company to meet its aspirations of creating a meaningful brand. The difference between customer expectations of the total experience and customer perceptions of the delivery of that experience is the gap in brand delivery. The brand is made up of identifiable components such as product quality, service quality, price, ease of acquisition, availability, quality of the relationship, etc., that adds up to the sum. Walt was always focused on the sum total, on the Disney brand, which was inclusive of the individual elements.

The idea of creating "rules of the land" to help guide the development of Disneyland would work equally well in defining and delivering on a corporate brand aspiration or strategy to define and influence brand expectations among customers. The basic technique is to start with the desired end-state—what you want the consumer to experience—and work backwards to identify the key elements required to deliver that experience, attempting to remove contradictions along the way. The guidelines have to be spelled out so employees can understand the result they are trying to achieve and "rules of the land" have to be developed and communicated as standard operating procedures and embedded in the business culture.

In the early years, when the business was struggling, Walt focused on animated cartoons as the basis for the Disney brand. Once he was able to establish through the Alice series that he could make competitive cartoons, he shifted to quality as the distinguishing brand feature. Walt put in place business processes (gag meetings to identify funny scenarios, story boards to visualize the story from beginning to end, daily sweatbox viewings of pencil drawings to identify flaws, etc.) and new camera technology to ensure that all of his films were of high quality.

Soon quality became a given, an expectation, but when the quality of Mickey Mouse wasn't enough to sell the series, Walt injected innovation by adding sound. Walt began to consider technological innovation as an important attribute to add value on top of high-quality animated cartoons. As the pattern continued, what were once innovations that enhanced the brand soon became brand expectations, putting pressure on Walt to maintain his high standards.

Walt was compelled by market forces to continuously move forward, as what started as an innovation soon became required table stakes. When he reached one plateau, he sought out what might be needed to climb to the next. When rubber-like characters and slapstick gags started to get tired, he raised the bar by demanding situational comedy and more realistic acting by his animated characters. With a full-length feature in mind, he initiated drawing classes for his artists, years before he felt they were ready and skilled enough to invest everything he had in the effort.

Walt was continuously extending and setting new expectations. This put pressure on his competitors to match his capabilities or establish their own unique brand characteristics. Without some point of uniqueness, customers will lose interest and stop buying a particular firm's product, thereby putting them out of business. Walt was consistent throughout his career in making the pursuit of customers in open competition his top priority.

Research and Planning to Succeed

As Walt progressed in his career, he began to place greater emphasis on market research to improve his offerings and by doing so to stay ahead of his competitors. He never lost sight of the fact that consumers determined his fate, and never let his employees forget it either. He believed that the public wanted, recognized, and rewarded quality, and made it his top priority.

From his earliest days in animation he would pre-test his silent cartoons in local movie houses before sending them to Winkler and Mintz in New York. This gave him first-hand insight into what audiences liked and didn't like which he used to guide enhancements and improvements. Before investing in the untried process of adding synchronized sound to cartoons, Walt gathered his workers and their wives together to test whether adding sound would sustain the illusion that the characters on the screen were talking. The requirement to create storyboards for each story sequence prior to any animation was also a type of research to identify story weaknesses and invite broader input from more people at an early stage in the production process to improve the experience of the viewing audience.

Walt also tested quality in other ways. He used the Silly Symphonies series to test whether artistic preparedness and technical ability was sufficiently advanced to begin production of *Snow White and the Seven Dwarfs*, or whether more training and development time was needed. He screened incomplete scenes for his artists and asked for their comments on cards as a way to gather additional ideas and improve on the existing content. While those who animated the scenes being shown later expressed mixed feelings about these showings (it was an opportunity for them to show their work, but also could result in additional work if Walt decided changes should be made), it allowed for shared learning and demonstrated respect for the ideas of the rest of the animation staff.

The notion that Walt was a freewheeling creative force uninterested in the discipline of thoughtful planning, which he left in Roy's capable hands, is not true. Walt understood that he needed research and planning to help him achieve his goals. "In fact," writes Disney biographer Bob Thomas, "Walt never entered any project without meticulous planning." If the research showed that the project had promise, Walt would "proceed with planning, which could take months or years. Sketches and models were prepared and carefully analyzed. Everything was mapped out before Walt would signal the go-ahead."[27]

There is a business truism that says, "Failing to plan is planning to fail." A characteristic of successful leaders is their ability to create primary and alternative contingency plans that extend into the future. As a person matures, his or her ability to integrate more information and manage higher degrees of complexity leads to longer planning-time horizons. The greater a person's ability to manage complex information, the greater their capacity for long-range planning and ability to successfully implement multiple projects simultaneously over long-term time horizons while overcoming a myriad of unforeseen problems that arise along the way. Walt demonstrated these characteristics continuously through the many aspects and phases of his career.

As the scope and stakes of projects increased, Walt sought to reinforce and validate his plans with a secondary reliable and objective perspective. As he had to justify his decisions to shareholders and partners, his reliance on third-party economic and planning analysis grew, as did the added value such research and analysis delivered to his own problem solving. Buzz Price cites almost one hundred projects that his firm, Economics Research Associates (ERA), undertook on behalf of Walt and Roy while Walt was alive, which included the entry into television production, development of Disneyland and EPCOT, the creation of theme park attractions including thost at the New York World's Fair, and other investment opportunities such as an indoor theme park at Riverfront Square in St. Louis, a Circarama attraction at Niagara Falls, a ski resort at Mineral King, and the creation of CalArts.

Lessons We Can Learn from Walt Disney's Business Success

- Quality is a reflection of moral integrity. Personal integrity pays dividends.
- Set your standards high and keep thing fresh and clean.
- People appreciate perfectionist quality when they understand that it's done for their benefit.
- Let quality and integrity to your own values, and those of your customers, serve as your guiding compass.
- Trading-off higher quality for lower costs is riskier in the long run than investing in excellence. Quality is an investment in success, not an additional cost.
- "Plus" to improve everything you do.
- Don't give up on good ideas that stall. Put them aside until a later time.
- Create products so good that the public demands them.
- Embrace life-long learning for yourself and make it a requirement for others.
- Be a "fiend" for quality. High quality standards will attract and retain high-quality people.
- Build quality into the production process to be rewarded for the extra effort.
- Demonstrate respect for your customers.
- Use creative tension to push new ideas beyond the comfort zone and explore new boundaries.
- Never begin a major project without meticulous planning.

1. Quoted in Nate Naversen, "Contagious Business Philosophy the 'Disney' Way!" themedattraction.com/disney_way.htm, accessed August 17, 2016.

2. Merritt and Kaufman, *Walt in Wonderland*, 82.

3. Jim Miles, "Lessons of Walt Disney," Jan. 8, 2004, laughingplace.com/news-ID180410.asp, accessed August 17, 2016.

4. Smith, *Walt Disney: Famous Quotes*, 80.

5. Thomas, *Walt Disney*, 9.

6. Thomas, *Building a Company*, 218.

7. Roy O. Disney in Green and Green, *Remembering Walt*, 182.

8. Green & Green, *Remembering Walt*, 69.

9. Merritt & Kaufman, *Walt in Wonderland*, 39–40.

10. Peri, *Working with Walt*, 6.

11. Peri, *Working with Walt*, 5.

12. Gabler, *Walt Disney*, 225.

13. Gabler, *Walt Disney*, 226; Lenburg, *Who's Who in Animated Cartoons*.

14. Thomas, *Walt Disney*, 110–111.

15. Barrier, *The Animated Man*, 87.

16. Barrier, *The Animated Man*, 88.

17. Barrier, *The Animated Man*, 82.

18. Barrier, *The Animated Man*, 88.

19. See Barrier, *The Animated Man*, 92.

20. Berry, *Discovering the Soul of Service*, 30.

21. Gabler, *Walt Disney*, 270.

22. John Hench, *The Language of Vision*, quoted in Gennawey, *The Disneyland Story*, 53.

23. Hench, *Designing Disney*, 78.

24. Hench, *Designing Disney*, 78.

25. Hench, *Designing Disney*, 79.

26. Hench, *Designing Disney*, 79.

27. Thomas, *Building a Company*, 251.

PRINCIPLE FIVE

Anticipate and Exceed Customer Expectations

Walt understood from his earliest days in business that people want their expectations to be exceeded. He despised standing still, and was forever looking for opportunities to innovate and dazzle audiences. Walt's authenticity and honesty, and his ability to introspect and connect with his intellect and his emotions, allowed him to investigate what mattered to consumers based on his understanding that most people hold the same underlying emotions, values, and general expectations.

Walt was driven to innovation in part by his boredom of repetition, and in part by his curiosity about new technology. Mostly, he was driven by his romantic belief that the application of technology could be used for the betterment of mankind, and that the only real constraints are the laws of nature and the limits of imagination. Walt saw it as his role to push the boundaries of human happiness and family entertainment. He believed that these values were deeply embedded in all mankind. For children, the value of maximizing life's enjoyment was bubbling at the surface. Adults, unfortunately, were prone to repressing their natural enthusiasm. Walt wrote his stories and created his movies and theme parks to appeal to both constituencies. Fun could be delivered through humor and entertainment, but the spark to rekindle the flame of childhood wonder in adults was *magic*.

The responsibilities of living and providing for oneself and one's family weigh heavily on most people, and occupy much of their time. The "Disney Touch" was the ability to create—through cartoons and storytelling, and later through the direct interactive experience of Disneyland—a gateway into a magic portal capable of rekindling a sense of wonder in the most jaded of souls, even if only for a brief moment. When people experience that moment of magic, it is so much more than they expect that it can touch them deeply and in ways they don't soon forget.

Such experiences are the basis for creating loyal brand advocates to drive additional and repeat business.

Learning to Adapt, Organize, and Deliver

From Walt's earliest years in animation, he was focused on being the best studio in the business. He studied the work of his New York competitors to learn their methods and benchmark the quality improvements of his studio staff.

When Walt left Kansas City, he chose California over New York because he thought he was too late to make his mark in animation, instead setting his ambition toward being a Hollywood movie producer. His passion was to earn a reputation for creating the best entertainment for audiences, not to be the most famous or the richest.

Following Walt's return to animation with Roy as his partner, Walt wrote, directed, animated, inked, and filmed the animation sequences of *Alice's Day at Sea* and *Alice Hunting in Africa* by himself in the latter part of 1924.[1] He had certainly proven his ability and tenacity to draw in that early environment, in which there was only he and Roy to do all of the work. Timothy Susanin writes in his book *Walt Before Mickey*:

> Walt wrote and directed *Day at Sea* and also "did all the drawings myself...I did—I had no help at all. I was all alone."
>
> The film required a few hundred drawings per day—thousands in all. ... Roy remembered that while "Walt did all the animation...I cranked the old-fashioned camera" used to film the live-action footage.[2]

According to Walt, he and Roy would finish up at their work at the studio, and then go home where "Roy did the cooking while I drew as late as possible every night."[3]

Walt ceased animating in early 1924, after the first few Alice films were completed. He shared the animation work beginning with *Alice's Spooky Adventure* with Rollin "Ham" Hamilton, whom he hired in February 1924. Walt was more interested in producing and directing films, which required the hiring of skilled personnel and organization of resources under his direction and leadership. Ub Iwerks replaced Walt as head animator when Iwerks joined the studio on July 23, 1924. Walt recognized that to provide an improved product and win over audiences and exhibitors, he needed the help of animators with considerably more skill than he himself possessed, and soon took on more animation staff to share the work and increase his production capabilities, among them Thurston Harper, Hugh Harman, and Rudolf Ising.

To compete with the best, you have to aspire to be the best. Walt was always focused on learning and working hard to that end. If he was going to succeed, he would have to learn to inspire, lead, and manage the creativity of others, finding ways for them to excel and take pride in their own work, while at the same time ensuring everyone was working together within an organized structure to create a product consistent with Walt's vision and high standards for quality and entertainment value.

Not everybody was up to that challenge. In the early years, many animators were looking to define their own characters and set up their own studios, just as Walt had done, hoping to cash in on what they thought would be an easy road to fame and fortune. What most of them learned was what Walt had learned, that making money in the animation business wasn't easy because of the need to simultaneously please three constituencies: distributors, movie-house exhibitors, and theatre patrons.

Walt retained final control of the studio's projects to ensure they conformed to his overall vision of story and quality. Different artists perceived this differently. Some described it as Walt's total control, while others looked upon it not as artistic control, but rather as final approval to ensure production coordination and continuity. The perceptions play on the question of how much license artists were given to exercise their creativity. As Friz Freleng noted, in the early silent Alice years, artists had broad discretion to develop scenes based on loosely defined situational outlines; there were no stories per se. Work was then shown to Walt for approval. According to Freleng, who described Walt's guidance and assertion of authority as bullying, "You'd show it to him, and sometimes he liked it and sometimes he didn't."[4]

Freleng quit the Disney Brothers Studio on September 1, 1927, claiming that his personality clashed with Walt. "Walt was just a hard person to work for," said Freleng. "I think a lot of people have said the same thing, you had to please Walt, you couldn't please yourself."[5] Hugh Harman, who encouraged Walt to have Freleng join the team from Kansas City and was part of the Winkler conspiracy against Walt over the Oswald films, sided with Walt when it came to Freleng. "Walt was very generous and kind with him. ... I don't think that [Walt] harassed him in any sense."[6] In fact, Harman indicated that it was the other animators who picked on Freleng relentlessly, to the point of building fires under his chair for laughs "almost every other day."

Nonetheless, Walt himself admitted that he was a tough boss at times, stemming from the relentless pressure of keeping from going under: "I used to be less tolerant in those days because there was more pressure of that payroll and getting that picture out, and I guess I was a pretty tough guy at times. ... I can look back and [realize] I used to get mad and blow my top."[7]

At the Disney studio, says Freleng, "Those people were really doing what they thought Walt would want to do, what Walt wanted to see, and not what *they* wanted to do. If they had a great idea they might tell Walt about it, and he'd say, 'Hey, that's a good one, let's develop it,' or something like that. But they never were on their own."[8] Walt had established and preferred to head a traditional command-and-control structure with the accompanying coordination of work and division of labor.

While Freleng appears to have harbored some animosity toward Walt for the control he perceived Walt to exert over his animators, Freleng's descriptions of how work was done during the studio's silent film years suggests animators were given wide latitude to develop their ideas within confined boundaries to come up with crowd-pleasing scenes. Walt didn't sit over them telling them what and how to animate. To ensure that the studio, which was perpetually suffering from cash-flow issues, was using its scarce resources effectively, Walt held his animators to short time-spans, often checking on their work at the end of each day to ensure that the work they were doing was appropriate and moving along to meet the distribution schedule. Later Walt would hire directors to oversee the shorter-term day-to-day operations of the animators so he could concentrate on managing multiple projects simultaneously and overseeing the longer-term strategic growth of the studio.

Freleng indicates that back in those early years the studios looked upon the cartoon shorts they were producing as throwaway material:

> It was just like newspapers, newsprint—what are you going to save it for? ... The art of animation was just something that you figured wasn't even going to last. ... You never even figured cartoons would ever have sound to them. I mean, they were just movement. The trick in the early days was just to make 'em move.... But you didn't distinguish one from another, they all did it the same. When Walt got into distinguishing one from another by personalities, then it changed the whole thing. ... He was the initiator of that.[9]

The Alice cartoons allowed Walt to establish himself and learn the art of filmmaking, how to run a studio, and most importantly, how to develop pictures that were appealing to audiences. But looking back, he didn't hold the body of work with much regard. "She was terrible," he is quoted as saying in a 1931 magazine article.[10] By the end, costs of production had risen and the studio was losing money on each new Alice release.

In later years, Walt would earn a reputation as being the best storyman in the business, thereby contributing to the enjoyment of Disney cartoons by audiences. But in the 1920s, audiences were enchanted by the magic and novelty of moving drawings themselves, and the general consensus was that people wanted laughs via sight gags, not stories. Walt was often asked by his distributors to provide more and funnier gags, and not get bogged down in story development. As his distributor of Alice Comedies, Margaret Winkler kept pushing for more audience laughs. In one letter to Walt, she wrote, "I would suggest you inject as much humor as you possibly can. Humor is the first requisite of short subjects such as Felix, Out of the Inkwell, and Alice." Walt later writes back, "We are...working for more laughs, leaving out little details of the story and putting in funny gags."[11]

Merritt and Kaufman write that in those early years, "the tyranny of the gag sharply restricted narrative development and characterization."[12]

Mel Shaw, who had worked for Harman and Ising before being hired by Disney in 1937, wrote in his memoir, *Animator on Horseback*,

> In reflection, it became apparent that the difference between working with Hugh and Rudy, and becoming part of Walt's vision for the medium, was found in their basic approach to story development. Hugh and Rudy developed cartoons and situations that were cleverly conjured up by storymen as well as animators. They animated one gag after another. On the other hand, from my first meetings with Walt, I could see that he immediately saw the possibilities of the characters having particular personalities.[13]

The Multiplane Camera as an Example of Customer-Pleasing Innovation

Walt was a master of discovering ways to enhance the customer experience. Improvement through innovation always started with an honest and realistic understanding of the current state, followed by a search for something that would provide greater appeal to consumers.

A major innovation that Walt brought to his craft as he planned and directed *Snow White and the Seven Dwarfs* was the multiplane camera. With few exceptions, animation had always been a two-dimensional process of flat characters on flat backgrounds. Animation in general lacked any feeling of depth. But with Walt's vision and desire to raise the standards of animation in the direction of live-action movies and to create greater realism, a solution to the problem of creating depth in the filming of scenes was desirable.

The solution was to create a camera in which animation cels and backgrounds can be separated by space, allowing each plane an element of independent movement, and a camera capable of zooming in and out, rather than having a fixed focus.

With the idea identified and the search for an innovative solution approved, the head of the studio's camera department, William Garity, developed what he called a "multiplane camera." Holliss and Sibley describe it:

> The multiplane was a huge construction with a number of levels on which could be placed foreground details, characters and backgrounds in order to create an illusion of depth. If the camera was required to move, say, through a forest towards a figure in a clearing, it became possible to remove various components of the picture to left or right as the camera got closer to give the appearance of moving *into* the scene. The multiplane camera was a major breakthrough in assisting the animators to create previously impossible effects.[14]

The possibilities of Disney's multiplane camera were first tested on the Silly Symphony *The Old Mill*, which was really a visual poem more than a story. Walt describes it: "The story was what happened to an old mill at night; nothing more. The first scene showed the old mill at sunset. Cows wandered home. A spider wove her web. Birds nestled. A storm came up and the mill went on a rampage. In the morning, when the cows wandered back, the spider's web was shattered and the birds' feathers were rumpled. The critics said 'poetic,' but the important thing was the proof that I had a feeling of third dimension."[15]

The Old Mill won an Academy Award in 1938 for Best Short Subject, Cartoons. Another was awarded to Disney in the Scientific or Technical category for the design and application of the multiplane camera itself.

Integrity Requires Settling for Perfection

The unfortunate truth is that it's very difficult to satisfy customers. To do so is an immense entrepreneurial and managerial achievement. To have our expectations satisfied—to experience perfection—is something each of us desires. The amount of complaining we do is evidence of this. While the desire to experience perfection may have a certain spiritual dimension, those rare occasions when we do experience it directly can often be attributed to the heroic efforts of individuals, working together, with a commitment to achieve a common result that we highly value.

When it came to the building of Disneyland, Walt was extremely customer-driven. He once said, "Everything I do I keep a practical eye toward its appeal to the public."[16] To be customer-driven, Walt required his artists and designers to seek out improvement opportunities by observing and interacting with guests. Disney Imagineer and author John Hench writes:

> To design most effectively for our guests, we learned that we had to observe them up close, waiting in lines with them, going on rides with them, eating with them. Walt insisted on this by saying, "You guys get down there at least twice a month. For God's sake, don't eat off the lot. Stay there...lunch with the guests...talk to them." This was new to us; as filmmakers, we were used to sitting in our sweatboxes at the studio, passing judgment on our work without knowing how the public might actually respond to it. Going out into the park taught us how guests were being treated and how they responded to sensory information, what worked and what didn't, what their needs were and how we could meet them in entertaining ways. We paid attention to guests' patterns of movement and the ways in which they expressed their emotions. We got an idea of what was going on in their minds.[17]

Perfection is a lofty goal that most people believe to be beyond their reach, so they never strive for it, either in their personal or professional lives. If business executives don't think they can organize and manage to reach a lofty goal, it is almost certain that they won't. Instead, they'll set the bar too low and celebrate their competitively insignificant achievements. Too many organizational leaders appear to subscribe to Woody Allen's humorous dictum that 80% of life is "just showing up." You didn't just show up if you worked for Walt Disney.

As one example of the culture of quality that Walt insisted upon, consider another observation by John Hench:

> I became aware of how radically different Walt's attitude to his customers was when I was loaned to another studio for a special-effects job. I was doing a film title that required an eagle to fly into a lighted foreground and land on a rock while folding his wings. I was provided with an eagle that was too old to do the stunt, and stumbled on the rocks. We watched the dailies in a dark sweatbox. When the lights came on, I saw that one of the studio executives was in the booth watching us. I said, "I'll do this over again. We'll get the eagle to land right, so that it looks like a conqueror." The executive said, "No! We'll use it. That's okay, the bastards won't know any different." That was his attitude toward the people for whom he was supposed to furnish entertainment and amusement. He didn't like them. He didn't care. I have often wondered how many people in business really like their customers.[18]

Consistent with this general cultural malaise and disdain for customers around the issue of quality in production, as consumers we seem to have been conditioned to accept "minimal acceptable effort" as the expected standard. As consumers, we have resigned ourselves to social and cultural mediocrity, and as a result we are disappointingly accepting when that is all we get from the organizations we deal with.

Why as consumers do we accept such low standards of behavior? Primarily because we have been led to believe that it costs more to deliver a better result, and we typically don't want to pay more. To satisfy consumers on the single dimension of price, conventional wisdom has executive managers controlling costs as the preferred way to increase profits, thereby disregarding the expectations and perceptions of customers, and delivering mediocrity.

In too many cases business executives conclude—sometimes correctly—that consumers don't want to pay more for that additional value. As a result, business owners and managers often build mediocrity into their business model, convinced that sound business wisdom calls for increasing profits by foregoing quality. Too often managers are encouraged to reduce costs and maximize efficiency at the micro level when what is needed is to demonstrate increased respect for customers by maximizing value creation for the system as a whole at the macro level.

Walt repudiated such destructive business practices as an economically unsound prescription for mediocrity. He held himself to very high personal standards from the start, recognizing early in his career that the public expected high standards from the Disney brand. He maintained a personal responsibility to the people who made him successful to meet those standards. Later, with regard to Disneyland, he said about the public: "When they come here they're coming because of an integrity that we've established over the years. And they drive hundreds of miles. I feel a responsibility to the public."[19] Walt paid attention to and understood that there was an implicit value equation, a relationship between the perceived value of what was being offered, and the price consumers were willing to pay for acquisition.

Walt demonstrated to anybody in the business world who was paying attention that any cost/benefit equation pointing to the sacrifice of values sought by customers is false. It is wrong on all accounts: moral, economic, and spiritual. As human beings, we pay an inordinately high price for abrogating our responsibility as consumers to set our standards high and reward those entrepreneurs that can best fulfill our pursuit of our own life-affirming values. Walt refused to tolerate employees and vendors who couldn't live up to his expectations and standards. Often these were standards of capability and integrity rather than results, as Walt was often willing to work with others through the discovery process of innovation, even when that entailed significant failures or rework along the way.

Walt's work with Arrow Development in creating and building unique custom-made attractions for Disneyland is an example of how he worked with others to achieve optimal results.

Arrow Development was a small machine shop located near San Francisco, owned by Ed Morgan and Karl Bacon, which came to Disney's attention when WED was seeking attraction manufacturers. Amongst other things, Arrow built playground apparatus and some amusement devices. Robert R. Reynolds, author of *Roller Coasters, Flumes, and Flying Saucers: The Story of Ed Morgan and Karl Bacon*, writes,

> Disneyland would be the catalyst in the transition of Arrow Development from a machine shop that, while an amusement supplier, was still multitasked and willing to take on any work in order to survive, to a full-fledged ride manufacturer. It would also begin a relationship between Arrow and Disney that would last for twenty years. During that period, Arrow Development would be responsible for building almost every ride system to enter Disneyland, and later, Walt Disney World.

The amount of work given to Arrow at the beginning of Disneyland's construction must have been daunting for a small shop. In addition to the Mr. Toad vehicles and track, they were also responsible for the Tea Cup ride, Dumbo the Flying Elephant, King Arthur Carrousel, Casey Jr., and Snow White.[20]

Walt found in the proprietors of Arrow Development two like-minded entrepreneurs who were committed to innovation, flexibility, and top quality, and capable of applying themselves and their organization to overcoming design and engineering obstacles standing between Walt and his dreams. Whatever the challenge and last-minute changes, of which there were many in the development of innovative custom-built attractions, Arrow was able to deliver. Walt recognized the contribution of Arrow Development in the success of Disneyland, and wanted to make sure that the business remained viable to ensure their contribution to Walt's future plans. Ed Morgan and Karl Bacon explained their situation.

> Karl: We had a fixed bid on all the Fantasyland rides. We lost money on every one we did. Walt Disney said after it was all over, "How did you guys come out on the rides?" I told him that we lost money. He said, "I don't want you to lose any money on my work, I'll cover your costs." And he did.

> Ed: He also said, "We couldn't have done it without you boys. What else can I do for you?" We said, "Nothing, it's just been a pleasure to work with you." But we could have probably received a concession such as hats or popcorn. They also gave stock at that time because they were broke. We should have taken stock instead of being paid.[21]

When it came to Disneyland, it wasn't just vendors that had to achieve high standards. Walt had the foresight and audacity to raise the bar on customers themselves. Walt's optimism about the inherent goodwill of people and an understanding of their deeper latent values gave him the courage to create a park that demanded their active participation in his vision to ensure its success.

Consider that few people believed Walt would be able to keep his park clean. Conventional thinking was that people naturally litter, and there's nothing to be done about it except to clean up their mess. Walt didn't believe it. When Walt told his wife he wanted to build an amusement park, her first reaction was that amusement parks were dirty and didn't make money. Walt allegedly replied, "That's the whole point. I want a clean one that will."[22]

During a press tour of the park led by Walt one week after it opened, a reporter predicted that Disneyland staff would never be able to keep the park clean and that it would soon be covered in litter, to which Walt replied that it would stay clean because "people are going to be embarrassed to throw anything on the ground."[23]

In time, Walt's commitment to cleanliness was shared by his guests, and redefined the standard of expectations elsewhere. People went home to ask the question in their own communities and places of patronage: if Disney can do it, why can't we/you? With downtowns decaying across America, and a lack of funding to repair crumbling infrastructure in the 1960s, city planners looked to what Walt had created for inspiration on how to develop cleaner, more functional, and safer downtown districts. Urban planner Sam Gennawey notes, "In many ways, Disneyland helped to save 'downtown' from the wrecking ball and established a higher value for preservation and rehabilitation."[24]

Architect of the Ford Magic Skyway exhibit at the New York World's Fair, Welton Becker, recalled the intense interest that Walt had, not only for what Disney was providing to the exhibit, but also for the surroundings that influenced the total experience of the visitors to the fair. Beckett noted that Walt was concerned people in line wouldn't have something to look at to keep their minds occupied. And he was concerned about the design of the washrooms. "I've never seen a great executive get down and take his coat off and really direct and work as he did on those exhibits," noted Beckett of Walt's enthusiasm and concern for the quality of the total guest experience.[25]

Executive-level concern for identifying and removing what Walt referred to as "contradictions"—which may be intangible to others and unarticulated by customers—and for enticing customers to contribute to the overall experience is a necessary though not sufficient condition for delivering an experience to customers that exceeds their common experience and perhaps even their expectations.

Consumers Pick Entrepreneurial Winners and Losers

Walt worked tirelessly to surpass consumer expectations, to a large degree because he set his own expectations for a minimum threshold exceedingly high. As a result, he invested more money in his business and his products than did his competitors, and, as theme park consultant Nate Naversen puts it, "much more than normal on items that financial-minded people find frivolous."[26]

That's why business success is, in its most fundamental aspects, a marketing endeavor, and not a financial endeavor. The value of Walt Disney Productions and WED was derived from the ideas originating and created in the mind of Walt Disney and his associates. Without Walt's almost intuitive sense of the role marketing must play as the leading force in business, all of Roy's financial skill could never have built the company. Walt was not an exceptionally talented cartoonist, even if he started out with aspirations to become one. He was, however, an intuitive genius when it came to marketing in the widest meaning of the term.

Walt understood that you become successful in business by thinking of great ideas and implementing them to create more value for consumers than they can easily obtain elsewhere. People will exchange money for perceived benefits at a level they judge to be commensurate. Business, at its base, is the art of organizing the means of production around an idea or solution, and trading value for value. Walt recognized that people are inherently excellent judges of value and quick learners. Market prices for goods and services reflect these values. The continuing ebb and flow of the success of Walt Disney's many creations—from cartoon characters, to movies, to theme park attractions and merchandising—always depended on the value that consumers placed on these creations at any point in time.

The Constant Search to Eliminate Value Detractors

To improve the customer experience, Walt didn't just focus on things that worked. He also had to be cognizant of negative factors that detracted from the creation of customer value.

In an article for the *Journal of the Society of Motion Picture Engineers* in 1941, Walt reflected on his perception of the future of the animation business circa 1928:

> The [Oswald] series was going over. We had built up a little organization. ... The cartoon business didn't seem to be going anywhere except in circles. The pictures were kicked out in a hurry and made to price. Money was the only object. Cartoons had become the shabby Cinderella of the picture industry. They were thrown in for nothing as a bonus to exhibitors buying features. I resented that. Some of the possibilities in the cartoon medium had begun to dawn on me. And at the same time we saw that the medium was dying. You could feel rigor mortis setting in. I could feel it in myself. Yet with more money and time, I felt we could make better pictures and shake ourselves out of the rut.[27]

The possibilities Walt envisioned eventually led to the creation of *Snow White and the Seven Dwarfs*. To get there required continuous innovation to capitalize on the possibilities while attracting audience interest. Walt had to slowly bring his staff, the public, and the industry around to supporting his vision for the development of more elaborate and entertaining animation. To succeed, he had to remove the barriers that stood in his way.

Other examples of Walt assessing and eliminating value detractors is evident in the addition and closure of attractions at Disneyland. Just after Disneyland opened, Walt added a number of attractions, including a circus with live animals. He also insisted on a parade down Main Street, like he remembered from his youthful days in Kansas City. Included in the parade was an old calliope restored to working order followed by restored old circus carts with circus animals. Walt found that the circus usually played to a half-full tent and that circus culture conflicted with the wholesomeness he was trying to portray in the park and so he got rid of it in less than two months (November 11, 1955, to January 8, 1956). He added puppet shows, but soon learned that people came to see what was unique about Disneyland, and weren't that interested in more traditional attractions.[28]

When customers didn't find attractions worth their time, Walt was quick to remove and replace them with another idea.

Walt was also of the mind that the under-delivery of value as perceived by customers was much more risky than over-delivery of value, be it quality, design, service, or the total guest experience. In financial terms, this translated to the notion that under-capitalization of a project was much more risky than spending "too much," although both can be dangerous if the return on investment doesn't materialize.

One of the difficulties of entrepreneurship is tracking consumer values to know when they change and to correctly anticipate how best to adapt one's offerings to cope. Walt accepted that progress was inevitable. Instead of fighting it, as did many of his competitors and other business executives, Walt constantly sought new technological innovations and thinking about how to leverage what consumers might soon enjoy in an effort to stay ahead of the changing demand curve. "You don't build it for yourself," Walt once said. "You know what the people want and you build it for them."[29]

According to Buzz Price, "Early on, the park installed an extensive interviewing program to measure visitor reactions, satisfactions, complaints, suggestions, and demographic makeup. This was a new idea in the industry."[30] Walt didn't presume to know what was best for customers. He was prepared to experiment and quickly adapt. At Disneyland, the standard of success was always established and measured by the happiness of the guests.

Walt was asked about the evolution of technology in his business during a Canadian Broadcast Corporation television interview in 1960, by interviewer Stan Hellenk:

> STAN: Has the evolution been a difficult thing? You foresaw that things were going to take a different track. For example, the development of television. You figured, "Well, this is inevitable and I must get into it."

> WALT: Yes, television will, in time, I think, become more or less an extension of the theater screen. I think there will always be things that are, say, perfect on television but could never compete on a motion-picture screen. In other words, the quality of the picture—the definition and things—I don't think will ever equal that of a good high-class movie theater. But it's another way of reaching the

people, another way of entertaining the people. I welcomed it. You can't fight these things. I learned that a long time ago. It's progress. You can sit back and try to fight it but it's stupid. I think, "Go with it."[31]

Lessons We Can Learn from Walt Disney's Business Success

- People want their expectations to be exceeded. Give them the magical moments they desire.

- People will reward with loyalty those who can consistently create experiences that exceed their expectations.

- Always keep a practical eye toward appealing to the public (or target audience).

- Seek out improvement opportunities by observing and interacting with your customers and the public. Find out what's going on in their minds.

- Pay attention to, and understand, customer perceptions of the relationship between value and price, and what it may mean for your business model.

- An honest exchange of values through trade is a moral, economic, and spiritual imperative.

- Demand more from you customers. Help them participate as partners in the value-creation process.

- Demand more from your organization to ensure they are creating happy customers. Pay attention to what your customers don't like and fix it.

- Help customers transact business and gain the values they want, the way they want. Don't confuse what's best for you with what customers think is best for themselves.

- It's riskier to under-deliver and fail to meet customer expectations than to over-deliver and exceed customer expectations.

- Don't fight progress. Go with it!

1. Merritt & Kaufman, *Walt In Wonderland*, 127–128.

2. Susanin, *Walt Before Mickey*, 92.

3. Susanin, *Walt Before Mickey*, 93.

4. Ghez, *Walt's People: Volume 2*, 23.

5. Susanin, *Walt Before Mickey*, 162.

6. Susanin, *Walt Before Mickey*, 163.

7. Susanin, *Walt Before Mickey*, 163.

8. Ghez, *Walt's People: Volume 2*, 27.

9. Ghez, *Walt's People: Volume 2*, 29–30.

10. Susanin, *Walt Before Mickey*, 160.

11. Merritt and Kaufman, *Walt in Wonderland*, 15–16.

12. Merritt and Kaufman, *Walt In Wonderland*, 16.

13. Shaw, *Animator on Horseback*, 93.

14. Holliss and Sibley, *Walt Disney's Snow White and the Seven Dwarfs*, 26.

15. Holliss and Sibley, *Walt Disney's Snow White and the Seven Dwarfs*, 26.

16. Smith, *Walt Disney: Famous Quotes*, 29.

17. Hench, *Designing Disney: Imagineering and the Art of the Show*, 21.

18. Hench, *Designing Disney*, 20.

19. *Walt Disney: Famous Quotes*, 65.

20. Reynolds, *Roller Coaster, Flumes, and Flying Saucers*, eBook loc. 375.

21. Reynolds, *Roller Coasters, Flumes, and Flying Saucers*, Loc. 495.

22. Gennawey, *Walt Disney and the Promise of Progress City*, 79.

23. Gabler, *Walt Disney*, 529.

24. Gennawey, *Walt Disney and the Promise of Progress City*, 81.

25. Barrier, *The Animated Man*, 293.

26. Naversen, "Contagious Business Philosophy the 'Disney' Way!", themedattraction.com/disney_way.htm.

27. Susanin, *Walt Before Mickey*, 166.

28. Thomas, *Building A Company*, 201–202; "Mickey Mouse Club Circus," davelandweb.com/mmcc/, accessed November 8, 2016; YouTube, "Extinct Attractions: Disneyland 1955 Circus," youtube.com/watch?v=dfrHyPoflyI, accessed November 8, 2016.

29. Smith, *The Quotable Walt Disney*, 255.

30. Price, *Walt's Revolution!*, 35.

31. Interview with Stan Hellenk, in *Walt Disney: Conversations*, 78.

Create Valued Experiences Through Business Design and Innovation

Walt Disney took great pride in thinking carefully about the best way to achieve the results he desired. He was a leader in developing and implementing innovative and often risky ideas, and was open to considering the best ideas in the context of a result he desired or problem to be solved. As an artist working with artists, design elements were always important to Walt and can be seen clearly in his films and parks. Design was an integral aspect of storytelling and creating consumer appeal.

Over a period of a few years in the early 1950s, the concept for Disneyland developed from a small park where tourists could meet Mickey Mouse to an interactive guest experience premised on bringing the beloved Disney stories to life. The challenge was given to artists with film and storytelling experience, not to architects and engineers with little or no experience in the kinds of aesthetics Walt was seeking. What evolved from Walt's unique need was a new discipline that didn't yet exist, one that could combine imagination, architecture, engineering, and artistic and environmental design to deliver a unique interactive and immersive entertainment experience.

Walt thought about the design of Disneyland through the lens of his own expertise in which the entire park would be a theatrical experience. By controlling and manipulating the entire environment, Walt could tap into deep-seated human values and emotions to positively affect behavior. Disneyland wasn't built *for* this purpose, but it was consciously designed *into* Disneyland's purpose, as an underlying premise and experimental element.

Karal Ann Marling, in her essay "Imagineering The Disney Theme Parks," observes of Walt:

> [A]s an entertainer, a creator of comic characters, a teller of fairy-tale fables meant to resolve the conflicts encountered in the world of toil and trouble, he did not believe for a moment that art—his art, the

picture-postcard kind—was obliged to be disturbing, challenging, unsettling. He believed instead that it ought to provide comfort and refuge from that world of woes he knew at first hand. His park was built behind a berm to protect it from the evils that daily beset humankind on all sides. It aimed to soothe and reassure. It aimed to give pleasure. Joy. A flash of sunny happiness. The small, sweet, ordinary, domestic emotions seldom implicit in the definition of aesthetic pleasure. The architecture of reassurance.[1]

The key to Walt's approach to any kind of design was to consider the environment that was being created for people. Walt had one overriding instruction for his WED staff charged with research, development, design, and engineering of attractions. According to Imagineer Marvin Davis, Walt instructed his staff: "All I want you to think about is when people walk or ride through anything you design, I want them to have smiles on their faces when they leave. Just remember that and that's all I ask you."[2]

Marling reminds the reader that at the time, "Disneyland was clearly a countercultural artifact"[3] in that it was a work of art that was meant to elicit happiness in a post-war culture of nihilism, moral skepticism, and the fear of a cold-war nuclear policy of mutually assured destruction:

[I]n marked distinction to Los Angeles in 1955, the buildings of Disneyland were meant to be seen at close hand by pedestrians, whose cars had been consigned to a distant parking lot, forgotten for the day behind a tall earthen wall. Disneyland was pretty. Blatant competition between store and store was banished. The scale of the place was homelike, as unlike the corporate skyscraper and the hulking mall as could be imagined. If the product being sold at Disneyland is not really shoes or soap or civic betterment but contentment and pleasure, there might be profit, too, in unmasking the faults of urban America—its dullness, tawdriness, confusion, its overbearing swagger. And substituting harmony, mild adventure, safety, and order—the order of art; the art of reassurance; the architecture of Disneyland.[4]

Designing for Visual Literacy

In studying the works of the new breed of urban planners, Walt discovered confirmation for his conclusion that environments affect behavior. This wasn't a new insight. The challenge Walt faced in building the self-proclaimed "happiest place on earth" was in the thoughtful creation of an environment with a degree of harmonious elements so powerful as to manipulate human emotions toward the requisitely positive: benevolence, friendliness, happiness, courage, wonder, pride. At the same time, the removal of the negative was also required to eliminate confusion, intimidation, confrontation, boredom, tiredness, anger, and feelings of isolation.

Walt put forth considerable effort to design his interactive environments so that they would have instant appeal to visitors. He wanted visitors to Disneyland to encounter a world set apart from their everyday concerns, where they could leave their troubles behind and experience a deeper level of enjoyment and relaxation. "I don't want the public to see the world they live in while they're in Disneyland," he said, "I want them to feel they're in another world."[5]

For many aspects of the park, designers were asked to do extensive research, often requiring travel throughout the United States and overseas, to identify design ideas like the most effective way to manage crowd flow or engage people standing in line, and find specific items for the park, such as gas lamps, door knobs, store fixtures, or period antiques. As an example of his quest for authenticity, Walt funded research to gather hundreds of photos and drawings of the details of railway stations built in the 19th century for study to give design authenticity to the main railway station at Disneyland.[6]

For Walt and many of his WED staff, the designing of Disneyland and later projects was a passionate international quest for knowledge driven by Walt's grand vision to build environments that create and deliver human happiness.

John Hench, who played an integral role in designing Disneyland, wrote that Walt "wanted Disneyland to be a place where adults and children could experience together some of the wonders of life and adventure, and feel better because of it."[7]

According to Hench, every aspect of Disneyland was purposefully planned to deliver an emotional experience using architecture and design as its central building block. Disneyland, said Hench,

> tried to present an undilutedly rosy view of the world; contradiction or confusion were qualities the planners of Disneyland associated with the defective, poorly planned, conventional amusement park. … Disneyland offered an enriched version of the real world, but not an escapist or an unreal version. We program out all the negative, unwanted elements and program in the positive elements. We've taken and purified the statement so it says what it was intended to.[8]

Reflecting back on his development work, Hench notes that the removal of visual clutter that creates visual contradictions also removes mixed messages and feelings of uneasiness and uncertainty that can create tension, stress, and even fear. "[Walt] understood people enough to know," said Hench, "that you don't give them problems to think about, but something to feel good about."[9] Further, said Hench, "Walt wanted all the details to be correct. What it amounted to was a kind of visual literacy."[10] Walt noted that Disneyland was in part built as a physical space to stimulate the imagination "and above all, a sense of strength, contentment, and well-being."[11] Walt's goal was to create a language of design by embracing a wider domain of detail that went beyond just architecture to immerse guests in an enhanced positive experience.

Walt viewed the physical design and layout of Disneyland in terms of movie principles, as if it was a permanent movie set. Each part of the park was to have its own authenticity and character that had to be protected and kept pure at all costs to preserve the illusion of the show. Attractions were to be thought of as movie experiences to guide their design, with the guest physically passing through scenes. The good, in the form of courage and cunning, was always to win out over evil and the abuse of power.

Passing from one area of the park to another, said Hench, was designed as a "kind of live action cross dissolve" where one scene slowly fades out while the next slowly fades in. "He would insist on changing the texture of the pavement at the threshold of each new land because, he said, 'You can get information about a changing environment through the soles of your feet.'"

Underground corridors were built with hidden entrances so that staff could appear and disappear without having to walk through areas of the park where their uniforms would introduce a contradiction to the guest experience.

Disneyland was designed and executed to be as much a state of mind as an amusement park, to evoke community among strangers, to inspire and lift the human spirit above the mundane and toward fun, imagination, and possibility. "What we are selling is not escapism but reassurance," noted Hench.[12]

The emotional response the public experienced at Disneyland was genuine. "I was fascinated and intrigued," writes Hench, "by the way Disneyland *would* make adults and children feel better for having used their imaginations while visiting the park, so that they would leave feeling more self-assured, stronger, alert, and much more alive."[13]

Harmonizing for Happiness

A result of Walt's attention to design detail at Disneyland was that things were often made to appear more real and authentic than the real thing being portrayed. The simulated age and beauty of turn-of-the-twentieth-century Main Street brought forth emotions of nostalgia and confidence. Marling writes: "The old-fashioned storefronts enhanced the prestige of the businesses inside and gave customers the confidence to shop in an unfamiliar setting. ... Main Street was a strip mall all dressed up in scintillating Victorian costume that made the products you shopped for at home—film, pianos, bathing suits, even real estate and shoes and lingerie in 1955—seem intriguing all over again."[14]

The ground floor of the buildings on Main Street are almost life-size, while the scale of the upper floors change with the altitude, creating the illusion of height in a more compact area. This use of forced-perspective allows the street to maintain its beauty and charm while removing the intimidation and shadows of a canyon-like street scene, allowing more sunlight and blue sky than would be the case if the street was authentic.

Building this way was more expensive, as Walt noted: "This costs more, but made the street a toy, and the imagination can play more freely with a toy."[15]

Walt was able to achieve the unprecedented guest response he desired by paying attention to a myriad of meaningful details that other business leaders were prone to overlook or ignore. What makes the show work, writes Hench, "is the sum total of all the thousands of little details of which the guests are never quite fully aware...details working at the subliminal level."[16] This multi-dimensional attention to detail was integral to creating a valuable and unique personal experience for each visiting guest and family.

Hench provides some insight into the precarious balance required to make it all work and the Imagineering success formula in a 1975 Walt Disney World employee handbook:

> What we create is a "Disney Realism," sort of Utopian in nature, where we carefully program out all the negative, unwanted elements and program in the positive elements. In fact we even go beyond realism in some cases to make a better show. Don't forget, people are coming here to be entertained...it is a show, you know. We create a world they can escape to...to enjoy for a few brief moments...a world that is the way they would like to think it would be.
>
> Interestingly, for all its success, the Disney theme show is quite a fragile thing. It just takes one contradiction...one out-of-place stimulus to negate a particular moment's experience. Take that street car conductors costume away and put him in double-knit slacks and a golf shirt...replace that old Gay Nineties melody with a rock number... replace the themed merchandise with digital clock radios and electric hair dryers...tack up a felt-tip drawn paper sign that says "Keep Out"...place a touch of AstroTurf here...and a surly employee there... it really doesn't take much to upset it all.
>
> What's our success formula? Well, it's attention to infinite detail...the little things, the minor picky points that other companies just don't want to take the time, the money, the effort, to do right. As far as our Disney organization is concerned...it's the only way we've ever done it...it's been our success formula in the past and it will be applied to our future projects, as well. We'll probably still be explaining this to outsiders at the end of our next two decades in this business.[17]

After Disneyland opened, Walt made it part of his routine to take an early Saturday morning walk through the park in earnest with about a half-dozen of his key people to scrutinize park operations. Walt would be looking for things that he didn't like and needed to be fixed as well as new ideas that would result in park improvements for the benefit of guests. Walt's staff would take notes and photographs, and then over the next few days work on ideas for modifications in the form of drawings. Walt would review them and indicate where he wanted changes or how to expand the ideas into something more effective.[18]

Rethinking Conventional Rules

Prior to Disneyland, there was an established paradigm for designing an amusement park. As a general rule, parks were set out in a grid, allowing maximum access from four directions. They were built to attract attention, so creating maximum visibility was important. In thinking about Disneyland and how to improve the experience for visitors, Walt had to rethink the conventional rules. The existing established conventions produced results he abhorred. Following them would have led Walt to the same unsatisfactory results.

Walt was an optimist and operated with beliefs and values that provided him with a genuinely benevolent sense of life—a conviction that the world is open and receptive to human efforts to remove barriers and reward actions that result in the improvement of our well-being. He believed that the vast majority of people are good, fair, and honest, and held the same common-sense life-affirming values that he did. When people were disappointed the most, it was because their expectations failed to be met due to a lack of imagination, creativity, and mental effort on the part of product and service providers. Too many business proprietors took their customers for granted, or worse, held them in contempt and treated them in an unfair, unjust, disrespectful, and sometimes demeaning manner.

From Walt's perspective, the first place to look when people are behaving badly is the environment in which they find themselves. By identifying and creating trust-inducing environments, he hoped to facilitate and encourage positive behavior. He believed that if you demonstrate respect *for* people by building environments that were respectful *of* people, they would reciprocate that respect with appropriate benevolent behavior that was good for business.

The conventional view amongst amusement park industry operators was to assume people were seeking opportunities to act out anti-socially in ways harmful to the proprietors and others, and therefore any show of respect toward customers would be wasted. Recall the advice of the leading park owners to Walt: don't provide customized rides because the public won't know the difference, they don't care, and worse, they will vandalize them no matter what you do; and don't bother with things like the castle and a horse-pulled trolley on Main Street or the fancy landscaping and authenticity of design because they don't generate any income and the customers won't really notice, so there is no reason to build and maintain them.

The prevailing wisdom of showing disrespect to customers, and people in general, was built right into the amusement park industry business model, and so no attempt was made by park owners and managers to strive for improvements. Instead, customer disrespect became a cynical excuse to exploit the "local yokels" and tourists who come to fairgrounds to satisfy their primal urge for sensual stimulation, danger, and an adrenalin rush. The challenge for the amusement park owner and carny was to separate as much money from the "marks" by any means and as quickly as possible. Designing a better environment was seen as harmful to their "proven" business model and thus a waste of time and effort.

Walt was convinced that he could use design principles and psychology to overturn convention and appeal directly to the best in people, and by doing so create a uniquely positive entertainment experience that families would find emotionally rewarding and for which they would be happy to pay more. Seen this way, Disneyland was just another extension of Walt's artistic dedication to lifting the human spirit and the human potential.

Another way in which Walt rethought conventional rules was to apply what he had learned in his study of modern urban planning techniques to produce healthier human environments. To create the relaxing and refreshing guest experience he sought, Walt sought to design a park where the maximum number of operational and maintenance elements experienced by guests could be controlled, hidden, or eliminated altogether. Walt worked backwards during the planning stage to develop innovative design solutions that would maintain the purity of the show.

One of the ingenious, paradigm-shifting solutions incorporated in Orlando was to build the park on the second floor of a two-story structure, thereby using design innovation to achieve a more unique and fully immersed guest experience. By building the park this way, writes Nate Naversen,

> Disney can quickly whisk supplies in and out of the park from below without having to bring a truck through the front gates. In medical emergencies, heart attack victims may be quickly taken off stage to a medical facility without disturbing most guests. ... Trash may be placed in an underground vacuum network at dozens of locations around the park, where it may be quickly vacuumed to a central receiving area, saving time and energy for custodial people. Lastly, cast members in costume can walk straight into their themed land without having to walk through another land.[19]

Walt's design innovations such as underground utility corridors, vacuum garbage disposal technology, and unique custom attractions and transportation systems added significant upfront capital investment for infrastructure. In return Walt was able to create an unprecedented positive guest experience that was critical to winning the endorsement of the public and justifying the investment and long-term payback.

Searching, Finding, and Learning from Best Practices

If you are going to create valued experiences, you have to understand the expectations of actual and potential customers and design processes, policies, and procedures to deliver on those expectations. Starting Disneyland from scratch as a greenfield project allowed Walt to avoid the complication of changing pre-existing embedded processes, habits, and corporate culture, and overcoming organizational inertia and employee resistance to change.

Walt made it a cornerstone of his ideation process to acquire knowledge of the current state of the industry and inspiration from the best available information. As the park was being built, Walt had to begin thinking about not just building the park, but how to operate it on a day-to-day basis. To gain a deeper understanding of what was going on in the amusement industry around the country, gather more detailed operational data, and establish benchmarks for business performance, Walt tasked SRI and his own WED staff in 1954 with visiting parks all over the country to gain first-hand observations of their operations and gather competitive intelligence. Harper Goff recalls: "Walt sent us all around to every amusement park in the country. We would take pictures and come back and tell Walt all about what they were doing. One of the main things we tried to get was their 'gate'...how much they charged, how many people came through, and how much they made. Also what kinds of operating problems they had, such as dishonesty."[20]

Best-practices research wasn't limited to amusement parks. Staff visited every kind of tourist attraction to gather ideas. They visited New York's Fifth Avenue where they measured from building line to curb, the Mall in Washington D.C., and the French Quarter in New Orleans. They visited themed restaurants and museums such as Chicago's Museum of Science and Industry, and reported back to Walt on five features of note including corporate sponsorships of flashy industrial exhibits, a General Motors sponsored "Yesterday's Main Street" circa 1900 with a real cobblestone street and gaslights, a moving sidewalk, a fairy castle doll-house exhibit, and a scaled-down Santa Fe train.[21]

Disney historian Michael Barrier notes, "Disney had an advantage in that his people were visiting more attractions, and scrutinizing them more carefully, than any operator preoccupied with his own business could hope to do."[22] By studying the operational methods and business designs of others attempting to do similar things, Walt was able to gain insight and pre-emptively apply his critical thinking to potential problems and solutions.

Designing Happiness Processes, Policies, and Procedures

Not only were landscapes, attractions, and facilities carefully designed and crafted to reflect their function, so were business processes, policies, and procedures.

Deliberate behaviors are required by staff to produce consistently reliable guest experiences and results, with little being left to chance. Attention to process detail is just as important to creating service quality excellence as it is to creating product quality excellence. As a result, policies for staff were established, some of which prohibited them from doing specific things while "on stage." For example, guests should never see cast members eating, drinking, smoking, sleeping, sitting down, chewing gum, leaning against a wall or railing, or folding his or her arms.

"Does this seem extreme?" asks theme park industry consultant Nate Naversen. "Of course it does. But when it comes to customer service, it makes perfect sense. Imagine how a potential guest would feel when walk-ing up to a cast member doing one of the above no-nos. Making sure the cast-member is courteous and efficient is key while 'onstage' at a Disney theme park. It helps create a positive guest experience whenever a guest interacts with an employee."[23]

Dedicating a company to the creation of customer happiness and pub-lically declaring a park to be the happiest place on earth requires the establishment and maintenance of extremely high standards that cus-tomers have come to expect from the Disney brand. Walt set for himself and his staff an immense responsibility, the achievement of which was, and continues to be, no easy task. For Walt, every interaction between cast members and guests—every "moment of truth"—mattered, and there-fore each had to be carefully thought out, planned, and trained for. Guest experiences were observed to ensure the desired outcomes were achieved. If not, then some specific aspect of the park design, business processes, or staff training was inadequate and had to be refined. Walt knew that to create the guest experience he wanted, nothing pertaining to the work that needed to be done could be left to chance—that staff would perform best when their roles were scripted, as if playing a part in a performance.

To achieve the high level of guest experience desired, Walt needed a staff training program. C.V. Wood hired Van Arsdale France for the job.

According to France, Walt was clear that people with previous amusement park experience were not to be hired as Disneyland employees because they would bring with them the wrong mindset. Walt's solution was to start from the ground up to define and develop a new breed of "show people" educated and trained in the Disney Way. As summarized by Steve Mannheim in *Walt Disney and the Quest for Community*, "Employees were taught the official Disneyland terms, such as guests, hosts/hostesses, audience, attractions, security officers, and costume. The following terms did not exist within the berm: customer, employee, crowd, rides, guard, and uniform. When dealing with the public, a cast member was 'onstage' and playing a 'role.' Disney also insisted that the organization operate on a first-name basis."[24]

As part of the training program for new staff, France created a booklet in 1955 titled "Your Disneyland: A Guide for Hosts and Hostesses." The guide, writes Mannheim, "outlines many of the original park guidelines."

> For example, "The Disneyland Look" consisted of natural-looking cosmetics, neat hair, clean hands and nails, shined shoes, a clean costume, and a fresh shave for men. Moreover, employees were instructed to "try a smile," use courtesy words, and "treat any question as if it were the most important thing in the world." ... There were also "Disneyland Taboos," like on-the-job consumption of alcoholic beverages. Finally, the guide states that teamwork is "essential."[25]

As with his movie stories and scenes, every sensory experience at Disneyland was subject to Walt's "customer delight" philosophy because it was all part of the total Disney experience, from fragrances and smells, to music, to the texture of the pathways. Even the process of parking cars at Disneyland was subject to Walt's scrutiny. Here Walt provides some insight into his total quality philosophy, noting:

> The first year (of Disneyland) I leased out the parking concession, brought in the usual security guards—things like that—but soon realized my mistake. I couldn't have outside help and still get over my idea of hospitality. So now we recruit and train every one of our employees. I tell the security police, for instance, that they are never to consider themselves cops. They are there to help people. The visitors are our guests. It's like running a fine restaurant. Once you get the policy going, it grows."[26]

When customer delight is your stated objective, the best business processes are those that customers themselves experience as right and reasonable. But they also have to make sense from the perspective of the employees who have to carry them out. Well-designed business policies create boundaries of accountability for employees and make their work personally meaningful. They provide guidance, a sense of purpose, and a standard by which to measure achievement and earn a sense of pride.

Every attraction at a Disney theme park has a multi-page description and explanation of the philosophy of the attraction so that cast members understand the context of their "performance." At Disneyland, employees aren't hired to just show up and hustle people on and off attractions like carnival midway ride jockeys. They are hired to perform a specific role in relation to achieving a defined, measurable end result, which includes making a positive contribution to the total guest experience throughout their visit and maintaining the magic.

To keep the park clean, all staff is required to pick up trash they see, even though street cleaners and custodial staff are hired to do this on a full-time basis. Given that these folks are the most visible and accessible to guests, they receive the greatest number of questions about the park and directions. As a result, they receive extra inter-personal skills training, and their primary job is to provide friendly service to guests. While they may appear to have a low job on the totem pole, they play a critical role in the overall guest experience; therefore, extra effort is made to prevent park guests from experiencing a "don't-ask-me-it's-not-my-job" attitude. Their secondary job is to clean up the trash.

Shortly after the park opened, a reporter checked up on Walt's claim about litter, and wrote that on average a discarded cigarette butt would be picked up and discarded in just twenty-five seconds.[27]

Walt was a leader and innovator in service delivery because he understood the importance of designing the guest experience into the product or service to create maximum value. He did it in his films, and he did it in his parks. In his own simple way, Walt was a marketing maverick because of his laser-like intuitive focus on giving customers what they wanted, even if they didn't know they wanted it at the time.

In the Safe Hands of Disney Daycare

To the public, Disneyland was some kind of new-fangled amusement park, and the reputation of amusement parks was not good. They were seen as unsafe and potentially dangerous. In the selling of Disneyland, Walt knew he had to change that perception. To help reinforce the message of safe family fun, early promotional material noted that forty-five full-time security officers would be on hand.[28]

In addition, the architecture of Disneyland was designed to entertain, sooth, and reassure guests. Almost everything was scaled down from full size to make it appear more toy-like and less imposing. An admission charge was implemented as a barrier against riff-raff. These features, notes Michael Barrier in *The Animated Man*, reinforced the message that Disneyland is safe "by subtly imposing calm and order on an environment, the amusement park, that can be coarse and chaotic. As Walt Disney knew, such landscaping is anything but a cosmetic garnish—it encourages people to behave better."[29]

The focus and feeling of safety and security portrayed through Disneyland's compelling architecture and environmental engineering resulted in an unexpected phenomenon during summer months.

Disneyland's first president, Jack Lindquist, writes in his memoir *In Service to the Mouse* that he noticed in the early days of the park many women would arrive in the summertime with small children aged six to ten, purchase admission tickets, and drop off the children. Lindquist writes:

> We started seeing the same people doing this day after day: buying tickets and dropping off their children.
>
> So I said, "Let's follow them and see what the kids do all day."
>
> They saw all the free shows, watched the band march down Main Street, and went to the Golden Horseshoe Revue, a western stage show in Frontierland. They did everything they could do for free. At lunchtime, they bought a hamburger or a hot dog and a soda at Carnation and would sit there to eat. They then wandered around the park until around five in the evening. At that time, they'd go outside the park and wait to be picked up by their mothers.
>
> We talked to some of these people and found that, for the most part, they were single moms. One woman told me, "I cannot afford a good babysitter. I wouldn't trust my kids with a babysitter I can afford, but for $5 a day, and $1.50 for food, I feel perfectly safe leaving my kids here."
>
> That was quite a statement about Disneyland.
>
> For less than $35 a week, from nine in the morning to around six at night, these kids stayed at Disneyland. And these kids were happy.[30]

Disneyland had earned an untarnished reputation for being clean and safe, so safe that mothers were willing to entrust their children to the park's care without further adult supervision. This was long before the days of easy and instant electronic communications through cell phones and instant messaging.

Urban planner and Disney historian Sam Gennawey confesses that he was one of those children. At that time there was a price for park admission and an additional price for the main attractions, but many of the park's attractions were free with admission, and among them was his favorite, the Carousel of Progress. When the Audio-Animatronics show was over, guests would make their way up the exit ramp and to a 115-foot diorama with a minutely detailed working model of EPCOT's Progress City. Gennawey recalls his amazement at the model: "I would listen to the narration as it promised that living in Progress City would mean a great, big, beautiful tomorrow where we would all lead rich and rewarding lives. It sounded wonderful, and I wanted to know more. What would life be like in Progress City? Was the project even possible? When can I visit?"[31]

Thanks to Walt, Disneyland was designed to be educational, inspirational, safe, and comforting to children, mothers, and millions of visitors.

The Importance of Organizational Design

One other area worthy of consideration is the design of Walt's organizations themselves, which evolved from a simple two-person operation in 1923 into a global, multi-faceted, multi-dimensional, exchange-listed organization.

Walt said he didn't like organization charts because as the head of the studio he felt the need and desire to talk to anybody at any time and to assign tasks without interference by others based on his best judgment. From the earliest days there was always organization because there was always process. In the beginning Walt was the animator and storyman, and Roy was business manager and cameraman. As the volume of work grew, others were hired to assume specific roles suited to their skill, knowledge, and ambition. Work processes were developed to ensure the efficient use of resources in the creation of films and the administration of the business. As new technologies were adopted, new skills were acquired and developed, and processes and workflows were worked out, adapted, and refined.

From the time he was CEO of Laugh-O-grams in Kansas City, Walt had ideas about how he wanted to run his organization which he refined over the years out of necessity and in response to changing business conditions and social environments.

As the business grew, the creation of new products increasingly required coordination of resources. Walt saw this as his role. He knew from his early experiments in animation back in Kansas City that he could delegate the animation elements and still produce a superior product. He also learned that the value-added aspects of the business resided in developing, managing, and delivering a product that audiences would find engaging enough to justify premium pricing. Reflecting back in 1959 to his early experiences, Walt recalled,

> And with some of the boys I'd worked with in Kansas City augmenting the set-up, I was able to eventually build an organization. And it reached a point that I had so many working with me, and there was so much time and attention demanded that I had to drop the drawing end of it myself. But I've never regretted it, because the drawing was always a means to an end with me. And so through these other boys, who were good draftsmen and artists in many different phases of the business...very talented people—and coordinating their talents

is what has built this business. And if I hadn't dropped the drawing end of it myself, I don't think I'd have built this organization.[32]

Following the phenomenal box office success of *Snow White*, at a time when Walt was overly enthusiastic and optimistic, he was asked by an interviewer in 1938, "How do you do it?" He responded:

> We're an organization of young men. We have licked every mechanical difficulty which our medium presented. We don't have to answer to anyone. We don't have to make profits for stockholders. New York investors can't tell us what kind of pictures they want us to make or hold back. I get the boys together and we decide what we want to do next. Now it's my ambition to set up the organization so that it will belong to the people in it. The revenue from *Snow White* gives us a chance to go ahead."[33]

Walt was cognizant of and attentive to the importance of organizational design and having a structure, workflow, and division of labor for effectively applying resources, achieving goals, and providing for the creative needs of his staff. Just as Walt was a proponent of learning by trial and error and accepting of the costs inherent in failure as an investment in future improvements, the same was true in the creation of an effective business operation. He was learning over time what was more or less effective. He noted in *Newsweek* in 1962, "I saw very early in the business one thing—that organization was where you had to put the emphasis. ... You have to break things down, specialize."[34]

He took great pride in attributing the success of the studio, including having won twenty-nine Oscars, to the quality of the organization he built and the dedicated work of his staff. Walt was asked in a 1963 CBC interview what had been his greatest reward to date. He responded, "Well, my greatest reward, I think, is that I've been able to build this wonderful organization...and also to have the public appreciate and accept what I've done all these years. That is a great reward."[35]

Lessons We Can Learn from Walt Disney's Business Success

- Use design elements to tap into human values and emotions to positively affect behavior.
- Use design to make a statement.
- Remove clutter and contradictions. Program out the negative and program in the positive.
- Don't give customers problems to think about; give them something to feel good about.

- Pay attention to the little things that other companies don't make the effort to do right.

- Seek ways to shift the paradigm and redefine the business model away from conventional or entrenched thinking.

- Understand and gain insight into critical aspects of your business and marketplace dynamics through competitive research and business intelligence.

- Create training programs and guidelines for employees so they think about and do things to achieve the desired results.

- Eliminate policies and procedures that disrespect customers and embarrass employees.

- Create boundaries of accountability for employees and find ways to make their work challenging and personally meaningful.

---

1. Marling, *Designing Disney's Theme Parks*, 83.

2. Green and Green, *Remembering Walt*, 156; also Marling, *Designing Disney's Theme Parks*, 83.

3. Marling, *Designing Disney's Theme Parks*, 85.

4. Marling, *Designing Disney's Theme Parks*, 85–86.

5. Walt quoted in Holliss & Sibley, *The Disney Studio Story*, 68.

6. Thomas, *Walt Disney*, 12.

7. Hench, *Designing Disney*, 1.

8. Hench quoted in Gennawey, *Walt Disney and the Promise of Progress City*, 66.

9. Hench in Green and Green, *Remembering Walt*, 102.

10. Hench quoted in Gennawey, *Walt Disney and the Promise of Progress City*, 65.

11. Hench quoted in Gennawey, *Walt Disney and the Promise of Progress City*, 66.

12. Hench quoted in Watts, *The Magic Kingdom*, 439.

13. Hench, *Designing Disney*, 1.

14. Marling, *Designing Disney's Theme Parks*, 79.

15. Walt quoted in Marling, *Designing Disney's Theme Parks*, 81.

16. Jim Korkis, "John Hench and the Language of Vision," mouseplanet.com/9594/John_Hench_and_the_Language_of_Vision, accessed November 5, 2014.

17. Jim Korkis, "John Hench and the Language of Vision," mouseplanet.com/9594/John_Hench_and_the_Language_of_Vision, accessed November 5, 2014.

18. Per Bill Martin, quoted in Barrier, *The Animated Man*, 259.

19. Naversen, "Contagious Business Philosophy the 'Disney' Way!", themedattraction.com/disney_way.htm, accessed August 29, 2016.

20. Goff in Barrier, *The Animated Man*, 246.

21. Marling, *Designing Disney's Theme Parks*, 64–66.

22. Barrier, *The Animated Man*, 246.

23. Naversen, "Contagious Business Philosophy the 'Disney' Way!", themedattraction.com/disney_way.htm, accessed August 29, 2016.

24. Mannheim, *Walt Disney and the Quest for Community*, 123.

25. Mannheim, *Walt Disney and the Quest for Community*, 123–124.

26. Walt quoted in Naversen, "Contagious Business Philosophy the 'Disney' Way!", themedattraction.com/disney_way.htm, accessed August 29, 2016.

27. Gabler, *Walt Disney*, 528.

28. Barrier, *The Animated Man*, 256.

29. Barrier, *The Animated Man*, 256.

30. Lindquist, *In Service to the Mouse*, 203–204.

31. Gennawey, *Walt Disney and the Promise of Progress City*, xviii.

32. Interviews by Tony Thomas, 1959, on the audio recording *Voices From the Hollywood Past*. From the Walt Disney Archives, in Jackson, *Walt Disney: Conversations*, 63.

33. "Snow White's Daddy," George Kent, from *The Family Circle*, Vol. 12, No. 25, June 24, 1938, 10–11, 16, in Jackson, *Walt Disney: Conversations*, 9.

34. *Newsweek*, Dec. 31, 1962, in Kathy Merlock Jackson, ed., *Walt Disney, Conversations*, 86.

35. Interview with Fletcher Markle in Jackson, *Walt Disney: Conversations*, 102; Smith, *The Quotable Walt Disney*, 258.

Minds Create Value, So Treat Them with Respect

Don Peri interviewed many of the top artists that worked directly with Walt for decades, and noted one thing they had in common. Peri writes, "They admired, respected, even loved Walt Disney, and yet all of them experienced the full force of Walt's personality. The word most often used to describe their feelings about Walt is 'awe.' They were then, and for the rest of their lives remained, in awe of him."[1] Peri continues,

> Part of the reason they were so affected by Walt was their devotion to work that they knew was on the cutting edge of animation advancement. They cared deeply about their contributions, and Walt's opinions about their work affected how they viewed their role. Those at the studio in the 1930s experienced the excitement of advancing a new art form with each discovery made and the camaraderie of sharing those heady times with Walt and with each other.[2]

From the beginning when Walt started Laugh-O-gram Films Inc. in Kansas City, he set out to create a friendly and inclusive atmosphere for those who worked for him. Walt very quickly recognized his shortcomings as an animator, and openly understood that he needed the ideas and cooperation of others to obtain the results he wanted and achieve his goals. He saw himself as an idea man, leader, and coach, and much later in his career described his role metaphorically as the conductor of an orchestra and as a bee that flittered from project to project to drop his pollen of wisdom and keep the hive productively buzzing.

Walt operated on a first-name basis, with an open-door policy and informal code of behavior for his employees. This atmosphere helped create a workplace of fun, good humor, respect, benevolent creativity, and internal friendliness that was conducive to the creation of cartoons with universal audience appeal. One writer commented, "No one can create the kind of friendly entertainment product we demand in a formal, unfriendly atmosphere."[3]

Wilfred Jackson, who was intimately involved with Disney animation and television for 35 years, noted that practical jokes at the office were part of the culture, and Walt didn't discourage it. "We didn't just clown around—we worked hard, but Walt didn't measure your value to the studio by whether you had your nose down to the grindstone for exactly eight hours every day. It was the contribution you made—as long as you got your job done and didn't interfere with anybody else getting their job done, how long you took and when you did it didn't matter."[4]

In his memoir, Charles Shows, a Disney writer, director, and producer in the 1950s and 1960s, recalls a humorous encounter with Walt:

> I had just finished lunch at the studio cafeteria when I felt sleepy. I paused while crossing the lot and sat down under the shade of a tree near the animation building. The next moment I was asleep.
>
> About 3 p.m., I felt a gentle tap on my shoulder. I yawned and opened my eyes. When I looked up, I saw a familiar face smiling at me. It was *Walt* who had interrupted my siesta.
>
> I gulped nervously and tried to scramble to my feet. *I'm in trouble this time*, I thought. Then I felt Walt's hand on my shoulder restraining me gently. "Don't get up, Charlie," he said. "I just wanted to tell you we'll be looking at some scenes from the space picture at four o'clock."
>
> He smiled and started across the lot. I stared after him, dumbfounded. I was so overwhelmed by Walt's show of thoughtfulness that I almost couldn't go back to sleep.[5]

Walt showed respect for his staff and did his best to take care of them and their families. Roy said of Walt, "Walt demanded a lot of people, but he gave a lot, too. When the depression hit, and it looked as though we might have to close the studio, Walt gave everyone a raise. Some thought him crazy, but it gave morale a big boost. He hated to fire anyone, and if someone didn't work out in one job Walt would try to find a niche where he was better suited. Once when we were faced with having to drop some animators, Walt found places for them at WED Enterprises...where he was secretly developing plans for what eventually became Disneyland."[6] In his roughly five years at Disneyland, Van Arsdale France noted, "I don't remember anyone getting fired for coming up with a dumb idea [or] making a mistake."[7]

Shows noted:

> Besides trying to be one of the boys around his own studio, Walt believed in treating his employees, especially those with talent, almost as through they were equals.
>
> If you were a writer, director, animator, or other talent, Walt would take you "off the clock." This meant you could come to work or go home at any hour—with no time clock to punch.

At times, some creative people took advantage of this freedom. ... Walt didn't seem to mind as long as they turned out good work.[8]

In addition to giving raises as the depression took hold, Walt also instituted a bonus program, handing out $32,000 in bonuses in 1934 based on his assessment of who made the biggest contributions. A more complicated system based on a pre-specified formula was put in place in 1936.[9] The work of each animator was assigned a grade based on the judgment of a panel of supervisors, and each grade was assigned a dollar amount. The total footage animated at each grade was multiplied by the assigned dollar amount to produce a total dollar value. The bonus paid equaled the dollar amount determined by the formula minus the animator's salary.

Walt's intentions were good in that he was trying to reward desirable outcomes in a positive way as a show of respect for exceptional work. Unfortunately, according to Ben Sharpsteen, sequence director of *Snow White* at the time, nobody really liked it. Around bonus time, people would reflect on their work and try to relate it to their bonus. The system tried to balance speed and quality, but for the most part disadvantaged slower workers, and brought to the foreground the issue of extra work done without bonus compensation, such as rework by better animators to improve the work of poorer ones. As with any bonus system, those that felt they benefited liked it, and those who felt slighted didn't like it. Overall, however, given the general sense of enthusiasm at the studio at this time, the bonus system reflected Walt's intent of focusing on creating a culture of high-quality work combined with efficiency, particularly in the production of the shorts. At the same time, it created an alignment of values and a sense that workers had a financial stake in the operations and success of the studio.[10]

In his speech accepting the Showman of the World Award in 1966, Walt paid tribute to his 3,000 employees, many of whom had been with the company for over 30 years. "They take pride in the organization which they helped to build. Only through the talent, the labor and the dedication of this staff could any Disney project get off the ground."

Walt said: "You can dream, create, design and build the most wonderful place in the world, but it requires people to make the dream a reality."[11]

Walt also said that "there is no corner on brains," meaning that everyone has the potential for creative thinking and the development of breakthrough ideas. Walt was known to solicit ideas from everybody, even restaurant waiting staff. Disney animator and director Wilfred Jackson recalled, "Walt talked to everybody about his pictures, he shaped them up that way. He talked to the gardener or the janitor or anybody he could get hold of. He worked the thing out in his own mind by telling and re-telling and re-telling the thing—and bouncing it off anybody. If you had an idea, he would listen to it."[12]

While the final decision about how to proceed on any matter was always Walt's, he was almost always open to discussion and testing of promising alternative ideas just out of curiosity to see what might be produced or what the outcome would be. "I've always had a feeling that any time you can experiment you ought to do it," said Walt. "You'll never know what will come out of it. ... When my boys come to me with an idea that sounds plausible, I try to go with them on the experiment. Because you'll never know what will happen."[13]

In the 1960s Walt created his first Audio-Animatronics exhibit, The Enchanted Tiki Room. But before it became an attraction for guests, it was just an experiment of effects that needed a story and some show-business flare. Lots of money and time was invested in creating something in the name of experimentation, with confidence on the part of Walt that it was somewhere along the road to a meaningful product without a clear path to the goal line. Studio songwriter Robert Sherman related his first point of involvement with the project, and is an example of how Walt liked to work in an inclusive manner:

> One day in 1962, Walt's secretary called us up, asking us to come over to Stage Two. When we arrived, we found ourselves in the middle of a magnificent new project called The Enchanted Tiki Room. The team of designers and engineers had set up a big room in the middle of the sound stage. There were four walls, dozens of exotic birds and hundreds of tropical flowers. We sat down among the Imagineers on chairs placed between the four colorful walls and the show began. ... It was a bit psychedelic and it basically made no sense at all. It was just strange. When it was over, Walt stood up and gave us his notes.
>
> "It's a great show, but nobody knows what the damn thing is about." Then he turned to Dick and me. "Any ideas, boys?"
>
> Dick or I suggested that one of the birds could be an "emcee" and that he could sing a calypso number which would explain what it was that the audience was watching. Walt loved the idea and added:
>
> "There could be four 'emcees.' They could each have different accents: Irish, Spanish, French and German."
>
> Walt was amazing like that. He would take an idea and make it even better. He did it all the time.[14]

Inspire Confidence in Others

Walt's staff may not have always liked his hard-headedness and relentless drive for improvements, but they admired and respected his deep first-hand knowledge of every aspect of his business, his insightful assessment of talent, and his confidence in the latent capabilities of his staff to rise up to face new challenges. An early but typical example of Walt's attentiveness to discovering the potential capabilities of staff is illustrated by Wilfred Jackson's experiences.

When Jackson joined the studio in 1928 as a graduate from the Otis Art Institute, Walt was just starting on Mickey Mouse. Jackson was eager to learn animation and offered to work for free. He began washing ink from cels so they could be reused. Later, Walt had him animating Minnie Mouse running along a riverbank. Every time he proved himself, Walt promoted him to a job with greater responsibility. Bob Thomas writes, "To Jackson it seemed that he was being pushed beyond his capacities; but he was so anxious to prove himself to Walt that he tried ever harder. One day he remarked to Walt: 'I'd sure like it if you would let me handle a whole picture myself.'"[15]

The young Jackson was eager and excited about being a contributing animator, but Walt knew he wasn't nearly as capable as his new cadre of experienced New York animators. Instead of letting him animate and fearing he would fail, Walt came up with a different solution and put a challenge before Jackson: "I've got a lot of loose ends that have been cut out of the Mickeys. Why don't you work up some kind of story that would tie all of them together?" Jackson did just that, creating *The Castaway*. In doing so, Jackson had demonstrated to Walt his value as a director, which he remained for more than thirty years.[16]

Another early Disney hire was artist Ben Sharpsteen, who was animating in New York in the late 1920s for one of the leading cartoon studios. Sharpsteen was discouraged as an artist by the low standards for work and poor general attitude throughout the industry, where the only thing that mattered was that the kids in the movie houses laughed at the gags. With ambitions to do more as an artist, he packed up, moved to San Francisco, and eventually made his way to the Disney Brothers Cartoon Studio in L.A., which he joined in 1929.

Sharpsteen met with Walt and was immediately impressed by two things: Walt's complete understanding of every aspect of the business, and his commitment to creating cartoons so good that the public couldn't deny them. Having just lost his Oswald series to distributor Charles Mintz, Sharpsteen says that Walt vowed to reach his audience in spite of the control film distributors exerted on the studios. "If he could establish himself with the public, then he could control his entire business and then the distributors would have to come to him and not he to them. It was an extremely ambitious statement to make," recalled Sharpsteen years later, reflecting on Walt's determination to solve his problems by professing his commitment to be the leader in quality.

Sharpsteen was ambitious but soon became discouraged about his ability to keep up with the newer crop of more skilled and experienced animators.

Recognizing this, Walt asked him to move from doing animation to teaching animation to the new hires. Sharpsteen showed initiative and leadership in establishing and managing the training program successfully, and when Walt needed another director, he moved Sharpsteen into that role based on his assessment of Sharpsteen's ability to handle the work.[17]

Disney artist Herb Ryman noted this talent of Walt's: "He was able to bring out hidden energies. Walt's enthusiasm and his curiosity and his affection for life and for all things were very deep, and he plumbed into the depths of the talents around him, which sometimes I thought were rather ordinary talents. But out of those talents—by encouragement, by stimulation, and sometimes by insult—Walt could bring things out that were phenomenal."[18]

Through his own enthusiasm for his work, Walt was able to garner respect from his staff and inspire them to put forth exceptional effort and achieve exceptional results. Disney art director and animator Ken Anderson reflected back on the relationship between Walt and his staff:

> He was just a man who was so gung ho because this whole thing was just a plaything. It was the highest kind of human endeavor because it was play...this was his amusement, his life, his entertainment. As a result, of course, he made us feel the same. We all got heads of steam just because of our proximity to Walt who had this tremendous enthusiasm for this thing he was doing.[19]

Disney artist Marc Davis noted that things changed after Walt's death in 1966: "If there is a change in the organization from Walt's time until now, it's this: there is nobody there who could make me feel as good by saying, 'I like that,' as Walt."[20]

By allowing and encouraging artists to stretch their capabilities and do their best work, often work they didn't think themselves capable of doing, Walt demonstrated a deep respect for their hidden and undeveloped human potential, and in return earned the love and respect of so many of his studio colleagues.

While many artists benefited and admired Walt's ability to pose new challenges and stretch their talents in unforeseen and unique ways, this admiration wasn't unanimous. As Disney luminaries such as Homer Brightman, Bill Peet, and others who experienced or witnessed Walt's sometimes capricious and volcanic style noted, at times his behavior bordered on abusive.

Brightman writes in his memoirs that Walt was a "hard driver" of people, "not very interested, perhaps, in the ones being driven, only interested in improving the stories."[21]

Walt once said, "People don't cause problems because they want to, but because they lack skills to succeed. Give them skills and never criticize people."[22] Walt demonstrated throughout his career his passion for, and commitment to, improving people, without regard to their place in the organization. John Hench recalled a story about Walt taking the time to instruct a Disneyland employee after watching him behave in a way he thought to be unsightly from the point of view of park guests:

> He would walk the park in disguise, wearing an old hat and dark glasses, observing how people were treated. On one of these walks, I saw him stop at the newly opened restaurant Plaza Pavilion, with table seating outside. A young boy was busing dishes, scraping them into a cardboard box at the table in front of diners—not a very appetizing thing to watch. Walt walked over to the boy, patiently and quietly explained to him that cleaning plates should not be exposed to the guests, and asked the boy to take the used dishes back to the kitchen to clean them. Walt waved his hand a bit; the boy nodded and removed the dishes. I watched the whole thing from a distance. I kept seeing this picture in my mind; I was really shocked by the whole thing. It did look bad from the guests' point of view, but Walt didn't raise hell with the busboy's boss; he spoke only to the boy. I am sure that neither the boy nor the diners knew that it was Walt. It was typical of Walt to go to the source of a problem in this way.[23]

The Illusion of Easy

The corollary to valuing and respecting people who contribute fully and effectively at work is to recognize when people are not contributing to the best of their ability, or worse, claiming abilities that they do not have or being dishonest about their ability to create and deliver the value they have promised. Walt had very little time for, and often displayed contempt for, those he put in the latter group. He was constantly reassessing his judgment of people based on their character and ability to deliver results.

Brightman recalled and related an amusing incident from the mid 1930s about animator Rudy Zamora, whom Walt had hired for his skill, in spite of his reputation in the industry for being reckless, rebellious, feisty, outspoken, and contemptuous of authority:

> [Rudy Zamora]…was assigned to animate Mickey Mouse [in the short feature *The Band Concert*]. He got into the right mood using the Actor's Studio method of animating by marching up and down in a drum major's uniform. Walt saw him strutting around the halls and told him to get to work. A day or two later, Walt ordered him to bring his animation up to his office.
>
> The animator took a stack of 500 animation pages up to Walt and told him this was the scene. Walt smiled; he was happy at this prodigious output. But, as he leafed through the pages, he found that only the

top page had a drawing. All the rest were blank. Walt went white. "Out!" he shouted, pointing to the door. The animator never worked for Disney again, but he had no trouble finding work. He was one of the most gifted animators in the business.[24]

There is ample evidence that Walt respected people who did their best on a task, even if in his opinion they may have underperformed because the task assignment was beyond their current capability or training. He was constantly asking his employees to engage in areas for which they had little previous experience, whether it was to direct movies, produce TV shows, or design parks, testing and measuring their ability to contribute in ways that create value for Disney customers. Former Walt Disney Imagineer and executive Marty Sklar wrote,

> Walt Disney's own genius lay not in the ideas he himself generated, but in the casting of talents—many of whom were Disney studio veterans embarked on "new careers" in the second half of their creative lifetimes.[25]

It was also a common practice for Walt to assign the same task to more than one person or group so that he would have multiple perspectives, alternatives, or options to consider and choose from. Knowing he didn't have all the answers, this would put real choices on the table for consideration, thereby sparking his own thoughts on the matter through a process of contrast, comparison, or integration. For example, Walt assigned the concept painting of the Disneyland castle to two artists in order to have variation and choice.[26] The same may have been true for the soundtrack to *Cinderella*.[27] Those that understood Walt's way of doing things praised and respected him for assigning the same work to multiple parties, recognizing their own positive contribution to the success of the studio, while those that didn't found working this way frustrating, feeling that Walt had wasted their time.

Walt respected the contribution of his staff, but never lost sight that the jobs of the employees at his studio existed largely because of his creative power and vision, and not the other way around. Walt saw himself as the prime mover that gave momentum to those who moved forward with him. Disney artist Mel Shaw joined Walt in 1937 and reflects in his autobiography, *Animator On Horseback*,

> [Walt] was seldom happy with the status quo. ... Even with the growth of the talent surrounding us, none of us could visualize the future of the Walt Disney Studios. How could we know that we were part of a studio that could crank out feature animation productions, live action, shorts, and merchandising? The reality of what Walt would create went far beyond anyone's imagination.[28]

As an entrepreneur and capitalist funding the production of his products, including an investment in the salaries of his staff ahead of completion and delivery of their work to the marketplace, Walt resented any notion of a sense of entitlement from his staff, including those who would take advantage of his generosity. From his earliest days in Hollywood, Walt wasn't shy about telling new hires that he was the boss, and that they should find work elsewhere if they couldn't accept that fact. Many, such as Harman, Ising, Iwerks, and Looney Tunes animation legend Chuck Jones chose to do so, recognizing that their own ambitions to hold leadership positions clashed with Walt's controlling style.

When Warner Bros. closed their animation studio in 1953, Walt hired Chuck Jones. Four months later, Warner reopened its animation department and rehired Jones. When Walt asked Jones why he was leaving, Jones replied, "Actually, there's only one job here worth having, and that's yours." To which Walt replied, "That's true, all right. ... Unfortunately, it's filled."[29]

Many of Walt's staff thought that what he did was so exceedingly simple that they could easily do the same thing. After all, as many rightly noted, he couldn't even draw well. Harman and Ising rode Walt's coattails for years in California, always plotting to leave and start their own studio. Whether or not they respected Walt's capabilities (their private letters seemed to indicate that they thought Walt a fool), they remained and schemed until hired away by Charles Mintz, demonstrating that they knew they needed Walt more than Walt needed them. Mintz too was convinced that Walt added little value to the Oswald cartoons, and thought that if he hired Walt's animators to continue drawing the pictures and oversaw their production, he could make the series more profitable, and thus more successful. Mintz also was of the mind that Walt needed him and his "renegade" animators more than they needed Walt.

Walt's original distributor for Mickey Mouse, Pat Powers, suffered from the same fundamental error, hiring Iwerks away from Walt after distributing his Mickey Mouse pictures for one year, and thinking that in Iwerks' animation skill and reputation lay the secret of Walt's success. Iwerks had been with Walt since their Kansas City days, and had learned every aspect of the art and business of animation as intimately as Walt. And yet when given the chance to prove himself with the financial backing of Powers, Iwerks was unable to succeed in running his own studio successfully, with many of his staff very critical of his leadership abilities.

Iwerks had a completely different studio management style that was almost 180 degrees from his perception of Walt as domineering, controlling, and paternalistic. Iwerks gave his artists more freedom and control over story and content, but it wasn't long before they began to resent Iwerks for the complete opposite reasons the "renegades" complained about. They felt

Iwerks was absent too often, occupied by other matters, and didn't provide enough direction and attend properly to the detailed matters required to run a successful studio in direct competition with Disney. After Powers shut down the studio to cut his losses, Iwerks later rejoined Walt Disney Productions where he was able to make significant contributions to the studio and soar creatively under Walt's guidance and leadership.

Many others left Disney for what they thought would be greener pastures and quickly came to realize that they had made a mistake, later admitting their regrets about leaving.

Walt's most successful and astute employees came to realize that those who resented working for Walt the most were also often the least capable of facing the challenges that Walt put before them. Homer Brightman captured the resentment of many of the more junior studio staff in his description of issues such as unfair treatment regarding *Snow White* bonuses and a general resentment of the working conditions at the new state-of-the-art Burbank studio that served to motivate the desire to strike for better employment terms.

There was also some resentment toward Walt regarding his reluctance to grant credit to the producers of his films, as was common at other studios. But in his own mind, he had good reasons for his decision. The *Ladies Home Journal* reported in 1941, "The fact that his employees rarely get public credit for their work is the result of a policy calculated to prevent inter-office jealousy rather than a desire on Disney's part to hog the show."[30] More than twenty years later, in 1964, Card Walker tried to feature the producers and their films in the annual report to show that the studio had filmmakers who could carry the company forward should something happen to Walt. Walt immediately vetoed the idea, saying,

> I don't mind sharing the pictures. But I don't want to talk about "a Bill Walsh production for Walt Disney," or "a Bill Anderson production for Walt Disney." I've worked my whole life to create the image of what "Walt Disney" is. It's not me. I smoke, and I drink, and all the things we don't want the public to think about. My whole life has been devoted to building up this organization that is represented by the name "Walt Disney." I don't want you breaking that down by doing this in the annual report.[31]

It's Not Just What You Do, It's Also How You Do It

There is an underlying theme in many of the stories told by Disney employees who wrote memoirs that they or others were often victims of Walt's capricious and disrespectful behavior as Walt engaged in a decades-long pursuit of innovation, creativity, and customer value creation. There is a perspective by some that they were under too much pressure, that the quality and effectiveness of their work was always being scrutinized, that Walt's expectations were too high and by implication he should have lowered his standards and put his relations with people and consideration for their feelings ahead of the unrelenting requirements of the work and the business.

Others disagreed, such as Disney promotional artist Gyo Fujikawa, who worked for Walt in the late 1930s and early 1940s, and went on to be a successful children's book author and illustrator. Fujikawa noted that Walt was right to set high standards and criticize sub-par work: "He was right to criticize them because…everything was going out under his name and he wanted to make sure the work reflected what he was thinking."[32]

Walt was careful to be judicious with his criticism of artistic work, as animator Frank Thomas noted:

> [H]e never came down to the room and criticized your drawings directly. He always did that in the projection booth, but he would never force you to show something until you were ready to show it to him. He was the best director we had as far as knowing how to handle people, knowing how to get the work out of them. Walt had the ability to make you work over your head.[33]

Artist Mel Shaw noted the trials and tribulations of a sweatbox session in the old Hyperion studio when he was working on *Bambi*:

> This small projection room was called a "sweatbox" for a very good reason. Some animators considered it akin to experiencing a medieval torture chamber. On the screen, through the smoke and heat, someone's animated scene, drawing by drawing, would be taken apart by Walt and the directors. This was probably a sequence the animator had sweated over for weeks or months. When the artist entered this little room, it was with the belief that he had created the scene that would make the picture. But when the critics were through, all that was left was a broken ego and reams of work ahead. This proved out to be the reason why Walt's pictures became the guideposts of animation and why only the heartiest of animators could be part of it.[34]

The best of the best were up to the challenge posed by Walt's high standards, and respected him for it. Animator John Lounsbery noted that not only did Walt have a way of "enthusing me with a new project," but he also "would convince you to throw out a whole sequence and make it better. He would send you back to it enthused."[35]

Disneyland TV show producer Bill Walsh said of Walt, "He never let you sit down without pouring a little turpentine on your rear end," meaning he was always looking to challenge ideas to drive more thinking, more creativity, more imagination, and ultimately, a better show.[36]

It can be difficult to come to work each day and face new and unique challenges, but it turns out that while stressful, it is also exhilarating to be pushed into success and to look back proudly on amazing work created or contributed in the process of achieving what others thought to be impossible. Walt provided such an opportunity to those who dared to grab it. Walt Disney Productions and WED earned reputations for excellence that became a magnet for the best minds in animation, filmmaking, and themed attraction design and engineering. Working for a proven leader is always more challenging and exhilarating than working for the rest, and not everybody was cut out for working to Walt's level of aspiration and intensity.

Walt produced an environment of perpetual change and challenge, and was constantly on the lookout for those relatively few special individuals who could cope with the adversity and, like Olympic sports competitors, were prepared to train and play at the top of their game. Walt didn't earn his reputation for world-class excellence by tolerating incompetence. Nor did he expect competence and success to happen by itself. Walt made sure that his staff, like himself, was constantly engaged in continuous learning, continuous improvement, and continuous customer delight. By doing so, he demonstrated and earned respect.

Walt took pride in being a tough, conscientious taskmaster. It was in many ways the means he had developed to achieve a specific end. It was his way of separating the best from the average. Walt was relentless in testing the capabilities of his staff to adapt to higher standards and expectations, always looking for people who could think independently and at the same time conform, who had a strong sense of shared passion and commitment for Walt's vision, and who could balance artistic creativity with personal and business discipline over extended lengths of time.

Those who were most successful in working with Walt were adept at walking this tightrope. They found the work exhilarating. Gabler captures some semblance of the atmosphere in 1936, when the studio was in its prime with *Snow White* in production and Mickey Mouse at the height of his popularity:

> To be one of the roughly five hundred employees at the Walt Disney Studio in the mid-1930s as it began *Snow White* was to be swept up in a frenzy of exhilaration. One observer said that it was "so far in advance of the times that it became a place of pilgrimage, not only for Mickey devotees but for anyone interested in the growth of a contemporary experiment in art and entertainment." Grim Natwick called it a "mythical sun around which the other studios orbited." "Each new picture contained breathtaking improvements," Thomas and Johnston would write, "the effects were better, the animation had more life, and the whole studio had an upward momentum. It was

like being a player on a winning team! To us, all this was pure magic." ... There was very little griping and virtually no competition among the employees, only camaraderie. Work was joy. "It wasn't that you had to do these things," Marc Davis said. "You wanted to do them. You were so proud. Every write-up the studio got, everybody went out and got it. Very few people have ever, as a group, experienced that kind of excitement."[37]

While the most talented and most ambitious in the field were attracted to the Disney studio to be part of something unique and exciting, the fact was that very few of Walt's staff had the flair or appetite for entrepreneurship. They came to Disney seeking jobs; paid employment. One reason they were so successful and trusted by Walt was their ability to produce amazing results under his direction and leadership. They were accustomed to taking approved chances and avoiding risk.

Even the best of them, such as Ward Kimball, was reluctant to lead when the opportunity arose, although when put to the challenge, he did so to great results, as Walt anticipated and expected. Disney historian Michael Barrier writes:

"When [Walt] got off on the park," Ward Kimball said, "there was no stopping him; you couldn't get him in to look at something. He'd just say, 'Go ahead and do it.'" Kimball himself benefited from Disney's inattention when he made several Tomorrowland shows about space travel for [the] *Disneyland* [TV show]. Kimball's shows were inventive and mostly serious in their approach to the subject, but they departed sharply from the mid-1950s Disney norm in their knowing use of modern design and their occasionally flippant tone.

Kimball was aware of how unusual—and how hazardous—his situation was: "This was a risk you never ran before; you never dared go ahead on your own, without the OK. What could you do? He was interested in something else."[38]

At the time Walt was only interested in his park, which he was thinking about all the time, and delegating more of the story work on his film projects to his experienced and capable staff. While the quote above makes it appear that Walt's most capable staff viewed him as a dangerous man and worked under fearful conditions, the exact opposite was true. Disney biographer Neal Gabler writes:

"Those were the days when he didn't have any contact with the picture," Ward Kimball said of Walt's lack of participation in *Man in Space*. He simply attended the screening, laughed throughout, and then asked, "How in the hell did you guys think up all that stuff?" Milt Kahl, who was working on feature animations at the time, had the same experience. He said that Walt would sit in on the story meetings but not as often as he once had. "[T]he difference was," Kahl believed, "that on weekends and evenings and sitting on the john and all that stuff, he wasn't thinking about our pictures. He was thinking about Disneyland."[39]

There were many instances in which Walt respected certain attributes of people, but as he learned more about their operating values and values-based worldview he refused to do business with them and broke off relationships. We can see this, for example, with his choice to abandon Mintz and Powers, and in his ongoing dissatisfaction with film distributors and the hiring and firing of C.V. Wood to manage the building and operations of Disneyland.

When the operating styles of Walt and Wood are contrasted, it becomes clear why Walt could not work with Wood once their underlying values surfaced. We learn from 'Buzz' Price in his book *Walt's Revolution!* that Wood lived his life in the tradition of P.T. Barnum; that much of his business life was built on showmanship and hucksterism. Price, who worked with Wood for a number of years at SRI before Wood was hired to manage the Disneyland project, relates, "Life with Wood was a succession of quotables" and shares some examples that provide insight into Wood's world view. "If you are caught red-handed in an act of impropriety, deny guilt. You are carryin' out research." "You and I are both con men, Buzz, but we deliver the goods." "Always walk fast, in a hurry, they'll think you are doin' somethin'." "When presentin', bring a big stack of books. It can be the Mexican Mining Laws of 1924 but bring a big stack."[40]

When asked about Wood, Disney Imagineer and Disneyland attractions designer Bob Gurr stated right out, "He was a con man and certainly behaved that way."[41] Price agrees, writing, "He was a bit of a con man, albeit a charming one. Walt reacted to him the way the farmer reacts to the fast city slicker. It was a completely immiscible personality conflict. ... Their clash of egos was oil and water and Walt was the boss."[42]

Walt worked successfully with many people that had strong egos. *Mary Poppins* author P.L. Travers comes immediately to mind, as does Walt's stable of leading artists and film directors, extending even to Salvador Dali and their abandoned *Destino* project. In the case of Wood, it was more than a clash of egos. It was a clash of fundamental moral and personal values revealed in Wood's apparent manipulative and deceptive modes of operation and lack of personal respect for Walt and his vision for the organization.

Designing with Respect

We have seen how everything about Disneyland and later EPCOT was thought about and designed in a humanitarian and human-centric manner. Walt was constantly seeking better ways to enhance the human potential and personal experiences, and to provide human psychological comfort through environmental design.

At the root of Walt's aspirations in this regard was his deep-seated respect for people, which even permeated his design aspirations for both the Hyperion and Burbank studios. *Snow White* animator Shamus Culhane reflected upon the new animation building that was constructed at the Hyperion studio in 1935, as related by biographer Neal Gabler:

> "In the first place, everything was painted in bright tints of raspberry, light blue, and gleaming white, no institutional greens or bilious browns like the other studios," recalled Shamus Culhane, a young animator then. Where furniture at the New York studios looked as if it "had been stolen from the Salvation Army," at Disney, "[e]ach animation team had its own room with three beautifully designed desks, upholstered chairs, cupboards for storing work in progress, and most amazing of all...each room had a moviola. ... The desk furniture was something!"[43]

The new Burbank studio was built years later following the heady days of *Snow White's* immense success, and is described by Sam Gennawey in *Walt Disney and the Promise of Progress City*:

> Walt and Roy's facility in Burbank was the first movie studio solely dedicated to the manufacture of animated films. All design decisions were based not on architectural interest or beauty but on how the solution could enhance the filmmaking process.

> Walt wanted to do everything he could to encourage the maximum creativity and efficiency of his artists. For example, to create the perfect animation desk, Walt asked Frank Thomas, one of his most trusted animators, to design one based on his experience. ... In *Building a Company*, author Bob Thomas claimed that "[Walt] planned the Burbank studio down to the contour of the chairs."

> In press releases, the studio was described as a "self-sufficient, state-of-the-art production factory that provided all the essential facilities for the entire production process." In *Walt Disney: The Triumph of the American Imagination*, Neal Gabler, said, "Walt saw the studio in psychological terms. From the moment he started talking about the planning of the studio, he always had in mind the psychological effect of the physical space, because Walt didn't believe good work came out of tyranny. Studio heads at that time believed...anxiety was the source of productivity. Walt didn't operate that way. He felt that if people were happy they would create well."

> The Burbank studio was designed to provide the artists all the comforts of home. There was a snack stand, barber, cleaners, a buffet-style restaurant, and health club. Every part of the facility was air conditioned by a custom-made General Electric system. This was very

rare at the time; it not only ensured the artists' comfort, but it kept dust off the painted celluloid sheets as well. ... The Disney studio's work environment was unique at the time, but it would become the prototype for modern-day high-tech companies and other high-performance organizations after World War II.[44]

Hey, Hey, I'm Okay

Because of his legendary status, Walt found that when he met with leaders of the biggest corporations in America they were somewhat star-struck and tongue-tied in awe of him, sometimes making it difficult to do business on equal terms. Walt tried to put people at ease by using his dress and mannerisms to indicate that he was just a normal guy. "He would deliberately dress down" when meeting corporate executives, noted Bob Gurr, "by undoing a button or slopping up his tie so it was askew. He tried to send a signal, 'I'm okay.' ... He knew he scared the daylights out of people and he didn't want to let that get in the way of being able to work with him. Otherwise all he'd have is a bunch of people agreeing with him and their expertise wouldn't show."[45]

Walt liked people who were productive, showed initiative, could think creatively on their own, and weren't afraid to take chances. Ken Anderson relates a personal story from the 1942 Disney-arranged research trip to Central America that provides insight into Walt's treatment of people. Walt brought his wife and 12 staff along, and after a few days of sitting around the hotel, Anderson and Ernie Terrazas, who was Mexican, rented a limousine to explore Mexico and make sketches of the countryside as inspiration for a yet-to-be-defined Central American-themed Disney animation project. Anderson neglected to clear the multi-day trip with business manager Jack Cutting. Anderson picks up the story:

> When I got back after having gone all over Mexico, I don't know how much money I spent, but I had book after book after sketchbook, luckily. I got back to the [hotel] and found that Jack was in a stew, a dither. He didn't know whether Walt knew about it or not, but we still had two or three days in Mexico City...and then there was no denying that I was in the doghouse, but Jack was fearful. He liked me and he didn't want to see anything happen but he was afraid something would and he didn't know how he would break it. Well, we got on the plane and there was no one but us, Disney people. It was a chartered plane. About over Guadalajara, Walt said, "Hey, Ken, I understand that you took off and went down to Mexico and made a bunch of sketches." And I said, "Yes, I did," and he said, "Where are they?" I had a lot of nice stuff and I got the sketchbooks out and passed them back to him and sat there with my teeth hanging out. He

looked at them and finally he said, "Goddamn it, why can't anybody else around here do like Ken? Go out and see things and do things. This stuff is great." (I heaved a sigh of relief.)[46]

Walt didn't take kindly to being directly challenged, but he often demonstrated respect for those who were willing to do so in an honest and thoughtful way. Walt's closest colleagues learned over their long careers that how you approached Walt was the key. Those who were more mature and understood Walt were able to use this knowledge plus a bit of psychology to their own advantage. According to Marc Davis, Walt was often contrarian because he resented being told by others what to think, preferring to do his own thinking and apply his own judgment independently. If told that he would like something when he saw it, he was more likely to find fault, and vice versa. For example, if an employee came into a story or sweatbox session telling Walt that something was great, you could be sure Walt would find fault. But the opposite was true. If staff came in verbalizing some apprehension, Walt might conclude that the work was acceptable.[47]

Master animator Frank Thomas noted that you couldn't talk back to Walt, but you could have a difference in opinion.[48] Artist Herb Ryman said he was able to change Walt's mind or "unsell" ideas he disapproved of "by doing a drawing to show what it would look like. You couldn't disagree with him, but you could make a drawing. He'd say, 'Why, that's terrible. We can't do anything like that.' Naturally, I'd agree."[49]

Another technique used to cope with Walt's decision-making style is related by Charles Shows in his discussion of the general methodology of creating and presenting work to Walt for his approval:

> As soon as a writer completed a project, all the other writers would come in and carefully go over the storyboard, generously offering suggestions that would improve the final product. There was no sign of the characteristic jealousy that is common among some creative people, particularly in the Hollywood film industry.
>
> One day after pinning up the last sketches on what I thought was a very good story, I invited my co-workers in for a nit-picking session to make sure my product was flawless before Walt saw it. As I read the story aloud from the sketches, I felt even more assured it was smooth and solid.
>
> But one of the veteran Disney writers in the crowd jumped up and said, "For Christ's sake, Charlie, don't let Walt see your story like *that*!"
>
> "What's wrong with it?" I reacted. "There's not a hole in it!"
>
> "That's exactly what's wrong with it," said the pro. "If Walt goes over your storyboard and can't find one thing to criticize, he'll be mad as hell. He's got to be able to find a few mistakes—and make a few changes—or he wouldn't be the big producer.

I got the point immediately and began to write in a few glaring mistakes. Sure enough, when Walt arrived to go over the storyboard with me, he spotted the weak points at once. For the next ten minutes he generously suggested ways to correct the "flaws," then walked out, beaming and whistling happily.[50]

Walt didn't like employees who tried to gain his favor by, as he put it, "polishing the apple," i.e., presenting themselves in the best light. After an in-house screening of one cartoon with which Walt wasn't very pleased, he called out for comments from the group in attendance. Roy recalled,

One after the other they spoke up, all echoing Walt's criticism. "I can get rubber stamps that say 'Yes, Walt,'" he snapped. Then he wheeled and asked the projectionist what he thought. The man sensed that dissent was in order. "I think you're *all* wrong," he declared. Walt just grinned. "*You* stick to your projector," he suggested.[51]

"We have no geniuses at the studio," Walt once said. "I have no use for people who throw their weight around, or for those that fawn over you because you are famous."[52] On the one hand, he made it very clear that he was running the studio, and on the other hand, he insisted on being treated the same as everyone else. Of course, this created conflict amongst his staff about how to treat him, and made dealing with him difficult at times. Bob Thomas writes of Walt in the later period of his career:

He refused to be treated as a special person because of his position as head of an ever-growing enterprise. ... Sycophantic employees lasted a brief time around Walt. When he visited a movie set or walked down a hall, he didn't like to be accosted; his time was limited, and he wanted to choose the person he talked to, whether it was a producer or a prop man. He especially disliked being burdened with others' personal problems.[53]

This story, told by Disney nurse and lyricist of over 90 Disney songs, Hazel George, captures some of Walt's attitude in this regard. Writer Bill Peet had worked with Walt for 27 years and was considered his best story man:

Bill Peet was a drinker. Hal Aldequist told [Walt] about Peet's drinking [problem].

Walt didn't like this (a snitcher) and replied, "Find out what he's drinking, I want you to start drinking the same." But once Peet got loaded and told Walt, "This is the way it should be." That was the end.[54]

Achievement Requires Respect within a Proper Context of Interests

Both Walt and Roy subscribed explicitly to the principle of treating others with respect as the basis for creating value, and recognized and appreciated the important contributions that people made to the company. Walt rarely complimented staff directly or publically, as modern management protocol would recommend, but he didn't see that as a matter of disrespect.

An extreme example of the respect Walt and Roy exhibited comes from an incident that pitted them against each other in a bitter 1963 family feud. It is instructive because it seems anomalous when compared to how they both treated others with whom they clashed over their careers. Even when relationships with outsiders ended badly, a certain level of decorum always prevailed toward the individuals involved, and in this case, in the end, the deeply held Disney value of respect for people once again prevailed.

By 1963, as preparations were being made to purchase land in Florida for what is now Walt Disney World, Roy had growing concerns about the propriety of the personal services contract between WED and Walt Disney Productions. A lot had changed in the ten years since the original agreement with WED had been signed. Disney stock was now freely trading on the New York Stock Exchange under changed securities laws, rather than being closely held and traded on the Over-the-Counter Exchange. What Roy feared most was a new shareholder challenge that would result in a media scandal and a public relations disaster for Walt personally as well as for the corporation, thereby putting the Florida expansion at risk.

In what was to become an acrimonious family weekend at Walt's Palm Springs retreat, Roy approached Walt with the reasons why it was prudent for the studio to buy out Walt's contract. Walt was enraged and became adamant that he deserved to be earning as much as other leaders in the industry, and the agreement with WED made that possible. But it was unlikely that this was just about money. An even greater underlying factor was Walt's fear that he would lose his autonomy and ability to function unencumbered by the restrictions and trappings of corporate constraints and meddling shareholders. Walt's bottom line was that he hadn't done anything wrong, so there was no need to alter the agreement.

As a result of the confrontation, the two brothers didn't talk to each other for months. Their lawyers conferred but little progress was made toward a satisfactory resolution. As the situation dragged on, Walt hired his own lawyers to analyze the personal services contract and provide advice. Their recommendation after careful legal analysis was to sell everything back to the studio, including the licensing of the Walt Disney name. Accepting this advice, Walt then hired the best lawyer he could find in Los Angeles to negotiate a settlement with the studio lawyers. When Walt's lawyer raised the possibility in the midst of negotiations that Walt might have to seek employment elsewhere, Roy exploded in anger at the threat that Walt would leave the company. According to Bill Cottrell, who was present, "This was like pouring gasoline on the fire. The conversation ended very quickly."[55]

Cottrell reported back to Walt, who by this time had heard enough. He wanted the matter settled. The lawyers for each side, however, remained intransigent. It is reported by Bob Thomas in *Building a Company* that one day Roy overheard a heated discussion between the lawyers for each side in the conference room next to his office, and intervened. The room fell silent. Roy addressed his team of lawyers: "Let me say a few words. You seem to forget how important Walt Disney has been to you and your lives. None of us would be here in these offices if it hadn't been for Walt. All your jobs, all the benefits you have, all came from Walt and his contributions. He deserves better treatment than what's being shown here."[56]

Roy's intervention altered the trajectory of the negotiations, and a settlement was soon reached. The studio would buy WED, which would eventually be renamed Walt Disney Imagineering, provide Walt with a ten-year extension on ownership of the trains and monorail, and allow the royalty contract on the Walt Disney name to stand. Walt would rename his new company Retlaw Enterprises.

With the dispute over and Roy's birthday at hand, Walt made his way to Roy's office with a birthday present of an Indian peace pipe. After a light-hearted meeting to put the acrimonious past few months behind them, a 61-year-old Walt returned to his office and wrote his older brother a letter:

> It was wonderful to smoke the pipe of peace with you again—the clouds that rise are very beautiful.
>
> I think, between us over the years, we have accomplished something—there was a time when we couldn't borrow a thousand dollars and now I understand we owe twenty-four million!
>
> But in all sincerity, Happy Birthday and many more—and—
>
> I love you.[57]

Lessons We Can Learn from Walt Disney's Business Success

- Create a friendly and inclusive high performance workplace culture with clearly defined values and norms that are meaningful to your customers and appropriate for your business.
- Succeed through talent and dedication of staff. It requires people to make a dream a reality.
- Work hard, measure, and reward results to ensure work is being done effectively and staff feels a sense of achievement.
- Demand a lot from people and give a lot, too. Discover and leverage the hidden talents and capabilities of others. Become an expert in the casting of talents.

- Give people the skill and knowledge they need to succeed. Encourage and expect life-long learning and the development of staff to benefit business aspirations and objectives.
- There is no corner on brains. Encourage creative thinking and the development of breakthrough ideas, always and everywhere.
- Don't delegate decision-making when the responsibility is yours.
- Use your enthusiasm and curiosity to raise the talent around you.
- When things aren't working out, go to the source of the problem.
- Provide reasons for controversial decisions so people know where you stand and why.
- Pour a little turpentine. Challenge ideas to drive more thinking, more creativity, and more imagination.
- Don't tolerate sycophants and people intent on "polishing the apple."
- Be respectful and show appreciation for the contributions people make to the company, its vision and purpose, and its customers.

1. Peri, *Working with Walt*, xv.

2. Peri, *Working with Walt*, xvi.

3. Merlin Jones, "Foundations for the Disney Business," January 11, 2007, imagineerebirth.blogspot.ca/2007/01/foundations-for-disney-business.html, accessed September 10, 2016.

4. David Johnson, "Wilfred Jackson Interview," animationartist.com/columns/DJohnson/JacksonInterview/jacksoninterview.html, accessed September 11, 2016.

5. Shows, *Walt: Backstage Adventures with Walt Disney*, 43.

6. Roy O Disney, "Unforgettable Walt Disney," Reader's Digest, Feb., 1969, 217; dix-project.net/item/2307/reader-s-digest-unforgettable-walt-disney, accessed September 6, 2016.

7. France, *Window on Main Street*, 68.

8. Shows, *Walt: Backstage Adventures with Walt Disney*, 49–51.

9. See Gabler, *Walt Disney*, 243.

10. Gabler, *Walt Disney*, 244.

11. Scott Madison Paton, "Service Quality, Disney Style," *Quality Digest*, atqualitydigest.com/jan97/disney.html.

12. David Johnson, "Wilfred Jackson Interview," www.animationartist.com/columns/DJohnson/JacksonInterview/jacksoninterview.html, accessed September 11, 2016.

13. Walt quoted in Greene & Greene, *Inside the Dream*, 168.

14. Sherman, *Moose*, 288.

15. Thomas, *Walt Disney*, 112.

16. Thomas, *Walt Disney*, 112.

17. Thomas, *Walt Disney*, 112.

18. Ryman quoted in Peri, *Working with Walt: Interviews with Disney Artists*, xxiii.

19. Andersen in Ghez, *Walt's People: Volume 10*, 131.

20. Davis quoted in Peri, *Working with Walt: Interviews with Disney Artists*, xxiii.

21. Brightman, *Life in the Mouse House*, 17.

22. Mike Vance, "Mike Vance 1987 Promo," youtube.com/watch?v=BdBOj2r-wIDE, at 3 min., 15 sec., accessed October 26, 2016.

23. Hench, *Designing Disney*, 30.

24. Brightman, *Life In The Mouse House*, 33; Rudy Zamora profile, agni-animation.com/fullerton/halloffame/Rudy_Zamora.html.

25. Sklar, "The Artist As Imagineer," in Marling, *Designing Disney's Theme Parks*, 15.

26. Gennawey, *The Disneyland Story*, 80.

27. See Charles Wolcott in Ghez, *Walt's People: Volume 8*, 170.

28. Shaw, *Animator on Horseback*, 95.

29. Wikipedia, "Chuck Jones," en.wikipedia.org/wiki/Chuck_Jones, accessed November 9, 2016; Greene & Greene, *Inside The Dream*, 175.

30. "Mr. And Mrs. Disney," *Ladies Home Journal*, 1941, in Jackson, *Walt Disney: Conversations*, 23.

31. Thomas, *Building a Company*, 249.

32. Ghez, *Walt's People: Volume 16*, 27–28.

33. Ghez, *Walt's People: Volume 16*, 27–28.

34. Shaw, *Animator on Horseback*, 99.

35. Quoted in Ghez, *Walt's People: Volume 10*, 76.

36. Gabler, *Walt Disney*, 514.

37. Gabler, *Walt Disney*, 236–237.

38. Barrier, *The Animated Man*, 269.

39. Gabler, *Walt Disney*, 523.

40. Price, *Walt's Revolution!*, 131.

41. Bob Gurr, Interviewed by Jim Korkis, in "Disney Legend Bob Gurr: Filling the Gaps," mouseplanet.com/9361/DIsney_Legend_Bob_Gurr_Filling_in_the_Gaps, accessed, October 20, 2014.

42. Price, *Walt's Revolution!*, 136–137.

43. Gabler, *Walt Disney*, 238.

44. Gennawey, *Walt Disney and the Promise of Progress City*, 29.

45. Gurr quoted in Greene & Greene, *Remembering Walt*, 90–91, also cited in Barrier, *The Animated Man*, 308.

46. Andersen, In Ghez, *Walt's People: Volume 10*, 133.

47. See Ghez, *Walt's People: Volume 10*, 110, bottom of page, for an example.

48. Ghez, *Walt's People: Volume 10*, 104.

49. Ryman, *A Brush With Disney*, 162.

50. Shows, *Walt: Backstage Adventures with Walt Disney*, 59–60.

51. Roy Disney, *Readers' Digest*, "Unforgettable Walt Disney," 216.

52. France, *Window on Main Street*, 135.

53. Thomas, *Walt Disney*, 231.

54. Ghez, *Walt's People: Volume 10*, 111.

55. Thomas, *Building a Company*, 261.

56. Quoting Cottrell, in Thomas, *Building a Company*, 262.

57. Thomas, *Building a Company*, 262.

PRINCIPLE EIGHT

Let Creativity Work for You

Walt Disney was extremely creative in ways that most business practitioners are not. One notable trait that set him apart from his contemporaries, noted journalist Vernon Scott, was that "[Walt] was a creative artist who was forced to become a businessman. Those other guys were businessmen who invaded the arts. ... He was always on the side of quality and art, not just the buck. ... [H]e wanted to put quality up on the screen."

"Those other guys" were studio heads like Harry Cohn (Columbia Pictures), Louis B. Mayer (MGM), Jack Warner (Warner Bros.), and Daryl Zanuck (Twentieth Century-Fox), and "they weren't creative men like Disney was," said Vernon.[1]

Walt well understood that freewheeling creativity without purpose and imposed structure had little value. From his earliest days, he developed specific processes to capture and transform creative ideas into things of value. "There was much more to his success than a blind faith in intuition," writes Christopher Finch, art curator and author of *The Art of Walt Disney*. "He knew that for intuition to mean anything it had to be implemented, and that this demanded a combination of stringent analysis and sheer hard work, backed up by the practical talents of the artists with whom he surrounded himself."[2]

The Walt Disney difference finds its roots in both his intellect and values. Walt was an idealist and romantic who wanted to be an artist but didn't have the patience for it. It allowed him to be sympathetic to the artistic disposition within the creative business process and to build a successful commercial arts-based organization and creative mecca.

Roy, who by his own admission typified the business-mind, commented about Walt in the May 1966 issue of *Fortune* magazine: "I just try to keep up with him—and make it pay. I'm afraid if I'd been running this place we would have stopped several times en route because of the problems. Walt had the stick-to-itiveness."[3]

Dream, Dream, Dream, and Then Retreat

The creative development processes developed by Walt Disney and his team was one of his secrets to creating wealth, and to this day remain a core competency of the company. Walt understood that creativity also requires discipline, which is why he was not only a dreamer, but also a planner. "In fact," writes Bob Thomas in *Building a Company*, "Walt never entered any project without meticulous planning." All of his Disneyland-related projects started with economic research. If the findings were favorable, "Walt proceeded with planning, which could take months or years. Sketches and models were prepared and carefully analyzed. Everything was mapped out before Walt would signal the go-ahead."[4]

One could say that Walt dreamed with both feet planted firmly on the ground. Mike Vance wrote, "One of the many ways Walt Disney amazed the world was by not only dreaming big dreams, but by dreaming doable dreams."[5] Reflecting back upon Walt's life, Roy said: "He was a practical guy. He would dream, dream, dream, but then he would come back to reality. The main thing was to get the job done. He would try for the utmost, and then he would retreat to a position he could handle."[6]

Walt originally created WED Enterprises to explore the concepts of television production and Disneyland, the latter starting with sketches in order to create something objective from intangible thoughts and ideas. As the Disneyland concept progressed, Walt took on all aspects of creating the final product through his WED team, with every square foot designed and engineered to appeal to the senses, from the color and materials used to construct the attractions, to the textures of the pavement, to the sounds and smells one experiences throughout the park. Walt held as a foundational premise that every frame of a Disney movie or aspect of a Disney park must make a contribution to the story. Walt invoked creativity in striving for total integration of ideas and execution. Everything was the result of a choice to enhance the human experience, and nothing was left to chance.

"Disneyland is a thing that I can keep molding and shaping," said Walt. "It's a three-dimensional thing to play with. But when I say 'play with it,' I don't mean that. Everything I do I keep a practical eye toward its appeal to the public."[7]

For Walt, creativity was just another facet of a culture of ongoing innovation and *discontinuous* improvement.

Creativity Requires Focus

Taking charge of one's curiosity and managing it into a creativity process requires a specific methodology, and a commitment to adhere to it and invest appropriately. Like the adage that to be a writer you have to write, to be creative you have to create.

Walt's creative power was derived from his unusual and heightened ability to focus all his knowledge and experience into a specific context and extract actionable conclusions. His ability to freely tap into his imagination in seemingly unencumbered ways was one of his unique and distinguishing characteristics and a source of awe and inspiration for his colleagues and others whom he worked with.

As one example, consider the iconoclastic act of the creation of *Snow White and the Seven Dwarfs*. Upon reflection, some who were involved with Walt in the creation of *Snow White* thought that the monumental and historic achievement it represented had everything to do with Walt and very little to do with the animators involved. Gabler writes:

> Wilfred Jackson believed that the animators were really irrelevant and that Walt was the only one who really mattered. "It is my opinion," he told [Frank] Thomas and [Ollie] Johnston, "that if Walt had started in some different place at the same time with a different bunch of guys, the result would have been more or less along the same lines." *Snow White* belonged to Walt Disney, just as Walt Disney belonged to *Snow White*.[8]

The results would likely have been the same because of Walt's ability to invoke awe and inspiration amongst his staff. Mel Shaw writes:

> In this highly charged and successful studio atmosphere, animators, artists, and storymen were continually vying for Walt's approval by trying to present him with their most superior work. This made the employees work harder than ever; no one had any doubt as to who was at the helm of this ship. We were all trying to please and impress Walt."[9]

For Walt, the creation of *Snow White and the Seven Dwarfs*, *Pinocchio*, and *Fantasia* weren't just about art and story and the technical aspects of filmmaking. Each was a multi-year project requiring new and unprecedented complexities including hiring, training, production coordination, expansion of the studio, financing, special-effects innovation, and lots more, overlaid upon Walt's already established business responsibilities and obligations to produce new and original Mickeys and Silly Symphonies to meet contractual obligations.

The Creative Recruiting of Creative Talent

One aspect of being creative is to surround oneself with creative people. That's what Walt did. He wasn't just a talent scout for his live-action films; he had always been a talent scout for all major roles across the studio's creative value chain.

He was a master at matching talent to his aspirations. When he had a project to work on, he would seek out the most appropriate talent and try to recruit them to the task, whether they were currently with the studio or outside of it.

For example, by the time it came to staffing WED, Walt had intimate knowledge of the backgrounds, interests, and capabilities of the staff at his animation studio as well as other talented people in the industry. With this knowledge, he began to recruit and redeploy them into new roles, asking them to undergo a mind-shift and apply the principles of two- and three-dimensional design for animated and live-action films to the creation of interactive environments for people. Often they were asked to do something they had never done before and didn't know how to do. They had to study, learn, create, and take chances together.

Walt understood that he needed show-business people for these roles, and assembled a powerhouse group of respected creative talent— Imagineers—that included Marty Sklar, Herb Ryman, John Hench, Peter Ellenshaw, Marc Davis, Bill Justice, Harper Goff, Alice Davis, X. Atencio, Ken Anderson, and many others who have become recognized for their pioneering work.[10] They were able to leverage the combined power of their creative imaginations to portray their own and Walt's ideas graphically and via sketches, paintings, and models, and further springboard to an even higher level of creativity.

In general, the task assignment of Imagineers was to develop ideas for theme park attractions that would dazzle customers, and then figure out how to build them to fit into the park and achieve the desired effect. Walt was confident that because of the unique skills and abilities of the people he recruited, they would be more valuable contributors at WED than at the studio, even when the individuals themselves weren't quite sure what Walt had in mind and what they were getting themselves into.

"Walt was gathering people almost like instruments in an orchestra," said Imagineer Bob Gurr. "He put us all together, but he never passed out the music. Oddly enough, I think he was the *only* one who knew where he was going to go. He knew the different skills that all the different folks had, and he put them together. But only he knew what the outcome was going to be."[11]

According to Imagineer Randy Bright, "The WED staff became a harmonic blend of talents that was unparalleled in the entertainment industry. It consisted of designers, architects, writers, sculptors, engineers, creators of special effects, and imaginative people from many other disciplines." Author Steve Mannheim writes that Walt's vision for WED was to gather together a diverse team of professionally trained "Renaissance men" capable of working effectively and creatively "alongside the many vocations in the motion picture business."[12]

Harrison "Buzz" Price, who reported directly to Walt for more than ten years as his trusted research consultant, recognized that Walt's ability to assemble, organize, and unleash great talent was a boon to creativity:

> Walt knew how to assemble a remarkable collection of talents, great egos to be sure, and they clashed from time to time as egos will, but the concept of working together usually over-rode such problems. He would accommodate anybody who could get the job done even though the style might be antagonistic to his own. The spirit and the loyalty that Walt manifested to his family and the people working for him channeled diverse views to a common commitment to the job at hand. There was this intangible spiritual glue."[13]

Creativity Requires the Removal of Constraining Barriers

Walt looked for hidden potential in ideas and abilities and thrived on pushing the limits of conventional thinking. He abhorred negativity and cynicism as detrimental to the creative process. This constant forward pushing and pulling often frustrated others who didn't understand his motives or methods, or lacked the disposition and courage to step outside their own comfort zone, thereby preventing them from contributing effectively under Walt's leadership.

Disney lawyer Bob Foster says he discovered Walt's disdain for negativity early in his career: "Walt didn't particularly like attorneys. The reason was that attorneys essentially are negative people, cautioning their clients about what not to do. Walt didn't like being told what not to do. I learned not to avoid him, but not to bother him. The important thing with Walt was to state things positively."[14]

Walt understood that a key element of creativity is barrier-free thinking to develop ideas. Later these ideas will have to be made practical, but starting the thinking process must proceed without stifling constraints.

According to Frank Thomas, Walt sought a positive atmosphere in idea-generation meetings. He observed, "If you said no to his proposal, he'd say, 'Why the hell can't I do that? We're trying to get ideas here. Maybe we won't get any good ones, but we sure won't if you take a negative attitude.'"[15]

As the old expression goes, Walt was not one to suffer fools gladly, nor was he prone to let time go lightly. When he attended meetings he demanded productive use of his time, and when they were over, or became non-productive, he left. Bill Cottrell reflected on Walt's participation in *Snow White* story sessions:

> He was such a dynamic personality himself that he made every story meeting, every meeting in a sweatbox an important one. He didn't

take anything for granted. It was as though he had something to do and accomplish and time was of the essence. He had a great ability to use his time."[16]

Walt was less strict about how others used their own time, within limits. According to Hazel George, Walt often said, "You can't put a guy in a room and say, 'Create!'" Walt's job was to motivate, inspire, and create a positive and challenging working environment that would allow others to get to where Walt needed to go. Charles Shows observed: "I believe...a key reason why his films were superior, was time: he gave his creative people the time to be creative. ... Disney never used the word *hurry*. He would let a writer develop a script until it was as near perfect as the writer and Walt could make it."[17]

Ollie Johnston was one among many who found story meetings with Walt to be "really marvelous." He would become so motivated by Walt's creative enthusiasm that "I couldn't wait to get back to my board."[18]

Homer Brightman provides an early example of Walt's mind at work in a 1935 Donald Duck story meeting in which storyboards were being presented to Walt. The meeting started at 8:30 a.m., and after three-and-a-half hours,

> The group seemed restless and tired, but Walt was just getting steamed up. He was able to do the whole story by himself. He didn't need any help; just a couple of cigar store Indians to bounce his stuff off of. He described everything clearly as if it had taken place on a picture screen in his mind. ... Walt went on in a rush, his eyes vacant as if he actually saw the picture animating before him and he was simply describing what he saw. ... Walt then went back over the whole story from beginning to end, never hesitating, adding new things as he went along. His mind seemed to be a kaleidoscope of ideas forever changing, sending new messages to him. I think his mind was something he couldn't turn off if he had wanted to.[19]

Not much changed over the years in this regard. Songwriter Richard Sherman, writing about his experiences with Walt in the early 1960s, noted, "We had learned from experience that when Walt was hot on a subject, one had to let him expound uninterrupted. He didn't tolerate interruptions at these moments. Those he was with were to merely act as sounding boards for his enthusiasm."[20]

Walt made it a long-standing practice to eliminate situations that created artificial constraints hindering his ability to produce effective results. For example, he learned to avoid joint ownership of projects through corporate partnerships where possible. When they were necessary to move forward, he would later negotiate a buy-out to regain control. The primary reason for sole ownership, from Walt's perspective, was that it expanded his ability to think creatively by eliminating unnecessary barriers. Walt liked to pursue his goals without concerning himself with others getting in his way and slowing him down, or encumbering him from leveraging his imagination to achieve his vision.

It was for this reason that he disliked general meetings, especially corporate board meetings, unless they were positive, purposeful, and productive. He found that too often they stifled creativity. Disney writer Jack Spiers provides some insight:

> Walt didn't like meetings. He told me that a meeting was a bunch of people pooling their common ignorance. So when I was writing the General Electric Carousel of Progress show for the World's Fair, about three or four times a month the honchos from General Electric would fly out to hold a meeting to discuss the project. Nothing would ever get settled at those meetings. Walt finally came in and stood at the head of the table and said, "All right gentlemen, what I want you to do is go down to the Coral Room and have a good lunch. Then I want you to go back to Burbank Airport and get in your Grumman Gulf Stream and fly back east where you came from and stay there until I've got something I want you to see. Then, I'll call *you*. Thank you, gentlemen" and he turned around and left.[21]

Walt was also skeptical about entering into agreements with governments for reasons of creativity and control. When Walt was working on plans to develop EPCOT, President Lyndon Johnson signed the Demonstration Cities and Metropolitan Act of 1966 to provide financial and technical assistance to improved inner-city revitalization. One stated goal of the program was to "promote the...application of new and improved technologies and methods of constructing, rehabilitating, and maintaining housing, and the application of advances in technology to urban development communities" and to develop "new and imaginative proposals." A study was initiated by Walt to investigate the best way to seek federal funds to support EPCOT. In the end he chose to forgo pursuing government assistance, having concluded that the control he would have to give up to conform to oversight by the Department of Housing and Urban Development (HUD) wasn't worth it.[22]

Everything Is Connected to Everything Else

Another aspect that defined Walt's method of creativity was his determination to extend the application of discovery and ingenuity beyond its initial scope by building on his successes. Walt often dabbled in ideas out of sheer curiosity without knowing where they would lead, while having some sense at the time that what he was creating may be a small step along a path to something better and more valuable that may only come to fruition somewhere off in the future.

Walt had an uncanny ability to visualize and imagine possibilities for successful commercial endeavors where others operating from a different context or paradigm were dismissive and disparaging. We saw this from those who thought the attempt to make a full-length animated feature was folly, and again in the mindset of amusement park owners and their initial reaction to Walt's plans for Disneyland. Walt was also operating in such a way that he was able to project his imagination further into the future than most. He possessed the rare cognitive ability to connect all his knowledge in the discovery of potential future paths and to break it down into identifiable stages extending forward in time.

Another example of Walt's entrepreneurial insight and ability to extend the scope of his creative commitment is evident in the development and application of Audio-Animatronics, which helped to make Disney attractions such a big hit at the 1964 World's Fair.

The Abraham Lincoln figure that was at the forefront of computerized three-dimensional staged entertainment can be traced back to a visit by Walt and Lillian to New Orleans, and a Disney family vacation to Europe.

On a 1946 train trip to the Atlanta premier of *Song of the South* with Lillian, at a stop in New Orleans, Walt discovered a 100-year-old French antique automated wind-up bird in a gilded cage. He was intrigued by the wide variety of small life-like actions the mechanical bird could exhibit which included whistling, and purchased it for his home.

A number of years later, in the summer of 1949, Walt combined a visit to England to observe the production of *Treasure Island* with an extended family trip to Ireland, Switzerland, and France. His daughter Diane recalled:

> When we went to Paris, Dad went off on his own and came back with boxes and boxes of these little windup toys. He wound them all up and put them on the floor of the room and just sat and watched them. You know, the dog that rolls over and stuff like that. He said, "Look at that movement with just a simple mechanism." He was studying; he could see Audio-Animatronics. We thought he was crazy.[23]

What intrigued Walt was the idea of how technology had advanced from complex mechanical birds to simple and inexpensive mechanical toys seemingly capable of acting on their own by means of a hidden mechanism. He began to wonder how much better his guys in the machine shop could do putting this kind of technology to use with the more advanced tools and technologies of today.

Around this time, Walt began to enjoy working with miniatures in the design and building of his trains. He also began to think about making automated miniature dioramas using the kinds of mechanisms contained in the bird and the toys. Before investing in that idea, Walt hand-built a miniature model of Granny Kincaid's cabin from the film *So Dear to My*

Heart. He installed lights that would come on when people stood in front of it to peer inside and recorded Granny telling her story. He then made plans to have it displayed at the 1952 Festival of California Living in Los Angeles where he could assess the audience reaction, which was generally boredom due to the lack of action.

In the meantime, Walt was interested in doing something more sophisticated and difficult to test the capabilities of his Imagineers to create animated models based on what could be learned from the mechanized toys.

In 1951 Walt assigned Broggie and sculptor Wathel Rogers to lead a team in creating a nine-inch tall mechanical figure that could dance on a stage and talk using cams and cables, and which became known as "Project Little Man." The project was relatively successful.

This was followed by the development of a barbershop quartet in which the figures moved and appeared to sing, but given the lack of miniaturization of technology at the time, it was impossible to build it as envisioned by Walt. If they were to use the technology then available, the animated figures would have to be bigger. Broggie recalled: "I told Walt that if we were allowed to build full-size figures, we could put the equipment inside the figure. We wouldn't have to go through cables and cams, we could build integrated figures."[24]

The mechanical projects were put on hold as Disneyland became Walt's top priority, only to be resurrected around 1960, at which time Walt delivered his clockwork bird to Broggie with instructions to reverse engineer it and figure out how it worked. "Walt gave it to me," said Broggie, "and asked me to look inside it. I was supposed to take it apart, and it was like taking apart a piece of jewelry. When I finally got it all apart and laid everything out I found a little bellows made of canvas, and some little cams and other parts."[25]

Walt instructed Broggie to develop the technology to animate mechanical devices, including plans for a life-size interactive fortune-telling Confucius to be placed in the lobby of a Chinese restaurant at Disneyland. Broggie and Rogers were able to build a head with blinking eyes and moving mouth before Walt stopped the project to work on something bigger and better: an animated likeness of Abraham Lincoln that could stand, move, and talk. All of this development over the span of years eventually led to the use of Audio-Animatronics in the development of Disneyland attractions, including the creation of animals for the Jungle Cruise and in the automation of birds and other inanimate objects for the Enchanted Tiki Room. Eventually, Walt's fascination with three-dimensional animation resulted in the creation of Abraham Lincoln and the Hall of Presidents using modern hydraulics, electronics, and early forms of programmable computer technology.

Walt was able to take a century-old idea he discovered in the mid-1940s and develop over a period of twenty years the ingenuity, skill, and vision to create a completely new form of mass entertainment that has survived and prospered to this day.

Focusing on What *Isn't* Thought of as Necessary

Walt was said to have been in love with Paris. According to author and friend Ray Bradbury, "[Walt had] learned that one of the great secrets of cities like Paris is that there are fountains everywhere, and flowers and more places to sit...and you surrounded yourself with people and beauty that isn't necessary."[26]

That there is a general lack of interest in making available "what isn't necessary" was a key discovery for Walt. He knew from experience the inspiration and deep emotional joy that can come from receiving or discovering something heretofore thought to be unnecessary, or impossible, or perhaps not thought about at all.

As an entrepreneur, Walt made a career of identifying new information that other business leaders and managers didn't think was necessary until he had proven otherwise. By creating and delivering the unexpected and the unarticulated, Walt was able to exceed customer expectations, set new standards of possibility, and raise the bar on himself and his competitors. An excellent example is the reaction of the leading amusement park operators to Walt's concept of a modern, clean, emotionally pleasing and psychologically refreshing amusement park. Industry leaders considered this to be impossible.

Focusing on what others didn't consider necessary—often because they believed that thinking about it and creating it meant extra work and wasted effort—didn't just apply to big ideas. It also applied to the smallest details, which Walt felt were integral to creating an enhanced and more authentic audience experience for both his film and non-film projects.

As a typical example, consider that in reviewing the designs for the various scenes in the GE Carousel of Progress exhibit for the New York World's Fair, the 1920s staging showed one of the characters sitting in a bathtub with his back to the audience. Walt took one look and in his usual way, was able to instantly improve the show by turning the tub around to face the audience. Walt proceeded to remove his shoes and socks and to sit in the tub with his feet sticking up and out of the end. Walt exclaimed, "He'd wiggle his toes, don't you think?" By projecting himself into the show, Walt was able to discover and reveal how focused attention to small seemingly insignificant details can improve the authenticity, quality, and admiration by customers for the show.[27]

Regardless of personal differences between individual staff and Walt, there was great mutual respect among them. Because Walt never lowered his standards, his staff enthusiastically put forward their best effort to make meaningful contributions and feel pride in their work. And because employees were engaged, Walt left them free to create and discover solutions to challenges in the manner they thought best, subject to review and approval by Walt at the appropriate time.

The recognized experts often criticized Walt for his attention to what they considered to be unnecessary and wasteful details, but time and again, customers proved Walt right and his critics wrong.

Creating and Managing a Pyramid of Capabilities

Many commentators have stated of Walt that he could not countenance any sort of disagreement with his own views. But the evidence indicates this is a misreading of Walt's character. Part of the contradiction in observing Walt's behavior over his career comes from the fact that he had immense respect for the creative talents of his colleagues in pursuit of the tasks at hand. At the same time, he was disdainful of those who wasted his time by failing to provide thoughtful solutions that pushed the limits of their capabilities. Walt was looking for ideas and results, not polite conversation. With Walt, everything was about the work.

Walt was overwhelmed in running the studio and coordinating projects, talent, and operations. He was providing oversight to everything that was going on while working out in his mind the next big project, or innovation, or the way out of a crisis to achieve his goals, commitments, and aspirations. He was focused on the realities of running a complex business and dealing with the unprecedented problems and opportunities that confronted him, while at the same time attending story meetings, reading scripts, and reviewing drawings and scenes with his animators at the end of most days.

Many of Walt's business colleagues started off in the same place as Walt in those early days in Kansas City when everybody was learning the business together, but that didn't last long. As a result of differences in cognitive maturation, information management capabilities, motivating values, and skilled knowledge, with time Walt and his Disney studio colleagues were managing their work from different modes of capability.[28]

The relative relation between the potential capabilities of individuals changes over time as individuals mature. Obvious differences emerge in their abilities to complete longer-term complex tasks, solve unprecedented problems, and effectively manage multiple projects simultaneously and weave them into a coherent whole to meet established deadlines. Walt rapidly progressed: from animator to business manager responsible for developing organization systems and design, oversight, and coordination of business units; to architect of market-driven business strategy; to overseeing the development and coordination of a portfolio of businesses; to influencing opinions and actions in the realms of politics, commerce, technology, and society on a broad basis to promote his vision, goals, and the financial well-being of his organization and its interests.[29]

When given the opportunity, people tend to find the level of work at which they are most capable and comfortable. Walt was constantly on the lookout for staff that exhibited higher potential capability than they were utilizing in their current roles by presenting them with new and unique challenges. If one ignored the hierarchy of authority and instead arranged Disney staff in a pyramid from highest information processing capability to the lowest, none of the staff would dispute that Walt's place was at the top the pyramid.

Individuals who are able to think at higher conceptual levels see the world differently than those at lower levels because they can identify more interconnections and develop higher-level integrations from what they see as lower-level data and information. While everybody is living in the same world, not everybody conceptualizes the world the same way because people bring different cognitive skills, information processing capability, mental horsepower, and passion to interpreting and applying what they see in the world.

Consider for example that where Walt may have been responsible for coordinating the efforts of 500 people to meet production schedules and distribution deadlines while managing business relationships with the outside world, at the same time an animator may be required to spend weeks or even months in his office absorbed in drawing a 30-second animated scene in coordination with the story and music departments. Where Walt may be juggling, evaluating, and prioritizing a hundred diverse tasks and ensuring that all elements of the many movies in production and projects being developed are advancing on schedule, dealing with a multitude of issues that arise constantly and people vying for his attention, the animator by contrast is more narrowly concerned with a specialized few tasks and scene deadlines.

As the weight of responsibility on Walt's shoulders for managing the immense complexities of the organization continued to grow significantly, the separation between Walt and his animators also necessarily grew. Where at one time when they were just starting out together, they were each sharing in the same work and engaging in whatever tasks needed to be done at the time, as the complexity of operating the business increased, work had to be organized into specialized roles with defined responsibilities under managerial control.

At one time it was possible for all staff to be in a room together and they could goof around and play tennis in the morning and baseball at lunch. Over time, as the seriousness of business obligations grew, when Walt walked into a room, there was very little small talk. Whether Walt liked it or not, there was too much to do and too little time, and it was Walt who bore the weight of responsibility for ensuring all the promises and commitments, internal and external to the business, were adequately fulfilled.

Both Walt and his artists were emotionally invested in their own work as well as that of the studio, but at different levels and in different ways. If an animator felt disappointed or slighted by a decision that was made, Walt had no time to listen to an expression of the artist's feelings or opinions about his dedication to the task and the amount of work he had done, for which he now had nothing to show. Nobody was working harder and doing more for the studio and the livelihood of its employees than Walt. Walt was situated at the top of the pyramid as the primary guiding and directing intelligence of the business. For Walt to lead the organization and do the work required of him within the context of the business, he often had to detach himself from such emotional connections with the people themselves to make the best decision based on the context at hand.

As an example, an artist may be upset at Walt for being critical or dismissive of what amounts to two weeks of work, and be disappointed that he now has to rethink a scene where he was hoping to put it behind him and move on to something else. Walt, on the other hand, may be frustrated that the lack of progress on a scene is putting pressure on the production schedule, and while he wanted to move this animator on to something else of pressing urgency, he now has to reassess all of his plans and find another solution while the scene is being reanimated.

A clear pattern emerges across the Disney literature: in almost every instance cited where there are personal conflicts between staff and Walt, it is related to a difference in perspective and context rooted in seeing the work from different levels of abstraction.

Those on the receiving end of Walt's ire will say that Walt couldn't take criticism. But Walt's mind was not closed to new and better ideas. In fact, the opposite was true. Walt would frequently throw out good work—work that was already *better* than what the competition could produce—to pursue something even greater. Those who were more astute understood that, rightly or wrongly, it was the approach one took with Walt that was of the essence, not the content of the discussion. Walt was prepared to deal with the facts, but had no time or inclination in such situations to deal with negative emotional arguments or ego-driven outbursts.

Many individuals found their own preferred ways to deal with Walt, but perhaps the most insightful observation was that of Buzz Price. When Price began working with Walt through SRI, he discovered the value of what he called "yes if" consulting, and avoiding "no because." "Yes if" was conducive to Walt's desire for positive creativity and avoidance of negativity. "Yes if" avoided the problem of telling Walt what couldn't be done. Price writes:

> If necessary to make a project work, "yes if" could contemplate and consider a partial or complete change in direction. "Yes if" was the language of an enabler, pointing to what needed to be done to make the possible plausible. Walt liked this language. "No because" is the language of a deal killer. "Yes if" is the approach of a deal maker. Creative people thrive on "yes if."[30]

Walt Disney's Tips on How to Produce Original Ideas

In *Break Out of the Box*, former Disney University dean Mike Vance summarizes nine points from his notes and recollections that encapsulate Walt Disney's views and opinions on what produces original ideas:

- *Avoid trite jargon and clichés.* Using jargon and bromides often becomes a substitute for really thinking through a problem.

- *Don't copy, steal, or plagiarize.* Respect the intellectual property rights of others and expect the same in return. Be aggressive in protecting what is yours.

- *Ask probing questions.* Be curious. Get to the core of the problem and opportunity through good research and development. "When we start a project," Walt said, "we really study it from every angle. We literally walk around it from every point of view in order to leave no stone unturned."

- *Use stories to communicate.* Stories draw people in, and require a beginning, middle, and end. They can tap into imagination and engage and motivate people to action.

- *Remember that the best answers are often the simplest answers.* Original thinking can be stifled or blocked by making a task or challenge too complex. Walt said, "Keep it so simple a child can understand it."

- *Be a nonconformist.* Have respect for tradition, laws, manners, and decency, but at the same time explore new approaches that might go against other people's deeply held preconceptions. Innovation requires breaking the rules.

- *Avoid sequels.* Once you've created something once, it's time to move on by expanding the boundaries and pursuing something more challenging. Walt believed in life-long learning.

- *Study creativity in nature.* Walt studied creativity in nature. He said: "I like to watch animals to find out how old Mother Nature handles a problem." Creativity requires a change of scenery and time to think about things in a fresh way.

- *Find connections between things.* Part of Walt's genius was his ability to link different stories and ideas together to come up with unusual and creative solutions. Walt said: "One thing leads to another thing. It's important to find the connection between the parts if we expect to come up with original solutions." As a way to get ideas out of people's heads, he would often say: "Show it to me. Don't tell it to me."[31]

Lessons We Can Learn from Walt Disney's Business Success

- Creativity requires hard work and stringent analysis. Do the work.

- Creativity requires discipline. Make research and planning a core element of your creative process.

- Dream big dreams—achievable dreams—with both feet planted firmly on the ground.

- Everything is the result of a choice. Don't leave important things to chance.

- Make choices that will enhance the human experience.

- Make creativity and innovation an important facet of your business culture.

- Be an active talent scout. Surround yourself with creative people.

- Study, learn, create, and take chances together.

- Channel diverse views into a common commitment to achieve the task at hand.

- Don't let negativity and cynicism destroy the creative process. Separate barrier-free thinking from practical refinement.

- Don't waste your time or the time of others in unproductive meetings.

- Provide customers with something valuable but not considered "necessary" to exceed their expectations.

- Give employees space to discover solutions, make meaningful contributions, and take pride in their work.

- Use "yes if" language of engagement to promote creativity, not stifling "no because" language that puts up barriers.

1. Vernon Scott quoted in Green and Green, *Remembering Walt*, 128.

2. Finch, *The Art of Walt Disney*, New Concise Edition, 1975, 12.

3. Thomas, *Building a Company*, 287.

4. Thomas, *Building a Company*, 251.

5. Vance and Deacon, *Think Out of the Box*, 71.

6. Roy Disney quoted in Bob Thomas, *Building a Company*, 302.

7. Smith, *The Quotable Walt Disney*, 45.

8. Gabler, *Walt Disney*, 246–247.

9. Shaw, *Animator on Horseback*, 100.

10. See Price, *Walt's Revolution!*, 51.

11. Greene & Greene, *Inside the Dream*, 132.

12. Mannheim, *Walt Disney and the Quest for Community*, xviii.

13. Price, *Walt's Revolution!*, 65.

14. Foster quoted in Thomas, *Building a Company*, 278.

15. Thomas, *Walt Disney*, 10.

16. Cottrell quoted in Ghez, *Walt's People: Volume 10*, 49–50.

17. Shows, *Walt: Backstage Adventures With Walt Disney*, 193.

18. Johnston in Ghez, *Walt's People: Volume 10*, 126.

19. Brightman, *Life in the Mouse House*, 17–18.

20. Sherman, *Moose*, 282.

21. Green and Green, *Remembering Walt*, 174.

22. Gennawey, *Walt Disney and the Promise of Progress City*, 139; Mannheim, *Walt Disney and the Quest for Community*, xiv.

23. Diane Disney Miller in Green and Green, *Remembering Walt*, 165.

24. Keith Gluck, "The Early Days of Audio-Animatronics," waltdisney.org/blog/early-days-audio-animatronics, accessed September 19, 2016.

25. Barrier, *The Animated Man*, 290.

26. Gennawey, *Walt Disney and the Promise of Progress City*, 122.

27. Source of story is Randy Bright, in Barrier, *The Animated Man*, 292.

28. See Jaques and Cason, *Human Capability: A Study of Individual Potential and its Application*.

29. See Jaques and Cason, *Human Capability*.

30. Price, *Walt's Revolution!*, 32.

31. Vance & Deacon, *Break Out of the Box*, 98–99.

Think Deeply from All Directions

Walt Disney was a maverick and an iconoclast. He wasn't an intellectual, but he was a practical and fiercely independent thinker with a proven ability to influence, challenge, and overturn the status quo. He had an immense respect for people with practical intelligence, skilled knowledge, and a passion for achievement, and was constantly seeking ways to connect people and resources to achieve extraordinary results.

In interviews, Walt spoke about the considerable time he spent thinking about opportunities and developing his ideas, often reflecting on them for years in an ongoing spiral of chewing, building, refining, adapting, sharing with others and incorporating input, and feeding his mind with research. On many occasions Walt created what James Collins and Jerry Porras, authors of *Built to Last: Successful Habits of Visionary Companies*, referred to as Big Hairy Audacious Goals (BHAG), i.e., a long-term goal that changes the fundamental nature of how a business competes.

Time after time Walt would envision an opportunity and its end state, define his goals strategically, think carefully and creatively about how to achieve them within an established timeframe, and take decisive action by aligning resources, talent, and managerial oversight.

Recall Walt's decision to leverage the latent value of his brand and products on television to attract investment capital and business partners in support of building Disneyland. Not only did he have the courage to stand up to the pressure of the movie industry studios to boycott television, he also demonstrated his ability to see beyond the obvious financial deal to a more profound, integrated, and disruptive long-term strategic vision for the entire corporation.

In an interview in 1959 published in *Think*, Walt was asked, "Do you find that TV is affecting your motion pictures in the theater?" Walt replied, "Not at all. ... We went into TV with one thing in mind. Not to go out of the motion-picture business, but to keep the audience aware of motion pictures. We lost $2,000,000 last year in TV. But we sold our motion-picture product."[1]

Walt's ability to think at a higher level and from all directions allowed him to confidently create and pursue opportunities that successful entrepreneurs of the day dismissed as reckless and crazy, such as ABC's Leonard Goldenson, the folks at film distributor RKO, and other financial types.

Create the Future Then Clear the Path

Walt dreamed about the future, and then thought deeply about how to connect his vision with the reality at hand in a practical manner. This skill helped to make him a successful business visionary. He was involved in all aspects of his business, but as he matured he tried not to become immersed and embedded in day-to-day firefighting. Instead, he was leading and inspiring his artists, Imagineers, and executives to create and influence the future to suit his corporate interests by negotiating to clear a pathway toward his vision with business partners, industry leaders, and governments.

To do this effectively, Walt had to consider the impact of his work from multiple perspectives. Robert Dilts, a trainer and educator in the field of neuro-linguistic programming, studied Walt's creative thinking process and identified three primary components of Walt's methodology, which he called *dreamer, realist,* and *critic.*

Generalizing, Dilts found that in the "dreamer" phase the thinker fantasizes creatively, abstractly, and without boundaries from his or her own personal perspective.

In the "realist" phase the thinker assesses the situation from someone else's personal perspective, such as customers, employees, or other interested parties.

In the "critic" phase the thinker reflects critically on the situation from a more removed objective perspective. This phase serves a different purpose than the first two phases. The dreamer and realist positions are experiential assessments from the inside. The critic is external to the process, and represents an evaluation based on a defined set of criteria, in this case business criteria. If phases one and two represent what the experience of the dream or vision might look and feel like, the third phase is about assessing how and whether the outcome can be achieved given the existing constraints.[2]

We saw this explicitly in Walt's thinking about the creation of Disneyland. He expounded a view from his own perspective as a father trying to find something to do together with his daughters (dreamer); the view from the experiences of a child going to an amusement park (realist); and later, a more fully considered and practical perspective such as that outlined in his proposal to the City of Burbank (critic). While he didn't use the language, Walt had developed a generalized process of thinking critically from all directions, including qualitative and quantitative research, before developing plans, and then cycling through the process to "plus" them with input from others that included concept drawings and models, until he had reached certainty about the best path forward.

"When we consider a new project," said Walt, "we really study it—not just the surface idea, but everything about it. And when we go into the new project, we believe in it all the way. We have confidence in our ability to do it right. And we work hard to do the best possible job."[3]

From Contrasts and Options to Commitment and Action

When Walt first explored the possibility of building a park for the studio, his intention was to create a recreational environment where parents and children could do things together in a clean, safe, stimulating, and fun environment. Walt set for himself the task of discovering such places so he could learn how to build such a park. To his amazement, with one or two exceptions, such places didn't exist. Walt realized that to create the kind of park he envisioned, he would have to invent his own blueprint. That there was no existing precedent was an indicator to Walt that whatever amusement park owners and tourist attraction operators thought to be the best way to do things, they were wrong.

Conventional thinking in this area failed to meet Walt's minimally acceptable standards. As he visited parks and observed the way they operated, he realized that what he was investigating was not how to run a successful tourist attraction, but rather the opposite: how to run an *unsuc-cessful* tourist attraction. In a way, discovering how not to do things made Walt's challenge easier, for it established a point of contrast and set him on a quest to figure out what was wrong with the existing amusement park business model in the context of his own unique vision for creating a fun and family-inclusive experience. His difficult challenge as an entrepreneur was to figure out a viable business model to justify the park's existence and create enough excitement and interest to entice outside investors.

As long as Walt was just thinking, it didn't cost him any money. But as soon as he required others to contribute their own thinking and exper-tise, he had to hire staff and pay wages. Many of the people he initially hired to work on the imagining and building of Disneyland came from Twentieth-Century Fox. According to Herb Ryman's biographer, John Stanley Donaldson, there was a good reason for this. Twentieth-Century Fox had a backlot that was "five times the size of Disneyland. Having everything—from temple to tenement. A period riverfront had been con-structed to thirty acres, replete with streets, buildings, and piers; a replica steamboat, the *Clermont*, side-paddled to a three-acre basin, excavated to depth of seven feet—filled with five million gallons of water. ... The place just needed a turnstile."[4]

In Walt's mind, designing and building a working studio backlot wasn't conceptually much different than building a working park. He sought and hired artists with experience in set design and storytelling, identified the gaps, and worked to close them.

Walt made a common practice of studying and learning from his own and others' mistakes and failures. It was almost habitual for him to quickly identify shortcomings, from which he would springboard to a creative solution that could be aligned with his own vision and values.

As an illustration of how Walt used this technique of contrast and extension, consider that in the estimation of animator Ward Kimball, Walt had two artists on staff in the late 1940s who were inefficient and incapable of doing good work. During a private discussion, Walt defended their contributions to Kimball, noting, "Homer and Harry are alright. By doing things wrong, I can tell the right way of doing things."[5] In other words, Walt understood that it was in part the perceived shortcomings of Homer Brightman and Harry Reeves that made them valuable members of Walt's team. In this regard, mistakes and failures served as a foil for Walt—as a point of contrast or demarcation against a more suitable alternative. Walt understood that in the realm of creativity, he would be worse off without such points of contrast upon which to build.

By investing in and embracing his own mistakes, failures, and disappointments as well as those of others, Walt was able to partake in valuable R&D and investigative techniques leading him to different options and perspectives on how to overcome difficult and sometimes seemingly impossible challenges. Walt is quoted in the *Chicago Tribune* in 1966: "I happen to be kind of an inquisitive guy and when I see things I don't like, I start thinking, why do they have to be like this and how can I improve them?"[6]

The World as It Could Be

There are detractors that accuse Walt of having suffered from a psychological need to embrace a flight from reality to cope with the world. Such psychologizing seems to be a complete misreading of Walt. If anything, Walt's lifetime of achievement in the face of critics who thought they were smarter and wiser than a self-educated eighth-grader proves the opposite. It demonstrates that Walt had clearer insights into the ways of the world, in the context of his work and creating commercial value in his field of expertise. Walt's differing viewpoint was an extension of his benevolent sense of life and insight that deep down all people hold roughly the same values and want the same basic things.

Walt's inherent optimism and belief in shared common-sense values is given support by the research of Christopher Alexander, a professor at University of California at Berkeley from 1963 to 2002, and expert in human-centered urban design.[7] As pointed out by Sam Gennawey in *Walt Disney and the Promise of Progress City*,

> One of the most fundamental and relevant discoveries from Alexander's research has been the realization that "human feeling is mostly the same, mostly the same from person to person, mostly the same in every person."…. Alexander's forty-year research has shown that those individual qualities account for only 10 percent of human feelings. The other 90 percent are the "stuff in which we are all the same and we feel the same things."

"One of Walt Disney's greatest gifts," writes Gennawey, "was his ability to understand and tap into those universal feelings." Because of this ability, "[Walt's] creations have crossed the boundaries of time and culture, and his work is still relevant today."[8]

It is also worth noting that many of the famous social psychology experiments of the 1960s and 1970s by people like Yale University psychologist Stanley Milgram and Stanford University's Philip Zimbardo helped to demonstrate that a large part of our behavior is conditioned by the situations in which we find ourselves and our preconceptions of how we ought to behave when placed in certain roles. Those experiments seem to provide support for Walt's approach to building human environments and embedding within them norms and standards based on shared human values.

Dick Nunis, who was head of Disneyland Park Operations at the time, tells this interesting story:

> Billy Graham came to the park in the early 1960s. He'd never been to Disneyland before and Walt escorted him around. I was with them to make sure everything went all right. We got off the Jungle Cruise and Billy stopped in the middle of Adventureland and said, "Gosh, what a fantastic world! What a marvelous fantasy world."
>
> Walt said, "Billy, look around you at all the people. All the nationalities. All the colors. All the languages. All of them are smiling. All of them are having fun together. Billy, *this* is the *real* world. The fantasy's outside."[9]

Walt was aware of the power that Disneyland had over people of all ages and cultures, and was trying to understand more about what he created and to build on it, which eventually drove his passion for the idea of EPCOT.

Over his career, Walt's thinking evolved from entertaining people and making them laugh by showing comical gag situations in movie houses around the world; to understanding how to create drawings of characters that could act to tell a story, set to sound and music to alter human emotions; to building a park that could change and enhance people's positive experiences. For Walt, EPCOT was the next step: a larger-scale experiment in creating a positive social environment to enhance the human condition.

Shifting Perspective for Insight and Understanding

Walt's ability to shift perspectives, to identify paradigm boundaries and constraints and apply imagination to move beyond them, was a hallmark of his creative methodology. He was able to take everything he knew pertaining to a challenge or opportunity, and over time spin the pieces around in his head like a Rubik's Cube, searching for a way to create alignment amongst the pieces, including their monetization. "I've got a lot of [ideas]," Walt once said. "I haven't worked them out and I haven't proved them out. I carry ideas around in my head for a long time."[10]

Once Walt did prove them out in his head, he was prone to action. For example, he rethought the reasons that film studios actively fought against the emerging technology of television to reach an opposing viewpoint, and once television was shown not to be a passing fad, he resisted the trend to license out his back catalog of films for the small screen. Author Charles Tranberg writes,

> By the mid-1950s many motion picture studios realized that television was here to stay and began selling many of their older films to TV to make an extra profit. Disney, on the other hand, felt that many of his classics could be re-released in theatres and make millions more. For example, *Twenty-Thousand Leagues Under the Sea* brought in $5.6 million in its initial release in 1954. When it was re-released in 1963 the film brought in another $2.5 million. *Snow White* grossed another $2.75 million on its fourth re-issue and the third time *Bambi* was released it brought in more money than its first two releases *combined*." Other films that did less well and were not strong candidates for theatrical re-release were edited and shown on the Disney television show.[11]

Russell Ackoff, Wharton professor of management science, refers to these kinds of creative leaps and qualitative changes as *discontinuities* in his 1994 book *The Democratic Corporation*, writing:

> Creative leaps are *discontinuities*. ... They involve three steps: identification of self-imposed constraints (assumptions); removing them; and exploring the consequences of their removal. This is why there is always an element of surprise when we are exposed to creative work—it always embodies the denial of something we have taken for granted, usually unconsciously. This is particularly true when we are exposed to the solution of a puzzle that we cannot solve precisely

because of a self-imposed constraint; hence the *aha!* experience when the solution is shown to us.

The point is that *creative but discontinuous improvements* are usually worth much more than a string of *small but continuous improvements*. This is not to say that continuous improvement has no value, but it can seldom elevate an organization into a leadership position. It should be used to augment, not to substitute for, a discontinuous improvement program.

Put another way: continuous improvement, valuable as it is when it does yield improvements, is at best a way of trying to catch up with a leader. ... Creative leaps are required to take the lead.[12]

While Walt was focused on discontinuous improvements in many different areas in his effort to build a new kind of amusement park, one area that turned out to be key was the discovery and application of urban design and planning principles that would deliver to visitors the positive experiences he intended and desired. Urban planner Sam Gennawey writes, "Disneyland did not start out to become a showcase for innovative urban design and planning policies, but that is exactly what has happened."[13]

The uniqueness and quality of the Disneyland experience immediately raised the level of expectations among consumers of other types of retail, entertainment, and leisure attractions. Gennawey observes: "Not only did Disneyland change the public's perception of what an amusement park could be, Walt's innovations have forever changed the public's expectations of the public realm and how we design these spaces."[14] With Walt having demonstrated that the lowly amusement park had so much potential for reformation and transformation, entrepreneurs and consumers began to follow Walt's lead by reimagining the possibilities for other less demanding environments.

The success of Disneyland as an example of a new innovation in large-scale environmental design of public space by story artists and movie set designers revealed a new and hidden core competency of WED. With Disneyland, Walt not only had the park that had consumed him for decades, he also began to realize he had something of greater significance. Seen as it had been intended, Disneyland was a singular attraction built to support the next stage in the expansion of the Disney business empire and the business interests of Walt Disney Productions. Walt saw it as his playground, and he could easily have rested on his laurels.

Instead of seeing Disneyland as just a successful park, Walt reframed his perspective by looking at it as its own experiment, as a "proof of concept" for something bigger. By reframing what he had done, he came to understand that he had successfully built a new kind of *environment* for people in the *form* of a park. It was only after the park was built that Walt and others came to recognize that in many ways Disneyland contained many of the elements that are needed in every safe and successful community. Architects and urban planners were taking notice and beginning to praise Disneyland as the leading example of new urban planning. Gennawey writes in *Walt Disney and the Promise of Progress City*,

> Born of a movie mogul's vision, the design of Disneyland is a reflection of Walt's cinematic and storytelling background. At the time, Disneyland set a new standard for cleanliness of public spaces. It also helped to renew public interest in historical central business districts. Pesky but vital infrastructure was cleverly hidden from the guests' view. Most importantly, Walt created through the park a special kind of public space that has connected emotionally with millions of guests.[15]

Walt was now curious about taking up bigger and more socially relevant challenges, asking: How can the concepts embedded in Disneyland be applied to solving the problems emerging from urban decay in American cities, and how can the principles of design that had been applied to Disneyland be expanded and repurposed to serve and improve the health, happiness, and well-being of the people that our cities and towns are built and governed to serve? Gennawey writes:

> The success of Disneyland convinced Walt that he might be able to take what he had learned and apply it toward building a beautiful, functional city where people not only played and worked but also where they lived. Walt had confidence in his creativity. He had already changed the world of animation forever. His studio was light-years ahead of other movie studios in function and design. His theme park redefined the world of amusement parks. Maybe now he could turn his attention to transforming the urban experience.[16]

In his final years, Walt was quietly exploring EPCOT as his prototype to transform urban living. While doing so, he imparted one final piece of advice about accomplishment and creativity. "Think beyond your lifetime if you want to accomplish something truly worthwhile," he said. "Put together a 50-year master plan. Thinking 50 years ahead forces you to engage in a quality of thinking that will also improve your present thinking."[17]

Lessons We Can Learn from Walt Disney's Business Success

- Understand your business model and discover ways to improve it to change the nature of how to create customers.
- Think widely beyond the obvious to identify longer-term strategic possibilities.
- Think backwards to connect your vision of the future to the realities of today, and work forward to build a bridge to tomorrow.

- Assess your aspirational plans from multiple perspectives, such as dreamer, realist, and critic.

- Use input from other sources, including qualitative and quantitative research, to assess ideas and develop the best path forward.

- Before you start a major project, study everything about it, believe in it, and have confidence in your ability and that of your team to do it right.

- Understand conventional thinking and explore moving beyond it. Deep down all people hold roughly the same values and want the same basic things.

- Reframe your achievements as a plateau on a longer and larger journey.

---

1. Jackson, *Walt Disney: Conversations*, p. 74.

2. See Dilts, "Walt Disney: Strategies of Genius," atnlpu.com/Articles/article7.htm, accessed October 26, 2016.

3. "Foundations for the Disney Business," imagineerebirth.blogspot.ca/2007/01/foundations-for-disney-business.html, accessed September 20, 2016.

4. John Stanley Donaldson quoted in Gennawey, *Walt Disney and the Promise of Progress City*, p. 52n.

5. Ghez, *Walt's People: Volume 18*, pp. 75-76.

6. Walt quoted in Steve Mannheim, *Walt Disney and the Quest for Community*, p. 46; original source, Norma Lee Browning, "Magic Cities For Young, Old Foreseen By Disney," *Chicago Tribune*, 25 October 1966; Smith, *The Quotable Walt Disney*, p. 252.

7. Wikipedia, "Christopher Alexander," en.wikipedia.org/wiki/Christopher_Alexander, accessed September 24, 2016.

8. Gennawey, *Walt Disney and the Promise of Progress City*, p. 13.

9. Green and Green, *Remembering Walt*, p. 167. See also Gennawey, *Walt Disney and the Promise of Progress City*, p. 66.

10. Smith, *The Quotable Walt Disney*, p. 251.

11. Charles Tranberg, *Walt Disney & Recollections of the Disney Studios: 1955-1980*, p. 5.

12. Ackoff, *The Democratic Corporation*, 99–100.

13. Gennawey, *Walt Disney and the Promise of Progress City*, 63.

14. Gennawey, *Walt Disney and the Promise of Progress City*, 63.

15. Gennawey, *Walt Disney and the Promise of Progress City*, 63.

16. Gennawey, *Walt Disney and the Promise of Progress City*, 64.

17. Walt Disney quoted in Mike Vance & Diane Deacon, *Break Out of the Box*, 13.

Roy O. Disney's Advice for Executives

One evening over dinner with Disney University executives, Roy discussed the advice he would want to see included in development training for Disney executives and managers. Disney University dean Mike Vance was there to capture these spontaneous comments.[1]

Most of these musings pertain to the understanding and utilization of emerging technologies. But on another level, they demonstrate an underlying thinking by Roy for the importance of management discipline and process as the foundation for managerial success. Roy learned these lessons from working at Walt's side for his entire career.

Stay knowledgeable about developing technologies.
Roy wanted information about the latest technological developments to be included in Disney's management development programs. He said: "It's our responsibility to know what technology is available to us right now, and what is being created in R&D labs around the world." The general principle is to keep on top of technological developments that can affect your business, and figure out a way to use them to your advantage to serve your customers and the business mission.

Identify emerging technologies.
It wasn't enough just to be aware of technologies, it was important to do something with the information. For Roy, it was important to actually make a list of emerging technologies with the possible applications or impacts on your area of expertise. Getting the ideas out of your head and onto paper requires thinking and capturing ideas so they can be worked with. For Roy, such work required answering context-specific business questions such as: "What direction will the computer take? How will it affect managing a theme park and movie studio? What advanced technology will help us automate through the use of robotics?"

Pick a technology wave to ride.
Roy wanted managers and executives to know enough about emerging technologies that they were able to make choices and take calculated risks. He said: "Pick a technology that you will bet on and believe in because of the research you've given to the subject. Convince all of us that we should join with you." Business cannot succeed if managers don't take calculated risks and make decisions. This process requires research to gain knowledge, application of business judgment within the longer-range context of the business function being managed, and the development of a rational argument that is strong enough to convince others and win them over to your own conclusions, thereby creating consensus amongst the management team while also educating others.

Don't be premature (or late) in picking your technology.
This was a warning from Roy to ensure the prudence of the investment. Being early or late with some technology investments can be costly. Roy was indicating that it is important to know through independent research the point in the development cycle at which the investment is being made. This will help guard against being fooled into a sub-optimal solution by overzealous promoters.

Keep personal skills in synch with technology.
Roy saw technology as a tool to support the work and increase individual creativity and productivity. To take advantage of the benefits, one has to be proactive in learning new ways of working to achieve results.

Go beyond money.
With the success of Disneyland and Walt's efforts to partner with the leading industrialists to create attractions, securing money for the Orlando project was not a major issue for Roy. "What we need," he told one investment banker, "is investors who will also make a contribution to the project." Roy thought it important to seek out partners who could bring additional value to the equation beyond the initial value being sought. In more general terms, don't just settle for the obvious—think more deeply about additional value that can be added, and understand the values of those with whom you choose to do business.

---

1. Vance and Deacon, *Break Out of the Box*, 99-100.

Walt used to say that Disneyland would never be finished, and it never will. I like to think, too, that Walt Disney's influence will never be finished; that through his creations, future generations will continue to celebrate what he once described as "that precious, ageless something to every human being which makes us play with children's toys and laugh at silly things and sing in the bathtub and dream."

—Roy O. Disney, "Unforgettable Walt Disney,"
Reader's Digest, February 1969, 218.

Bibliography

Ackoff, Russell A. *The Democratic Corporation: A Radical Prescription for Recreating Corporate America and Rediscovering Success.* New York, NY: Oxford University Press, 1994.

Anderson, Christopher. *Hollywood TV: The Studio System in the Fifties.* Austin, TX: University of Texas Press, 1994.

Barrier, Michael. *The Animated Man: A Life of Walt Disney.* Berkeley, CA: University of California Press, 2007.

Baxter, John. *Disney During World War II: How The Walt Disney Studio Contributed to Victory in the War.* New York, NY: Disney Editions, 2014.

Berry, Leonard. *Discovering the Soul of Service: The Nine Drivers of Sustainable Business Success.* New York, NY: The Free Press, 1999.

Brightman, Homer. *Life in the Mouse House: Memoir of a Disney Story Artist.* Windermere, FL: Theme Park Press, 2014.

Collins, James, and Jerry Porras. *Built to Last: Successful Habits of Visionary Companies.* New York, NY: HarperCollins, 2002.

Crafton, Donald. *Before Mickey: The Animated Film 1898–1928.* Chicago, IL: University of Chicago Press, 1993.

Culhane, Shamus. *Talking Animals and Other People.* New York, NY: St. Martin's Press, 1986.

Disney, Roy O. "Unforgettable Walt Disney." *Readers Digest*, February 1969, 212–18.

Drucker, Peter. *Management.* New York, NY: Harper & Row, 1973.

Drucker, Peter. *The Practice of Management.* New York, NY: Perennial Library, 1986.

Eliot, Marc. *Walt Disney: Hollywood's Dark Prince.* New York, NY: HarperPaperbacks, 1993.

Emerson, Chad Denver. *Project Future: The Inside Story Behind the Creation of Disney World.* Ayefour Publishing, 2010.

Finch, Christopher. *The Art of Walt Disney, From Mickey Mouse to the Magic Kingdom*. New Concise ed. New York, NY: Abrams, 1975.

France, Van Arsdale. *Backstage Disneyland: A Personal History*. Buzz Price Archives, University of Florida, 1989.

France, Van Arsdale. *Window on Main Street: 35 Years of Creating Happiness at Disneyland Park*. Windermere, FL: Theme Park Press, 2015.

Gabler, Neal. *Walt Disney: The Triumph of the American Imagination*. New York, NY: Alfred A. Knopf, 2006.

Gennawey, Sam. *The Disneyland Story*. Birmingham, AL: Keen Comm., 2014.

Gennawey, Sam. *Walt Disney and the Promise of Progress City*. Windermere, FL: Theme Park Press, 2014.

Ghez, Didier. *Disney's Grand Tour: Walt and Roy's European Vacation, Summer 1935*. Windermere, FL: Theme Park Press, 2014.

Ghez, Didier, ed. *Walt's People: Talking Disney with the Artists Who Knew Him, Vol. 1*. Windermere, FL: Theme Park Press, 2015.

Ghez, Didier, ed. *Walt's People: Talking Disney with the Artists Who Knew Him, Vol. 2*. Windermere, FL: Theme Park Press, 2017.

Ghez, Didier, ed. *Walt's People: Talking Disney with the Artists Who Knew Him, Vol. 6*. Windermere, FL: Theme Park Press, 2017.

Ghez, Didier, ed. *Walt's People: Talking Disney with the Artists Who Knew Him, Vol. 8*. Windermere, FL: Theme Park Press, 2017.

Ghez, Didier, ed. *Walt's People: Talking Disney with the Artists Who Knew Him, Vol. 10*. Windermere, FL: Theme Park Press, 2017.

Ghez, Didier, ed. *Walt's People: Talking Disney with the Artists Who Knew Him, Vol. 16*. Windermere, FL: Theme Park Press; 2015.

Ghez, Didier, ed. *Walt's People: Talking Disney with the Artists Who Knew Him, Vol. 18*. Windermere, FL: Theme Park Press; 2016

Goldenson, Leonard H. *Beating The Odds: The Untold Story Behind the Rise of ABC*. New York, NY: Charles Scribner's Sons, 1991

Gordon, Bruce, and David Mumford, eds. *A Brush with Disney: An Artist's Journey Told Through the Words and Works of Herbert Dickens Ryman*. 2nd ed. Santa Clara, CA: Camphor Tree Publishing, 2002.

Green, Howard E. and Amy Boothe Green. *Remembering Walt: Favorite Memories of Walt Disney*. New York, NY: Disney Editions, 2002.

Greene, Katherine, and Richard Greene. *Inside the Dream: The Personal Story of Walt Disney*. New York, NY: Disney Editions, 2001.

Haden-Guest, Anthony. *The Paradise Program*. New York, NY: William Morrow & Company Inc., 1973.

Heide, Robert, and John Gilman. *Mickey Mouse: The Evolution, the Legend, the Phenomenon!* New York, NY: Disney Editions, 2001.

Hench, John. *Designing Disney: Imagineering and the Art of the Show*. New York, NY: Disney Editions, 2003.

Holliss, Richard. *Walt Disney's Mickey Mouse: His Life and Times*. New York, NY: Harper & Row, 1986

Holliss, Richard, and Brian Sibley. *Walt Disney's Snow White and the Seven Dwarfs*. New York, NY: Simon & Schuster, 1987.

Holliss, Richard, and Brian Sibley. *The Disney Studio Story*. New York, NY: Crown, 1988.

Imagineers. *Walt Disney Imagineering: A Behind-the-Dreams Look at Making the Magic Real*. New York, NY: Hyperion, 1996.

Iwerks, Leslie, and John Kenworthy. *The Hand Behind The Mouse*. Disney Editions, New York; 2001.

Jackson, Kathy Merlock, ed. *Walt Disney: Conversations*. University Press of Mississippi, 2006.

Jaques, Elliott and Catherine Cason. *Human Capability*. Falls Church, VA: Cason Hall & Co., 1994.

Jaques, Elliott, and Stephen D. Clement. *Executive Leadership*. Cambridge, MA: Blackwell Publishers, 1994.

Kaufman, J.B. *The Fairest One of All: The Making of Walt Disney's Snow White and the Seven Dwarfs*. San Francisco, CA: Walt Disney Family Foundation Press, 2012.

Kaufman, J.B. *Snow White and the Seven Dwarfs: The Art and Creation of Walt Disney's Classic Animated Film*. San Francisco, CA: Walt Disney Family Foundation Press, 2012.

Korkis, Jim. "Chuck Jones: Four Months at Disney." MousePlanet. September 9, 2009. mouseplanet.com/8944/Chuck_Jones__Four_Months_At_Disney.

Korkis, Jim. "Disneyland '59." MousePlanet. May 27, 2015. mouseplanet.com/11023/Disneyland_59.

Korkis, Jim. "Horsing Around with Walt and Polo." MousePlanet. July 11, 2007. mouseplanet.com/8203/Horsing_Around_With_Walt_and_Polo.

Korkis, Jim. "Walt in His Own Words." Jim Hill Media. April 6, 2005. jimhillmedia.com/alumni1/b/wade_sampson/archive/2005/04/06/1256.aspx.

Krause, Martin, and Linda Witkowski. *Walt Disney's Snow White and the Seven Dwarfs: An Art in Its Making*. New York, NY: Hyperion, 1994.

Kurtti, Jeff. *Walt Disney's Imagineering Legends and the Genesis of the Disney Theme Park*. New York, NY: Disney Editions, 2008.

Lenburg, Jeff. *Who's Who in Animated Cartoons*. New York, NY: Applause Theatre & Cinema Books, 2006.

Lesjak, David. *Service with Character: The Disney Studio and World War II*. Windermere, FL: Theme Park Press; 2014.

Levitt, Theodore. *Innovation in Marketing*. New York, NY: McGraw-Hill, 1962

Lindquist, Jack. *In Service to the Mouse*. Orange, CA: Chapman University Press, 2010

Lipp, Doug. *Disney U*. New York, NY: McGraw-Hill, 2013.

Maltin, Leonard. *The Disney Films*. 3rd ed. New York, NY: Hyperion, 1995.

Mannheim, Steve. *Walt Disney and the Quest for Community*. Burlington, VT: Ashgate Publishing Co., 2002.

Marling, Karal Ann, ed. *Designing Disney's Theme Parks: The Architecture of Reassurance*. New York, NY: Flammarion, 1997.

Merritt, Russell, and J.B. Kaufman. *Walt in Wonderland: The Silent Films of Walt Disney*. Baltimore, MD: John Hopkins University Press, 2000.

Miles, Jim. "Lessons of Walt Disney." Laughing Place. January 8, 2004. laughingplace.com/news-ID180410.asp.

Miller, Diane Disney. *The Story of Walt Disney: A Fabulous Rags to Riches Saga*. New York, NY: Dell Publishing, 1959

Mises, Ludwig von. *Human Action: A Treatise on Economics*. 3rd revised ed. San Francisco, CA: Fox & Wilkes, 1966.

Naversen, Nate. "Contagious Business Philosophy the 'Disney' Way!" Themed Attraction. themedattraction.com/disney_way.htm.

Paton, Scott Madison. "Service Quality, Disney Style." Quality Digest. January 1, 1997. qualitydigest.com/jan97/disney.html.

Peet, Bill. *An Autobiography*. New York, NY: Houghton Mifflin Company,1989.

Peri, Don. *Working with Walt: Interviews with Disney Artists*. Jackson, MS: University Press of Mississippi, 2008.

Pierce, Todd James. *Three Years In Wonderland*. Jackson, MS: University of Mississippi Press, 2016.

Polsson, Ken. Chronology of the Walt Disney Company. kpolsson.com/disnehis/.

Price, Harrision "Buzz." *Walt's Revolution! By the Numbers*. Orlando, FL: Ripley Entertainment, 2004.

Rand, Ayn. "Galt's Speech." *For the New Intellectual: The Philosophy of Ayn Rand*. New York, NY: Signet, 1961.

Reisman, George. *Capitalism: A Treatise on Economics*. Ottawa, IL: Jameson Books, 1990.

Reisman, George. "Classical Economics vs. The Exploitation Theory." Mises Institute. January 24, 2005. mises.org/library/classical-economics-vs-exploitation-theory.

Reisman, George. "Overthrowing Smith and Marx: Profits, not Wages, as the Original and Primary Form of Labor Income." February 21, 2014. georgereismansblog.blogspot.ca/2014/02/reismans-remarks-at-conferral-of-his.html.

ReImagineering Blog. "Foundations for the Disney Business." January 11, 2007. http://imagineerebirth.blogspot.ca/2007/01/foundations-for-disney-business.html.

Reynolds, Robert. *Roller Coasters, Flumes, and Flying Saucers: The Story of Ed Morgan and Karl Bacon*. Northern Lights Publishing, 2013.

Rogers, Bob. "The Coming Revolution in Themed Entertainment." Themed Attraction. 1997. themedattraction.com/future.htm.

Schnaars. *Marketing Strategy: A Customer-Driven Approach*. New York, NY: Free Press, 1991.

Schumpeter. Joseph A. *Capitalism, Socialism and Democracy*. New York, NY: HarperPerennial, 1975.

Shaw, Mel. *Animator on Horseback*. Windermere, FL: Theme Park Press; 2016.

Schmidt, Chuck. *Disney's Dream Weavers*. Windermere, FL: Theme Park Press, 2017.

Sherman, Robert B. *Moose: Chapters from My Life*. Bloomington, IL: AuthorHouse, 2013.

Shows, Charles. *Walt: Backstage Adventures with Walt Disney.* Windsong Books, 1979.

Sito, Tom. *Drawing The Line: The Untold Story of the Animation Unions from Bosko to Bart Simpson.* Lexington, KY: University Press of Kentucky, 2006.

Smith, Dave, ed. *Walt Disney: Famous Quotes.* The Walt Disney Company, 1994.

Smith, Dave, ed. *The Quotable Walt Disney.* 1st ed. New York, NY: Disney Editions, 2001.

Susanin, Timothy S. *Walt Before Mickey: Disney's Early Years, 1919–1928.* Jackons, MS: University Press of Mississippi, 2011.

Thomas, Bob. *Disney's Art of Animation: From Mickey Mouse to Beauty and the Beast.* New York, NY: Hyperion, 1991.

Thomas, Bob. *Walt Disney: An American Original.* New York, NY: Hyperion, 1994.

Thomas, Bob. *Disney's Art of Animation: From Mickey Mouse to Hercules.* 2nd ed. New York, NY: Hyperion, 1997.

Thomas, Bob. *Building a Company.* New York, NY: Hyperion, 1998.

Thomas, Frank, and Ollie Johnston. *The Illusion of Life: Disney Animation.* New York, NY: Disney Editions, 1981.

Tranberg, Charles. *Walt Disney & Recollections of the Disney Studios: 1955–1980.* Albany, GA: BearManor Media, 2012.

Vance, Mike. "Management By Values." Tape 1, Side A. Cleveland, OH: Intellectual Equities, Inc., 1985.

Vance, Mike, and Diane Deacon. *Think Out of the Box.* Franklin Lakes, NJ: Career Press, 1995.

Vance, Mike, and Diane Deacon. *Break Out of the Box.* Franklin Lakes, NJ: Career Press, 1996.

Walt Disney Family Museum. *The Man, the Magic, the Memories.* New York, NY: Disney Editions, 2009.

Watts, Steven. *The Magic Kingdom: Walt Disney and the American Way of Life.* Columbia, MO: University of Missouri, 1997.

Williams, Pat. *How to Be Like Walt.* Deerfield Beach, FL: Health Communications Inc., 2004.

Young, Jordan. *Dali, Disney and Destiny: The Inside Story of "Destino."* Past Times Publishing, 2012.

About the Author

Barry Linetsky has had a long-time interest in Walt Disney and his innovative business practices which, after years of painstaking research and writing, has resulted in the book you now hold in your hands.

For more than two decades, Barry has been an entrepreneur and a partner with the Toronto-based advisory firm The Strategic Planning Group, working with business and government executives across a wide-range of industries throughout North America to develop customized products and solutions that address the strategic, marketing, and organizational-related business challenges they face.

Barry holds an MBA from the Rotman School of Management, University of Toronto, and an MA in Philosophy and BA in Sociology from York University. He has had a number of business articles published in Rotman Magazine and the Ivey Business Journal, including "The Project Management Paradox," which was republished as an Executive Briefing by the Economic Intelligence Unit in partnership with Harvard Business School Publishing.

You can read more about how to think like Walt Disney and other business topics by visiting BarryLinetsky.com. Follow Barry on Twitter @BizPhilosopher (twitter.com/bizphilosopher).

More Books from Theme Park Press

Theme Park Press is the largest independent publisher of Disney, Disney-related, and general interest theme park books in the world, with over 100 new releases each year.

We're always looking for new talent.

For a complete catalog, including book descriptions and excerpts, please visit:

ThemeParkPress.com

Walt Disney and the Pursuit of Progress

Walt Disney is well-known for animation, theme parks, and Mickey Mouse. But his real passion was technology, and how he could use it to shape a better, prosperous, peaceful future for everyone.

themeparkpress.com/books/great-big-beautiful-tomorrow.htm

Learn the Secrets of Walt Disney's Success

Acclaimed Disney expert Jim Korkis tells the stories of what Walt did right, what he did wrong, and how you can follow in his footsteps. Drawing upon his internal knowledge of the Disney company and its legacy, Korkis distills the essence of Walt Disney's leadership principles into an exciting narrative of popular history and self-help.

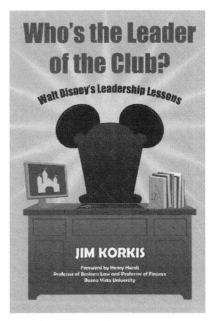

themeparkpress.com/books/leader-club.htm